ALAN TAYLOR

Liberty Men
and Great Proprietors

The Revolutionary Settlement

on the Maine Frontier, *1760–1820*

Published for The Omohundro Institute of

Early American History and Culture, Williamsburg, Virginia,

by The University of North Carolina Press

Chapel Hill & London

This volume received indirect support from an unrestricted book publications grant awarded to the Institute by the L. J. SKAGGS AND MARY C. SKAGGS FOUNDATION of Oakland, California.

The Omohundro Institute of Early American History and Culture is sponsored jointly by the College of William and Mary and the Colonial Williamsburg Foundation.

Manufactured in the United States of America

Taylor, Alan, 1955–
    Liberty men and great proprietors : the revolutionary settlement on the Maine frontier, 1760–1820 / Alan Taylor.
        p.   cm.
    Includes bibliographical references.
ISBN 0-8078-1909-3
ISBN 0-8078-4282-6 (pbk.: alk. paper)
    1. Maine—History—1775–1865.   2. Frontier and pioneer life—Maine.   3. Land settlement—Maine—History.   4. Maine—History—Colonial period, ca. 1600–1775.   I. Title.
F24.T39   1990   89-24790
974.1—dc20   CIP

Artwork by Richard Stinely

cloth   05   04   03   02   01   5   4   3   2   1
paper   05   04   03   02   9   8   7   6

LIBERTY MEN AND GREAT PROPRIETORS

General Henry Knox. By Gilbert Stuart, circa 1805. *Deposited by the City of Boston. Courtesy, Museum of Fine Arts, Boston*

FOR MY PARENTS

Ruel Edward Taylor, Jr.

Virginia Craig Taylor

ACKNOWLEDGMENTS

As with the settlers, my debts are many and can never be repaid in full. Fortunately, the debts of scholarship are pleasant to acknowledge. My graduate education and the initial research for this book depended on the generous financial assistance from the Irving and Rose Crown Fellowship Fund to the History of American Civilization Program at Brandeis University. Further research and much rewriting were possible because of a postdoctoral fellowship at the Institute of Early American History and Culture supported by the Colonial Williamsburg Foundation, the College of William and Mary, and the National Endowment for the Humanities. A grant from the Humanities Foundation of Boston University subsidized the illustrations for this book.

Several considerate and thoughtful people enriched my research trips to Maine. Julia and Robert Walkling, Jane Hunter, Joel Bernard, Hal and Dorothy Raymond, and Hank and Pam Gemery shared their hospitality and ideas with me. I also thank Elsie Adams, Margaret Clifford, Millard Howard, Phyllis Gardiner, and Martha and George Vaughan for making the papers of their ancestors available to me. For their generous and helpful advice, I thank the genealogists Robert Charles Anderson, Carolyn Ballantine, the late Priscilla Jones, Roger Joselyn, Isabel Maresh, Betsey Moshier, David Nichols, Danny D. Smith, and Robert Taylor. As supervisors of the Maine Humanities Council's "Maine at Statehood" program, Karen Bowden and Julia Walkling provided me with opportunities to present my research to schools and historical societies in Augusta, Camden, Damariscotta, Hamden, Portland, Saco, South Paris, and Waterville. Along the way, Linda, Maria, and William Rodgers were kind and caring friends.

I often asked archivists to search in the deepest, darkest corners of their archives for their most obscure collections. I appreciate the patience and dedication of the staffs at the Goldfarb Library of Brandeis University, Colby College's Miller Library, the Bowdoin College Library, Swem Library at the College of William and Mary, the Maine Historical Society, the Maine State Archives, Special Collections at the Fogler Library of the University of Maine at Orono, the Kennebec County Courthouse, the Lincoln County Courthouse, the Lincoln County Cultural and Historical Association, the Church of Jesus Christ of Latter-Day Saints Branch Library in Weston, Massachusetts, the Massachusetts Historical Society, the Boston Athenaeum, the New England Historic Genealogical Society Library, the Suffolk County Courthouse, the Essex

Institute, the Massachusetts State Archives, the Library of Congress, and Mugar Memorial Library at Boston University. I am particularly grateful for the extra pains taken to assist my research by Martha Clark of the Massachusetts State Archives, Norma Moore and Jeffrey Brown of the Maine State Archives, Eleanor Barrie of the Lincoln County Courthouse, David Dearborn of the New England Historic Genealogical Society Library, and Tom Gaffney of the Maine Historical Society. I also appreciate the excellent support I received from the staffs of the computer centers at Brandeis University, Colby College, and the College of William and Mary. Alan Melchiore, a fellow graduate student, also offered astute advice on statistical methods.

I have been especially fortunate in the scholars who have taken the time to teach me their craft. When I was an undergraduate at Colby College, Harold B. Raymond's wisdom and humane purpose inspired me to try to become a historian. At Brandeis University David Hackett Fischer encouraged me to launch this project; David Kaplan taught me the value of anthropology to historical inquiry and was ever generous with his time and insights; Alex Keyssar inspired by example and challenged with criticism; and Marvin Meyers was the ideal thesis director: demanding and encouraging, skeptical and reassuring, uncompromising in his standards but tolerant of diversity. At the Newberry Library's summer program in family and community history William Cronon introduced me to quantitative methods with his trademark enthusiasm and thoroughness. He and John Brooke, Charles Clark, Christopher Clark, Samuel K. Cohn, Hank Gemery, David Hall, Barbara Karsky, Gordon Kershaw, Rachel Klein, Peter Knights, David Konig, Gregory Nobles, Thomas Purvis, Thomas P. Slaughter, Alfred Young, and, especially, Laurel Thatcher Ulrich carefully read and commented upon parts of this work in challenging and perceptive ways. Through my drafts and redrafts, Robert A. Gross, then of Amherst College, held me to his high standards for vividly recapturing the lives, cares, and struggles of ordinary people engaged in extraordinary undertakings.

My fellowship at the Institute of Early American History and Culture introduced me to another set of thoughtful and demanding critics. As the Institute's director, Thad Tate maintained a scholarly climate that was supportive and stimulating. Michael McGiffert's close evaluation of two essays taught me much that improved the whole book; no editor works harder and with greater skill. Richard Bushman and Christine Heyrman evaluated the book manuscript with precision and care. Gil Kelly supervised the manuscript's final preparation with his characteristic thoroughness, tact, and wit. Others associated with the Institute who provided valuable support and advice include Cynthia Carter Ayres, Nina Dayton, James P. P. Horn, Anne Kelly, Kevin Kelly, Jean Lee, Fredrika Teute, and Danny Vickers. I cannot adequately express my gratitude to (and sense of loss over the death of) Stephen Botein, who served as the Institute's Visiting Editor of Publications; all who knew him recall his kindness, decency, humor, judgment, and integrity.

I dedicate the book to my mother and to the memory of my father for their unfailing support.

CONTENTS

ILLUSTRATIONS AND TABLES

Plates

Figure

Maps

Tables

LIBERTY MEN AND GREAT PROPRIETORS

A View of Paris Hill. Settlers Clearing Land, with a New Town Emerging in the Background. Overmantel from the Lazarus Hathaway House, Paris Hill, 1802. *Courtesy of the Hamlin Memorial Library and the Paris Hill Historical Society. Photograph by Abelardo Morell*

INTRODUCTION

Equality of property is the life of a Republican government; destroy that equality and the principles of the government will be wholly corrupted, while the form remains a cloak for oppression and tyranny. Those people who are acquainted with the settlement of the eastern country, can bear witness to the evils arising from the large patents, grants, and Indian deeds in these parts; and I trust from a sense of duty to generations yet unborn, will be vigilant to suppress the progress of that Hydra.—"Scribble-Scrabble," *Cumberland Gazette*, 1786

ON NOVEMBER 20, 1885, Benjamin Tibbetts of Liberty, Maine, celebrated his one-hundredth birthday. Two days later a newspaper reporter from coastal Belfast traveled west into the hilly backcountry to interview Tibbetts, the last survivor from the generation that settled mid-Maine after the American Revolution. Flanked by the Androscoggin River, on the west, and the Penobscot River, to the east, mid-Maine lay in what had been known as the District of Maine, or the Eastern Country, until separation from the Commonwealth of Massachusetts in 1820. Born in coastal Boothbay, Maine, to a Continental army sergeant originally from Dover, New Hampshire, Tibbetts had worked as a sailor and served in the War of 1812 before moving inland to settle in Liberty in 1815. He and his wife reared twelve children, who produced fifty grandchildren, "but how many great grand-children he did not know as they were scattered all over the continent from Aroostook County, Maine, to California." Here was vivid testimony to how rapidly whites had occupied the continent.[1]

Tibbetts delighted in the chance to talk about his life. Twin themes dominated his conversation with the reporter—a lifetime spent in hard labor to provide for his family and a sense of ultimate fragility before the awesome power of God. Proud of what he had accomplished, Tibbetts boasted:

> I have done some things that are worthy to be recorded. In my day I was the stoutest man in these parts. I was the best axeman for miles around. I felled in one day in June between 9 a.m. and sunset, one acre and eight rods of trees of mountain growth. I was then fifty years old, and if you doubt it there are men now living by whom I can prove it and I will do so tomorrow if you say so. I hoed in one day 3,200 hills of corn and hilled it up in the old-fashioned way. I helped fell the trees on every farm around this mountain.

1

But Liberty's poor soil, bad roads, and short growing season meant that Tibbetts's lifelong labor brought his family a competency, but no prosperity. Hard labor for small returns sustained his sense of living in a cosmos where human achievements paled before God's unbounded power.

> I was out one day when about 60 years old trying to break a pair of steers and they behaved so badly that I became very angry with them and swore at them fearfully. Suddenly I thought what if God should send a great white cloud and burst it over my head and kill me dead for my wickedness. I was so frightened at the thought, that I looked around to see the cloud, and I thought I saw it coming, and I held down my head and covered my face with my hands, expecting every moment the cloud would strike me. But after remaining in that position for some time and finding I was not hurt, I lifted my head and found the cloud had passed by. I then and there promised God that if he would help me I would never swear another word as long as I lived, and would you believe it, I never had the least inclination to swear from that day to this.[2]

Tibbetts did not mention—or at least the newspaper did not publish—the most dramatic moment of his life. About seventy years earlier, on the night of September 5, 1815, Tibbetts and a dozen other Liberty settlers donned Indian blankets, blackened their faces, and armed themselves with guns, bayonets, and swords. Each man placed a small wood chip in his mouth to disguise his voice. They quietly walked to Marshall Spring's hotel in adjoining Montville, where lodged Joseph H. Pierce, Jr., one of the Eastern Country's Great Proprietors—wealthy land speculators who claimed legal title to most of mid-Maine and who demanded purchase payments from the settlers.[3]

Poor and living atop an infertile soil, Liberty's settlers thought one dollar per acre more than fair as a purchase price, but Pierce demanded twice that and threatened ejectments. Benjamin Tibbetts and his neighbors regarded Pierce's intransigence as imperiling their hard-earned property in parcels of rocky Maine soil. Reaching Spring's hotel, the White Indians' leader rapped on the door. Opening it, Spring saw the armed crowd. He tried to slam the door shut, but Tibbetts thrust his foot into the opening, and his companions wrenched the door open. Shoving Spring aside, the White Indians burst into Pierce's room, destroyed his papers, and roughly dragged the terrified proprietor outside. They threatened to kill Pierce unless he took an oath to lower his price to one dollar per acre and also swore to prosecute no one. He promised, and they set him free, naively expecting Pierce to take his oath as seriously as they did.[4]

But Pierce hastened to the county seat and secured grand jury indictments against the seven men he recognized. Most, including Tibbetts, evaded the warrants by temporarily slipping away to Canada or to sea. Two men were arrested, tried, convicted, and sentenced to three years in prison. Fortunately, Pierce, the attorney general, and the governor concurred that pardons would produce "a good effect on that part of the Country." Then Pierce and the settlers compromised at $1.50 per acre, and the resistance in Liberty came to an end.[5]

THIS STUDY EXAMINES four phenomena that converged in Benjamin Tibbetts's life: migration to the frontier, labor applied to wilderness land to create property, a spiritual search for divine meaning, and organized resistance to the Great Proprietors. Widespread in mid-Maine, the settlers' resistance began in the 1760s, lapsed when the Revolution seemed to sweep away the proprietary claims, and revived in the 1790s, after the proprietors reasserted their demands for payment. Initially the insurgents called themselves Liberty Men or Sons of Liberty: defenders of a Revolution betrayed by America's great men. But their foes called them White Indians, on account of their disguises and their supposed savagery. Over time, especially after 1800, the most militant settlers adopted the name of White Indians and elaborated a protest culture of mock-Indian costumes and rituals. This study also narrates the resistance in order to explore the interdependence of migration, labor, religion, and politics in the settlers' lives. The mid-Maine land conflicts generated an extraordinary volume of richly detailed documents, which offer a special opportunity to explore the language, ideas, and behavior of rural people in post-Revolutionary America.

Mid-Maine's unrest was decentralized and slowly simmering, a diffuse resistance to specific land laws rather than an overt rebellion against all government. The resistance never had a pivotal climax, a crucial confrontation like General Benjamin Lincoln's forced march through a February 1787 snowstorm to rout the Massachusetts Regulators (also known as Shaysites) at Petersham. In mid-Maine, resistance activity occurred sporadically in the midst of lives ordinarily preoccupied with improving their homesteads to acquire property and with evangelical worship to secure salvation. Resistance activity surged on the infrequent occasions when a community's proprietors made special efforts to break the stalemate, pressing lawsuits and surveys with new vigor. Then settlers temporarily devoted themselves to mass meetings, protest petitions to the General Court, military patrols of community bounds, and the intimidation of suspected traitors within. The pressure momentarily relieved, settlers once more confined their resistance to logging wherever they pleased and to tavernroom and hearthside talk. Benjamin Tibbetts spent far more days felling timber, hoeing cornfields, and breaking steers than he did mobbing land agents, but from time to time he had to become a White Indian to defend the property his labor created.

Backcountry Resistance

Mid-Maine's conflict was part of a national pattern of backcountry resistance. From the mid-eighteenth century to the mid-nineteenth century in at least ten other areas, yeomen seeking free or cheap access to wilderness land confronted gentlemen who had exploited their political connections to secure large land grants. In New Jersey during the 1740s and 1750s yeomen resisted land laws that favored their proprietors. During the 1750s and early 1760s some settlers in South Carolina's Rocky Mount District violently obstructed surveyors working for nonresident speculators. At the same time, settlers in North Carolina's Granville District rioted against unscrupulous land speculators. Beginning in the 1750s and recurring intermittently until about 1860, tenants in upstate New York rebelled against their landlords. From 1762 to 1808, Wild Yankees in northeastern Pennsylvania challenged that state's proprietors. Beginning in 1764 and persisting through the Revolutionary war, western Vermont's Green Mountain Boys rebelled against their New York landlords. In the 1770s, settlers around Pittsburgh with cheap Virginia land titles violently resisted Pennsylvania's jurisdiction and land speculators. During the 1780s, Ohio squatters evaded federal land laws and federal troops. From 1795 through 1810, squatters in northwestern Pennsylvania waged gang warfare against land speculators' hired hands. Finally, during 1835–1836, settlers in western New York's Holland Purchase rioted against the land company that held their burdensome mortgages.[6]

The costs and mode of administering justice represented a second focal point of conflict over the surplus produced by common farmers. Heavy taxes, burdensome debts, excessive judicial fees—or the government's failure to protect farmers from marauding outlaws and Indians—threatened to impoverish freeholders, raising the dreaded specter of tenancy. In ten more rebellions rural folk organized to protect their liberty (equated with secure and egalitarian possession of freehold property) against apparent extortions by, or indifference from, outside great men. In 1763 and 1764 central Pennsylvania's Paxton Boys massacred government-protected Indians and started (but did not complete) a march on Philadelphia. Beginning in 1764, North Carolina's Regulators challenged their rulers until crushed at the Battle of Alamance in 1771.

During the late 1760s South Carolina's Regulators defied their colony by establishing vigilante justice in the backcountry. During that same decade New Jersey's Liberty Boys rioted against their county courts. Similarly, from 1770 through 1775, rioters in eastern Vermont frequently closed the courts. From 1774 until ratification of a new state constitution in 1780, western Massachusetts' Berkshire Constitutionalists kept their courts from sitting. In 1782 Ely's Rebellion rallied yeomen in parts of western Massachusetts and northern Connecticut against their judges. In 1786–1787, the New England Regulation (or Shays's Rebellion, as dubbed by its foes) shut down the courts and hindered tax collection in portions of Massachusetts, Vermont, New Hampshire, and Connecticut. In much of the backcountry, and especially western Pennsylvania, Whiskey Rebels defied federal excise taxes during the 1790s. And in 1799, farmers in central Pennsylvania mounted Fries's Rebellion against a new federal land tax. In most of these ten insurgencies, the aggrieved people also expressed anger over inequities in the distribution of land.[7]

Agrarian resistance climaxed during an unprecedented surge by America's white population into the backcountry. The period from 1760 to 1820 was pivotal in the occupation and agricultural development of the American continent by white settlers. Benjamin Tibbetts was but one among thousands throughout the American backcountry who combined frontier migration, hard labor, evangelical seeking, and property contention. Except for the first colonists in the early seventeenth century, neither before nor since has such a high proportion of America's population lived in newly settled communities. Nowhere else in the world, during the late eighteenth and early nineteenth centuries, did laboring families create so much new property. The conflicts over the distribution of that new property would determine what sort of society would be reproduced over time as Americans expanded across the continent.[8]

The surge of settlers into the backcountry occurred at the same time that the American Revolution encouraged heightened aspirations among the common folk. The Revolution did not cease in 1783 when the Treaty of Paris ended the war with Great Britain; during the 1780s and 1790s the diverse people who had united against British rule fell out over the social and political implications of their Revolution. The agrarian conflicts represented a new, internal, and attenuated stage in the continuing American Revolution, as yeomen and gentlemen, in certain select hillcountry pockets, came to blows over the nature of property, the local diffusion or central consolidation of power, and the legitimacy of extralegal crowd violence in the new Republic.[9]

Gentlemen of property and standing favored a limited reading of the recent Revolution as simply a war for national independence, a war intended to place America's government in their own hands and to safeguard their extensive property from arbitrary parliamentary taxation. They expected the new order to honor pre-Revolutionary legal contracts, especially large land grants. Distrusting the political judgment of the common people, most gentlemen sought to consolidate political decision-making as much as possible: in counties rather than towns, in states rather than counties, in a new federal government rather than the states. Then the commercial centers' discerning gentlemen could govern, exercising their superior judgment independent of popular pressure (except at elections, when they expected the electorate to choose between gentlemen). Convinced that social order was dangerously fragile, gentlemen worried that any extralegal resistance would doom the new Republic. Urging the Pennsylvania legislature to send militia to suppress the Wild Yankees, Thomas Fitzsimons insisted, "If the frontiers are suffered to insult your government, the contagion spreads more and more wide, by the accession of all the disselute and idle, until it may reach the centre, and all be anarchy, confusion, and total ruin." To safeguard their limited Revolution, gentlemen parried the "popular license" of backcountry agrarians.[10]

Wild Yankees, Anti-Renters, Whiskey Rebels, Regulators, and Liberty Men believed in a different American Revolution, one meant to protect small producers from the moneyed men who did not live by their own labor, but, instead, preyed on the many who did. Agrarians dreaded prolonged economic dependence as tenants or wageworkers as the path to "slavery." They sought an American Revolution that reinforced their fundamental drive—to maximize their access to, and secure their possession of, freehold land. This meant minimizing the levies of great men: taxes, rents, legal fees, and land payments. Convinced that republican government could not survive (except as an oppressive sham) unless property was widely and equitably distributed among adult white males, agrarians regarded free access to frontier land as essential to liberty's survival. They feared that, unless the great could be checked in their demands, America would ultimately replicate Europe's oppressive societies of arrogant aristocrats lording over impoverished, landless, and powerless masses. To protect their freeholds for transmission to their children, agrarians insisted on the right of local communities to check forcefully the encroaching power of wily great men. In 1771 a land agent explained to New York landlord James Duane why the Yankee settlers on his manor resisted tenancy: "Their whole fear was, drawing their Posterity into Bondage. Silly People!"[11]

In discussing the early American land rioters, I have avoided the labels "radical" and "conservative" in favor of the more appropriately ambiguous "agrarian." On the one hand, the land rioters do not seem "radical," in the twentieth-century sense of the word, because they counted on a defensive localism to protect their interests, instead of pressing a systematic program for restructuring social institutions. On the other hand, the label "conservative" does not fit comfortably atop settlers who nurtured a labor theory of value and who perceived a chronic class struggle between laboring producers and parasitical gentlemen. The agrarians behaved and thought neither as radicalized proletarians nor simply as backward-looking traditionalists. They hoped that their relatively diffuse and restrained tactics (dictated by their limited means and rural dispersion) would be enough to secure important social consequences: the preservation of America as a land of small producers able to support their families free from domination by an employer or landlord. We need to recognize both how rare such a society was in the eighteenth century—when powerful landlords directly exploiting tenants and laborers were the rural norm in Britain, the European continent, and most of the other New World colonies—*and* how far that dream has receded in our own industrial capitalism, where workers and managers are organized into complex, hierarchical, and bureaucratic structures. To understand agrarian resistance in the early Republic, we should avoid two misconceptions: that settlers were a proletariat, and that there can be no class conflict without one. As small freeholders engaged in manual labor, the settlers were not a proletariat, but they belonged to a class distinct from the great land speculators, who were mercantile capitalists living off the land payments levied on the fruits of the yeomanry's labor.[12]

In recent decades, historians of the American Revolution have shown the importance and sincerity of the fearful rhetoric that moved colonial America's political leaders to resist Britain's imperial rule; far more than insincere propaganda, the language expressed a compelling worldview that made the Revolution both possible and essential. Yet there persists a tendency to trivialize the agrarianism of humbler men as hypocritical cant. Certainly there were canny opportunists like Vermont's Ethan Allen who exploited agrarian rhetoric to serve their own competing land speculations, but it is misleading to conclude from conspicuous but isolated examples that the language served most rural folk simply as a convenient cover for their crypto-capitalism. For every Ethan Allen, there were hundreds who sought no more than farms for themselves and for their children, hundreds whose behavior was compatible with their rhetoric. An Ethan Allen could enjoy great popular support because, in addition to promoting his own self-interest, he so eloquently expounded, and so effectively defended, agrarian ideals that secured the small farms of hundreds of less flamboyant Green Mountain Boys. At a time when debts and hardships threatened many rural Americans' family independence, when most rural folk elsewhere in the British

Empire endured wage labor or tenancy, and when the most conspicuous social trends moved New England's circumstances closer to Britain's, the yeomanry's fears of losing their economic autonomy were far from groundless. Surely we ought to take the agrarians' language and ideas as seriously as those of the Revolution's whig leaders.[13]

The preoccupation of rural Americans with achieving economic autonomy also suggests an ambiguous answer to another, related historical debate: were they promoting, or resisting, America's development as a capitalist society? If we define capitalism in neoclassical terms as the avid pursuit through market exchange of improved circumstances, the yeomanry were eager capitalists. They readily bargained and swapped, bought and sold, in part to gratify immediately, as far as possible, their passion for store-bought goods but also, in part, to acquire and develop land to support their families and sustain their security in old age. When and where the natural economy could not supply their needs, many turned to a supernatural economy—employing magical techniques to search for buried treasure—as a supplement. But if we perceive capitalism as a system of social relations of production in which most people must sell their labor for monetary wages to capitalists who own the means of production, then the yeomanry were determined to avoid such a fate, were determined to cling to the land that sustained them in cherished "independence." They wanted to live in a society where many small producers engaged in exchange as equals, where no white man had any dominion over another. Indeed, they were ready to believe that free market exchange and equality of dominion would preserve one another, perpetuating America's unique society of independent producers. Agrarians hoped to sustain American capitalism at a simple stage of development where households bought and sold the fruits of their labor without having to sell their labor itself.[14]

The Great Proprietors, in contrast, insisted that America's commercial development required the emergence of a more efficient, complex, and hierarchical social order where property would become concentrated in the hands of the capitalists who best understood how to employ it to create more property. General David Cobb insisted that economic development required "a total change of public opinion, and perhaps of government too," for "*so long as it is a crime for any one to improve more than 1 or 2 hundred acres of land, so long will it be that none but a farmer's family can be cloathed in woolen, and they but partially.*" The proprietors believed that putting a price on unsettled land would accelerate the restructuring of American society by forcing out inefficient farmers.[15]

Nonetheless, frustration of the agrarian vision of equal producers united by simple commodity exchange resulted less from elite pressure than from a fundamental contradiction in the yeomanry's way of life.

Because rural Americans were determined to work their own farms, hired labor was scarce and unreliable; to have enough hands to develop a new farm, rural families sired as many children as possible. This was good for the parents, but, in any given settlement, the surging population quickly exceeded the supply of land. Most of the founders' grandchildren had to move on in search of their own frontier land or forsake independence for either tenancy or wage labor. To sustain their way of life, every generation needed vast and increasing quantities of land; the yeomanry purchased its autonomy by destroying that of the native Americans in their way. The society of agrarian producers was only possible where there was a continent that could be readily wrested from its aboriginal inhabitants. And such conditions were temporary. Contrary to Thomas Jefferson's optimism that North America's land could sustain yeoman autonomy "to the hundredth and thousandth generation," the supply would prove insufficient by the end of the nineteenth century. By 1885, when Benjamin Tibbetts's great-grandchildren were scattered from Maine to California, few of their offspring could expect to obtain farms. Eight years later, Frederick Jackson Turner would conclude that the 1890 census marked the end of America's frontier of "free land": "And with its going has closed the first period of American history."[16]

The early Republic's land conflicts pivoted on whether, in a given region, the inevitable decline of the agrarian dream would be accelerated, or postponed, by a single generation. By minimizing what they had to pay for the land, a community's settlers hoped to secure sufficient land for themselves and for their children. Recognizing the pace at which their population growth consumed land, they knew that most of their grandchildren would have to move on. Where proprietors succeeded in imposing prices for their titles, it was difficult for settlers to procure enough land nearby for their sons; in such circumstances the children, rather than the grandchildren, felt the pinch. Because the nearby presence of their children contributed to parents' security in old age, one generation was no small difference to mid-Maine's settlers.[17]

THIS WORK EXAMINES in detail one of the episodes of agrarian conflict: the Maine frontier, where Liberty Men defended their version of the Revolution against Great Proprietors. In Maine, the process of frontier settlement intersected with America's Revolutionary settlement: the resolution of whose values and whose property interests would be legitimated by the Revolution. In the immediate wake of the war, thousands migrated from southern New England to mid-Maine in pursuit of autonomy as small farmers. In their new settlements they gradually acquired improved property in the land, and they developed evangelical meetings hostile to the commonwealth's Congregational establishment. When, in the 1780s and 1790s, the proprietors revived their dormant land claims, the settlers exploited their distance from political and religious authority to organize a resistance that safeguarded their new property. But the Great Proprietors were committed to a more hierarchical and paternalistic worldview. They worried that the combination of frontier migration, evangelical religion, and the recent Revolution had produced a centrifugal force that would tear social order apart. As was the case throughout the American backcountry between 1790 and 1820, the conflict between agrarian and elite ways of defining the Revolution produced a deadlock that became an opportunity for a new breed of political leaders to gain power; Jeffersonian politicians reframed political ideology in a manner that permitted compromise legislation and defused the confrontation. The conflict between Great Proprietors and Liberty Men and the ultimate triumph of the Jeffersonians were symptomatic of a more widespread social and political transformation: the making of a liberal social order.[18]

CHAPTER ONE

Origins of the Conflict

You must remember in the first place, that the eas[t]ward country (as it is called) has been Settled in a very illegal manner. It has been the practice to give the settlers a hundred acres of land for settling, after they have been quarrelled with and irritated a long time, and this has learn't their neighbours to snarl and mutter at the proprietors.—Elisha Sylvester of Greene, January 19, 1801

No part of the United States affords such solid grounds of proffit to capitalists, as the District of Maine.—General Henry Knox, November 11, 1795

ON THE AFTERNOON OF May 2, 1811, a special commission, appointed by the Massachusetts General Court to investigate the land controversies, held a hearing in the town of Bristol on the mid-Maine coast. Eighty-six-year-old William Jones hobbled forward to testify for his neighbors and against the Great Proprietors' claims to their farms. Born in 1724 to Scottish parents in northern Ireland, Jones had migrated in 1730 with his family to New England and settled in Bristol. Jones attested that the troubles of the settlers had begun in 1731, when the Great Proprietors of that generation had secured the demise of Colonel David Dunbar's scheme to establish a new crown colony on the coast of mid-Maine.[1]

As commander of His Majesty's fortress at Pemaquid on the mid-Maine coast, Dunbar drew the Jones family and about three hundred other Scotch-Irish settlers to the then virtually unsettled northeastern frontier with promises of free homesteads. His settlements later became known as the towns of Edgecomb, Boothbay, Newcastle, Nobleborough, and Bristol. By securing settlers, Dunbar meant to hold the region as a new colony, in defiance of Massachusetts' claims to jurisdiction and the Great Proprietors' claims to title. He led his armed settlers on raids that seized and destroyed the Great Proprietors' boats, garrison houses, and sawmills in the region—a precedent for the subsequent resistance. But in 1731 Massachusetts' General Court, royal governor, and Great Proprietors successfully pressured the imperial Board of Trade to order Dunbar to forsake his colonization scheme. He surrendered his fort at Pemaquid to Massachusetts authorities and left the settlers without titles, but the abandoned settlers resisted the victorious proprietors' demands for land payments. Dunbar had warned the Board of Trade, "There will be a kind of warr 'tween these pretended proprietors and those that will go to settle upon the King's terms, for they will not quit the possession."[2]

11

Josiah Little. *From George Thomas Little,* The Descendants of George Little . . . *(Auburn, 1882)*

Three major proprietary claims, based on letters patent issued between 1629 and 1632 by the Council for New England of Charles I, covered almost all of mid-Maine. On the west the Pejepscot Proprietors claimed the *Pejepscot Patent:* the land four miles back on both sides of the Androscoggin River from its mouth to its "uppermost falls." In the center the Kennebeck Proprietors (also known as the Plymouth Company) laid claim to the *Plymouth Patent:* about three million acres located fifteen miles deep on each side of the Kennebec, Maine's central and most important river. To the east, Brigadier General Samuel Waldo and two companies of his partners, the Ten Proprietors and the Twenty Associates, claimed the *Waldo Patent:* about one million acres located between the Medomac and Penobscot rivers.[3]

The Great Proprietors did not possess clear legal title to the lands they claimed. Drafted in England by lawyers who had never seen the Eastern Country, the three major patents were vague and overlapping. Worse still, the three major patents were also in conflict with ten smaller proprietary claims: the royal Pemaquid Patent and nine claims based on Indian deeds. With no notion of exclusive, private, hereditary property in land, Maine's Indians repeatedly sold the same turf to different whites. Moreover, the vague metes and bounds of the royal patents and the Indian deeds encouraged creative surveying by aggressive proprietors determined to stretch their claims, which compounded the overlaps.[4]

Because they did not possess clear titles, the Great Proprietors were reluctant to sue one another directly for fear of a legal decision that would invalidate their entire claim. To preclude direct tests, most proprietors refused to warrant their deeds, because the purchaser of a warranty deed could introduce it in his defense if sued by another proprietor, thereby bringing the seller and his title into the suit. Moreover, if the defendant lost the suit, his warranty deed rendered the original seller liable to refund not only the purchase price but the defendant's legal costs and the value of his improvements as well. Consequently, the wary proprietors usually sold only quitclaim deeds or grants, neither of which protected the buyer from a suit by another proprietor with a competing claim. The settlers sorely felt that lack of protection because the proprietors, instead of directly suing one another, competed by suing the settlers who bought from the competition. The settler who bought one company's title invited ejectment suits from other proprietors eager to prevent the competition from gaining the upper hand. Thus, in 1800 the Pejepscot Patent's settlers complained: "Each claimant comes producing pompus Parchmints of royal patents or fragments of Antient Indian Deeds. He who purchases of one is considered as the enemy of the other, being the tenant in possession. He is sued and at the end of seven years law suit it is of no consequence to him whether he gains or loses his cause, he is ruind in either case."[5]

Anticipating ruin from the proprietors' multiple demands for payment and their aggressive litigation, settlers feared that they would ultimately be reduced to tenants beholden to haughty landlords. In fact, the Great Proprietors wanted to sell freehold titles, rather than dictate leaseholds, but many settlers were skeptical. In 1760 Job Averell "alarmed" his Pownalborough neighbors by insisting that the Kennebeck Proprietors meant "to bring them all into a lordship and to make them all tennants under them. . . . They will do as they please with them and one of the company has confest that this is their scheme." Similarly, in 1772, Boothbay's inhabitants detected a proprietary "design of reducing the settlers to rack rents on leases of years, or turning them off entirely." During the 1760s, to defend their apparently imperiled liberty as freeholders, mid-Maine's coastal settlers organized armed bands determined to enforce community solidarity against proprietary claims.[6]

The dread of tenancy, so common in the eighteenth-century American backcountry, expressed new settlers' sense of how tenuously they held their cherished independence as freeholders. The freeholder's direct access to nature's productive resources freed him from dependence on an employer, a landlord, or a master. Wage labor and tenancy were tolerable only as youthful way stations for accumulating enough money to acquire freehold land. Without freehold land, fathers could not pass on liberty and prosperity to their offspring; they could not retain their adolescents' labor and would suffer in old age. The New England yeomanry knew that tenancy was the unhappy lot of most of the world's peasants. Dunbar's Scotch-Irish settlers had fled from the rigors of Old World tenancy. Recognizing the uniqueness of America's widespread freehold land, the settlers feared their vulnerability to aristocratic ambition.[7]

Revolution

Fears of impending tenancy also helped catalyze the American Revolution. In Massachusetts in 1774 the yeomanry worried that the loss of their charter liberties to Britain's Coercive Acts exposed them to uncontrolled domination by corrupt imperial officials and their American allies. The common people believed that such unchecked power would ultimately reduce them to "slavery" as tenants to aggressive "great men" who meant to "reduce the country to lordships." This alarm assumed particular urgency because southern New England's small farmers were profoundly disturbed by their region's economic stagnation and their inability to provide adequate homesteads for their children as a growing population pressed against the local supply of land. In April 1775, at Lexington and Concord, New England's yeomanry struck back at the most visible aspect of their eroding circumstances: the drive by imperial authorities to centralize and tighten their control over the colonies.[8]

The war stimulated settlement of mid-Maine's backcountry. Cut off from external commerce by British warships, the coastal settlers (who had lived primarily by harvesting the forest) had piles of slowly rotting lumber and cordwood instead of desperately needed provisions. Because the coastal soils were ill suited to agriculture and because British raids afflicted the seaside settlements, the war encouraged hundreds of families to move inland, where game was more plentiful, the soil better, and raids unknown. After the war's end in 1783 with the Treaty of Paris, the coastal settlers who led the movement into the backcountry were joined by thousands of newcomers from southern New England, families hard-pressed by the postwar depression, people in search of new lands where they could directly appropriate their own food and fuel. Many were war veterans left penniless by their hard service and the virtually bankrupt state and national governments' inability to pay them. Between 1775 and 1790 Maine's population tripled to almost one hundred thousand. In 1770 there were only eight incorporated towns in mid-Maine; in 1780, twenty-four; and in 1790, thirty-four.[9]

Settlers thought that the backcountry lands were free for the taking. The loyalism of the four principal Waldo heirs, the most conspicuous Kennebeck Proprietors, and a few Pejepscot Proprietors inspired widespread rumors that the Commonwealth of Massachusetts would confiscate their patents to bestow free homesteads on impoverished families. Settlers insisted that loyalists' property ought to be the just reward of those who, in the words of Bristol's William Rogers, "fought under the idea that they were to have the lands they were defending." New settlers encountered little opposition, because the wartime dispersal of many leading proprietors as loyalist refugees paralyzed their land companies for the duration and because the commonwealth's Supreme Judicial Court ceased to meet in war-torn mid-Maine (and so could hear no ejectment or trespass suits). In March 1780 Colonel Jonathan Bagley, one of the Pejepscot Proprietors, toured their claim and reported, "I can Do No more without Help for the people say the Proprietors are all Turnd Torrey and the Proprietors' Claim is Good for Nothing." Despite his loyalism, William Gardiner, the son of a leading Kennebeck Proprietor, persisted in the Eastern Country throughout the war trying in vain to preserve his father's estate from the squatter invasion. When Gardiner complained too much, the settlers had him jailed for loyalism. He lamented, "My crime was too much Estate, and too much Power." He bitterly denounced the settlers as "those who had flown gaols for the most abandoned crimes . . . a sett of wretches that was and are a disgrace to humane nature."[10]

The rumors that the backcountry lands were free for the taking were more firmly rooted in settler hopes than the commonwealth's policy. The historical moment when the mid-Maine backcountry was settled had important and enduring consequences, because the recent Revolution had encouraged many common people to question long-standing sources of authority. Temporarily freed from the constraints of precedent and tradition, men's thoughts were alive to new possibilities. In 1781, Jonathan Sayward of York, Maine, wrote in his diary:

In the present struggle every bodys imagination is exercised, and hath produced new disorders. Distraction is become . . . common, new kinds of sicknesses, new sectaries in religion, various opinions: yes I do not know but there must be new heavens and new earth before all these things shall be finished. I had almost forgot to add we have new pollitions and new polliticks, almost as strange as the other disorders.

He concluded that the common folk were "remarkably unsettled in religious as well as political principles." Similarly, in 1788 the merchant William Frost of York caustically commented on the political contagion among the lower classes, "There is nothing but tumult and noise and free thinkers, prognosticators, lawmakers and the Deavil knows what stiring about now a days, but I hope the time is near at hand when every lowsey fellow shall not be a lawmaker."[11]

In particular, the Revolution encouraged men to call for a more egalitarian distribution of frontier land, as essential to the new Republic's survival. During the late 1770s and early 1780s, some of the more radical whigs sought "agrarian laws" to confiscate large landholdings for redistribution to the landless. A proposed 1779 draft for the Massachusetts state constitution would have required the General Court to confiscate all landholdings in excess of one thousand acres to provide farms for the landless, thereby preserving an egalitarian distribution "in all future generations." The *Boston Gazette* described the defeat of the draft by conservative interests at the state constitutional convention in 1780 as a victory for "those who may aim to bring our country into Lordships." Four years later the Reverend John Murray of Newburyport, the popular evangelical Presbyterian who led New England's largest congregation and who had preached in Boothbay on the Lincoln County coast during the 1770s, found oppression in the land "when *Agrarian Laws* cannot be obtained; or must pass unexecuted—when individuals are permitted to purchase or possess such enormous tracts of land as may gradually work them up to an influence, dangerous to the liberty of the state." In 1786 "Scribble-Scrabble" wrote in the *Cumberland Gazette* that Europe's large private landholdings "produced lords and barons, with their opposites, slaves and dependents. Luxury and poverty have stalked thro their land in every age since, as their constant attendants. . . . Let us come nearer home and view this eastern territory. Do we not discover the seeds of the foregoing evils just beginning to take root, and which, unless checked in season, will in time sprout into existence?"[12]

In mid-Maine, the agrarianism of the 1780s was seconded by the heritage of resistance rooted in the coastal towns established by Colonel Dunbar. Most of the backcountry's new settlers migrated from or through those towns, where they learned to challenge proprietary claims and justify violent resistance. In 1801, after visiting the new settlements upstream from Dunbar's towns, two proprietary agents reported:

> The settlements from Ballstown to Davistown (both inclusive) are chiefly filled up with emigrants from the towns below on Sheepscot and Damascotta Rivers. In general when they went into the woods they were very indigent and very ignorant and in too great a proportion very unprincipled. If that country has been the field of honest industry to some it has also been the "City of Refuge" to many wretches whose poverty and crimes had rendered their longer continuance in places where they were well known inconvenient if not impracticable.

In 1801 Elisha Sylvester, a proprietary informant among the settlers, confirmed the influence of coastal experience and traditions on back-country resistance:

> I have lately travelled through part of the Plymouth claim (so called) and find the notions of the settlers to be—that they are the sole owners of such lands as they have made themselves the possessors of, and that the easterly line of said tract not being run, they have a good right to hold their possessions by the firelock and will kill any person who offers to run a compass thro' their possession. This they say is no Murder! This is the education which they have received from the practice and parental instruction which they received at Boothbay, Edgecumb, and other places near Damariscotta and Sheepscott rivers, not to mention Kennebeck.

The Revolution seemed to have restored and expanded Colonel Dunbar's promise of free land for actual settlers.[13]

The agrarian notions that proliferated in tavern talk and newspaper columns during the Revolution and immediate aftermath became discredited in southern New England during the late 1780s when the region's great men succeeded in suppressing the New England Regulators (or Shaysites) and in ratifying the new Federal Constitution. But the disgruntled yeomen who fled to mid-Maine could cling to their convictions that wilderness lands ought to be freely available to the needy and that the common folk had the right to resist laws they perceived as unjust. Mid-Maine's settlers dubbed several new settlements on proprietary land Freetown, Freedom, Unity, New Canaan, and Liberty Mount to express their hope that they had obtained free land and to identify their new communities with the Revolution. In 1808, Fairfax's settlers remembered, "Many of us were soldiers in our revolutionary war, that we faithfully served our country in its struggles for freedom, that we lost our all in the momentous contest, that we fled to the wilderness as a refuge from poverty and oppression and that by our toils, industry and cares that wilderness now buds and blossoms like the rose."[14]

Consequently, the settlers nurtured the agrarianism of the 1780s, long after it had been driven from political discourse in southern New England. In August 1810, Elliot G. Vaughan visited Bristol to record Colonel William Jones's persistent sympathy for Daniel Shays and his fellow Regulators of 1786–1787:

> The Col. said there was no proprietor [who] owned any land, and that the government was corrupt in allowing any title, and instanced amongst many other things the injustice of the government in confirming and establishing the Waldo Patent; . . . and said that Shays and the party that were with him were the only party that was right in government, and said that no proprietors had any right, for God gave the earth to the sons of men, and that no man had a right to more land than he could improve, and named 200 acres. I then ask'd him what could be done. . . . His answer was that God Almighty had it in his power to settle it in two ways. One was to serve all the proprietors as he did the first Born of Egypt (cut them all off in one Night). The other was to raise up some man like Cyrus who would purge the Land.

Vaughan noted with alarm that the colonel's neighbors, who had gathered to listen, vigorously assented.[15]

Reaction

Contrary to settler hopes, the commonwealth failed to confiscate the Great Proprietors' claims. The war's end in 1783 brought the slow and incomplete confiscation proceedings to a halt. Thereafter three powerful men in the commonwealth's new political order—Major General Henry Knox, Governor James Bowdoin, and Colonel Josiah Little—assumed control of the three great land companies with the grudging consent of their loyalist partners. Taking the legal offensive, the resurgent proprietors successfully parlayed their political connections and savvy into legislative confirmation of their claims, which enabled proprietors to prevail in court suits against settlers who claimed they lived on public lands. Henry Knox privately conceded that, without legislative confirmation, the Waldo Patent "was entirely nugatory as no action of trespass could lye where there was no legal description of boundaries." Indeed, the original patent "was so obscurely worded and written with so little knowledge of the subject that no person could possibly make out the boundaries." By exercising his considerable political talents and contacts, Knox converted his legally dubious patent into a precise tract of land endorsed by the commonwealth. The General Court obliged "in great haste" (the words of one of Knox's supporters) on July 4, 1785, the last day of a session, after the few representatives from settler communities had left for home. In November 1788, the General Court granted the Kennebeck Proprietors a similar confirmation of their patent. The General Court was willing to give the Pejepscot Proprietors a similar confirmation, but the two parties could not agree on whether that patent extended one or twenty miles above head tide on the Androscoggin. In 1793, negotiations stalled, and the General Court instructed the commonwealth's attorney general to commence a lawsuit to test the Pejepscot title. But, because the General Court's Eastern Lands Committee refused to grant to the settlers the commonwealth's title to the land, the settlers were vulnerable to the Pejepscot Proprietors' lawsuits during the twenty years that elapsed before the Supreme Judicial Court resolved the controversy.[16]

The proprietors prevailed in the General Court during the 1780s because they overmatched the limited political influence of the poor and remote settlers who were virtually unrepresented. Many settlers lived in unincorporated settlements ineligible for representation, and most incorporated frontier towns preferred to save the burdensome expense of sending a representative to the General Court. In part, they were inhibited by the belief that only towns that could pay their taxes should vote, and during the 1780s most of mid-Maine's settlements sought tax abatement. In 1788, when the General Court confirmed the Plymouth Patent, only five of the thirty-six mid-Maine communities had any General Court representation. In contrast, mercantile Suffolk and Essex counties (where most of the Great Proprietors dwelled as social and political leaders) counted fifty-nine members serving sixty-three towns in 1788. In February 1795 Waterman Thomas, Waldoborough's representative, bitterly complained:

> Your petitioner is sorry to remind the Honorable Court that his constituents have for ten years past been praying this court for relief, and their petitions have been referred from session to session, and year to year, and can obtain no relief. Consider their situation two hundred miles distant from the seat of Government. . . . and no friend in the General Court. They say that the heirs of Brigadier Waldo can always be heard and attended to on the first day of the Court meeting, or last, can get their request granted without notifying the settlers on this patent, notwithstanding it takes from them their property and priviledges, wherefore your petitioner prays their case be taken up and equal justice done them.[17]

The General Court could have taken the sting out of its failure to confiscate the patents if it had directed all of the Great Proprietors to grant small farms at token prices to those squatters already on the land. The General Court mandated such a policy—known as "quieting"—in eastern Maine, where the legislators feared that disgruntled settlers might decamp for nearby British New Brunswick, which offered free land grants. Quieted settlers paid five to twenty cents per acre, fractions of the two to three dollars per acre sought by their proprietors in the 1780s. Consequently, eastern Maine largely escaped the agrarian unrest that prevailed to the west in mid-Maine. There would have been little, if any, resistance in mid-Maine if the General Court had required the Great Proprietors to quiet the settlers there. But because mid-Maine was much more densely settled than eastern Maine, the Great Proprietors in the former region stood to lose far more land if they quieted their settlers; so they fiercely opposed the idea. Wealthier and more politically formidable than their eastern Maine counterparts, mid-Maine's Great Proprietors could successfully oppose quieting acts in the General Court.[18]

The General Court could also have reduced settler anger if it had used the cheap sale of the remaining public lands to hold down the prices the Great Proprietors could charge. In March 1784 the General Court enacted a democratic sales policy for the public lands to the north and east of mid-Maine. In most public townships buyers could purchase only 150 acres apiece and would not receive deeds unless they settled their lots within a year. Moreover, half the lands in the interior townships would be freely granted in 100-acre lots to actual settlers who would have to settle within a year and clear 16 acres within four. The policy favored actual settlers and discouraged land speculators. It did not last long. Four months later the General Court resolved to sell entire townships and groups of townships at the highest possible price to wealthy speculators. The commonwealth's staggering Revolutionary war debt and the popular discontent over high taxes dictated selling the public lands for an immediate revenue. The Court maximized the short-term public income by selling to the one group that could afford down payments in cash. Ultimate payment would fall on the most powerless: on the marginal yeomen who most needed new lands. The new land policy entrusted profit-seeking middlemen with retailing lots to actual settlers, sparing the General Court the associated bureaucratic difficulties and administrative costs. By adopting a public land sales policy that favored landed oligopoly, the commonwealth enhanced the Great Proprietors' ability to charge premium prices for their lands in mid-Maine.[19]

For their part, mid-Maine's proprietors might have minimized opposition to their postwar resurgence if they had continued and extended the generous prewar policies that they had pursued in a few selected locales before the Revolution. To attract substantial farmers (rather than the poor loggers and scratch farmers who had previously prevailed on the Maine frontier) to new townships, some of the Great Proprietors had spent liberally on community improvements—forts, schools, meeting-houses, gristmills, sawmills, and roads—and had given away half the lots to those applicants who met their standards. After the war, the propri-etors saw no need to apply such policies—intended to attract the right sort of people to unsettled areas—to the new backcountry settlements that were inhabited by poor men the proprietors disliked and that were growing rapidly without assistance. It seemed only just to the Great Proprietors that such presumptuous squatters provide a profitable re-turn on the prewar investments. Consequently, after the war the Great Proprietors demanded the highest prices in the history of their cartels from those settlers least able to pay and most determined to obtain homesteads by right of first possession. The towns that benefited from the liberal prewar policies (mostly prosperous communities along navi-gable rivers) did not participate in the postwar resistance that thrived in the backcountry's new settlements.[20]

The Great Proprietors meant to reap a rich harvest from the Revolu-tionary interlude in their control over the land. During the late 1770s and early 1780s the promise of free land drew settlers to the region in numbers far exceeding those that the proprietors had introduced be-fore the war. It was ironic that an illusion of free land created the settler population from whom the resurgent proprietors meant to profit. Hav-ing invested labor in their lands, settlers were vulnerable to proprietary lawsuits. If ejected, the settler's home, barn, fences, and cleared fields would all pass uncompensated to his proprietor, affording the latter with powerful leverage to demand premium prices for the land. Be-cause wilderness land was virtually worthless without men to improve it, the settlers created the value that the proprietors demanded from them.[21]

Law

The resurgent Great Proprietors pressed their claims in the courts, where they enjoyed every advantage. Because lawsuits over land titles were long, complex, and expensive, wealthy proprietors could often outlast the penurious settlers they prosecuted. Often the threat of long, involved litigation was sufficient to bring settlers to terms. If a suit did come to trial, the proprietors could depend on the justices to support their claims. The proprietors exercised their considerable influence with the governor and council to secure the appointment of sympathetic justices. In February 1799 James Bowdoin III, a Kennebeck Proprietor and the son of the late governor, spoke to Governor Increase Sumner about appointing his land agent, Daniel Cony of Augusta, as one of the three justices of the Court of Common Pleas in the new county of Kennebec, "which he did a few minutes after it took place." The Kennebeck Proprietors secured a second seat on the court's bench for one of their own, Joseph North of Augusta. When John Chandler, the county's sheriff, toured the backcountry in April 1808 to sound out settler complaints, he repeatedly heard that "one Judge sits on the bench who is himself one of the proprietors, and another who is agent for the proprietors, and thus they say they canot obtain justice, but that their destruction appears sure." The Pejepscot Patent's settlers justified their resistance on similar grounds; in 1800 a group of armed mock-Indians violently halted a proprietary surveyor and explained, "Col. Little is a great man, and he will get such men appointed as he Pleases and we poor fellows must suffer unless we now resist and not suffer any lines to be run."[22]

Appeal from the Court of Common Pleas to the Supreme Judicial Court brought the settler no relief, for the high court's justices were all staunch Federalists determined to safeguard the claims of great propertyholders from anticipated anarchy. Isaac Parker and Theophilus Parsons, the lawyers for Henry Knox and Josiah Little, became Supreme Judicial Court justices who used their grand jury charges to denounce the resistance. The proprietors almost always prevailed when they brought a suit to final judgment in the Supreme Judicial Court; between 1798 and 1808 the Kennebeck Proprietors won possession in fifty of the fifty-five ejectment cases they sued to final judgment.[23]

The Great Proprietors felt that only the Supreme Judicial Court's prestige and authority preserved great property's rights in the semi-civilized Eastern Country. One proprietor boasted that the Supreme Judicial Court was "the grand axis on which our social compact turns." In September 1797 General David Cobb, a proprietary land agent, reported that "the great body of the people of this country" possessed no "regard to the rights of private property." He explained that the only reason why jurors ordinarily sustained proprietary lawsuits was "the opinion generally entertained of the great abilities of the judges of the Supreme [Judicial] Court, and the respect and regard, or rather fear, they have for or of the laws of the old government of which they are a part *only*. But remove this restraint, and you will have little justice in the District." He added:

> The principle of levelism is so strong in man that it requires a length of time for him to be habit[ua]ted to the principles of civil order before it can be so far subdued (it can never be eradicated) as to admit of his doing justice to others. . . . The only mode by which

large property in new settling countries can be protected and pre-
serv'd is to have those countries a part of an old organiz'd
government.

In February 1804 Isaac Parker, newly risen to the bench of the Supreme
Judicial Court, wrote to his mentor, Henry Knox:

> As it respects the District of Maine, its morals and habits, its reputa-
> tion, its prosperity how much depends on the dignity, independ-
> ence and correctness of principle in the chief branch of justice! As
> it respects proprietors of land, the subject is equally important.
> What would your land or any land be worth, if this court did not
> spread respect and even awe for itself? It would not be property,
> 'twoud be occupancy which is the only property of a savage country,
> which this would become were it not for the *Sup. Court.*[24]

The importance of the commonwealth's judiciary to the Great Proprietors was especially evident in the Pejepscot Patent. Successive legal continuations delayed a trial of the commonwealth's lawsuit against the
Pejepscot Proprietors until July 1796. During the trial, the proprietors
presented testimony that in the mid-seventeenth century their original
claimant, Thomas Purchase, had dug a cellar and built a house beside
the Twenty-Mile Falls on the Androscoggin River in the town of Lewiston. If so, the Pejepscot Proprietors' claim extended at least that far
upriver. When the jury retired, one member denounced the proprietors' evidence: "What a piece of work they made in giving in their
evidence about the *cellar!* . . . I sware I dug that *cellar* myself about
fourteen years ago when I was there log[g]ing." A second juryman
added: "Yes, I always knew they had no right there. I could bring more
people, to prove they have no right there, than this house would hold.
Those papers were all hatched up within a few years past. I wonder that
any one would give the cause to injure so many people." The jury found
for the commonwealth. But, when called to affirm judgment, one member, David Sewall (a gentleman from the commercial, riverine town of
Hallowell who would become a proprietary land agent), dissented on the
grounds that the two vocal jurymen had prejudiced the case. The justices agreed, declared a mistrial, and scheduled a new trial for July
1797. Again a jury ruled for the commonwealth, but the justices set the
verdict aside, on the grounds that it did not accord with the legal facts as
they saw them.[25]

Rather than hazard a third trial, the commonwealth's attorney general
(James Sullivan) and Josiah Little agreed in July 1798 to submit the
dispute to three court-appointed arbitrators. If the arbitrators ruled in
his favor, Little consented that the governor would appoint three commissioners to set the price each Pejepscot Patent settler should pay for a

one-hundred-acre lot. In February 1800, the arbitrators ruled in favor of the bounds claimed by the Pejepscot Proprietors. The governor then appointed commissioners who set modest prices—one to two dollars per acre—on 405 settlers' lots. Although Little eagerly accepted the arbitrators' decision, he announced that the Pejepscot Proprietors would not honor the commissioners' awards to any settlers living on the company's "divided lands"—those lands already distributed to member proprietors. Little claimed that most settlers within the patent lived on divided lands, but refused to let Sullivan check the company's books to confirm this. Little avoided settler representatives who tried to deliver the awarded sums. Instead, he commenced a new spate of ejectment suits against many of the same settlers. Little also refused to pay his half-share of the commission's costs and declined to deliver to the commonwealth a valid deed renouncing all claim to lands above the Twenty-Mile Falls. He then boldly announced that his failure to deliver that deed voided the original agreement, freeing him to do as he pleased with the settlers within the awarded bounds, *while retaining the Twenty-Mile Falls' boundary awarded by the court-appointed arbitrators.* Sullivan was incredulous: "No lawyer ever yet conceived that where property is awarded on the performance of conditions, that he to whom it is awarded shall refuse to perform the conditions . . . and yet shall hold the property." But in August 1807, the Supreme Judicial Court endorsed the Pejepscot Proprietors' daring action by ruling against a settler who, in his defense, presented his commission award and proof he had tried in vain to pay Josiah Little.[26]

To frustrate the proprietors' legal advantages, settlers revived their resistance during the 1790s. Aggrieved settlers sought to keep the land controversies out of the courts either by disrupting the surveys the proprietors needed to extend their claims over new settlements or by obstructing the visits of deputy sheriffs bearing writs summoning settler defendants to attend a lawsuit. The settlers hoped to forestall proprietary ejectments in the hope that the General Court would reconsider its land policies and extend quieting to the Great Proprietors' patents.[27]

Property

Proprietors and settlers contested for shares in the property white men created on the frontier by laboring to improve the land. The two groups competed to determine who would establish survey lines on the landscape wrested from the Indians, survey lines that subdivided the terrain into townships and private plots. This was a struggle between two different sets of rules defining access to wilderness land—rules (in anthropologist Sally Falk Moore's words) "about what is settled and what may be competed for, about the conditions of competition and access to resources and the like." Contrary to proprietary rhetoric, the settlers were not lawless "banditti" determined to destroy private property. Proprietors and settlers shared a devout commitment to private property but fundamentally disagreed over how it was legitimately made. Each group saw itself defending its property (and so its liberty) from the other's aggression.[28]

The Great Proprietors maintained that real property was *a legal right*, a chain of documentary "title" originating with a deed from the domain's sovereign (English king, colonial legislature, or Indian sachem). Such titles were projected onto the wilderness *in advance of settlement*. Anyone who settled or logged a piece of land, without purchasing the legal proprietor's title, was a "squatter," or "intruder," subject to an ejectment or trespass suit. Successful judgment invested the proprietor with a writ directing the county's deputy sheriffs to evict the squatter or seize sufficient personal property from the trespasser to answer the assessed damages and costs. In effect, title endowed the proprietor with access to the state judiciary's power to coerce. In effect, the settlers who bought a Great Proprietor's title obtained immunity from his ejectment and trespass suits. Therefore, the value of a proprietary title depended on the ability of the courts to make and enforce legal decisions.[29]

Throughout Maine, settlers asserted their right to the virgin timber and defied the Great Proprietors' efforts to confine logging within purchased bounds. In September 1743 Job Averell, a land agent for the Draper heirs, accosted two brothers he found cutting staves, house frames, and cordwood for export to market in Boston. When he asked "whether they had bought the lot they answered no, hang the proprietors. They said they were nothing but rogues that had no right and they would cut where they pleased." Similarly, in January 1767 James Wilson of Topsham justified his logging on the Pejepscot Proprietors' claim by insisting that the wilderness "was common land and hee had as good a rite to cut timber thair as anney man." In 1795 a visiting proprietor complained: "Not a stick of Coard Wood or Lumber will be Left in a few years. . . . And the People begin to think that no one has any Right but them selves." As loggers, the settlers were elusive and, even if caught and successfully sued for damages, usually evaded payment. As a rule, the first settlers stripped and marketed the virgin timber without ever paying the proprietors for it.[30]

In mid-Maine, settlers also insisted on their right to the soil, on holding their homesteads without paying for the Great Proprietors' title. In 1761 several Sheepscot Valley squatters declared that "for them possession was the best title" and that in regard to wilderness land they "had as good a right to have it as any body else." Such settlers maintained that real property was fundamentally *a material asset*—the product of labor applied to improve the previously "common" wilderness: the running of

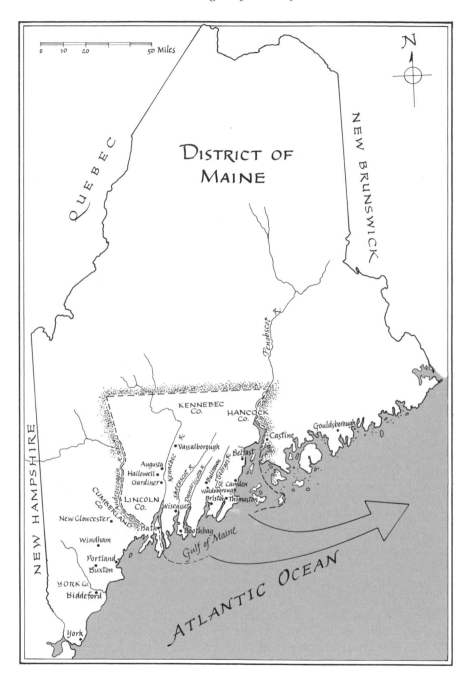

Map 1. Maine in 1800

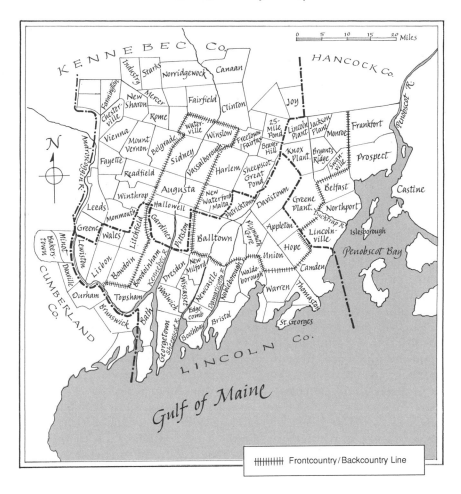

Map 1. Maine in 1800 (Inset)

survey lines through the forest to set off one man's exclusive holding from another's; the fencing, clearing, and cultivation of fields of hay, grain, and pasture; and the erection of barns, dwelling houses, grist-mills, and sawmills. Therefore, the settlers held that title properly began with the man who commenced improving possession.[31]

The settlers were certainly *not* averse to exclusive private property held by legal title. They held no brief against buying and selling land or against accumulating extensive acreage so long as this property began with labor on the land. In their view, early comers and industrious families deserved all the property they could create and manage; late arrivals would have to accept smaller portions or move on in search of their own frontier opportunity. The hard-earned prosperity of older, longer-settled families and the stark poverty of younger newcomers meant that property was not evenly divided in the settlements. Settlers simply disputed how title was legitimately created. They insisted that their mode of creating real property was more equitable because it rewarded actual labor and eased the access of poor families to independence as small producers. Accordingly, they perceived proprietors as corrupt parasites attempting to feed on the property created by laboring families.[32]

To claim private possession of a piece of the wilderness, the settler hastily erected a crude log camp known as a "possession camp" and ran a "possession fence" around the lot by felling small trees and laying them end to end. Thus, in May 1806 in Greene, Deputy Sheriff Nathaniel C. Allen found, "It appeared from the statements of the settlers that what they called pitching lots and getting possessions had been very much practised and that a greater part of the settlements made had passed through one or more sales by a kind of bill of sale or quitclaim deed and delivery of possession, as a kind of traffic, and that several of the settlers had made several pitches each and had sold out their possessions."[33]

The exclusivity of possession claims and the frequent contentions over them testify to the settlers' devotion to private property. But because several settlers usually arrived on a ridgetop simultaneously, because neighbors were desirable, and because cultural expectations of rural equality taught that a man should hold only what his family could improve, most settlers limited their claims to about 50–150 acres per working male. A few aggressive early arrivals fenced in tracts of 1,000 acres or more, but newcomers often felt free to intrude and settle within the larger tracts run in violation of community norms. Migrating from Stonington, Connecticut, in 1769, Shubael Williams was one of Islesborough's first settlers. Having four adolescent sons and first pick of the township's lands, he claimed a tract of 670 acres, no more and no less. He divided the tract into five farms, one for each of his sons and himself. In 1784, when newcomers asked whether he claimed any additional land beyond his possession fence, Shubael Williams "answered, no, he did not for if he could hold what land he had enclosed it was enough for him and his children." To hold that land, Williams led Islesborough's resistance against the Great Proprietors.[34]

Some settlers made a meager living as "possession speculators" by staking claims for sale to newcomers. In September 1803 Samuel E. Dutton, a proprietor's lawyer, investigated settler claims in Newburgh and reported of one lot, "One Moses Walton, a great possession specula-tor (who by the way settled nearly half the lots in this township) had taken it into his head to fell a tree or two at this place by the side of the road until he had made what he called a *possession*." Walton was "a strug-gling fellow that never settled a lot in his life, and at the time he worked on this [lot he] had nearly a dozen more under way." Walton took up the lot in March 1797 by cutting down an acre of trees and running a pos-session fence around its one hundred acres. By year's end he sold the lot to Abel Hardy, who in 1798 raised some corn and potatoes there. He soon sold out to Daniel Livermore, who in June 1803 sold to Samuel Mudgett, who turned around and sold possession to Ezra Beals, the occupant Dutton found on the land.[35]

Few original possessors persisted on a lot to develop its agricultural potential; possession claimers and homestead settlers were usually dis-tinct, successive groups. Most mid-Maine settlers who defied proprietary claims in the 1790s and subsequent decade belonged to the second, more permanent breed of settlers who had already purchased their lands from the more footloose original possessors. In three selected mid-Maine communities active in the resistance—Ducktrap–New Ca-naan, Balltown, and Sheepscot Great Pond settlement—the 1790–1800 decadal persistence by heads of household was remarkably high and uniform: 71 percent, 79 percent, and 78 percent, respectively. As stayers and improvers, the newcomers were especially apt to organize resistance to proprietary demands for additional payment. The newcomers pre-ferred to buy from the possession speculators because they sold their titles for less than a dollar per acre, far less than the Great Proprietors demanded. By resisting, the second-breed settlers hoped to secure first possession, rather than proprietary title, as the legal basis of property in the Eastern Country.[36]

In this preference for cheap, legally suspect titles, mid-Maine's settlers resembled their counterparts in Vermont, eastern New York's border-lands, north-central New Jersey, and northern and western Pennsylva-nia who latched onto dubious Indian, possession, or competing colony titles as a quasi-legal basis for resisting their proprietors or landlords. As the next chapter will argue, the Great Proprietors of mid-Maine re-garded the settlers' competing mode of creating property as a threat to the very foundation of civilized order.[37]

Charles Vaughan. *Courtesy of the Maine Historical Society*

CHAPTER TWO

The Great Proprietors

Mildness ever beamed in his countenance ... and equity and generosity always marked his intercourse with his fellow-men. The poor, he never oppressed; the more obscure citizen, I believe, could never complain of injustice at his hands. With all classes of people, he dealt on the most fair and honorable principles; and would sooner submit to a sacrifice of property himself, than injure or defraud another.—The Reverend Alden Bradford's funeral sermon for Henry Knox, November 2, 1806

In the settlement of the complicated concerns of his property in this part of the country, his munificence and liberality shone with the brightest splendor. His soul was too great for selfishness, too noble for avarice.—Colonel Samuel Thatcher's eulogy for Henry Knox, October 28, 1806

We resolve that there is on this land claimed by K[nox], above seven hundred children, in our judgment, which never had a shoe or stocking to wear from the womb to nine years of age, but their extreme poverty is no defence against an abusive cruel nabob who is continually crying pay me for my land or I will drive you from your bark huts.—Davistown resolves, 1796

ON SEPTEMBER 20, 1758, in Boston the Reverend Thomas Barnard, Congregational pastor of Salem's prestigious First Church, delivered the annual sermon to the Society for Encouraging Industry, and Employing the Poor. For a decade the society had sought to turn a profit, reduce Boston's expenditures for poor relief, and do good (roughly in that order) by putting paupers to work in a linen manufactory. But as Barnard spoke, the society was near dissolution because its product could not compete with the cheaper linen imported from Ireland or produced by northern New England's Scotch-Irish households. The Gentlemen Subscribers blamed their losses and Boston's continued high poor rates on the reluctance of the poor to submit to the factory discipline then so novel in North America. The Gentlemen Subscribers were angry at the apparent ingratitude of the poor who declined to become clients to their would-be patrons.[1]

Barnard addressed his sermon to "Gentlemen of Influence, possessed of important offices in the Commonwealth," for the society's register of subscribers was a roll of the provincial establishment, including some of the preeminent Great Proprietors. The latter were indeed wealthy and powerful men. The Pejepscot Proprietors included two royal governors:

Benning Wentworth of New Hampshire and Thomas Hutchinson of Massachusetts. Brigadier General Samuel Waldo's heirs included Samuel Waldo, Jr., Cumberland County's judge of probate; Francis Waldo, collector of His Majesty's Customs at Falmouth (Portland); and Thomas Flucker, the colonial secretary for the Province of Massachusetts. The Kennebeck Proprietors enrolled Massachusetts' preeminent merchants, including James Bowdoin, William Brattle, Dr. Silvester Gardiner, John Hancock, and Benjamin Hallowell. Thus in 1768 a French visitor found that Kennebeck Proprietors owned fourteen of Boston's twenty-two carriages—symbols that distinguished the province's aristocrats. In 1731 Brigadier General Waldo could travel to London and employ his considerable influence with the imperial bureaucracy to destroy Colonel David Dunbar's scheme for a new royal colony in mid-Maine. When Jonathan Belcher, Massachusetts royal governor, failed to support Waldo's encroachment on the Penobscot Indians' lands, Waldo again sailed to London, where he secured the appointment of his lawyer, William Shirley, to replace Belcher. To no one's surprise, Shirley reversed Belcher's Indian policy. The new governor also promoted the interests of the Kennebeck Proprietors; one of their subsequent lawyers noted, "The claim was in the hands of men of great influence in the government, to whom Shirley, who was then governour, was very attentive."[2]

Barnard felt at home with his genteel audience. He was the son of a slaveowning Congregational minister in Andover, educated at Harvard (socially ranking eighth in 1732's class of twenty-nine), an avowed foe to New Light evangelicals, a member of Salem's genteel literary and philosophical clubs, formerly a lawyer, and recently one of Salem's General Court representatives. He shared his audience's concern over the commonwealth's increasing numbers of the poor; in Salem he was embroiled in a controversy with the town's overseer of the poor, who charged the minister with engrossing two cow leases that belonged to the town poor. And, like many of the proprietors in his audience, in the approaching imperial crisis he would cautiously cling to the loyalist cause.[3]

Barnard's sermon blamed the indiscipline of the poor upon their direct access to natural resources in the Eastern Country. "Too much Land has proved more inconvenient than too little." "Thrô such a Plenty of Land, Numbers are supported by the spontaneous Products of Nature with little Labour." Land "plundered of the Products of Nature, by Men of desperate Fortunes and idle Habits, perpetuates Idleness, Intemperance, Ignorance, a savage Temper and Irreligion; and all the Time their Protection [from Indians] is a dead Weight on Society." Such men forgot the "Submission they owe to civil Rulers, and Gratitude to them for their Care and Protection." Barnard assured the Gentlemen Subscribers that it was their duty "to forward Industry with all our Might, in those who are fit for Labour."[4]

There was something odd about Barnard's sermon. After all, the society employed widows and pauper children, not the laboring families who ventured to the Eastern Country. And at least the poor who lived off nature's bounty did not draw on Boston's taxpayers for relief. But Barnard and his audience feared the opportunity poor folk found on the northeastern frontier to live independently. The Gentlemen Subscribers perceived the frontier as an escape hatch that allowed men and women to evade discipline, morality, and law. So long as that outlet existed, the poor would remain saucy and uncooperative, and the frontier would sustain a squatter anarchy where quasi-Indian whites squandered nature's bounty to live in idle dissipation. By preempting the continent, indolent squatters threatened America's orderly development into a mature commercial society like the mother country.[5]

Barnard implied that independence was too easily available, that it had spread beyond the deserving, thereby imperiling social stability. The solution was to raise the entry costs of becoming a frontier householder; imposing land payments to proprietors would limit frontier freeholds to those with sufficient labor discipline to obtain the needed funds. Until they completed their payments, settlers would serve probationary apprenticeships as clients to proprietary patrons. Only the deserving would eventually obtain their cherished independence. Less disciplined men would remain in, or return to, the older towns under the needed supervision of gentlemen employers. This system would enlarge the labor pool, enabling capitalists to establish profitable manufactories like those emerging in England. Land payments collected by proprietors would create capital for investment in commercial ventures, including manufactories.[6]

The Great Proprietors shared Barnard's desire to stitch social authority into an unbroken web from southern New England's old towns to northern New England's new settlements. Poor and turbulent men could not then escape discipline by fleeing to the wilderness; instead, orderly development would prevail on the frontier. The Kennebeck Proprietors instructed their agents to allow none to settle on their patent "but those that be well recommended for their honesty, sobriety and industry by the selectmen of the town where they live, or the minister of said town."[7]

Barnard's dream of imposing hierarchy and stability on the frontier's turbulent poor survived the Revolution. In the commonwealth, indeed throughout postwar America, virtually all of the preeminent land speculators were Federalist gentlemen committed to centralizing power to promote social order and regularity. Maine's Great Proprietors were well-educated, well-connected gentlemen convinced of their intellectual and moral superiority and of their paternalistic duty to direct the process of settlement. When viewing their claims, commencing lawsuits, and reporting the settlers' "outrages," proprietors carried in their minds a blueprint for an orderly, prosperous, moral, stable, and stratified society where a natural elite guided the improvement of the common folk and the continent. The proprietors feared that, if they failed, squatters would preempt the vast American frontier for an asylum of the turbulent poor lost forever to commercial civilization, a threat rather than an asset to the older centers of trade, culture, and governance. The proprietors regarded land payments as the means to compel improving labor and moral restraint from common folk who would otherwise squander frontier abundance on indolence and alcohol. Proprietary supervision and exactions would school lesser folk in their duties while generating from their labor the capital needed to underwrite America's commercial future. It would vest that capital in the hands of the superior men who would employ it wisely. For this service to society, proprietors deserved to profit from the settlers' labor. Some of the more cautious and deferential settlers shared this perspective. In January 1785 Nathaniel Fales of Thomaston wrote to Henry Knox, "I am greatly rejoyst to hear that your Honer thinkes of coming to live amonst us which I beleve will be much for your entrest and a great blesen to the inhabints as we shall have a head ovr us."[8]

The lives of three leading proprietors—the visionary Charles Vaughan, voluble Henry Knox, and contentious Josiah Little—illuminate how financial interest and ideological commitment reinforced each other among the Federalist Great Proprietors and how the proprietors promoted hierarchical networks of dependence that contradicted the settlers' fundamental drive for economic autonomy.

Charles Vaughan

Charles Vaughan of Hallowell, a Kennebeck Proprietor and the company's principal land agent, belonged to a family of international investors with sufficient wealth accumulated over several generations to disdain mere profit seeking. English Unitarians smitten by the Enlightenment's promise that liberally educated men could rationalize human society, the Vaughans committed themselves to disseminating reason among their fellow men. They wanted to expand their capital while employing it in ways that uplifted humanity. Of course, when moralizing and the family capital came into conflict, the latter quietly took precedence: a Jamaican sugar plantation worked by black slaves was the cornerstone of the Vaughans' mercantile empire.[9]

The family's formidable patriarch, London merchant Samuel Vaughan, closely supervised his sons well into adulthood to ensure their devotion to the family principles. Like so many enlightened gentlemen, he regarded the American frontier with a mixture of fear and excitement: fear that unregulated contact with the wilderness would allow settlers to revert to savagery, excitement at the fresh opportunity, free from the past's burdens, for gentlemen to shape a rational, benevolent, and stable social order. Samuel Vaughan acquired his cherished chance to practice his ideas on American settlers from his wife Sarah, the eldest daughter of Benjamin Hallowell, a wealthy Boston merchant, loyalist, and Kennebeck Proprietor. She inherited a substantial interest in the Plymouth Company's "undivided lands" and valuable divided lands in Hallowell, a promising commercial town on the Kennebec River.[10]

The task of planning the new society on those lands fell to their son Charles. Born in London in 1759, Charles Vaughan grew up on the family plantation and in 1785 migrated to Boston to represent the family firm, commence his own mercantile business, and look after the Kennebec lands. Born to great wealth, Charles Vaughan never learned how to manage money carefully and always took it for granted that he could draw on his father to cover his losses. This negligence provided Samuel Vaughan with the grounds to badger and instruct his son in long letters written from London. In April 1789, he directed Charles to make a suitable marriage alliance and remove to Hallowell. Samuel Vaughan expected a good match "especially as your Family, Connections, Education, Character and expectations will enable you to address the first character and fortune in the State." Samuel Vaughan was extremely pleased with his son's choice, Frances Western Apthorp of Boston, the daughter of John Apthorp, an old friend and another Kennebeck Proprietor. In March 1790 Samuel Vaughan congratulated "both families on the expected Union, as it promiseth every thing that can be expected from the most elevated and useful state of Rational Beings."[11]

Later that year Charles Vaughan and his new bride removed to Hallowell, where they continued to receive Samual Vaughan's demanding letters from distant London. In February 1793 the patriarch rebuked Charles for pursuing business speculation rather than social uplift. Wounded by this charge of betraying the family mission, Charles replied in March that he had lavished money to improve the valley's settlers. To encourage their conversion from immoral lumbering to commercial agriculture, he erected a flour mill. To enlighten the locals, he supervised and subsidized construction of a boy's academy and a Congregational church. To discipline the unenlightened, he helped plan and finance a new courthouse and jail. Charles Vaughan characterized his expenditures as "sacrifices to counteract bad habits and prejudices; building to promote Industry and Oeconomy" and certainly "never in themselves an object of Revenue." This welcome news sent Samuel Vaughan into raptures. In June 1793 he praised his son for "having by your philanthropy, kindnesses and disinterestedness, gained the full confidence of a new tho' rapidly encreasing community and laid a foundation for Improvement of Agriculture, Industry, Morals and the Education of the rising Generation and become an arbitrator to reconcile differences and to render the Community prosperous and happy and I would ask was there any situation upon Earth more Godlike or enviable[?]" Employing the Great Proprietors' favorite analogy, he characterized his son as "the father to an infant but growing community." But Charles never remained in the family's good graces for long. In 1797 he incautiously muttered, "I have no objection to do good, but I desire to profit by it." This may have been the family's de facto credo, but they were shocked to hear it expressed so bluntly.[12]

The family worried needlessly about Charles Vaughan's motives. Although an avid speculator, he also invested in every venture calculated to reform the locals. Had they known, the Vaughans would have taken pride in Judge Daniel Cony's March 1801 ridicule of Charles, brother Dr. Benjamin Vaughan, and brother-in-law John Merrick, all Hallowell residents: "There is not probably a family on the globe more fond of experimenting and of novel revolutionary ideas, of dabbling in almost every kind of business, say Plymouth Company matters, tontine buildings, canals, land speculations, navigation, agricultural societies, India trade, turnpikes, physic, brick machines, bridges, bank stock, Society to Direct Foreigners, aquaducts, etc. etc. etc." To temper the settlers' taste for potent rum, Charles Vaughan constructed a brewery that produced a mild beer from spruce buds. He raised funds for academies, explaining: "The first settlement of a country is chiefly made by needy men of enterprize, with habits of hard labour, without property and without education. The children of this part of the settlers, unless means of public education are furnished, will remain like their parents uninstructed and ignorant and the children of the others cannot but fall off." He helped organize and finance a female academy to train women as schoolteachers, reasoning that because women instructors received half the pay men did, enlarging the supply of female schoolteachers would allow more poor towns to sustain schools for longer periods of time. Determined to reform the settlers' "cultivation which has been hitherto that of necessity and has caused its disrepute," Vaughan took the lead in organizing, incorporating, and financing the Kennebeck Agricultural Society, a gentlemen farmers' club that promoted agricultural improvements. In 1801 he obtained assistance from the Kennebeck Proprietors by insisting that the society would encourage "the more able men, who are now moving into the country, or who have acquired a property by their past residence." As an example to the settlers, Vaughan maintained a model farm, where he experimented in the latest crops, techniques, and livestock breeds described in English agricultural books and journals. To improve the settlers' scrawny cattle, he granted free access to his breed stock. To turn the settlers' tastes from rum to cider (if not spruce beer), he gave away thousands of apple scions.[13]

The Vaughans should have worried more about the money Charles Vaughan squandered on his multiple unprofitable enterprises. The Hallowell flour mill failed because he built it on a small stream without adequate waterpower. Almost no one would buy his spruce beer. A major investment in commercial wharfage, warehouses, and stores at Jones's Eddy on the lower Kennebec went sour because it could not compete with nearby Bath and Wiscasset as a commercial center. In September 1807 he lost his position as the Kennebeck Proprietors' agent, resigning in anger at their subordinating him to the company's lawyers, James Bridge and Reuel Williams. He lost more money on his own frontier townships as taxes, lawyers' fees, and survey costs mounted while the settlers refused to pay and stripped the local timber. Fellow Kennebeck Proprietor Robert Hallowell Gardiner avoided Vaughan's advice because "he was so entirely deficient in all method, his papers were kept in so confused a manner, that he could never find at the proper time what was wanted, and as he had never succeeded in any thing he had undertaken."[14]

Henry Knox

General Henry Knox was a parvenu elevated by a fortunate marriage, his timely involvement in a successful revolution, and his talents for political and business intrigue; yet, to secure his new standing, he longed to impose perfect order and stable hierarchy on the world around him. He sought to bring the Maine frontier into harmony with his rational and hierarchical vision of the cosmos. He prefaced his revealing last will and testament:

> First—I think it proper to express my unshaken opinion of the immortality of my soul or mind; and to dedicate and devote the same to the Supreme Head of the Universe—to that great and tremendous Jehovah who created the universal frame of nature, worlds, and systems in number infinite and who has given intellectual existence to the rational beings of each globe, who are perpetually migrating and ascending in the scale of mind according to certain principles always found on the great basis of morality and virtue—to this awfully sublime Being do I resign my spirit with unlimited confidence of his mercy and protection.

Confident that he had risen to the top of mankind's "scale of mind," Knox thought himself one of God's viceroys responsible for employing his superior abilities to civilize lesser mortals.[15]

Like so many other Federalists who had held Continental army commands, Knox insisted that the officers had proved their unique worthiness to serve as the new Republic's ruling meritocracy. He believed in a Revolution that preserved a governing elite based on demonstrated "morality and virtue" rather than simply on inheritance. Knox had not engaged in the Revolution to promote an egalitarian society without social distinctions. Such a society would have debased what he had achieved. Having risen from modest origins through military service to new wealth and power, he wanted to preserve and enhance the social distinctions traditionally enjoyed by the colonial elite. By striving to maintain the full value of his new status, Knox also meant to prove to himself and to others that he belonged at society's pinnacle, because he understood the importance of a natural aristocracy.[16]

After the war, Knox and his Federalist compatriots feared that the Revolution would escape their control as it invited common people to strive for more money and power. He was the quintessential Federalist gentleman who lived luxuriously and speculated avidly in land and commerce while denouncing the common folk for disrupting society with their "extravagant" consumption and "licentious" aspiration. Self-blinded to their own aggressive pursuit of self-interest, Federalist gentlemen expressed an inner anxiety over their own disruptive behavior by blaming the lower orders for social turmoil. By lashing out against self-interest among the yeomanry, gentlemen bolstered their self-image as conservators of a stable society.[17]

Born in Boston on July 25, 1750, Henry Knox was the son of William Knox, a Scotch-Irish master mariner, and his wife Mary Campbell. His father died when Henry was twelve. Apprenticed to a bookbinder, Henry Knox opened his own stationery and book shop in July 1771. Smitten with military ambition, Knox voraciously read books about military discipline and engineering, and he eagerly served as an officer in Boston's elite militia units drawn from the most respectable tradesmen and merchants. When the Revolutionary war began, Knox was one of the few whig officers with a sound technical knowledge of artillery and military engineering. He parlayed this and his ebullient personality into a lifelong friendship with George Washington and rapid promotion through the Continental ranks, rising to brigadier general within eighteen months and to major general by the war's end. Among the officer corps and war contractors he developed an extensive network of useful friends who enjoyed powerful positions in the post-Revolutionary order. Appointed the United States secretary of war in 1785, Knox held the post, at first under the Confederation and later under George Washington's administration, until 1794. Gregarious, gracious, charming, flamboyant, lavishly generous, and physically imposing at nearly three hundred pounds, Knox was extraordinarily popular with the gentlemen and ladies of Federalist high society in Boston, New York, and Philadelphia. He used his influence and patronage to nurture his friends and garner extensive interests in an array of speculative land companies spread along almost the entire frontier arc from the Scioto and Ohio companies through New York's Saint Lawrence Valley to the Eastern Country.[18]

Knox obtained his interest in the Waldo Patent from his 1771 marriage to Lucy Flucker, the high-spirited daughter of Thomas and Hannah (Waldo) Flucker and the granddaughter of Brigadier General Samuel Waldo. On the eve of the Revolution, Lucy's parents owned three-fifths of the Waldo Patent. Loyalists, the Fluckers fled to England during the war. The commonwealth confiscated their property but, because of General Knox's influence, honored Lucy's claim to one-fifth. Despite their loyalism, the other Waldo heirs escaped confiscation of their two-fifths by quietly remaining in the commonwealth for the war's duration. The Suffolk County judge of probate conveniently appointed Henry Knox's good friend, the Boston merchant Joseph Pierce, as agent to dispose of the confiscated two-fifths. Pierce avoided either satisfying Thomas Flucker's many creditors or selling the estate on the public's behalf.[19]

With the end of the war, Henry Knox turned his attention to securing the Waldo Patent. In 1784, at Knox's signal, Joseph Pierce resigned his agency, and the general secured his own appointment to the vacancy. The estate's chief claimant became the public's agent to administer its confiscation and sale. On July 4, 1785, Knox secured legislative confirmation of the Waldo Patent as a thirty-mile-square tract (576,000 acres) and the islands within three miles of its coast. He later recalled, "Until this was effected there did not appear to be any estate at all." During the late 1780s and early 1790s the General Court's few settler spokesmen repeatedly protested the confirmation and insisted that the General Court should quiet the Waldo Patent's settlers. But Knox's legislative servants knew how to bottle up settler petitions for session after session in dead-end committees run by their friends. Although Knox had secured confirmation of the Waldo Patent, the two-fifths interest confiscated from Thomas Flucker remained the commonwealth's property, temporarily entrusted to the general's safekeeping. As the estate's agent, Knox was bound to satisfy the creditors' claims that threatened to eat up the entire value of the two-fifths share.[20]

To forestall the creditors and ultimately obtain the prize, Knox put a characteristically serpentine plan in motion. On June 17, 1791, at Boston's Bunch of Grapes Tavern, a favorite gathering place for Great Proprietors and other members of Boston's mercantile elite, Joseph Pierce publicly auctioned the commonwealth's two-fifths share to Dr. Oliver Smith, a close friend of Knox's brother William. The general's insistence on money down and the advertisement's gross underestimation of the acreage involved as 65,000–70,000 acres (in fact, two-fifths of the remaining undivided lands represented about 180,000 acres) kept the price down to a mere three thousand dollars. This was an incredible bargain; two years later Knox would pay twenty-five thousand dollars for the remaining two-fifths of the patent's undivided lands. Dr. Smith was a front for Henry Knox. Seventeen days after the sale Pierce reassured the anxious general that the sale had been "well conducted and . . . I believe not more than two in the room had the least idea that it was purchased for you and I assure you not one possible reflection or insinuation has been or can be made, as it respects you in this business." Within six months Smith sold the property for the same three thousand dollars to Henry Knox's frequent intermediary, General Henry Jackson, who ten months later deeded the tract to his close friend, completing the property's carefully arranged transit into Knox's hands. Moreover, the sale obliged the creditors to accept payment from the auction's paltry three thousand dollars in proceeds, less Knox's considerable expenses as agent. In the end the commonwealth netted nothing from its confiscation of Flucker's estate, because Knox's expenses and a small part of the creditors' claims exhausted the entire three thousand dollars. By adding the commonwealth's two-fifths to his wife's one-fifth, Knox reconstructed the three-fifths interest held by Thomas and Hannah Flucker before the Revolution. Determined to rid himself of an increasingly distasteful partnership with the remaining Waldo heirs, Knox bought their two-fifths for twenty-five thousand dollars in October 1793, reuniting the patent for the first time since Brigadier Samuel Waldo's death (except for the portions Waldo's heirs had set off to his partners, the Twenty Associates and the Ten Proprietors, before the war).[21]

Recovering and reuniting the Waldo Patent was not enough to satisfy Knox's virtually unbounded hunger for land. In partnership with New York's William Duer, one of America's most ambitious and unscrupulous land speculators, Knox tried to corner the entire market for public lands in the Eastern Country. To hide their identities, Knox and Duer worked through two intermediaries: General Henry Jackson and Royal Flint. In their June 1791 instructions to their agents, Knox and Duer outlined their purpose: "It is more than probable that four millions of acres well located will cover all considerable tracts of cultivable land, in which case the purchase of half would operate as a monopoly of the whole and enable us to fix the price." Knox employed his considerable political capital to persuade the General Court to waive its one-million-acre limit on land sales. It helped that his close friend and wartime colleague, General David Cobb, was the General Court's speaker of the House. By March 1792, Knox and Duer had purchased nearly three and one-half million acres located in two parcels—one in eastern Maine and the other at the head of the Kennebec—for less than twenty cents per acre. They masked from the General Court their inability to pay for such a vast wilderness empire; after making a relatively small down payment, the speculators planned on future sales to settlers at enhanced, monopolistic prices to meet all subsequent payments to the commonwealth. In this manner, the settlers would finance the land monopoly held over them by Duer and Knox.[22]

But Knox had overreached himself. In March 1792, bankruptcy landed William Duer in debtors' prison. Almost equally insolvent and unable to meet upcoming payments, Knox desperately cast about for a new partner. He found America's wealthiest capitalist, William Bingham of Philadelphia, who bought out Duer and took over all future payments and management of the lands, advancing Knox a loan and promising one-third of the eventual profits. Because Knox never repaid the loan, he gradually faded from the enterprise his political skill had put together, and the domain became known as the Bingham Purchase. But, as proprietor of the Waldo Patent, Knox reaped indirect benefit, as did the other Great Proprietors, from the restricted competition in land sales wrought by the concentration of so much land in a fellow proprietor's hands. David Cobb became Bingham's land agent.[23]

As in his massive purchase of public lands, Knox chronically courted financial disaster with heedless, ambitious investments in multiple, grandiose, ill-conceived, and poorly managed ventures. Driven to accomplish prodigious feats hurriedly, Knox developed an astonishing array of businesses in Thomaston and Warren along the lower Saint Georges River. His barrel works, saw- and gristmills, wharves, coasting and West India vessels, stores, lime quarries and kilns, brickworks, fisheries, gardens, orchards, grain fields, canals, and breeding farms employed dozens of men—many specially imported from Boston—as mechanics, fishermen, shipwrights, sailors, carpenters, masons, millwrights, blacksmiths, coopers, tanners, shoemakers, gardeners, limeburners, brickmakers, and loggers. Dozens more found work supplying Knox's operations with cordwood, staves, and hoop-poles. Overextension in multiple directions meant that no single enterprise was ever adequately capitalized; all suffered when frequent flirtations with bankruptcy compelled drastic contractions in employment that wasted expensive preparations.

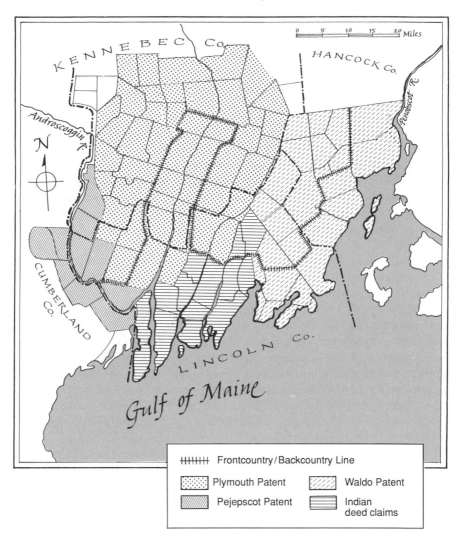

Map 2. Proprietary Claims, circa 1790

The general persisted in his many losing enterprises not only because he daily expected them to yield rich returns but also because they created extensive webs of patronage rendering most of the people in the lower Saint Georges Valley, directly or indirectly, his clients. But Knox's paternalism should not be confused with indulgent generosity, especially in regard to the prices he sought for his title. Other proprietors felt that the general was "too enthusiastic" in assessing his land's value.[24]

Henry and Lucy Knox also obsessively squandered their resources to demonstrate their wealth, power, taste, and enlightened benevolence to the watching world. Robert Hallowell Gardiner, a fellow proprietor, observed that Henry Knox lived "in the style of an English nobleman." In Thomaston the Knoxes designed and had built a palatial mansion they dubbed Montpelier. Neither graceful nor beautiful, Montpelier was, like its owners, massive and powerful in its bulky dimensions. According to Knox's good friend Henry Jackson, at 3,025 square feet per floor, four stories, nineteen rooms, and twenty-four fireplaces, Montpelier "covers more ground, has more rooms in it, and larger rooms, more windows, doors, fireplaces and is a much larger house in every respect than any other private house from Philadelphia to Passamaquoddy." And it was used only as a summer residence. In August 1806 Leverett Saltonstall visited and observed, "It seems to fancy the seat of a prince with an extensive establishment." In an ironic and aristocratic touch, Knox tried to buy deer to stock a game park he planned to establish where wild deer had recently abounded. The imposing mansion sat upon a hill with a commanding view downriver to the sea and inland over Thomaston's small cabins and new clearings. The onlooker could not but walk away awed by the gap between his circumstances and Henry Knox's. On July 4, 1794, the Knoxes roasted a whole ox, erected temporary tables that sat one hundred at a time around the piazzas, and threw open their doors to a gaping throng of curious men, women, and children who, summoned by a public announcement, had gathered outside the grounds at dawn. "The house was so much larger than anything they had before seen, that everything was a subject of wonder. Every object around had all the attraction of novelty," one of the Knoxes' daughters later recalled.[25]

Montpelier's symmetry expressed the general's search for immutable, hierarchical order. Balanced windows braced a central entrance; a double piazza surrounded and elevated the mansion. On each side, west and east, at a slight distance from the mansion, two matching crescents of nine outbuildings—cookhouses, stables, and carriage houses—formed a sweeping semicircle that reached inland. The symmetry of rooms and furnishings within matched the balance displayed without. The front entrance opened into a skylit, oval room pivoting around a crystal chandelier that hung from the ceiling four stories above. To the left a visitor saw a portrait of George Washington, the father of his country, and to the right a portrait of Henry Knox, the father of the people on the Waldo Patent. Beside the portraits stood matching globes, one of the earth, another of the heavens—the entire cosmos caught and depicted in Henry Knox's parlor. Two flying staircases, one on each side, led to the upper rooms. But the mansion mocked Knox's dream of stable superiority; Montpelier was so poorly designed and so expensive to maintain that by his death in 1806 it was already well on its way to ruin. The need to prove his wealth and power so ostentatiously plunged Henry Knox ever deeper into the debt that eventually pulled him down.[26]

Knox delighted in elaborate schemes of hierarchical order. In the spring of 1783 he developed the Society of the Cincinnati, a hereditary organization of Continental army officers that had aristocratic touches; members received elaborate badges and diplomas, and membership passed by primogeniture. The society sought to perpetuate the superior status that the officers felt they had earned; critics smelled a plot to subvert the Republic. In 1786 and again in 1790 Knox proposed a sweeping "Plan for the General Arrangement of the Militia," classifying the entire male population, eighteen to sixty, by age group into three "corps," under the direction of an extensive, professional officer corps. In the most controversial feature, Knox planned to enroll all men eighteen to twenty into an "Advanced Corps" of three-thousand-man "legions" that would convene in "Annual Camps of Discipline" for a month's unpaid service every year. Knox designed the scheme to indoctrinate young men in nationalism and industrious labor as well as provide for the national defense. They would certainly advance on "the scale of mind" beyond the temptations of agrarian rebellion. But because of its elitism and exorbitant expense, the plan died quickly in Congress on both occasions.[27]

Knox's hierarchical schemes expressed his dread that the common folk were prone to anarchy. He doubted whether the new American republic could survive unless firmly ruled by "the good, the rich, and the wise," by gentlemen of self-discipline, wealth, and education. Convinced that the common folk lacked sufficient moral and intellectual discipline to restrain their allegedly innate violence and greed, he dreaded pure democracy. With an enthusiasm rare for a Federalist, he celebrated Napoléon Bonaparte. "What think you of the democracy now? Bonaparte ought to receive the admiration of every body, for bringing this lawless monster to the guilliotine," Knox wrote to David Cobb. Naturally, Knox especially admired Napoléon's grand conscription schemes, because obliging so many "to subserve to his will and power, argues greatness of mind." Betting hats with his Federalist friends on Napoléon's chances in impending battles, Knox rarely lost.[28]

Certain that the common people lusted for their chance to plunder the rich, the general read into them a destabilizing greed that he seems to have feared finding within himself. He did not consider his own acquisitive intrigues with army contracts and land speculations when he wrote with unconscious irony, "The aspirations of the people of America after money are so strong that I tremble to think of the consequences." In 1790 Knox worried that the new American constitution could not endure, because the common folk were so impatient of "the acquisition of wealth by the slow progress of industry. . . . I have been apprehensive that the mass of New England seeing that the operation of government brought no wealth or honor to each individually would become sour and ripe for new extremes." As secretary of war, he helped suppress the New England Regulation (Shays's Rebellion) and instructed army officers to roust the squatters on the Ohio frontier, warning that "the evils of usurpation and intrusion" imperiled federal control of the West. From Knox's perspective, agrarian rebels were not protecting their own property; they were a propertyless rabble bent on usurping his.[29]

The general frequently announced that he, not the agrarian, was the industrious settler's truest friend. "My relation to the settlers as a father and guardian and my reputation ought to be the security in the mind of every settler that my intention is to be their close friend and protector and they are to be assured that all my conduct shall conform to this idea and it will be a duty they owe to themselves to suspect the man to be their enemy who shall make a contrary suggestion," Knox wrote in 1801. He insisted that the people could secure their property and well-being only by purchasing his title. In 1786 he assured Thomaston's settlers that he supported their patriarchal ambitions: "When every man shall be convinced that he holds his land by the best right and title according to the laws of his land on which he may have bestowed much labor . . . he will be animated by hope to an industrious cultivation of the soil and none shall make him afraid. His children like his plants shall grow up around him a comfort and blessing to his old age." Knox liked to boast that he never brought lawsuits against his settlers, that men accepted his terms simply because they recognized how just and reasonable they were. In August 1800 he informed the commonwealth's governor, "I have in no instance attempted to turn off a settler nor have I yet brought a suit against an individual, deeming it most preferable to give the usurpers full time to inform themselves of the conduct that would best secure their true and permanent interests."[30]

Knox cherished his self-image as the benevolent proprietary father, but he confronted many settlers who declined to play their appointed roles as grateful clients. To harry selected squatters from the land without sullying his paternal identity, Knox enlisted the services of an unscrupulous alter ego: Dr. Ezekiel Goddard Dodge. Knox preserved his image by subcontracting to Dodge the overt aggression inappropriate to a true gentleman. A Congregational minister's son cast out of Harvard for disciplinary reasons, Dodge migrated to Thomaston in 1789 to make his fortune as a doctor, petty land speculator, and investor in commercial shipping. Sharp-witted, opportunistic, and ambitious, Dodge did not let any paternalistic notions complicate his relentless pursuit of individual advantage. At bargain prices, Knox sold Dodge title to lots possessed by recalcitrant squatters. Dodge then applied his considerable talents at intimidation to oust the occupants; he hired men to topple fences, seize cabins, and forcibly mow the targeted settlers' hayfields; he engaged lawyers to conduct protracted litigation that exhausted the targets' finances. The arrangement allowed Knox to highlight the disasters befalling those who failed to buy his title, and it enabled Dodge to acquire valuable land at reduced rates.[31]

Convinced he was the champion of social stability, Knox was blind to the irony in his employing Dodge's disruptive, confrontational talents. Knox worked himself into magnificent piques of righteous indignation whenever he thought a settler was about to cheat him of a piece of land, once writing, "Having been much conversant with the animal man I am not much surprised at frequently finding him attempting to benefit himself at the expense of others and exercising dirty little tricks for that end." One of Dodge's victims, Frederick Reed of Thomaston, saw what Knox could not: the contradiction with the general's paternalistic solicitude for settler well-being. Confronting a lawsuit he could ill afford, Reed begged Knox to call off "that informors bosting cruill monster of a Ezekill G. Dodge hows hart is harder then flint ston how wold if he cold drive all gods creation down the steep plase into the sea." Reed reminded Knox of his stock paternalistic speech eloquently expressing his desire for the settlers to "be at peas . . . under our own vine and fig tree and have non to make us afrad." Reed insisted that this should have meant "no Dodges to torment us nor our hairs [sic]." But Reed complained in vain and in 1802 lost two-thirds of his land to Dodge's lawsuit.[32]

Claiming a superior capacity to bring order, security, and prosperity to lesser men, Knox obtained none of these in his chaotic and often tragic personal life. The gross mismanagement that reduced the general's vast resources to bankruptcy made a mockery of his claims that the settlement process could not produce civilization without his supervision. Death at birth or in infancy claimed an appalling ten of the

Knoxes' thirteen children, repeatedly putting a morbid pall on their customary gaiety. It may also have fueled their excessive consumption. In his penchant for drink, scandal, and extravagance, Henry Jackson Knox—their only son to survive to adulthood—severely disappointed his distressed parents. Henry Knox vowed to "civilize" the settlers on his lands, but he could not inculcate virtue in his own son. The general's greatest single humiliation occurred in 1801 when the Senate refused to promote his son from midshipman in the United States Navy on account of his drunken excesses. Knox wrote a pathetically candid letter to President Jefferson, hardly an intimate: "I have lost ten children and I have been embarrass'd in my pecuniary affairs, all these, however, have not affected me so keenly as this recent disgrace."[33]

What impelled Henry Knox's manic empire building, conspicuous consumption, dreams of immutable hierarchy, and dread of tumultuous striving among the common folk? He struggled relentlessly to prove to himself, to his wife, and to the other Waldo heirs that Lucy had married a natural aristocrat, the one man capable of carrying on where Brigadier General Samuel Waldo had left off. Knox built Montpelier atop the ruins of the old fort that had begun Waldo's development of the patent; within the mansion he symbolically hung a full-length portrait of the brigadier. Knox could never forget that the aristocratic Fluckers had resolutely opposed their daughter's marriage to a social inferior, to a man who worked with his hands as a bookbinder. Lucy Knox once took their young son Henry Jackson Knox on a visit to a fellow member of Boston's elite. When the child "disarrange[d]" the hostess's books, Lucy explained, "Henry must not be restrained; we never think of thwarting *him* in anything." When the hostess retorted, "But I cannot have my books spoiled, as my husband is not a bookbinder," Lucy stormed out of the house. No doubt she expected her husband to spare her such humiliation by conspicuously displaying his wealth, power, and considerable social graces. Henry Knox knew that the other Waldo heirs—loyalists who had been obliged to sell their interest to the general—thought him an upstart usurper of their property and privileges. Knox's language is revealing; other proprietors maligned the settlers as "yahoos," "timber pirates," "land-thieves," and "squatters," but only Henry Knox called them "usurpers."[34]

Josiah Little

Colonel Josiah Little inherited his controlling interest in the Pejepscot Proprietors from his father, Colonel Moses Little of Newbury, an avid land speculator who also held shares in several Vermont and New

Hampshire townships. A devoted Congregationalist and commander of the local militia regiment, Moses Little was a power in Newbury, a conservative, long-settled, farming community in Massachusetts' Essex County. In 1781 he lost his speech to a crippling stroke, which settlers interpreted as the just desserts of his aggressive ambition. Adam Cotton of Bakerstown said, "The riteous judgement of God had overtaken him by striking him with the num palsy in the midel of his grasping after that which was none of his own." But Josiah Little took command of the family's land claims and proved even more iron-willed and hard-driving than his formidable father. Josiah Little also invested in commercial real estate and shipping, dominated Newbury town government, and, as a zealous Federalist, represented his community in the General Court for twenty-five years.[35]

Any opposition only inflamed Josiah Little's stubborn determination to press on without compromise. When he decided that Lewiston's Androscoggin rapids were an obstacle to navigation, he personally supervised their blasting and lost a hand to a premature explosion. Relentless and meticulous, Little refused to give in to age or infirmity, driving himself forward on annual tours of his far-flung land claims past his eightieth birthday. Oblivious to threats, he routinely visited every settlement at will to harangue the settlers about paying, to note newly settled lots, to seek out timber trespassers, and to take depositions for use in court cases. He regularly returned to the cellar hole allegedly dug in the seventeenth century by Thomas Purchase, whose Indian deeds sustained the Pejepscot claim. For Little this was part quasi-religious pilgrimage and part legal search for stray nails and rusty tools meant to prove that the cabin site was more than a century old. Pausing only on Sundays, he religiously kept the Sabbath and attended the nearest Congregational church. His entry for September 23, 1800, the day after Lewiston settlers violently attacked his lodging, demonstrates his undeviating attention to business: "The windows was all Broken in with stones, guns fired, my bed shot into and set on fire, myself wounded with stones. In the morning I set up an advertisement at William Garcelon's store. . . . My expenses were $5.00."[36]

Two letters written twenty-nine years apart about a black man named Cambridge, who had been Moses Little's slave, tell much about Josiah Little. During the war Cambridge concluded that the Revolution ought to save blacks as well as whites from slavery. The Littles disagreed. In February 1778 Josiah Little informed his father: "Cambridge Refuses to be Governed by me and would not do as he was bid. . . . I threatned to Lick him and then he Dared Me to Strick him which I Did and no sooner than I struck he Come at Me and hove me Down but Did [not] hurt me and now is Run away and carried of[f] all his close. Where he is

I know not but hope to find him. . . . Send word what is Best to Do about the Black whelp." Set free by the 1783 Supreme Judicial Court decision liberating slaves in Massachusetts, Cambridge moved to Dracut, where in March 1807 a racist crowd demolished his house. Josiah Little promptly hired a lawyer to investigate, explaining, "He is a poor black man and justice ought to be done." Convinced of his utter rectitude and superior judgment, Little refused to brook any insubordination from men he saw as his ignorant inferiors, white squatters as well as black slaves. But when those men approached him with the proper deference, Little felt duty-bound to assist them. He concurred with Knox and Vaughan that society properly had hierarchical gradations, where superiors had added responsibilities to guide their lessers as well as the perquisite of reaping some of their labor.[37]

Civilization versus Nature

The Great Proprietors regarded civilization as a hard-earned, easily lost triumph over man's natural savagery. They saw the frontier as the front line in a chronic struggle to preserve fragile order from collapsing into brutal anarchy. In August 1802 the proprietary lawyer William Minot returned from a visit to Penobscot Bay and spoke of "the wild regions of Maine where nature contends with civilization." The proprietors insisted that only their direction of settlement could secure society's orderly development on the frontier. James Bowdoin III of the Kennebeck Proprietors bestowed one thousand acres of land possessed by squatters on newly incorporated Bowdoin College in Brunswick. The settlers' land payments would help liberally educate the sons of the region's leading men. James Bowdoin thought the new college would "determine the fate of a country; whether it shall be virtuous, prosperous and happy; or vicious, unfortunate and wretched. The Godly work cannot be too soon set on foot." Fresh from a frustrating tour of his family's squatter-occupied claim along the Penobscot River, wealthy young Leverett Saltonstall attended Bowdoin College's commencement in 1806. He found the "genteel and respectable company of gentlemen and ladies" a welcome respite from his stubborn settlers. "Several of the graduates were sons of men of property and large and respectable connexions," he noted with approval. "The College is very respectable in its infancy and I hope it will grow in advantages and become a very important seminary. All their efforts are necessary to civilize the country about them."[38]

Gentlemen insisted that they needed to control settlement because, when left to their own devices, the poor could not resist quasi-Indian lives of wasteful indolence wherever minimal work assured their subsistence. As Henry Knox's guest, Talleyrand visited Maine in 1794 and wrote: "We must admit that what pleased us least in the province of *Maine* is the moral disposition of the inhabitants. Indolent and grasping, poor but without needs, they still resemble too much the natives of the country whom they have replaced." William Morris, a proprietor's land scout, toured the Kennebec Valley and reported that "among these people the habits of contrivance and expedient supply the place of regular industry; this produces intemperance and restlessness among the lower class of people, and a desire to gain much by little labor." After traversing the Kennebec Valley, Edward Augustus Kendall concurred. "Where the fishery or the chase is present to the poor, the poor cannot be induced to submit themselves to daily labour." He explained: "All that distinguishes commercial society springs out of the habit of daily labour. It is regular and daily labour that alters the face of human affairs; but regular and daily labour was never submitted to, at the first, but from necessity: it is maintained (as is evident from the history of all the labouring classes of society) only with extreme difficulty, and by the aid of necessity; and it is abandoned as soon as necessity withdraws her stern and tyrannous control." When poor men escaped the discipline of labor, society lapsed "into an abject and vicious state, the wreck and ruin of the commercial state."[39]

According to genteel observers, innate indolence abetted by natural abundance left most settlers satisfied with basic subsistence. Talleyrand reported, "The adventurous spirit which led them to seek a living far from home gave them for two or three years the activity necessary to make a small clearing, but when they had cleared seven or eight acres destined for the cultivation of potatoes and corn, and when they had cleared some places to pasture their livestock, then the first needs appeared to them to be almost satisfied, slackness appeared, and they did nothing more to push back the wilds which surrounded them." Robert Hallowell Gardiner, a Kennebeck Proprietor, agreed: "If the surplus would supply them with other necessaries, pay their taxes, and keep their buildings in repair, they were satisfied without inquiring whether the product of their labour should not have been much greater." The duc de La Rochefoucault Liancourt, another of Henry Knox's guests, contemptuously described a Waldo Patent settler who put subsistence first: "He is content with his lot, and is full of the ordinary prejudices of all the old, ignorant husbandmen of the district of Maine."[40]

Inexplicably convinced that their eastern Maine tract was unusually fertile and promising, William Bingham, his partner Alexander Baring, and their agent General David Cobb blamed the region's laggard development on the vicious inhabitants who disfigured its landscape and perverted its economy with their malignant behavior. Bingham complained,

"Whilst from their idleness and dissipation, they present such an appearance of wretchedness, such misery is attributed to the poverty of the country and not to its true cause." Baring added that the Eastern Country's low land values resulted from the "opinions of the people in the country" who formed their ideas "insensibly from habits, and a dull round of experience and custom. . . . They have been accustom'd to consider waste lands worth nothing because they have always been neglected and plunder'd, but when we commence agricultural improvements it is to us to tell them what land in that state is worth and not to learn it from them." Formerly an officer who helped suppress the New England Regulators, Cobb agreed: "Every inhabitant here is now a depridator—a trespasser—plunderer. They live by it, and therefore they will not cultivate the finest soil in the world. Their not doing this, is the chief cause why the reputation of the country has been damn'd in the opinion of those cursory observers who have seen it." He explained: "If a people who live by lumbering, are indulged in cutting the forrests wherever they please, they will have but little more estimation of the value of the soil than the savage who hunts them for his living. . . . Prevent depredation and you may raise the prices of land to what you please."[41]

Discipline versus Cunning

Noting the duality of the settlers' economic life—their simultaneous, reinforcing pursuit of long-term homestead security *and* short-term market gain—proprietors and travelers found the settlers' economic cunning just as distasteful and dangerous as their presumed sloth. Genteel complaints depicted the settlers as indolent *and* grasping, undisciplined *and* devious. Gentlemen considered the settlers' aggressive haggling and shrewd bargains as elemental to their flawed characters, along with their wasteful ease. Proprietors nurtured a stereotype of the proper settler as dutifully attending only to improving his farm, forsaking all temptation to speculate. By this standard many settlers appeared presumptuous upstarts behaving with a speculative cunning inappropriate to their humble means and status, proof that a little commercial knowledge was a dangerous thing in poor men without a restraining sense of their proper subordination. Their betters needed to teach them, not simply to have commercial aspirations, but to pursue them *in a manner appropriate to their class*, to yoke their desires to a patient, disciplined labor.[42]

Proprietors wanted only that sort of ambition that would keep their settlers at work improving their farms, raising land values. Nothing so exercised a Great Proprietor's fury as competition from lowly possession speculators horning in on the middleman's profits that justly belonged exclusively to gentlemen. Alexander Baring instructed his land agents: "A tract of land laid out for a farm should not exceed 160 acres. It is as much as any settler can want, unless to speculate on, which among this class of people I woud check as much as possible." For speculation distracted the settlers' "attention from agricultural improvement." Similarly, Baring reserved mill seats for sale only "to some steady character whom we can depend on and who wou'd probably become a leading man in the little community which woud form around it." Only men who *appeared* "very respectable" could be allowed larger land purchases or mill seats. The Kennebeck Proprietors claimed three million acres but tried to restrict the acreage they sold to individual settlers because "few farmers can conveniently manage more than one hundred acres."[43]

Henry Knox also wanted settlers with enough commercial drive to turn the wilderness into profitable farms, but not so much that they would speculatively preempt some of *his* profits from rising land values. His role was to supervise the settlement and distribution of the Waldo Patent; they were supposed to keep at work improving their farms. Unfortunately for Knox's plans, many settlers proved far cannier in the ways of the market than the general had banked on. Knox's land agents issued "signing-rights" and "permits" allowing the recipient one hundred to two hundred acres to be "pitched" by the settler within a specified settlement, then run out by one of the general's surveyors, and eventually paid for at a stipulated price per acre (usually one to three dollars). At the same time that the settlers resisted paying Knox, they carefully saved, or shrewdly bought and sold, his signing rights and permits. Because the documents required no down payment, many settlers concluded they had nothing to lose in taking out permits and signing rights as an insurance against rising prices in the event that Knox's claim prevailed. This attempt to have it both ways infuriated the general, who felt that the settlers publicly assailed his honor as a gentleman while privately depending on it to maintain the value and validity of their signing rights and permits, should their resistance fail.[44]

The settlers' "multiplied instances of deception" with permits and signing rights kept Knox and his agents in a confused, frustrated lather. About 1797, at Knox's direction, George Ulmer investigated the disposition of the signing rights and permits issued during the previous decade for land in his vicinity. Only forty of one hundred still belonged to the original grantees or, if deceased, to their heirs. Knox and his agents complained bitterly that, by turning the documents into a medium of exchange, the settlers perverted their purpose to encourage improving settlement. Some procured signing rights and permits that stipulated a relatively low price, because presumed to apply to a settlement with inferior soil or poor access, but applied them to claim a lot in a better settlement. Other settlers sold their signing rights or permits to newcomers, then squatted anew on Knox's backlands. Knox cluttered his "Land Record Book" with memos like this about James Perkins, Jr., of Northport: "It appears on the whole that this young man has been playing a double game and selling lands under my permit which was never in his [improving] possession."[45]

One transaction particularly galled the general. A black man named Richard Ryatt obtained a permit, but, without improving any land, sold the document for twenty dollars to Prospect's Deacon Zenas Lothrop, "who," in Knox's jaundiced words, "is famous for buying everything he can without money," exactly the sort of settler that infuriated the general. To add a further edge to Knox's resentment, he had employed the deacon as a caretaker for his Brigadier Island (now Sears' Island) farm until John Rynier, one of the general's agents, "found him out, not only to be dishonest in his work, but [an] instigator and concerned with the others, in getting into the cellar and stealing rum, with the connivance of Mrs. Lothrop, by means of taking out a board in her bed room in the night." Rynier insisted that the deacon stop stealing Knox's rum and sign a written pledge that he would no longer "allow any crews of vessels to bring their liquor into the house, or make frolics"; the deacon took offense, "saying he would not be tied down by any man," and quit. Confronted with Ryatt's transfer to Lothrop, Knox proclaimed the permit invalid and issued a statement "in order that my justice may also appear conspicuous": "The permits were intended solely for actual settlers and no others. Not for speculation. The consideration, besides the small sum specified, was the industry and labor bestowed on the land by a regular settler. . . . There is neither political, moral, equitable nor legal principle to oblige me to give validity to a piece of paper which has no value attached to it. No money was ever paid or offered."[46]

The Prescription

Proprietors and their supporters hoped to reclaim the settlers from nature for civilization by inculcating a more complex, hierarchical economy directed by men with capital. According to the proprietors and their guests, the settlers' avid pursuit of economic independence rather than commercial agriculture obstructed maximum exploitation of the frontier's resources. The settlers needed to accept their properly specialized and subordinate role. Having read Adam Smith, the proprietors and their traveler guests knew that the division of labor together with the market's "invisible hand" multiplied productivity, knew that commercial transactions improved the participants' intellectual awareness and moral steadiness. Talleyrand concluded:

> The interest of the state is evident, it must make farmers of the greatest part of these men who are today farmers, fishermen, and lumbermen, or rather who are neither the one nor the other. The division of labor must be established among them. Then the land will produce more fruits and the sea will favor fishing as much; for men who are really fishermen by condition and not from laziness will go to seek their fishing farther, if necessary, on better stocked fishing banks; they will endure more fatigue, they will undertake longer absences, but they will employ fruitfully for themselves and more usefully for their country the days which today are consumed almost uselessly in inadequate fisheries. It will be the same with wood, more work will be done by fewer men and in less time. The rest of the efforts and of the days will be given to the land to which it belongs rightfully. . . .
>
> In a word the province of *Maine* is not agricultural enough and work is not divided enough there.

Talleyrand insisted, "This marvelous and demonstrated effect of the division of labor cannot be accomplished without an increase in capital."[47]

Genteel commentators believed that obliging settlers to purchase proprietary titles would redeem them from indolence and cunning and thereby rescue the Eastern Country from barbarism. Because the settlers were not working as diligently and efficiently as possible, land payments would not burden anyone willing to mend his ways. Compelled by the pinch of new land payments to obtain increased returns for their labor, settlers would forsake their lethargy and petty speculating and devote themselves to commercial agriculture's hard work. Introduced to commercial civilization's moral and social benefits, settlers would learn to honor their contracts, respect the wealthy, appreciate schools, support regular preaching, avoid excessive drinking, and disdain violence. Anyone who refused to adapt to the new order would lose his land and have to move on. Some of the new fruits of this more intensive and efficient labor would flow as land payments into the hands of gentlemen who could be trusted to employ the money as capital for reinvestment. In this view, the Great Proprietors were economic trustees, who would oblige their settler charges to adopt behavior essential to their own well-being as well as to that of the nation.[48]

The Great Proprietors practiced what they preached. Confronted by formidable resistance to his claim over Greene Plantation, Benjamin Joy of Boston proposed affording the settlers "constant employ at all times both winter and summer," constructing roads and harvesting timber for him to pay for their lands. In August 1810 David Sewall of Hallowell, Joy's land agent, presented the proposal to the settlers, observing that "as he was about to give them extensive business, he was sure that commerce would civilize them." But the settlers wanted no part of Joy's plan to "civilize" them. As their regular trips to Belfast's market with shingles and clapboards attested, they were not averse to commerce; they simply preferred to work for themselves and retain the proceeds to improve their homesteads, rather than part with their labor further to enrich Benjamin Joy. So they mobbed David Sewall.[49]

To transform eastern Maine's settlers into orderly, profitable, commercial farmers who would pay for their land and confine their logging to what they had bought, David Cobb pursued a dual policy. First, by precept and example he strove to convince the settlers of William Bingham's dictum "that the pursuits of agriculture are much more productive, as well as more respectable." Cobb repeatedly traversed the region "preaching the principles of civilization to the people" and "explaining the rights of property to them." Falling prey to his own vociferous enthusiasm, he prematurely reported in December 1796, "In a short time the present passion for plunder will cease and agricultural industry succeed." He supplemented his sermons with a model farm established at Gouldsborough "solely, for the purpose of distroying the prejudices of our poor ignorants" by "teaching the Yahoos here, these log stealing scoundrels, how to get their living by cultivating the soil." The wheat-damaging "blast" and local oxen who balked at plowing complicated Cobb's educational efforts, probably to the delight of his skeptical neighbors. The ill-conceived, poorly run farm ran at an annual deficit of six hundred dollars.[50]

Second, Cobb demanded that the settlers either cease logging on Bingham's land or pay one-eighth of the planks, boards, shingles, spars, staves, and clapboards produced from the logs cut on his tract. But the persistent and elusive loggers repeatedly frustrated Cobb's efforts. Feeling alone in a hostile and barbaric land, and never one to mince words, he denounced the settlers as "the worst of boors" and observed, "You have, with a smooth face and fair words, to bare the vilest insults from the most vicious scoundrels that ever disgraced civil society." Fed up, in April 1799 he declared: "Prosecutions must be commenced against these depridators or this country will be unfit for any civilized character to live in. I have persued every mild measure for three years past to no effect. We must now draw the sword of the law and we are determined to thro' away the scabbord." But trespass prosecutions availed little against poor settlers who could "swear out" of jail by taking an oath that they possessed insufficient property to satisfy the legal judgment.[51]

Unable to transform the settlers, Bingham, Baring, and Cobb tried to recruit an entirely new set: farmers from southern New England who could be planted in their tract's unsettled interior "removed from the vicious habits and bad example of the lumbermen." Cobb believed that interior settlement along roads would prevent prized newcomers from degenerating into "lumber men, and thence be a curse to the country and themselves." Expressing the Great Proprietors' conviction that the lower orders lacked the self-discipline to resist the wilderness's siren song, Cobb wrote, "The farmer who setts down on a river in this country turns as naturally to a log stealer as the civiliz'd man does to a savage, and a thousand such settlers will give us no more value to the soil than so many Indians residing upon it, but he who settles upon a road and cannot with ease convey his lumber to markett, will cultivate the soil and give substantial value to the country he resides in." Cobb hired and supervised work crews to construct an extensive network of roads into and through the tract and to build mills, houses, and inns as "hothouse settlements" intended to attract the sort of prosperous newcomers who would not endure the first settlers' stark hardships in confronting the wilderness. Alas, despite Bingham's and Baring's investments and contrary to their illusions, eastern Maine was so cold, infertile, and remote that, unlike mid-Maine, the region attracted very few agricultural settlers and remained sparsely settled by loggers and fishermen.[52]

As secretary of war, Henry Knox argued in 1789 that the key to civilizing the Indians was encouraging "a love for exclusive property." This was also his plan to civilize the Waldo Patent's presumably quasi-Indian settlers. By steadily and conspicuously increasing his land prices, Knox consciously promoted speculative thinking among the settlers. He believed that the proper sort of commercial aspiration, in addition to being good for the settlers, would break down their resistance as they recognized a common interest with their proprietor in enhancing the local price of land that subsequent purchasers would pay. But Knox ran up against many settlers' preference for low land prices because they wanted their children to obtain nearby vacant lands cheaply. Because, the general noted, "many people on the patent viewing the subject on a contracted scale are far, very far from considering our interests as the same," he set out "to convince them of their error." He instructed Thomas Vose, his agent in Thomaston: "On all occasions impress on the people our full conviction that by promoting their interests we shall promote our own. That by making their lands rise in value we shall enhance the price of our own. In short, that our interests are inseparable."[53]

Determined to drive out those settlers who were unfit for commercial redemption, Knox tried to winnow the upright from the licentious. He swore (in vain) to sell land only to "moral, industrious young men and who shall be able to obtain certificates of character as such from the selectmen and minister of the town to which they belong." Attentive to the rumors about past crimes that pursued some settlers to the frontier, Knox wrote of Greene Plantation's John Drew, a suspected forger, "This fellow has been a pest to society in New Hampshire and must be driven out of the country." Of course, the settlers Knox disliked so much were in no hurry to buy his title.[54]

He particularly disliked the very poorest settlers, who recurrently squatted, logged, and sold their possession rights to newcomers. Knox directed his land agents to sell no land to "those unprofitable people who are stripping the land of its lumber and then quitting it, first having deceived some new comer with a deed of no validity and for what the plunderer may have obtained a valuable consideration." In 1786 the general assured Thomaston's more propertied men that their interests lay with the proprietors rather than with their poorer neighbors:

> You have in the course of your experience seen many men take up lands merely for the sake of stripping it of its lumber, and then for a small pittance selling their possessions, and remove to act the same scene over at another place. You have seen these men and their families struggling with wretchedness and want, and their children springing up without education, torments to their old age. But we rejoice that the people of Thomaston are of a different character, that we have found them moral and upright, and their possessions in general flourishing under the vigor of their industry, and we are anxious that nothing may arise to retard or frustrate their laudable pursuits.

More bluntly, Knox told Northport's selectmen in 1796 that he was the best friend of "the industrious and moral part of the settlers. The idle and wicked can not benefit any new country, and the sooner they depart the better for the settlement."[55]

Order versus Anarchy

Regarding themselves as civilization's champions against barbarism's temptations, the Great Proprietors concluded that the settlers' resistance threatened to destroy social order. Savage anarchy loomed if settlers could steal land with impunity and the government's collusion. Knox's land advertisements wooed "respectable *Emigrants*" by insisting that he governed the land "on principles promising them great prosperity and the establishment of harmony and *good order* throughout that fertile region." By imposing prior surveys and land payments he promoted "orderly settlement," precluding the "unauthorized intrusions" of squatters that were "entirely subversive of the blessings of the social compact." He urged "every regular settler . . . to discountenance and discover lawless persons—It would be deemed madness among *farmers* to suffer a wolf to enter among their sheep, much more so would it be for regular settlers having legally engaged valuable consideration for their lands to suffer an audacious usurper to enter and remain among them, SCATTERING THE SEEDS OF DISCORD, MISERY, AND INSURRECTION WITH BOTH HANDS." In a pamphlet assailing the settlers' resistance, John Merrick— Charles Vaughan's brother-in-law and a proprietary land agent in his own right—criticized their insistence that the common folk could extralegally judge and locally nullify laws they regarded as inequitable. He argued that this doctrine "would carry us back to a state of nature where the will of the strongest is the sovereign law." Anarchy would give way to tyranny as violence led "to civil war, and from civil war to civil and military confusion, and its universal follower *despotism*." In this view, far from defending liberty, the insurgents were its greatest enemy, imperiling the republican government that could survive only if men rigorously honored the laws made by their legislators.[56]

According to the Great Proprietors and their supporters, resisting the commonwealth's property laws was futile as well as evil; immutable, divinely ordained laws governed society as well as nature, producing the existing distribution of wealth and authority. In January 1808 Deputy Sheriff Pitt Dillingham visited backcountry Fairfax (Albion) to exhort the settlers that their hopes of forcible redress were illusory. Addressing a crowd of armed and disguised White Indians, Dillingham counseled resignation to their hardships and to the insistent demands of their merchant-creditors and Great Proprietors:

> That so long as there were evils in the natural world so long there would be evils in the moral [world]. That when we could prevent our corn from being cut off by frosts, our ships being overset by hurricanes, our cities sunk by earthquakes. When we could controll the elements, keep the trees ever green and make the Streams forever murmer, then, not untill then, could we eradicate evil from the moral world by taking pain, sickness, poverty, etc. from among men. That we all knew it could not be done. We must therefore submit to those evils with the fortitude of men and the resignation of Christians, and not by rebellions against the laws make our situations more miserable.[57]

But the settlers who endured nature's hardships doubted that they should suffer their Great Proprietors in silence. Convinced that they were already working diligently to establish prosperous farms, most settlers scoffed at the notion that parting with much of their wherewithal to pay a Great Proprietor would hasten the advent of civilization on the frontier. The proprietors' vision of hierarchy and control clashed with the settlers' pursuit of family autonomy as freeholders.

Maine Log Cabin. The structure to the right is a "hovel," which housed the settler family until they could construct a more substantial dwelling. The hovel
then became a barn for livestock. Northern Maine, later nineteenth century.
Courtesy of the New Brunswick Provincial Archives (reference no. P4/1/42)

CHAPTER THREE

The Settlers

Let us your Properties explain;
Your Loggin Houses dropping Rain;
The fruitless scheming, and the Toil;
Your Fire won't Roast, nor Water Boil.
Thro' all your Forests, Hills and Plains,
The Goddess Want, in Triumph reigns;
And her chief Officers of State,
Sloth, Dirt and Theft, around her wait.
Your C[our]t is such a partial Whore,
To spare the Rich, and plague the Poor.
If these of all Crimes are the worst,
What Place was ever half so curst?
When tired by Day attending Law,
At Night when we together draw,
There's neither Feathers, Chaff, nor Straw,
Whereon to lay a weary Head,
Not One in Ten, can get a Bed.
—Gershom Flagg, on the Kennebeck Proprietors, 1767

OVER THE COURSE OF the eighteenth century, as population grew and New England's older towns became crowded, the yeomanry needed new lands on the frontier if they were to preserve their society of many independent family farms. New land presented new hope that farmers could pass on their freehold prosperity and status to their children and thereby preserve them from tenancy or wage labor in a crowded land. In his almanac for 1763, Nathaniel Ames of Dedham celebrated the victory over the French and their Indian allies, a triumph that opened northern New England to settlement: "But now behold! the Farmer may have land for nothing. . . . Land enough for himself and all his Sons, be they ever so many." The Great Proprietors also noted the settlers' patriarchal goals. General Benjamin Lincoln assured those that "have a family of children, they have it in their power to settle those around them; a circumstance very important to parents, and especially as they approach the evening of life." The earl of Sterling addressed his advertisements for his Eastern Country lands "to Farmers who have large Familis of Children, and who have no great Stocks to provide them with." Henry Knox wooed "the sensible yeomanry of New England, who are confined

61

in their situation by an overpopulation." But, contrary to Nathaniel Ames's wish, the Great Proprietors did not intend for the farmer to obtain wild land "for nothing"; they meant to profit from the land needs of New England's rapidly increasing yeomanry.[1]

Settling

Until the Revolution, William Allen, Sr., had prospered as a master mariner, trader, and clothier on Martha's Vineyard, an island off the southeast coast of Massachusetts. But during the war, a British privateer seized a vessel containing a cargo he owned, a loss that plunged Allen's family into poverty. After the war, the Allens faced a difficult future if they chose to remain on Martha's Vineyard, for population growth and careless exploitation had wrought worsening scarcities of land, hay, fish, lumber, timber, and firewood in southern New England's old towns. Desperate for a little more land, the "poorer class of people" in Compton, Rhode Island, had the "bad habit of filching part of the road and fencing it in." In 1796 the English visitor Alexander Baring was shocked to find that firewood in Massachusetts seaports was "dearer than it was in France and Germany" as a result of "a total want of any system of preservation of forests." Bemoaning the wood shortage in Raynham, Massachusetts, in 1794 the Reverend Peres Fobes noted, "This has already occasioned emigrations, and will probably produce more."[2]

The 1800 federal census return for half of one mid-Maine county confirms that the Eastern Country was settled primarily by hard-pressed families from eastern Massachusetts and New Hampshire. The census enumerator recorded the place of origin for the heads of households in western Hancock County. Most emigrated from small towns on or near the coast, rather than from the more prosperous major ports of Boston, Salem, Newburyport, and Portsmouth. Tracing the 206 men who lived in the adjoining settlements of Ducktrap and Northport in 1800 to tax valuations for their premigration towns, one finds that most came from poor families. The valuations disclose how much improved land (acres tilled for grain, mowed for hay, or pastured with livestock) each taxpayer owned. In 1771, twenty improved acres was the median holding among Massachusetts farmers and the threshold of rural prosperity. Only a quarter of Ducktrap-Northport's settlers came from families meeting that standard. A matching proportion came from families with no improved land at all. The average settler's family owned eleven improved acres, or about half the level of prosperity. Because limited improved acreage undercut their ability to raise livestock, the average settler came from a family that owned no horse, one ox, two other head of cattle, and a single pig: not enough to sustain a typical family of husband, wife, and three children without supplemental wage work for others.[3]

The Eastern Country attracted the poor rather than the prosperous. Late into the eighteenth century, the region's thin, stony soil, long, cold winters, deadly Indian wars, and conflicting land titles discouraged settlement by farmers of steady habits and substantial means. Most Yankees who could afford longer journeys headed for a more promising frontier: for Vermont or western New York. But from southeastern New England the quickest and cheapest route to the frontier was by sea to the coast of Maine, no small consideration to people with few resources. With good weather and favorable winds, a day's sail brought a family from Boston to mid-Maine. During the warm months, dozens of small vessels, known as wood coasters, regularly plied the waters between Massachusetts' coastal towns and Maine's many coves, offering migrants cheap transport. In 1801 passage on a wood coaster from Boston to Penobscot Bay cost two dollars, the equivalent of four days' wages for a laborer. Moreover, the fleet of wood coasters permitted those who settled along the coast and rivers to obtain an immediate, albeit scanty, subsistence by harvesting cordwood and timber for shipment to market in southern New England—important for people who otherwise lacked the means to survive until their first crop.[4]

In the words of a Mount Vernon settler, the Eastern Country served as "an assalum for people to come and settle on that could not live any where else." In 1797 Boston merchant John Southack visited and found Maine "peopled in general by the lower order of the people, who are not of much consequence any where else." In 1789, Penobscot Valley settlers maintained that "no people ever venter'd to settle an inhospitable wilderness, in more needy circumstances, than this people without money, provisions or farming utensils." Norridgewock's inhabitants explained, "Fatal necessaty not cureosity brought the greatest part of the inhabitants into this cold, distant and uncultivated wilderness." Had they not migrated, they "must have remained a public charge in the respective towns" they came from.[5]

In early 1792 William Allen, Sr., was thirty-seven years old with a wife and six children, aged two to twelve. With the onset of middle age, a father who had yet to prosper in his hometown realized that he was less and less likely to do so in the future. An understanding bound the generations; sons labored for their parents until age twenty-one; then or within a few years, prosperous parents provided sons with a shop, a fishing boat, or a farm; finally, sons maintained their parents in old age once they were "past their labor." But, with little property as an incentive to keep their sons at home, the Allens risked losing their security in old age. Migration to the frontier offered such families an eleventh-hour chance to develop a substantial homestead where sons could invest their labor in lands they stood to inherit.[6]

In the spring of 1792 William Allen, Sr., left his children and his pregnant wife to journey northeastward to Farmington in mid-Maine's Sandy River valley, a tributary of the Kennebec and a haven for migrants from crowded, depressed Martha's Vineyard. He sought out a promising piece of wilderness land. In 1799 the geographer Thomas M. Prentiss described mid-Maine's topography: "When a traveller attains the summit of a hill, the whole around him appears like an Ocean of woods, swelled and depressed in its surface like the great Ocean itself." Aside from the meadows, settlers preferred the uplands to the lowlands. Valuable lumber—cedar, pine, spruce, hemlock, and fir—filled the troughs, but settlers disdained the soil there as almost worthless; in addition, the hemlocks were very difficult to cut down, the pine stumps slow to rot and hard to remove, and the lowlands more susceptible to frosts. In the uplands, hardwoods prevailed, frosts were less frequent, and the soil yielded superior hay. Settlers selected the best uplands on the basis of the trees growing there. Large, old hardwoods, especially maple, ash, bass, beech, and white birch, indicated a rich soil. Smaller hardwoods mixed with softwoods—spruce, fir, and pine—testified to a mediocre soil. Where hemlock, spruce, larch, cedar, pine, and fir prevailed, the settlers found inferior soil.[7]

Finding a piece of land he liked, Allen bought a possession claim to it and felled five acres of trees for a clearing. It usually took a man two weeks to clear five acres, but a skilled axman could cut down an acre a day by using the "driver tree" method. The axman selected a semicircular line of trees with a particularly large tree at the head to serve as the "driver." He then cut each of the trees in the line about halfway through so that, when he cut the driver down, it would not only topple every tree in succession but bring them down in a semicircle with their tops together, convenient for burning.[8]

Over the summer Allen built a log cabin while he waited for the dead trees to dry. In the late summer, with borrowed oxen and chains, he hauled the deadwood and brush into piles that he set ablaze. Known as a "good burn," the technique covered the clearing with a soft, fertile layer of fine ashes ready for winter rye or Indian corn seed without plowing. For the first few years the per-acre crop yields on new clearings prepared with good burns doubled those of long-tilled lands. By enabling settlers to raise crops of grain during their first year on the land with relatively little labor, and less capital, the good burn dramatically enhanced poor families' opportunities to renounce wage labor and migrate to the frontier in search of economic autonomy. Isaac Parsons, who introduced the method to the Eastern Country in 1762, boasted that it "proved a greater encouragement or inducement to the settling of the state of Maine, than any one thing, except the withdrawing of the Indians." In 1790 the agricultural writer, Samuel Deane of Portland, Maine, wrote, "The invention of this kind of culture has been of essential advantage to the poorer sort of people: And it has been conducive to bringing forward rapid settlements in our new towns and plantations." The occupation and burning of new lands in northern New England became so extensive that it produced the famous "dark day" on May 19, 1780, when a vast cloud of smoke combined with a thick cloud cover to plunge northern New England into nearly total darkness.[9]

Allen returned to the Vineyard and on September 1, 1792, loaded his wife and seven children (including a four-month-old baby), some of their household furniture, and their horse, cow, heifer, hog, and six sheep onto a small, forty-ton wood coaster crowded with other passengers and their effects. The vessel proceeded "downeast" to the mouth of the Kennebec and ascended to Hallowell, where the Allen family disembarked. Driving the livestock before them and hauling their possessions in a hired ox-drawn cart, they traversed fifty miles of tortuous roads to reach the Sandy River valley.[10]

On September 29, nearly a month after they had started, the family reached the cabin and clearing. The eldest son, twelve-year-old William Allen, Jr., later recalled the inauspicious sight:

> We found it in a rude, forbidding, desolate looking place. The trees about the house and opening were mostly spruce and hemlock. They had been cut down on about five acres, a strip forty rods long and about twenty wide on the first of July, and burned over. The whole surface was as black as a coal. The trees on the north side of the opening were burned to their tops, and the timber on the ground was burned black. A small bed of English turnips on a mellow knoll, sown after the fire was the only green thing visible on the premises. A log house forty feet long and twenty wide had been laid on the bank of a small brook. The building was formed of straight spruce logs about a foot in diameter, hewed a little on the inside. It was laid up seven feet high with hewed beams and a framed roof, covered with long sheets of spruce bark secured by long poles withed down. The gable ends were also rudely covered with bark. The house stood near the felled trees, there was neither door nor window, chimney nor floor but a space had been cut near the centre of the front side for a door.

During the next week, the family floored the cabin with split basswood logs, built a door and interior partitions, cut a window, constructed a stone hearth, and sawed a hole in the roof for the smoke to escape. On October 8, 1792, they moved in, as William Allen, Jr., remembered, "not to enjoy the comforts of life, but to suffer all the hardships that pioneers must undergo in a hard battle with poverty for more than five years, in that desolate place, without friends or neighbors."[11]

Hardships

The Allens learned that isolation, wilderness predators, periodic pest infestations, and crop-damaging climatic changes prolonged the poverty most settlers brought with them to the frontier. During their first autumn on their new homestead, the family harvested the corn planted by the elder Allen and hurriedly prepared for the approaching winter; they caulked the cracks between the cabin logs with moss on the inside and clay on the outside, constructed a stone chimney up through the hole in the roof, and built a crude, log "hovel" roofed with evergreen boughs to house their livestock. After a cold and often hungry winter, the family labored to wrest a living from their new land. William Allen, Jr., recalled:

> Our fare was coarse and scanty and our work hard. The land was hard to clear and unproductive when cleared, not one eighth of it being fit for cultivation, and that a mile from the house. Our clothes were worn out and torn to pieces going through the bushes; our bare feet and ankles scratched, and our necks bleeding from the bites of flies and mosquitoes. When we cleared the land and planted corn on the further end of our lot, the bears ate it up, and we seemed to be doomed to suffering and poverty.

The family lost ground as mounting debts obliged the elder Allen to sell off his livestock and rely on a rented cow.[12]

Debts were oppressive, and cash was painfully scarce among the settlers, because so many lived too far from navigation profitably to haul their bulky grain or lumber to market and because merchants usually paid for the settlers' produce with goods rather than specie. In August 1788, Norridgewock's seventy-nine taxpayers collectively possessed a mere seven dollars in coin; as they explained, "There is no market that we can go to, and if there were, we have nothing to send." Alexander Baring found that in the early 1790s "there was so little money in this country that dollars were shewn about among the farmers as curiosities." In 1794 Talleyrand observed: "In very long stretches of completely settled coast there is no specie. . . . There all transactions are in the form of barter. Six thousand feet of boards are exchanged for a cow, a gallon of rum for 6 days labor, etc. Even prostitution is bought more or less publicly and is paid for with pins; that is the small coin of the country." In 1803 the Augusta lawyers Reuel Williams and James Bridge reported that "the scarcity of cash at all times experienced by the greater part of our Eastern people" resulted in interest rates of 20 to 30 percent.[13]

The settlers also suffered from the loss of precious livestock and crops to wild predators. By advancing into the forest and overhunting the deer and moose that predators had eaten, settlers invited attacks on the domesticated animals and crops they introduced. Wolves preyed upon poultry, sheep, and swine while bears posed a dual threat, attacking livestock and devouring Indian corn. In their warfare with bears and wolves, settlers resorted to special mass hunts, poisoned carcasses, steel-jaw traps, Indian-designed traps that crushed a predator's skull with a falling log, nocturnal fires around corn patches, guns set with trip wires (with occasional fatal results for hungry neighbors), and troughs of rum set out to intoxicate prowling bears, rendering them easy marks for settler guns in the morning (with occasional inebriating effects on thirsty neighbors who got to the troughs before the bears did).[14]

Smaller predators—black flies and mosquitoes—fed on the settlers' blood and often drove them from their work in the spring and early summer. In July 1795, David Cobb informed William Bingham: "The surveyor and those who came to view the country . . . have as frequently returned almost blind by the bites of flies and musketoes. You have no conception of the hosts of these devils that infest the thick forrest at this season." Often farm work in the settlers' forest-surrounded clearings became unbearable. "We had hard times during the winter, 1792–1793," William Allen, Jr., remembered, "but suffered more intensely the next summer, under our severe tasks and privations, and from the torment of black flies and mosquitoes. Our camp was near a large swamp that swarmed with these pests, which tormented us day and night. We could scarcely see, our eyes were so swollen. Sometimes the boys had their necks bitten till there were raw sores with flies imbedded in them." In search of some surcease from the biting insects, settlers maintained day and night "smokes," straw and brush fires, at their doors; these filled their cabins with a dense, almost choking smoke that, even in the hottest weather, was preferable to their tiny but innumerable foes.[15]

Settlers periodically lost entire harvests to invasions of grasshoppers and "army worms," so named because they marched in a direct line like the ranks of a voracious army. In November 1779 Lincoln County's magistrates lamented:

After having struggled through the miseries of a hard and pinch
ing winter, the people's countenances pale, and their bodies be

come feeble, through want and hunger, they were in the spring of
the year, from the first appearance of things, in great hopes of a
fruitfull summer, but their early hopes were soon cut off, by amaze-
ing swarms of grasshoppers, and other insects which in many parts
of this county almost covered the face of the ground, and distroyd a
great part of the grain and grass and almost all vegetables that grew
out of the earth.

Another devastating infestation occurred in 1793, when, in the words of
one settler, the grasshoppers "destroyed almost every green thing." The
infestations were not more serious on the frontier than elsewhere in
rural America, but the settlers felt them more severely because they
rarely possessed any surplus of grain to draw upon in adversity.[16]

Maine's short growing season, between spring's last and late summer's
first frosts, rendered crops especially vulnerable to climatic variations.
During the twenty years 1791–1810, either June or August frosts occurred in at least five years. Especially hot and dry weather in midsummer could stall crop growth, preventing maturation before the late summer frosts. Paul Coffin's journal entry for September 14, 1796—"Fine
season, corn almost beyond danger"—expressed the settlers' watchful
anxiety over their crops as the earth began to chill in late summer. In
1810, Surry's settlers raised 570 tons of hay and 760 bushels of Indian
corn; the next year drought and frost cut their hay crop to 190 tons and
the Indian corn to 379 bushels. As a result, the town selectmen reported, "a large proportion of the stock have been or must be sold or
killed."[17]

Because the land produced grass during only six months of the year,
northern New England's settlers strained to harvest as much fodder as
possible during the summer to maximize the number of livestock they
could sustain through the long, cold winter. During the hay harvest,
settlers put aside all other work and enlisted every available pair of
hands, including those of adolescent girls and young women. In the best
years fodder supplies barely met the settlers' needs; when droughts or
frosts depleted hay and corn crops, settlers had to sell off or slaughter
much of their stock in the late fall. Unusually cold winter weather increased the cattle's caloric demand, accelerated their consumption of
fodder, exhausted many settlers' supplies, and obliged them to sacrifice
their stock. By postponing the date when settlers could turn their livestock out to pasture again, a late spring also produced fodder exhaus-
tion and stock destruction.[18]

Many settlers could not escape from the vicious cycle of inadequate
fodder. When spring arrived, farmers needed to wait three weeks for
the grass in their pastures to mature, but Jeremy Belknap noted that

"scarcity of fodder obliges the poorer sort to depart from this rule," reducing the pastures' subsequent capacity to support livestock. Worse still, many settlers turned their starving cattle into mowing fields, undercutting their yield at hay harvest and perpetuating the fodder shortage. Spring malnutrition diminished the cattle's strength and stamina, increasing their vulnerability to disease and reducing their ability to work. Weak and hungry oxen often could neither haul lumber nor pull a plow for planting until dangerously late in the spring.[19]

At times, many people also lacked enough to eat. The predominance among the settlers of young couples with several young, dependent children increased food needs while providing little compensating labor. Mid-Maine's fertility ratio—the number of children under ten for every woman aged sixteen to forty-four—was 2.1 (2.3 in the backcountry towns), versus 1.5 for Massachusetts. Settlers regarded daily meat as the standard of prosperity. William Crosby of Belfast recorded a conversation with a settler from backcountry Beaver Hill (Freedom):

"How is it out at Beaver Hill?"
"Bad enough just as much as we can do to keep from starving."
"All poor? Not one rich man among you?"
"Wall—yes. There *is* one rich man—very rich: Squire S[mith]."
"What do you mean by *very* rich?"
"Wall, Squire S[mith] can afford to have pork with his beans every
    day of the year."

In the good times of fall, a brown bread made from a mixture of rye and Indian cornmeal, known as "rye and Injun," served as the settlers' staple. This they augmented, as available, with beans, fish, game, molasses, milk, rum, puddings, barley cake, pork, some beef, and potatoes. The last they boiled in an iron kettle or roasted in their hearth ashes. In the Waldo Patent the duc de La Rochefoucault Liancourt characterized "rye and Injun" as "the ordinary food of the people in this neighbourhood, but which, in other places, would be given to the dogs." Winter brought on a season of increasing deprivation, as many parted with their grain and livestock to meet their taxes and annual fall payment to the furnishing merchant. The traveler Edward Augustus Kendall noted, "Nothing, as I am assured, is more common than for families to live for three months in the year without animal food, even that of salt-fish, and with no other resources than milk, potatoes and rum." Such a diet was especially pinching for people engaged in the heavy manual labor of logging and farming.[20]

By spring and early summer many settlers had exhausted their potatoes and turned to a variety of stopgap substitutes. William Allen, Jr., recalled: "Many expedients were resorted to, to allay the cravings of hunger; some lived for several days at a time on greens; some dug up their potatoes after they were planted, cut out and replanted the eyes and ate the rest. After three or four months, when green corn was fit to pick and potatoes large enough to dig, all were relieved essentially." In 1792, the selectmen for the town of Blue Hill explained to the General Court that, because of the prevailing early-summer hunger, the inhabitants' "peas and beans are generally made use of before they arrive to maturity." Because families reserved most of their food for the laboring husband and older boys, the younger children suffered the most. According to John Langdon Sibley, some children in the town of Union "were constantly gnawing the under bark of the white birch, and eating it, till it brought on constipation and disease."[21]

Some years were especially hard. A cold, hard winter following the summer drought and early frosts of 1789 produced famine in the spring of 1790. In the fall of 1789 Thomas Vose of Thomaston observed: "It is a melancholy time with the people in this country, on account of the drouth, which has been more severe the summer past, than it has been for many years. Not any rain of consequence from the middle of June untill the latter part of August. The people in general will be obliged to kill or put off one half of their stock." On March 12, 1790, Samuel Nasson of Sanford wrote: "Country news always the same —poverty and complaint. But it is generally thought it will be a hard spring for you know that corn and pork makes us cheerfull and pleasant but it is thought that they will be scarce more so than for many years past." He predicted, "Many horses and oxen with other creatures will die." Eight days later Henry Sewall of Hallowell observed, "The month of March has hitherto been uncommonly severe, and there is a great cry for bread corn, but especially for hay." At month's end Thomas Vose estimated "that one third of the cattle will die this spring for want of hay." Finding that not one in twenty of his neighbors had enough to eat, Samuel Goodwin of Pownalborough begged Boston's gentlemen to enter a subscription to provide the Eastern Country with emergency food shipments. In April, Daniel Cony reported, "*Man* and *beast* in this Eastern Country are realizing at this present day what may properly be called *starvation*." In June, a group of farmers from southwestern Maine informed the General Court: "Abundance of cattle have died for want of food and it hath been with great dificulty that those that are alive were saved. People were obliged to give what little corn they had to them, to the great distress of their familys; and those cattle that are alive are of but little use at present being mere skeletons: so that no lumber can be halled for some considerable time." To compound the settlers' woes, that spring also featured, in the words of Nathaniel Wells, an "astonishing number of devourers, I mean the grasshoppers which were vastly more numerous than was ever before known."[22]

Frontier life was especially hard for women. They particularly lamented the initial loss of their social and economic networks of female kin and friends with whom they had exchanged work, produce, and visits. Because these exchanges were difficult in the newest settlements, where the closest neighbors might be a mile or more away, women sometimes resisted being uprooted from their hometown kin and friends. After cutting a clearing and building a cabin in backcountry Davistown, Ezekiel Knowlton married his pregnant twenty-eight-year-old second cousin, Mary Knowlton, on September 18, 1794, in their hometown of Nobleborough, near the mid-Maine coast. They wintered in Nobleborough, where she gave birth to their first child, a girl named Abigail. In April 1795, Ezekiel went back upriver alone into the wilderness to their new cabin beside Saint Georges Great Pond, where he tapped maple trees for their syrup. On the fourteenth he drafted a letter informing Mary that he would come for her and the baby in three weeks.

> It is tedious living here alone. It is a great time of scarcity here, and I must go down after seed corn for there is neither corn or grain to be had here in this place. It will be very difficult getting bread here but it is difficult and costly living here alone, and maintaining two families . . . and we shall both enjoy more satisfaction by living together than apart . . . I suppose you will be loth to leave your friends, but you may remember what I have often told you—that I am the only friend you have on earth's world according to the laws of matrimony, and if there is any other that you set more by than you set by me, I must look out for another housekeeper, for I cannot live alone. I don't write this to grieve you, my dear, but because I would wish to be just.

He signed, "Your loving friend and partner till death." Mary and Abigail joined him.[23]

Poverty

Hardships prolonged the settlers' poverty. During the 1780s and early 1790s, petitions from throughout mid-Maine flooded into the General Court with pleas for abated taxes. In 1790 William Scales of Bowdoin wrote that his fellow settlers were "as destitute of food and raiment as the Vagabonds of Affrica." He concluded, "A few families excepted, were all their goods thrown out into the streets many men would not think it worth their while to gather them up." In September 1791 Bristol's selectmen wrote, "We are a poor people in general and the one half of our houses is small hutts not sufficient to shelter us from the storm nor are we able to get better and many poor famelys has none at all."

Life was no easier in Canaan, where most settlers were "forced to live for weeks together with out any bread, and without meat for more than half the time, a very few excepted, and to go almost naked, even in this severe climate, and to live in huts incomparably worse, than ordinary stables to the westward [in Massachusetts]." Gray's settlers wrote that "a great part of the town, the greater part of the year, live like hermits, being painfully destitute both of food and clothing." Condeskeag's settlers assured the General Court "that no part of the United States are so needy as we." "Could your honors come into our huts, fare as we do, and look upon our half naked children, we should need no other petition to have [our] taxes postponed."[24]

Should we discount this testimony, for all its universality and eloquence, as self-interested? Men who want their taxes abated might exaggerate their poverty. But the General Court found compelling evidence to accept these petitions. During the ten years 1783–1792, virtually every settlement in mid-Maine had its taxes abated after careful, on-the-spot examination of their circumstances by special General Court committees. And the pressing need to pay the commonwealth's staggering Revolutionary war debt made the General Court's committees tough judges. Few of the hard-pressed hill towns in western and central Massachusetts received similar relief, although their burdens were sufficiently heavy to provoke the violent New England Regulation of 1786–1787. Lincoln County's abated taxes (£20,033) were eight times those of Berkshire County and almost four times those of Hampshire County and Worcester County, all more populous counties in western Massachusetts. The General Court believed that the lot of settlers on the northeastern frontier was far worse.[25]

Tax valuation returns for the commonwealth's towns corroborate the General Court's conclusion. According to the valuation returns for 1784, no Eastern Country town ranked in the top decile of wealthholding, but twenty-seven of the thirty-six towns in the last decile were new settlements in Maine: the commonwealth's very poorest communities lay on its northeastern frontier. The 1802 report of the General Court Committee on Valuation indicates that, on average, the mid-Maine settler possessed less than half as much property as the inhabitant of Massachusetts: dividing mid-Maine's aggregate wealth by its ratable polls—able-bodied men and boys over the age of sixteen—yields a per poll figure of $22.43, less than half of the similar figure for Massachusetts proper, $46.36 per poll.[26]

With virtual unanimity, visitors were struck forcefully by rural Maine's widespread poverty. Foreign visitors found the older communities of eighteenth-century America refreshingly free of the vagrants and beggars commonly seen in Europe and Britain. This impression led many to conclude (and some historians to accept) that poverty did not exist for whites in early America. But those travelers who ventured to the frontier periphery found poor families, who, by leaving older communities, contributed to the core's thriving appearance. In 1771 the Reverend Jacob Bailey of Pownalborough, Maine, noted the conditions of his parishioners:

> I might here add many affecting instances of their extreme poverty—that multitudes of children are obliged to go barefoot through the whole winter, with hardly clothes to cover their nakedness,—that half the houses were without any chimneys,—that many people had no other beds than a heap of straw,—and whole families had scarce anything to subsist upon, for months together except potatoes, roasted in the ashes.

In 1787, the Reverend William Bentley of Salem found the Maine backcountry "inhabited by poor people, whose cottages could not be exceeded in miserable appearance by any of the most miserable in Europe." After a 1795 tour of the Waldo Patent, the duc de La Rochefoucault Liancourt concluded:

> [The settlers] are universally poor, or at least live as if they were so in an extreme degree. The habitations are every where poor, low huts. Every where, you find a dirty, dark-coloured rye-meal, and that not in sufficient quantity. . . . In short, of all America, the province of Maine is the place that afforded me the worst accommodation. And, considering how little reason I found to praise the accommodations of many other places; what I have now said of Maine must be regarded as an affirmation, that the condition of human life in that place is exceedingly wretched.

In 1797 John Southack observed: "Human nature, in some parts of the eastern country, makes a dreadful picture. Existence, I have often thought to myself, was rather a curse than a blessing. To go into their log houses, and see half a dozen children almost naked and almost starved, cannot fail to excite pity in a feeling mind." After touring the upper Kennebec Valley in 1807, the English traveler Edward Augustus Kendall expressed his disgust at "the representations that are often made, on the ease of living in *new countries.* . . . Nothing can be more fantastic."[27]

Hope

In the face of such daunting hardships, what sustained the settlers and continued to attract newcomers? The Eastern Country offered many hard-pressed families their last, best hope of securing their liberty as independent producers. Settlers sought freedom from economic dependence as wage laborers in southern New England's seaports and commercial farms. William Allen, Jr., explained, "The hope of obtaining a freehold on which they can support their rising family, cheers on those who have been compelled to work on hire for their daily bread." Settlers preferred frontier hardships to life without hope of economic independence. Endurance had its eventual rewards, as settlers gradually acquired the property that they could obtain nowhere else. Most of the 128 taxpayers who persisted in Balltown between 1791 and 1801 modestly increased their improved acreage, their mature livestock, and their annual grain production; during the decade the average taxpayer added about nine improved acres, three head of mature livestock, and nine bushels of grain annually produced.[28]

Endurance rewarded the Allen family. Hoping to recoup their fortunes, the Allens sold their Farmington homestead in 1797 and moved four miles deeper into the forest, into the future town of Industry within the Plymouth Patent. The Allens and the other settlers of Industry gambled that they could fend off the Kennebeck Proprietors' claim and secure free title by possession. The new farm bore good crops of corn, wheat, and rye; the lot's abundant sugar maples yielded hundreds of pounds of sugar during late winter and early spring; and by buying calves the family slowly "raised up a good stock." They began to "look forward with good hope of better times from year to year."[29]

The family competency secured, the elder Allen began to prepare his oldest son, William Junior, for independence. In April 1801, on his twenty-first birthday, he passed "from minority to freedom." He became a voter and a taxpayer, and he began to keep his own account book to record exchanges of labor and goods with his neighbors. The elder Allen had set aside a hundred uncleared acres for his son, who recalled, "I owned a good axe and had possession of a hundred acres of wild land, without a title; but I had no whole suit of decent clothes." William Allen, Jr., conducted a good burn, sowed five acres of Indian corn, two acres of wheat, and one of rye with seed borrowed on credit, and he erected a barn to hold his harvest. The grain served him in good stead in local exchanges, but to earn cash and manufactured goods, Allen made shingles and shoes for sale in the outside market or served as an itinerant schoolteacher (at the time he had a grand total of one month's schooling, but his mother had taught him to read and write, which made him one of the better-educated young men in the settlement). His prospects of independent prosperity looked bright, provided he and his neighbors could hold their lands without paying large sums to the Kennebeck Proprietors.[30]

Agriculture

As agricultural reformers, gentlemen faulted the New England yeomanry for their reluctance to maximize their profits by specializing in a marketable crop. Agricultural reformers (who were often Great Proprietors) urged the Eastern Country's settlers to cultivate winter wheat. Sown in the fall, rather than the spring, winter wheat yielded a heavier grain that produced a whiter, more commercially valuable flour. Proprietors believed that winter wheat would increase local land values by putting more cash in settlers' pockets, enhancing their ability to buy title at higher rates.[31]

But most settlers defied the reformers' advice and dedicated their agriculture to family subsistence rather than to the market. They raised little more grain than their own families required, devoting most of their homesteads to a woodlot and to pastures and mowing fields for their livestock. The 1791 valuation return for Balltown (located on the Sheepscot River in the Lincoln County backcountry, and an important center for the resistance) reveals that the average taxpayer possessed 138 acres, but only 7 had been improved, principally for pasture or mowing. Only six taxpayers had crossed the twenty-improved-acre threshold of rural prosperity. About a quarter of the taxpayers had not yet improved any land. Livestock holdings rarely exceeded immediate household needs; two-thirds possessed no horses, and no one had more than two; almost no one possessed more than two oxen; few men had more than five adult cattle; only a handful of families owned more than two adult pigs. Moreover, the settlers preferred a mixed tillage, where corn predominated, rather than wheat. In 1791 Balltown's 156 families raised 3,001 bushels of grain: corn, summer wheat, winter rye, barley, and oats, in that order, and *no winter wheat*. The average of about 19 bushels per family fell well below the 30 bushels a year necessary for family self-sufficiency. Potatoes, and imported provisions bought with lumber, bridged the gap, when it could be bridged at all. Corn was king, constituting more than two-thirds (2,008 bushels) of the settlement's grain crop. During the next decade the settlers expanded their improved lands and increased grain production faster than their population grew. In 1801, Balltown's 235 families raised 6,562 bushels of grain, or nearly 28 bushels per family—near family self-sufficiency in grain. Instead of shifting away from corn and toward winter wheat, as reformers and proprietors hoped, the settlers of Balltown increased their reliance on corn to more than 85 percent of all the grain they raised.[32]

The settlers' preference for a mixed agriculture of summer wheat, winter rye, Indian corn, and potatoes helped ensure family subsistence. They were wary of gambling their daily bread on the market and the vagaries of Maine's climate. Winter rye, summer wheat, and potatoes (a leading crop but not included in the tax valuations) did well in the cold summers that damaged Indian corn, and the latter grain prospered during the hot summers that hurt the first three crops. By planting both types, the settler prepared for either sort of summer, assuring his family's sustenance through the approaching winter. Although less marketable because of its bulk and its abundance throughout New England, Indian corn predominated in the settlers' fields because it provided the greatest number of uses and was the most prolific grain, yielding thirty to forty bushels per acre, compared to wheat's fifteen to twenty. Unlike wheat straw, cornstalks were a valuable supplement to chronically short hay, enabling settlers to winter more livestock. And winter wheat seed was more expensive than Indian corn seed. The Reverend Samuel Deane of Portland, a Congregational minister and agricultural reformer (a common combination in eighteenth-century New England), conceded: "The cheapness of seed, being next to nothing, greatly recommends to the poorer sort of people, the culture of this corn. For it is often the case, that they are scarcely able to procure other seed for their ground."[33]

Most important, New England's small farmers preferred mixed agriculture because it best suited the social order they cherished, a social order of many small but roughly equal farms run by family members with occasional neighborly help. This ideal was incompatible with the reformers' proposals, which required too much labor for family farms to implement. Indeed, the reformers implied the need for a more inegalitarian organization of agricultural production: fewer men would be independent small farmers, and fewer, larger farms run by well-capitalized men able to command sufficient wage labor would effect the needed improvements. The Reverend Mr. Deane acknowledged that few hardscrabble farmers could afford experimentation and specialization, "for the failure of one crop, would reduce them to beggary." So, the Reverend Samuel Tenney, another Congregational minister and agricultural reformer, insisted that the time had come "for gentlemen of the highest ranks (for ranks there ever will be in society) to value themselves on being (as they may with propriety be considered) a kind of *humble assistants* to the Deity, in the *work of creation*." Gentlemen could "enjoy the godlike pleasure" by assuming "direction of the various operations of husbandry; then shall we, probably, see a spirit of enterprise and emulation infused into our farmers." But a third Congregationalist agricultural reformer, the Reverend Jeremy Belknap, recognized that there was formidable rural resistance to agricultural specialization for market. It stemmed "partly from the ideas of *equality* with which the minds of husbandmen are early impressed, and partly from a want of education, that no spirit of improvement is seen among them, but every one pursues the business of sowing, planting, mowing, and raising cattle, with unremitting labor and undeviating uniformity."[34]

Markets

But living by subsistence agriculture alone meant a mean existence that no settler wanted. To obtain tools, West India goods, and cash for their taxes, settlers needed to produce commodities for the external market. "We all could make shingles, baskets and brooms to sell and I made shoes for the family and some for others when I could find no better employment," William Allen, Jr., remembered. Settler families tried to maximize both their self-sufficiency within the local community's context of mutuality *and* what they could sell to outsiders. Given their marginality, they could ill afford to neglect either side of their economic equation. They needed market connections to get by, but few were well placed to prosper from them. The current debate among historians over whether eighteenth-century New England farmers were committed to or hostile to the market obscures the economic dualities of rural life. In Maine the settlers pursued two complementary economic strategies that ebbed and flowed with three sets of alternations: between warm and cold seasons; youth and old age in the life cycle; and night and day.[35]

Settlers tended to work to secure provisions during the warm months and to produce marketable commodities during the cold seasons. In the spring and early summer, men turned their livestock out to pasture in the forest, planted gardens, caught coastal and river fish, netted pigeons, or worked in the sawmills on shares. In midsummer they cut marsh and meadow hay to feed their cattle through the long winter. In late summer they harvested their gardens and in the fall slaughtered a pig and one of their cattle. Most men spent their winters in the forest either hunting for moose, deer, and beaver to obtain marketable pelts as well as food or logging to procure boards, planks, clapboards, staves, shingles, hoop-poles, house frames, masts, spars, and ship's timber, all principally for market. Hunters and lumbermen ascended the frozen rivers with oxen and a load of hay to live in crude camps while they harvested pelts and logs. The hunter bore his rewards home on sleds, and the logger hauled his felled trees with oxen across the snow onto the river ice (each log blazed with his particular mark) to await the spring thaw that bore them over waterfalls and through rapids to downstream mills that exploited the spring's high water to saw night and day. Some settlers, especially young, unmarried men, hired out for wages in the frontcountry's older, more commercial towns during the winter and spring when food was scant in the hill country. They made shoes, worked on commercial farms, labored in shipbuilding yards, shipped out as mariners on voyages to the West Indies, or engaged in fishing voyages to the Grand Banks. Late-winter and early spring maple sugaring provided many families with a marketable commodity. To supplement the family income, boys scoured the woods for ginseng that they packed and sold to merchants for export to distant China. But, as with so many other forest commodities, harvesting rapidly exhausted and destroyed the supply. The settlers' work followed a seasonal, preindustrial cycle, where periods of intense labor amid great hardships alternated with interludes of hard-drinking ease.[36]

In addition to the seasonal ebb and flow, reliance on the market waxed and waned as part of a family's life cycle. Because they ordinarily began with few resources, young single men and new couples had to rely on commodity production and the sale of their labor. They meant, in time, to acquire their own farms and strive for family self-sufficiency. As men and women aged, they grew more concerned with their future security. They tried to diminish their dependence on wage labor or market production, working instead to put sufficient land in the hands of their children to assure their own support in old age. Except for the dreaded poorhouse, their society made no provision for the decaying strength and health of the landless man and woman. Those who failed to acquire property and pass it on to their children died alone, in want, and in humiliation. The fate of William How, an Irish-born laborer in Bristol, Maine, represented the yeoman's deepest fear; without land or kin and "being always in the capacity of going from place to place where he could get employ," as an aged and infirm man How became a public pauper. The most respected man looked after his sons' independence by ensuring their inheritance of sufficient freeholds. William Allen, Jr., admired his father-in-law, Stephen Titcomb, Farmington's first permanent white settler, who "reared up a family of eight children, was able to give each of his four sons a good lot of land, and to endow his daughters, in a farmer's way, with a decent outfit, a cow and six sheep."[37]

Malachi Elwell, a settler in Belfast, Maine, nicely expressed the search for a balance between short-term gain and long-term security. In 1794, in return for a commitment for life support, Elwell deeded the family homestead to his son-in-law, Owen Callahan. Elwell promised that if it was "found best for the family at large to sell and remove elsewhere I will give up my obligation on this lot having one as good wheresoever you may purchase again." Selling and moving might be in the family's immediate interest, and Elwell was ready to cooperate if it did not imperil his ultimate security.[38]

In addition to the seasonal and life cycles, there was a third dimension of economic duality in the settlers' world: a movement back and forth between a supernatural and a natural economy, between the realms of night and day. The modest circumstances of his neighbors and kin defined a young man's expectations within the natural economy. He strove to become a "middling liver," the man who had secured a "competency," which usually meant a farm of 50–150 acres. Of his parents when they married, Levi Leighton wrote: "What their plans for the future were I do not know, but they built no castles in the air. They had no trade or profession but to get a living in the same way their fathers and mothers did." Naturally, when Levi came of age: "My chief ambition . . . was to earn money enough to buy a small farm and stock it with sheep and cattle, and secure a good and agreeable [marriage] partner to help carry it on. Of course this was all I knew of the world. . . . I had no trade or profession but farming, and that in its most simple and rude manner." Hard experience taught the settlers that the mundane world was grudging in its rewards. John Low of Lyman explained: "We get our liveing by the Sweat of our Brow, all husbandmen. We are obliged to Rise early, set up late and Eat the Bread of Carefulness." Less charitably, A. H. Giddings of Danville described his neighbors: "Habits of population: industrious of necessity. None wealthy. Many parsimonious. A few intemperate. Very little enterprise." Most settlers were capable of quick exertion but averse to prolonged effort: Dr. Porter said of his townsmen, "If the inhabitants of Fryeburg wished to remove Stark's Hill and could do it in a day—the Hill would be removed; otherwise, it would not!" The natural economy was a place of modest expectations, hard labor, and respites of drunken ease.[39]

But at times many settlers shifted nocturnally into a second, supernatural economy to exercise their dreams of wealth. The settlers' economic marginality encouraged a pervasive fantasy that their farms lay atop treasure troves buried by pirates and guarded by evil spirits. The fantasy flourished even among settlers who lived dozens of miles from the coast. In 1807 Edward Augustus Kendall toured the upper Kennebec Valley and found that "the settlers of Maine like all the other settlers in New England, indulge an unconquerable expectation of finding money buried in the earth." Locating and recovering a treasure required occult skills. A dream repeated three times guided seekers to a suspected trove; apparently, the rural Yankee's subconscious was peculiarly concerned with finding money. At the suspected spot, treasure-seekers employed divining rods—forked witch-hazel branches—to detect the precise place to dig. To ward off attacks from guardian spirits, the seekers laid out protective magic circles by scooping out a groove with a silver spoon or by dripping animal's blood around the digging-ground. To preserve the magic circle's efficacy, the seekers strictly adhered to "the rule of silence," for any spoken word would, at least, cause the suspected treasure to settle beyond their reach into the bowels of the earth or, worse yet, imperil their lives by unleashing enraged spirits: the ghosts of men sacrificed by the pirates to guard the trove. Most suspected treasures escaped capture because of a careless seeker's hasty words of triumph, fear, or frustration. Even if the seekers reached a trove, they usually failed for lack of sufficient countermagic to break the protective enchantment: spirits attacked, and the chest plunged from reach.[40]

Encounters with treasures and guardian spirits were frighteningly real to those who experienced them. Settlers' exposure to treasure tales from impressionable childhood on and their careful performance of elaborate preparatory ceremonies at the digging-ground built anxious anticipation. Convinced that only night digging could succeed, the seekers exhausted themselves with long hours of strenuous labor by flickering lanterns in dark, remote, and cold locales. Strict procedures, especially the rule of silence, sustained tension. Finally, seekers drank freely to fortify their nerves and warm their bodies. These circumstances stimulated their anxiously expectant frame of mind to the point that one participant's suggestion, or any unexpected sight or sound, could trigger a group hallucination. Subsequent repeated narration to others confirmed, refined, and elaborated the experience in the seekers' minds.[41]

Northern New England proved fertile ground for practicing the supernatural economy, if not for its promised rewards. The migrants usually settled in backcountry districts where poor soil, a harsh climate, and relative isolation from market slowed their material progress. In such locales, there was a certain logic to believing that economic success depended on an ability to win battles with spirits. Vulnerable to nature, settlers supposed they were buffeted by powerful, supernatural forces that circumscribed what men could accomplish in their daylight hours. Malevolent witches, demons, and spirits complicated construction, sickened livestock, and sowed mental distraction among the people. To neutralize evil, rural folk strove to live by a detailed list of behavioral rules, or "superstitions." In September 1800, while touring the upper Kennebec, the Reverend Paul Coffin wrote: "Here in Fayette was *witchcraft* in plenty. A man had been troubled six months and it was thought he must die. He is emaciated and often horribly distressed. A Mr. Billings, a baptist teacher, soon to be ordained, has lost his milk for some time. The end of a cheese would come and go and boil off the fire, and finally come to nothing." From Thomaston in July 1805 William Scales wrote, "The belief of witches, pharies, apparitions, hobgobblings and all manner of ridiculous fables prevail in these parts." The belief that supernatural beings hemmed in the settlers' success in the material world led many to conclude that fortune could be purchased only by taking the fight into the spiritual realm to plunder specters of the riches they hoarded.[42]

Treasure chests symbolized the longed-for prosperity that settlers hoped lay all about them beneath the stony ground that so slowed their advance. The fantasy's image of chests stuffed with coins reflected the settlers' compelling desire for scarce specie. Kendall quoted a Sandy River valley settler who exclaimed: "We go on toiling like fools; digging the ground for the sake of a few potatoes, and neglecting the treasures that have been left in it by those that have been before us! For myself, I confess it, to my mortification, that I have been toiling all my life, to make a paltry living, and neglecting, all the while, the means that have long been in my hands to make a sudden and boundless fortune." Persistent hardships bred a frustration with the natural economy that encouraged dreams of a sudden windfall from an alternative, supernatural economy. The promise of imminent riches helped many settlers cope with sustained hardships by assuring them that they were almost wealthy, rather than permanently poor.[43]

Treasure beliefs usually lay dormant, awaiting someone's vivid dream or the arrival of a charismatic treasure seer with special occult skills. At such moments, dozens of settlers would turn to treasure-seeking, neglecting their farms for weeks as they devoted their nights to digging. Kendall described an 1804 outbreak in the upper Kennebec Valley when a treasure seer named Daniel Lambert gave "new food to the credulity of the multitude, and a fresh excitement to the inclination, constantly lurking in its mind, to depend for a living upon digging for money-chests, rather than upon daily and ordinary labour. The belief in the existence of these buried money-chests, and the consequent inclination to search for them, is imbibed in infancy; and there wants nothing but the slightest occasion to awaken both."[44]

The town of Canaan spawned "Lambert's folly," mid-Maine's most extensive and intensive treasure-seeking episode. Belying its Biblical name, Canaan became "a byword and synonym for poverty and drunkenness." In a postscript to their 1801 tax valuation, Canaan's selectmen insisted that local poverty exceeded even the miserable statistical appearance. They maintained that "a considerable number" of the inhabitants were "very poor and [had] their whole taxes abated." Only 48 of the 144 taxpayers owned frame houses, and most of those were "of little value, without windows or chimneys, there being not more than 10 or 12 houses of the 48 of much value and the residue consist of log huts." The local saw- and gristmills were "of an ordinary quality indeed and will scarce pay the annual repairs." Only half the taxpayers possessed barns, and most of those were "destitute of doors and underpinning and rapidly decaying." The inhabitants' horses, oxen, steers, cows, and swine were "of a small size" and "of a mean and ordinary quality." Men did not become rich in Canaan through any ordinary chain of events. Frustrated in the hopes that led them to name their town a Canaan, the settlers needed an alternative, supernatural economy. Sure that they deserved a better fate, many settlers did night battle with the spirits who denied them their just rewards.[45]

Treasure-seeking was no unchanged legacy from a timeless, irrational past; it developed and proliferated in the American backcountry after the Revolution in association with the expanding culture of capitalism. A syncretism of traditional superstitions and new impulses, the treasure fantasy attests to the settlers' ambivalent response to capitalism. They had begun to succumb to its promise that every hardworking man deserved not merely sustenance but riches (and to its anxiety that those who did not acquire wealth had proved themselves unworthy); yet they remained skeptical of its injunctions to pursue sustained, disciplined labor and to delay gratification as the means to certain reward. Rewards had never been certain in their experience. So they practiced capitalism where its promise of unlimited returns seemed to make the most sense: the realm of spirits and treasure chests. Of course, gentlemen committed to encouraging greater labor discipline among the common folk regarded treasure-seeking as a perversion of true enterprise, as disturbing evidence that rural folk were all too ready to forsake the sustained industry that was their proper duty. Kendall quoted a disgusted gentleman, that treasure-seekers "become insolent and saucy, neglect economy and industry, and every benefit to society; and moral habits decay wherever these ideas prevail." As with the Great Proprietors reacting to settler speculations in possession rights, this indignant gentleman thought that the poorer yeomanry needed to be taught to subordinate their acquisitiveness to purposeful, mundane labor.[46]

Mutuality

Settlers ordinarily operated within the confines of the natural economy where common experiences with hard labor and hardships encouraged mutual sympathy and cooperation. John Marden of Palermo remembered that his neighbors "were all laboring men," who shared common problems and perspectives. "These settlers were all very poor, but as 'happy as clams' and as friendly to each other as monkeys." Timothy Dwight also found a "general spirit of good neighborhood" in northern New England's new settlements.

> These things grow naturally out of their circumstances. . . . Such offices become peculiarly valuable and necessary by their situation. Every case of distress is easily realized by all, because all have been sufferers. . . . Like sailors, these people learn from the evils of life mutually to feel and relieve. This vivid sympathy mightily contributes to lighten the evils and soothe the sufferings incident to a new settlement, and spreads cheerfulness and resolution where a traveler would look for little else besides discouragement and gloom.

Mutual support sustained the settlers' tenuous hold on their liberty as freeholders. Their cherished concept of independence meant freedom from domination by a superior, rather than an aversion to interdependence with equals. Indeed, settlers knew that to preserve their independence as freeholders they needed to practice the mutuality of neighbors.[47]

By no means did they abandon their faith in the liberating qualities of private property if available to all; but, to assure their survival and well-being, settlers frequently pooled their resources and labor. Neighbors customarily exchanged labor, a system they called "changing works." To provide fresh meat to the maximum number through the fall and winter, settlers staggered their butchering and shared the meat with neighbors. Similarly, a successful hunter summoned his neighbors to partake in the butchering and in the meat. In hungry times, men with surplus grain shared with those who had none. The settler whose rye ripened first enjoyed the eager assistance of his hungry neighbors in hastily harvesting and grinding his crop for common distribution. The owner received recompense in ensuing weeks as the other settlers' crops matured. When fire destroyed a settler's cabin, his neighbors united to help him rebuild and to contribute spare furniture and tools. To wage war on predators or to search for lost children, settlers conducted mass hunts that involved hundreds to sweep dozens of square miles.[48]

Collective work parties were essential to the settler ethos of "good neighborhood." In November 1793 Hezekiah Prince, a twenty-two-year-old newcomer to mid-Maine, wrote: "One thing I can but admire in all these new settlements is the kind neighborly feeling that exists. It is in some respects like one large family. They assist each other in all their heavy work, all the neighbors and settlers for miles around joining their forces and uniting their labor in husking bees, house building, wood clearing, etc., and the women in quilting and the like." Given the locally abundant land and the almost universal determination to live as independent producers, there was little labor available for wage sale within settlements, and few settlers could afford to buy any. Through work parties, settlers rotated their labor, providing all with needed assistance in the largest tasks.[49]

Mixing recreation with work was a hallmark of preindustrial labor. The settlers' collective work parties met their taste for social companionship as well as their need for labor. During the day's work the host provided abundant rum; and once the task was completed, he supplied a supper, usually followed by a dance. Settlers cherished the sociability of work parties as respite from mundane, often harsh routine on lone farms. The greatest undertakings, particularly church or mill raisings, attracted hundreds drawn from all the nearby settlements. Twice on his autumn 1800 preaching tour of the upper Kennebec Valley, the Reverend Paul Coffin could not convene listeners because all of the nearby settlers were at a raising.[50]

Widespread intemperance lent a dark undercurrent to their sociability. In eighteenth- and early nineteenth-century America, the poor drank prodigious amounts of alcohol. Many believed that they could not perform their heavy physical labor unless partially intoxicated, particularly when the weather was unusually hot or cold. The settlers' origins in poverty and their military service during the Revolution—when rum was part of the soldier's daily ration—prepared them to drink heavily. On the frontier, their arduous work in damp, cold conditions without adequate shoes and clothing encouraged their heavy consumption of warming alcohol. And, because they lacked orchards, because their lumber fetched West India goods in return, and because they needed a beverage that was not too bulky to carry to work deep in the forest, the Eastern Country settlers consumed rum rather than the more benign cider that prevailed in southern New England.[51]

Settler sociability also promoted heavy drinking. Offering and accepting alcohol was the most important ritual of neighborliness, particularly in a region where the people possessed so little else to share; refusing to offer or to accept was an affront. Every visit, work party, election, funeral, marriage, militia muster, and birth called for sharing alcohol. The more liquor a man could give, the higher his local standing; leading men cemented their local reputations with the "liberality" of their "treating." Social exposure to drink began at birth; belief held that "every child had to be soaked in rum inside and out, or it would be a fool, or not live, or some other bad sign." Few could resist the social pressures to drink. Colonel William Jones of Bristol remembered that when his father "got into company he drank freely and it always wrought on him like a physic, and he would be as sick as if he was at the point of death, and many times for some months could not endure the smell of liquor, yet if in company he would drown his health." Drunkenness allowed men to vent the jealousies and resentments that "good neighborhood" suppressed. Men who ordinarily had to cooperate with one another could, when drunk, become violently competitive and delight in cruel, practical jokes. Work parties often featured wrestling matches and belittling humor that vented the individualism and aggression that men ordinarily had to control to honor their community's demands for mutuality. The morning after, settlers could mend strains on "good neighborhood" by blaming any unpleasantness on the alcohol.[52]

Widespread intemperance had pathological consequences. Poverty and sickness promoted the settlers' drinking, which in turn, for many, worsened their health, increased their debts, and paralyzed their industry, perpetuating their marginality. Alcohol damaged the reputation of the settlers, confirming the Great Proprietors' conviction that they needed elite guardians. General Benjamin Lincoln (a proprietor to eastern Maine lands as well as the commander who suppressed the New England Regulation) insisted that the settlers' intemperance "enervates and infeebles their bodies, the object of which must be that the next generation will be in a degree effeminate and puny." Proprietary agent General David Cobb of Gouldsborough wrote: "The greater part of the inhabitants of the town follow lumbering and fishing and like all other places where lumbering is persued, they are very intemperate, very lazy and very poor. It may be said in truth, altho' disgraceful to the town, that a majority of the inhabitants are drunkards."[53]

Resistance

As a result of their marginality, of their chronically imperiled "liberty" as independent producers, settlers were profoundly anxious over any new exaction. Throughout eighteenth-century America, a hunger for autonomy brought poor men to backcountry regions where harsh circumstances dictated constant vigilance in defense of their new farms. Possessing little else, settlers clung with stubborn and fearful pride to the land that promised an independent subsistence, if little more. A plague of grasshoppers, a summer drought, a late spring or an early fall, a new tax, or the demands of a proprietor or landlord could suddenly plunge them into the dependence of debt and ultimately deprive them of their land. In stressful times, they spoke with foreboding of falling into "slavery" or lapsing into the "wooden shoes and uncombed hair" of peasants.[54]

When the Great Proprietors sought to contain the Revolution's social consequences and restore their control over the Eastern Country, the settlers saw a fundamental assault on their liberty as freeholders. In October 1788, Ducktrap's settlers explained to Henry Knox and the other Waldo heirs that they could not afford land payments: "We are each and every one of us very uneasy—that when we survey our naked families hear our creditors allso and [have] little or no provision to support us through the approaching winter and that we have to pay for the land that most of us payed largely for before [to original possessors] we find our difficulties to be such as is not equalled in any part of the Eastern Country (except in your Honrs. Patent)." In January 1789 Waldoborough's alarmed settlers assured the General Court that they could never pay the Waldo heirs' price of four shillings per acre (twenty pounds per hundred acres):

> We have no lumber but cordwood which (to get one cord to market) will take one man and four oxen two days and then fetch but three shillings which the petitioners want to purchase clothing for their children or pay their taxes which is more than they are able to pay, that with an addition of twenty pounds will involve many families in distress and misery, as they have no other resource, many having but one cow, and some not so much as a cow and large families of small children.

They concluded: "We have nothing to hope for but to be slaves to a sett of men . . . which have attempted to bring us into bondage."[55]

Because settlers customarily united in acts of mutuality when confronted with hardship or danger, the settlers responded to proprietary pressure with a cooperative resistance that they understood to be a sort of work party. In 1796 a New Milford (Alna) settler referred to an ambush set for a proprietary agent as a "frolic," the term for a community work party that culminated in hard-drinking festivity. In 1801, when asked why the Plymouth Patent settlers opposed proprietary surveys on the adjoining Waldo patent, one Liberty Man explained "that their interference was of the nature of 'changing work'—that they expected the time would come when they should need the assistance of their neighbors on the Waldo Patent to drive off surveyors from the Plymo. patent." A house-raising or cornhusking could evolve through heavy drinking and animated discussion of grievances into a crowd action against any wayward neighbor who supported the proprietors' claims. So, in December 1800, proprietary supporter Stephen Chase of Lewiston worried, "There is to be a frolick at Josiah Dill's on Christmas Day and I feel afraid of the consequence for that is the rendezvous, for all the black tribe." As with their other forms of mutuality, settlers cooperated in acts of resistance in order to protect the private property of each and every family. But mutuality belonged to but half of the settler's economic culture; in time the privatism of the other half would come to the fore and complicate the resistance.[56]

Courtroom, Pownalborough Court House. Built at expense of the Kennebeck Proprietors, 1760–1761, for Lincoln County. *Courtesy of the Maine Humanities Council*

CHAPTER FOUR

Liberty Men

The cry of the two counties of Lincoln and Hancock is Liberty! Liberty!

Court: Who is that that cries for liberty?

People: It is the peasants.

Court: There is no liberty for you, return to a sense of your duty or you shall fall under irretrievable ruin, you and your families, we will chain you to your oars.

People: What, are we in Algiers?

Court: You shall presently see where you are, we will send our armies and destroy you.

People: Why, what have we done?

Court: You have rebelled against our laws!

People: Your laws! Have you made laws to play pranks with them, for traps and snares to catch men that are seeking after liberty?

Court: There is no liberty for you; it is we that have the power, that have the liberty.
—Samuel Ely, 1797

ON THE MORNING OF July 18, 1800, in Lincoln Plantation (now Thorndike), seven surveyors employed by Henry Knox stumbled into an ambush laid by armed settlers "blacked and disguised like Indians." Bullets ripped into the surprised surveyors' ranks. They retreated to the coast bearing their three wounded. Determined to build his fortune by retailing land to settlers, the general had sent the surveyors into the backcountry to subdivide his claim into townships and lots. But the backcountry settlers wanted neither to pay him for their new homesteads nor to have neighbors who would. In June 1801 Knox sent a second survey party into the backcountry, but it too fell into an ambush that sent the members reeling back to the coast with one badly wounded man. "Our defeat occasioned exultation among the greater part of the people in the suspected regions," reported George Ulmer, Knox's principal land agent. Ever the paternalist, Knox could not fathom opposition to his plans. "My object is to fill the country with industrious settlers and to make it flourish in all respects. A few wretches may from the darkness of ignorance oppose my views but they cannot be many," he argued. But his agitated assistants warned the governor of Massachusetts that "banditti" had formed "a settlement of men in opposition to the rights of property and the utter subversion of all laws relative thereto."[1]

89

The Seed-Plot of Sedition

Knox's surveyors had run into trouble because they had penetrated the cockpit of the resistance: the Sheepscot backcountry. Two of the general's men dubbed the region "the grand seed plot of sedition and insurrection." Located in the eastern half of mid-Maine, the Sheepscot backcountry included the upper reaches of the Sheepscot, Damariscotta, and Saint Georges rivers that flowed southward to Dunbar's towns along the coast. The area was situated between Maine's two largest and longest valleys, the Kennebec, to the west, and the Penobscot, to the east. In 1801 three counties intersected in the Sheepscot backcountry: the southern third belonged to Lincoln County, the northwestern third lay within Kennebec County, and the northeastern third was part of Hancock County. Proprietary claims also subdivided the Sheepscot backcountry between the Plymouth Patent on the west and the Waldo Patent on the east. Proceeding from south to north through the militant settlements within the Plymouth Patent, a traveler passed from Balltown through Hunt's Meadow, Pinhook, Patricktown, Cunninghamtown, Sheepscot Great Pond settlement, Claytown, Smithtown, Beaver Hill, Freetown, and Sandy Stream to Twenty-Five-Mile Pond settlement. Returning from north to south on the Waldo Patent side, the traveler passed through Bryant's Ridge, Lincoln Plantation, Jackson Plantation, Davistown, and Quantabacook.[2]

A newly settled and heavily forested landscape of hills and long ridges rising between lakes, ponds, and damp lowlands, the Sheepscot backcountry was well suited for a settler resistance against the intrusions of unwanted outsiders. Indeed, in 1801 the Sheepscot backcountry had only tenuous links to the wider world: to the older and more commercial, prosperous, and populous frontcountry towns along the coast and the two major valleys. In 1801 there was but one road through the region between Belfast, on Penobscot Bay, and Augusta on the Kennebec River. Only six years old, the road was little more than a stump-strewn path running, in the words of one settler, "through a wilderness of swamps without any bridges. The horses had to all go in one track through the swamps with a ridge between their stepping places, to give a foot person a chance to walk over the wet places without wading through the mud and water." In August 1796 the settlers carefully provided the Reverend Paul Coffin with "pilots" to keep him from losing his way on the "new and crooked path" as he traveled from one settlement to another. In 1802 William Crosby, a young Belfast lawyer, got completely lost on one of the region's roads: "The mire was so deep I had to dismount and drive my horse before me, and finally came to Tilden Mills, where I got so entangled among fallen trees that I had to

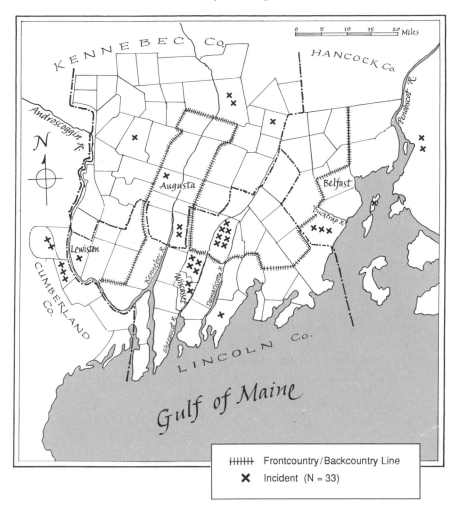

Map 3. Resistance Incidents, 1790–1799

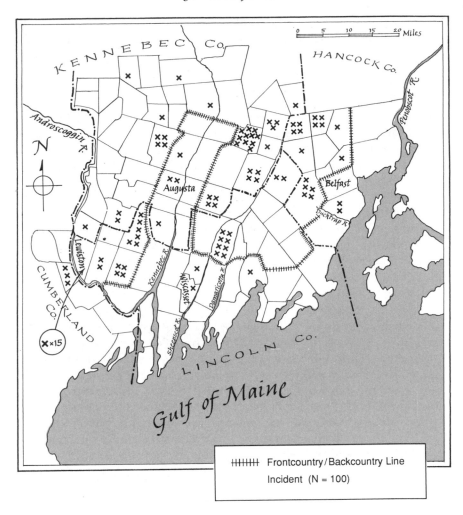

Map 4. Resistance Incidents, 1800–1809

get the millmen to haul me out." The backcountry's difficult access created a sense of common isolation from the outside world, a sense that bound settlers together and encouraged their confidence that they could hold external great men at bay.[3]

Backcountry isolation complicated the Great Proprietors' efforts to assert their claims. Indeed, they were often at a loss for ways to cope with the resistance, for want of the most elementary information about the backcountry settlements. In 1796, some sixteen years after Davistown was founded on the upper Saint Georges River, Thomas Vose, Henry Knox's land agent who dwelled in the lower Saint Georges Valley, wrote: "I am told that there is a considerable . . . settlement by the name of Davistown on the Twenty Associates' land. . . . I cannot as yet give a very full account of them." Poor information and vague patent, county, township, and lot boundaries within the backcountry undermined proprietary efforts to bring lawsuits for trespass or ejectment. In 1803 the Plymouth Company lawyer Reuel Williams of Augusta reported that he had been frustrated in his attempt to prosecute one settler: "No one knows where his house or his settlement is. All we can as yet learn, is that when he comes out of the woods he comes from that quarter and when he returns he goes in that direction." Moreover, a Sheepscot backcountry settler could readily evade a warrant issued in one county by temporarily slipping across the convenient border into one of the other two counties.[4]

Because remote settlements offered little to attract men of property, standing, and education, backcountry settlers found few, if any, squires or orthodox ministers to influence their notions of what was "orderly" and what "licentious." In 1800, only nine of the thirty-nine backcountry communities in mid-Maine had a justice of the peace; conversely, twenty-nine of the thirty-six frontcountry towns had a resident esquire. "No men of wealth, influence or public spirit have ever thought fit to take up their abode amongst us. The keeper of a store is in the way, if any there is, to attain to all the distinction that is attainable in this town," one settler observed. In 1800 only two of the backcountry settlements had a Congregational church, in contrast to the frontcountry, where fifteen towns had organized parishes. The Reverend Alfred Johnson, a Congregational missionary on the Maine frontier, complained to his superiors: "I have no assistance from those habits of age and honor [that] you have to bring your people to worship. These people are removed from all they used to fear."[5]

As a result, gentlemen worried that migration to the frontier compounded the recent Revolution's destabilizing potential by removing thousands from older districts where social and political authority combined in the same traditionally recognized and respected families.

Timothy Dwight—a Congregational divine, staunch Federalist, and president of Yale College who visited mid-Maine—wrote:

> In most new settlements a considerable proportion of the adventurers will, almost of course, consist of roving, disorderly, vicious men. In the regular, established society in which they were born, they were awed and restrained. On the new grounds to which they resort, they are set loose, and usually break out into open licentiousness of principle and conduct.

In this view, the surging frontier migration came at the worst possible time, when common folk, newly agitated by the Revolution, most needed elite counsel to calm their expectations.[6]

The Great Proprietors strove to break down the isolation from authority that helped sustain the resistance. They hoped that improved roads would corrode the settlers' independent notions. Henry Knox subsidized construction of the first road through the Sheepscot backcountry. Charles Vaughan urged his fellow Kennebeck Proprietors to finance additional roads into the backcountry, "as it will facilitate a settlement with the squatters by putting them in the way of better information than what they possess." General David Cobb, Knox's close friend and William Bingham's land agent, insisted that better roads would replace "disorganizing squatters" with more orderly newcomers and "smother for ever the confiscating avarice of Democracy." The proprietors also sent men of property and standing from the frontcountry towns into the backcountry as emissaries to upbraid the settlers for their seditious thoughts. Such itinerant squires and ministers were temporary substitutes for the resident superiors that the settlers lacked. Two of those emissaries for Henry Knox went among the settlers to denounce the resistance as licentious "in the eyes of all virtuous, good citizens, in the eye of government and of the world and if persisted in could not fail to bring down wretchedness and ruin on themselves and families." In the longer run, Knox hoped to establish "squires of excellent character" on his backlands in the conviction that their presence would "tranquilize" resistance. In effect, the proprietors meant to shrink the backcountry "seed plot of sedition" by expanding the frontcountry realm of orderly subordination.[7]

To obtain information about the Sheepscot backcountry and rebuke the settlers for ambushing his surveyors, General Knox sent the Reverend Thurston Whiting and Major Benjamin Brackett into the disaffected region in August 1801. They found themselves in a strange and hostile land.

> In Sheepscot-great-pond settlement, Patrickstown and Claytown we remarked a striking similarity of temper and vein of talking among

the inhabitants. Our address, tho' studiedly mild and soothing, irritated. They flinched under the touch of the gentlest hand that could be applied to them. It was evident we touched a sore that would not patiently endure rubbing. . . . Their long and deep rooted repugnance to proprietors (whom they view as their natural enemies) and to every one that advocates their pretensions, the apprehension they must have of the precarious tenure by which they hold their lands and their habitual fear of being at some time or other disseized of them, has absolutely perverted their understanding and judgement and . . . induced a certain ferociousness in their countenances, gestures and language whenever *title of land* is the subject of conversation.

In addition to a striking consensus, the emissaries warned Knox about the settlers' deep conviction: "They appear to have contracted an inflexible perversity and obduracy of mind which renders them callous to all argument and persuasion. They are determined to prevent the survey of lands on your patent as well as that of the Plymo. Company at the hazard of everything dear and valuable on Earth."[8]

In the Sheepscot backcountry Whiting and Brackett found defiant settlers who considered and called themselves Liberty Men: defenders, of their notion of the American Revolution from betrayal by the Great Proprietors.

Instead of reasoning they resort to harangue. All old and young, husbands and wives, mothers and sons have gotten the same story by rote and two or three demagogues in and about Sheepscot Pond Settlement deliver it with a great deal of impassioned and boisterous eloquence. "We fought for land and liberty and it is hard if we can't enjoy either. We once defended this land at the point of the bayonet and if drove to the necessity are now equally united, ready and zealous to defend it again in the same way. It is as good to die by the sword as by the famine and we shall prefer the [former]. Who can have a better right to the land than we who have fought for it, subdued it and made it valuable which if we had not done no proprietor would ever have enquired after it. God gave the earth to the children. We own no other proprietor. Wild land ought to be as free as common air. These lands once belonged to King George. He lost them by the American Revolution and they became the property of the people who defended and won them. The General Court did wrong and what they had no right to do when they granted them in such large quantities to certain companies and individuals and the bad acts of government are not binding on the subject."

The "harangue" summarized the three propositions at the heart of an agrarian persuasion: that laboring men had a God-given right to claim and improve wilderness land, that the American Revolution had been a collective enterprise securing that natural right, and that communities could resist laws traducing the Revolution's meaning.[9]

Their degree of isolation had left the settlers relatively free to develop an agrarian persuasion. At root, the land controversy in the Eastern Country was a class conflict that pitted yeomen, who were small producers living by family labor, against Great Proprietors, who were mercantile capitalists intent on levying land payments to extract some of the yeomanry's surplus. But, although rampant through the American backcountry during the later eighteenth and early nineteenth centuries, this class tension did not always culminate in armed conflict. Only specific cultural circumstances enabled particular settlers to develop the moral conviction and confidence they needed to stand against the wealthier, more powerful men of the wider world. Resistance by the hard-pressed is never simply an automatic response to oppression: often they are in no position to hope for better or to organize to resist. But the post-Revolutionary settlers of mid-Maine were well situated in time and place to develop their own notions about the nature of property and authority. Proprietary pressure on impoverished families created the need for ideas to sustain resistance; traditions inherited from Dunbar's settlers provided the substance of their ideas; the Revolutionary moment lent moral urgency and legitimacy to the effort; and a degree of cultural autonomy from the wider world governed by great men sustained the opportunity to develop agrarian notions. When drawn together at mills, frolics, taverns, and religious services, settlers shared their ideas about how and why they should resist the proprietors' demands. Particularly articulate, thoughtful, eloquent, and visionary men helped to focus these explorations and rally a conviction and consensus that could withstand challenges from encroaching authorities.[10]

Marginality alone did not create land rebels; the men who served as the rank and file in Henry Knox's surveys and posses were at least as poor as the backcountry's settlers. By paying a dollar per day—twice the premium rate for day labor—the general recruited guards and chainmen among the many landless transients in Belfast, a coastal, commercial town with no legacy of warfare against the Great Proprietors. As the principal market town on Penobscot Bay's western shore, Belfast attracted poor, young newcomers seeking wage work as farmhands, dockworkers, land-clearers, and journeymen artisans while they familiarized themselves with opportunities to obtain land in the adjacent hinterland. In 1801 a third of Belfast's taxpayers were landless, twice the proportion in adjoining (but less commercial) Northport and three times that of

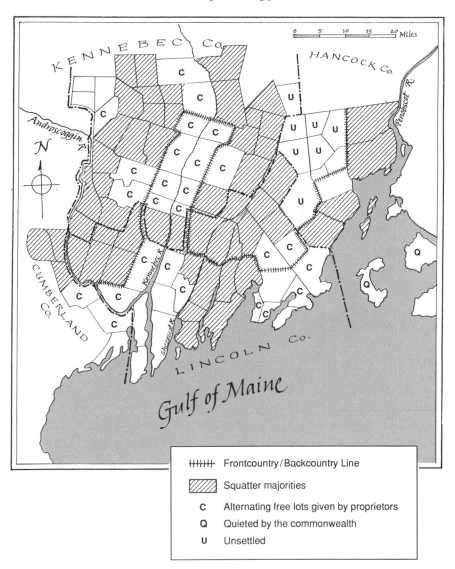

Map 5. Extent of Resistance, 1795

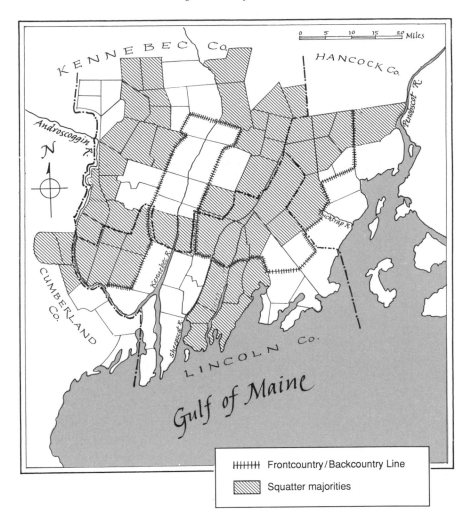

Map 6. Extent of Resistance, 1800

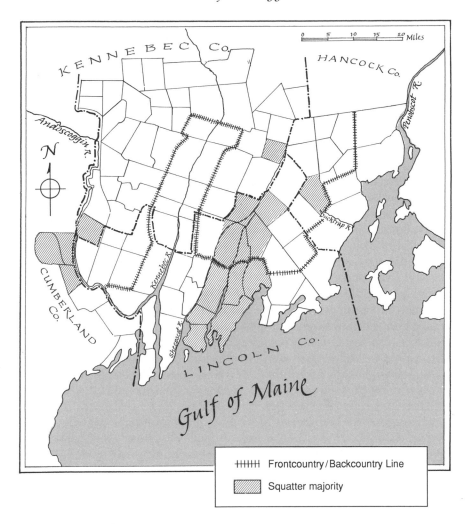

Map 7. Extent of Resistance, 1810

Balltown in the Sheepscot backcountry. It is revealing that Knox could recruit so few assistants in Northport and Lincolnville, poor coastal towns near Belfast. Having recently given up their own resistance and agreed to buy Knox's title, the inhabitants of the two towns desperately needed cash for their payments. They must have been sorely tempted by the generous wages Knox paid, but their legacy of resistance invested their sympathies with the still-militant backcountry.[11]

In contrast to the backcountry settlers who had passed through the Lincoln County coastal communities with a tradition of hostility to proprietors reaching back to Colonel Dunbar's day, most survey recruits came directly from older communities in southwestern Maine where land could be acquired only by purchase. Not used to trust in one another to act against gentlemen of wealth and standing, the recruits dared not directly occupy the homesteads they needed. They had never known the cultural distance from authority that allowed the backcountry's settlers to develop their own notions about property and power. Knox invited poor newcomers to conclude that their best opportunity lay in serving the certain victors; they could earn generous wages and relatively favorable terms for the lands they helped to wrest away. Knox banked on the newcomers' limited sense of the possible, the assurance that, because the Great Proprietors were wealthy and influential men, they would inevitably prevail. Only in extraordinary circumstances can laboring families transcend the received realism that ordinarily sustains every society: backcountry Liberty Men enjoyed unusual cultural leeway, and the survey recruits did not.[12]

The newcomers' pursuit of individual advantage came at the expense of the Waldo Patent's backcountry settlers. The survey assistants owed their good wages to the Liberty Men; without their resistance, Henry Knox would never have hired so many assistants at such an expensive rate. But the general knew that the wage he paid survey guards and assistants was a pittance compared to the land payments their work would wrest from the settlers. In September 1801, Waterman Thomas, who sympathized with the resistance, struck up a conversation with the working men gathered at a Belfast blacksmith's shop. He asked, "Who would go on surveying land for General Knox and raising the price to 5 dollars p[er] acre?" A newcomer named William Stewart replied that "he would for one and why should he not have five dollars p[er] acre if the settlers were willing to give it?" Speaking for the backcountry's moral economy, Thomas asked who could undercut the claims of fellow laboring men. Stewart saw it as a simple matter of supply and demand; Henry Knox deserved whatever the market would bear, just as the Belfast laborer should make the best of any artificially inflated wage. The devil could take the backcountry settlers; Stewart would follow Henry Knox in driving the hardest bargain. A similar perspective prevailed among the poor urban men who served under gentlemen officers to suppress the insurgent small farmers involved in the New England Regulation of 1786–1787 and the Whiskey Rebellion of 1794. Similar hardships did not suffice to unite the urban poor and the rural smallholders of the early Republic in the absence of a shared ideology.[13]

James Shurtleff

In a January 1801 letter to the Pejepscot Proprietors, Elisha Sylvester of Greene, a schoolteacher, farmer, and proprietary informant, explained why his neighbors had the resolve to resist:

> And the misfortune of education, which prevails amongst them leads them to think unfavourably of that government which has sold lands to certain land-jobbers, who make, or at least have sometimes made, the indigence and ignorance of the insipid settlers subservient to their avarice. Their insidious Demagogues have stimulated their enthusiasm by telling them that the celebrated *Lock* says, that he who makes any improvements on lands in a State of Nature has a better claim to it than any pretended purchaser can have etc., without any regard to the relinquishment of natural rights for those of a political nature.[14]

James Shurtleff of nearby Litchfield was the principal ideologue who drew upon a selective reading of John Locke's writings to justify the settlers' possession claims. Born in Plymouth, Massachusetts, in 1745 and married there in 1783 to Priscilla Torrey, Shurtleff began adulthood in poverty. In 1771 he owned a workshop worth but one pound in annual rent, no livestock, and no improved land. Only 9 of Plymouth's 255 taxpayers who owned any real estate were as poor or poorer. About 1783 Shurtleff migrated to Litchfield, a new backcountry settlement located on the contested border between the Pejepscot and Plymouth patents. The town's settlers insisted that neither proprietary company owned *their* community. A farmer, Shurtleff also served his neighbors as an elder in the town's Calvinist First Baptist Church, as a schoolteacher, as a land surveyor, and once as a General Court representative. By migrating to the frontier and developing a piece of wilderness land, Shurtleff improved his circumstances, but he could ill afford to pay a proprietor for title. In February 1799 a sympathetic justice of the peace withheld a writ "because Shurtleff was poor." In 1810 he was a man of modest means with a frame house and barn, nine improved acres, sixty-eight more unimproved, a horse, three pigs, and three mature cattle.[15]

To defend his "competency," Shurtleff synthesized ideas useful to the settler cause. His 1798 pamphlet, *A Concise Review of the Spirit Which*

Seemed to Govern in the Time of the Late American War, Compared with the Spirit Which Now Prevails; With the Speech of the Goddess of Freedom, Who Is Represented as Making Her Appearance upon the Alarming Occasion, insisted that free settlement by the poor efficiently transformed the wilderness into a landscape of prosperous farms and villages, added to the commonwealth's tax base, and lightened older towns' tax burdens for supporting paupers. Referring to his fellow settlers, Shurtleff explained, "They have abandoned the thronged sea-ports or towns, in which they could not find proper employment, and where many of them must have become burthensome by becoming beggars." Instead, "with great labor and difficulty, they have supported themselves and families in a way evidently advantageous to the public." By seeking their own support in the wilds and reproducing New England's cherished social ideal of many modest farms, settlers alleviated the inequality that accompanied population growth and commercial development.[16]

According to Shurtleff, land payments to proprietors hindered the transformation of the wilderness into homesteads and of the poor into substantial citizens. Every dollar that went into a proprietor's pocket depleted the resources a poor farmer needed to improve his farm and advance his family's prosperity. "If the settlers are obliged to involve themselves in debt to purchase their land, the surplus of what is wanted to support their families . . . in order to their making further improvements, is extorted by their landlords." Similarly, in 1802 the settlers on Plymouth Gore wondered why they should make land payments "to enrich those who need it much less than we do ourselves." Arriving during or after the Revolution, most settlers established their homesteads without proprietary assistance. The Great Proprietors deserved no land payments because, in Shurtleff's words, settlement was the result "of the painful exertions of the settlers, and not that of the proprietors."[17]

Shurtleff insisted that laboring families had a natural and divinely ordained right to free wilderness land, a right that preexisted and morally superseded all subsequent human acts and legislation. God created men equally, endowing none by birth with any superior claim to the earth and its fruits. In the beginning, all land was wild and common, the collective possession of all men. No one had any right to own unimproved wild land, but every man had the complete right to the property created by his labor. Consequently, a man obtained exclusive, rightful ownership over a piece of the common land by applying his labor to improve it, transforming wilderness into a productive farm. Shurtleff wrote, "In order to detach any part of the common mass and give it the stamp of exclusive right, he must not only claim it, but annex his labor to it, and make it more fit for the use of man; till this is done it remains in the common stock, and anyone who needs to improve it for his support, has a right." Shurtleff drew upon the prevailing consensus, derived from John Locke's highly influential *Second Treatise of Government*, that all private property rights had originated in improving labor upon a wilderness during mankind's original state of nature. To counter Shurtleff's argument, the Great Proprietors pointed out that Locke had proceeded to insist that civilized people had left the state of nature long ago and entered social compacts; in civil society, written laws defined property and protected the unequal distribution of wealth that had developed over the centuries. But, as Locke had noted ("in the beginning all the World was *America*"), the American frontier lay at the murky intersection of the social compact and the state of nature. Where Great Proprietors argued that civil society extended over the forests of Maine to protect their patent titles, settlers countered that they had entered a state of nature and created property in advance of the social compact.[18]

According to the agrarians, labor created all value, all property. In 1789, Bowdoin's settlers claimed that, when they arrived, the lands "were only bare creation [and] by their industry they have brought them into a cultivated state, and feasted themselves with the hope that they were serving the state and laying up an inheritance for their little ones." In 1797, Prospect's settlers asked: "Who made these lands more valuable than when in the state of nature? Was it not the settler?" In 1800 the Androscoggin Valley's settlers explained:

> We could not exist without drawing Subsistence from the earth, we could not do this without great expense of Labour, this could not be had but by a Reduction of the wilderness; the lands adjacent to those we are now on would be at this time, if in a Wilderness state, of greater value than it was when we came into the country, but this rise in value, has its origin in our labours so that to give as much now, for what we Possess as the Ajacent wilderness is valued at, would be to give to others the great advantage of our labour, but even this is tolerable, when compared with the plan of these Proprietors to drive us from our houses and fields.

Because unimproved wilderness lands were not property, proprietors had no right to sell title to them. The landed magnate who levied tolls on the settlers' access to wild land stole part of their labor. William Scales of Bowdoin explained this to Josiah Little of the Pejepscot Proprietors:

> If your claim comes by the original Indians, in the first place, they were cheated in the venditure, by the purchaser, in the second place, the properties of mere nature, especially lands, never were the object of venditure. O why do you not sell the rain, dew, frost and Sunbeams also[?] If your claim comes by the [General] Court, they have granted to an individual the inheritance which the Al-

mighty gave and sealed to his people in the beginning, which will bring upon them [the General Court] an eternal curse, and upon you for making use of it, to destroy the people and as you destroy them so you will destroy yourself.[19]

Unfortunately, mid-Maine's agrarians lamented, not all men were content with living upon their own labor, upon their own deserved piece of property. Some lusted for the superior wealth and power possible only by exploiting their brethren. Human parasites who did not live by their own labor preyed on the many who did. Pejepscot Patent settlers denounced the Great Proprietors as avaricious men "continually prowling for the hard earnings of industry," who "by prosecuting some and threatening others have succeeded in swindling the people of this District to a larger amount, than it is believed the people of every other portion of the United States have been cheated by every description of rogues whatever." According to Shurtleff, "instead of applying themselves to labor," proprietors dedicated "their genius to stratagem and artifice, buying for a trifle old Indian writings they call deeds" and "imposing upon the ignorant." Shurtleff insisted that the earth could sustain all in comfort if every family enjoyed equal access to the resources they needed, if cooperation supplanted possessive individualism:

> But avarice contracts this spacious ball,
> And makes it for the inhabitants too small,
> While each, tenacious, fain would grasp it all.[20]

Shurtleff argued that inequality began in the distant past, when rapacious aristocrats seized control of the earth and reduced the peasantry to self-perpetuating powerlessness, poverty, ignorance, and degradation. By revealing America's abundant wild lands, God offered Europe's exploited laboring folk a second chance, an opportunity to escape from landed tyranny. But the colonists could not seize that second chance without a struggle during the pre-Revolutionary "times of political darkness," because Great Proprietors, entranced by "visions of manors, and the magnificence and splendor of foreign landlords," used Indian deeds and royal grants to extend the Old World "mode of tyranny" over New World lands. Indeed, it was difficult to alter the tyranny of "custom and habit" whenever "men in place and of great influence, are the proprietors."[21]

According to Shurtleff, the American Revolution awakened the common people to demand their equal rights to the earth. Throughout America the yeomanry understood the Revolution as a struggle to escape from the impending "slavery" implied by unchecked parliamentary taxation. The Eastern Country's settlers perceived proprietary demands for payment as a similar threat derived from the same source—the incessant drive by the powerful to exploit the weak. The yeomanry endorsed the Revolution to rescue America from Ireland's fate as a landscape of miserable cottages for the many and grand manor houses for the landed few. Fear mobilized men to consider new possibilities. "Good God! how were the poor people animated with the hopes of a turn of times in their favor, when a revolution should take place," Shurtleff recalled, "and a constitution established upon the principles of the equal rights of man." The Revolution allowed the people to recognize their natural right to free land. "The shades are dispelled, and freedom has displayed her enlightened beams [and] all men are called upon to repent and reform; and those who have thus engrossed, or derived lands from the titles of these engrossers, to give up the overplus of what they want for their own use, to them who are poor and want to improve it," he concluded.[22]

Samuel Ely

Because the Great Proprietors failed to repent, an agrarian preacher named Samuel Ely found a receptive audience among the settlers for his gospel of violent resistance. During his contentious and peripatetic life spent in the poor towns of New England's hill country, Ely preached that the Revolution presented an opportunity for the yeomanry to escape exploitation by their genteel rulers. During the 1780s and 1790s, he tapped a profound and pervasive anxiety that great men innately sought to "enslave" the common folk. The Reverend Timothy Dwight knew and detested Ely for betraying orderly principles in favor of demagoguery: "He was voluble, vehement in address, bold, persevering, active, brazenfaced in wickedness, and under the accusation and proof of his crimes would still wear a face of serenity and make strong professions of piety. At the same time he declared himself everywhere the friend of the suffering and oppressed and the champion of violated rights. Wherever he went, he industriously awakened the jealousy of the humble and ignorant against all men of superior reputation as haughty, insolent and oppressive."[23]

Dwight's charge of brazen hypocrisy does not fit a man who clung to his dangerous principles through severe hardships. Profoundly troubled by his understanding of how power functioned, Ely filled his emotionally charged writing with violent images that evinced his traumatic, lifelong struggle against powerful men. Late in life, Ely would slip into the commonwealth's State House and secretly lay a petition on the speaker's rostrum in the House of Representatives. Alarmed over his nation's fate, Ely symbolically dated his petition, "Amarica, January 2,

1797." Filled with a tortured sense of impending doom, Ely labeled his petition "The last petition of an innocent man, a plaintive worm, involved in one continual round of distress, miseries, and torture, or a man persecuted in the bowels of a free Republic by a systematic junto of luxurious sons, patentee land jobbers, and voluptuous jo[w]les." He had been "stabed," "dismembered," "crushed," "ruined," and "drove from my poor innocent family" by General Henry Knox and his land agents as "a sacrifice of both person and property to gratify the avaricious appetite of men who are strieving to be independent Lords in a glorious Republic." Lordship-hungry proprietors meant "to engross the property of God's poor, to ruin me and my family."[24]

No scion of poverty, Ely began his troubled life in 1740, the son of a respected squire who belonged to one of the preeminent and longest-resident families of North Lyme, Connecticut. As a youth Ely may have been disturbed by his hometown's economic stagnation. He studied for the Congregational ministry at Yale and graduated in 1764. A year later he began to preach "on probation" in the northeastern Connecticut town of Somers, where the congregation was "distracted with feuds and disorder." In 1767 Connecticut's Congregational establishment refused to ordain Ely, but Somers's evangelical New Light majority conducted the ceremony themselves, despite fierce opposition by the town's orthodox minority.[25]

The division persisted, and foes from Somers's leading families hounded Ely with rumors of moral indiscretions, sharpening his self-righteous sense of persecution by the great for championing God's poor. In 1771 he published two sermons about Job's travails. In the introduction Ely described himself as "much dispised by the great, and by the fashionable world." Implicitly likening his travails to Job's, Ely claimed that "sanctified afflictions" proved that Job / Ely belonged "to the sacred, select progeny and family of God," while the fortunate "who enjoy a continual spring of pleasure, justly bear the title of bastards instead of sons." The insistence that men in difficult circumstances stood closer to God, while wealth and ease marked enmity to him, frequently recurred in evangelical writings. The sermons maintained that, because "earthly judges many times will not hear a poor man out, altho' they believe his case to be just," Job / Ely appealed "to God's tribunal for a trial." God pronounced him "a holy, pious, good man one that feared God and eschued evil in all ways" and whose "boldness in pleading was an honor to him, as his cause was just." This insistence that the righteous poor could defy corrupt earthly authority and ground their actions in a direct appeal to God lay at the heart of rural New England's post-Revolutionary insurgencies. In the Eastern Country, James Shurtleff made the same argument.[26]

Dismissed by the dissension-weary congregation in October 1773, Ely patched together a meager living as an itinerant preacher in several of the new hill towns in western Massachusetts' Hampshire County, returning periodically to his wife and young daughters in Somers. In 1777 his preaching took him to Vermont, where settlers resisted nonresident proprietors from New York, a resistance coterminous in the inhabitants' minds with the Revolution against British "enslavers." Enlisting in their dual revolution, Ely fought at the battle of Bennington. Subsequently tried by court martial for collecting booty on the battlefield, he was acquitted on the grounds that he had served as a volunteer unconnected to any unit.[27]

Reappearing in Hampshire County in January 1782, he led Ely's Rebellion, a precursor by four years of Daniel Shays's more famous insurgency in the same region. The county's hill farmers complained of the numerous debt suits brought by their mercantile creditors and of heavy taxes to sustain an expensive government. Suits and taxes threatened to deprive yeomen of their land and, so, of their liberty. They insisted that their genteel rulers perverted the Revolution for their own benefit and deprived the poor soldiery of their just pay by embezzling tax receipts— that, in short, "it cost them much to maintain the Great Men under George the 3rd, but vastly more under the Commonwealth and Congress." In April at Northampton, club in hand, Ely exhorted a crowd to close the Court of General Sessions of the Peace, the county conclave of squires: "Come on my brave boys we'll knock their Grey Wiggs off and send them out of the world in an instant." Northampton's leading whig, Joseph Hawley, estimated that two-thirds of the farmers in the hill towns of western Massachusetts and northeastern Connecticut stood by the parson.[28]

To behead the rebellion, the county magistrates arrested, tried, and convicted Ely of "treasonable practices." But in June 1782, 130 armed men broke open the county jail in Springfield and liberated Ely, who fled across the state line to Vermont. There, to expand his rebellion, he exploited local resentment among the small farmers against that state's new land tax. In September 1782, Vermont authorities tried and convicted Ely of sedition and turned him over to Hampshire County magistrates. To prevent a second rescue, they incarcerated Ely in Bristol County's cold and filthy jail in southeastern Massachusetts. He pitifully petitioned the Supreme Judicial Court for an early release: "I am alive and that is all as I am full of boils and putrefyed sores all over my body and they make me stinck alive besides having some of my feet froze which makes it difficult to walk." In March 1783 the General Court ordered Ely's release upon his posting a one-thousand-pound bond— with his father and brother as sureties—that he would forfeit if he did not keep quiet and stay out of the commonwealth.[29]

Instead of leaving the commonwealth, Ely settled in the Eastern

Country. The 1790 federal census detected his presence with wife and daughter in Pownalborough's North Parish (Alna), a community with a long history of land troubles with Great Proprietors. His next-door neighbor, Asa Andrews, later figured prominently in the violent mobbing of a proprietary agent. By June 1792 Ely moved eastward, settling within the Waldo Patent on the north side of Ely's Brook (now Shaw's Brook) at Northport's Saturday Point. Again living as an itinerant preacher among new and poor settlers, Ely learned of his new neighbors' hardships, hopes, and grievances, all so similar to what he had known among the hill folk of Vermont, northeastern Connecticut, and western Massachusetts. At a time when the Great Proprietors resumed and pressed their claims, the settlers received into their midst an eloquent man who understood their fears and aspirations. Ely's personal history of open defiance to great men combined with the settlers' frustrations for an explosive mix.[30]

Taking up the settlers' cause, in 1797 Samuel Ely wrote a pamphlet, *The Deformity of a Hideous Monster, Discovered in the Province of Maine, by a Man in the Woods, Looking after Liberty.* He argued that, to succor the ambitions of Great Proprietors, the commonwealth's rulers sacrificed the settlers' aspirations to attain sufficient land to live out their lives as comfortable patriarchs settled amid their prospering children:

> We will say here is a poor man that hath a number of sons that are but young; the father wishing to make some provision for them, and as we say, puts his life in his hand and turns out into the wilderness with his family upon King's land, where he knows he has liberty, where he has a thousand difficulties to go through, but in hopes of something future, he beats through them all; he takes possession, we will say, of five hundred acres, for himself and his sons: But lo! when the war is ended, his sons not being of full age, the [General] Court says he shall have but one hundred acres, although he took it when it was King's land, and is the first possessor. But if a man produces a deed from a native of ten thousand acres, dated a hundred and forty years ago, executed ten years ago, let it stand, it may make him a gentleman.

Ely concluded, "If one that conquered and defended the land against the King, presumes to take a lot of land, he may not hold it, say the rulers (we want it to make gentlemen)." He charged that the General Court confirmed and sold lands to proprietors as part of a plan to reduce the settlers to tenancy by driving up the price of land to a prohibitive level.[31]

The Rulers and the Ruled

To preserve the Revolution and save themselves from lordships, the Liberty Men concluded that they had to take up arms. They did not intend to overthrow the state government, but simply meant to suspend the execution of particular "oppressive" and "unconstitutional" laws until their "political fathers" in the General Court could rectify their mistakes. James Shurtleff justified violence whenever "a man has learning, money, wit and sagacity, and uses them against his neighbor in an unjust cause and against the spirit of law, consequently against law (for law subverted is not law)." Ely concurred with the New England Regulators that local communities must protect natural rights by determining the legitimacy of legislation passed by the General Court.

> It is a good law that children should obey their parents, and that parents should not provoke their children to wrath; and so it is a good law that the people should obey their rulers in laws that are founded on the word of GOD, but not otherwise, and the common people have a just right to judge of laws. . . . And so if they make or pass resolves that I shall oppress or destroy my neighbor, I have no warrant to obey them; or if rulers make a law to dispossess me of my just property, I have a just right to resist; and if any man comes to trespass in my enclosure, I have a right to stop him; if a man has no right to defend his field, what may he do?

Convinced that their resistance upheld the state constitution, Davistown's settlers urged their neighbors, "Consolidate all your hearts like David and Jonathan into a living band of brothers to arise and stand forth like heroes in defence of your invaded rights and lands; fear not the terrors of thirsty land-jobbers, but remember [that] the intention and purity of our constitution was made to defend the poor from the rich, the weak from the powerful, the industrious from the rapacious, the peaceable from the violent, the tenants from the lords, and all from their superiors."[32]

During the 1780s and 1790s the settlers clung to the pre-Revolutionary conception of politics as a "protection covenant" between "the rulers" (drawn from gentlemen of property and standing) and "the ruled" (the common folk who worked with their hands). Rulers were supposed to provide benevolent protection, and the ruled to return grateful deference. But the protection covenant implied that, when the rulers failed to protect the people's property and liberties, the ruled could suspend their obedience and riot until wayward gentlemen resumed their proper role. Consequently, there were two starkly different faces to the settlers' politics. When locally confronted by an immediate and pressing grievance, settlers could quickly gather to exercise

their violent resentments on suspected "traitors"—as they had done in
1774 and 1775 against the region's loyalists. But General Court politics
seemed a distant realm, approachable only by humble petition.[33]

Preoccupied with securing their immediate subsistence and self-con-
scious about their limited education, most settlers felt they had no business participating in extralocal politics. In May 1780, General Peleg
Wadsworth described the settlers as "small in their own eyes." In a 1790
letter to Congressman George Thatcher, Samuel Nasson of Sanford
expressed awe at the federal government then housed in New York City:
"You soar in quite another region. You flow in wealth. We suffer with
extrem poverty." Sanford's residents could not scrape together enough
money to hire a schoolteacher. "But you can, they tell me give your
doorkeepers five times that sum. Where do you get so much as to wallow
in wealth? If all that we hear is true I shall expect soon to hear you own a
Pallace to set in." In 1821, Ephraim Rollins of Nobleborough recalled
the settlers' former notion that state politics was the exclusive concern of
gentlemen. In 1788, when the inhabitants sought incorporation, their
proprietor, Arthur Noble of Boston, "the then Oricle of the times and
Monarch of the East, offered the settlers to assist them in the business if
they would give him the privilege of naming the town and fearing his
opposition they consented and submitted the whole business to him and
when their act of incorporation came beheld the name of their town was
Nobleborough—many of the petitioners were dissatisfied but few dared
to complain."[34]

Irregular communication with the outside world prolonged the settlers' disengagement from state and national politics. For lack of any
postal service east of Casco Bay, few settlers ever saw a newspaper or
received any mail in the 1780s. A Blue Hill settler observed, "We are so
as it wore out of the wourld that we don't hardly know wether we do rite
or rong but we mean to do as well as we can." In January 1788, when
Massachusetts ratified the Federal Constitution, newspaper publisher
Thomas B. Wait of Falmouth (Portland) noted, "It is an important period and they are almost totally ignorant of every public transaction."
Four months later the young lawyer Silas Lee arrived in the town of
Penobscot: "The new constitution is scarcely named here. The people in
general appear to be totally unacquainted with it and equally indifferent
as to its establishment." Similarly about state politics: "They care very
little. . . . The greatest and almost only object of their concern are the
sheriffs and justices of the peace. These are often looked upon with
dread."[35]

Consequently, during the 1780s, when the General Court confirmed
the proprietary patents, the settlers did little more than regularly petition their "political fathers" for redress. Few voted in state elections, and

their towns rarely sent representatives to the General Court. During the 1780s and 1790s, low voter turnout and town unanimity characterized politics throughout the commonwealth, but political participation was acutely minimal in the Eastern Country. When townspeople did vote for governor or lieutenant governor, unanimity usually prevailed as the voters followed the lead of one or two local leading men with a broader awareness of the outside world. In 1794 Talleyrand observed, "Placed at a great distance from the general government, separated from the seat of the state to which they belong, poorly supplied with public papers, little prepared to read them, they leave their opinions on men and things in the hands of a small number of men who dispose of the votes, each in his district; they . . . have no idea of the law except the fear which a judge inspires in them." In the important 1787 gubernatorial election between James Bowdoin and John Hancock (both men were Kennebeck Proprietors), only twelve of mid-Maine's then twenty-two incorporated towns bothered to return votes. In all, only 998 men voted, less than one-fifth of the region's adult males (versus one-third for the rest of the commonwealth). Seven of the twelve voting towns cast *all* of their ballots for a single candidate. In the other five at least 85 percent of the votes went to but one of the candidates. And yet, compared to previous years, this election represented a large turnout and a close contest. The settlers' disengagement from extralocal politics during the 1780s assured the proprietors' success in securing confirmation of their patents; that success obliged the settlers to assume their other political face as rioters.[36]

Instead of participating in the General Court's politics, most settlers hoped to defend their interests by locally obstructing those laws that they deemed oppressive. Agrarians distrusted any extralocal establishments, religious or political, as the natural preserves of parasitical gentlemen ever bent on expanding their power and property at the expense of the many. As a last resort, agrarians upheld the right of local communities to check the encroaching power of the great men by nullifying the local operation of oppressive legislation until their rulers could reconsider. Only in this manner could humble people defend themselves against unscrupulous men of wealth and learning adept at subverting and manipulating concentrations of extralocal power. By clinging to the ruler-ruled dichotomy of the colonial era's political culture, Liberty Men denied that the Revolution had established a truly republican order, where the common farmer was as politically potent as the moneyed magnate. Agrarians doubted that equality of dominion—where no man controlled another without his consent—could exist beyond the town level. Unless power was diffused to the towns, where men of limited means and education could directly participate in governance, great men would inevitably abuse the power they accumulated as county and state establishments operating behind the facade of republican government.[37]

No radicalized proletariat, the settlers could not conceive of dispensing with their elite rulers. Living within a preindustrial class structure, agrarians employed preindustrial forms of resistance intended to obstruct aggression by the powerful and restore the proper balance of power between producers and great men. Like the South Carolina, North Carolina, and New England Regulators, the Eastern Country's Liberty Men saw themselves as engaged in a legitimate, temporary intervention intended to restore the necessary equilibrium between central power and local liberty. Balance restored, agrarians were ready and eager to return to their farms, leaving governance to the chastened gentlemen until they next transgressed.[38]

Defending the Revolution

Convinced that they had fought the Revolution to obtain free access to wilderness land and to enhance local autonomy, the Liberty Men felt betrayed by their rulers. James Shurtleff explained:

> I say, for one man to thus hold thousands of acres, and others pursued and hunted about, and threatened with the utmost severities, who are endeavoring to draw their support by taking possession of, and occupying a single lot, . . . is a despotism so apparent, that it is shocking to humanity, especially in such a country as this, who have separated from others for the sake, as is pretended, of enjoying freedom in its purity: for whether these proprietors drive off the settlers, or demand obligations for sums which are unreasonable, and which they can never hope to satisfy, will amount to the same thing.

Similarly, the settlers of Davistown raged: "In the name of wonder where do we live? Not in the land of freedom, but in Algiers, for we are clogged, shackled and fettered with a loaded demand, which three quarters of the people can never pay no more than they can create a world." They could understand no right that allowed the commonwealth to endorse the claims of a handful of already wealthy men to vast tracts of land needed by great numbers of humbler men for their own survival. "Indeed idiotcy itself cannot believe in piling up property in such a manner on one man, to the robbing of thousands."[39]

Samuel Ely argued that a revolution betrayed into the hands of the rich was far worse than no revolution at all. Referring to the crown's policy of granting free land to settlers in nearby Nova Scotia and perhaps to the memory of David Dunbar's grants, Ely insisted that, contrary to the hopes of laboring folk, the Revolution wrought "a restriction of the liberty which the poor people had while the British King held the claim, for then a poor man was allowed to take a piece of land without control; but if he has taken State's land, now he must pay for it at an extravagant price, or he may not hold it, or the Court will release it to proprietors who will plague him like the despots of Europe, one set or company after another." Ely continued: "The power has already taken away our liberty, and now we must be content or they will take away our lives also. . . . We fought for liberty, but despots took it, whose little finger is thicker than George's loins; the cry is violence and wrong; O that George held the claim still! for, before the war, it was better with us than now; when we were under the British King we had liberty; but what liberty have we now?"[40]

Convinced that the Revolution was more than a struggle for national independence, the Liberty Men insisted that it was a collective venture meant to perpetuate an egalitarian society of autonomous, small producers by guaranteeing free wilderness land to the neediest. This expressed their historical experience as poor men who had fought in the war and migrated to the frontier in search of free land unavailable in older communities. They did not seek a redistribution of existing improved property, merely the right of laboring families to create their own titles by freely claiming and improving wilderness land. Then the new property created by the steady progress of settlement across the American continent would lift the poor into prosperity rather than increase the elite's wealth and power.[41]

The settlers felt engaged in a critical struggle, at a pivotal historical moment, for America's future as a truly democratic society. By requiring laboring families to buy wilderness land, proprietors threatened the foundation of liberty in an egalitarian distribution of property. James Shurtleff argued: "Freedom cannot hold impartial sway in such a country as this, at the same time when large tracts of wilderness land are held by individuals or companies, to be entirely at their disposal, who may retard or prevent a settlement at will—prevent the lands being appropriated to the use for which they were originally designed; or if they submit to have them settled, may insist upon such terms which must entirely discourage or subject the settler to servitude for life." Because proprietors meant to "become the haughty lords of a race of beggars," settlers endured "the pressures of tormenting suspense, whether they shall be freemen or slaves; for slavery must be the fate of the greater part, should their opponents carry their point." In a plea to the General Court's backbenchers, Samuel Ely wrote: "Forgive me my dear brother farmers if I say three patents in the hands of three men ill disposed can subvert the best constitution of any *state* as property always has a commanding *power*." He insisted: "I am pleading for the people not only of the Province of Maine, but for [those of] the [Massachusetts] Bay. There are many poor people in the western parts as well as here that want lands, that have hazarded their lives in the war, and got nothing but miserable trash for their pay, yet they may not have land without money, or giving a mortgage, which is worse, though they should have a share in the conquest."[42]

Pressured during the 1790s by renewed proprietary surveys and lawsuits, the settlers revived the faltering American Revolution by defending their landholdings. In a letter to Josiah Little of the Pejepscot Proprietors, William Scales, a settler in the town of Bowdoin, explained: "You will remember how the people were kindled into rebellion against the british authority with blazing promises and engagements of theocracy, universal liberation, and gospel liberty but they have found the image of the british tyranny and a more dreadful usurpation, deception and imposition. Therefore by the same rule their rebellion against Britain is justified, their rebellion against the american tyranny and usurpation is justified." James Shurtleff warned the Revolution's betrayers: "A people who have been tutored in the school of freedom, and who have had the rights of humanity instilled with bloody strokes in the late American war, cannot easily forget the interesting lessons they have been thus taught, and consequently feel, with the keenest sensibility, the rough and heavy hand of oppression. And what mode of oppression ever took place among a people more fatal to the natural rights and liberties of man, than the monopolizing of wild lands?"[43]

Inspired by such rhetoric, backcountry settlers who called themselves Liberty Men or Sons of Liberty armed for the Revolution's last skirmishes. In the fall of 1795 the Twenty Associates, Kennebeck Proprietors, and Waldo heirs provoked a series of confrontations by aggressively pressing surveys into the backcountry. "This chafed the minds of the people as a bear bereaved of her whelps," Samuel Ely said. In November 1795, Balltown's settlers warned surveyor Benjamin Poor to be gone, explaining that "they were determin'd that no surveyor should run any line there at present, for the Plymouth Company was endeavoring to take their land from them, that they, meaning the inhabitants of Ballto[w]n and the vicinity, had fought for it once and were determined to fight for it again." In December 1795, Simon Brown of Clinton demanded that Gershom Flagg cease his survey for the Plymouth Company, "as the land was the people's and not the company's." Brown added that "he had been in the service 6 years and fought for the land, and would have it."[44]

Confrontations

Two series of confrontations, one focused on New Milford (Alna), the other on Lewiston, illuminate how the Liberty Men conducted their resistance. In early 1796 the Draper heirs, a proprietary company based upon a supposed Indian deed, sued several New Milford settlers for ejectment. One defendant, Isaac Prince, invited John Trueman, the Draper heirs' agent, out to his farm to discuss terms. On July 8, 1796, as Trueman rode north along the Sheepscot River from his lodging in Wiscasset into New Milford, Prince mustered a dozen neighbors in the woods beside the road. They dubbed the occasion a "frolic" or "caper," terms for any sort of collective work and recreation party. As expected on such occasions, the host provided "victuals and drink" in return for his neighbors' help. Apparently, drinking the host's rum committed a man to the "caper," for, to clear himself, one participant, Asa Andrews, later testified that Prince "asked me to drink some rum and . . . on my refusing he offered to force me." The Liberty Men put on old clothes and dipped their fingers into a hat filled "with powdered charcoal or camp black mixed with grease" and smeared the black concoction on their faces.[45]

Trueman rode up over a hill and into the waiting ambush. Bursting from the bushes on the east side of the road, Prince halted Trueman by presenting a loaded musket to his chest. The other Liberty Men leapt out, dragged the agent from his horse and into the bushes, where they tore off all his clothing but one sleeve and a lone stocking, cut him on the ears with a penknife, beat him with bundles of tree branches, and repeatedly bellowed their intent to kill him. When they felt he was sufficiently terrorized never to return, the men let Trueman break away and flee back down the road to Wiscasset. The settlers then rifled his saddlebags and shredded his papers, including legal executions and settlers' notes of hand promising payment for their land. They stuffed the scraps beneath a rock. Basking in their neighbors' congratulations, the assailants boasted of their determination, in Andrews's words, to "kill all the proprietors who should come there." But Trueman had recognized Prince, and an investigation by Manassah Smith, the Drapers' Wiscasset lawyer, identified ten others. In March 1797, deputy sheriffs caught three suspects and locked them into Wiscasset's wooden jail.[46]

The arrests aroused settlers throughout the Sheepscot Valley. In the last week of March "a great body of men" mustered in New Milford, filling Daniel Clark's yard. They threatened to kill the suspected informants, including Asa Andrews, and to burn the buildings belonging to Stuart Hunt, a resident "gentleman" who owned an interest in the Draper claim. Feeling springtime's pinch, they told Clark "they were hungry and must have something to eat, that Mrs. Clark had been baking." Given the bread, they heeded Clark's advice to disperse. But a day later they remustered, swelled by additions from "the upper settlements of Sheepsgut and Damariscotta ponds" to two hundred to three hundred men "well armed and suitably provided with axes and bars to pull down the gaol." Before dawn on the morning of March 29 they marched on Wiscasset. With a military precision probably learned from service in the Revolution, the armed settlers divided into three parties. Two guarded Wiscasset's principal approaches while the third party hastened into town, surrounded the jail, and awoke and prodded the jailer at bayonet-point to open the cells, releasing the three captives. The settler brigade marched triumphantly out of town back to the backcountry, where the men dispersed. To evade recapture, the liberated men temporarily fled the area, signing on as sailors on mercantile voyages to the West Indies.[47]

To forestall arrests of the suspected rioters, the Liberty Men systematically harassed the proprietors' supporters within and the authorities without. In early May armed crowds harassed Stuart Hunt's house three times, firing shots and hurling rocks through the windows. The Liberty Men had a long reach; fearing for his life, the government's principal informer, Asa Andrews, fled to Westford, Massachusetts, where he insisted that "the very rioters" tracked him down and "ambushed his house." The settlers also strove to frighten Wiscasset's residents into restraining proprietary agents and legal authorities. In May 1797, Manassah Smith reported, "The New Milford boys, as they call themselves, have wrote and droped letters round the point [Wiscasset], threatening that if any of them are further molested they will destroy all the point by poisoning the provisions, water etc., and by burning all the buildings on the point and of all those who shew themselves on the side of government etc." To acquaint Smith with his vulnerability, one night "the New Milford mob" slipped into his Wiscasset stable, stole his horse, and held it until the lawyer paid them fifteen dollars in ransom. "This is the way we are to be governed by mobs, highway robbers and thieves and the major part join with them. God deliver us from such a banditti of Devils," Smith raged.[48]

The New Milford boys succeeded in intimidating Wiscasset's authorities. Heeding his townsmen's fears of retribution, Lincoln County's sheriff followed the governor's orders to send out a posse but made sure that the backcountry settlers knew of their planned march a week in advance. This satisfied both the suspected settlers, who went into hiding, and the posse, who returned home safely after a pleasantly fruitless ride upriver to Balltown and back. The Draper heirs were less pleased.[49]

A similar spate of incidents occurred in and around Lewiston from 1796 through 1801. Lewiston's majority felt bitterly frustrated by the Supreme Judicial Court's refusal to invalidate the Pejepscot Patent and angry at Josiah Little's high price for land and increasing resort to law-suits. Winslow Ames, a Lewiston selectman, regarded Little as "an en-emy to the Country and he thought it was as right to fight an enemy at home as to fight a foreign enemy. He looked on Col. Little as oppressing the people and if they could [not] obtain their rights by fair means they must take foul." Indeed, "when he looked at the conduct of Col. Little, he felt as though he could fight like a Horse. On the whole, he said he could not compare himself to any thing but a mad dog." Ames con-cluded "that the best way to deal with an enemy was to deprive him of the means of subsistence," by intimidating Little's local supporters.[50]

Anticipating a showdown with Little, Lewiston's majority sought com-munity solidarity by intimidating the minority who assisted the propri-etors: Robert Anderson, William Carvill, Stephen Chase, Amos Davis, Joseph Eveleth, and Ezra Purrinton of Lewiston, and Peter Merrill of Little Gore (Auburn) on the other side of the Androscoggin River. When Eveleth told Abel Allen to let the courts decide the land contro-versy, Allen "said he did not care any thing about the Law for they had a New Law of their own." Eveleth ignored Allen's warning; one night Liberty Men plundered his logging camp of tools and another night torched his haystack. Peter Merrill reported that David Hildreth "called to me asking if I had my Guns ready, telling me that there was Indians in the woods." Employing tactics identical to the Green Mountain Boys', the Liberty Men beset the proprietary supporters' homes at night, star-tling the occupants with sudden deafening volleys into the night air, stray shots into the houses, a hail of stones through the windows, and loud yelling. In the morning the victims found their fences leveled and their livestock roaming free. A crowd broke into Merrill's barn, where Josiah Little had stored his chaise, a symbol of wealth; hauling it across the winter snow to the Androscoggin River, the crowd smashed the chaise to pieces that they hurled into the dark water. One of Merrill's neighbors later confided "that Colonel Little ought to be served in the same way." Another night some settlers stripped Stephen Chase's Lewis-ton sawmill and gristmill of their tools.[51]

Intimidation within sustained the solidarity needed to obstruct Josiah Little's surveyors. In May 1800, in Lewiston's woods, the surveyor Lo-throp Lewis and his assistants pulled up short before the sudden ap-pearance of a dozen "sons of darkness" garbed in old ragged blankets, armed with muskets and clubs, speaking "in the Indian tone," their faces smeared with blacking. Lewis recalled their performance: "They now appeared to be in the greatest rage imaginable, Demanding of me my papers etc., Demanding of me where Col. Little was. 'If,' sd. they, 'we coud catch him in the woods he shoud not get out again. We find he means to ask a great price for his Land and for our Part we had as good Die by the Sword as by famine and are Determined never to have any Lines run upon our hunting Ground.'" From pacific southwestern Maine, Lewis had never seen men "so compleatly Disguised as to their Colour, Habit, etc. as they were and that appeard to be so Lost to all Sense of Decency, Order, and good Government, railing and reviling against the Government in a most Shocking manner." Illiterate, or pretending to be (as real Indians were), they ordered Lewis to read aloud his survey memorandum book. Then they seized the book to erase its writing. Returning the book, they ordered the surveyors to depart, suspending Little's surveys for another year.[52]

The climactic confrontation came four months later, one night in September 1800, when Josiah Little visited Lewiston and lodged with Ezra Purrinton. Shortly after midnight a crowd led by David Hildreth and Josiah Dill gathered outside the house, fired shots into the air, called Purrinton a "Damd Harbourer," and loudly demanded that Little come out. With characteristic theatricality, the crowd, in Ezra Purrinton's words, "uttered many threatning speeches against said Little and Demanded the Body of Josiah Little, Declaring with horrid Oaths that if said Little was not delivered up they would have the Deponent's Bones and the Bones of his family all together by burning the house." The crowd pelted the house with stones, smashing the windows and injuring the colonel. Someone fired a shot into the house; the bullet set ablaze the bed Little had just risen from. With that, the Liberty Men dispersed into the night as suddenly as they had gathered. In subsequent weeks the Liberty Men continued to harass the Purrintons and three sympathetic neighbors. William Carvill, a neighbor, testified, "Abraham Jordan told me that I must look out for Breakers and another said he guessed they would break prety white upon me." As prophesied, both Carvill and Purrinton had their rail fences toppled in the night, stones thrown through their windows, and shots fired about their houses by crowds who used "high and threatning Language" and "made a Headious Noise."[53]

The New Milford and Lewiston episodes demonstrated that the resistance had two interdependent dimensions: intimidating proprietary supporters within while sealing off their communities from authority without. Internal intimidation constituted about two-fifths (63 of 148) of the resistance's known acts of violence: burning barns, shooting livestock, stealing tools, torching haystacks, toppling fences, and besetting houses at night with cowbells, gunshots, hurled stones, and bloodcurdling yells. Obstructing intruding deputies, surveyors, and land agents composed the rest (85 of 148) of the acts. The same pattern of enforced solidarity and community isolation characterized resistance elsewhere in rural America by New York's Anti-Renters, Pennsylvania's Whiskey Rebels and Wild Yankees, and Vermont's Green Mountain Boys.[54]

Successful resistance to external authority required internal solidarity.

In 1796, Davistown's settlers addressed their neighbors, "Your deliverance from final poverty, from infamous oppression, from entailed miseries to posterity now depends upon the union of the people." They resolved "that one inhabitant shall not break in upon the survey of another, and where they have done it, they shall quit the premises, or we will drive them off by force, that the people may have peace among themselves." The resisting communities chose three-man "landed committees" (or "people's committees") to survey their townships, suffer no one to take up land without community permission, and allow only residents to sell any land within their bounds. Resisting communities adopted the principle that, so long as the local majority favored resistance, no individual settler could assist, or come to separate terms with, the Great Proprietors. Instead, the majority required all to assist in shutting their communities off from the operation of the distasteful land laws that promoted proprietary control. Often a community's settlers assembled in mass meetings to formalize their mutual contract by entering written bonds to unite against the proprietors and to kill any signer who broke ranks. Sometimes the signers drew blood from one another for the ink. The settlers' folk tradition insisted that anyone who violated so solemn a covenant signed his own death warrant.[55]

Settlers ostracized and intimidated those who betrayed the community. Equating their resistance with the Revolution, the Liberty Men considered proprietary supporters "Tories" who deserved coercion. For assisting the Kennebeck Proprietors, Richard Meagher, a leading man in New Waterford (later Malta, now Windsor), had his house burned by men he described as "a set of lawless ill-minded fellows who dress in Indian dress to kill proprietors, sherifs and Tories (meaning I)." At the very least, the settler who alienated his neighbors lost the important benefits of communal sociability and neighborly help. His life became lonelier and harder. One night at a cornhusking in New Waterford the crowd suddenly pelted with ears of corn "from all parts of the barn" a settler who had spoken against the resistance. Tories faced rituals of public degradation intended to humiliate and discredit them in their neighbors' eyes. In June 1806 a party of Liberty Men led by Nathan Barlow disciplined John Harvey of Fairfax. They "forcibly took him and placed him naked astride a rail and in that position forcibly carried [Harvey] along the highway for . . . three miles, and then and there threw [him] on the ground and besmeared his naked body with dirt and filth and in that condition exposed [him] to contempt and derision." Liberty Men also menaced the Tories' property. In 1795 a surveyor reported that when the settlers of Hunt's Meadow began to waver, their Balltown neighbors threatened "to come and take their cattle to support their army and then come and burn their barns." Barns were symbols of frontier prosperity possessed by the more comfortable settlers, who provided most of the proprietors' clients; a barn burning sent a clear message to property-conscious men that they held their possessions at community sufferance and that the security they sought did not lie in a separate peace with the proprietors.[56]

Just as community defense hinged upon unity within, to maintain their solidarity the settlers needed to demonstrate their ability to withstand external pressure. Poor, preoccupied with laboring on their homesteads, and dispersed over a rough, heavily timbered landscape, settlers necessarily pursued a limited and defensive strategy. In contrast to the New England Regulation of 1786–1787, when thousands of aggrieved yeomen swarmed down from the hills to shut down county courts and intimidate state legislatures, mid-Maine's Liberty Men usually stuck close to home and tried to seal off their communities from outside authorities enforcing the commonwealth's land laws. Each community conducted its own resistance, procuring munitions, sending out spies, and organizing covert militia companies to patrol their bounds. Patrols employed an elaborate system of signals with tin horns to alarm their neighbors and turn out, in the words of one chagrined deputy, "a number sufficient to effect any of their purposes." The Liberty Men intercepted and repelled intruders: surveyors running proprietary lines or deputy sheriffs serving proprietary writs. Interlopers who ignored warnings to halt risked volleys of musketry discharged into their horses (sometimes wounding the riders as well), beatings with fists and sticks, and painful rides on rough, wooden rails while the Liberty Men shredded any writs or survey plans. When settlers needed larger numbers to rescue some of their brethren from jail, a network of night riders spread the word to adjoining settlements. In response, hundreds of armed men drawn from various companies gathered at a backcountry tavern to cast bullets, elect field officers, fortify their courage with rum, and, ultimately, march on the county seat.[57]

Although decentralized and intermittent, under pressure the resistance could suddenly appear extensive, formidable, and elaborate. Deputy Sheriff Henry Johnson of Winslow testified that the Liberty Men (or White Indians) "had every appearance of military discipline and subordination, and obeyed the commands of a person they called their chief. Centinels were regularly posted and relieved and . . . every avenue to their settlement was strictly guarded to prevent the approach of any officer, and [they] emphatically declared they would kill any officer who should serve any writs of ejectment or upon whom any such writs were found." The Liberty Men stockpiled ammunition in special magazines, sought out legal advice, levied taxes to meet their expenses, administered local justice, and held periodic mass meetings to promulgate their "laws," burn effigies, and whip up fervor for the cause. In 1801 Charles Vaughan warned his fellow Kennebeck Proprietors that in most of the

backcountry mass ejectments availed nothing, "for they are so well organized that a stick of fire would be put to all buildings recovered by law
and threats of future attack would keep off purchasers." Until the proprietors could pacify the "violent set," more prosperous and peaceable
men "would not accept the land as a gift, with an obligation to reside
there in person." In January 1808 Deputy Sheriff Pitt Dillingham returned from negotiations with the Liberty Men and described their resistance as "a very generall and serious combination [that] had been
entered into by several thousands in the county." Three months later
John Chandler, Kennebec County's high sheriff, toured the backcountry and reported: "The opposition or disaffection is much more formidable than I expected. It extends at least over the whole of the Plymouth claim."[58]

Although less dramatic than venturing out to close the courts, the
settlers' decentralized tactics secured the same end. Unless deputy sheriffs could serve writs on settlers and unless proprietary surveyors could
run their lines proving that the defendants dwelled within a particular
claim, proprietors could not successfully prosecute the ejectment
and trespass cases necessary to reestablish their control. Samuel Ely of
Northport warned that completed surveys enabled proprietors to "en-
snare poor men that have no money to defend their rights, and so take
away their right of liberty." If a proprietary survey preceded settlement
or eluded settler vigilance, the settlers destroyed the surveyors' boundary stones and corner markers, substituting their own. The Liberty Men
hoped that their resistance would encourage their rulers to intervene
and mandate a farm for a token price to every settler. If not, the settlers
knew that they might obtain the same if they could fend off the proprietors' surveys and lawsuits for three decades because, according to the
commonwealth's statute of limitation on ejectments, a settler obtained a
title by adverse possession if he was not ejected within thirty years after
his particular lot was first taken up (usually by an earlier claimant). To
break the impasse, the Great Proprietors needed to prosecute the Liberty Men for their violent acts. But it was difficult to arrest suspects,
harder still to find willing witnesses against them, and nearly impossible
to keep prisoners in mid-Maine's flimsy, wooden county jails so easily
broken open by determined crowds. The Kennebeck Proprietors complained, "Convictions, the only remedies offered by the courts, are
scoffed at, derided, and dispised."[59]

So long as the settlers could sustain their "seed plot of sedition"—their
degree of cultural distance from authority—the resistance would remain
formidable. Competition between two versions of Christianity helped
delineate the battle lines separating great men from Liberty Men.

Montpelier. Summer Residence of Henry and Lucy Knox, Thomaston. Constructed 1793–1794. *Courtesy of the Maine Historical Society*

CHAPTER FIVE

Seekers and Preachers

Ignorant, wandering, and unprincipled preachers. . . . too lazy to labor, and therefore hopeless of any other than a wretched subsistence in their own proper spheres, often blown up with spiritual pride, believing themselves as peculiar favorites to receive immediate communications from heaven, assume the character and employment of religious teachers. The precarious pittance furnished by this business, miserable as it is, they consider as better than starving at home.—The Reverend Timothy Dwight, Congregationalist, 1807

The only persons who opposed [the revival] were GOG and MAGOG, viz. the enemies of Liberty and Equality; or, in more explicit terms, the Drones of Society, i.e. the persons who wish to live wholly on the earnings of others. These were very much opposed to the reformation. They called it *delusion, enthusiasm.*—John Buzzell, Freewill Baptist elder, 1811

ON JANUARY 8, 1801, Nathan Barlow and his Freetown (Albion) neighbors gathered to hear an itinerant evangelical preacher. He warmed the winter-chilled audience with a vivid picture of hell's horrors. Barlow recalled leaving the company "much agitated about it . . . for reflecting on the life I had lived, I considered myself in the most imminent danger, and begged of God to convince me of it if it was so." Shortly after Barlow returned to his crude log cabin, the early winter twilight crept over Freetown. Barlow remembered that at that moment he was "taken all at once with a strange kind of feeling, and laid me down: I began to grow stiff and to lose the power of moving by degrees, till I was totally unable to stir. I am very clear that I did not fall asleep." Suddenly Christ appeared "with a glorious countenance" and took Barlow by the hand. He recalled that Christ "carried me away as quick as a flash of lightning (my spirit I mean, for I was sensible at the time that I had left my body behind, and had no feeling of weight, but light as air)." Conducted to hell, Barlow witnessed the tortures of the damned. Then Christ took Barlow· to the gates of heaven to see God and the saved in all their ecstatic glory. Christ returned Barlow's spirit to his body charged with a mission: to narrate his vision to local gatherings of religious seekers. Regaining his senses, Barlow doubted the experience, whereupon Christ wrenched him back into the trance for a second whirlwind tour of hell and heaven. Restored once again to his body, Barlow forsook his doubts and accepted his mission on earth. He recounted his experience to local audiences and had it transcribed for publication by a literate neighbor

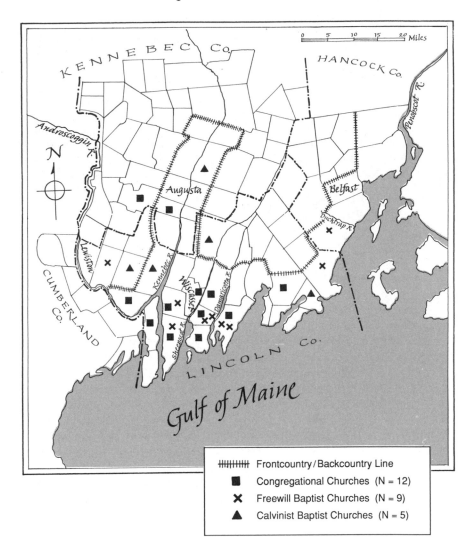

Map 8. Mid-Maine Churches, 1790

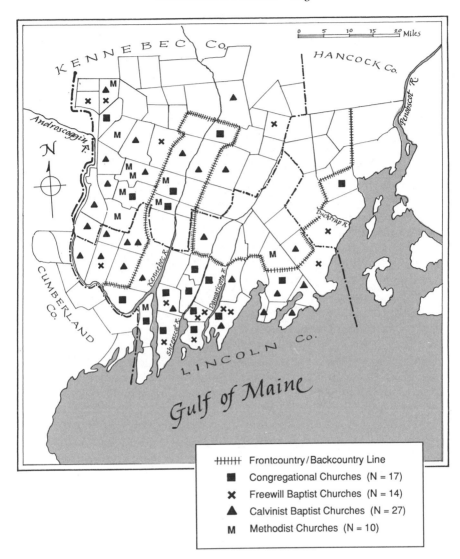

Map 9. Mid-Maine Churches, 1800

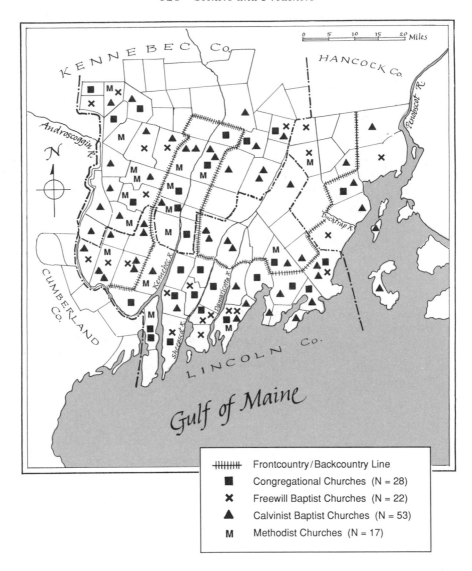

Map 10. Mid-Maine Churches, 1810

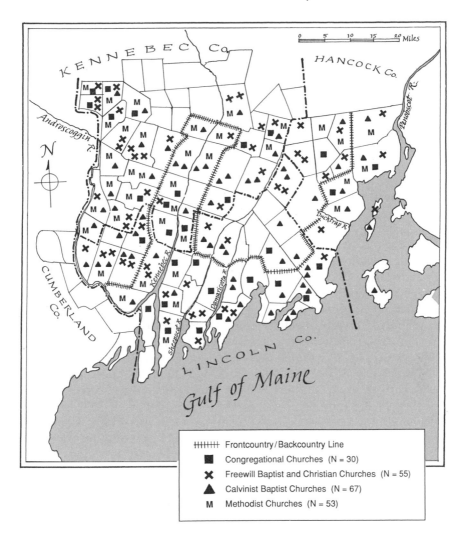

Map 11. Mid-Maine Churches, 1820

named William Taylor. And, whether Christ intended it or not, after his mystical experience Barlow emerged as a paramilitary leader in the settlers' resistance. He led armed patrols of White Indians who drove off approaching sheriffs and disciplined local men who assisted the proprietors.[1]

The Mystic and His Judge

Nathan Barlow's origins were humble. Born about 1775 on Cape Cod, Nathan was the son of Obed Barlow, one of the poorest men in the town of Sandwich. In 1784 Obed Barlow owned only a shop and a lone cow, no house. Seven years' labor did not significantly improve his lot; only 128 of the 1791 tax list's 427 taxpayers were as poor as or poorer than Obed Barlow. In 1792, at age forty, Obed disappeared from the Sandwich tax rolls to reappear later that year in a new Sheepscot backcountry settlement called Freetown (later incorporated as Fairfax and now known as Albion). The name announced the settlers' determination to pay no outside proprietor for their lands. Obed laid possession claim to one hundred acres of wilderness land and gradually cut a clearing and erected a cabin. Mounting debts burdened his efforts to develop a new farm. Acting on a creditor's behalf, a deputy sheriff tried to seize some of Obed Barlow's livestock in June 1803; Obed did "beat, wound and evilly entreat" the offending officer. After losing three successive suits for debt brought by his trader-creditors, Obed Barlow sold his homestead and moved eastward into the adjoining Beaver Hill settlement.[2]

Nathan first appeared as an independent householder in March 1799, when the federal direct tax assessors found him dwelling just south of Freetown in Harlem (China). His property was meager: a one-hundred-acre squatter's lot assessed at $186 and a rough log cabin worth a mere $30; he ranked thirty-ninth among Harlem's forty-nine taxpayers. Nor was he able or willing to pay the modest tax; in March 1801 the federal government advertised the property for sale to meet the unpaid tax. Nathan moved northward into Freetown to squat on a new lot of land. Shadowed by his own debts and lost lawsuits, Barlow sold his Freetown land to his creditors and in 1805 followed his father eastward into the Beaver Hill settlement to claim a new lot of land. When he died in 1817 in the prime of life, he owned no legal title to any real estate and held a mere $100 in personal property; one cow, a single mare, a yoke of yearling steers, eight sheep, a pig, and a set of blacksmith's tools comprised almost all of his small property. Poor and illiterate, Barlow would never have become influential but for his vision and his neighbors' need for his message.[3]

The Eastern Country's agrarians wanted to believe that the commonwealth's rulers would embrace the settler cause once they learned the full measure of proprietary perfidy. Persistent rumors expressed this optimism. Many claimed that the Supreme Judicial Court's chief justice let it slip that the Kennebeck Proprietors' title was worthless and would not stand up in court. In 1796 the Waldo Patent's settlers insisted that the governor and General Court quietly favored their plans to burn the buildings of Henry Knox and his agents. Similarly, in August 1801 David Gilpatrick of Patricktown (Somerville) told two of Knox's agents that the General Court "had determined that proprietors and settlers should 'fight it out' and passed an act or resolve to that effect." The supposed law thoughtfully stipulated that the combatants could use "guns and swords." In 1820, Freedom's inhabitants believed that "a Gentleman of high standing" had urged them to persist in the resistance because "the Legislature was doing something *handsome* for them." In the short run, such rumors encouraged resistance, but, because they reiterated their rulers' legitimacy, the agrarian cause flagged whenever the governor, General Court, or Supreme Judicial Court explicitly condemned the settlers' violence.[4]

To persevere in the face of their rulers' hostility, the settlers needed to convince themselves that they obeyed a higher law. This is what Nathan Barlow provided his neighbors. Barlow's vision and divine mission fortified his neighbors against despair and compromise. In their minds, opposition from the courts, the legislature, the governor, the trading town squires, and the county sheriff carried little moral weight when matched against a man who had traveled with Christ.

In June 1808 Justice George Thatcher of the Supreme Judicial Court sentenced Nathan Barlow to two years' hard labor in the state prison for his White Indian activities. Because Chief Justice Theophilus Parsons usually declined to undertake the long journey, Thatcher generally presided over the Supreme Judicial Court during its two annual tours into the Eastern Country. Like the Barlows, Thatcher was born on Cape Cod (in Yarmouth in 1754) and migrated to Maine to better his lot. There the similarities end, for Thatcher earned a Harvard degree and studied law before removing to Biddeford, Maine, in 1782. From 1788 to 1801 Thatcher represented the District of Maine in Congress, resigning to assume his seat on the Supreme Judicial Court. During the mid-1780s he maintained cordial ties with Maine's Antifederalist leaders and criticized land patents as oppressive anachronisms that threatened the Republic's survival. But, shaken by the New England Regulation of 1786, Thatcher reassessed and concluded that inequality was natural and immutable. In April 1789 he pronounced the classic conservative dictum: "If [people] are indolent, ignorant, and poor it is their own fault. If they are well informed, rich, virtuous and agreeable it is the effect of their own exertions."[5]

Thatcher became an outspoken and inflexible Federalist. Except for a stubborn, principled sympathy for Quaker abolitionists' right to petition Congress, Thatcher favored an energetic national government that brooked no popular insubordination between elections. Dismissing agrarians' fears of centralized power, Thatcher insisted that the greatest threat to ordered liberty came from "democratic mobs, by the erection of whiskey poles and liberty poles." He felt the Bill of Rights unnecessary, wanted to tax immigrants because America had "too many foreigners," and favored ignoring popular uproar to levy a stamp tax. Not content with defending the controversial Alien and Sedition Acts that tried to suppress domestic dissent, Thatcher proposed making them permanent and called for more vigorous prosecution. He especially disliked and distrusted frontier settlers as unruly ignorants who threatened orderly government with their agrarian prejudices. Thatcher opposed printing and freely disseminating copies of the Constitution in the new western states because it would only encourage frontiersmen's seditious readiness to judge the constitutionality of federal laws for themselves. "It was not political information which these people were in want of but moral information, correct habits, and regular fixed characters," he added. Thatcher thought "that a pair of spectacles might as well be put upon the nose of a dead man, as that information should be sent among these people." Subsequently, as a Massachusetts Supreme Judicial Court justice, his stern bearing, rigorous treatment of debtors, and conservative rulings in favor of the Great Proprietors antagonized the Eastern Country's settlers.[6]

Thatcher subscribed to a religious rationalism at complete odds with Nathan Barlow's visionary faith. In 1817 Thatcher explained, "The Religion of Jesus is a religion of reason addressed exclusively to the understanding." True religion would triumph "as people progress in civilization, knowledge, arts, and sciences, that is, as reason and the understanding assume the lead of mankind." He concluded, "The christian temper, manners and character are the children of education; they require constant schooling, teaching, chastening . . . in the same general manner the arts and sciences are taught and perfected."[7]

Naturally, evangelical mysticism disgusted Thatcher, who ascribed it to the inherent laziness of the uneducated. Employing the same language used by the Great Proprietors to criticize the settlers' work culture, Thatcher insisted:

All people are naturally averse from hard work; and will rarely labour hard six days in a week if they can get enough for a comfortable support by working four or five. . . . Hence it is, I believe, that most people seem ready to hear, believe and resort to any principles that promise to excuse them from the task of being disciplined and instructed in the way of Gospel morality or true holiness . . . and seem ready to follow almost any man or mountebank who will but tell them their salvation does not depend upon their virtuous life at all; and the moment they can bring themselves to believe that *God* or the *Holy Ghost only* is able to produce the change of heart, that ought to be effected by discipline, they will lie by and watch the movements of the spirit.

Thatcher denied the legitimacy of the spiritual journeys that played such an important role in the settlers' religious culture.

Hence while some man is bawling out these delusions in a thousand forms of repetition, men, women and children jump up, clap their hands and cry out they see Jesus—They behold God face to face, singing Halalujahs—Others in seeming distress and agonies of mind fall on the floor and lay some time in a seeming state of insensibility; and, after a while, on coming to their senses again they declare they have been translated to Heaven—Some to Hell; but all have seen God, conversed with Angels or departed friends and seen visions of various kinds—till the Assembly may be said to resemble Bedlam more than Christians worshiping Jehovah in spirit and in truth. . . . Indeed, my friend, there is no setting bounds to delusion, when reason is abandoned and the regular and established course of the natural and moral world is interrupted and made to give way to *miraculous grace* and *special interpositions*.

The tension between Barlow's mysticism and his judge's rationality suggests that the struggle over mid-Maine's lands broke along cultural lines defined by starkly different approaches to knowing God.[8]

The Orthodox and the Evangelical

The Revolution dramatically undercut Congregational religious authority—as well as proprietary control of the land—in the Eastern Country's many new settlements. During the colonial era, the General Court had mandated a system known as the Standing Order, where every town was to levy taxes to maintain a substantial meetinghouse and support an "able, learned, and orthodox minister," by whom the legislators meant a college-educated Congregationalist. Sanctioned by the General Court, endowed with a then rare liberal education, befriended by gentlemen, and garbed in impressive black robes, most Congregational divines were authoritative men who channeled and shaped much of the information that reached their communities from the wider world. But the Revolutionary war disrupted the colleges that trained Congregational ministers, and an increasing proportion of the young men from good families preferred to study law instead of divinity: the number of orthodox ministerial candidates dwindled at the same time that the Revolution spawned an unprecedented number of new frontier settlements. Moreover, Harvard graduates were increasingly loath to endure the hardships, isolation, and poor pay of a frontier parish when so many more desirable parishes lay vacant in southern New England's older and more prosperous communities. At the same time, hard-pressed frontier settlements were ever more reluctant to incur the expense of meetinghouse, parsonage, and salaried minister. Consequently, during the 1780s the number of Congregational ministers lagged ever farther behind the rapid growth and northward expansion of New England's population, removing an increasing number from the reach of orthodox preaching and reproof. In 1790 only one-fifth of mid-Maine's sixty communities had organized a Congregational church. Congregationalism remained virtually confined to the more prosperous and populous commercial towns of the coast and valleys; only one of the twenty-four backcountry communities supported a Congregational church.[9]

Congregationalists recognized that the accelerating pace of frontier settlement imperiled the Standing Order. According to the orthodox ministers, social order decayed when common people moved beyond the restraining influence of their superiors. "A town destitute of the [orthodox] ministry is like a field, deserted by its cultivator, and left to produce a rank spontaneous growth," observed the Reverend Stephen Chapin. In language akin to that of the Great Proprietors, the Reverend David Thurston of Winthrop worried that expansion into the wilderness sapped self-discipline and subverted civilization. Addressing the orthodox Maine Missionary Society, Thurston explained:

Every one knows the manner in which our *new settlements* are formed. The first settlers are men of little or no property, dependent upon their daily labor for support. They go into the wilderness and fell the forest and clear the land for cultivation. It is usually several years before they are able to erect a comfortable dwelling house: and many more before they can enjoy some of the common privileges of older settlements. During this whole period, they are from necessity without schools, without ministers, without any of that influence, or those institutions which contribute so essentially to form the sober, steady, sterling character of older parts of the country. By the time they are able to support these institutions, long habit has made them easy without them. . . . In such a soil, we should naturally suppose, that infidelity and every species of error would take root and flourish. Every account represents the state of these settlements, as deplorable for ignorance and irreligion. Let it be remembered, that the people who have grown up in these habits, are giving birth to other settlements beyond them, which are of course still more barbarous and less favorably disposed to the institutions and character of their ancestors.

He concluded gloomily that, by "the very nature of a spreading population" on a wilderness continent, "our country has a strong tendency to degenerate, and to degenerate rapidly. . . . *The population of the country outgrows its institutions.*" Thurston estimated that it would take 130 Congregational missionaries at an annual cost of sixty-five thousand dollars to reclaim the Eastern Country's settlers.[10]

The few Congregational ministers who settled in the Eastern Country before 1800 tended to be poorly disciplined men tainted with some personal scandal that denied them employment elsewhere. Such wayward clergymen embarrassed and discredited the Congregationalist Standing Order among the settlers. The Reverend Seth Noble of Bangor was a powerful preacher equally adept at heavy drinking and improper "anectdote and levity." One congregant concluded, "When out of the pulpit he ought never to go in, and when in never to go out." Noble exhausted his parishioners' patience when he delayed marrying his housekeeper until her pregnancy was conspicuous. The Reverend John Urquhart of Warren had to forsake his controversial ministry when, to his parishioners' surprise, a first wife unknown to them arrived and "in a great rage ordered the second wife away, and took her place at the head of the table." The Reverend Nathaniel Whitaker of Canaan stood trial for raping a young congregant, but escaped on a legal technicality. In 1794 Bath's new Congregational minister proved to be an impostor who had previously performed the same deception in Berkshire County. The hard-drinking Reverend Alfred Johnson of Belfast ventured into the backcountry to marry a young couple in Greene Plantation (Belmont, Morrill, and Searsmont). "They all took so freely of the good cheer that the priest forgot his verses, so after trying several kinds of poetry and ditties he gave it up and said to the parties, 'You may consider yourselves married and I will come out some other day and finish the ceremony.'"[11]

Such wayward clergymen discredited Congregational orthodoxy. The Reverend Alexander MacLean, a Congregational missionary, lamented:

The Reverend Mr. Johnson last year did more to prejudice the serious people of every denomination against the society and their missionaries than all who had been sent before. Hardly an individual, whether Saint or Sinner whom I heard mention his name, but reprobated his conduct and if he had studied to defeat the design of his mission, he could not have used more effectual means than he did.

The Reverend Paul Coffin, another Congregational missionary, reported that, when a New Sharon man complained that many orthodox ministers "hurt the cause of religion by careless and worldly conduct which did not show an heart engaged for God and his cause, I was obliged to say, amen!" Given the many sorry examples, few settlers felt in any hurry to establish the expensive Standing Order in their midst.[12]

Absent or discredited Congregational authority created opportunities for settlers to seek their own path to the Holy Spirit as "Christian primitivists." Hoping to recapture the simplicity and spirituality associated with the original, apostolic Christian church, the frontier's religious seekers deemphasized creeds, articles, doctrine, and church governance in favor of "experimental religion," moments of intense communication with the divine, moments where the "new born" obtained a precious new understanding of themselves, God, and the Scriptures. That moment secured their salvation, their resurrection to an eternal life of bliss in heaven, their rescue from eternal damnation. New births had a pattern: initial despair, resignation to Christ, an ecstatic vision of heaven's marvels, and a culminating sense of wonder at how differently the world looked when they emerged from their trance. Thus Colonel William Jones of Bristol ecstatically described his new birth at age nineteen.

> The Lord was pleased to deliver me instantaneously from the jaws of a gaping hell. The change was amazing; [I was] raised in an instant from the deepest misery, to the glorious hope of eternal happiness. . . . As much of heavenly joys was sent into my soul as this earthly vessel was able to bear: except the Lord had enlarged and strengthened it to receive more. O! the joy and rapture that came to my soul; for a space of time I cannot tell how long; but I may with St. Paul say: I did not know whether I was in the body or out of the body; but suppose all bodily objects disappeared and heavenly objects filled their places. . . . Such a change must take place in every one that comes to heaven.[13]

A creative, anarchic ferment prevailed among the seekers in the new settlements. Encouraged by their neighbors and confronting no orthodox minister's opposition, "exhorters" emerged among the settlers and "improved" their oratorical and prophetic gifts. Collected together around local exhorters, seekers met in cabins for exhortation, prayer, and reading the Bible aloud. Seekers' explorations were simultaneously highly personal and collective. In animated exchanges with one another and with itinerant preachers, religious seekers defined, shared, compared, and defended their personal investigations. The settlers' cooperative ethos encouraged the believers to build their faith around collective support and validation. Just as they often needed their neighbors' help in improving their farms or in defending them from proprietary writs, settlers gathered together to provoke and compare their individual conversions; every seeker found God on his own but needed collective support to prepare for that moment and to confirm its validity.[14]

Evangelical preachers and Congregational missionaries toured the backcountry, competing to win the allegiance of the proliferating groups of seekers. Mid-Maine's four leading evangelical denominations—the Calvinist Baptists, Freewill Baptists, Methodists, and the Christian Connection—renounced the Congregationalist reliance on coerced taxes in favor of individual choice and voluntary contribution. But the evangelical and the orthodox differed most fundamentally over how a seeker could find God. Evangelicals insisted that Christ continued to communicate with his children and that no one properly understood the Scriptures without experiencing the Holy Spirit in a new birth. Conversely, the orthodox distrusted mystical experiences; they insisted that God had completed his revelation to mankind with the New Testament. Where evangelicals encouraged the settlers' inquisitive dabbling in experimental religion, the orthodox insisted that the laity needed careful scriptural guidance from a learned minister wise to human folly and Satan's delusions. The orthodox were especially suspicious of sudden new births by men who had previously been conspicuous sinners, exactly the sort of conversions that so impressed evangelicals with the saving power of the Spirit. The orthodox were not averse to new births, but insisted that true conversion required careful preparation: a sound morality and a clear understanding of the Scriptures. True conversion demanded equally careful behavior thereafter: a reconciliation of the event with Scripture and an undeviating dedication to morality and good works.[15]

Evangelicals rejected the learned, orthodox clergy. By seeking worldly honors, knowledge, and salaries, the orthodox ministers lost sight of their own depravity, precluding spiritual experience with the divine. The orthodox ministry stood as misguided beacons luring many to eternal destruction, for their abstract preaching put men's souls to sleep, ensuring their damnation. In the words of Colonel William Jones, they were spiritually dead "worldlings" or "hirelings" devoted to "the god of this world, money." They were deceiving parasites bent on fleecing their flocks for salaries rather than provoking the new births essential to their salvation. During his missionary tours of the backcountry, the Reverend Alfred Johnson endured the epithets "humbug, college made minister, dull formality, dead letter and dumb dog."[16]

In contrast, the evangelicals offered a humble, ill-educated, impoverished ministry, distinguished only by their superior gifts for provoking new births. The evangelical preacher appeared as the newborn man relieved of the sin oppressing so many in his audience. In search of "gospel liberty"—a spontaneous sense of God's power within—the evangelical preached without notes and cared little for grammar, consistency, or logic. He sought simply to become a conduit of divine energy that would immediately jolt his listeners into a comprehension of their eternal peril and suddenly inspire their search for divine exaltation. He wore "a plain uniformity of dress" and employed a simple, direct discourse intended to reach as broad an audience as possible. The most radical evangelicals—the Freewill Baptists and the Christian Connection—encouraged preaching by charismatic women and adopted ritual foot washing to display their renunciation of worldly inequality.[17]

Frontier evangelicals encouraged a collective worship, where the distinction between preacher and laity virtually dissolved. Promoting "Christian freedom, equality, union, and brotherly love," Elias Smith of the Christian Connection insisted, "In the church of Christ no one has a right to set himself up to rule all the rest, and say who shall speak and who shall hold his tongue." He celebrated worship where "every one has a right to preach, pray, exhort, or sing one by one. And when they cannot avoid it, they have a right to pray all at once, as they did in the times of the apostles." The Reverend Daniel Oliver, a Congregational missionary, was both fascinated and repelled by the worship conducted by a Methodist in Northport:

> His manner was very disgusting to me. He preached from the Text, "Blessed are the pure in heart for they shall see God." The *pitching* of *breath, sighs* and *groans* of preacher and hearers was *awful* and *tremendous*. I know not what to compare it to, unless a number of swine shut up in a yard, with furious mad-dogs rushing upon 'em . . . all wallowing in their distress, groaning, squaling and pausing for life. Still the preacher appeared serious and the people inquisitive.[18]

Congregationalists insisted that by failing to test dreams and visions against scriptural knowledge the frontier evangelicals peddled dangerous nonsense. The Reverend Alexander MacLean lamented, "I have observed that those who have only had a common education are ready to chuse the most mysterious passages of Scripture to discourse from and to find a mystical spiritual meaning in every such passage and of consequence often make havock of Scripture, make it speak whatever their imagination suggests." The Reverend Daniel Little wrote, "Such men are to be pitied and prayed for, who take the flights of a wild and disordered brain for the genuine dictates of wisdom and the much to be desired noble elevation of the holy spirit of God." Another Congregational missionary, the Reverend John Turner, complained of northern New England's evangelicals: "The more there are speaking at once, and the louder they scream, the greater, in their opinion, is the power of the Spirit. The word of God is despised, when it opposes revelations, communicated to them." He was especially horrified at their familiarly addressing Christ as "brother Jesus." He concluded: "As a body they may be considered, as the scum of the earth, the filth of creation. Lying, drunkenness, uncleanness, Sabbath-breaking, fraud and theft may be found among them, without close scrutiny."[19]

According to the orthodox, by elevating the spirit to the neglect of Scriptures, the frontier evangelicals imperiled souls in two ways: they discouraged people from making the proper preparations for conversion, and they gave those who had experienced visions a false sense of confidence in their salvation. All of the evangelicals courted the second danger; the Calvinist Baptists (mid-Maine's predominant denomination) were especially prone to the first. Their preoccupation with the sudden new birth as a miraculous intervention by God led many to an extreme fatalism that rejected the importance of the moral law. They were inclined to tolerate sin among the unconverted and to denounce a reliance on Scriptures to seek salvation, because no one could be saved until God willed it. The Reverend Stephen Chapin enumerated the hyper-Calvinist heresies that led so many settlers to Antinomianism, a rejection of all authority in this world:

> 1 All days are equally holy. 2 The dictates of the spirit are the rule of life. 3 That the spirit strives only with the elect. 4 That the Bible is of no use to the impenitent. 5 That the unconverted have lost natural ability to do duty. 6 The atonement is limited and therefore the invitation is not universal. 7 That there is no propriety in using means with the unrenewed. 8 Above all, the antinomian leven is secretly and widely diffusing.

In 1797 the Reverend Paul Coffin returned from a missionary tour to report that a Baptist "said he had *prayed before conversion;* the tho't of which sin was a dreadful Burden to his Soul. . . . Many such things I heard." Three years later Coffin added, "When a supposed convert behaves amiss and is reminded of it, 'it is decreed,' is the Answer. The most abandoned Sinner is more likely to enter the Kingdom than the most virtuous man. . . . These and many like Things are current with many People, among the untaught Inhabitants of *Maine*."[20]

For the Congregationalists, the fundamental problem in frontier Maine was that the settlers were too poorly educated to prefer Scripture to visions. In November 1797 the Reverend Coffin complained: "'Tis as much to be lamented in Maine perhaps, as anywhere, that people lack good christian education. . . . Better measures to promote the Kingdom of Christ and more scriptural, are much wanted in this country in general." In 1812 the Reverend Richard Hazeltine assured the president of the Congregationalists' Massachusetts Society for Promoting Christian Knowledge that Maine's Baptists "manifest sufficient zeal for *preaching*, such as it is, [but] are extremely indifferent with respect to *teaching*; their children know nothing about such a branch of family discipline as religious instruction; and by such families is the Sabbath most shockingly profaned." Only improved education by Congregational missionaries freely distributing the printed word could save Maine's deluded seekers: "The people here have never, or not till of late, enjoyed much advantage from schools; of course they have never acquired much taste for books, nor derived much benefit from reading. To christianize a people it is necessary they should first be civilized and humanized."[21]

Consequently, the Congregationalist missionary conceived of himself as a teacher of the written word. In contrast to the evangelical itinerant, the orthodox missionary stressed knowledge of the Scriptures as part of a necessarily gradual process of Christian preparation. He appeared as the learned expert doling out free tracts and reading his carefully written sermon; it elucidated a particular scriptural text and concluded with an "improvement" that drew moral lessons for the listeners to apply to their lives. Banking upon education to rescue the settlers but recognizing their inability to support schools on their own, the Congregational missionary societies allocated funds to subsidize teachers in the new settlements. And, to increase the supply of teachers in mid-Maine, the missionary societies invested funds in the Hallowell Academy founded by Charles Vaughan. In 1792 the Reverend Daniel Little gushed, "Twenty grammar Schollars for english school masters through the county proceeding from the Academy with virtue by their side will effect a revolution and date an era of science and virtue not to be forgotten till the sun shall in the east rise no more." In fact, the future was less heroic for Congregational virtue. The funds allocated by the societies for town schools were woefully inadequate; the morals and abilities of the teachers usually disappointed their patrons; and, in many towns, the evangelical majority rejected Congregational aid as a Trojan horse. The Reverend Alexander MacLean complained, "I know some places where the people are very poor and the children are brought up in ignorance, but they chuse to have it so and shut their Ears against . . . those who are not of their persuasion . . . and I believe they would use fire and sword to extirpate such as Heretics of the worst kind."[22]

In sum, the Eastern Country's religious contest pitted those who stressed the scriptural word against those who relied principally on the inner spirit, those who insisted upon an end to divine revelation with the Bible and those who sought their own latter-day revelations, those who insisted the common people needed teachers and those ready to trust in their spiritual impulses, those who insisted the Revolution had gone too far and those who felt it was still incomplete. Cyrus Eaton of Warren explained, "Two religious parties were formed . . . the one rejoicing in the clearness of head, the other in the warmth of the heart, and each stigmatizing the other's religion as learned coldness, or misguided fervor." Where the evangelicals gloried in their seekers' spiritual self-assertion (subject to collective validation by fellow seekers), the orthodox sought a restoration of the colonial era's more deferential religious culture. Where the orthodox regarded the evangelicals' explosive growth as a dangerous side effect produced by the Revolution's disruption of respect for authority, the evangelicals perceived the Standing Order as a tyrannical anachronism that must fall to complete the Revolution's democratic promise. Where Elias Smith of the Christian Connection exhorted his readers to esteem preachers "for their works, as servants, but never submit to them as masters," the Congregationalist Paul Coffin sought audiences who were "teachable and modest."[23]

The Evangelical Triumph

The evangelicals got the better of the bitter competition for Maine's settlers. In 1790 only a third of mid-Maine's communities had any organized church; most settlers lived without religion or participated only in informal seekers' meetings. By 1800, two-thirds of mid-Maine's communities had at least one church; by 1810, four-fifths. During the 1790s the slow-growing Congregationalists established churches in only five new towns, compared to the Calvinist Baptists who organized in twenty-one new communities, the Methodists in nine, and the Freewill Baptists in five. In 1800 the three leading evangelical denominations collectively outnumbered the Congregationalists' churches in mid-Maine by three to one. And the Congregational churches were so small that one orthodox missionary conceded that in mid-Maine "not more than a twentieth part of the professors of religion are Congregationalists." Between 1800 and 1810 the evangelicals established new churches in almost three times as many towns as the Congregationalists. Congregationalism remained largely confined to the more prosperous communities located in the frontcountry, where, by 1810, three in every five towns had an orthodox church, versus only one in every eight backcountry communities.[24]

The sustained efforts of Congregational missionaries were largely fruitless. The Reverend Jotham Sewall, mid-Maine's leading Congregational missionary, calculated that between June 1803 and May 1807 he traveled 7,330 miles and delivered 907 sermons but admitted only 35 adults to Congregational fellowship: 209 miles and 26 sermons per new member. By contrast, during the three years 1806–1808 the Freewill Baptist itinerant Ephraim Stinchfield of New Gloucester traveled about 7,500 miles, preached 1,257 times, and baptized 370 adults, for a far more efficient 20 miles and 3 preachings per convert.[25]

In part, the evangelicals prevailed because a worsening doctrinal controversy among the Congregationalists undermined the effectiveness of their missionaries. After the Revolution, some Congregationalists hardened in their allegiance to Calvinist predestination, and others embraced the Arminian notion that God had endowed man with the free will and reason to seek salvation. As a result, missionaries from the different wings of Congregationalism discredited one another with their dissension.[26]

More important, the evangelicals prevailed because they harmonized better with the frontier's conditions and culture. Afflicted by hardships, frontier seekers were drawn to an emotionally rich faith that expressed their sense of impotence before God's power; they hungered for the visionary new birth and latter-day revelations encouraged by the evangelical. During the 1790s the Calvinist Baptist itinerant James Potter of Bowdoin found "great scarcity" in "the new settlements" but insisted that ecstatic worship helped the settlers cope with their physical as well as their spiritual hunger: "Thus were these poor people fed, first upon a promise and then the effect of it supplied the wants of their bodies." Evangelical preaching without notes impressed settlers committed to the spirit within, settlers who insisted, "Reading is not preaching." Requiring convincing testimony of a new birth for church membership, evangelicals insisted upon adult "believer's baptism" by public immersion (versus the orthodox satisfaction with infant baptism). Believer's baptism was a dramatic public ritual that the Congregationalists could not match. Curiosity and careful advance notice drew dozens, sometimes hundreds, to the appointed river, pond, or cove; often the drama and the converts' fervor deeply impressed many in the audience, producing more conversions.[27]

The evangelicals' fluid denominational structures favored aggressive proselytizing among a rapidly expanding frontier population. A variety of itinerants rotating through the settlements appealed to the settlers' taste for variety and novelty in a way that one settled, learned minister could not. The evangelicals created new churches far faster than the Congregationalists could; an evangelical itinerant quickly organized his converts into a church without waiting for the settlement to obtain legal incorporation as a town. Rather than waiting for Harvard to graduate a learned minister willing to live on the frontier, an evangelical denomination recruited a local exhorter to serve as the new church's elder, deacon, or class leader. Evangelicals reaped existing seekers' groups by recognizing and recruiting poorly educated but enthusiastic and religiously

ambitious men like James Potter who could not find similar encouragement from the Standing Order that insisted upon a liberally educated
ministry. Impoverished settlers could afford the evangelicals' inexpen-
sive ministry. Evangelical preachers made do with meager voluntary
contributions and with services conducted in barns, homes, and fields,
in contrast to the Congregational insistence on substantial salaries, par-
sonages, and meetinghouses all sustained by compulsory taxes. Evangelical preachers lived in poverty or supplemented their income by con-
ducting their own farms or trades. Understanding their neighbors'
material hardships and spiritual longings better than learned outsiders,
evangelical preachers were adept at communicating with their fellow
settlers.[28]

By reversing the secular world's celebration of material success and
contempt for the poor, the evangelicals' otherworldliness provided impoverished settlers with a new sense of self-worth. Evangelicals insisted
that the fruits of an innately evil material world discouraged attention to
spiritual salvation. John Colby, a Freewill Baptist itinerant active in mid-
Maine, saw heaven's wonders and concluded that the "riches of this vain
world" were nothing but the devil's lures, meant to distract men from
"the glories of that better, fairer, brighter world above." In March
1784 the Freewill Baptists' circular letter to member churches warned:
"Now if any of you will go on in sin, indulging in pride and fashions,
. . . worldly-mindedness, worldly honors, Rabbi-greetings, uppermost
rooms and chief seats—choosing all or any of these, is choosing the way
to hell, because they are the things that lead there. They are in opposition to the teachings of God's spirit, which alone can lead the soul to rest
and peace." To attain heaven, seekers were supposed to live at war with
the world. This attitude sustained an egalitarian suspicion of the wealthy
and powerful, for the greater a man's attachment to the material world,
the less likely he was to recognize his spiritual worthlessness without
Christ. James Potter observed: "In visiting the rich professors of religion, I found that they had much to say about the world; but in visiting the poor I heard them converse much upon the riches of divine
grace. . . . I now realized the truth of this scripture, 'God hath chosen
the poor of this world, rich in faith and heirs of the Kingdom.' "[29]

Consolation for the hard-pressed rather than a call for an alternative economic system, evangelical otherworldliness made poverty more
psychologically endurable, provided a useful critique of the material
world's powerful men, encouraged contributions to the "church stock"
for charity to the poorest members, and discouraged lawsuits between
brethren. Otherwise, it deterred few evangelicals from pursuing more
property, privately owned. In mid-Maine there was but one noteworthy
attempt to carry evangelical otherworldliness to a collectivist conclusion.
In 1779 Edward Lock of Gilmanton, New Hampshire, helped found

the Freewill Baptists in New England. He migrated to Chesterville in Maine's Sandy River valley, where his powerful preaching attracted a considerable following. About 1799 Lock revealed a dream that Christ intended his followers (in the words of William Allen, Jr.) "to establish a community of goods for Christians to have all things in common." Lock's plan enjoyed important support from other influential Freewill Baptists in the area, especially elder John Whitney. But the plan generated divisive suspicions that Lock had designs on the collective property. Alarmed by the dissension, the Freewill Baptist annual meeting renounced the scheme and reluctantly ousted Lock, who retired to his farm. His loss temporarily devastated that denomination's influence in the Sandy River valley; by 1804 half the valley's affiliated churches had lapsed.[30]

Religion and the Resistance

In December 1808 the Reverend Stephen Chapin returned from a frustrating tour of mid-Maine as a Congregational missionary. He filed a report that blamed the hostility to orthodoxy in the backcountry partly on the agrarian resistance.

> The want of good titles is a source of unceasing difficulty. Many of the back settlers are in law termed squatters. They view themselves as oppressed by the proprietors. They are jealous of professional men and men in affluence; viewing them as combined to oppress the poor. They feel hostile to such characters. They are exasperated. Hence many of them resort to the savage practice of dressing in the Indian habit, and seeking the woods to prevent surveyors and civil officers from performing their duty. . . . So long as these difficulties remain the state of society will be unhappy. It will remain a kind of medium between barbarism and civilization.

A fellow Congregational missionary, Edmund Eastman, concurred: "The unsettled state of the soil is a subject of great anxiety and continual contention which greatly damps the spirit for agricultural improvement and greatly lessens their exertion for the promotion of religious order."[31]

As Chapin and Eastman recognized, the contest over religious culture paralleled the struggle between proprietors and settlers over the labor newly invested in the Eastern Country's lands. This is not to say that either visionary religion or the resistance caused the other. Of the two, evangelical religion was the more fundamental and the more extensive and enduring. The intersection of visionary religion and agrarian resistance in mid-Maine belonged to a subset of a far larger, essentially otherworldly phenomenon. During the post-Revolutionary generation, evangelical religion proliferated throughout the American backcountry, regardless of the presence or absence of agrarian grievances. Instead, we should regard agrarian protest and evangelical seeking as initially independent but compatible responses to similar circumstances: a growing population of hard-pressed people living in new independence from traditional authority and challenged by the recent Revolution to think for themselves. In mid-Maine, agrarian protest and visionary religion grew side by side and proved mutually reinforcing as each promoted a more decentralized and egalitarian culture that seconded the settlers' growing distrust of centralized authority and elite expertise. Conversely, Great Proprietors and Congregational divines understood their own affinities and shared interest in restoring a more organic and hierarchical order in the turbulent Eastern Country. It was more than coincidental that the resistance and evangelical religion flourished in the same backcountry milieu while Congregationalists did well only in the frontcountry towns.[32]

Liberty Men seized upon and adapted the evangelical message to empower their resistance. Direct access to the Holy Spirit allowed settlers a sense that, despite, perhaps because of, their poverty, they were spiritually superior to outsiders with greater wealth, power, and education. Evangelicals encouraged men and women to follow their inner impulses, which led seekers concerned over the land conflict to a Christ who favored the settlers' struggle. Visionary religion offered the resistance a style, a stock of symbols and arguments, borrowed and adapted by agrarians to define and sustain their cause. When Great Proprietors demanded land payments, settlers could identify themselves as seekers serving God, and their opponents as worldlings serving Mammon. And the settlers could place their conflict in the millennial context of a supernatural struggle between Christ and Antichrist. Thus James Shurtleff wrote:

> For religion and freedom, of old 'twas decided,
> Springs both from one root, and can't be divided.

Shurtleff depicted Satan enraged over the settlers' struggle for landed liberty because it imperiled his control over the earth exercised through the agency of great men:

> Yet now 'tis disputed, for what do I hear?
> Strange rumor of late, which alarms and affrights,
> Strange rumor of freedom, and human rights;
> Tho' men are but squatters, vile squatters, you see,
> Who settle on earth, holding not under me;
> But, alas! human rights, as urg'd by the squatter,
> Makes my kingdom and hell's foundation to totter.

In 1800 Major Joel Thompson of Lewiston assured his neighbors that it was "doing God service to kill Col. [Josiah] Little or any other person concerned in the line which he is in." In August 1810 a Bristol settler cursed a proprietary supporter as someone who "carried the mark of the beast on his forehead."[33]

Seekers who synthesized resistance and spirituality helped their neighbors justify resisting legal authority. In this way, Nathan Barlow, a poor, illiterate blacksmith, obtained important influence among his fellow settlers. It is unlikely that he would have acquired such influence had he remained in Sandwich, Massachusetts, where the orthodox minister's authority loomed so large. Indeed, mid-Maine's leading agrarian ideologues all claimed religious authority—Samuel Ely was a minister, James Davis an exhorter, James Shurtleff a Calvinist Baptist elder, William Jones a Methodist class leader—and all insisted that the resistance harmonized with God's purpose. As the settlers most experienced and skilled with written and spoken words, they naturally came to the fore when their neighbors needed speeches, pamphlets, notices, and petitions. Among a rural people who were used to reasoning from Biblical analogy, no other rhetorical style could have been as effective. It would have been unusual if they had not assumed this role, for religious men writing in a spiritual vein were conspicuous in other agrarian resistance movements throughout the American backcountry.[34]

Colonel William Jones of Bristol combined leadership in his town's resistance with a passion for evangelical religion. As a young man he knew his full share of poverty and hardships and received an enduring scar from an attacking Indian in 1747. He prospered as a farmer, a skilled carpenter, and a wintertime schoolteacher (although his only education came from his parents and their Bible). His early and zealous commitment to the Revolution enabled Jones to advance into important new political offices: militia lieutenant colonel, Bristol's General Court representative, and delegate to the January 1788 Massachusetts state convention to ratify the Federal Constitution. In contrast to many other leading men, new honors did not alienate Jones from his neighbors; culturally he remained a neighbor, committed to evangelical piety and agrarian localism and convinced of a magical cosmos alive with the evil work of demons, witches, and warlocks as well as with God's active intervention. He clung to the resistance, declining a proprietor's bribe of a free homestead. An outspoken Antifederalist critic of the Federal Constitution as unchristian and undemocratic, Jones particularly denounced its failure to include a religious oath for officeholders. He continued to work with his hands, crafting the furniture for Bristol's first Methodist church. He retired from his political posts, began preaching, gathered a seekers' group, and, in 1793, committed their allegiance to the Methodists. Headstrong, he soon broke with the Methodists for disagreeing with his opinions.[35]

His perspective was starkly Manichaean; men were either "sent of God and in his employ, or they were sent of the devil and in his employ, for there are but these two masters." To find salvation, men had to forsake pride in their worldly honors and possessions, for "while their minds are carnal they cannot receive the things of the spirit, while that carnal mind remains it is at enmity against God." This was easier for the hard-pressed. "The poorest may have [salvation] if he will freely give up his all, and the richest cannot have it short of his all; this is one great reason why not many rich, not many learned, not many noble, attain this prize and miss of eternal happiness, they will not part with their great all." Jones insisted that the "little and humble soul that will see himself poor and come humble to the foot of free grace and beg and find mercy and grace, while the rich and full are sent empty away." When wealthy and well-educated proprietors sought land payments from Jones and his neighbors, the colonel had little difficulty identifying the settler cause with God's.[36]

Similarly, in Twenty-Five-Mile Pond settlement (Unity), Deacon Stephen Chase was at once the community's preeminent exhorter and the leader of its Liberty Men. Recognizing the connection between resistance and visionary religion, George Ulmer chose Abraham Welch, a Quaker, to infiltrate Chase's Liberty Men. Like the radical sects associated with the English Civil War of the 1640s and early New England's Puritan fringe, Chase's seekers were Antinomians who interpreted the Bible allegorically to conclude that Christ was in fact the spark of divinity within every man, rather than a distant deity. The Reverend Paul Coffin toured Twenty-Five-Mile Pond and complained, "Father Chase talked so much of the double meaning of every text of sacred writ, and so mixed heterogeneous matter that I left him after dinner." The Reverend Jotham Sewall, another Congregational missionary, visited Chase and reported: "He appeared to hold that all things were predestined and that sinners were not to blame for their wickedness and yet seemed to make high pretensions to religion. . . . He appears in some things to agree with Quakers." Chase's seekers shared the Quakers' meditative search for Christ's voice within and the application of that inner voice to interpret Scripture. But, when dealing with proprietary surveys, they did not practice the Quakers' pacifism. According to these seekers, once a man experienced the new birth, he became Christ and could do no wrong. In September 1803 Sewall had a disturbing conversation with a Twenty-Five-Mile Pond settler who held: "All the Bible is to be misunderstood; spiritually there is no such thing as the Garden of Eden, nor even such a man as Moses; the Patriarchs, or even such a being as Christ literally. That the way Christ was born again was by being born in the hearts of everyone that is born again. After conversing awhile I told him I thought he was led away with a delusion of the devil." The Antinomian belief in the Christ within must have reassured settlers that they did no evil in violently smiting the Great Proprietors' surveyors.[37]

Chase initially welcomed Coffin in the naive hope that the Congregational missionary would publicly endorse his unorthodox notions. Coffin demurred and recorded Chase's disappointment: "He went home sober, and never asked me again to call on him. O, how I sank from high esteem to nothing in the space of two hours!" Chase's alienation undercut the efforts by Coffin and Sewall to organize a Congregational church in Twenty-Five-Mile Pond settlement. Sewall could gather only nine members, all but two of them women. Soon that feeble church was riven by internal dissension and disciplinary problems when the men failed to keep their hands off the women. Significantly, Benjamin Rackliff, an active Liberty Man, ignored his wife's pleas and refused to allow the tiny Congregational band the use of his tavern for their services. Instead of joining the Congregationalists, Chase's seekers and Liberty Men affiliated with the Freewill Baptist itinerant John Whitney, an adept at visionary religion who had supported Edward Lock's collectivism.[38]

Congregationalist missionaries repeatedly found the most unorthodox religious concepts—those which they considered Antinomian—in the very places where the resistance was strongest. The Sheepscot backcountry between the Kennebec and Penobscot rivers was the cockpit of resistance; according to the Reverend Alexander MacLean, it was also the region "where Missionary labours are needed more than any [other] part of the District of Maine . . . as there are a great body of Freewill Baptists there who are the greatest Enemies to the truth and more enthusiastical than any other Denomination." MacLean was especially shocked by the seekers organized by Captain John Harvell in Bernardstown (Madison and Cornville), Clinton, Canaan, and Norridgewock.

> I met Capt. Harvell of Bernardstown, a sensible man with whom I conversed about three Hours, much at a loss to determine whether he was crackbrain'd or not, never having heard of him or his sentiments before. He professed to have had Revelations since he was ten years old, maintained that all the Elect were God, that when one died the body was damned, but the Soul which was God returned to him, that Christ's body when he died was damned and his prayers when on Earth was damned and that nothing which he Harvell did was sinful.

Such doctrines and visions resemble those of Chase's seekers and those promoted by Elias Smith of the Christian Connection, the most radical evangelicals of the early Republic.[39]

Just as there were strong affinities between agrarians and visionaries, Great Proprietors and Congregationalist divines recognized that they shared the same worldview and the same opponents. Proprietors and Congregationalists concurred that the Revolution had created a discontinuity between the old, southern New England and the new, northern New England by spawning turbulent settlements in desperate need of closer guidance from their betters. Both were profoundly disturbed by the emerging pluralism and voluntarism of frontier culture because both believed that society must be an organic whole organized in a hierarchical fashion. In religion as in politics, the common folk should defer to an elite of learned men administering a uniform set of laws, moral and civil. Otherwise, the Reverend Stephen Chapin warned, "The turbulent and ferocious tempers of men would be unbridled and the world be converted into a place of anarchy and slaughter." In this view, great men were the cement that held society together and held the chronic threat of anarchy at bay. Therefore, he insisted that it was "vain and highly criminal" for people to ignore or reject the teachings of orthodox ministers.[40]

Disturbed by the resistance's association with the evangelical ferment, the Great Proprietors shared the Congregational clergy's sense that backcountry settlers had lapsed into a religious anarchy that tolerated delusion and crime; it seemed that disorderly religion sustained disorderly behavior. Proprietors and Congregationalists agreed that the common people needed a scriptural creed that promoted moral discipline and temporal resignation rather than a visionary faith that could spill over into millennial fantasies. The Reverend Edward Payson, a Portland Congregationalist active in missionary societies committed to reclaiming frontier settlers, assured his wealthy patrons:

> Keep your wealth; enjoy your possessions; give us but the Bible to smooth the path of life, and the bed of death; and we will envy none their possessions, but living, and dying, will bless you; though we should perish with hunger. Such *is* the language of the pious poor. Such, were it not for their vices or their ignorance, would be the language of all the poor; and who will deny, that their vices and ignorance render it still more necessary, that they should be put in immediate possession of the Bible.

In April 1808, three weeks after an attempt to burn the Kennebec County courthouse in Augusta, that town's Congregationalist minister preached against the Liberty Men's right to judge and suspend the law: "While you have rulers, you are bound to submit to them; and when you have laws enacted, you are bound to obey them. . . . It is not your opinion of the wisdom of a law, that lays the foundation of your obligation to obedience." Just as evangelicals and agrarians shared an antiauthoritarian localism, orthodox Congregationalists and Great Proprietors sought a more hierarchical, more stable society by inculcating deference to temporal expertise and status.[41]

Perceiving a common problem, the Great Proprietors and the Standing Order concurred on the solution: substituting a learned clergy expounding Scripture for the evangelical itinerants who promoted visionary indulgence. A Great Proprietor and the commander who suppressed the New England Regulation of 1786–1787, General Benjamin Lincoln wanted to increase the Eastern Country's Congregational missionaries and settled ministers: "These things will have the best effect upon the minds of the people; and bring them into a state of order." Lincoln's close friend Henry Knox recruited the Congregational Reverend Daniel Little to preach in the Waldo Patent. Little agreed that his message would bring "prosperity to the patentees, a reformation among the present settlers and felicity to after generations." Convinced, Knox also subsidized the Congregational churches in Thomaston and Warren, supplying the ministers' room, board, and salary. He occasionally employed those ministers on missions into the backcountry to preach both orthodoxy and submission to his claims. After Knox's death, his proprietary successors continued to finance Congregational preaching in the Waldo Patent.[42]

The Cultural Divide

The careers of William Scales, a Christian primitivist, and Thurston Whiting, a Congregationalist, delineate how the cultural divide between the visionary and the orthodox shaped how men responded to the agrarian resistance. Born into a poor family at Bath on the lower Kennebec in 1741, Scales attended Harvard on a charity scholarship. In the eighteenth century, Harvard ranked its graduates according to the social status of their families; Scales graduated in 1771 with a social standing of next to last in his class of fifty-six. Life in the often turbulent college located near cosmopolitan Boston shocked the lonely man from a rustic community. "I went to college alone. A new scene now opened to my view! A strange country! A strange people! Great pride and vanity! I began to be afraid that I should be led aside from my God." He denounced the worldly curriculum as "dead languages in themselves of no more worth than the noise of owls and infinite heaps of worthless stories more worthless than the effluvia of rotten cadavers." As a cruel prank, a fellow student named Thurston Whiting stole and defaced Scales's "hebrew psalter." Disgusted with the faculty as arrogant worldlings and with the students (several of them proprietors' sons and heirs) as impious "young devils," Scales turned inward in search of "the extraordinary gift of the Holy Spirit: For my desire to reform the world was great."[43]

In revulsion against the orthodoxy and high style he saw in fashionable Cambridge, Scales became a Shaker and led an eccentric, ascetic, itinerant life, preaching for charitable contributions on the frontier. Like many other religious outsiders, Scales removed to the northeastern frontier in search of an asylum from orthodox authority. He settled as a squatter in Bowdoin, a backcountry town claimed by and named for Governor James Bowdoin, one of the Kennebeck Proprietors. Perhaps Scales became a squatter there as an act of revenge on one of the "young devils" who had tormented Scales at Harvard, for the governor's son and heir, James Bowdoin III, had been one of Scales's classmates. On his 640-acre tract Scales dreamed of establishing a utopian school that would be everything that Harvard was not; he proposed offering the common folk a pragmatic curriculum in "industry and economy" intended to enlighten and liberate their minds, rendering a new, more egalitarian and pious society possible, transforming Maine into "a temporal Paradise."[44]

Scales insisted that seekers would find God within rather than through clerical authority above. In his 1780 pamphlet, *The Confusion of Babel Discovered*, he explained: "True religion is not known through the excellency of man's wisdom, but in demonstration of the spirit and power. . . . Nor is this good spirit far from any of us (except such whose day of grace is over) but is near, even within us, reproving the disobedient, and comforting the obedient." Salvation came by discovering the Holy Spirit within. "They who are the real disciples of CHRIST . . . *are sealed with the Holy Spirit of promise*, as Paul hath it: that *they have drunk into that Spirit*: that *they are led by him*, and *the same mind is in them as is in* JESUS CHRIST." The convert achieved sudden perfection in this life: "He reproves men for sins, and makes them give them all up before he takes possession of their souls; and when he does so, the old man, or body of sin in them is crucified and nailed to the cross, that it may be wholly destroyed." This notion had egalitarian consequences; people who could merge with God could dispense with worldly authority, ushering in a utopian Christian anarchy. Scales assured his readers that, by obeying "the truth as it is manifested in yourselves," liberation "from your spiritual and temporal task masters" would follow. "But let me beseech you to see for yourselves; don't give up your understandings to other men." This was the sort of reasoning—from an inner Christ, to perfection in this world, and a dispensation with spiritual and temporal rulers—that the orthodox assailed as Antinomianism.[45]

Naturally, Scales opposed the proprietary claims, drafting petitions for his Bowdoin neighbors to the General Court and an extended epistle addressed to Colonel Josiah Little of the Pejepscot Proprietors. In the epistle Scales located the fundamental problem in man's entrapment within structures of inherited authority that enabled a few to delude and exploit the many. Scales's labor theory of value assigned the region's land to the settlers who improved it. "In supporting your claim you will inevitably distress the Settlers inexpressibly, who, in settling and improving the lands have endured hardships and penuries indescriptible and through the Labors of the people at their lives' end the land, which once was of no more value than the Sandbanks of Taara, are become only worth living on in cases of no other alternative, which consideration alone clearly demonstrates the injustice of your claim, however you came by it." Scales considered proprietary patents to be marks "of the beast" that served the Antichrist's drive to deprive the yeoman of "the darling right to live by his own labor in peace and quietude without the intollerable burdens of the beast, or to dispose of his earnings in freedom, or to buy, or to sell, or to have the least privilige in law or Society, except he has some mark . . . and pays some officer that hath a mark of ordination, or corronation, or commission, etc." Scales called on Little and his fellow proprietors to renounce their corrupt patents: "Now therefore make your choice to perish with the beast or to escape by rid[d]ing yourselves of the mark of the beast and of his name and the number of his name." Ever eager for an audience, Scales concluded his cover letter: "I could wish all the lines I deliver may be published and I called on to answer for them properly. I am ready at all times." But Little neither renounced his "mark of the beast" nor published Scales's words.[46]

Scales was certainly not a typical evangelical. In fact, he was mad, and defiantly so, as he conceded in a June 1790 memorial to the General Court: "Insanity, or a fracture in the intellect, makes no odds, as to reason in a petition, or, the reasonableness of a petition of a people." Indeed, that was his point; it required a "fracture in the intellect," a defiant rejection of social norms, to escape psychologically from a corrupt, vain, deluded, and exploitative world; this sort of "insanity" *increased* true "reasonableness." Scales believed that the people could free themselves from exploitation if they could change their way of perceiving the world. He assured Josiah Little, "For people are utterly deceived in their ministers, governments, and professed regenerations, and if they were wholly liberated, they would become mad."[47]

Scales mixed lucid insights into a defiantly odd rhetoric, a stance partly calculated to attract attention and partly intended to jolt listeners and readers into a sobering recognition of the fundamental disorder in their social relationships. To express his alienation from the prevailing discourse in his society, Scales had entitled his first pamphlet *The Confusion of Babel Discovered.* He confessed, "Some words I use are indeed something singular, and one or two of them I formed myself." He explained that "the wickedness of the present day" obliged stretching the language to describe "the tricks of deceivers." In February 1790 the Reverend William Bentley of Salem recorded in his diary: "A crazy man by the name of *William Scales* came along, dispersing Advertisements to *The virtuously disposed*, begging Charity for the Town of Bowdoin. He was partly educated at Cambridge, intimately connected with the Shakers, and preaches through the streets. He is decently dressed, has a clear and manly voice, and excites public curiosity." Scales was neither out of control nor oblivious to the world around him; although "crazy," he dressed decently, spoke effectively, and knew how to capture public attention.[48]

Scales was born a generation too soon. But for his passion for apocalyptic speculation, he would have felt at home among the mid-nineteenth-century transcendentalists, with their faith in God's universal presence, their renunciation of materialism, their commitment to the individual soul's potential for perfection, and their desire to escape from a commercial society that suppressed personal fulfillment. He was not so different from a later Harvard graduate and fellow eccentric, celibate recluse: Henry David Thoreau. Like Scales, Thoreau wanted to speak "*without* bounds; like a man in a waking moment, to men in their waking moments; for I am convinced that I cannot exaggerate enough even to lay the foundation of a true expression." Thoreau added, "Sometimes we are inclined to class those who are once-and-a-half witted with the half-witted, because we appreciate only a third part of their wit." So it was with William Scales.[49]

William Scales's opposite was the Reverend Thurston Whiting of Warren, who served as one of Henry Knox's emissaries sent into the backcountry to preach orthodoxy and denounce the agrarian resistance. Throughout life, Whiting parlayed keen opportunism and pleasing manners into patronage from worldly men with superior power and status. Cyrus Eaton of Warren described his acquaintance as "a young man of a prepossessing appearance, agreeable manners, a cultivated mind, and of the orthodox faith." But he possessed an "amiable and too facile" personality with "a lurking love of mischief at other people's expense." Born at Wrentham, Massachusetts, in 1753, Whiting began Harvard College when only thirteen. In January 1768 Whiting curried popularity by defacing a book belonging to an unfashionable and much older undergraduate: William Scales. Later that year Whiting was expelled for catalyzing a student uprising by fabricating charges of brutality against an unpopular tutor. Migrating with his parents to mid-Maine, Whiting ingratiated himself with Lincoln County's leading magistrates, Harvard graduates, and Plymouth Company allies: Sheriff Charles Cushing (Harvard 1755, first socially in a class of twenty-five) and Justice Jonathan Bowman (Harvard 1755, sixth of twenty-five).

They secured Whiting a parish as Newcastle's Congregational minister, despite his educational deficiencies.[50]

Suspicious of Whiting's sudden pretenses to piety, Colonel William Jones of nearby Bristol delighted in a display of divine power at the ordination: "At the very instant they were giving him the charge" a violent "tempest of wind and storm" arose to blow the clergymen's hands away from Whiting's head. He soon fulfilled Jones's worst expectations. Devoted to cards, drink, company, gossip, business speculation, and adultery, Whiting was disfrocked for his "irregularities" by a church council in January 1782. Marriage to proprietary heiress Martha Brown rescued Whiting's fortunes; after preaching as a temporary "supply" in Edgecomb, in 1786 Whiting removed to Warren to develop his wife's property, including a valuable gristmill. There he zealously promoted Federalist political candidates, especially Congressman George Thatcher. Whiting also cultivated a powerful new patron in Henry Knox, who helped him obtain temporary positions as a minister in Warren, Thomaston, Cushing, and Vassalborough. He also found a kindred spirit in Dr. Ezekiel G. Dodge of Thomaston, who (according to Cyrus Eaton, who knew both men) drew his close friend "into excesses unbecoming the clerical character." Whiting must have been among the Congregational clergy that William Scales referred to in asking the General Court in 1796, "And why are bad characters supported as teachers of the people, such as bucks, wags, adulterors, fornicators, drunkards, rape[r]s?" Usually in partnership with proprietary land agents and lawyers, Whiting avidly speculated in proprietary titles, for he planned to profit from the defeat of the agrarian resistance.[51]

While Scales urged his listeners to defy authority and find their Christ within, Whiting insisted that divine authority came from above, filtering down to the common people through intermediaries higher up on the social scale. His two published works addressed Federalist sentiments to voluntary societies (Wiscasset's Masonic lodge and Thomaston's Friendly Society) composed of gentlemen from Lincoln County's commercial towns. Both pamphlets lauded genteel societies for providing lesser men with needed guidance. Oblivious to the ironic contrast with his own collegiate behavior, Whiting celebrated deferential order as he likened his Masonic lodge to the prophet Elijah's seminary:

> There is something charming in the idea of a well regulated society, established and calculated for infusing and disseminating useful knowledge, and cultivating the best principles of human nature, and grafting upon them the principles of pure religion,—where the MASTER presides with dignity and gracefulness and is equally feared and loved—Where subordination is duly maintained and submission to discipline and decorum, from a sense of the propriety and love to the MASTER, is as delightful as it is useful and ornamental.

His language bespoke a genteel world: charming, well regulated, useful, pure, dignified, graceful, subordinated, disciplined, decorous, proper, delightful, and ornamental. The hierarchy preserved these attributes of a civilization that represented a difficult triumph over man's innate brutality: "A state of savage, uncultivated nature, instead of that peaceful, happy state, by some romantic writers represented, is but a scene of lawless violence, or of abject and wretched slavery. It will be found, moreover, that learning, liberty and religion go hand in hand." Where the alienated William Scales denounced social complexity and sought to recapture the presumed simplicity and equality of the primitive Christian church, the well-connected Thurston Whiting celebrated respect for hierarchical gradations as essential to civilization's tenuous triumph over the worst instincts he believed innate to the anarchic lower orders.[52]

Encouraged by Knox, Whiting preached the principles of hierarchical order to the settlers of the militant backcountry. In September 1801, after touring the Sheepscot backcountry, he and Major Benjamin Brackett reported:

> We labour to convince this deluded short sighted people that their views and plans, if realized would be totally subversive to all justice and order and even of the very existence of society—that property depended on laws—That to prevent a general scramble and universal anarchy it was necessary that general precise rules for the partition of property be fixed and established and strictly adhered to. That it was of little consequence to government (as such) in whose hands these general fixed rules placed any particular portion of property; but that it was of the last importance that these rules be sacredly and inviolably maintained. The very existence of government, of civil society and all its blessings depended upon it.

The allegiance to legal precedent that Scales sought to shatter—to destroy the proprietary claims—Thurston Whiting forthrightly defended, to put down the resistance. Whiting zealously championed legal precedent as the glue that held society together, preventing a catastrophic relapse into savage brutality.[53]

But Whiting and Brackett found the wrong sort of religion all too evident in the backcountry. Captain Daniel Clay of Sheepscot Great Pond (Palermo) showed them a copy of a 1796 pamphlet written by James Davis and Samuel Ely to justify the resistance as divinely sanctioned. Clay invited the emissaries to read it. After scanning the pamphlet, Brackett indignantly urged the settler to burn it. "God forbid," said Clay. "I believe it to be as true as my Bible and if there is a Christian in America the man who wrote that book is one."[54]

The Sawmill and Milldam at Ducktrap. In Lincolnville, originally constructed by George and Philip Ulmer. *Courtesy of the Lincolnville Historical Society*

CHAPTER SIX

Leading Men

Another evil . . . is found in the character and influence of many of those who are considered as principal men in every newly settled country. . . . Those who acquire this influence are in many instances both ignorant and licentious. It is, therefore, frequently exerted in favor of loose principles and practices, and against those which are better.—Timothy Dwight

The supreme Lion sends a letter to the great ones in the County of Lincoln, directing them to undeceive those that were deceived by artful men. . . . For it seems it must be a crime not to fall down and worship the golden image which they have set up.— Samuel Ely

IN JANUARY 1789 George Ulmer of Ducktrap rode into Waldoborough, his birthplace, on a dangerous visit. Waldoborough's settlers did not appreciate the recent decision by George Ulmer and his older brother Philip to support Henry Knox's claim. George Ulmer found "a large body of people" waiting for him. "They told him he was the enemy of the people; and that he shou'd not leave Waldo[borou]gh alive." Ulmer staunchly defended his stand and escaped without harm, dissipating the remaining doubts among Knox's minions. William Molineux of Camden, a squire who had long suspected Ulmer of "acting an artfull part," concluded that he could "render us more service than any man on the patent." Delighted, Knox wrote: "I am glad to hear from you of the firmness of Capt. Ulmer. We must cultivate the two brothers." As leading men in their community, George and Philip Ulmer were prized acquisitions in the proprietors' efforts to break down the settlers' resistance from within.[1]

Mediators

According to traveler Timothy Dwight, most migrants to the Eastern Country were poor men "having large families and small farms" seeking sufficient land "for the sake of settling their children comfortably"; but an important minority were more speculatively minded men "allured by the prospect of gain presented in very new country." Aggressive ambition and access to capital enabled a few men to stake out the most strategic economic positions on the frontier, to emerge as the mediators between, on the one hand, their neighbors as small producers and, on the other hand, external markets and supplies of trade goods. Such a man could expect, in time, a coveted appointment by the governor and council as an esquire, a justice of the peace responsible for maintaining order in his settlement. He became a political mediator between his neighbors and the commonwealth's rulers.[2]

In Ducktrap the Ulmer brothers secured a dominant standing by obtaining a valuable tract combining timber, waterpower, access to the sea, and settler labor. The brothers were the sons of Captain John Ulmer, "a man of property and energy" among Waldoborough's German settlers. Officers in the Revolutionary war, the brothers served in a small post of Massachusetts state troops at Camden. A few miles to the north at Ducktrap the brothers saw their main chance: several promising mill seats along the Ducktrap River that stretched back into a richly timbered interior and emptied into a small but snug harbor ideal for wood sloops and lumber schooners. An illiterate squatter named James Getchal had already occupied the land beside the harbor, but, lacking the capital to develop the site, he sold his possession claim to the brothers for thirty pounds in September 1784 and moved further down the coast to squat again. The Ulmers greatly enlarged Getchal's possession claim by boldly running new survey lines around the entire basin's several hundred acres. Thereafter, all of the watershed's lumber would have to be cut at their mills and shipped from their wharves. As a trader's sons and as military officers, the brothers could secure trade goods on credit from Boston's merchants to stock a store. Eager for store goods and tempted by easy credit, many settlers became the Ulmers' debtors. Settlers sustained their credit by delivering cordwood, ship's timber, mill logs, staves, shingles, clapboards, and spars to the Ulmers' wharf. The Ulmers ran sawmills to cut the logs into planks and boards, built vessels from the timber to carry all to market in Boston or the West Indies, and managed a store to sell the West India and English goods that their ships returned with. With the forest commodities garnered from the Ducktrap watershed, the brothers paid back their creditors and secured new capital (principally more store goods) to continue expanding.[3]

As traders and mill owners, the Ulmers operated on a grander scale than their neighbors, but the brothers were still squatters exploiting the Revolution's disruption of proprietary power in the Eastern Country. Before the Revolution, the Waldo heirs would have quickly suppressed the Ulmers' occupation of such a valuable tract. During the colonial era the Great Proprietors tried to establish mercantile empires by monopolizing the profits as middlemen standing between the settler producers and the outside market. They meant the forest's commodities to pass through their hands in return for trade goods dispensed from their stores. They hoped to control the harvesting of wilderness resources and set the prices settlers paid for imported provisions and tools. This plan promised immediate returns at a time when the poor and scattered settler population could not yet pay for their lands. Accordingly, the Great Proprietors usually refused to sell mill seats; either they built and ran the mills themselves, or they leased out a few to trusted subordinates. In this way the Great Proprietors hoped to minimize competition, maximize their profits, and control where settlers logged. By suspending proprietary control, the Revolution created new opportunities for mercantile men as well as for "the people." In the 1780s the returning proprietors found that entrepreneurial newcomers had usurped their positions as middlemen. This posed a dilemma; restoring their lucrative commercial monopolies would pit the Great Proprietors against the most influential settlers, but failure to do so would concede some of their patents' most valuable lands.[4]

After initial, abortive attempts to restore the prewar mercantile monopolies within the Waldo Patent's coastal settlements, Henry Knox reassessed and shrewdly concluded that obtaining land payments from "the people" and regaining control over the Waldo Patent's unsettled backcountry districts were more important and more attainable goals. The settlers' organized resistance rendered foolhardy any attempt at legal ejectments until Knox could disrupt their united front. Settler unity both shielded leading men from prosecution and gave them something valuable to sell to Henry Knox—influence over their neighbors. Knox conceded the leading men their local positions as middlemen in return for their influence over their hardscrabble neighbors. The leading men who supported Knox emerged as the Waldo Patent's greatest beneficiaries of the American Revolution and the settler resistance it spawned. Revolution and resistance enabled them, first, to stake out valuable positions at proprietary expense and, subsequently, to preserve those positions by selling their influence.[5]

In August 1788 Henry Knox framed terms that appealed to the leading men's longing for secure title to their particularly valuable tracts of land. He agreed to sell them their lime quarries, mill seats, and harbor lots for 4s. ($.67) per acre: the same price per acre he charged a common settler for a poor lot of stony soil in a settlement's recesses. Knox also renounced the Waldo heirs' prewar practice of forbidding the erection of any sawmill or limekiln on the premises sold. The purchaser of Henry Knox's deed became the complete master of that piece of property. About half of the six hundred squatter families who dwelled in the Waldo Patent's coastal settlements, including virtually all of the leading men, submitted to Knox's terms in August or September 1788. By conceding a fraction of his vast wilderness empire to the coastal settlements' leading men at bargain prices, Knox reaped substantial payments from "the people" (in 1788 the Waldo heirs received commitments to pay $21,856) and regained control over the patent's unsettled lands. At the conclusion of his successful 1788 tour of the patent to intertwine his "interest" with that of the area's leading men, Knox drafted a memo outlining a "narrative" he planned to write: "It will appear how invariably people are governed in their conduct by what they conceive to be their pecuniary interest."[6]

George and Philip Ulmer were among the leading men who benefited from selling their influence over their neighbors to Henry Knox. In 1785 one of Knox's agents advised breaking up the Ulmers' monopoly over the Ducktrap watershed. Instead, Henry Knox readily sold them 1,165 acres, including the entire harborfront, in 1788. Furthermore, Knox appointed George Ulmer his principal land agent and surveyor to supervise new settlement in the backcountry and obtained, from the governor's council, coveted commissions as justices of the peace for both brothers. The general exercised his influence in the General Court to secure an act of incorporation for the toll bridge the Ulmer brothers erected over the Ducktrap River. Knox also obtained George Ulmer's appointment as the collector of the federal direct tax of 1798 in Ducktrap, Northport, and Belfast. The general even intervened to exempt George Ulmer from the medical examination legally needed to obtain a state pension for a supposed war wound. Capitalizing on their lucrative patronage from the general, the Ulmer brothers developed the largest mercantile establishment on Penobscot Bay's western shore and constructed impressive frame houses, one on each side of their harbor. In 1798 George Ulmer was Ducktrap's wealthiest taxpayer, with 1,900 acres valued at nearly $4,400 and a house worth $1,200. His brother and partner was second, with an $800 house and 1,024 acres worth nearly $2,800. The two brothers ranked far above their neighbors; the settlement's next most valuable house was worth $350, and the next most valuable landholding was worth $936. The visiting Reverend Paul Coffin partook of the new genteel style enjoyed by George Ulmer: "The Squire and his very comely wife, treated me with liberal hospitality. We had bloated eels, pigeons, fresh mackerel, cucumbers, wine, etc."[7]

As Knox anticipated, winning over the Ulmer brothers discouraged resistance among their poorer neighbors, who brought logs to their mills and obtained goods from their store. Before the Ulmers enlisted in his camp, Knox noted that the residents of Ducktrap and adjoining New Canaan had been the Waldo Patent's "most hostile" settlers. But, once the Ulmers and their immediate Ducktrap neighbors accepted Knox's terms on September 24, 1788, the rest of the settlers in the twin communities anxiously embraced the proferred terms six days later: testimony to the value of the brothers' influence.[8]

The brothers continued to pay dividends on Knox's invested patronage. During the early 1790s most of the settlers in Ducktrap and New Canaan delayed paying Knox in the hope that the General Court would intervene to quiet them with one-hundred-acre homesteads for five dollars. The majority took heart in 1792 when Samuel Ely settled at Saturday Point, a few miles north of Ducktrap. He encouraged his neighbors to drive off Knox's land surveyors and discipline those in their midst, including the Ulmer brothers, who spoke for the Great Proprietors. In February 1793 Ulmer publicly struck his new competitor and then challenged him to a duel. In April 1793 Ely and his supporters obtained vengeance with axes and crowbars, tearing down the Ulmers' milldam on the Ducktrap River, depriving the brothers of their sawmill in the midst of the all-important spring sawing season. In the winter of 1795–1796, while George Ulmer was away on business, Knox's other agents nervously reported that "the people" in Ducktrap and New Canaan planned to burn down Montpelier and the buildings belonging to the general's supporters. In March 1796 Ulmer returned from Boston to find that "the combination was general with a few exceptions." But a warrant from Boston for Ely's arrest preceded Ulmer's return and sent the parson into precipitous flight. Thrown into disarray by Ely's sudden disappearance, the settlers failed to obstruct Ulmer's return as they had planned. Making the most of their confusion, Ulmer immediately restored his vigorous presence among the people. Later that month Ulmer informed Knox, "I have endeavourd to mix in all the company I possibly could since my arrival, without the least fear and if they continue to shrink from their resolutions of opposition as they now appear to, by the time you arrive there will not be a man found that will own that he was in the least dissatisfied." The settlers' public conversation took on a new tone, stressing their love of order rather than their readiness to fight. Within a month Ulmer confidently informed Knox, "All is intirely tranquil . . . amongue the people, there is not a person that appears to be the least opposed to your intrist, and but few that will own that they ever were."9

Resentment against Knox and Ulmer continued to fester beneath the newly placid surface. In July and again in September, George Ulmer awoke to see hundreds of spars, which he had stored for Knox, "drifting about the bay" because overnight someone had secretly cast off the booms, allowing the tide and currents to scatter the contents far and wide. In March 1797 Ulmer arrested Harris Ransom, who had boarded with Ely's family at Saturday Point. In a letter to Knox, Ulmer reported Ransom's confession that, during Ely's brief, furtive return in September 1796, eighty-two men joined with the parson in written bonds "to burn yours and many other people's houses, rob the stores, and burn the goods before the owners' faces, poison their cattle by mixing poison with salt, and putting in their fodder, and many other matters were to be done." In this plan the settlers' grievances as squatters against Knox merged with their resentments as debtors against their creditors who supported the general. Ransom pleaded guilty "in order to prove him-selfe a good fellow as he term'd it" but refused to name any names, saying "he would rather die than make any further discovery." Ulmer hustled Ransom across the bay to jail in Castine. Ely disappeared, never to return.[10]

In Ducktrap and New Canaan, settler resistance decayed into grum-bling, applause for the backcountry settlers who attacked Knox's survey-ors in 1800 and 1801, and prolonged delays in meeting their land pay-ments. Most of the coastal settlers who had not yet agreed to terms took advantage of a special commission established in 1797 by the General Court, at Knox's suggestion, to set compromise prices lot by lot; forty-two settlers from Ducktrap and New Canaan submitted their home-steads and on average received awards that stipulated a price of eighty-two cents per acre, a bit more than the 1788 submittees had agreed to pay. The settlers who compromised with Knox in 1788 and 1797 felt more at ease with their terms as they watched local land values soar in the late 1790s. At last, in the fall of 1801, the Waldo Patent's coastal settlers trooped by the dozen to Montpelier to complete their payments or deliver mortgage security. Ecstatic with relief and vindication, Henry wrote to his wife Lucy: "It confirms my judgment of the measures I have pursued. This you will call vanity. I own it and rejoice therein. But when the lowest acre will command obligations for 5 dollars with the good will of the people, and when hope points to no distant period *at ten* and higher, the heart that has been compelled to endure anguish . . . has a well founded claim to dance a little. But this [is] between ourselves." Resistance continued in the backcountry.[11]

Rewards and Threats

George Ulmer proved to Henry Knox the value of cultivating leading men. By 1797 the general already knew what his agent John Lillie ad-vised: "If you get the friendship of one good man it will be the means of bringing three of those lawless rascals to terms who wish never to pay you any thing." Knox preached this policy to his fellow proprietors. In June 1801 he pressed his friend Joseph Pierce, Sr., the leader of the Twenty Associates, to offer unusually attractive terms to Major Samuel Mooers and Lieutenant Humphrey Hook, Davistown's two leading men, who were ready to desert their neighbors. "It would be madness not to give those people favorable terms and an immediate answer through me," he explained. "Long arguments on this head are needless, to one of your knowledge of the human character. Let a few influential characters agree and all the rest will feel miserable until they do the same." By 1802 Charles Vaughan reached the same conclusion, advising his fellow Kennebeck Proprietors, "The Company cannot strengthen itself in a more certain way, than by an accommodation to the *most substantial men* in each settlement; which will render it easy to effect the object of the Company with the *remaining* settlers." He found resistance leaders, those most "active and spirited in opposition to the Co.'s interest in past times," most capable of "equally active measures in favor of the Co. in future" once their allegiance had been properly cultivated.[12]

When patronage seemed inappropriate or did not work, the Great Proprietors targeted leading men for prosecution. As agent and lawyer for the Kennebeck Proprietors, Reuel Williams sued those who "ought to be dealt with rigorously because they can pay and have some influence upon others." Henry Jackson explained to Knox, "It's only necessary to prosecute a few of *the great fish* and a stop will be put to their plundering immediately." In December 1806 Joseph Pierce of the Twenty Associates learned that John Meservey of Appleton had "endeavored to stimulate others in his neighbourhood *to combine* to fix their own terms for such land as they have trespassed upon." Pierce instructed Silas Lee, the company lawyer: "As our prosecuting such sort of *leaders* heretofore, has been attended with salutary effects, we request that you would immediately send him a writ of ejectment." Five years later another Appleton Ridge leader (a man named Keene who, Pierce noted, "writes an excellent hand and no doubt was once something more than his present appearance indicates") offended the Twenty Associates by drafting a petition for his neighbors. Pierce's son and agent, Joseph H. Pierce, Jr., secured several of Keene's promissory notes from third parties, as "they might serve at least to keep him under a little, if necessary."[13]

To resist the Great Proprietors, a community needed the allegiance of its leading men. New England communities counted on their most prosperous residents for political leadership. The yeomanry did not begrudge their leading men's influence and property so long as their first loyalty was to the local community rather than to more powerful, cosmopolitan outsiders. For the yeomanry counted on their leading men to preserve the autonomy, the "liberty" of "the people," from external "great men" bent on engrossing the poor man's property. Rural folk worried when their leading men lost their sense of kinship with their humbler neighbors, when their leaders' developing class consciousness as "gentlemen" superseded identification with their home communities. In 1799 an Augusta newspaper writer addressed "the common people and those of little information . . . who believe that our government [is] determined to take away our liberties, step by step, and at last bring us into lordships and slavery." He discerned widespread prejudices "that the rich were all villains" and "that for many years past there has been a settled plan among our great men and rulers to deceive and cozen us out of our liberties and constitution." He lamented, "No sooner does a man become rich or is elected to office, than you chalk him down as a rogue and unfriendly to the poor."[14]

Politically reliant on leading men but sometimes suspicious of their intent, New Englanders resorted to crowd violence when they believed that there was no other way to recall them "to a sense of their duty." Crowd actions were short, sharp rebukes on those rare occasions when leaders violated community expectations in a particularly flagrant manner. In their wake, people expected the chastened leader to alter his course and return to a proper solicitude for the common good. In 1766 Richard King, the leading man in Scarborough, Maine, angered his neighbors by embezzling parish funds and by aggressively prosecuting his many debtors. A crowd broke his house's windows, wrecked his furniture, destroyed his business papers, shot or mutilated some of his livestock, and burned his barn. Members of the crowd explained that their violence "was a good thing, and would do *King good*, and *make him a better man*." They saw no contradiction in violently recalling King to his duty while continuing to elect him to the town offices that no one else in Scarborough could perform so well. A successful crowd action restored a wayward leader, who had become a conspicuous threat to his people's liberty and well-being, to his proper role as their guardian. Then the community could benefit from, rather than fear, his special skills and superior education. Then, and only then, could the community consider itself safe from powerful outsiders who might attempt to exploit them. A luckless deputy who ventured into Maine's backcountry knew he was in for a long day when the confident locals could boast "that they had all the town to join them, that they had *the first men* in town and were determined that no property should be attached . . . and they would defend it at the expense of their lives." He returned home with his unserved writs.[15]

The Eastern Country's agrarian unrest was a conflict between differing means of defending two different notions of liberty. The resisting settlements resorted to the traditional extralegal mechanisms to pressure their leading men into performing their expected role: leading their communities' defense against encroaching power. This time the threat came from Great Proprietors, rather than British imperial officials. But the Great Proprietors felt that their notion of liberty—protecting their extensive property claims from squatters—necessitated defeating communitarian opposition. Proprietors wooed and cajoled frontier leading men to prove their worthiness as gentlemen, as deserving leaders in the new republican order, by delivering their neighbors away from their traditional "prejudices" and inculcating the "good principles" of orderly submission to the formal law in all cases. Leading men had to decide whether their primary allegiance lay with the settlers as neighbors or with the Great Proprietors as gentlemen. The agrarian struggle pivoted on the contest for the allegiance of each community's leading men, a contest between local and class notions of elite duty.[16]

The Great Proprietors were most successful in winning over those leading men with genteel aspirations and commercial ties to the wider world: men like George and Philip Ulmer. The few settlers who regularly engaged in commerce with the wider world could claim the status of "gentleman" in court cases and land deeds. Such men were far more solicitous of the Great Proprietors' interest than were their humbler neighbors. As emerging economic and political mediators, such leading men were relatively independent from the social pressures of their neighbors, but more dependent on sustaining external recognition of their standing as reputable gentlemen committed to orderly principles. For example, in 1800 there were 6 men recognized as gentlemen among the 123 heads of household in the adjoining settlements of Davistown and Sheepscot Great Pond; 4 of them actively supported the proprietors: Humphrey Hook, Dr. Abner Meiggs, Major Samuel Mooers, and Jonathan Greeley. A fifth, Jonathan Bagley, was Hook's business partner and probably shared his allegiance. Only 1 gentleman, Sheepscot Great Pond's Jacob Greeley, cast his lot with the resistance. He paid for his decision when Knox intervened with the governor and council to frustrate his ambition for an esquire's commission; instead, his brother Jonathan, a proprietary supporter, received the appointment. Among the two settlements' 35 identifiable Liberty Men, Jacob Greeley was the only "gentleman."[17]

The resistance was more enduring in the backcountry, where most of the leading men were substantial farmers without genteel aspirations or mercantile connections. Sheepscot Great Pond settlement's 6 leading Liberty Men were quite prosperous by backcountry standards, ranking first, second, fifth, eighth, tenth, and thirteenth on an 1806 highway tax list of 108 taxpayers. According to Palermo's 1811 valuation return, they all possessed a frame house and barn (emblems of frontier prosperity), at least 20 improved acres (the threshold of rural prosperity that was so rare in such settlements), another 150 (or more) unimproved acres, and at least 10 head of mature livestock. But their property was exclusively agrarian; they possessed no commercial property: no securities, no stock-in-trade, no shipping, no annual factorage, no money-on-hand, no bank stock, no ounces of plate, and no toll bridge or turnpike shares. Men who owned such things were rare in the backcountry. Palermo's commercial property consisted of a gristmill, a sawmill, and one hundred dollars in money at interest, held by three different men, none a resistance leader.[18]

Sometimes the Great Proprietors forfeited the support of the backcountry's leading yeomen by default, because they could not recognize mere farmers, however influential in their settlements, as worthy of considerable patronage. Even Henry Knox, the shrewdest proprietor at co-opting settler leaders, allowed class bias to cloud his perception of men he could not recognize as gentlemen. As Knox's land agent, George Ulmer cultivated the support of Greene Plantation's first and most influential settler, Daniel Dollof. Afflicted by economic setbacks, Dollof needed a special deal to buttress his eroding position. Ulmer informed Knox that Dollof had supported the proprietary stand among his neighbors "and is now a very poor man and his wife insane—if any settler is an object of pity he is one." At the Dollofs' cabin Ulmer found their "six children entirely naked" and "the wife could by no means prevent shewing her skin in many places that ought [to] be coverd." Ulmer promised Dollof a price of no more than $1.33 an acre. But Knox did not share his agent's sympathy or sense of Dollof's importance. Across the bottom of Ulmer's letter he scrawled, "He must fare as the other settlers, in the same circumstances should fare." Explaining that Dollof had "run out 200 acres [of] excellent land" which "I then thought as I now do that this was a good grab for a pauper," Knox doubled Ulmer's promised price to $2.66 an acre. Unable to recognize Daniel Dollof's leadership among men of similar, or still greater, poverty, Knox alienated the Dollof family, stiffening Greene Plantation's resistance. At odds with their proprietor until the early 1820s, Belmont (eastern Greene Plantation after its 1813 incorporation) was the last community in mid-Maine to come to terms.[19]

The resistance was a coalition between the settlements' poor majority and those leading men most responsive to calls for community solidarity (or those most afraid of their poorer neighbors' retribution). In backcountry settlements the leadership pool of prosperous settlers divided their allegiance between the Great Proprietors and the resistance, whereas almost all of the poor were decided Liberty Men. Court records and proprietary papers identify 104 rank-and-file insurgents ("Indians"), 24 resistance leaders ("Chiefs"), and 40 local foes ("Tories") who can be linked to surviving tax valuation lists. Chiefs and Tories possessed similar propertyholdings, superior to the poorer Indians'. By the standards of eastern Massachusetts' older communities, the Chiefs and Tories held barely enough improved land and livestock for rural prosperity. The average Chief possessed about 22 improved acres, another 143 unimproved acres, and 11 mature livestock. The average Tory held

19 improved acres, another 168 unimproved acres, and 8 mature livestock. The average Indian lagged well behind with but 10 improved acres, another 86 unimproved acres, and 5 mature livestock. An overwhelming majority of both Chiefs and Tories possessed frame barns and frame houses—emblems of prosperity—compared to only half the Indians.[20]

The wealth differences between leading men and the Indians reflected age differences. In rural communities, men gradually acquired prosperity as they matured, reaping the accumulated fruits of their hard labor, and, perhaps, inheriting property from the previous generation. Indians tended to be poorer, younger men, those least able to pay for proprietary title, those who pursued the cycle of squatting, improving, and selling that proprietors particularly detested. By preserving this economic strategy, poor settlers hoped to acquire the prosperity of their older, more substantial neighbors. As with the New England Regulators, the Liberty Men drew their fighting force from young men: those settlers most anxious about their future because their material circumstances in the present were so tenuous.[21]

Observers differed over whether the poor soldiery or the more prosperous community leaders propelled the resistance. Thurston Whiting and Benjamin Brackett found that the poor "banditti of the wilderness" enjoyed encouragement, material support, and leadership from those "who are as destitute of principle, tho' not of bread." In 1808 Deputy Sheriff Pitt Dillingham reported that prosperous men "of sober habits" encouraged those "destitute of morals and property" to serve as "good dogs to hunt of[f] Plymouth Company agents." But one of those agents, Charles Vaughan of Hallowell, felt that the resistance began with those "too poor to buy their land" who cowed the more prosperous into quiescence. A proprietary supporter in Winslow concurred that the insurgency originated among "men of desperate characters and fortunes with whom new settlements particularly abound." Obstructed at Damariscotta Bridge by an armed crowd in April 1806, surveyor Charles Turner, Jr., observed, "[No one] of apparent age and respectability came to our assistance, or to endeavour to quell the riot, and appease the people, whether they were deterred by fear of suffering in their persons or property, or [were] well-wishers to our being stopped, I did not know; I have since learned that the former reasons operated with them to keep them out of sight."[22]

In fact, each half of the settler coalition needed the other. Poorer, younger men composed the armed bands. In confrontations, outsiders were less likely to identify poorer, younger men than the better-known community leaders; and, if indicted, poorer, younger men could better afford to flee temporarily to Canada or to sea. More prosperous men advanced provisions, bought ammunition, drafted petitions to the General Court, and negotiated with land agents and legal authorities. Indians provided the muscle that preserved settler property while the Chiefs negotiated relief from outside authority.[23]

Leading men were the least stable element in the settlers' coalition. Pressed between their neighbors' expectations and the proprietors' power, the backcountry's substantial farmers found themselves in an ambiguous position, playing for high stakes. They wanted to protect their hard-earned property, but often wondered whether security lay in resistance to, or accommodation with, the proprietors. On the one hand, because they possessed particularly valuable homesteads, leading men could save a lot of money if the resistance parried proprietary demands. On the other hand, they were better placed to buy proprietary title if prudence so dictated. And, as older men committed to long-improved homesteads, they were less reliant on the squat-and-sell cycle pursued by younger, poorer men to accumulate resources. The prosperous settlers, even the most overtly zealous for the resistance, chronically worried that their moment to strike a favorable deal was ebbing away and that, once it passed, a proprietary lawsuit would oust them from their hard-earned property. The shifting prospects of the resistance weighed heavily upon their minds; ever mindful of their purchasing option and that they had the most to lose if they were too late in exercising it, they kept a wary eye open for signs that the resistance was failing.

In contrast to their poorer neighbors, who were most concerned over the price of title, the prosperous settlers worried more about the Great Proprietors' reluctance to warrant their deeds. Thurston Whiting and Benjamin Brackett visited resistance leader Nathan Parkhurst of Twenty-Five-Mile Pond settlement (Unity) to find that he had "a noble farm" of five hundred acres and fifty head of cattle. "Uneasy in his present situation," Parkhurst was willing "to pay a reasonable and handsome consideration" for "an undisturbed title." Charles Vaughan sympathized with this concern, noting, "Settlers having in many instances been obliged to pay two proprietors, and being now called upon to pay a third, without having recourse by warranty on any one . . . and till it is proved that the Plym[outh] Co[mpany] is superior in title, the objection to purchase is not to be wondered at." By mollifying leading men with warranty deeds, Henry Knox was the first Great Proprietor to quiet resistance on his claim, bringing most settlements to terms by 1802.[24]

Precariously perched, backcountry leading men could fall into either camp. Charles Vaughan urged his fellow Kennebeck Proprietors to offer Moses Stevens of Sheepscot Great Pond (Palermo) special terms. "He is an active man, and in the improvement of roads etc. is praiseworthy. He has made spirited improvements which he ought not to lose. This man may be active for or against the Company. Disappointment or despair will rouse him to active measures, by which the Co. may suffer some inconvenience." Stevens's neighbor, Captain Daniel Clay, reflected the stress of conflicting pressures. Conversing with Thurston Whiting and Benjamin Brackett, Clay initially extolled Henry Knox as his beloved Revolutionary war commanding officer, but suddenly broke into "a violent passion" where he "clap[ed] his hands, stamp[ed] with his feet, and bawl[ed] out 'We fought for land and liberty and it is hard if we can't have either.'" Thoroughly confused, Whiting and Brackett concluded: "His character is a perfect medley of ignorance, contradiction, conceit and folly. He can be tranquil and outrageous, an advocate for religion and shockingly profane. He can advance and retrograde on any subject all within the compass of five minutes. A man might as well attempt to reason with a whirl wind as with him."[25]

Because canny settlers perfected a double face, proprietary emissaries often returned from the backcountry impressed with leading settlers' moderation and, so, astonished that the resistance endured. When before Great Proprietors, their agents, and legal authorities, a settler needed to mask his sympathies for, knowledge of, and activities in the resistance by proclaiming his love for the law and eventual readiness to purchase proprietary title. But among his backcountry neighbors it was not wise for a settler to arouse suspicions that he might strike his own deal with the proprietors. Neither face was necessarily more real than the other; settlers could rapidly swing from one to the other as circumstances dictated. Elisha Sylvester of Greene was a substantial farmer, respected schoolteacher, and poet who periodically bore his neighbors' protest petitions to the General Court. But to shield himself from prosecution and buy time, Sylvester secretly corresponded with Greene's proprietor, Josiah Little. Impatient and humorless, Little must have gritted his teeth when perusing Sylvester's chatty letters full of excuses, flattery, procrastination, and moral admonition. An October 1792 letter began:

> Friend Little! I am very poor, but I trust in mending circumstances. My Boys are coming forward and [I] am in hopes that if thou should not disturb me by hasty demand for payment for land I may purchase the lot I now possess.

He urged patience:

> I beg leave to remind thee of human frailty and the common misfortunes of life; Rich today and poor tomorrow and how this transitory existance is but a perpetual revolution of pain and pleasure. That it is essential to the peace and happiness of Moral agents, to be Moderate in commerce with their fellow servants; and that to be

lenient, instead of oppressive and avaricious, betokeneth a great mind. . . . As to the dispute about title I trouble not myself. I acquiesce with the principles of Nonresistance and passive obedience. And am thy friend and Servant (if the Service is not too hard).

Fourteen years later, Sylvester had still not paid for his lot, but continued to write buoyant letters to Little.[26]

Perils and Opportunities

No one had to exercise greater care and skill in wearing this double face than Davistown's preacher, William Pickles. His neighbors saw Pickles as an evangelical preacher who would conduct their godly crusade against the demonic proprietors. The courts and the Great Proprietors perceived Pickles as an educated gentleman who should deliver his flock over to "good principles," restoring them to "a sense of their duty." Memory of Samuel Ely's recent failure to navigate between these conflicting expectations must have lurked in William Pickles's mind. Playing a dangerous double role, Pickles masked his leadership in Davistown's Liberty Men by secretly feeding partial information to the Great Proprietors.[27]

Like Samuel Ely, William Pickles was a well-educated man uprooted by controversy from a more comfortable living in an older town and obliged to take to the wilderness in search of his daily bread as an itinerant preacher among new settlers. Born and married in Wales, he and his wife migrated to Philadelphia. About 1787 they moved to Bedford, New Hampshire, a Scotch-Irish community, where he "excited great attention by his power of preaching." In December 1790 Matthew Patten of Bedford described Pickles, an evangelical Presbyterian, as "one of the greatest, best and sensiblest preachers that I ever heard." But like Samuel Ely in Somers, Pickles found in Bedford a faction determined on his ouster, charging in March 1790, "The said Mr. Pickles since he came to Bedford has been disorderly in using spirituous liquors to excess, in using opprobrious language and that his behavior in several instances has been such that modesty forbids particular description." As powerful preacher and excessive drinker Pickles early displayed a striking duality.[28]

Apparently tired of the dissension, Bedford's majority gave in and declined to renew Pickles's appointment in late 1793. Like many a man out of options in the long-settled world, Pickles headed northeastward into the Eastern Country. In 1794 he succeeded Thurston Whiting as the preacher in Edgecomb and Newcastle, predominantly Scotch-Irish towns on the Lincoln County coast. Two years later Pickles moved inland to Davistown, where many Edgecomb and Newcastle families had removed to squat in defiance of the Twenty Associates. Settling beside the new county road that crossed through the settlement on its way from Belfast to Augusta, Pickles earned a scanty living preaching for contributions in Davistown and her sister settlements.[29]

In 1800–1801 the Davistowners joined their brethren in the nearby Plymouth Patent settlements to attack Henry Knox's survey parties in the adjoining Waldo Patent backcountry. Two ambushes wounded several surveyors. On July 4, 1801, hundreds of armed men (estimates ranged from two hundred to five hundred) mustered at Reed's tavern in Davistown for a march on the Hancock County jail in Castine to liberate three Liberty Men recently arrested for ambushing the surveyors. The Fourth was the twenty-fifth anniversary of American independence and the sixteenth anniversary of the General Court's controversial confirmation of the Waldo Patent. The Liberty Men elected officers, including Captain John Cunningham of Patricktown as their commander, cast bullets, filled their canteens with rum, and prepared to march. At the last minute William Pickles interceded, insisting that there was no need to proceed because the prisoners had been released on bail. The settlers agreed to wait a day before marching. When, the next day, one of the released prisoners arrived to confirm Pickles's information, the Liberty Men dispersed to their homes.[30]

At first, Pickles successfully played his difficult role. In June 1801, George Ulmer assured Knox that the preacher "privately promised me that he would use his influence to convince his acquaintances of the justness of your claim. I think he may be serviceable." Two weeks after the Liberty Men mustered in Davistown on the Fourth of July, Pickles lodged at Ulmer's house in Ducktrap. The preacher related that during the preceding week he had quieted four Davistown crowds intent on punishing the Tories in their midst, especially Major Samuel Mooers, who had assisted Knox's surveys. Dreading the witness stand, where he would be under the simultaneous scrutiny of neighbor and proprietor, Pickles fed information to Ulmer in return for the squire's promise not to call for his testimony in court. A month later, when Thurston Whiting and Benjamin Brackett visited Davistown to denounce the resistance, Pickles performed masterfully. The emissaries reported: "Mr. Pickles was their chief organ of communication. He asserted that the people of D[avistown] had ever been peaceable good citizens, friends to government and order and particularly had never been opposed to Genl. K[nox]'s surveying his lands, that they had a proper abhorrence of insurrections and mobs . . . and therefore he (Mr. P.) thot it very extraordinary that we should come to Davistown on such an errand." Nervously noting the crowd's "rising choler and clamor," Whiting and Brackett hastily insisted that their visit implied no censure. Despite the Davistowners' professions of obedience, no one accepted the emissaries' offer of good pay to guard Knox's renewed surveys.[31]

Pickles's carefully maintained appearance unraveled in late September 1801 when George Ulmer, under pressure from Knox, broke his promise and summoned the preacher to testify before the Lincoln County grand jury investigating the July Fourth Davistown muster. Pickles stood to damn himself in the eyes of Knox, Ulmer, the justices, solicitor general, and grand jury if he seemed to dissimulate. But he risked antagonizing the Liberty Men if his testimony imperiled a neighbor. Pickles had never faced a sterner test. In October 1801 Daniel Davis, the solicitor general, reported Pickles's failure to Knox:

> I have enjoined it upon Ulmer not to summon witnesses unless he be well assured that they not only possess, but will communicate their knowledge of the men and of facts. Of the twelve or fifteen which he brought there, not more than 4 were of any importance. Some of them really knew nothing, others probably lied before the Jury. Of the latter, the Revd. Mr. Pickles was the most eminent. He swore unequivocally that he knew not the names of a single man, concerned in the riot of 4th July or any other time. But it appeared before the Jury that [Captain John] Cunningham had said he recd. his orders and commission from this teacher of peace and righteousness. Upon the disclosure of this, the fellow pretended that his *conscience* required that he should say something more to the jury; but I refused to let him be re-examined from a persuasion that the testimony of so eminent a scoundrel as he appears to be can be of no service to a good cause.

Pickles's awkward performance also undermined his standing with his neighbors and eroded their confidence in their capacity for united resistance. Expecting the worst from the approaching Supreme Judicial Court trials of two ejectment suits brought by the Twenty Associates against Davistown settlers, the Davistowners capitulated in August 1802. They permitted proprietary surveys and agreed to pay about two dollars per acre for their homesteads.[32]

Seeing no future for himself in Davistown, Pickles removed to Vermont, where he died in obscurity about 1812. His departure left a community leadership vacuum filled by newcomers Timothy Copp and Ebenezer Everett. Both acquired esquire status, and both served as the Twenty Associates' agents, collecting settler payments and watching for timber trespasses. Shortly after arriving, Copp allied with the local Tories by marrying Major Samuel Mooers's daughter Mary and by naming their firstborn David Mooers Copp.[33]

At the grand jury inquest where Pickles committed perjury, another leading man, Robert Foye of Sheepscot Great Pond (Palermo), emerged as the prosecution's star witness. Thurston Whiting and Benjamin Brackett described Foye as "a rational moderate man who abhors the principles and measures of the insurgent settlers." There was nothing in his material or familial circumstances to set Foye apart from his neighbors and account for his proprietary allegiance. He was one of Sheepscot Great Pond's first settlers, arriving in 1787. Raised in Pownalborough's troubled North Parish (Alna), Foye knew the land controversies of the Lincoln County coast that had schooled most backcountry folk for resistance. Kinship ties should have pulled him toward the insurgency; his wife, Basheba Hutchens, was the sister of Hollis Hutchens, Sheepscot Great Pond's leading early settler and father of four zealous Liberty Men. Nor was there bad blood between Hollis Hutchens and Robert Foye, who named one of his sons Hollis Foye. Apparently temperament—an innate caution, a greater reluctance to oppose men of wealth and power and their legal institutions, and a greater fear of extralegal actions—led Robert Foye to espouse submission to the proprietary claims. Pessimistic about the resistance, Foye decided that assisting the Great Proprietors was his best chance to secure enough land for his sons: the same patriarchal goal that led his more daring neighbors to become Liberty Men. Because almost all of his neighbors supported the resistance, Foye's proffered support to the Great Proprietors was a rare and valuable commodity that promised to earn him favorable terms.[34]

Foye's testimony led the grand jury to indict twelve Liberty Men, including two of his wife's nephews, David and John Hutchens. The nephews escaped conviction in October 1802, but two other men were less fortunate. Later that month, about thirty settlers went to the Wiscasset jail to free the two by paying their fines. They also scouted the jail's security, for that evening armed Liberty Men marched into Wiscasset. Breaking open the jail, they liberated John Bumford of Balltown, who, in a separate June 1802 trial, had been convicted on Foye's testimony and sentenced to ten years at hard labor for setting fire to a Tory's barn. Bumford and his liberators returned to the backcountry. Later that night Robert Foye's barn and attached shed burned to the ground; the flames consumed his hay, grain, tools, and sleigh. Such was the price of betraying neighbors.[35]

Jonathan Bartlett lived near Robert Foye on the western side of Sheepscot Great Pond, but their positions on the resistance could not have been farther apart. Raised in Balltown, Bartlett moved up the Sheepscot River about 1787 to settle at Sheepscot Great Pond's outlet, where he erected the new settlement's first sawmill and first gristmill. But as the community's settlement proceeded northward away from the mills, their southernmost location became increasingly inconvenient; in

1806 Charles Vaughan described them as "not enough used for profit." By 1811 neither mill remained in operation. Nonetheless, Bartlett was one of the settlement's most substantial farmers, owning a frame house, a barn, 20 improved acres, 205 unimproved acres, a horse, 4 oxen, 2 mature cows, and 4 swine. It is revealing that Bartlett clung to "yeoman" status in court records and land deeds, although, as a large landholder and miller, he could have claimed to be a "gentleman." Thus did Bartlett demonstrate a sense of identity with his poorer neighbors, in contrast to Robert Foye, who, although slightly less prosperous than Bartlett, increasingly assumed the label "gentleman."[36]

Bartlett's intelligence and eloquence commanded great influence among his neighbors and grudging admiration from his proprietary foes. Charles Vaughan noted, "Jona. Bartlett has been considered as the best informed and most correct in his judgements of the [Kennebeck Proprietors'] title and the weakness of it has been supported with great warmth and success by him." In August 1801 Thurston Whiting and Benjamin Brackett visited Sheepscot Great Pond and convened the settlers at Christopher Erskine's tavern. Labeling Bartlett "the great gun of squatters' law," the emissaries observed: "He appears to be possessed of all the cunning, talents and impudence of an old practised pettifogger. He was the chief speaker and the most open and explicit advocate for the expediency and necessity of insurrections and mobs. From the deference paid to him by his neighbors and from all that we could collect from *them* about *him* we may consider him as the barometer of the atmosphere around him." Bartlett backed his words with money and action, provisioning and serving as an officer in a Liberty Man company that in September 1801 unsuccessfully hunted in the Waldo Patent backcountry for a proprietary survey party commanded by George Ulmer.[37]

Robert Foye probably set in motion the chain of events that undermined Jonathan Bartlett. About two weeks after Bartlett returned from his expedition to the Waldo Patent backlands, Foye apparently led a delegation that secretly approached Charles Vaughan about coming to terms. The delegation claimed to speak for thirty settlers, about a third of Sheepscot Great Pond's households. According to Vaughan, most "were not the original intruders but [newcomers] who have purchased from them for valuable considerations" and felt uneasy over their "uncertain tenure." They presented an opportunity to break up the solid settler front and oblige the rest to sue for terms. Vaughan recognized that Sheepscot Great Pond was the geographic linchpin of the resistance, lying in the very center of the Sheepscot backcountry astride the strategic east-west county road linking Augusta with Belfast.[38]

To capitalize on the Foye group's opening, in January 1802 the Kennebeck Proprietors proposed that the General Court appoint a three-man commission to visit the Plymouth Patent and set lot-by-lot prices that each settler should pay for proprietary title to secure no more than one hundred acres. Modeled on Henry Knox's Waldo Patent Commission of 1797, the proposal stipulated that the longer a lot had been settled, the lower the award price—a conscious bias in favor of the older, more prosperous, most influential settlers. Poorer, newer settlers would pay more. By presenting the commission as the utmost that the General Court could do for the settlers, the Kennebeck Proprietors meant to foreclose hopes that the commonwealth would quiet every family with one hundred to two hundred acres at token prices. The General Court passed the proposal, and the Kennebeck Proprietors secured commissioners whom they could trust: Peleg Coffin of Nantucket, Elijah Brigham of Westborough, and Thomas Dwight of Springfield. They were wealthy Massachusetts gentlemen from old, established families, men who socialized and sympathized with the Great Proprietors, men determined to "produce more correct ideas of the rights of property among said settlers."[39]

Two very divergent assessments of the Plymouth Patent Commission's awards survive: one by Charles Vaughan, the Kennebeck Proprietors' land agent, and another by William Allen, Jr., a young settler who paid an especially high price. Vaughan insisted that the commissioners were too generous. Citing the awards to William Allen and his son William Allen, Jr., both of Industry, for $120 and $190 for their two one-hundred-acre lots, Vaughan insisted that they should have paid at least $200 apiece. The younger Allen disagreed. It infuriated him that, instead of personally inspecting the settlers' hardscrabble homesteads, the commissioners held hearings in a comfortable Augusta tavern and relied on proprietary agents' reports to set their awards. Allen bitterly felt the wide gap between his penury as a settler and the commissioners' comfort as gentlemen. Working and lodging in Hallowell at the time, in October 1802 he "went up to Augusta on the east side of the river, more than twice the distance of the road on the west side, to avoid paying toll over the bridge, not having money to pay the toll." Presenting his submission in Thomas's tavern, Allen saw the commissioners, Charles Vaughan, and the Plymouth Company's lawyers dine on roast beef "but [I] could not eat of it, for I had no money to buy a dinner. I bought a good-sized cracker for a cent, and made a dinner of this, and walked back to Hallowell the same way that I came." The commissioners' awards to Industry settlers averaged $1.18 per acre (before interest and surveying fees), twice what they had expected. Allen fumed:

> They were not aware of the stubborn nature of the soil in Industry
> nor of the absolute poverty of the settlers who often had to live on

bread alone for days, and sometimes to make a dinner of herbs. . . . They saw some fertile gardens near the beautiful Kennebec, received the glowing descriptions of the settlers' lands from the proprietors' agents and made up their prices accordingly. If they had come as far as Industry, and seen for themselves the land covered with stones, and roads so rude that no wheeled carriage could pass a mile in any place in town and if they had seen the evidence of our poverty everywhere apparent, I am sure they would not have set the price of our land half as high as they did.[40]

Allen barely procured enough specie to meet the June 1805 deadline for completing the payment of his "award." "By great exertion, selling my oxen and all the grain and corn I had, and borrowing of a friend in Winthrop ten dollars I made the payment. I was obliged to pay two dollars to send the money to Boston. Thus my lot cost me two hundred and seven dollars, instead of fifty dollars which I expected to pay." In return, he received no warranty deed, only the Plymouth Company's grant, worthless should a competing company bring suit. But in meeting the deadline, Allen was relatively fortunate; he knew the experiences of thirty-one other submitting settlers: only six had the resources to pay (usually by liquidating their precious livestock), another fifteen mortgaged their farms to third parties to borrow the necessary cash, and the final ten "gave all up and abandoned their possessions."[41]

Despite its limitations, the commission secured 536 settler submissions, cutting the extent of the resistance within the Plymouth Patent in half. Nine-tenths of Sheepscot Great Pond's settlers submitted, securing one-hundred-acre homesteads at an average price of ninety-one cents per acre (a lower average than Industry settlers paid because Sheepscot Great Pond was an older settlement). Almost all the holdouts dwelled around Jonathan Bartlett in the settlement's southwestern corner, near still-defiant Patricktown and Balltown. Two holdouts, Rufus Plummer and Joseph Hutchens, had married Bartlett's daughters and held their lands by his sufferance. Vaughan believed that Joseph Hutchens wanted to submit but could not "for he then improved the land as Bartlett's and had rec'd from him no evidence of gift, and perhaps knowing the temper of the old man he thought it most prudent to remain quiet."[42]

With the loss of community solidarity, Sheepscot Great Pond's holdouts were dangerously vulnerable to legal action. In Vaughan's words, the holdouts had been reduced "to a number that may be controuled." Formerly the proponent of conciliatory measures intended to disrupt backcountry unity, Vaughan exhorted the Kennebeck Proprietors in February 1803: "As the Co. have now settled with the bulk of the intruders on the undivided lands, the settlers of Ballstown, parts of Smith-

[town] and Patrick[town] excepted, the Co. need not from motives of policy offer further indulgences. Vigorous measures will soon bring the refractory to their senses, and lead to some general arrangement which may close all difficulties." In May 1805 he noted that the Sheepscot Great Pond holdouts, including Jonathan Bartlett and his sons-in-law, helped interrupt surveyor Lothrop Lewis's attempt to run the lines defining the Plymouth Patent's southeastern corner. Three months later the company brought ejectment suits against five of the Sheepscot Great Pond holdouts, including Bartlett, Rufus Plummer, and Joseph Hutchens. Armed with musket and bayonet, Plummer prevented Deputy Sheriff Josiah Norris's first attempt to serve the writs summoning the five to court, but a subsequent attempt must have succeeded, for by January 1806 the five cases stood on the docket for Lincoln County's Court of Common Pleas.[43]

Vaughan skillfully pursued a shrewd policy designed to deaden the settlers' willingness to resist. The ejectment suits brought defendants to the brink of economic destruction—the loss of their farms—and established in onlookers' minds the full extent of proprietary power. During the suspenseful interval before trial, Vaughan offered the defendants a limited, last-minute reprieve by agreeing to sell them their homesteads. He acted simultaneously as stern avenger and as benevolent patron, as an awful but just father withholding his impending wrath when treated with proper respect by hitherto wayward children. Vaughan knew that, in combination, the two steps taught settlers the dangers of resistance while inculcating a grateful relief at the limited exercise of proprietary mercy.[44]

Rather than lose their farms, the five defendants agreed in March 1806 to pay the Plymouth Company's legal costs to sue them and four dollars per acre in three annual installments, starting in June 1808. In return, the company dropped its lawsuits. The price was more than four times what the holdouts would have paid had they submitted to the Plymouth Patent Commission in 1802. Vaughan frankly told them that the price "was intended to inflict a punishment for their past violent conduct." Vaughan proudly confided to the Kennebeck Proprietors that the price was "more than is just" and "had the desired effect of humbling them." He explained:

The settlement made is the most important under all circumstances to the Co. of any that has occurred, because it gives a strong impression by price that the Co. has confidence in their title, and this price is given by men who acknowledge they have merited the smart put upon them, and by men some of whom are of the worst habits and most violent in their opposition and one of whom had more influence in exciting and directing the opposition in Patricktown and Ballstown and because that influence will by this settlement be directed to a better use.

Vaughan noted that, because Bartlett had been the most able and determined leader of the resistance, "his purchase will be the strongest evidence of a conviction of his own errors and will weaken others in their opposition and give courage to the well disposed to be active in a settlement with the Co."[45]

In late March the Kennebeck Proprietors sent Charles Turner, Jr., to try once again to survey their patent's southeastern corner: a venture that had been repeatedly interrupted by armed Liberty Men. On this occasion Vaughan "required" a public demonstration of Bartlett's "sincere repentence." Turner reported that Bartlett "rode night and day through Balltown and Patricktown to prevail with the Setlers to cease their opposition—and on Saturday morning joined us." At Damariscotta Bridge settlers again obstructed the attempt, but never before had the company's surveyors proceeded so far, for which Vaughan credited Bartlett's exertions. Grateful, Vaughan promised to rescind one-quarter of the price demanded from Bartlett and one of his sons-in-law, Joseph Hutchens. When the company procrastinated in approving Vaughan's promise, the agent worried that further delay would "revive in him those feelings that will be thousands of dollars damage to the Co." The Kennebeck Proprietors acceded but, to keep Bartlett under control, declined to issue his deed until 1818 (just as Bartlett himself had withheld deeds to control his sons-in-law).[46]

Defeat undermined Jonathan Bartlett's control over his two sons-in-law, wrecking his patriarchal dream. Lacking sons, Bartlett dominated his daughters' husbands by withholding deeds to the lands they improved within his possession claim. Because both were well past their majority (in 1805 Plummer was twenty-six and Hutchens thirty-three), his retention must have generated tensions that preexisted the lawsuits. The Plymouth Company's price-break to Joseph Hutchens, but not to Rufus Plummer, may reflect Bartlett's favoritism to one son-in-law over the other. Perhaps Plummer opposed the family's reluctant accommodation with the Plymouth Company. In any event, he soon manifested his bitter alienation from Jonathan Bartlett and the Hutchens family. On January 18, 1808, he stole a gelding from Bartlett, and eight days later he wrote, to Reuel Williams, a lawyer for the Kennebeck Proprietors, to inform on the timber trespassers active in his area, including Jonathan Bartlett, Joseph Hutchens, and one of Joseph's brothers, Daniel Hutchens. A year later, in January 1809, Rufus Plummer shot and "grievously and dangerously wounded" Daniel Hutchens, and profanely threatened to do the same to Bartlett. A justice of the peace ordered Plummer thrown into the county jail, where he remained until his two June trials, when he received sentences of two months' solitary imprisonment followed by five years' hard labor at the state prison in Charlestown, Massachusetts. With the death of his daughter Mary sometime before September 1812, Bartlett lost his other son-in-law: Joseph Hutchens promptly sold his Palermo homestead for $650 and joined his father and brothers in migrating to Morgan County, Ohio.[47]

Jonathan Bartlett's setback was Robert Foye's triumph. He became Palermo's most successful patriarch, settling five sons in Palermo or adjoining Montville (formerly Davistown). He succeeded where others failed by bargaining his support to the proprietors, splitting the local resistance. Foye succeeded by frustrating his neighbors' pursuit of similar aspirations by different means. Robert Foye had the resistance to thank, for without it he had nothing of value to offer the Kennebeck Proprietors and Twenty Associates. In this way Jonathan Bartlett contributed to Robert Foye's success, just as Foye helped bring down Bartlett.[48]

Fortunately, Jonathan Bartlett lived long enough to reconstruct his patriarchal dream with the next generation, with Rufus Plummer's two sons, Washington and Peasley, who were raised by their grandfather. In August 1829 Bartlett and his wife divided their ninety-eight-acre farm between the two grandsons in return for $400 from Washington Plummer and a formal covenant from Peasley Plummer to maintain his grandparents comfortably for the rest of their natural lives. Having disposed of his land, Jonathan Bartlett died in 1830 possessed of only $53.05 in personal property. Two years later his grandson's grandson Charles Plummer Tidd was born in Palermo; inheriting his great-great-grandfather's fighting spirit and sympathy for the hard-pressed, Tidd would fight with the abolitionist John Brown in Kansas and again at Harper's Ferry.[49]

Triumphant in Sheepscot Great Pond, Charles Vaughan felt confident that the remaining pockets of the resistance in the Plymouth Patent were doomed. Almost all of the Waldo Patent's settlers had come to terms, and resistance on the Pejepscot Patent seemed about to crumble. In October 1806 he assured his fellow proprietors that a complete survey of all the company's unsold, undivided lands was at last within reach. "I find the most influential and leading settlers are highly in favour of it, and thro' their influence, if properly treated much may be done," he observed. To prepare for the projected survey, in August 1807 the Kennebeck Proprietors announced their plans to sue and evict all remaining squatters who refused to take one-year leases from the company. Reviving the dreaded specter of lordships, this provocative announcement combined with the depression wrought in late 1807 by President Jefferson's Embargo to produce the dramatic final efflorescence of the resistance, culminating with Paul Chadwick's death in September 1809. (The next chapter will explore the climactic two years of the resistance, 1808–1809.)[50]

Postscript: Daniel Lambert's Treasure Chest

In the spring of 1804, Daniel Lambert of Canaan seemed to have found the solution to his neighbors' pressing need for cash to pay their Plymouth Patent Commission awards. According to the traveler Edward Augustus Kendall, Lambert, like most of his neighbors, was a poor farmer and logger "in a very abject condition of life." Canaan tax lists for 1798 and 1801 confirm his poverty; land deeds indicate Lambert was a squatter and so illiterate he could not sign his name. So in the spring of 1804 it attracted intense and widespread interest when he and his two grown sons suddenly appeared in public mounted on good horses and wearing expensive clothes: twin marks of successful gentlemen. They ceased working on their homestead and idled their days away in the taverns of Canaan and adjoining Norridgewock. Daniel Lambert added immeasurably to his local popularity by buying round after round for his neighbors who gathered there to drink and gape at the Lamberts' fine appearance. He compounded their consternation by ostentatiously lighting his pipe with burning bank notes. Despite Canaan's location dozens of miles inland, his neighbors attributed Daniel Lambert's sudden wealth to the discovery of buried pirate treasure, because of his reputed occult skills with divining rods. Initially, the Lamberts remained guardedly mum, but in time hints of discovered treasure escaped from Daniel's lips. He needed to say no more. Soon "nothing was talked of but Lambert and his gold; and every day gave birth to new histories of the chest that had been found, and of its immeasurable contents." Lambert confirmed the reports by publicly demonstrating his divining ability to locate a gold coin buried, as a test, in a field.[51]

At a time when several hundred Kennebec Valley settlers were scrambling for some of the region's chronically short specie to pay for their awards, Lambert's treasure chest packed with gold seemed a godsend. The submittees included Daniel Lambert, who was probably particularly militant, for he had once lived in Balltown and was the very last settler in all the patent to submit his lot to the commission. But his timely discovery promised to more than pay the $112 the commissioners had set as his payment to the Kennebeck Proprietors.[52]

Lambert's apparent good fortune inspired his cash-strapped neighbors' fervent hopes of discovering, and intense efforts to secure, their own treasure chests. Kendall quoted an eyewitness to the intense excitement. "All hands are digging in search of money, to the neglect of tilling their lands, and securing their crops. Days and nights are spent by many persons, in digging up old swamps and deserts, sixty, seventy and eighty miles from *navigation*. . . . 'What a stupid clown must he be,' say they, 'who will toil all day for a dollar, or for what he can raise on his farm, while a chest of money can be dug up in one night and he become rich at once.'" Lambert encouraged the mania by assisting several digging parties. In 1851 John W. Hanson recalled, "Gradually, he inoculated the entire population of the Kennebec valley with a treasure-seeking mania, and people in all conditions of life, were found digging from Anson to Seguin, and all along the coast, even to Rhode Island." Hanson concluded, "The excitement so universal and intense, can hardly be realized at the present day." But guardian spirits frustrated every attempt, snatching the chests away at the last moment. "Doleful sighs and dismal noises are heard; the chest moves in the earth, almost out of their very hands," Kendall's source reported.[53]

Settlers with more property and less patience for treasure-seeking hoped to cash in on Lambert's good fortune in another way. Lambert agreed to swap his gold for his neighbors' produce and livestock at generous prices, but, because he had sent the gold to the United States Mint in Philadelphia for conversion to coins, for the moment he offered bank notes and notes of hand in return for his neighbors' property. He promised to honor all the notes and celebrate the return of his gold on September 1, 1804, with free rum and a public dinner at Ware's store in Norridgewock. Dozens took advantage of Lambert's generous offer to share in the specie he had wrested from the spirits. William Allen, Jr., recalled, "A poor man living twenty miles off went to see him and got promise of $50 . . . and tried to obtain wheat of me on the strength of it assuring me that I might depend [on it] for all in Canaan and Norridgewock believed Lambert's story." In the general euphoria over the providential resolution of their cash crisis, none of Lambert's neighbors gave it a second thought when he quickly resold their livestock and produce at a substantial loss to third parties. However wise in the supernatural economy, Daniel Lambert seemed an innocent in the ways of the material world.[54]

An eager crowd gathered at Ware's store in Norridgewock on the appointed day. It did not bode well that no free rum and no public dinner awaited them. When word arrived that Daniel Lambert and his sons had fled across the border into Canada bearing the cash they had made by selling their neighbors' property, cherished visions of treasure chests vanished as quickly as they had appeared a few months before.

The angry crowd burned Daniel Lambert in effigy, perhaps using their worthless notes for tinder. Kendall's informants estimated the losses at more than twelve thousand dollars, a considerable blow to so poor a district. The losses may account for the failure of more than one-quarter of the Norridgewock-Canaan submittees to pay their awards to the Kennebeck Proprietors. In time a better humor developed about the episode, and for several years the locals convened in Norridgewock on September 1 to celebrate "Saint Lambert's Day" with a public dinner and mock toasts to their patron saint.[55]

The settlers eventually learned that the Lamberts belonged to a ring of counterfeiters who used the carefully contrived illusion of discovered treasure to disseminate their forged bank notes (Daniel Lambert's outside partners had provided the fancy clothes and fine horses). Daniel Lambert dissolved the elaborate mirage of treasure chests and guardian spirits to reveal yet another exaction on the settlers' industry. The settlers' wishful dream of an overnight escape from debt sustained a credulity that Daniel Lambert exploited; his gain worsened the poverty that spawned the fantasy. Initially hailed as a savior bearing the cash needed to rescue his neighbors' homesteads from proprietary demands, Daniel Lambert ultimately emerged as a poor man's Josiah Little, yet another opportunistic "rogue and deceiver" preying upon the property of laboring men. Indeed, Daniel Lambert exceeded the Great Proprietors by levying payments on the settlers' dreams, on their escapist fantasy.[56]

CHAPTER SEVEN

White Indians

The most prominent feature in their character is a violent and implacable hatred to the law. . . . They threaten, they prophesy. The sheriff of the county and his officers they have marked out and doomed as victims for sacrifice and the hated name of execution is to terrify them no more. They declare the profession of law must come down, that lawyers must be extirpated and their offices prostrated with the dust. The court house they say must fall and the gaol share a similar fate.—Lemuel Paine, Winslow lawyer, February 1808

IN THE EARLY MORNING OF January 28, 1808, Pitt Dillingham steered his horse-drawn sleigh northeastward away from his Augusta home toward Fairfax, deep in the backcountry. Located at the head of navigation on the Kennebec River, Augusta was a thriving, populous market town of merchants, lawyers, shopkeepers, artisans, laborers, and commercial farmers. Augusta boasted two Congregational churches, the county courthouse, the county jail, a row of fine, new Federal mansions on the bluff, a riverfront district of taverns, warehouses, stores, and wharves busy with commerce, and a decade-old toll bridge over the river. As a deputy sheriff, merchant, the county jailkeeper, and a leading man in town meetings, Dillingham knew Augusta uncommonly well for someone who had lived there for only three years. On Augusta's rural eastern outskirts Dillingham passed by broad, neatly fenced fields and sturdy frame farm buildings—white houses and red barns—a landscape attesting that a generation had already labored to improve the valley lands and that their heirs enjoyed a solid prosperity based on inherited improvements and proximity to Augusta's merchants.[1]

As Dillingham drove his sleigh beyond the valley into the hilly interior, man's dominion over the landscape became less evident; the forest grew larger as the roadside clearings shrank. Dillingham's sleigh frequently shuddered as a runner struck some half-buried stump, log, or rock in the middle of the increasingly winding road. Many fire-blackened stumps and bushes poked up through the snow cover in pastures surrounded by brush or rail fences rather than by stone walls. The outbuildings became low, log hovels roofed with spruce bark, housing a handful of scrawny cattle, sheep, and pigs wary for the sight or smell of a wolf. Augusta's two-story frame farmhouses with white-painted clapboards, glass windows, and brick fireplaces gave way to the backcoun-

Pitt Dillingham. *From James W. North,* The History of Augusta . . . *(Augusta, 1870)*

try's one-story log cabins with stick-and-clay chimneys and no glass in the lone "window," an opening closed tight with a shutter on this January day. In Fairfax the deputy saw neither store nor meetinghouse; there was not enough business to sustain a merchant in Fairfax, and, lacking funds to build a church, the local Calvinist Baptists met in private homes or the recently erected one-room schoolhouses. Fairfax's settlers had not been on the land long enough to mark prosperity on the landscape. Given time, they meant to replicate Augusta's prosperous farms; it would help if they could avoid paying a proprietor, as had done about half of the early settlers in Augusta, where the Kennebeck Proprietors gave away every other lot before the Revolution.

Fairfax's settlers needed time to pay off their debts to Augusta's store-keepers and to parry the Great Proprietors' demands for land payments. In late 1807 they ran out of time with the conjunction of two events: a commercial depression, induced by President Jefferson's Embargo on foreign trade, forced creditors to collect from their debtors at the same moment that the Kennebeck Proprietors commenced a legal offensive against the settler holdouts. In November and December 1807, deputy sheriffs fanned out across the countryside to serve dozens of writs for creditors and proprietors, writs attaching settler livestock and homesteads to oblige their owners to stand trial for debt or ejectment. In the best of times, few settlers could afford suddenly to pay their debts in full, or buy their homesteads, or employ a lawyer to defend their interests in court. Fewer still could do so when a commercial depression undercut the value of their livestock, grain, and lumber. The Embargo reduced the price of pine boards—upon whose sale the settlers chiefly relied to obtain cash and store goods—by almost two-thirds, from $14.00 per thousand board feet in early 1807 to $5.50 in January 1808. To buy needed time, backcountry settlers revived their resistance. Kennebec County sheriff Arthur Lithgow reported that most of the 140 writs obtained by the Great Proprietors in his county were intercepted and destroyed by parties of armed men in Indian disguise.[2]

Increased legal pressure and intensified resistance coincided with an unprecedented surge in evangelical revivalism. During the year August 1807–August 1808, mid-Maine's Calvinist Baptists increased by 676, more than ten times as many net converts as the preceding year, and more than twice as many as any previous year. Ephraim Stinchfield, mid-Maine's preeminent Freewill Baptist itinerant, baptized an impressive 548 converts in the two years 1808–1809, compared to only 125 during the preceding two years, and but 47 in 1810. Flushed with millennial enthusiasm, in June 1808 he reported: "The Lord is working. Satan is roaring; wicked men are opposing." In 1812 his fellow Freewill Baptist, the Reverend John Buzzell, remembered the years 1807–1809 as the "most remarkable for reformations in the District of Maine." Evangelical preaching, with its stress on the imminent millennium, provoked widespread conversion crises in mid-Maine because so many were profoundly disturbed by distressing events in the material world: several years of severe summer drought, the Embargo's commercial depression, fear of war with Great Britain, and the surge in proprietary prosecutions. Many concluded that the temporal world was coming unhinged and the Last Days were hastening upon them, creating a desperate desire for salvation before it was too late. In turn, the unprecedented conversions struck many as yet more evidence that the Last Days drew near, as Christ recruited his forces for the climactic struggle against Antichrist.[3]

The friends of order feared that the White Indians had come to believe that they could accelerate the impending transformation of the evil temporal world by toppling the corrupt legal system run by and for Antichrist's minions. In early January reports reached Sheriff Lithgow that the settlers planned to march on Augusta to destroy the public buildings and kill the Kennebeck Proprietors' lawyers and the officers of the law. Alarmed, Lithgow called out four hundred militia men to guard Augusta and sent Dillingham, his most trusted lieutenant, to Fairfax to negotiate "a peaceable and quiet understanding" with the settlers. Lithgow authorized Dillingham to promise that no deputy would serve any proprietary writs without posting prior notice at Broad's Tavern in Fairfax of the serving officer's name, the date and time he would venture into the backcountry, the name of the settler-defendant, and a list of the property to be attached to command his court appearance. Such advance notice would enable the settler to hide himself and his movable property. The officer would then play out the charade by calling in vain on the settler's homestead. Finding no one there and no livestock to attach, he would dutifully endorse the writ as incapable of service and return it to the chagrined agents and lawyers for the Kennebeck Proprietors, who would be stuck with the deputy's fees. The proposal was a face-saving device meant to maintain the fiction that Lithgow vigorously enforced all the laws. In return, he asked the settlers to cease assaulting his deputies, forsake marching on Augusta, and allow his deputies to resume serving routine writs for debts.[4]

Reaching Wilder Broad's Tavern in Fairfax, Dillingham found a waiting crowd of four hundred people, "who," he observed, "were without doubt nine-tenths as good Indians as any of them." Within an hour seventy-four men armed with muskets and disguised as White Indians appeared on the crest of an adjacent hill. They advanced in ominous silence and in single file behind "an elegant standard" toward the tavern, Dillingham, and the crowd. With military precision, they wheeled in front of the tavern to fire a deafening volley into the air. Marching into an adjoining field, they formed a half-circle and summoned the deputy to enter and address them. He stepped gingerly forward while the crowd pressed up behind to close the other half of the circle around the unnerved deputy. Dillingham described the scene:

> They were dressed with caps about three feet high, masks, blankets, moccasins on their feet. Their caps and masks were decorated with the most uncouth images imaginable. The masks were some of bearskin, some sheepskin, some stuck over with hog's bristles, etc. To give a true description of them is impossible. The frantic imagination of a lunatic in the depth of desperation could not conceive of

more horrid or ghastly specters. Their savage appearance would strike terror in the boldest heart . . . and in that situation with about seventy-four of those horrid visages on one side under arms, about four hundred spectators on the other and encircled in this ring I was ordered to speak.

He added that their appearance "shook every fibre of my frame." Collecting his wits, Dillingham outlined Lithgow's proposals and then withdrew to the tavern. After an hour's consultation the White Indians summoned Dillingham to reenter the circle. Their chief told the deputy, "All injum like very much your talk, all injum agree as you say." He promised that on the ensuing Thursday they would send a "committee [of] white men" to Augusta to close the deal with the sheriff. "After this they formed a circle, sang two songs of their own composition relative to the hardness of the times and then marched off. The utmost order and regularity was observed among them the whole day," Dillingham concluded.[5]

The White Indian King

Pitt Dillingham apparently returned from his difficult day in Fairfax clutching a White Indian recruiting notice he probably found posted on the wall at Broad's Tavern. Back in Augusta he and Lithgow strained to read its tiny, cramped script replete with innovative spelling and grammar by someone unpracticed at writing. The notice concluded with the cryptic signature "Teckarb Leinad." If the sheriff and his deputy reversed the spelling, they recognized the author as fifty-year-old Daniel Brackett, Fairfax's leading White Indian.[6]

Brackett's life displayed that combination of Revolutionary war service, migration, religious unorthodoxy, and White Indian activity so commonly found in mid-Maine. Born in April 1757 in coastal Falmouth, Maine, Brackett served three years in the Continental Line during the Revolution, enduring hardship and danger at Saratoga, Valley Forge, Monmouth, and the New York Highlands. Two of his brothers also served in the Revolutionary armies. Another brother became a Shaker. After the war Brackett returned to Falmouth. In 1798 he migrated up the Kennebec River and into the backcountry to claim and settle a one-hundred-acre lot in Fairfax—then called Freetown by its inhabitants because they meant to remain free of proprietary control. In September 1801, one of Henry Knox's informers identified the elder Brackett as the second-in-command of a company that ambushed the general's surveyors in Lincoln Plantation (Thorndike). In 1804, Daniel Brackett's lone son, Daniel Brackett, Jr., married Lydia Whitney, the daughter of the Reverend John Whitney, a Freewill Baptist preacher who promoted visionary religion and Edward Lock's collectivist plan. And on November 30, 1807, the younger Brackett led a White Indian party that fired at, captured, and beat a deputy sheriff, seizing and destroying his writs. Years later the son became a preacher in the radical Christian Connection.[7]

Lithgow found disturbing contents in Daniel Brackett's recruiting notice. It began by invoking the White Indian myth that a benevolent Indian king had come to the settlers' rescue, a myth Brackett merged with the millennial expectation that Christ would soon destroy Antichrist and his papacy:

> To Aall The settlers on the Kennebeck Claim and Elsewhere That has been imposd upon with Quit Claim deeds and deeds of teen years duration: and other agravations of Robberry to impoversh the people And to Bring them under lordships and slaveourey and as we poor indians did see your situation and did see it was a plan of pollicy and rogurey in great men and unjust: we poor indians did pitty you and was willin to spend our life for you because we all won brother: and our indian King beggs a favour of every settler and inhabbatant that is infriengd upon or like to be: that is to tell every indian that you see that Their king desires them to aquipp themselves with a Capp and blanket and a gun and tommahawk and Visit him at the first opertunity and take Directions: for he means to Cut Down all poopery and kill the Devil and give the world of mankind some piece by stopping the progres of Rogues and Deceivers and helping every man to his right and privilidges and libertys: the same as our indian nation injoys.[8]

Brackett then warned those settlers who opposed the resistance:

> And every indian that is absent and dont Come into a leigence with the rest will be Lookt upon as an einimy to the Cause of Justice and a trator to our indian king and a distroyer of our indian rights and privilidges and an einimy to his indian brethern and a desertor from the indian Crown and Countrey and a spy among the indians friends where they trade for [tobacco] and other nessasereys: Calld English subjects: and a friend to poopery Viz pollicy and Deceit and a suppotr of the devil and a brother to rogues and is a decivour by looking like an indian in the face and pretencesis and aynt in their alleigance to abide by their king in the Defenc of Justice and helping his friend[s] the english subjects to keep their rights and privilidges and libertyes from the Devil and rogues and Deceivours.

Brackett's Indian king demanding local solidarity against external great men echoed rebellious English farm laborers' Captain Swing and the Pennsylvania Whiskey Rebels' Tom the Tinker.[9]

Brackett's notice belonged to a particular moment in late 1807 and early 1808 when, unusually harassed by the law and especially excited by millennial anticipation, the White Indians expressed an unprecedented degree of alienation from the material world's social and political structures. Disappointed by the Revolution's unfulfilled promise, Brackett denied that national liberation had occurred by addressing his fellow settlers as "English subjects." His notice invoked notions long discarded by the better-educated men who directed the commonwealth's political institutions. The talk of king, crown, and subjects belonged to the colonial era's political culture, which justified extralegal violence as the common folk's essential last bulwark against exploitation by "great men." The insurgents' dread of falling "under lordships and slaveourey," the intervention of a benevolent monarch to protect the oppressed poor, and the location of their struggle within a cosmic war against popery and the devil evoked the Reformation's militant popular Protestantism. The tenacity with which Daniel Brackett nurtured the concepts and vocabulary of Gerrard Winstanley's day attests to his rebellion against the prevailing social order, as does his cultivation of imagery associated with the Indians—an oppressed people ordinarily regarded by whites as the backward dregs of humanity. In the Indians' more communal and egalitarian ethos ("we all won brother") Brackett found a useful image for criticizing the larger society. By bonding a venerable Protestant militancy to a new Indian identity, Brackett drew a cultural line between the backcountry folk and the outside world where "great men" prevailed.[10]

Brackett borrowed the millennial discourse, so prevalent among the Eastern Country's evangelicals during that season of emotional revivals, to cast settlers and great men as the saints and demons in a cosmic confrontation. In September 1808, at the crest of the millennial anticipation, the Calvinist Baptists' association for Lincoln County convened at Balltown, the most important resistance center. The association endorsed the circular letter prepared by Phineas Pilsbury from neighboring Nobleborough, another resistance community then in the midst of an emotional revival. Pilsbury's militaristic vision of the approaching millennium bore a remarkable resemblance to Daniel Brackett's notice; both promised the people that they would inherit the earth by rallying to a king's efforts to topple Antichrist by smiting the mighty. Pilsbury exhorted:

Put on your regimental dress, and rally under the standard of King Jesus, and come up to the help of the Lord against the mighty....

What wonderful inroads he hath made of late among his enemies—what a vast multitude he hath slain in the late war within the limits of this Association. Old Babylon is falling quite fast; she appears to totter very much; we think she is on her last feet, and they appear mostly clay. We hope the time is not very far distant when the pure Gospel shall meet with no obstruction from Antichrist, when true Evangelical preaching and apostolic practice shall be universally acknowledged by all professors of religion.

Pilsbury anticipated "the time spoken of in Daniel the Prophet; when the stone cut out of the mountain without hands shall become a great mountain, so as to fill the whole earth, and the kingdom, and the dominion, and the greatness of the kingdom under the whole heaven will be given to the people of the Saints of the Most High." He urged the people, "Put your cockades in your hats, and let an unbelieving, scoffing world know on which side you are, under whose banner you are fighting, and for what King (if called to it) you mean to die." Pilsbury referred to an otherworldly struggle; but in a time and place when and where rural folk declined to segregate the supernatural from daily involvement in the temporal world, the White Indians could easily identify their armed struggle with the approaching millennium.[11]

Brackett concluded his notice with an agrarian notion of a class struggle between the "Cultivators of soil" and the "great men" who monopolized "monney." According to Brackett, the great men were parasites who meant

> to git away all they [the settlers] have got and to turn them out of house and home by a pollitick Craft of roguery for in the first place they pick up all the land and Call it theirn and then they make monney and buy all the property out of the Countrey that Can be spard and people settles on the land as they are Cultivators of soil and Dont git their living by making monney nor Drawing sallaries nor fees and then they Come and Demand pay for the land [at] a price of their own and so gits all their monney back into their own hands again and then all sallaries and town and County Charges Demands monney and their is none or scarce enough to pay them and then all the debts of the Community that coms by trading must be paid and their must be monney and their is none in the Countrey and then Comes law Charges and fees and and the honest Debt together in an execution and Vendues and demands monney and for want of it they take all a man has and give it to another for a third part of its Value and so robbs him and turns him out of house and home for he gits no title to the land only a quit Claim or a teen year leeas.

According to Brackett, great men drained rural districts of circulating money by extorting "a price of their own" for suspect titles and by simultaneously pressing the people to pay their burdensome debts and oppressive legal fees. The twin pressures threatened to turn settlers "out of house and home," as their property passed into the hands of the great men. Therefore, donning Indian garb to waylay deputy sheriffs and proprietary surveyors was the only means by which "every man" could secure "his right and privilidges and libertys."[12]

Brackett's recruiting notice and Dillingham's description of his Fairfax encounter jointly illuminate the White Indians' careful organization and cultural innovation. They maintained a strict secrecy, adopted elaborate costumes, composed songs, designed their own flag, chose chieftains, executed complicated military maneuvers, displayed striking discipline, and crafted a distinctive ideology. After 1800, the settlers imaginatively elaborated the mock-Indian identity that they originally adopted simply to disguise their identities as a shield from criminal prosecution. They gradually began to call themselves White Indians rather than Liberty Men. A similar resort to Indian posturing and costuming had characterized the agrarian resistance by Vermont's Green Mountain Boys and Pennsylvania's Whiskey Rebels and Wild Yankees. Maine's White Indians wore moccasins and ragged Indian blankets. At first, they simply blacked their faces, but when this proved an inadequate disguise, the White Indians donned masked hoods with pointed peaks, a disguise akin to that of the subsequent New York Anti-Renters and the Klansmen and White Cappers of the South. To disguise their voices, the White Indians affected a guttural, pidgin English, in imitation of Indian speech. To supplement the effect, a White Indian might place a wood chip in his mouth.[13]

The White Indian counterculture expressed the settlers' sense that they too were a persecuted people at odds with the most powerful whites. Under a proprietary legal siege that threatened their possession of Maine's lands, the settlers felt a new sense of kinship with the dispossessed Indians. By designing and engaging in elaborate and distinctive costumes and rituals, White Indians set themselves apart from the outside world that harbored their proprietary foes and that was not privy to the culture of the resistance. Thereby, the White Indian counterculture encouraged the settlers to stand together rather than with external authority and its laws. Moreover, by donning Indian costumes, settlers doffed their inhibitions; as Indians they could engage in violence inappropriate to white men; taking off their costumes, insurgents became peaceable settlers once again, shorn, in their minds, of responsibility for what they had done as Indians. In an important psychological sense, the settlers meant it when they insisted that *they* did not commit the "outrages," the Indians did.[14]

There was more than a little ironic hypocrisy in this mock identity. Employing similar tactics of agrarian resistance, the settlers' forebears blocked authorities' occasional attempts to prosecute men who killed Indians in times of official peace. Balltown, the largest and most important center of the resistance, was named for Samuel Ball, who in 1749 murdered an unarmed Indian in peacetime but escaped judgment because no frontier jury would convict a white for such a crime. In 1808 many White Indians were the sons and grandsons of mid-eighteenth-century settlers who had wrested the land away from Maine's real Indians. For example, Davistown settler David Cargill was the son of Colonel James Cargill of Newcastle, an Antifederalist, a violent foe of proprietary land claims, a Revolutionary war militia officer, a sternly devout Scotch-Irish Presbyterian, and a cold-blooded scalp hunter in the French and Indian wars. By massacring a party of peaceful Indian men, women, and children at Owl's Head near Thomaston in 1755 to obtain their scalps, Cargill sparked the war that crushed the Penobscot tribe and opened the backcountry to settlement. With the Indians reduced to an impoverished and ineffectual few dwelling on a restricted and shrinking reservation along the Penobscot River, the settlers who replaced them on the land could afford to identify with their plight and appropriate their identity for use against the proprietors. On one occasion the irony of the identity turned to misfortune, when "a number of lumbermen in mock Indian dress" assaulted and almost killed a real Penobscot Indian who guided a state land agent to their trespassing ground.[15]

Horrid Visages

In addition to its internal, cultural purpose, the Indian identity presented a meticulously contrived "horrid visage" to outsiders. As Dillingham's account so clearly demonstrates, the White Indians took unusual pains to perform frightening rituals and display a terrifying attire to outsiders. Backcountry settlers knew that their poverty, relative isolation, hardships, and limited education led gentlemen to consider them as little better than savages, as literally White Indians. The settlers turned this stereotype to advantage to inculcate an inhibiting dread among their foes.[16]

When undisguised and facing authorities or proprietary servants, the settlers resorted to a carefully crafted rhetoric that mixed caution with implied threat. In March 1796, after Henry Knox's agents drove Samuel Ely from the Waldo Patent and momentarily suppressed open resistance in Ducktrap and New Canaan, George Ulmer reported, "Some still persist in heaving out threats, but in such a manner that it would be verry difficult to take hold of them." One group visited Ulmer's store and, "after drinking freely," dropped hints that Knox "would sicken and die soon." Rattled, Ulmer hastily wrote Knox in Boston to beware of an attempt to poison him. It seems far more likely that some frustrated and bitter settlers found recourse in a psychological war of suggestion to sow a measure of restraining fear in Knox's camp. In February 1801 Lewiston's Stephen Chase, a miller and proprietary supporter, reported, "The majority of the inhabitants of this town wishes that all the friends of the Proprietors of the Land were drove out of the town." But wary of prosecution, the Lewistonians assumed an ambiguous tone: "I find so many double minded, double tongued Persons which turn their faces to all parties and their backs to Justice." In August 1801 in Davistown (Montville), Thurston Whiting and Benjamin Brackett found: "Everyone had his cue. Not a single one knew anything in particular about past aggressions. . . . This language of reserve and evasion was doubtless preconcerted." At the same time, the settlers missed no opportunity to frighten their enemies with ominous suggestion. "In general they are cautious and guarded in their manner of expression, or at least they mean to be so and think that they are. They tell us that they would not advise Gen. Knox to send any more surveyors in the woods which are infested with Indians whose numbers have greatly increased since the arrest and commitment of some of their neighbors," Whiting and Brackett reported. In Smithtown (Freedom) the emissaries conversed with settler leader Stephen Smith "He asked us why Gen. K[nox] sent his agents and missionaries and did not come personally to inspect his own business? The same question has several times before been put to us and once or twice we thot the manner in which it was done carried a dark and dreadful intimation. Maj. B[rackett] usually replied that the Gen. was very corpulent and heavy on which account he was unable to perform long journies on rough roads on horseback."[17]

There was a noteworthy exception to this careful but threatening style. Where most men cautiously communicated their purposeful antipathy in what Whiting and Brackett described as "significant grimaces and sly innuendoes," women did not mince their words. They were unlikely to face criminal prosecution, and they were especially concerned with the threat to their security in old age posed by the proprietors' demands for payment, a security that hinged on retaining as much of the fruits of their life's labor as possible. Pursuing their families' activities in the broader world, men could be slightly more composed about the prospect of giving up and moving on, if need be. Because women kept closer to home, relied heavily on nearby networks of fellow women for emotional and economic exchanges, and had already, with some reluctance, undergone at least one leap into the frontier unknown, they were even more determined to stand and fight. Women who could shoulder muskets to shoot crop-ravaging bears could also stiffen their husbands' and sons' resolve when a proprietor's demands for payment similarly threatened their family's tenuous economic security. When Henry Knox's Brigadier Island farm laborers mutinied and plundered his rum supply, John Rynier, the farm manager, blamed the caretaker's wife, Mrs. Zenas Lothrop. She was "as fond and *can drink as much rum*, as any of them, and [h]as caused more differences in the house than ever I met with in my life—spurring up the work people not to mind me, but to do in the house what they liked . . . and she would do as she pleased in spite of the old man, as she is pleased to term me." Rynier complained, "She is like many others in the world—when taken from a state of starvation to good living, they do not know how to be too profuse."[18]

In their August 1801 backcountry tour, Thurston Whiting and Benjamin Brackett repeatedly encountered women who spoke their minds more forthrightly than did their sons and husbands. In Twenty-Five-Mile Pond settlement, Nathan Parkhurst spoke in a "calm and moderate" manner despite his recent arrest and imprisonment as a suspected White Indian. In contrast, "his wife with all the copiousness and with all the strokes and signs of female eloquence dilated on the subject of her husband's arrest and confinement." At Sandy Stream the emissaries lodged with Benjamin Rackliff, who, although a White Indian, said nothing to rankle his guests. But his aged mother "delivered a harangue" defending the squatters and assailing proprietary greed. In Davistown, the Reverend William Pickles chose his words carefully, but his wife Margaret filled the emissaries' ears with bitter complaints. "She wished that the Genl. knew how very unacceptable his agents (Ulmer and Houston) were among the people and how hardly they treated the settlers, threatening to burn their camps and drive them from their lands without allowing them any compensation for their labor. Vengeance, she said, was denounced against Esq. Ulmer and would undoubtedly be executed when opportunity afforded." In Patricktown, David Gilpatrick's mother repeated the Liberty Men's credo, pointedly telling the emissaries "that it was as good to die by the sword as by the famine and that if the men were all of her mind they would prefer the latter."[19]

When shielded by disguise or anonymity, men expressed more forthrightly their supposed readiness to spill blood by performing theatrical displays of violence. To shock, some White Indians killed, roasted, and ate the horses of persistent deputies before their eyes. At night they crept into shire towns to drop dreadful anonymous letters around the homes of sheriffs, lawyers, and land agents. These simultaneously threatened the recipients with destruction and demonstrated their vulnerability to secret nocturnal visits. The Kennebeck Proprietors' Augusta lawyers received sketches of themselves dangling from the gallows between matching tomahawks dripping blood. Colonel Samuel Thatcher, Henry Knox's son-in-law and Lincoln County's sheriff, awoke one morning to find that overnight the insurgents had thoughtfully left an open coffin on his doorstep. Three nights after Deacon John Neal of Litchfield assisted a proprietary survey, his barn went up in flames. A few days later, notices written in blood appeared around the town warning that, if Neal "was not easy with what he had got his house should go [next] and him in it." While canvassing the backcountry for timber trespassers, Charles Vaughan encountered a board posted to a tree addressing him by name and (in his words) "assuring me that there are Indians ready to fire at me with guns doubly charged and with a hand (*over death*) pointing to the trespassing ground, and another hand (*over life*) pointing to the road I came from." Suddenly feeling underpaid, Vaughan followed the hand of life homeward and devoted the afternoon to an angry letter demanding more money from his fellow Kennebeck Proprietors. Worn down by the tension and frustration of his "literal warfare with the individual settlers," Vaughan bitterly assured his fellow Kennebeck Proprietors in 1806, "I would undertake [searching out trespassers] on no terms; no price would tempt me to engage again in such a business."[20]

Reminiscent of the Green Mountain Boys, and especially the infamous Ethan Allen, the White Indians employed peculiarly violent and blasphemous language, expressions of a popular culture where words, especially oaths, carried an almost magical power to frighten or harm. In 1795, ten armed men burst upon the campsite in Balltown (Jefferson) of Ephraim Ballard's survey party for the Kennebeck Proprietors, awakening them just before dawn with deafening shots into the air. Pressing a loaded musket to Ballard's chest, the leader bellowed, "Deliver up, deliver up all, God damn you, deliver the compass, deliver up the cannister, God damn you, take nothing out, if you do you are a dead man." Ballard delivered. When Elliot G. Vaughan, a proprietary agent, visited Bristol in 1810, a crowd gathered to warn him, "Never show your head in Bristol again." Vaughan remembered that one settler angrily "wish'd to god he could see my blood on the burying ground above there where a number of their friends and relatives were who had been wounded and killed by the Indians and in the most irritating manner added God Damn you I wish I could meet you in some convenient place." The inhabitants ritually escorted Vaughan out of town, making "considerable noise" with cowbells. Vaughan spent that night in a house just across the Damariscotta River from Bristol. Long after midnight a crowd kept the terrified agent awake by "stoning the house and making almost every noise that can be conceived of." Vaughan did not return.[21]

As with western Pennsylvania's Whiskey Rebels who threatened Pittsburgh, the Paxton Boys who menaced Philadelphia, and the Anti-Renters of 1766 who marched on New York City, mid-Maine's backcountry settlers merged their grievances against proprietors with their resentments as debtors to intimidate the commercial and judicial centers that housed proprietary agents, lawyers, and sheriffs. Such threats alarmed Arthur Lithgow of Augusta in 1808. Belfast also feared settler vengeance. Although they needed their commerce with Belfast's merchants, the settlers resented that the town grew so conspicuously rich so fast, seemingly at their expense. During the ten years 1796–1805, Belfast residents confronted backcountry settlers in 134 debt cases in Hancock and Lincoln counties' Courts of Common Pleas. Nine times out of ten the Belfaster was the plaintiff and the settler the defendant. Two-thirds of such suits pitted high-status Belfast plaintiffs (gentlemen, traders, merchants, esquires, and doctors) against low-status backcountry defendants (yeomen, artisans, or laborers). The plaintiffs won every case. Only once did a backcountry yeoman, artisan, or laborer sue a Belfast gentleman, and that suit failed. In June 1801 the backcountry settlers were infuriated by the arrest and rough treatment of several suspected insurgents by a militia troop drawn from Belfast, provisioned by Knox, planned by George Ulmer, and led by Colonel Thomas Knowlton. Armed men "dressed in the Indian stile and perfectly black" appeared on Belfast's outskirts. On the morning of the twenty-sixth they briefly seized and interrogated a blacksmith named John Clark, when he ventured out with a basket to collect coal. The Liberty Men sent him back to Belfast with their threat to burn the town to the ground unless the inhabitants released their prisoners. "This place," Ulmer wrote from Belfast, "is in constant alarm." But the authorities' quick removal of the prisoners across Penobscot Bay to Castine and the continued presence of militia men under arms in Belfast's streets persuaded the Liberty Men to disperse.[22]

Restraint

Despite their horrifying threats, the White Indians practiced a purposeful restraint that allowed all of their foes but one, the traitor Paul Chadwick, to live out their natural lives. Ephraim Ballard, Colonel

Thatcher, Elliot G. Vaughan, Deacon Neal, Charles Vaughan, Augusta's lawyers, and Belfast's merchants all survived the settler resistance. Nor did the settlers put the torch to Belfast or Augusta (although a suspicious fire damaged the Kennebec County courthouse in Augusta in 1808). Preindustrial crowds in England and America characteristically acted with a purposeful restraint that assailed property but spared life. As with New York's Anti-Renters, slipping a hot coal under a barn served as the Liberty Men's favorite means of teaching Tories a lesson. Detached from a settler's house, barns were easier to approach in secrecy; fire would rage out of control before anyone could notice, but no one would be killed. It is striking testimony to settler self-discipline that decades of armed confrontation over very high stakes claimed but a single life.[23]

There were compelling reasons behind the gap between the settlers' terrible threats and their restrained deeds, between their frightening displays and their cautious actions. From the crushing defeat of their Regulator brethren in 1786–1787, the White Indians learned the folly of overtly challenging government with a military offensive. The settlers could ill afford open warfare with the state. Estimating Kennebec County's White Indians at one thousand armed men, John Merrick, a proprietary land agent, astutely noted in October 1809: "If the thousand insurgents persist in their object, it is probable that their farms must suffer, their winter lumber must remain uncut, their provisions for the winter be spent, and the gifts of their friends come to an end. . . . War in the mean time we know is costly, and is commonly decided by those who have the stoutest purse; and this does not belong to the insurgents."[24]

By avoiding offensive actions that fitted the legal definition of an "insurrection," the White Indians strove to deny their foes the grounds for calling out the militia. To minimize overt confrontations, settlers staged frightening spectacles along the fringes of advancing survey parties or sheriffs' posses. Undisguised settlers who fell in with interlopers dropped dire hints of the many enraged Indians lurking in nearby ambush—usually enough to send the visitors scurrying home. If not, the White Indians increased their psychological pressure. Hidden in the woods around the advancing party, they startled the visitors by suddenly firing loud volleys into the air and by periodically displaying themselves in their frightful attire. The further the party advanced, the more frequently settlers discharged their muskets and showed themselves, creating the impression that every step brought the intruders closer to a deadly ambush. If the visitors camped, they faced a sleepless night guarding their horses from theft and enduring the most hideous noises that the settlers could imagine. A day or so of this treatment generally sufficed to send the unnerved interlopers fleeing from the backcountry. If not, as a last resort, armed and disguised settlers stepped in force across the visitors' path to forbid any further advance. The settlers' decentralized tactics combined with frightening performances to sustain the resistance within a legal gray area short of insurrection.[25]

With neither illusions about their capacity to wage a protracted war against the state nor ambitions to become martyrs, the White Indians planned to melt quietly into the background if the militia invaded their communities. Aware that considerations of expense forbade a long-lasting occupation, settlers felt confident that any militia expedition would quickly withdraw. Charles Hayden of Winslow, a surveyor for the Kennebeck Proprietors, noted: "They appear in their disguise, committ an outrage and disappear. I think if the sheriff, officers and magistrates should go into that section of the country they would not find any body of armed men to read the riot act to; all would appear in peace." In February 1808 a Bowdoin tavern keeper boasted to George Bender, an emissary from the governor, that, even if he sent the militia against them, "tho a body of 500 Indians were assembled yet when the troops reached the spot they would find nothing to fire at but trees, nobody would know who the Indians were, or where they had gone to." The settlers counted on the government's commitment to the common law and civil liberties; they were confident that the frustrated militia would simply go away rather than arbitrarily destroy buildings and imprison bystanders. Settlers could conduct such a restrained strategy because the authorities behaved in such a predictably limited manner. Indeed, when Sheriff Arthur Lithgow called out Augusta's militia on his own authority in January 1808 without first consulting the governor in Boston, the governor's council rescinded the order and rebuked and sacked the sheriff for overstepping the letter of the law.[26]

In addition to sustaining a useful legal ambiguity, restraint helped preserve the solidarity critical to the settlers' resistance. Many older, more prosperous settlers lay tenuously poised between loyalty to their neighbors and adherence to the law. Already uncomfortable with the White Indians' intimidation of wayward neighbors, the cautious were unprepared for open rebellion. To preserve their coalition, the White Indians carefully avoided the acts of bloodshed that would drive the fence sitters into cooperation with the authorities as the lesser of two evils.[27]

But the White Indians saw no need for their foes to know those limits. Through terrifying displays the White Indians inculcated in their foes an inhibiting dread beyond their actual danger. In this way, the settlers sought maximum leverage at minimal risk. They meant for outsiders to expect the worst and so treat them with great caution. By shrewdly manipulating terrifying imagery, they meant to enjoy the paralyzing effect of town burnings and revenge killings, without their corrosive consequences for the settlers' coalition.

Fear

For years the settlers' performances worked, convincing their foes that they stood in imminent danger of death from a savage folk who could not control their passions. Six days after his ordeal, Pitt Dillingham wrote, "No earthly consideration would tempt me to go among them again provided they wore the same appearance they then did." In November 1809 Philip Bullen of Hallowell, a surveyor for the Kennebeck Proprietors, wrote:

> I can say that it was many a time that I have traveled in the dead of night to gitt on to certain lines by the dawn of day, and it is many a day that I have run my line not dareing to make any noise for fear of being discovered by the ill-disposed inhabitants and when night came on have built a little fire with barks and sticks to cook a little food by, not presuming to make any noise by cutting wood, and then put out the fire to avoid discovery and then lay all night on the cold earth without sleep on acct. of the expectation of being discovered and being fired upon if not killed and twice in particular actually been fired upon . . . and shurly it is impossible to describe the feelings of one's heart in such situations to any person who has not experienced the same.[28]

Authorities and townspeople chronically feared that the hill folk were about to descend in violent force to disrupt court sessions and set shire towns ablaze. In August 1804, the alarmed proprietary lawyer Benjamin Whitwell of Augusta breathlessly warned Newburyport lawyer (and future chief justice of the Supreme Judicial Court) Theophilus Parsons that Kennebec County stood on the brink of an overt insurrection:

> Our adversaries are vigilant and active. They dare to threaten an insurrection in the county if opposed in executing their projects. Such discontents exist . . . that we are seriously apprehensive that threats will be executed. It has been their favorite object to obtain the controul of militia. This they have completely effected. One or two desperate and unprincipled characters have lately been elected to the command of regiments and reports are now circulating that

an armed force will be collecting for the purpose of preventing the county courts transacting business at their session of the ensuing week.

Belfast's residents became so anxious over repeated threats by back-country settlers to put their town to the torch that, in November 1807, when some young men fired guns on the outskirts of town as a prank, the town's men tumbled out of bed to spend the long night under arms, starting at every sound in anticipation of a White Indian attack that never came. A delighted backcountry poet, Daniel Dollof's son Joseph Dollof of Greene Plantation (Belmont), penned a mock epic entitled "The Greene Indian War," ridiculing the fright, zeal, greed, and pomposity displayed by Belfast's town fathers, prosperous merchants whom the settlers knew as disagreeable creditors as well as proprietary supporters.[29]

Dread rewarded the settlers with circumspection from their foes. In early June 1801 George Ulmer toured the backcountry to warn the inhabitants of their impending ruin if they dared attack Henry Knox's surveyors again. Unappreciative of this concern, on June 7, 1801, in Davistown a party of armed Liberty Men led by James Smith of Smith-town (Freedom) briefly seized Ulmer to "threaten him the said Ulmer to kill and murder." They allowed Ulmer to flee back to Ducktrap, but their words apparently gave pause, for at the last moment before the survey party set out on June 20, 1801, Ulmer wrote to a surprised Henry Knox, "And I very much regret that my business is such that I cannot be in the woods myself until the business is fully accomplished." Knox had to get another agent to lead the dangerous survey routed by an ambush on June 22 in Lincoln Plantation (Thorndike) that left one man severely wounded.[30]

Pitt Dillingham's mission for Arthur Lithgow also testified to the effectiveness of settler posturing. It was a startling concession for a county sheriff to negotiate with and appease what, by law, was a criminal conspiracy. But Augusta's worried lawyers supported Lithgow's proposal, and Edmund Bridge, Lincoln County's sheriff in 1808, applied to the governor for permission to suspend the service of all writs, those for creditors as well as those for proprietors, in that county's backcountry. Not subject to the same pressures, Governor James Sullivan in distant Boston apparently felt that Maine's magistrates had taken leave of their senses; he rebuked Bridge for even broaching the idea and allowed his council to replace Lithgow. Nonetheless, Edmund Bridge and John Chandler, Lithgow's successor, quietly restrained writ service in the backcountry during the ensuing year.[31]

The Great Proprietors were frustrated by the settlers' success in deterring surveyors and law officers with threats and small patrols, neither of which constituted clear-cut evidence of an insurrection. Proprietary surveyors and deputy sheriffs repeatedly abandoned forays into the backcountry at the first sign of trouble, but, despite repeated pleas, the Great Proprietors could not persuade the governor and General Court that an actual insurrection—requiring militia—existed in mid-Maine. Wary of a militia expedition's costs and of provoking more extensive violence, the authorities in Boston preferred to believe settler protestations that the outrages were the work of a small minority. "At present," Henry Knox fumed in August 1801, "a shapeless rumour exists." He explained: "Our great object is to oblige them to avow their designs. At present they act by dark sayings and equivocal conduct." In October 1809, John Merrick denounced the insurgency conducted by "unknown men, who dare not *name* or *shew* themselves . . . who are one day said to be *many and powerful*, when it is designed that they shall *inspire terror*, and next day are represented as *few and contemptible*, when it is intended to *prevent any force being kept up against them*." As James W. North, a proprietor's grandson, wrote in his 1870 *History of Augusta*: "This mode of guerrilla warfare was worse than open and formal insurrection. In the latter, a crisis would soon be reached, and a remedy provided; but in the former, disguise and secrecy prevented the notoriety which would call for the intervention of the strong arm of government, and the guerrillas as effectually attained their object." The settlers' resistance to the land laws remained formidable so long as their visages seemed convincingly horrid.[32]

Bloodshed

But the performances grew steadily less effective over time as proprietors and their lieutenants gradually learned to call the White Indians' bluff. Familiarity with the settlers' "horrid visages" slowly bred contempt. Benjamin Joy's experienced land agent, David Sewall of Hallowell, learned to ignore the settlers' theatrical posturing. In Greene Plantation (Belmont and Morrill), Sewall and his new assistant, John Conner, passed through twenty White Indians who, in Conner's words, "lined the sides of the road, making sounds and articulations different from the English language." Sewall calmed his frightened assistant's nerves by observing that "he had seen these things before." They continued on their rounds. Late in the resistance a deputy sheriff reported that he and a posse confronted White Indians in Freedom, "who ordered us to *stand*, but not minding their command, they cocked and aimed their guns at us when passing near them. Their guns were presented at the breasts of my horse and the breasts of the aid with me, but we received no injury and passed by them, they threatening however to blow us thro if we passed on." Such persistence increasingly presented the White Indians with the painful choice of backing down or actually taking life. In either case the White Indians stood to lose; backing down conceded defeat, and deaths would alienate the more cautious settlers, dissolving the essential solidarity. Three incidents accelerated the decay of the effectiveness of horrid visages: the November 1807 assault on Deputy Sheriff Henry Johnson, the April 1808 beating of constable Moses Robinson, and the climactic September 1809 assassination of Paul Chadwick in Malta.[33]

A resident of Winslow, a river town on the upper Kennebec, Deputy Sheriff Henry Johnson dwelled just beyond the usual reach of White Indian intimidation but close enough to suspect his adversaries' weakness. His saddlebags filled with writs attaching backcountry settler homesteads for the Kennebeck Proprietors, he rode eastward away from the river toward Beaver Hill (Freedom), deep in the backcountry, on November 24, 1807. En route he entered hostile Fairfax (Albion). Five sentries "disguised in a most heidious garb, their faces completely masked," stepped out from the woods, leveled their muskets, and brought Johnson to a halt by demanding "in the Indian dialect" his name and purpose. Johnson lied that he bore writs for creditors but none for proprietors. The sentries replied that because they meant to "guard poor white men's property . . . they would serve the writs 'as the devil found sixpence, all in a heap.'" Seizing and examining Johnson's writs, the White Indians discovered his deception. Enraged, they ordered him on pain of death to strip off his clothing. Johnson retorted "that if his cloaths came off before he went to bed that they must be at the trouble of taking them off after [he] had become a corpse." After a prolonged exchange of threats and refusals, the sentries tired of the confrontation, gave back Johnson's writs, and told him to go home and never return. Spurring his horse, Johnson hurled a parting insult and defiantly proceeded on at a gallop to Beaver Hill. Despite brushes with four more White Indian patrols—one of which fired shots to startle him—Johnson successfully served his writs. About midnight he turned toward home, only to run into another Fairfax patrol sufficiently enraged by Johnson's persistence to shoot at him. Four shots grazed his coat, and two bullets struck him in the foot and killed his horse. Thrown clear, Johnson hobbled off, dodging death once more when two other sentries' muskets snapped but failed to discharge.[34]

Johnson's brush with death hinted that it was but a matter of time before the armed patrols mishandled one of the many confrontations with their increasingly persistent enemies. This happened in April 1808, when Fairfax constable Moses Robinson arrested his neighbor Daniel Brackett, Fairfax's principal White Indian, for debt, only to find himself surrounded by the muskets of an Indian-attired rescue party. Quite sensibly, Robinson released his man and surrendered his writ. Less sensibly, he proceeded to the nearest magistrate and obtained a new warrant to arrest Brackett for resisting arrest. Reinforced by a deputy sheriff, Robinson again found and arrested Daniel Brackett. En route back to the magistrate with his prisoner, Robinson ran into an eight-man White Indian patrol, from neighboring Beaver Hill, commanded by Nathan Barlow. One man fired "a brace of balls" through Robinson's horse, which reared and cast the constable to the ground. Barlow seized Robinson's pocketbook, removed the writs, and tore them to "attoms." The patrol then exercised rough retribution on Robinson for betraying his neighbors. The White Indians carried the struggling constable into a nearby cabin (probably Brackett's), where they tore off his clothing "at the points of six bayonets," shredded those clothes into rags, and beat him "in a merciless manner, with sticks prepared for that purpose." They turned Robinson "naked as he was born, into the woods, in which situation he was obliged to travel three miles to his family, in an inclement season of the year."[35]

Barlow went too far in visiting such a savage beating on Moses Robinson, a man respected by Fairfax's more cautious settlers, who, as a consequence, quickly reassessed their support for the resistance. The new Kennebec County high sheriff, John Chandler of Monmouth, reported that the incident had disrupted the settlers' united front; many who had "once countenanced the opposition . . . now see that they are not safe among themselves, and [I] have no doubt they will aid in securing the offenders." Barlow's arrest, successful prosecution with the aid of several Fairfax witnesses, sentence of two years at hard labor, and the failure of backcountry folk to rescue their compatriot before his safe removal to state prison in Charlestown proved Chandler prophetic about the crippling division in settler ranks. Deputy sheriffs safely resumed their rounds in Fairfax; in May—immediately after Barlow's arrest—the town's leading men agreed to negotiate with the Kennebeck Proprietors. Late in 1810, Fairfax's settlers at last permitted a comprehensive survey of their lands by the Kennebeck Proprietors and began to make land payments.[36]

Barlow's fate signaled the beginning of the end for the resistance. His removal must have profoundly discouraged those who had counted on his divine charisma, and it must have buoyed those who favored reaching an accommodation with the proprietors that would put an end to violent incidents. Too much had hinged on a millennial confidence in impending triumph with divine assistance, a confidence fed by the rapid accession of numbers and the successful maintenance of community solidarity. But any reverse to the resistance's momentum imperiled the millennial illusion in which many had come to trust. Millennialism facilitated rapid recruitment but was easily frustrated, and an equally rapid dissolution set in.

In September 1809, a climactic third incident claimed a life and sounded the death knell of the resistance. The Kennebeck Proprietors had long sought to survey Malta (formerly New Waterford, now Windsor) so that they could compel the settlers to purchase or move on. The company breached the local solidarity by enlisting the assistance of Job Chadwick, a farmer, preacher, and schoolteacher. He had emigrated to the frontier from Falmouth in Massachusetts after he had been "stript of all his worldly property" by "a variety of misfortunes." To recoup his fortunes and provide an inheritance for his sons, he had obtained a possession claim to 250 acres in New Waterford. Although nominally a Calvinist Baptist, he had been engaged by a Congregationalist missionary society "to moralize and civilize" the settlers, "most of whom are very poor and . . . very rude and loose in their lives." Sympathizing with his new neighbors but subscribing to his employers' concern for social order, Chadwick reported in 1804: "The inhabitants of these parts are in low and distressing circumstances, partly owing to the new state of the country and partly because they have not obtained titles of their lands. . . . I believe that no people need teaching and preaching more than these." As he aged and as his family invested labor in their claim to develop a substantial farm, Job Chadwick grew increasingly anxious about his lack of secure title and about the White Indian violence. In 1807 he was fifty years old and concerned for the character and prospects of his two adolescent sons, aged fourteen and nineteen. The elder son, Paul Chadwick, belonged to the settlement's White Indian company, led by Elijah Barton. Seeking peace, Job Chadwick wrote to the Kennebeck Proprietors requesting terms; he claimed to speak for the "distressed inhabitants of the settlement called New Waterford [who] by reason of many speculators and pretended claims or agencies are in a perplexed state not knowing what to do or what to believe [but] wanting titles of the new lands we have lately taken in possession." If the Kennebeck Proprietors offered clear titles and "reasonable terms," Job Chadwick would purchase and assist their survey. In April 1809, when the Kennebeck Proprietors offered one hundred free acres "to some enterprising man in Malta" who would help survey that "turbulent township," Paul Chadwick volunteered.[37]

Dissenting from the Chadwicks' new faith in the Kennebeck Proprietors, Malta's majority continued to obstruct the company's attempted surveys. In late June 1809, the "Malta Indians" chased away a Plymouth Company survey party led by Isaac Davis. Paul Chadwick survived that confrontation, but in August, on the eve of another attempt, the company inflamed tensions by commencing suits for ejectment against five Malta settlers. On September 8, 1809, the survey resumed under Davis's leadership, with Chadwick as one of the chainmen. In mid-afternoon, eight armed men burst from the woods, surprising the surveyors. The White Indians "were all in disguise; their caps were of different colors, some were red and white and blue, and some all of one color; they were mostly green," a witness recalled. "Some of them had on blankets and cloth caps, and surtouts, with veils over their faces," another added. One White Indian demanded of Chadwick: "Damn you, how came you here? This is good enough for you!" Three men discharged their muskets at close range on Chadwick, who died the next day.[38]

As in the Robinson incident, Chadwick's murder frightened the most influential local men into breaking with the resistance by seeking the assailants' arrest, trial, and conviction. Major Abner Weeks of adjoining Harlem (China) and Squire James Brackett took the lead in tracking down the suspects. Mistakenly believing that the eight men had fled toward Canada, Weeks and Brackett convened "a consultation of several magistrates and other principal inhabitants" in Weeks's tavern on September 10; the leading men directed Captain Owen Clark of Vassalborough to go in pursuit. While Clark was off on five days of futile pursuit, Elijah Barton's father-in-law "consulted with a number of the most respectable men in that quarter," who insisted "that the prisoners had better come forward and give themselves up." The next day, September 15, Barton and six other suspects (the eighth man fled the area) heeded the advice and surrendered to Brackett. Several confessed to the attack, expressing their "great shame and confusion." Brackett arrested and dispatched the suspects to Augusta for incarceration in the county jail, pending trial for murder before the Supreme Judicial Court in November.[39]

Noting the split in settler ranks, John Merrick of Hallowell quickly wrote a pamphlet that urged the more prosperous settlers to renounce the resistance once and for all. Addressing "the considerate inhabitants" and "the older inhabitants of the county," Merrick stoked the leading men's wariness of higher taxes to pay for criminal trials, militia levies, and stronger jails, appealed to their increasing concerns over the region's external reputation. "Whenever [an insurgency] happens, lands cannot sell high; personal credit must lessen; and the inhabitants will meet reproach when they visit other parts. Females of prudence and of timid tempers will unwillingly stay there."[40]

Hoping to win the settlers' submission to a ritual reinforcing the majesty of the law, Merrick made two unusual promises. First, he assured the White Indians that the justices would heed "the prevailing temper of the leading men in the state, and in the county" by confining the trial to Chadwick's murder, precluding a wider investigation of other incidents. But Merrick warned that a rescue riot would only invite that broader inquiry, exposing others to prosecution. Second, he pledged that the leading men could secure pardons from the governor for most of the suspects, once convicted. "Public security and public example" demanded the execution of one or two, but the others would surely escape the halter. Power exercised and then partially withheld would simultaneously teach the settlers obedience to the law and gratitude for its merciful restraint. In sum, he promised the other White Indians immunity from prosecution and the lives of most of the suspects, provided they allowed the state its trial and execution or two, that "the solemnity of it may help to make their penitence lasting."[41]

On the night of October 3, the "Malta Indians" mounted a feeble effort to rescue the prisoners, marching to Augusta's eastern outskirts, only to be deterred by the town militia's rapid mobilization. In mid-November, an eight-day trial before a packed courthouse presented compelling evidence that Barton and his codefendants had killed Chadwick. But, in Robert Hallowell Gardiner's words, the defense lawyers had shrewdly excluded "the most respectable members"—those most likely to convict—from the jury. The defendants clung to their solidarity and chose to face trial as a body, none agreeing to testify against the others, preserving the mystery of which three had discharged their muskets. Those who had not fired risked their lives to stand in silence with those who had. The gamble saved all of their lives. Unwilling to send seven men to the gallows—at least six of them innocent of the one fatal shot—to atone for a single death, the jury shocked the justices, prosecutors, and crowd by acquitting all the defendants.[42]

Although the friends of order were disappointed in their hope of an exemplary execution or two, according to Gardiner, the trial increased "the number and zeal of those desiring to support the laws." The resistance crumbled in Malta, allowing Isaac Davis to complete his survey without interruption in April 1810. The Kennebeck Proprietors awarded one of the town's lots—the promised one hundred acres—to Chadwick's posthumous daughter Lois. The ending was less happy for Paul's father, Job Chadwick, who could not meet the mortgage payments on his homestead to Gardiner, who repossessed it in December 1814, with Captain Owen Clark as one of the legal witnesses.[43]

In fact, because settler solidarity depended so heavily on sustaining a terrifying illusion without actually shedding blood, the resistance died before the trial began, expiring with Paul Chadwick on September 9, just as New York's Anti-Renters would crumble after two deaths in December 1844. Shortly before the trial, Gardiner observed, "So little fear have I [of further resistance] that I have accepted some land in Malta for land the Plymouth Co. owed me and have had it surveyed this present week without any difficulty." Much had changed in the year and a half since March 1808 when, at the peak of the resistance, Gardiner had expected the White Indians to shut down the courts, writing, "The people perceive [that] the government have been obliged to succumb and they are therefore willing to keep the controul." By alienating the "principal inhabitants," Moses Robinson's bruises and Paul Chadwick's blood shattered the community unity against external great men.[44]

White Men

At their January 1808 rendezvous with Pitt Dillingham, Fairfax's White Indians promised to send a committee of "white men" to meet with Arthur Lithgow. Governor James Sullivan's personal envoy, George Bender, attended the February 1808 meeting. To his surprise, the six settler representatives "appeared to be quiet, sober, intelligent men." Their chief spokesman assured Bender that "no men were better disposed to the government than they were. No men could like a quiet life more than they did. That they did think they had been hardly dealt with. That they had frequently petitioned but no notice had been taken of them, and they had been forced upon the measures they had pursued." As White Indians, settlers practiced their terrifying theater to nullify unwanted land laws. As "white men" negotiating with outside authorities, they presented an alternative—but every bit as real (or unreal)—face: quiet, humble, obedient, and industrious citizens burdened by oppression and deserving legislative redress. Settlers displayed one or the other as circumstance and advantage dictated.[45]

Settlers felt the tension between the two faces, between the horrid visages necessary to parry encroachment and the insistent obeisance useful to arguing for redress. To discredit proposed land reform, proprietors exploited the White Indian image, insisting that the settlers were harbingers of social collapse. The settlers confronted a dilemma:

they could not simultaneously resist external authority and cultivate a peaceable image. They could not suspend their resistance without risking their liberty as landholders, but they could attain no more than a tense stalemate so long as the General Court, governor, and judiciary upheld proprietary claims. By 1808–1809, the settlers confronted a stark choice: resort to open insurrection or surrender armed resistance and gamble on institutional politics. The declining effectiveness of the resistance and the increased integration of the backcountry into the wider world tipped the balance toward the gamble, particularly among the more prosperous, the more cautious. Leading men found defection easier because, at the same time that horrid visages began to fail, new Jeffersonian politicians procured limited land reforms in the General Court. The new promise of institutional politics both fed upon and accelerated the resistance's collapse.[46]

The resistance tried to nullify certain oppressive land laws while honoring the commonwealth's legal authority in all other areas. This task proved easiest where bad roads and rough terrain insulated new settlers from the outside world. Unwittingly, the settlers gradually undercut the isolation that facilitated their resistance. Their drive to escape hunger and dependence impelled accumulating property as well as resisting proprietary claims. But the relative isolation that facilitated the settlers' resistance complicated their efforts to procure prosperity. Isolation meant springtime hunger and shoeless, shirtless children, a poverty that was as much their foe as proprietary claims. However much they might complain of traders' extortion, no one volunteered to forgo commerce. Despite their dislike of lawyers, deputies, and justices, only in times of extreme crisis, such as 1807–1808, did the settlers talk about dispensing with the laws governing commerce.[47]

During the first decade of the nineteenth century, settlers grew in numbers, improved their homesteads, and removed the stumps, brush, roots, and rocks from the roads linking them to the frontcountry market towns; and thus they increased their involvement with the outside world that ill understood their grievances. Because horses consumed more hay than the other livestock types, were rarely eaten, and were useless for plowing the Eastern Country's stony, stump-ridden soil, there was only one reason for keeping them: they made it easier for settlers to travel longer distances. In 1791, two-thirds of Balltown's settlers had limited mobility for want of a horse. By 1811, almost two-thirds of the taxpayers owned a horse. Most of the increase occurred after 1800. The settlers increased the number of their horses more than of any other livestock, underscoring the importance they placed on wider horizons. By 1810, most knew far more about the world beyond their settlement because by horse they could venture farther, more often. The external, commercial world's judgments about right and wrong assumed greater importance in settler lives, particularly among the older, more prosperous men. For increasing numbers, preserving their ties with the outside world qualified loyalty to the resistance.[48]

In January 1808, Jonathan Wilson of Belfast, a land agent and lawyer for Benjamin Joy, noted the settlers' loss of buffering isolation. Wilson advised Joy that there was no need to send deputies with writs into the well-patrolled backcountry; he could easily serve Joy's writs of ejectment on the settlers "when they come into this place to market where an officer will have an opportunity to see the whole of them in a short time at this season." By 1808, the settlers were neither as independent nor as invulnerable as they hoped.[49]

William King. *Photograph courtesy of the Maine State Museum*

CHAPTER EIGHT

The Jeffersonians

He that gives to the rich shall surely come to want; and another text should follow, As the partridge setteth on eggs and hatcheth them not, so he that getteth riches and not by right, shall leave them in the midst of his days, and at his end he shall be a fool.—Samuel Ely, 1797

[William King's] Bingham land was a source of trouble and expense; he derived no benefit from the conveyances to him, and the taxes and costs consumed his property, perplexing contention with town officers and trespassers drove him to insanity, so that he was placed under a guardian the last years of his life . . . and his estate was insolvent.—William Allen, Jr., 1876

BY 1804, Thomaston's Dr. Ezekiel G. Dodge—the unscrupulous entrepreneur who served as Henry Knox's cat's-paw against difficult settlers—had milked the general's patronage for all it was worth. He realized that his further advance to community preeminence necessitated undercutting his patron, and he saw an opportunity in the emerging challenge to the commonwealth's Federalist establishment brought by Jeffersonian politicians. Dodge recognized the leading Jeffersonians as kindred spirits: aggressive men from middling backgrounds, men in a hurry to become political insiders by encouraging popular resentments of the existing elite. Like many another Federalist grandee (or one of the Romans they so admired), Knox was undone by an ambitious man who had once been his mercenary.[1]

Mid-Maine's Jeffersonians coalesced in reaction against Henry Knox's power. In 1789, General Henry Dearborn of Monmouth coveted the new position of federal marshal in the district of Maine. But Henry Knox, as the secretary of war in George Washington's Federalist administration, controlled dispensation of the national patronage in the commonwealth, and he secured the post for his lawyer, Isaac Parker. Enraged, Dearborn won election to Congress and enlisted in the Jeffersonian opposition. When Thomas Jefferson captured the presidency in 1801, Dearborn obtained a gratifying reward—appointment to Knox's former post as secretary of war. Securing control of the national patronage in the Eastern Country, Dearborn enlisted ambitious young leading men from frontcountry towns into a new political network committed through him to Thomas Jefferson's administration. William King, a wealthy Bath merchant with his own ax to grind against Henry Knox, became Dearborn's chief lieutenant. He had been a Federalist, as befitted his origins as the son of Richard King, the wealthy merchant mobbed by his Scarborough debtors in 1766, and as the younger brother of Rufus King, the Federalist senator from New York. Impatiently ambitious, William King broke with the Federalists in 1802 when Colonel Samuel Thatcher of Warren, Henry Knox's son-in-law, declined to step aside in the race for Lincoln County's congressional seat. King declared himself a Jeffersonian, ran against Thatcher, and lost, but he subsequently won repeated election to the state senate as a Jeffersonian representing Lincoln County. Thereafter, King helped Dearborn recruit aspiring men determined to challenge each locality's Federalist elite. One of those recruits was Dr. Ezekiel G. Dodge.[2]

If Dodge had any principles, they accorded with the Jeffersonians' liberal individualism rather than with the Federalists' elite paternalism. The commonwealth's leading Jeffersonians argued that an impartial, minimal government would secure equal opportunity for all. Such government would, they argued, permit the market to reward the industrious poor rather than the parasitical rich, steadily eliminating hierarchy from American society, American culture. Freed of elite privilege, the market would produce a classless society with prosperity and esteem for all men of industry and merit. In capitalism's heady youth, before industrialization consolidated capital's power, most Americans shared the Jeffersonian confidence that the market could be freed of political manipulation by the great, to promote (rather than corrode) an egalitarian society of independent producers. Some common folk preferred the Federalists' promised stability within a hierarchical society; Jeffersonian liberalism appealed to America's Dodges—ambitious outsiders without sufficient "interest," "connections," and "tone" to win full acceptance among the Federalist gentry. Cyrus Eaton of Thomaston, who knew both the doctor and the general, later explained that because Dodge was "naturally predisposed toward the Jeffersonian or Democratic party, as embodying greater latitude in thinking and action, [he] could not but chafe under the overshadowing prestige and influence of Knox. He accordingly did not scruple to foster the suspicions and charges of unfairness which he found existing in certain quarters, in regard to the manner in which the Waldo property had come into the gentleman's hands." Displacing settler resentments onto Knox, Dodge used the Jeffersonian party "as a stepping stone" to become "the acknowledged leader in the town."[3]

Far less at peace with himself and with his commercializing society, Henry Knox was the quintessential Federalist driven by his unacknowledged, self-interested deeds to nurture his self-image as a benevolent patron to the common folk. The more aggressively he behaved, the more insistently he clung to his belief in a hierarchical and stable society guided by tradition and governed by a superior few self-cleansed of self-interest. The greater the challenge to his supremacy, the more vociferously he sounded alarms of impending anarchy. By weaving his neighbors into networks of patronage and dependence, Knox hoped to control and manage the economic ambitions he found so frightening in other, less genteel men. An uncomfortable creature of capitalism's upward mobility, the Federalist gentleman wanted to freeze America's social flux before it elevated newer, cruder men—men like Ezekiel G. Dodge.[4]

As his town's preeminent gentleman, Knox regarded public office as his due. Refusing personally to solicit votes from the common folk, Knox felt that hints properly placed by his "friends" ought to suffice with the Thomaston town meeting. For, far more than the office, Knox wanted the townspeople's honorific recognition that he was their "political father"; to mean anything, this recognition had to come reflexively, without overt solicitation. Because Knox would pay his own way, because his business enterprises employed so many townsmen, and because they still concurred that their representative should be their principal gentleman, Thomaston's citizens routinely sent the general to represent them in the General Court.[5]

Thomaston's adherence to traditional, nonpartisan, elite-dominated politics was the norm in mid-Maine through 1803. In the 1803 gubernatorial election one-quarter of mid-Maine's communities returned no votes. In most voting towns virtual unanimity (casting better than 90 percent of their ballots for one candidate) prevailed, as the inhabitants voted in accord with their leading men's advice. The Federalists benefited from this pattern; they won four of every five voting towns, including almost all the nearly unanimous communities, and captured a lopsided 71 percent of the region's votes. Federalism prevailed in every sort of community (indeed, the Federalists won two-thirds of the votes cast in resistance towns) but was especially strong in those with a justice of the peace or a Congregational minister. Resistance communities' Federalist votes reflected the traditional dichotomy of the settlers' political worldview: they accepted that only gentlemen could govern the commonwealth but reserved the right to resist any of their actions deemed oppressive. Hence James Shurtleff could champion the resistance and celebrate Federalist President John Adams in the same pamphlet.[6]

Henry Knox exploited his General Court seat to safeguard his land claims from legislative interference. In 1803 some Waldo Patent settlers again petitioned the General Court for redress. The Federalist leadership assigned the petition to a committee chaired by Knox, who rejected the appeal on the grounds that the legislature had "no constitutional rights to interfere in the premises."[7]

Such examples of political privilege created a receptive audience for Jeffersonian politicians with a new message. They exhorted: "Turn Out!

Turn Out! Therefore to the election. EVERY MAN, TURN OUT! Let no one stay at home through sloth or cowardice. If you will turn out, you will carry the point, you will secure your cause, and these haughty, selfish Aristocrats will be no longer in office, to controul your meetings." Unlike their fearful Federalist rivals, the Jeffersonians were confident they could manage an expanded electorate. Posing as the common man's tribunes crusading against aristocratic Federalists, the Jeffersonians became the champions of a broad coalition of outsiders uneasy with a variety of privileged establishments. For debtors, this suggested mercantile creditors and their lawyers; for religious dissenters, this meant the orthodox clergy; for many shopkeepers, fishermen, artisans, and sailors, this implied the major mercantile wholesalers; and for mid-Maine's backcountry settlers, this meant the Great Proprietors, whom the Jeffersonians denounced as "supercilious Lordlings, whose haughtiness, folly, and vanity you find on trial to be so insufferable." As squatters *and* evangelicals, many settlers had two reasons for enlisting with the Jeffersonians. The evangelicals' stress on individual conversion, dedication to an egalitarian worship, and insistence on free choice in religious affiliation harmonized with the Jeffersonians' exaltation of individualism, democracy, and voluntarism in politics. On the other hand, Maine's Congregationalist minority clung to the Federalist vision of an organic, hierarchical, and deferential society. It is revealing that when Balltown—a stronghold of the resistance—divided and incorporated as two towns, the inhabitants chose the names Whitefield (western half) and Jefferson (eastern); both towns were overwhelmingly Calvinist Baptist in religion and Jeffersonian in politics.[8]

Jeffersonian rhetoric struck a responsive chord in localities throughout the Eastern Country. The Federalists of Buckstown (now Bucksport), a frontcountry market town, bitterly complained that "many attended who never attended the election before," because the Jeffersonians so aggressively awakened "the jealousy of the people in the remote parts of the town, against the men of influence and property in this village." In 1803 the Federalists had crushed the Jeffersonians within the district, 5,718 votes to 2,002. The hotly contested 1804 campaign increased the Federalist vote in the district by 1,037 votes to 6,755, but the Jeffersonian vote leapt by 4,583 votes to 6,585. A year later the Jeffersonians handily won most of the district's votes, 9,378 to 7,201, a majority they retained every year until Maine's separation from Massachusetts in 1820.[9]

In Thomaston, Dodge cultivated the public's new longing to refute Federalist elitism and assert their own equal access to respect by symbolically smiting their preeminent gentleman. The shrunken employment at Knox's financially battered enterprises helped the doctor's efforts. Yet, in a straight contest with Isaac Bernard, Dodge's Jeffersonian candidate, Knox's reelection seemed certain, until the doctor split the town's Federalists by persuading Joshua Adams, a blacksmith and moderate Federalist, to run. Regarding possible defeat in open town meeting as an unendurable humiliation, Knox withdrew his name, and Adams prevailed. A year later the town meeting extended the Jeffersonians' gains, replacing Adams with Bernard. In March 1805 Henry Jackson Knox broke the news to his father. "The Jacobins of this town turn out so strong and the Federalists are so lukewarm that at March meeting all the Federal officers were turned out, and such men put in (as dismal to relate) who cannot neither *read nor write* intelligibly." Persistent, but a proper Federalist gentleman to the end, Knox penned a plaintive note to his business manager on the eve of the 1806 Thomaston town meeting. "I suppose the representative will be a democrat. . . . But if it should be otherwise and the town should think proper to choose me I should not decline but good previous arrangements ought to be made. Of this hint you will make a discreet use." Not thinking Knox's candidacy proper, the townspeople reelected Bernard. They could not regain their land payments, but with Dodge's help the Thomastonians learned to deny the general any political honor. They no longer wanted a "political father."[10]

A few months later, impending insolvency forced Knox to surrender almost all of his unsold Waldo Patent lands (117,700 acres) to his four leading creditors—the wealthy merchants and land speculators Benjamin Joy of Boston, Israel Thorndike of Beverly, David Sears of Boston, and William Prescott, Jr., of Salem. Virtually bankrupt, stripped of his wilderness lands, and rudely toppled in his own town by an upstart doctor, Knox was no longer useful to his fellow Federalists. In the summer of 1806 Charles Willing Hare, executor of William Bingham's estate (Bingham had died in February), traveled from Philadelphia to compare accounts with the general. Finding Knox "insolvent" and "perceiving that his political and private influence was gone and therefore that there was no use in being longer connected with him," Hare canceled the general's debts to the Bingham Estate in return for the surrender of his one-third interest in the Bingham Purchase. Henry Knox did not long outlive the demise of his wealth and power. On October 28, 1806, the massive general, who delighted in food, met an ironic end after he swallowed a small chicken bone that caused a fatal infection. After an ornate funeral added to his estate's debts, probate commissioners found that the general's $139,246.51 in debits exceeded his $121,146.81 in remaining assets.[11]

A master of intrigue among his fellow gentlemen at the General Court, Knox was undone by his reluctance to stoop to politicking among the common farmers and artisans at the mundane town meeting level, where he expected deference as a matter of course. But in town after town, county after county, throughout America, Jeffersonian electoral guerrillas of Dodge's stripe changed the rules, rendering the old Federalists' aloof style politically suicidal. The political culture changed, as aggressive Jeffersonians steadily weeded out Federalists unwilling to compete openly for votes at the local level. America's future belonged to the Dodges.[12]

The Jeffersonians' fierce competition with the Federalists for power and patronage dramatically transformed voter behavior throughout mid-Maine. In the 1807 gubernatorial election, only one community in eight failed to vote. The unanimously Federalist town, so conspicuous in 1803, ceased to exist in mid-Maine by 1807. The Jeffersonians captured 62 percent of the votes and prevailed in forty-nine mid-Maine towns to the Federalists' fifteen (one town, Augusta, was evenly split). The Jeffersonians won in all types of towns—navigation and backcountry, large and small, prosperous and poor, orthodox and evangelical—but did especially well in backcountry towns, wherever the Calvinist Baptists had organized a church, and in communities that had not had a justice of the peace in 1800. The Federalists held their own only in the older navigation communities, especially if they had a Congregational church, or had had a justice of the peace before 1800.[13]

Following the Jeffersonians' lead, settlers gradually reached a new, less passive understanding of the commonwealth's government as a forum for conflicting interests rather than as a conclave of political fathers. The settlers recognized that they could gain nothing unless well represented. In 1800 about three of every ten adult males in mid-Maine voted; in 1810 more than half the region's adult males voted. In 1800 only about one-quarter of mid-Maine's communities sent representatives to the General Court; in 1810 nearly three-fifths of the region's towns were represented. In 1800 mid-Maine had one General Court representative for every 2,641 residents; in 1810 there was one representative for every 1,465 residents.[14]

Involvement in institutionalized politics was double-edged; settlers obtained some new political influence, but only by conceding leverage within the backcountry to government. Upon joining the Jeffersonian network, the backcountry's leading men felt a new engagement with the commonwealth's political institutions. To reward leading men for their partisan services, governors nearly tripled the number of mid-Maine's justices of the peace (from 82 in 1800 to 218 in 1810). In 1800 there was one justice for every 644 people in the region; in 1810 there was one justice for every 390 people. The new appointments democratized the office, as Jeffersonian administrations rewarded some substantial farmers who would never have won Federalist recognition as esquires—James Shurtleff, for example. The new appointments spread justices of the peace, men charged with dispersing rioters, throughout the region.

In 1800 fewer than one-quarter of the backcountry communities had a squire; by 1810 almost two-thirds did. Because they owed their coveted commissions to external authority, these new esquires needed to maintain the good opinion of the outside world. Because their reputations suffered when resistance persisted in their communities, they exhorted their neighbors to trust instead in institutional politics and "to appear what you are—the substantial, the regular, the valuable part of society."[15]

The Settlers' Friends

Like Congregationalists reacting to the evangelicals' rapid proliferation on the frontier, the Federalists were stunned and alarmed by the Jeffersonians' sudden transformation of the Eastern Country's politics. Ever fearful that society lay on the brink of popular anarchy, Federalists expected the worst from any change they could not control. They regarded the Jeffersonians as irresponsibly ambitious, as shortsighted demagogues arousing dangerous resentments and inappropriate ambitions in an unthinking populace. In Federalist eyes, the menace and the stakes were compounded along the frontier, where the licentious tended to gather and where their expanding population created America's future. Samuel S. Wilde, a proprietary lawyer and Federalist, warned: "There is a spirit in the people of Maine hostile to all correct notions respecting title to lands. To flatter this spirit would be the business of unprincipled and ambitious men. No large proprietors would be safe either in their persons or their property."[16]

They worried needlessly. There was a gap between the Jeffersonians' fiery, election-eve rhetoric, intended to convince the electorate that they smote the Great Proprietors by voting Jeffersonian, and what they would deliver in the General Court. Neither agrarians nor revolutionaries, the commonwealth's leading Jeffersonians were ambitious doctors, lawyers, and merchants from the frontcountry's commercial towns. Most had substantial real estate speculations and no intention of weakening the legal defenses around great property. Indeed, they believed that their election was all the common people needed to secure, in James Sullivan's words, "the Path to Riches." Moreover, because the resistance towns were less populous than the frontcountry towns beyond the resistance, squatters were a minority of Maine's electorate, so what the party leaders would do for them was limited. Despite their campaign promises to stop at least the cheap sale of more public lands to speculators, the Jeffersonians failed to alter public land policy when they gained control of the commonwealth's government in 1807. And the General Court's leading Jeffersonians cooperated with the Federalists to frustrate radicals in the party's lower echelons who were agitating for structural legal reforms that would have swept out the conservative judiciary in favor of elected town courts.[17]

The Jeffersonians cheaply obtained backcountry support with sympathetic rhetoric and mild reform measures. They succeeded because their Federalist competitors rigidly opposed all land reform, whereas the penurious and localist settlers could not develop, from within, their own politicians able to operate effectively at the state level. The localism essential to the settler resistance discouraged the development from the grass roots of a political movement competent to capture the state government. Instead, after 1803, settlers accepted state leadership from the Jeffersonian politicians who had emerged in the commercial towns of the frontcountry. So, in 1807 a settler appealed to William King to alleviate the "want of some kind of system among the people, and without some kind of system it is to be feared that they will often be deceived and led away by our enemies." The Jeffersonians offered what the agrarians so desperately needed—a leadership class with sufficient wealth, self-confidence, and political savvy to challenge the Federalists for control of the state government. But, committed to commercial ambitions, the Jeffersonian leadership was unwilling fully to satisfy agrarian desires. Moreover, the settlers' devotion to private property and their improving ties with the wider world meant that they were eager to believe the pleasing Jeffersonian promise that all injustice could be easily set aright and rich opportunities opened to all simply by eliminating a few undue legal privileges. The Jeffersonians convincingly argued that this formula, applied through electoral politics, was a surer strategy for frustrating Federalist aristocrats and for safeguarding a republican society of independent producers than was the traditional resort to extralegal violence by autonomous communities. By staking out the position as "the settlers' friends," the Jeffersonians prevented the reemergence of the more militantly agrarian politics that had appeared in the commonwealth during and immediately after the Revolution but that had withered with the Antifederalists' defeat in 1788.[18]

The Federalist Great Proprietors should have known that they had little to fear from the new politicians, because so many of the leading Jeffersonians used to work for them. James Sullivan, the commonwealth's first Jeffersonian governor, was the principal proprietor of the town of Limerick, Maine, and he had been a lawyer for both the Plymouth Company and Henry Knox. Recognizing Sullivan's formidable legal talents and political influence, Joseph Pierce approached him in 1791 with a retainer fee from Henry Knox, "which he accepted and said that he should always be ready whenever called upon and in any part of the government." An avid land speculator in his own right, Henry Dearborn served as Kennebeck Proprietor James Bowdoin's land agent and later married his widow. Perez Morton, the Jeffersonians' first speaker of the General Court's House of Representatives, was a proprietary land agent in the 1790s. Dr. William Eustis, Boston's principal Jeffersonian, had served during the 1790s as one of Knox's legislative managers; as a Jeffersonian, he subsequently led the fight against radical legal reform. In the Eastern Country the Jeffersonians' county-level leaders also tended to be former proprietary servants. Henry Knox's three principal lieutenants—Thurston Whiting, Ezekiel G. Dodge, and George Ulmer—all became leading Jeffersonians. Upwardly mobile, they rode Knox's patronage as far as they could before turning on their mentor and to the Jeffersonians in pursuit of further rewards. Only at the town level could Jeffersonian leaders be found who were associated with the resistance: men like Luther Robbins of Greene and James Shurtleff and Deacon John Neal of Litchfield.[19]

George Ulmer exemplified the making, and the limitations, of a Jeffersonian politician. Zealous for wealth and power and eager to please, he carefully emulated Henry Knox, his grandiose patron. Mimicking Knox's grand style meant that Ulmer bore his subordinate status as a client with increasing unease. As the general's land agent, Ulmer assumed more and more of the decisions regarding the terms granted to particular settlers on Knox's patent. But the general wanted a grateful client, not a junior partner. In October 1801, Knox suddenly reined Ulmer in, vetoing terms he had negotiated with several settlers. Humiliated, George Ulmer suddenly resigned, blurting out his long-submerged resentment at his subordinate status by insisting that his service "sprang from the pure principles of friendship, and not slavish fear. I therefore had not ought to expect contempt in return." No doubt Knox found that presumption amusing, for even in resigning, Ulmer's dependence persisted; he closed by requesting a letter of recommendation.[20]

Ulmer's hasty resignation threatened his access through Knox to state patronage, threatened to cost him the cherished status of "esquire" that accrued to the local justice. To safeguard and perhaps enhance his status, Ulmer united with like-minded leading men throughout the commonwealth in the emerging Jeffersonian network. With the same sense of timing that netted the Ulmer brothers the Ducktrap watershed just as the Penobscot region began to develop, George Ulmer staked out the politically strategic position as Hancock County's first important Jeffersonian. At first this gamble left him isolated in the county's political community, composed largely of more cautious leading men who clung to the deeply entrenched Federalist state government. But, when the political tide turned, Ulmer was the first in line to reap Hancock County's share in the spoils. Upon securing election in 1807 as the commonwealth's first Jeffersonian governor, James Sullivan rewarded Ulmer with the county's richest patronage plums: commissions as county sheriff and militia major general.[21]

Employing his "natural and happy eloquence," Ulmer posed as the settlers' champion against the Great Proprietors. Of course, as the owner of more than three thousand acres obtained by assisting Knox's subjugation of settler resistance in the Waldo Patent, Ulmer was reluctant to meddle with the laws protecting great property. Nonetheless, his new, critical stance toward the proprietors weighed more heavily with backcountry voters than his past deeds against them, particularly since his Federalist competitors remained avowed proprietary supporters. In an 1805 race for the state senate, George Ulmer defeated General David Cobb, Henry Knox's close friend and William Bingham's land agent. Backcountry voters, some of whom had gone "bear hunting" for the squire when in Knox's service, overwhelmingly voted against Cobb, if not for Ulmer; Davistown, Balltown, and Sheepscot Great Pond gave Ulmer 161 votes to but 38 for Cobb.[22]

George Ulmer could never fully free himself from his long association with Henry Knox. In the summer of 1801, while in Knox's service, Ulmer had organized a militia party that marched into the backcountry to arrest suspected Liberty Men. In April 1806 Ulmer reminded Knox (who, in fact, needed no reminder), "You advised me . . . to represent some [other] person as haveing advanced the provisions observing [that] you did not wish to have your name mentioned." Dutifully accommodating Knox's desire for secrecy, Ulmer made out the account for provisions in the name of his son-in-law, John Russ of Belfast. When the commonwealth compensated Russ for the provisions, he turned the funds over to Ulmer, who, at Knox's direction, kept the money. But in April 1806, General David Cobb encouraged the commonwealth's treasurer to investigate Ulmer for fraud. Ulmer nervously wrote to Knox: "My dear sir what can it mean? Am I at last to be destroyd for having been your faithfull servant[?] I know you do not approve of it but it is verry strange that those who appeared to be my best friends while I was in your service have become inveterate enemies." Having got Ulmer's attention, Knox stepped in as his patron one last time, taking aside the treasurer, a fellow Federalist gentleman, to convince him that the matter required no investigation. There were clear limits to Ulmer's willingness or ability to challenge the Great Proprietors.[23]

Similarly, William King, the Eastern Country's foremost Jeffersonian, championed the settlers with more sound and fury than results. In the winter of 1805 he pressed the General Court to repossess half of the Bingham Purchase because its proprietors had failed to fulfill their 1792 contract with the state to establish twenty-five hundred families on their tracts in eastern Maine and at the head of the Kennebec River by 1803. If held to the letter of the contract, William Bingham's heirs stood to pay a penalty of seventy thousand dollars or forfeit about 1,750,000 acres. Proprietors previously confronted with similar (but much smaller) problems received routine extensions from their fellow gentlemen in the General Court. But the Jeffersonians had promised to put an end to the close relationship between legislators and land speculators. King's motion to investigate the contract alarmed Harrison Gray Otis of Boston, a Federalist state senator and staunch proprietary ally. He fumed: "The spirit of insubordination to the legitimate rights of property which is hourly increasing in the civilized parts of the country, is of consequence, more violent and dangerous among the semi-savages who steal land from non-residents and hide from justice in the recesses of the wilderness. These are also very convenient instruments in the hands of designing men who disdain not to encourage their outrages and defend their depredations." In January 1806, King's proposal passed in the Jeffersonian house of representatives but ran into trouble in the Federalist state senate, where General David Cobb, the Bingham heirs' land agent, presided.[24]

Once he had raised the issue, William King was eager to translate his political power into his own proprietary land. After all, he had entered politics to force his way into the commonwealth's elite, among whom proprietary land was an important status symbol. In March 1806 he approached General Cobb and secretly intimated a readiness to abort his efforts against the Bingham Purchase if the heirs would sell him several townships at a bargain rate. King even agreed to enter a partnership with the strangest of political bedfellows, Harrison Gray Otis. In December 1806, Charles W. Hare concluded the deal. Working on their respective political allies, the unlikely partners persuaded the General Court to pass a six-year extension of the troublesome settler requirement, which Otis and King then assumed and so freed the Bingham heirs of any further concern with establishing the requisite number of settlers. In return, the heirs sold Otis and King the best three townships, those located in the Kennebec Million's southwestern corner (the present towns of Kingfield, Lexington, and Concord), a total of about sixty-five thousand acres for a mere $5,000 (about eight cents per acre). Hare calculated that in selling lands then worth $16,250 for $5,000, the bribe cost the heirs a mere $11,250, or about one-seventh the penalty that the General Court could have collected, or one-fortieth the value of the acreage it could have repossessed. Better still, he concluded, "we have created a common bond of interest with some of the popular leaders in Massachusetts who have promised to support us against all future injustice."[25]

King's new proprietary lands proved nothing but a sop to his formidable vanity. In 1816 he procured incorporation of the largest settlement as the town of Kingfield and promptly informed his land agent Nathaniel Dudley, "In all your doings in future, that name will of course be adopted." Otherwise, the acquisition proved unhappy, as the self-styled "settlers' friend" sought to impose *his* land payments and timber rents on the restive squatters in his township. In January 1815, he was horrified to discover that his settlers insisted that the tract had reverted to the commonwealth because King had failed to satisfy the settler requirement. King angrily wrote his agent, "I am quite of your opinion that the persons who are disposed to make difficulty had better be kept *out* of the town, and you may be assured of my determination to do it." Throughout his life King's mounting expenses for surveys, agents, and taxes exceeded the slow and paltry returns from his tract's uncooperative settlers.[26]

The Betterment Act

Once the deal with Hare became public knowledge, the Eastern Country's Federalists made the most of William King's hypocrisy, but the issue appeared too late to dent the momentum that carried the Jeffersonians to a complete sweep in the spring 1807 elections; they strengthened the hold they had won over the General Court's two houses in 1806 and added the governorship. The Eastern Country provided a 4,419-vote Jeffersonian surplus that enabled James Sullivan to prevail despite a 1,384-vote deficiency in Massachusetts. In the wake of the Bingham deal and electoral victory, the Jeffersonians, in general, and William King, in particular, needed to resolve the land controversy. Inaction would alienate mid-Maine's backcountry voters, and, if the resistance persisted during a Jeffersonian state administration, the Federalists would scream about impending anarchy, which might cost the Jeffersonians precious votes in Massachusetts. The dramatic rise in violent backcountry confrontations late in 1807 increased the pressure on King to craft land reform legislation at the General Court's winter 1808 session.[27]

King developed an idea that had emerged among those more cautious settlers who had grown sufficiently uneasy with the resistance to seek some accommodation with the proprietors. Dividing land value in two, these settlers conceded that the land's value "in a state of nature" belonged to the proprietors, but insisted that the value of any improvements or "betterments" effected upon that land belonged to the settlers.

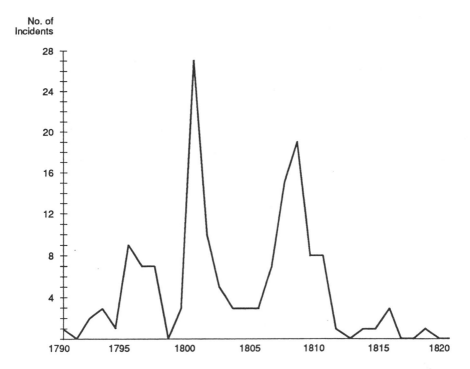

Figure 1. Resistance Incidents, 1790–1820

They would pay for the "state of nature" value, provided they obtained secure title and could stretch their payments over several years. Probably with King's encouragement, from November 1807 through January 1808, leading men throughout the backcountry drafted petitions, signed by hundreds, describing their grievances and advancing the betterments formula as the basis for reform legislation. Naturally, settlers and proprietors differed over just what the "state of nature" value was. The former regarded it as the roughly one dollar per acre that backcountry land commanded when first opened to settlement at the close of the Revolution. Proprietors preferred to consider it as the then-prevailing price of four to five dollars per wild acre, a price that represented the increased value imparted by settlers' improvements on adjoining lots. At issue was who—settler or proprietor—should reap the enhanced value created by the region's post-Revolutionary population growth.[28]

In January 1808, William King proposed the Betterment Act, to allow local juries to settle the issue lot by lot. When legally ejected by a proprietor, any settler who had been on the land at least six years could ask the jury to ascertain both the value of the property as wild land and the increased value imparted by his improvements. The proprietor then had the option of obliging the settler to pay the wild land value or of obtaining possession by purchasing the improvements. If the proprietor chose to sell and a competing proprietor subsequently ejected the purchaser with a new suit, the settler could sue to regain his money with interest.[29]

The Great Proprietors feared that local juries would exploit the Betterment Act to achieve de facto confiscation, by, in Harrison Gray Otis's words, assessing the wild land value as "before the flood if they saw fit." Despite the Jeffersonian majority in both houses, the Federalists attached two amendments to eliminate that danger. The first allowed the settler-purchaser but one year to pay in full; the proprietors knew that this hardship would severely reduce a settler's willingness to invoke the law. Second, Israel Thorndike, a Federalist state senator from Essex County as well as the principal purchaser of Henry Knox's Waldo Patent, introduced an amendment to require the juries to ascertain the enhanced wild land value that prevailed at the time of the trial (rather than at the time the settler moved onto the land). Thorndike's amendment awarded the enhanced land value imparted by settler population growth entirely to the proprietors. His amendment obtained enough Jeffersonian defections to pass by a single vote. Governor Sullivan signed the drastically altered bill into law on March 2, 1808. Equally important was the Federalists' success at the same session, again with critical support from moderate Jeffersonian leaders, in stymieing radical proposals to supplant the conservative state judiciary with a new system of elected town courts. Had this agrarian legal program triumphed, Maine's settlers would not have had to make do with the Betterment Act.[30]

When the Betterment Act passed, the waning effectiveness of the resistance had already opened a rift between cautious men of some property and the poorer majority. Because they could ill afford land payments, the poorer, younger men adamantly opposed negotiating a settlement with the proprietors. But those settlers who had slowly accumulated enough property to consider paying the proprietors felt increasingly uneasy over their insecure title to their much-improved homesteads, ever more fearful that proprietary triumph would oust them from their hard-earned property. And they had grown uncomfortable with the violent acts that increasingly accompanied the resistance as "horrid visages" ceased to deter the ever more aggressive proprietary agents, surveyors, and officers of the law. Noting the worsening divisions among the settlers and nervous over his farm's security, Elisha Sylvester of Greene wrote to Colonel Josiah Little in July 1806: "I find things have terminated as I have long anticipated. The people are confused, duped by the demagogues, drove about by every wind of doctrine, most of them in dispair, hating each other for their different recourses to safety, and I believe by all appearances are about giving up any further struggle. I consider all I have done as nothing, if I get security of the land." Perhaps these divisions extended into Sylvester's household, for he concluded: "P.S. I have at last got a bill of divorce . . . from my wife for her Adultery with two men." Between mid-December 1805 and May 1808, twenty-one Greene settlers broke with their neighbors to accept Little's terms, which averaged $4.19 per acre.[31]

A similar split developed in nearby Litchfield, where the leading men had grown weary with, and pessimistic about, the long struggle. One of those leading men, James Shurtleff, explained that he had lost hope that the government would quiet the settlers in free possession of their homesteads:

> The torrent of influence which has and I presume will be employ'd to prevent this wish'd for event has caus'd me to despair of its accomplishment. And contemplating the destructive tendency of legal controversy and that the lands in dispute are rising in value, together with the cost which must arise from protracted legal disputes which must fall upon us if we should fail of our hopes with respect to help from government and which must plunge us in distress from which we must despair of emerging, considering this I concluded it would be safer and best to purchase, provided we could be secur'd in the premises by good warrantee deeds if a reasonable price should be affix'd.

Yet most of his neighbors remained attached to the resistance: "The utmost discontent still possesses the minds of the settlers." Deacon John Neal, Litchfield's principal leading man, decided to press the issue by directing the Kennebeck Proprietors' renewed attempt to survey the town. Neal was a storekeeper, farmer, Litchfield's General Court representative, town clerk, and frequent selectman, a new esquire for his services to the Jeffersonians, and a deacon in the Calvinist First Baptist Church. He also must have known a lot about his town's resistance, for in September 1800 his brother, Lemuel Neal, was arrested for firing upon a proprietary survey but was rescued by several armed neighbors, including the Neals' maternal uncle, Calvin Hall. In November 1807, Litchfield's majority violently disrupted Deacon John Neal's survey for the Kennebeck Proprietors.[32]

The Betterment Act widened the rift. The more cautious settlers, who were already resigned to purchase, and who could pay the necessary amounts within a year by borrowing from third parties on mortgage security, regarded the law as insurance for their substantial improvements. Poorer men who could afford neither one hundred to two hundred dollars that a lawsuit cost under the Betterment Act nor to pay within a year, and who had yet to effect substantial improvements, found no advantage in the new law. As James Shurtleff warned William King, "most of the settlers' hopes greatly exceed all the benefits which can result from this act, expecting government will espouse their cause against the proprietors." In another letter to King, Deacon John Neal celebrated the act as "more than ever I expected to be don for us" and insisted, "The understanding men in the town is with me in oppinion as we have but little hopes that we are on the land claimed by the Commonwealth." But he conceded that the act "did not give my constituents the satisfaction that I expected that it would." In vain he advised "the unfortunate settlers in this part of our country . . . to settle with the propriators in the best way they could . . . for which I was surverly sencord by many of my townspeople altho my motives was good, was to save them . . . as I thought, but there is a number in this place that are igneranent and wilful." He complained: "It is a fact I cannot make them understand the act nor nothing that is reasonable. . . . It appears that nothing in reason will satisfy them and any one that speakes a word in favour of settling with propriators or reproves them for there rashness is condemned for a trator. I find it very dificult to git a long with such kind of people." Indeed, in November 1808, armed men obstructed a new attempt by Neal to survey Litchfield for the Kennebeck Proprietors. A few nights later, just before midnight, Neal bolted awake to "the rowaring of fire which he found to be his barn." He estimated his loss for the barn and its contents—hay, grain, flax, and cartwheels—at five hundred dollars. Men who believed they fought to preserve the Revolution, save themselves from tenancy, and advance Christ's millennial kingdom did not quickly adjust to the notion that a Betterment Act would suffice.[33]

To render the Betterment Act more palatable to the settlers, in March 1810 the General Court and governor adopted a bill drafted by William King to extend the term for payment from one year to three. The revised Betterment Act strengthened the hand of those leading men who sought to persuade their neighbors that further resistance was futile and that the settlers' friends in high office had extended all the relief that was possible. Four days later the General Court passed companion legislation intended to crush any remaining resistance. Thereafter, whenever violence interrupted a proprietary survey, any Supreme Judicial Court justice could call out the militia—without applying to the governor—to protect a renewed attempt. Anyone who opposed the renewed survey faced up to one year in jail and a fine of as much as one thousand dollars. Militia men who failed to obey their orders on such service confronted similar fines and prison sentences. Anyone who donned Indian disguise to obstruct a deputy sheriff was subject to one year in jail and fines as high as five hundred dollars. By enacting the new criminal penalties, the General Court told settlers to cease their resistance and make the best of the revised Betterment Act.[34]

Coming to Terms

Trusting in the Betterment Act and the influence of local leading men, the proprietors aggressively pushed their surveys into the resistance's remaining outposts during the years 1808–1812. The relentless pressure severely strained the resistance at a time of mounting internal division and new self-doubts. In July and again in December 1808, White Indians broke up Bradstreet Wiggins's attempts to survey northern Palermo for the Kennebeck Proprietors; but in February 1809 the Plymouth Company's clerk noted with approval that Wiggins had completed his work after many of "the inhabitants turned out to protect the surveyor." In September 1809, when a White Indian asked Isaac Marsh of Malta why he had allowed the Kennebeck Proprietors' surveyor to run out his lot, he replied wearily that "it was useless to stand out against so many." Settlers had begun to see too many proprietors, too many officers, too many surveyors, too many judges, too many people elsewhere in the commonwealth who supported the law and did not understand the settlers' grievances, and too many neighbors who had accepted proprietary terms. Increasingly engaged in the wider world, settlers were newly sensitive to the warning delivered by Justice Isaac Parker to the jury trying Chadwick's assailants: "Suppose the rioters should be successful in effecting their purposes in this remote section of a great and flourishing commonwealth, would the whole state sit down quietly under the inroads made on their laws and venerable usages, which are guaranteed by all the sister states?—But, gentlemen, such opposition to the laws is vain, it cannot prevail to any considerable extent."[35]

Times had changed; the remaining White Indians were increasingly on the defensive. Montville's nineteenth-century historian, N. E. Wells, recorded the local tradition that the town's remaining insurgents "caused those who bought the land from under them much trouble," apparently by surreptitiously killing or maiming livestock in the night. The holdouts eventually fell victim to their own tactics: "Demolishing the dwellings of these unwelcome tenants in their temporary absence seems to have been a popular method of disposing of them." A dwindling number of known confrontations attested to the decaying resistance; thirty-four violent incidents occurred in the two years 1807–1808, only sixteen in 1809–1810, and but one in 1811–1812. Freedom (the name Beaver Hill took upon incorporation in 1813) was the last Plymouth Patent community to come to terms: the hometown of Nathan Barlow allowed a survey in 1818, the year after his death. It was probably more than a coincidence that this was the year that the Kennebeck Proprietors finally released to Jonathan Bartlett the deed he had paid for eight years before; with the demise of the resistance, the company no longer needed to keep Bartlett under such tight control. His American Revolution was over.[36]

In 1813 the Supreme Judicial Court finally resolved the dispute between the Pejepscot Proprietors and their settlers. Colonel Josiah Little adamantly refused to deliver deeds to the settlers at the price of one to two dollars per acre awarded by the governor's commissioners, to pay his half of the commission's costs, or to release to the commonwealth the lands above Twenty-Mile Falls (see Chapter 1). So the attorney general commenced a new suit against the Pejepscot Proprietors before the Supreme Judicial Court in July 1808. The justices permitted the Pejepscot Proprietors successive continuations that postponed trial until May 1813. In the interim the justices allowed Little to press his ejectment suits against individual settlers left legally defenseless by the legal limbo of the commonwealth's title. In May 1813, at Little's insistence, the justices heard the commonwealth's suit in Cumberland County, rather than Lincoln County, where most of the disputed lands lay and where most jurors sympathized with the settlers. The Cumberland County jury ruled for the Pejepscot Proprietors, obliging the patent's settlers to permit surveys and fall back on the Betterment Act's limited protection.[37]

Completed surveys obliged settlers to come to terms or face lawsuits they could not win. It was Philip Robbins's misfortune to lose an ejectment suit after the resistance collapsed in his settlement, Appleton. Lacking either the money for legal costs (that ordinarily exceeded one hundred dollars) or the six years on the land to qualify, he could not invoke the Betterment Act. The settlement's proprietor, Joseph H. Pierce, Jr., of the Twenty Associates proudly noted: "To remove such intruders is to bring an action of ejectment. . . . To recover is certain unless he may claim under the Betterment Law. . . . But the intruders seldom avail themselves of this mode—in which case judgement goes agt. them—and a writ of possession issues. I have recovered of many, not one of 'em availing himself of the Betterment Act." In December 1811, as Christmas approached, Pierce supervised Robbins's ejectment by a deputy sheriff and the Twenty Associates' lawyer. Momentarily touched by the scene's pathos, Pierce reported: "He has 10 children, six of them had neither shoe nor stocking to their feet and abt. three inches [of] snow on the ground. It is impossible to conceive of more wretchedness than he and his whole family represented. He had killed his only pig however and they were going to roast some for our dinners but I excused the matter." Pierce formally served the notice affording the

Robbins family six months to depart their homestead and leave behind all of the labor they had invested in it.[38]

Such tragedies taught most settlers that it was wiser to accept proprietary terms whenever they fell below $4.00 per acre, the prevailing backcountry value of unoccupied wild land. A handful of ejectment cases per locale usually sufficed to set the price that most settlers there quietly accepted. The terms agreed to by thirty-one Malta settlers in August 1810 were probably typical of the Plymouth Patent backcountry; on average, they agreed to pay the Kennebeck Proprietors $2.56 per acre. The prices accepted by sixty-nine Greene settlers between August 1813 and January 1818 were probably representative of the entire Pejepscot Patent: an average of $3.59 per acre. This was about $.60 less per acre (17 percent) than twenty-one Greene settlers had paid Little in 1805–1808, before the Betterment Act. The modest difference reflects the act's limited impact on the terms negotiated between settlers and proprietors. Although far from the $1.00 per acre that backcountry settlers had hoped for, prices between $2.00 and $4.00 per acre were more attractive than running the risk of an ejectment suit, even with invocation of the Betterment Act.[39]

Only the settlers in seven Lincoln County towns—coastal Bristol, Edgecomb, Boothbay, Newcastle, Nobleborough, Waldoborough (only the western half), and adjoining, inland Jefferson (Balltown's recently incorporated eastern half)—obtained more than the Betterment Act. They secured what they had long sought: clear title from the commonwealth at a token price. Their triumph was fitting justice, for most of their towns began in the 1730s as Dunbar's settlements, subsequently became staging points for settling the militant backcountry, and for decades endured the region's most severe legal tangle involving the largest number of conflicting proprietary claims.

In June 1810, Justice George Thatcher of the Supreme Judicial Court ordered a survey of the "Brown claim" based on a vague (and fraudulent) Indian deed. In August 1810, in Bristol, Captain Samuel Tucker and sixty neighbors obstructed the survey. Furious at this affront to his authority, Thatcher invoked the March 1810 revision of the riot act to call out five hundred militia men to guard a renewed survey. To command, he appointed Colonel Samuel Thatcher, Henry Knox's Federalist son-in-law. Bristol's inhabitants stockpiled arms and ammunition for the confrontation, but on draft day all of Thatcher's assembled militia men deserted when resistance sympathizers seized a drum and "beat up for volunteers to join Bristol." When the General Court reconvened in January 1811, the seven affected towns sent a full legislative delegation, including the formidable Captain Tucker, and pressed for relief from proprietary suits.[40]

Timing smiled on the Lincoln County settlers' pressure. Convinced that the leading Federalists were traitors ready to betray the United States in the impending war with Great Britain, Elbridge Gerry, the new Jeffersonian governor, conducted his administration with unprecedented partisanship. More receptive to settler arguments than any previous governor, Gerry suspended Thatcher's militia order and persuaded the Jeffersonian legislature to repeal the provisions of the March 1810 law authorizing justices to call out the militia on their own authority (the penalties against Indian disguise remained). At Gerry's prompting, the General Court also appointed commissioners, who reported in January 1813 that only the Kennebeck Proprietors and Pemaquid Proprietors, by virtue of their crown grants, possessed valid legal titles to any part of the seven towns. The commissioners ruled that none of the Indian deed claims possessed any legal basis but that the William Vaughan heirs (no relationship to Charles Vaughan) had effected sufficient improvements to qualify for some consideration. On the commissioners' recommendation, the General Court compensated the Kennebeck Proprietors with one wilderness township in northern Maine, and the Pemaquid and Vaughan proprietors with half a township each. The other proprietary claimants to the seven towns received nothing. These included Thurston Whiting as one of the Brown Claim proprietors. Because the compensatory wilderness townships lay far away in the distant and infertile recesses of Maine's interior where the tide of settlement never arrived, the Kennebeck, Pemaquid, and Vaughan proprietors received practically nothing for their claims in the seven Lincoln County towns.[41]

Freed of these claims, 1,384 families in the seven towns received new deeds from the commonwealth, almost all for about thirteen cents an acre. Secure title for pennies an acre was everything the region's settlers had ever sought, but only the inhabitants of these seven towns—a small minority of mid-Maine's settlers—benefited from this de facto confiscation of proprietary claims. By February 1813, when the final legislation passed, the unpopular War of 1812 with Great Britain had enabled the Federalists to recapture the General Court's House of Representatives; they accepted the necessary resolve with the explicit proviso that its principles were "not to be considered as furnishing a precedent for any other cases." Because the Federalists retained control of the General Court and governorship until after Maine's separation in 1820, the settlers in the rest of mid-Maine knew no further initiatives on their behalf from the state government. The great majority of mid-Maine's settlers had to content themselves with far less, with the Betterment Act's principle that they owned their improvements but had to pay their proprietors for the wild land value.[42]

The National Pattern

Agrarian discontent peaked in the American backcountry during the Federalist ascendancy of the 1790s as part of a fundamental crisis in America's political culture, a deadlock between Federalist and agrarian interpretations of the classical republican heritage that had temporarily united the American Revolution's disparate supporters. In addition to Maine's Liberty Men, the Federalist rulers of the 1790s confronted Anti-Renters in New York, Wild Yankees and Fries's Regulators in Pennsylvania, and Whiskey Rebels in the entire backcountry from Pennsylvania to Georgia. The Federalists responded to resistance with troops and prosecutions intended to stifle agrarian protest and establish government's monopoly on violent coercion. Federalists were intransigent partly because so many of them owned large, speculative land claims throughout the nation. But more important, agrarians and Federalists were loath to compromise, because both groups operated from divisive premises rooted in the classical conception of politics. Federalists and agrarians concurred that society necessarily consisted of divergent social orders with different capacities, distinctive rights, and clashing interests. The most fundamental distinction was between "the rulers" (or "gentlemen," or "great men") and "the ruled" (or "the people"). Both Federalists and agrarians saw conflict at the center of political life; driven by innate human corruption, rulers and the ruled struggled to encroach on the other's sphere, rulers to enslave the people, the ruled to plunder their betters. Equally suspicious of human nature, agrarians and Federalists believed the worst about the other. Backcountry folk felt they defended republican liberty against encroachment by unscrupulous aristocrats, and Federalists insisted that they protected ordered liberty from the anarchy of licentious mobs.[43]

During the 1790s agrarians and Federalists reached a stalemate. Ultimately, the Federalists lacked the power to impose their will while, for want of education and wealth, the agrarians could not produce leaders sophisticated enough to operate successfully at the state or national level to alter the legal structure. But the social collapse into disunion, civil war, and anarchy that many observers forecast in the 1790s on the basis of agrarian discontent, sectional rivalry, political partisanship, and urban rioting was averted by the Jeffersonians' sweeping national triumph in 1800. America's more imaginative and entrepreneurial gentlemen saw Federalist intransigence as both a national danger and a political opportunity. Confident in their ability to conduct republican governance in a manner that channeled and managed popular grievances, these more flexible gentlemen rallied around Thomas Jefferson to shatter the Federalists' predominance. Few Jeffersonians were agrarian ideologues. Most meant to give just enough ground to popular discontents to assure a domestic stability that would permit every white man to pursue his commercial ambitions. Such was the world sought by Ezekiel G. Dodge, George Ulmer, and William King. America's liberal political economy emerged in response to the internal conflicts engendered by the Revolution.[44]

In the process of exploiting popular grievances for political gain, the Jeffersonians shattered the classical politics based on a protection covenant between the rulers and the ruled; in its place they advanced a liberal vision that offered a more stable basis for Americans to interpret and conduct their contests for political and economic resources. The Jeffersonians perceived a natural harmony of interests among all men when they were equal competitors regulated only by voluntary association and free exchange. The Jeffersonians maintained that concentrations of wealth were no threat to the Republic once *they* were in office. In the process of assuring the rich that they were safe from widespread electoral participation, the Jeffersonians insisted that concentrated wealth need no longer alarm the many. Consequently, the Jeffersonians dissolved the troublesome distinction between "the rulers" and "the ruled." As politicians became the "Friends of the People" rather than the "Fathers of the People," great men could no longer justify formal privilege, and rural communities could no longer nullify political authority. Once politicians were obligated to heed the people, the people were obligated to obey all the laws passed by their representatives. In adopting liberal rhetoric to smite the Great Proprietors, the settlers also undermined their agrarian notions. They forsook their consciousness as "the ruled," their sensitivity to struggle with "the great men," and the legitimacy of local nullification against central power. By denying that the gentlemen were a distinctive ruling order, the settlers also denied themselves any special rights distinct from any others in political society, including the right to resist outsiders. The Federalist landlords may not have liked their Jeffersonian competitors for offices, corporate privileges, political favors, and land grants, but they owed them no small gratitude for eroding the settlers' capacity to resist. Josiah Little, the Kennebeck Proprietors, and Henry Knox's successors were safe in the possession of their patents, not only despite but because of the advent of the Dodges.[45]

Throughout the American backcountry, Jeffersonian leaders played a role similar to the one they performed in mid-Maine. Indeed, William King probably modeled his Betterment Act on similar legislation enacted in 1797 by Jeffersonian legislatures in Kentucky and Tennessee. Capturing the national government in 1800, and almost all the state governments within a few years, the Jeffersonians worked to compromise the agrarian controversies. Thomas Jefferson's administration mollified Pennsylvania's Whiskey Rebels and Fries's Regulators by lifting the offending excise and land taxes levied by the previous Federalist regime. Albert Gallatin, a western Pennsylvanian who served as Jefferson's secretary of the treasury, modified national land policies. He made it easier for settlers and small investors to obtain western lands by extending credit on purchases and by multiplying the number of land offices located near the frontier. During the 1790s, Pennsylvania's Federalists had upheld the controversial land claims of large speculators to the state's northwestern corner. The new Jeffersonian state regime reversed that policy in 1800, but the intervention of the Federalist-dominated United States Supreme Court in February 1805 secured the speculators' triumph in that region. In 1801 Pennsylvania's Jeffersonian legislature and governor resolved most of the Wild Yankee agitation in northeastern Pennsylvania by appointing commissioners, headed by Thomas Cooper, to sell state title to most of the settlers (those with claims predating 1783) for an average of thirty-two cents per acre; the state drew on these payments and additional funds to compensate the affected proprietors. The legislature coupled this commission with legislation mandating draconian penalties against new squatters and the leading men who abetted them. In the 1810s Pennsylvania Jeffersonians led the fight for, and Federalists against, a betterment act for those settlers in northeastern Pennsylvania with post-1783 claims. In New York, Governor John Jay, a Federalist, suppressed renewed antirent resistance in 1798. Thereafter Columbia County's Jeffersonian leaders—especially the young lawyer and future president Martin Van Buren—periodically challenged the landlords' titles with petitions to the legislature and suits in the courts. Unfortunately for the tenants, the Jeffersonian legislators from nonrent counties were indifferent to land reform, and the Federalist judiciary was hostile; the obstructed reforms ensured the great wave of antirent violence in the 1830s and 1840s.[46]

The Jeffersonians dealt with the three fundamental disputes at the heart of agrarian resistance in mid-Maine and elsewhere in the American backcountry. First, confronted with contention over whether labor or title was the soul of new property, Jeffersonians crafted betterment acts predicated on a mix of the two in the value of any new farm. Consequently, settlers could not evade paying something for title, but proprietors could not use their legal advantages to extort the settlers' improvements. Second, the Jeffersonians faced the issue of whether extralegal crowd violence retained any legitimacy in the new Republic. By advancing a compromise, mixed definition of property coupled with tightened state laws against organized rural violence, Jeffersonians sent a clear message that redress could and must come through constitutional institutions. Their confidence in those institutions deepened once they captured control of the national and most state governments; they saw no need for violent crowds of Regulators once "the people's friends" were in power. Third, the Jeffersonians confronted whether political decision making should be diffused locally or consolidated centrally. During the Federalist ascendancy of the 1790s, alarmed Jeffersonians dabbled with Antifederalist notions of state and even local nullification of central authority. After 1800, most Jeffersonians continued to pay lip service to states' rights, but in practice behaved as if their advent to national domination rendered the distribution of power a moot issue.[47]

The Aftermath of Resistance

[The Great Proprietors] ought never to have had a foot of soil on this side of the Atlantic Ocean. But, alas! Justice does not always take place. Therefore, an honest man may be supplanted by a rogue from off his farm because power seems to give him right so to do or the Supreme [Judicial] Court may have guaranteed those rights which it seems at a future period never ought to have been given to such men, men in whose breast the cause of freedom and independence as it respects the United States never found a residence.—James Robinson, Jr., of Jefferson, 1820

[Moses Little and Josiah Little] were fine business men, broad-minded, energetic, and . . . much of the success in establishing proprietors' and settlers' claims was attributable to them, through wise, efficient counsel and square dealing; and many of the earlier settlers of Greene have much to thank them for.—Walter Lindley Mower, town historian, 1938

NO LONGER SCREENED BY the resistance from proprietary surveyors and officers of the law, during the 1810s the young men of the back-country who wanted land had to meet their proprietors' terms or move on. Where proprietors charged prices in excess of three dollars per acre, sons and daughters tended to move away in search of cheaper and often better land, to the dismay of their parents, whose security in old age depended on the proximity of their children. By January 1812 Palermo's settlers regretted their decision in late 1808 to suffer the Kennebeck Proprietors to survey Palermo into lots. Once the survey was complete, the proprietors prosecuted anyone they detected logging or clearing any land within the two-fifths of the town still retained by the company. Before he could safely fell a tree, a settler had to agree to buy the lot, posting the double security of a promissory note for the payments *and* a mortgage deed to the premises. Although the Kennebeck Proprietors would not warrant any deed to a settler, they insisted that he warrant the mortgage that secured his payment. The proprietors' demands of more than three dollars per acre were more than thrice the average price paid by those Palermoites who had submitted to the 1802–1803 Plymouth Patent Commission (and despite the decline in local land values that began in 1810). About a third of the recent purchasers could not meet their payments and had their grants canceled. In January 1812 the selectmen of Palermo complained:

A great many of us were forced to buy on these conditions as we knew we could not possibly git our living in this new country with-

Lincoln County Jail. Wiscasset. Constructed 1809–1811 in response to the White Indians' rescue riots. *Courtesy of the Maine Historic Preservation Commission*

out felling and clearing and we could not git the money to maintain a lawsuit so we concluded to give up all for the purpose of living quietly on our possessions for a few years. Some of us they have sued and that makes it bad for the poor settler: to pay the expense of a lawsuit and then lose his land and labour. Others have taken leases for one year and are debarred the priviledge of cutting a stick of wood on sd. land. Others have not bought at all. . . . And under all these circumstances we are entirely discouraged and afraid to build, set out orchards, make fences, or any other expense necessary for farms for fear they will be taken from us immediately. [Some settlers] have been moving away rapidly for about two years to the Ohio and Nova Scotia and the young are going away too, some leaving their lands after they have bought, others quiting their possessions etc.

The selectmen begged the General Court to adopt some measure "to encourage the young men so as to put a stop to their leaving their native country as soon as they arrive at the age of twenty-one years and going to a foreign government for that protection which they might reasonably expect from our own." It must have been a bitter irony that so many of their sons migrated to British Canada in search of the free land that their fathers had thought they had won by the Revolution against British rule.[1]

Palermo's selectmen insisted, "It is not only this town but the country all around us [that] is in the like situation." In December 1819, Boardman Johnson of Jackson (one of the Waldo Patent backcountry towns obtained from General Knox by Thorndike, Sears, and Prescott) reported that fewer than half of the inhabitants owned title to their farms, because they could not afford the three to five dollars per acre charged by their proprietors. Some tried but failed to meet the burden.

> The method of let[t]ing people have land is to let them go on under a bond for a deed when paid for. The possessor pays ¼, ½ or more as his circumstances will admit, spends his life in hard labour, makes a farm and some buildings. If he should dye before he has paid for the land the young family are hardly ever able to pay the residue and the farm returns to the original owner, together with what is paid, instead of a wild lot.

In 1820–1821 at least 1,731 men signed petitions charging that the Betterment Act did not adequately protect settlers from extortionate proprietary practices. Some signers had previously promoted accommodation with the proprietors: Deacon John Neal, James Shurtleff, three of Robert Foye's sons, and even George Ulmer, who (having lost his fortune and political offices) had retired to the backcountry.[2]

Some settlers briefly revived overt resistance when they felt pushed too hard, too fast for payment. In June 1820, Reuel Williams, a Kennebeck Proprietor, suddenly and vigorously pressed ejectment suits against ten Freedom settlers at a time when specie was especially scarce. The settlers again donned their White Indian attire to chase away twice a deputy bearing Williams's hated writs. Anson and James Barlow, probably Nathan Barlow's sons, apparently led this renewed resistance. But because the Freedomites had already permitted a survey, their revived resistance could only postpone their payments until the commercial depression lifted. By 1823 almost all of the men sued by Williams had come to terms. In May–June 1825 some Albion (formerly Fairfax) settlers burned two barns—one lay on a farm recently recovered by Williams in an ejectment suit, and the other belonged to one of his local supporters. Once again the revived resistance proved short-lived, and Williams's other local supporters never needed to collect on the fire insurance policies that he hurriedly procured for them from a company in Augusta.[3]

Accommodation

Although broad, the settlers' unease with the terms of accommodation was not deep. They complained, petitioned, stole proprietary timber, and directed the assessors of their towns to levy disproportionate taxes on proprietary lands, but only rarely did the settlers resume armed patrols or the intimidation of proprietary supporters. Indeed, given the previous volume and anger of their protests, it is striking how quickly most settlers adapted to the resistance's aftermath. Most reasoned that there was no advantage in mourning the resistance too long; the barn needed a new roof, the cattle wanted a larger pasture, and there was always wood to cut for the long winter. In June 1787, early in the resistance, Josiah Little visited the settlers in Bakerstown (Poland and Minot) and demanded how they dared to take up land within his claim without permission. "Their answer was: they Expected to git it. The Question was ask'd: how? Answer: of the State [and] . . . if we cannot git it any other way will buy of you." The important matter was securing the land, freely if possible, by paying if necessary. Paying a proprietor was not pleasant, but it had become necessary to keep the farm.[4]

Indeed, the prosperous settlers who were more concerned about clear title than low price could regard the resistance as a qualified success; they could conclude that it had secured all that was feasible and that the time had come to desist. The resistance had bought valuable time for the settlers to accumulate the resources to pay for their lands, rent-free time to harvest and sell the region's virgin timber without compensating the proprietors. The resistance obliged proprietors, through special commissions, the Betterment Act, or their own modified offers, to moderate their prices. Most settlers may not have secured their homesteads for a dollar or less per acre, but neither did most have to pay the four to seven dollars per acre sought by the Great Proprietors. The resistance induced the General Court (in resolving the Lincoln County claims) and the Supreme Judicial Court (in eventually adjudicating the Plymouth Patent's disputed bounds with the Pejepscot and Draper proprietors) to clear away the conflicts between proprietary titles before most settlers began their payments. Consequently, the older, more prosperous settlers could conclude that their resistance had secured mid-Maine as a region of middling farmers and had fended off their nightmare—lordships worked by exploited tenants. Few of the Great Proprietors sought to impose tenancy, because they anticipated that Yankee yeomen would not stand for it; by resisting the slightest hint of lordships, mid-Maine's settlers played their expected role and guaranteed the predominance of freehold tenure.[5]

Other settlers accepted the demise of the resistance because of the increasing influence of conservativism within mid-Maine's evangelical denominations, a trend that encouraged a new resignation in the face of temporal difficulty. During the 1790s, when evangelical itinerants were intent on recruiting seekers' groups, they paid less attention to doctrinal consensus and moral discipline than to cultivating spiritual fervor. But after 1800, tensions emerged within each denomination between the Christian Primitivists (or Antinomians, as their opponents called them) and conservatives who coveted the Congregationalists' respectability. Foot washing, collective worship, women preachers, and the search for visions and revelations had no place in the more respectable and disciplined denominations sought by the conservatives. Regretting the declamations of previous evangelicals against learned "hirelings," conservatives envied the Congregationalists' financially comfortable, authoritative, and educated ministry delivering written sermons. Seizing the initiative from the Christian Primitivists, who were more localist and anarchic, the conservatives tightened the internal discipline and codified the doctrines of the older, more centrally organized, most numerous denominations in mid-Maine: the Calvinist Baptists and Methodists.[6]

The conservatives attacked Antinomianism, the religious culture that had been compatible with the resistance. Uncomfortable with the Antinomian insistence on the perfection of the converted, conservatives stressed the enduring sinfulness of all flesh. So, like the Congregationalists, the conservative evangelicals urged believers to defer to their ministers, practice strict morality, and rigorously test the spirit by Scripture (rather than the reverse). The conservative Sylvanus Boardman exhorted his fellow Calvinist Baptists: "Remember, brethren, that the most dangerous enemies are within you, and of all your enemies, these will require the most watchful and vigorous resistance. These subtle foes are in league with all the enemies without, and when a communication between them is effected, dangerous consequences ensue." According to the conservatives, Satan, not God, lurked within. Consequently, they demanded that the faithful adopt a more austere and disciplined personality. In particular, the conservatives discouraged the festive communal work parties, the frolics that had played such an important role in sustaining mutuality and that had often turned into resistance musters. The conservative evangelicals sought revivals where converts confronted their innate sinfulness without the visionary encounters and emotional outbursts associated with Christian primitivism. In December 1809, just seven months after Deacon John Neal successfully surveyed Litchfield for the Kennebeck Proprietors, bringing that town's resistance to a close, his minister and fellow conservative, the Reverend Henry Kendall, closely supervised an extensive revival throughout the town: "This work has been carried on with the greatest regularity and order, without noise or confusion." By exalting ministerial authority and discrediting spiritual spontaneity, the conservatives attenuated the fer-

vor and diversity that had allowed Nathan Barlow to command attention. Mid-Maine's evangelicals increasingly became consumers of codified religious ideas approved by the denominational leadership dwelling
outside the region, rather than the recipients of divine messages speaking to their peculiar circumstances.[7]

The calming effect of the conservative trend on settler unease was
evident in Malta, where in September 1809 the White Indians had assassinated Paul Chadwick, the son of a conservative Calvinist Baptist
preacher. A year later, the Lincoln Association, to which Job Chadwick's
Harlem (a town adjacent to Malta) church belonged, convened for its
annual meeting and adopted an unusually long circular letter written by
John Baker of Chadwick's congregation. As was usual with evangelical
writings, the circular letter referred to no particular worldly events, but
it is significant that Baker exhorted, "The *person* of our neighbor must
be held inviolable by us," and explicitly denounced Antinomianism. Baker also insisted that believers could do nothing to advance the millennium aside from preserving their own morality and sustaining their
churches as oases of embattled belief: a passivity at odds with the active
millennialism promoted by Nathan Barlow and Daniel Brackett. In 1811
the Reverend Isaac Case, another conservative Calvinist Baptist, conducted a successful revival in Malta, "a place that has been almost a
Sodom for wickedness." The fifty new converts included "three men
that were tried for their lives for the murder of Mr. Paul Chadwick,
about 2 years ago." There had been no organized churches in Malta
when Chadwick died; within a decade the Congregationalists, Methodists, Freewill Baptists, and Calvinist Baptists organized churches there.[8]

Those settlers who could not adjust to the aftermath of resistance
moved on to another frontier in search of opportunity. The most discontented sought redress in out-migration rather than in revived resistance. Had there been no frontier to move to, the 1810s and early 1820s
would not have been so peaceful in mid-Maine. As Frederick Jackson
Turner argued, in the nineteenth century (if not the eighteenth) the
frontier served as a "safety valve" for the disgruntled white men of rural
America. Out-migration from mid-Maine tended to draw off the poor
young men and women who lost the most with the passing of the resistance. With them went any prospect of revived resistance. During the
1810s about half the identifiable Liberty Men departed their communities, a marked change from the previous decade, when two-thirds had
persisted in their towns. In contrast to the previous decade, when Liberty Men outlasted their local foes, during the 1810s proprietary supporters had the higher persistence rate, evidence that the tables had
turned.[9]

The out-migration of the disaffected was catalyzed by the advent of
hard times in mid-Maine during the 1810s, when a series of unusually

cold years (especially 1816) and the commercially disruptive War of 1812 with Great Britain produced widespread hunger and undermined land values. In April 1813 Alibeus Partridge of Camden described the bleak situation to his two sons, who had removed to Licking County, Ohio:

> The times are exceeding dark, scar[c]ety and war. Hundreds and hundreds have neither bread nor potatoes to eat and the back country seems to be worse of[f] than the seaports by reson of the frost being more sevear than last seson and that makes it more harder upon the seacost by reson that the co[a]sting is almost cut off. The British take and carey of[f] and burn numbers of them so that . . . the southern trade is so stopt that no provisions is brought from thence to help the difucalty.

He exhorted his sons: "Don't spare to write all you can for your leaters are red til they are almost wore out so that we want new wons. We want to know how the winter wather in general is with you and the spring seson. . . . If you can hold your own thare and live in any measure cumfortable you are much better off than here." A year later, William Parkman of Camden observed: "As to the times they are very hard. The District of Maine is going [to] wreck as fast as ever a country did. Farms can be purchased for less than half of what they could [have] been 5 or 6 years ago. A great many is moving away to Ohio."[10]

By compounding the difficulties of families newly burdened with land debts, the hard times encouraged marginal settlers to abandon Maine for a new start in the West. The cold years and wartime hardships diminished the settlers' ability to pay for their homesteads and raised new doubts about the wisdom of paying more than two dollars per acre for such marginal lands, especially when better lands for comparable prices were available in Ohio and western New York. Glowing reports promised that, in the Midwest, men did not have to slave for half the year procuring barely enough fodder to succor small herds of bony livestock through the winter. During the 1810s the "Ohio fever" drew as many as twenty thousand Mainers westward. More prosperous folk traveled in convoys of covered wagons that gathered together in Augusta before proceeding west. Lacking livestock or selling them to pay their debts, the poorer folk trudged hundreds of miles west, drawing their small children and smaller possessions along on handcarts in summer and sleds in winter. "War and adversity had cast upon some a heavy weight of debt, and poverty had always been the lot of a still greater number;—both classes having nothing to leave and little to carry with them. . . . The lower orders of society were put in motion, and nothing could break the spell," William D. Williamson of Bangor observed.[11]

In 1815 the Kennebeck Proprietor Robert Hallowell Gardiner of Gardiner, Maine, noted the "general discontent with the climate and country." He was tempted to say good riddance to most of the out-migrants, observing: "Multitudes are moving [to Ohio]. . . . It is certainly true that the necessaries of life can be raised there with much less labor; and the indolent will be rejoiced to exchange a cold hard country for one that is mild and easy." But some emigrants were settlers defaulting on their contracts with Gardiner, forfeiting their lots to seek new homesteads in the "mild and easy" West. Concerned, Gardiner hoped to retain and reeducate "the indolent" rather than see mid-Maine stagnate economically. "We continue to [expand] our manufactures here. A large and extensive tannery has been established here this summer. I am about erecting a furnace and our cotton and nail works are encouraging. We must try in these ways to keep some of our people from runing away into the western world." In contrast to the "indolent" settlers fleeing westward in continued pursuit of liberty as autonomous small producers, Gardiner promoted a characteristically paternalistic remedy where benevolent, enlightened men of wealth gathered humbler, less able men into webs of beneficial, disciplining dependence. Employing his capital garnered largely from settlers' land payments, Gardiner created new factories to better the workers while profiting the capitalist.[12]

The Brackett family was among those who ignored Gardiner's advice and ran away to the western world to preserve their independence. Feeling the infirmities of his wartime service and lifelong labor, in June 1807, fifty-one-year-old Daniel Brackett sold his Fairfax (Albion) homestead to his twenty-three-year-old son, Daniel Brackett, Jr., with whom he continued to live. But arrest warrants for the younger Daniel (for a November 1807 assault on a deputy sheriff) and his uncle Thomas Brackett (for assisting Nathan Barlow's April 1808 rescue of the elder Daniel) made continued residence in Fairfax dangerous, especially after the local resistance crumbled with Barlow's arrest, trial, and conviction in June 1808. That month young Daniel hastily sold the family homestead to their neighbor John Bradstreet, a fellow White Indian. The Bracketts moved eastward across the county line to Lincoln Plantation in Hancock County, where the Kennebec County arrest warrants could not be executed. A few years later the family decided to leave their painful memories behind, probably because of the demise of the resistance, the cold years, troublesome debts, and the death in infancy of young Daniel's three children. The Bracketts migrated, via a brief sojourn in northwestern Maine, to a new frontier community of poor settlers in western New York (then part of Sweden, Genesee County, now the town of Clarendon, Monroe County), where they reappeared in 1815.[13]

Because their new wilderness homestead could not entirely support the family, Daniel Brackett itinerated through the county in search of work as a shoemaker, boarding with his farmer customers. This was exactly the sort of insecure, rootless old age he had fought in the resistance to avoid. As an indigent Revolutionary war veteran, he appealed to the federal government for a pension in November 1820:

> I have not sufficient clothing to make me comfortable. . . . My occupation has formerly been that of farmer, but from old age, the rheumatism and general debility I am unable to do much labour. I am totally deaf in one of my ears and very thick of hearing in the other which was caused by my having the smallpox in the revolutionary war and is a great inconvenience to me.

The county clerk attested to Daniel Brackett's ill health and severe poverty. His enumerated property consisted of an ax, a handsaw, a square and compass, a scythe, a razor and case, and a set of shoemaker's tools (hammer, knife, and four awls) collectively worth $3.88. He possessed neither land nor livestock. He did own three debts: fifteen days' labor from Asahel Whittemore, a barrel of salt from William Whitney, and $52.00 in cash from his son, who was "too poor to pay me anything." Obtaining a pension of $8.00 per month, Daniel Brackett gave up shoemaking and returned to his son's Clarendon household, where he died in 1826.[14]

In western New York the Bracketts had again settled as squatters on a large proprietary claim: that of the Pulteney Estate. According to the town's nineteenth-century historian, every settler "was compelled to pay . . . or leave and lose his labor." During the 1830s, Daniel Brackett, Jr., ransomed his 137-acre homestead in three separate deeds. He gave part of his land to the town's Christian Connection church, a congregation he organized in 1815 and served as preacher. The local "Christians" sought "to shake off the authority of human creeds and the shackles of prescribed modes and forms, and to make the Bible their only guide; claiming for every man the right to be his own expositor of it . . . and in practice to follow more strictly the simplicity of the apostles and primitive Christians." By sustaining Christian primitivism, Daniel Brackett, Jr., attained what the family had sought in their spiritual life, if not what they wanted from the temporal world.[15]

Maine's separation from Massachusetts in 1820 climaxed the decade of transformation and accommodation. Revitalized by the Jeffersonians' association with the unpopular War of 1812, the commonwealth's Federalists won every gubernatorial contest and dominated every General Court from 1812 through 1820, despite continued Jeffersonian majorities in the District of Maine. Despairing of any Jeffersonian revival in Massachusetts, Maine's Jeffersonian leaders pressed for separate statehood. In 1819, Massachusetts' Federalist leadership accepted separation in the hope that it would rid them of the potential staging ground for any Jeffersonian revival in the commonwealth. Maine's Jeffersonians acceded to the demand that Massachusetts retain half of the Eastern Country's unsold public lands. William King assured Maine's Federalists of a share in the new state's patronage; and he reassured his fellow proprietors that as governor he would keep the tax valuation of wild lands low, precluding any use of the new state's tax power to confiscate their property. By 1819 the Federalists were willing to permit separation, because they had come to recognize that Maine's Jeffersonian leaders were not agrarians, did not intend to confiscate the large private landholdings, and could be trusted to appoint a judiciary solicitous of great property.[16]

To discourage revived resistance, the Jeffersonians who dominated Maine's new state government pursued a dual policy. On the one hand, the legislators mandated a public land policy favorable to actual settlers. The legislature reserved five ranges of wilderness townships in north-central Maine as "settling lands," where the first forty families per township could acquire one-hundred-acre homesteads for a mere thirty cents per acre. On the other hand, beyond reforming proprietary abuses of certain loopholes in the Betterment Act, the legislature declined to meddle in the proprietary lands of mid-Maine. Determined not to reawaken settler unease, the legislators hesitated to undermine the settlers' acquiescence to the notion that nothing more than the Betterment Act could be done for them. Indeed, to prevent any resurgence of the squatter population, in February 1821 the legislature passed a stern new law authorizing any two justices of the peace, upon receiving a written complaint, to convene twelve men as a jury to try suspected squatters; the convicted paid the full costs of suit and were ejected from their homesteads with no right of appeal to any higher court. The legislature attended to this bill *before* it reformed the Betterment Act. The state's dual policy discouraged settler hopes of a new Jeffersonian deal within the proprietary tracts, but held forth the public "settling lands" as a safety valve to draw off the discontented (and, the legislators hoped, dissuade them from migrating to Ohio). Unfortunately, the new policy benefited few, because most of the new state's unsold wilderness lay far in the northern interior where poor soil, especially long winters, and isolation from market discouraged settlement. Maine became a state long after Indian deeds, crown grants, and Massachusetts' land sales had transferred most of the best lands to Great Proprietors.[17]

Population turnover, increasing conservatism among evangelicals, and Maine's separation combined to encourage the widespread conclusion that the resistance was gone and best forgotten. Malta's settlers were especially eager to consign the resistance to oblivion. In September 1809 the town had hosted the resistance's climactic incident: Paul Chadwick's murder. But by 1820 Malta was dramatically altered, as half of the residents of 1810 had departed, including most of the town's White Indi-

A Morning View of Blue Hill Village, September 1824. By the Reverend Jonathan Fisher. *Courtesy of the William A. Farnsworth Library and Art Museum*

ans. They had been replaced by a larger number of new householders, most of whom must have been outsiders, because they bore surnames not present in the community ten years earlier. Those who remembered the resistance were a minority in the midst of latecomers and children coming of age, groups that knew from the start that they would have to buy proprietary title to obtain land in the community. Sensitive about their town's external reputation, the majority desperately wanted to change the name of their town, because it had become notorious for violence. In an 1821 petition to the Maine state legislature, the selectmen explained:

> That by reason of the unhappy disturbances in this town soon after its incorporation in which disturbances one Paul Chadwick was killed . . . the town acquired a bad character which appears to be connected with the name Malta and altho' there are no more than four of the persons remaining in the town who were concerned in that wicked plot, time has not worn off the stain by reason of which many good citizens are deterred from settling in the town and many of the good citizens of the town when abroad often have their ears saluted with the disagreeable sound of "Malta Indians."

By 1821 Malta's residents were eager to put behind them an unpleasant legacy that complicated their lives. In March the Maine state legislature renamed the town Gerry in honor of Massachusetts' late Jeffersonian governor who had done the most to assist the aggrieved settlers. But this did not satisfy the selectmen, who felt no attachment to the governor's memory. They complained that Gerry's similarity to Gray, another Maine town, resulted in misrouted letters. The complaint reiterated

their new engagement with the outside world of commerce and authority, a world whose encroachment had doomed the resistance. To the
town postmaster's relief, the legislature changed Gerry to the more distinctive Windsor in January 1822. The name change marked the demise
of the agrarian resistance in Maine.[18]

Postscript

In the summer of 1837 Nathaniel Hawthorne visited Thomaston and
pondered Montpelier's sadly dilapidated remains.

> The house and its vicinity, and the whole tract covered by Knox's
> patent, may be taken as an illustration of what must be the result of
> American schemes of aristocracy. It is not forty years, since this
> house was built, and Knox was in his glory; but now the house is all
> in decay, while, within a stone's throw of it, is a street of neat, smart
> white edifices of one and two stories, occupied chiefly by thriving
> mechanics. But towns have grown up, where Knox probably meant
> to have forests and parks. On the banks of the river, where he
> meant to have only one wharf, for his own West-Indian vessels and
> yacht, there are two wharves, with stores, and a lime-kiln. Little
> appertains to the mansion, except the tomb, and the old burial
> ground, and the old fort. The descendants are all poor; and the
> inheritance was merely sufficient to make a dissipated and drunken
> fellow of the one of the old General's sons, who survived to middle
> age.

This was the accepted wisdom of the age, recorded by Tocqueville as
well—that partible inheritance, political democracy, and a volatile free
market rendered wealth and power impermanent, undermining the social bases for an enduring aristocracy and promoting a republic of thriving mechanics and small farmers.[19]

Thirteen years later Hawthorne drew upon what he had learned
about Henry Knox in Thomaston to craft the character of Judge Pyncheon for the early pages of *The House of the Seven Gables*. Military officer, powerful politician, founder of a troubled family, and target of the
squatter Matthew Maule's curse, Judge Pyncheon held, in addition to his
Salem estate, "a claim through an Indian deed, confirmed by a subsequent grant of the General Court, to a vast and as yet unexplored and
unmeasured tract of Eastern Lands." Like the actual Waldo Patent, the
fictional Pyncheon claim "comprised the greater part of what is now
known as Waldo County, in the State of Maine, and [was] more extensive than many a dukedom." But Hawthorne rewrote the Waldo Patent's history to accord the settlers a happier ending: they successfully

"laughed at the idea of any man's asserting a right—on the strength of moldy parchments, signed with the faded autographs of governors and legislators long dead and forgotten—to the lands which they or their fathers had wrested from the wild hand of nature by their own sturdy toil." In Hawthorne's fiction, labor justly triumphed at title's expense. An ironist adept at masking his profound discomfort with America's inequities, Hawthorne probably knew the discrepancy between what should have been and what had actually happened on the northeastern frontier. Robert Clark notes, "His conviction that the American past contained buried wrongs, that the foundation of the Puritan colonies had involved authoritarian persecution of the heterodox and the expropriation of the poor by the rich (like Matthew Maule by Judge Pyncheon), and his belief that the crimes of the past were transmitted into the present by the very act of denying their existence; these prevented any simplistic agreement with the prevailing optimism about the regeneration of human nature and the inherent perfection of the United States which dominated social thought in his day."[20]

By embracing labor as the proper basis of property and by denouncing proprietary title, Hawthorne rebelled against his own heritage. Judge Pyncheon also owed much to Hawthorne's great-great-grandfather, Colonel John Hathorne (1641–1717) of Salem. Remembered as one of the witch trial judges, Hathorne was also an Indian deed proprietor to a mid-Maine claim. Nathaniel Hawthorne had a still closer tie to Maine's proprietors. After his father's death and his family's relocation in 1814 to Raymond, Maine, the young Hawthorne had a stormy relationship with his uncle and guardian, Robert Manning, who was a justice, a storekeeper, and the town's principal proprietor. Denouncing title's "moldy parchments" was a slap at the Mannings as well as at Colonel Hathorne.[21]

On his tour of mid-Maine in 1837, Hawthorne saw another scene that suggested that the demise of Henry Knox's aristocratic pretensions had not secured the republic of independent small producers. Traveling to Augusta, Hawthorne visited his best friend and Bowdoin College classmate Horatio Bridge, a successful lawyer and entrepreneur. That summer, Bridge supervised the construction of a dam across the Kennebec River to harness its waterpower for textile factories. The project's laborers lived in earth and log huts huddled beside the river on Bridge's property. Suspecting that the workers had stolen some of his wooden rails for firewood, Bridge threatened to pull down one of the shantytowns. "It seems queer that a man should have the right, unarmed with any legal instrument, of tearing down the dwelling-houses of a score of families, and turning the inmates forth without a shelter. Yet Bridge undoubtedly has this right; and it is not a little striking to see how quietly these people contemplate the probability of his exercising it—

resolving, indeed, to burrow in their holes as long as may be," Hawthorne mused.[22]

Horatio Bridge inherited his wealth and power from Kennebeck Proprietors. Both of his grandfathers—Edmund Bridge, Lincoln County's high sheriff, and Colonel Joseph North, a Kennebec County Court of Common Pleas justice—had held interests in the Plymouth Company and had employed their offices to subdue the settlers' resistance. James Bridge, Horatio's father and the Kennebeck Proprietors' Kennebec County lawyer, grew rich from legal fees and shrewd speculations in real estate and bank stocks. He and his law office partner, Reuel Williams, bought most of the Plymouth Company's unsold lands when the corporation dissolved in 1816. James Bridge earned a reputation for the cunning frugality with which he built and preserved his fortune. When the representative of a charitable society assured Bridge that a donation would bear enduring testimony to his wealth and standing, the lawyer "cooly replied that he could not agree with him, for from his experience in life, which had been considerable, he had found that people were more respected for what they had than [for] what they gave away." Because paternalism did not tincture his self-interest, James Bridge left behind an impressive blufftop mansion rather than a crumbling Montpelier. The Kennebec Dam Company's five officers bore witness to the origin of its capital in the previous generation's land payments from settlers to proprietors: Reuel Williams, his brother Daniel Williams, Horatio Bridge, and his brothers James, Jr., and Edmund. As the Reverend Thomas Barnard had hoped in his 1758 sermon to Boston's Society for Encouraging Industry, and Employing the Poor, putting a price on wilderness land had accumulated capital for industrial development. But Hawthorne could have written a tragedy about the dam's ultimate consequences; poorly sited, it gave way in May 1839 and redirected the river to eat away the west bank, suddenly tumbling the Bridge family mansion one hundred feet into the raging waters. But for the mis-sited dam, the river could never have consumed Horatio's patrimony.[23]

Before the flood, James Bridge's mansion and the shanties below bore witness that the failure of aristocratic culture in America did not preclude concentrations of wealth and power in the hands of those who mastered the market and the law. The passing of mid-Maine's resistance was but one of the early landmarks in the steady erosion of the republic of roughly equal small producers, the republic sought by the American Revolution. Over the course of the nineteenth century, industrial capitalism increasingly concentrated the wealth it created, widening the gap between the richest and the poorest. Most laboring people lost their independence as small producers to become the economic dependents of private corporations. Richard L. Bushman notes: "Republican princi-

ples were preeminent in the realm of words, not in the making of policy. In direct confrontations with powerful interests, independence and
equality yielded." In reaction, during the nineteenth century, hard-
pressed workers and farmers sustained a producers' ideology to damn
the rich and defend the workingman's right to the property his labor
created. In 1845 George Henry Evans's National Reformers attracted
considerable support in the upper Kennebec Valley; William Allen, Jr.,
approvingly cited their creed so reminiscent of what the Liberty Men
had said in his youth:

> Resolved, That the earth belongs to God, and he has given to every
> man an equal natural right to the use of light, air, earth, and water;
> and as it is from the earth we draw our subsistence, so any indi-
> vidual has a natural and inalienable right to the use of a sufficient
> quantity of land to afford him a comfortable subsistence, and it is
> not in the power of any government to make any just law which
> shall destroy that right.

But, after rapid but localized surges of fervent optimism, the populist
and workingman's movements of the nineteenth century collapsed, victims of the compelling Jeffersonian hope that the next election would
elevate the people's friends, would be enough to secure at last the elusive republic of small producers. By the early twentieth century most
Americans learned to accept inequality and dependence as essential to
the growing material prosperity that partially reached the middle and
working classes. Today the yeoman myth that we are a nation of the
economically autonomous has outlived its original congruence with material circumstances, as the plight of the few remaining family farmers
attests.[24]

In 1830, seven years before Hawthorne visited Augusta, a publisher
in the adjoining town of Hallowell issued a plain little book entitled *A
Narrative of Some of the Adventures, Dangers, and Sufferings of a Revolutionary Soldier*. The book's author, Joseph Plumb Martin of Prospect, had
lost the revolution he had sought. He was the son of a ne'er-do-well
Congregational minister whose unorthodox ideas cost him his parish
and forced him to become a cooper. In 1777 at age seventeen, Martin
enlisted as a private in the Connecticut Continental Line, and he served
to the war's end in 1783, rising in rank to sergeant. Left with nothing
but his musket, tattered uniform, and then worthless pay certificates,
Martin migrated to the Waldo Patent in search of a free homestead.
Regarding the Great Proprietors' claims as a threat to his tenuous, new-
found independence, Martin signed a protest petition to the General
Court in May 1790. Seven years later he accepted submission to the
Waldo Patent Commission as the best terms that he and his neighbors

could obtain; the commissioners assessed a $170 price for his one-hundred-acre homestead on Cape Jellison (now within the town of Stockton Springs).[25]

Wartime hardships had impaired his health. Further burdened by a retarded son and a sickly wife, Martin was hard-pressed to meet the December 1801 deadline for the submitting settlers to pay for their lots. When a September 1801 letter to Henry Knox begging for some remission went unanswered, Martin drafted a second plea:

> I have nothing more to add, for fear of offence, though Sir my heart is full enough. I throw myself and family wholy at the feet of your Honor's mercy, earnestly hoping that your Honour will think of some way, in your wisdom, that may be beneficial to your honor and save a poor family from distress. If your Honor can find it consistent with your own good to consider me, I again repeat my promise that I will do all within the compass of my small abilities to further your intrest in this place.

But, because Prospect's settlers had already come to terms, the general had little use for Martin's influence. In swallowing his pride to beg Knox for favor, Martin had humbled himself in vain. By 1811 his farm had shrunk to fifty acres—only eight improved—that yielded but ten bushels of grain and supported only three steers and two swine. He owned a frame house but no barn, no oxen, and no horse. By 1818 Martin had lost his homestead. Applying for a Revolutionary war veteran's pension, he deposed: "I have no real nor personal estate, nor any income whatever, my necessary bedding and wearing apparel excepted, except two cows, six sheep, one pig. I am a laborer, but by reason of age and infirmity I am unable to work. My wife is sickly and rheumatic. I have five children. . . . Without my pension I am unable to support myself and family." He procured a pension of eight dollars a month.[26]

Martin served in the Continental Line to secure free land as well as a free country, not a meager pension to hold off starvation. Martin's blasted hopes make sense of the biting humor and flashes of anger that characterize his reminiscences. Although General Knox is strangely absent from the volume, it seems likely that Martin's humiliating postwar relationship with the Great Proprietor shaped the memoir's emphasis on the soldiers' hardships and their disgust with their generally selfish and callous gentlemen officers. Martin repeatedly describes officers' helping themselves to the best housing, clothing, and food while ignoring their soldiers' plight. In the summer of 1780 when the enlisted men were without food, Martin saw butchers killing cattle "for the general officers (for they must have victuals, let the poor men fare as they would)." All Martin got that day was "an old ox's liver" that made him violently ill. "The liver still kept coming, and I looked at every heave for my own liver to come next, but that happened to be too well fastened to part from its moorings." He later concluded that the officers "did not feel the hardships which we had to undergo, and of course cared but little, if anything at all, about us." His wartime experiences anticipated the postwar land controversy in the Eastern Country, where, as proprietors, Generals Knox, Cobb, Jackson, Dearborn, and Lincoln demanded payments from settlers who frequently had been enlisted men.[27]

Martin felt that the common soldiery should have obtained free land after the war.

> When those who engaged to serve during the war enlisted, they were promised a hundred acres of land, each, which was to be in their own or adjoining states. When the country had drained the last drop of service it could screw out of the poor soldiers, they were turned adrift like old worn-out horses, and nothing said about land to pasture them upon. Congress did, indeed, appropriate lands under the denomination of "Soldier's lands," in Ohio state, or some state, or a future state, but no care was taken that the soldiers should get them. No agents were appointed to see that the poor fellows ever got possession of their lands; no one ever took the least care about it, except a pack of speculators, who were driving about the country like so many evil spirits, endeavoring to pluck the last feather from the soldiers. The soldiers were ignorant of the ways and means to obtain their bounty lands, and there was no one appointed to inform them. The truth was, none cared for them; the country was served, and faithfully served, and that was all that was deemed necessary. It was, soldiers, look to yourselves; we want no more of you. I hope I shall one day find land enough to lay my bones in. If I chance to die in a civilized country, none will deny me that. A dead body never begs a grave;—thanks for that.

He drew a radical lesson from his unfortunate experience. "The country was rigorous in exacting my compliance to *my* engagements to a punctilio, but equally careless in performing her contracts with me, and why so? One reason was because she had all the power in her own hands and I had none. Such things ought not to be."[28]

Mid-Maine Towns

Town	First Appearance in Census; Date of Incorporation	Frontcountry/ Backcountry; Resisting/ Nonresisting in 1800	Principal Patent
		Lincoln County	
Alna	1790; 1794	FC; NR	Plymouth
Appleton	1800; 1824	BC; R	Twenty Associates
Bath	1790; 1781	FC; NR	Indian deed claim
Boothbay	1790; 1764	FC; R	Indian deed claim
Bowdoin	1790; 1788	BC; R	Plymouth
Bowdoinham	1790; 1762	FC; NR	Plymouth
Bristol	1790; 1765	FC; R	Indian deed claim
Camden	1790; 1791	FC; NR	Twenty Associates
Cushing	1790; 1789	FC; NR	Waldo
Dresden	1790; 1794	FC; NR	Plymouth
Edgecomb	1790; 1774	FC; R	Indian deed claim
Friendship	1790; 1807	FC; NR	Waldo
Georgetown	1790; 1716	FC; NR	Indian deed claim
Hope	1790; 1804	BC; NR	Twenty Associates
Jefferson	1790; 1807	BC; R	Plymouth
Lewiston	1790; 1795	BC; R	Pejepscot
Liberty	1810; 1827	BC; R	Twenty Associates
Lisbon	1790; 1799	BC; R	Pejepscot
Litchfield	1790; 1795	BC; R	Plymouth
Montville	1800; 1807	BC; R	Twenty Associates
Newcastle	1790; 1775	FC; R	Indian deed claim
Nobleborough	1790; 1788	FC; R	Indian deed claim
Palermo	1790; 1804	BC; R	Plymouth

Patricktown	1800; —	BC; R	Plymouth
Putnam	1810; 1811	BC; R	Plymouth
Saint Georges	1790; 1803	FC; NR	Waldo
Thomaston	1790; 1777	FC; NR	Waldo
Topsham	1790; 1764	FC; NR	Pejepscot
Union	1790; 1786	BC; NR	Waldo
Waldoborough	1790; 1773	FC; R	Waldo
Wales	1790; 1816	BC; R	Plymouth
Warren	1790; 1776	FC; NR	Waldo
Whitefield	1790; 1809	BC; R	Plymouth
Wiscasset	1790; 1760	FC; NR	Indian deed claim
Woolwich	1790; 1775	FC; NR	Indian deed claim

Kennebec County

Augusta	1790; 1797	FC; NR	Plymouth
Belgrade	1790; 1796	BC; R	Plymouth
Chesterville	1790; 1802	BC; NR	Plymouth
China	1790; 1796	BC; NR	Plymouth
Clinton	1790; 1795	BC; R	Plymouth
Dearborn	1800; 1812	BC; R	Plymouth
Fairfax	1800; 1804	BC; R	Plymouth
Farmington	1790; 1794	BC; NR	other
Fayette	1790; 1795	BC; R	Plymouth
Freedom	1800; 1813	BC; R	Plymouth
Gardiner	1790; 1803	FC; R	Plymouth
Greene	1790; 1788	BC; R	Pejepscot
Hallowell	1790; 1771	FC; NR	Plymouth
Leeds	1790; 1801	BC; R	Pejepscot
Malta	1800; 1809	BC; R	Plymouth
Monmouth	1790; 1792	BC; R	Plymouth
Mount Vernon	1790; 1792	BC; R	Plymouth
New Sharon	1790; 1794	BC; R	Plymouth
Pittston	1790; 1779	FC; R	Plymouth
Readfield	1790; 1791	BC; NR	Plymouth

Rome	1800; 1804	BC; R	Plymouth
Sidney	1790; 1771	FC; NR	Plymouth
Temple	1800; 1803	BC; R	Plymouth
Troy	1810; 1812	BC; R	other
Unity	1790; 1804	BC; R	Plymouth
Unity Plantation	1810; —	BC; R	Plymouth
Vassalborough	1790; 1771	FC; NR	Plymouth
Vienna	1800; 1802	BC; R	Plymouth
Waterville	1790; 1802	FC; NR	Plymouth
Wayne	1790; 1798	BC; R	Plymouth
Wilton	1800; 1803	BC; NR	other
Winslow	1790; 1771	FC; NR	Plymouth
Winthrop	1790; 1771	BC; NR	Plymouth

Western Hancock County

Belfast	1790; 1773	FC; NR	Waldo
Belmont	1800; 1814	BC; R	Waldo
Brooks	1810; 1816	BC	Waldo
Frankfort	1790; 1789	FC; R	Waldo
Islesborough	1790; 1789	FC; NR	Waldo
Jackson	1810; 1818	BC	Waldo
Knox	1810; 1819	BC	Waldo
Lincolnville	1790; 1802	FC; NR	Waldo
Monroe	1810; 1818	BC; R	Waldo
Northport	1790; 1796	FC; NR	Waldo
Prospect	1790; 1794	FC; NR	Waldo
Searsmont	1800; 1814	BC; R	Waldo
Swanville	1800; 1818	BC; NR	Waldo
Thorndike	1800; 1819	BC; R	Waldo
Vinalhaven	1790; 1789	FC; NR	other
Waldo Plantation	1820; 1845	BC	Waldo

Tables

Table 1. Wealth Distribution in Two Mid-Maine Communities, 1791–1815

Quintile	Total Wealth	Proportion of Overall Wealth	No. of Taxpayers
	Balltown, 1791		
Wealthiest	$ 10,258	45.7%	38
Upper middle	5,795	25.8	38
Middle	4,008	17.8	38
Lower middle	1,962	8.7	38
Poorest	443	2.0	38
Overall	22,466	100.0	190
	Jefferson-Whitefield (Balltown), 1810		
Wealthiest	392,441	44.5	75
Upper middle	237,960	27.0	75
Middle	148,497	16.8	75
Lower middle	85,128	9.7	75
Poorest	18,026	2.0	76
Overall	882,052	100.0	376
	Ducktrap-Northport, 1798		
Wealthiest	36,343	50.3	35
Upper middle	15,441	21.4	35
Middle	10,346	14.3	35
Lower middle	6,317	8.8	35
Poorest	3,740	5.2	35
Overall	72,187	100.0	174

Lincolnville-Northport, 1815			
Wealthiest	80,314	46.0	57
Upper middle	40,216	23.1	57
Middle	27,038	15.5	57
Lower middle	18,518	10.6	57
Poorest	8,366	4.8	57
Overall	174,452	100.0	285

Sources: Balltown Tax Valuation Return, 1791, MSL; Jefferson and Whitefield Tax Valuation Returns, 1810, MSL; Ducktrap and Northport Federal Direct Tax Returns, 1798, NEHGSL; Hancock County Federal Direct Tax Returns, 1815, MeHS.

Table 2. Persistence in Three Mid-Maine Communities, 1790–1820

Status	1790–1800		1800–1810		1810–1820	
	No.	%	No.	%	No.	%
Balltown (Jefferson and Whitefield)						
Persisting	132	79.0	171	59.2	237	65.1
Departing	35	21.0	118	40.8	127	34.9
Total	167	100.0	289	100.0	364	⁓100.0
Sheepscot Great Pond Settlement (Palermo)						
Persisting	18	78.3	40	56.3	66	51.6
Departing	5	21.7	31	43.7	62	48.4
Total	23	100.0	71	100.0	128	100.0
Ducktrap–New Canaan (Northport and Lincolnville)						
Persisting	56	70.9	130	62.5	155	58.7
Departing	23	29.1	78	37.5	109	41.3
Total	79	100.0	208	100.0	264	100.0

Sources: Balltown, Sheepscot Great Pond settlement, Ducktrap, and New Canaan Manuscript Census Returns for 1790, M637, reel 2; Balltown, Sheepscot Great Pond settlement, Ducktrap, and Northport Manuscript Census Returns for 1800, M32, reels 6–7; Jefferson, Whitefield, Palermo, Northport, and Lincolnville Manuscript Census Returns for 1810, M252, reels 11–12; Jefferson, Whitefield, Palermo, Northport, and Lincolnville Manuscript Census Returns for 1820, M33, reels 34, 36. All four series are in the Records of the Bureau of the Census (RG 29), NA.

Table 3. Landholdings in Balltown (Jefferson-Whitefield)

A.	1791		1801		1811	
			Taxpayers			
Acres Owned	No.	%	No.	%	No.	%
0	15	7.9	17	9.3	56	14.9
1–50	17	8.9	21	11.5	51	13.6
51–100	84	44.2	55	30.2	132	35.1
101–150	26	13.7	46	25.3	80	21.3
151–200	26	13.7	21	11.5	21	5.6
201+	22	11.6	22	12.1	36	9.6
Total	190	100.0	182[a]	99.9	376[b]	100.1

B.	1791	1801	1811
Measure		No. of Acres	
Total	26,225	20,633	35,992
Mean	138.0	113.4	95.5
Standard deviation	118.2	84.5	86.5

Sources: 1791 Balltown, 1801 Balltown, 1811 Jefferson, and 1811 Whitefield tax valuation returns, MSL.

[a] 75 cases missing because of illegible portions of the valuations.

[b] 1 case missing because of illegible portion of the valuations.

Table 4. Improved Acreage in Balltown (Jefferson-Whitefield)

A.	1791		1801		1811	
Size of Acreage Owned			Taxpayers			
	No.	%	No.	%	No.	%
0	51	26.8	27	14.8	87	23.1
1–10	97	51.1	56	30.8	134	35.6
11–20	36	18.9	62	34.1	100	26.6
21+	6	3.2	37	20.3	55	14.6
Total	190	100.0	182[a]	100.0	376[b]	99.9

B.	1791	1801	1811
Measure		No. of Acres	
Total	1,259	2,340	4,029
Mean	6.6	12.9	10.7
Standard deviation	6.8	10.9	11.6

Sources: 1791 Balltown, 1801 Balltown, 1811 Jefferson, and 1811 Whitefield tax valuation returns, MSL.

Note: Deviations in totals from 100.0% in tables are due to rounding.

[a] 75 cases missing because of illegible portions of the valuations.

[b] 1 case missing because of illegible portion of the valuations.

Table 5. Mature Livestock Ownership in Balltown (Jefferson-Whitefield)

A.	1791		1801		1811	
Size of			Taxpayers			
Herd	No.	%	No.	%	No.	%
0	35	18.4	37	17.4	66	17.6
1–5	68	35.8	66	31.0	134	35.6
6–10	68	35.8	69	32.4	114	30.3
11+	19	10.0	41	19.2	62	16.5
Total	190	100.0	213[a]	100.0	376[b]	100.0

B.	1791	1801	1811
Measure		No. of Livestock	
Total	973	1,337	2,150
Mean	5.1	6.3	5.7
Standard deviation	4.4	5.1	4.5

Sources: 1791 Balltown, 1801 Balltown, 1811 Jefferson, 1811 Whitefield tax valuation returns, MSL.

Note: Mature livestock includes horses, oxen, cattle, and swine.

[a] 44 cases missing because of illegible portions of the valuations.

[b] 1 case missing because of illegible portion of valuations.

Table 6. Frame Structures Owned by Balltown (Jefferson-Whitefield) Taxpayers

Structures Owned	Taxpayers					
	1792		1801		1811	
	No.	%	No.	%	No.	%
Houses						
0	156	82.1	139	54.1	158	41.9
1+	34	17.9	118	45.9	219	58.1
Total	190	100.0	257	100.0	377	100.0
Barns						
0	109	57.4	126	49.0	159	42.2
1+	81	42.6	131	51.0	218	57.8
Total	190	100.0	257	100.0	377	100.0

Sources: 1792 Balltown, 1801 Balltown, 1811 Jefferson, 1811 Whitefield tax valuation returns, MSL.

Note: Those taxpayers that did not own frame houses lived in log houses.

Table 7. Grain Production per Balltown (Jefferson-Whitefield) Taxpayer

A.	1791		1801		1811	
Bushels Harvested	Taxpayers					
	No.	%	No.	%	No.	%
0	87	45.8	59	26.3	144	38.2
1–29	34	17.9	65	29.0	105	27.9
30+	69	36.3	100	44.6	128	33.9
Total	190	100.0	224[a]	99.9	377	100.0

B.	1791	1801	1811
Measure		No. of Bushels	
Total	3,934	6,106	7,608
Mean	20.7	27.3	20.2
Standard deviation	26.9	24.6	21.0

Sources: 1791 Balltown, 1801 Balltown, 1811 Jefferson, and 1811 Whitefield tax valuation returns, MSL.

[a] 33 cases missing because of illegible portions of the valuations.

Table 8. Mid-Maine Valuation Aggregates, 1793–1811

Region (No. of Towns)	Polls	Valuation	Per Poll
	1793		
Frontcountry (34)	5,273	$124,495.82	$23.61
Backcountry (14)	1,431	23,953.68	16.74
Overall (48)	6,704	148,449.50	22.14
	1802		
Frontcountry (36)	7,674	185,685.50	24.20
Backcountry (28)	3,800	71,732.37	18.88
Overall (64)	11,474	257,417.87	22.43
	1811		
Frontcountry (36)	11,676	313,506.89	26.85
Backcountry (47)	8,024	150,065.57	18.70
Overall (83)	19,700	463,572.46	23.53

Sources: *Abstract of the Report of the Committee of Valuation* (Boston, 1793; E 25771); *Report of the Committee of Valuation* (Boston, 1802; S-S 2625); *Report of the Committee of Valuation* (Boston, 1811; S-S 23322).

Table 9. Mid-Maine Population, 1790–1820

| | Distribution | | | | | | | |
| | 1790 | | 1800 | | 1810 | | 1820 | |
Region	No.	%	No.	%	No.	%	No.	%
Frontcountry	22,296	73.3	33,810	64.0	49,902	58.7	61,078	56.3
Backcountry	8,110	26.7	19,016	36.0	35,074	41.3	47,454	43.7
Overall	30,406	100.0	52,826	100.0	84,976	100.0	108,532	100.0

| | Percentage Growth | | |
Region	1790–1800	1800–1810	1810–1820
Frontcountry	51.6	47.6	22.4
Backcountry	134.5	84.4	35.3
Overall	73.7	60.9	27.7

Sources: Lincoln and Hancock (western half) County manuscript census returns for 1790, M637, reel 2; Lincoln, Hancock (western half), and Kennebec (southern two-thirds) County manuscript census returns for 1800, M32, reels 6–7; Lincoln, Hancock (western half), and Kennebec (southern two-thirds) County manuscript census returns for 1810, M252, reels 11–12; Lincoln, Hancock (western half), and Kennebec County manuscript census returns for 1820, M33, reels 34–36. All series belong to the Records of the Bureau of the Census (RG 29), NA.

Table 10. Mid-Maine's Age Structure, 1800–1820

Age Group in Years	1800		1810		1820	
	No.	%	No.	%	No.	%
	Frontcountry and Backcountry					
1–9	19,856	37.6	30,741	36.2	35,589	32.8
10–15	8,195	15.5	13,661	16.1	17,845	16.4
16–25	8,992	17.0	15,375	18.1	21,694	20.0
26–44	10,615	20.1	16,135	19.0	20,171	18.6
45 +	5,168	9.8	9,064	10.7	13,233	12.2
Total	52,826	100.0	84,976	100.0	108,532	100.0
	Backcountry					
1–9	7,690	40.4	13,286	37.9	16,302	34.4
10–15	3,011	15.8	5,637	16.1	7,858	16.6
16–25	2,973	15.6	6,076	17.3	9,092	19.2

26–44	3,935	20.7	6,480	18.5	8,709	18.4
45+	1,407	7.4	3,595	10.2	5,493	11.6
Total	19,016	100.0	35,074	100.0	47,454	100.0

Sources: Lincoln, Hancock (western half), and Kennebec (southern two-thirds) County manuscript census returns for 1800, M32, reels 6–7; Lincoln, Hancock (western half), and Kennebec (southern two-thirds) County manuscript census returns for 1810, M252, reels 11–12; Lincoln, Hancock (western half), and Kennebec County manuscript census returns for 1820, M33, reels 34–36. All series belong to the Records of the Bureau of the Census (RG 29), NA.

Table 11. Propertyholdings of Insurgents and Their Local Foes

A.	Property Owned			
	Indians	Chiefs	Tories	Overall
Woodland acres owned				
Mean	86.4	142.8	167.9	113.9
Standard deviation	81.2	79.1	225.0	134.3
Improved acres owned				
Mean	10.1	22.2	18.7	13.8
Standard deviation	10.6	14.7	14.0	13.0
Livestock owned				
Mean	5.4	10.5	8.4	6.8
Standard deviation	4.1	3.6	4.5	4.5

B.	Ownership of Property			
	Indians (N = 104)	Chiefs (N = 24)	Tories (N = 40)	Overall (N = 168)
Frame barns				
No. owning	56	21	36	113
% owning	53.8	87.5	90.0	67.3
Frame houses				
No. owning	53	20	31	104
% owning	51.0	83.3	77.5	61.9

Source: Tax valuation returns for Mid-Maine towns, 1791–1811, MSL.

Table 12. Age Distribution of Insurgents and Their Local Foes in 1800

Age Group	Indians		Chiefs		Tories	
	No.	%	No.	%	No.	%
0–25	16	12.6	2	6.2	0	0.0
26–44	98	77.2	16	50.0	29	70.7
45+	13	10.2	14	43.8	12	29.3
Total	127[a]	100.0	32[b]	100.0	41[c]	100.0

Sources: Lincoln, Hancock (western half), and Kennebec (southern two-thirds) County manuscript census returns for 1800, M32, reels 6–7, Records of the Bureau of the Census (RG 29), NA.

[a] 2 missing because of illegible portions of the census returns.

[b] 1 missing because of illegible portions of the census returns.

[c] 1 missing because of illegible portions of the census returns.

Table 13. Persistence of Insurgents and Their Local Foes, 1800–1820

Status	Indians		Chiefs		Tories	
	No.	%	No.	%	No.	%
	1800–1810					
Departing	46	35.7	8	24.2	17	38.6
Persisting	83	64.3	25	75.8	27	61.4
Total	129	100.0	33	100.0	44	100.0
	1810–1820					
Departing	81	49.1	13	39.4	22	42.3
Persisting	84	50.9	20	60.6	30	57.7
Total	165	100.0	33	100.0	52	100.0

Sources: Lincoln, Hancock (western half), and Kennebec (southern two-thirds) County manuscript census returns for 1800, M32, reels 6–7, for 1810, M252, reels 11–12; Lincoln, Hancock (western half), and Kennebec County manuscript census returns for 1820, M33, reels 34–36; all series belong to the Records of the Bureau of the Census (RG 29), NA.

Table 14. Occupational Status of Male Residents of Palermo, 1790–1820

Status	1790–1800		1800–1810		1810–1820	
	No.	%	No.	%	No.	%
Laborer	0	0.0	4	2.6	3	1.8
Yeoman or artisan	47	97.9	133	85.3	147	87.5
Gentleman or trader	1	2.1	18	11.5	15	8.9
Esquire	0	0.0	1	.6	3	1.8
Total	48[a]	100.0	156[b]	100.0	168[c]	100.0

Sources: 1790 Sheepscot Great Pond settlement, 1800 Sheepscot Great Pond settlement, 1810 Palermo, and 1820 Palermo manuscript census returns, Records of the Bureau of the Census (RG 29), NA; all deeds recorded by Palermo residents, 1790–1810, LCRD, LCC; all cases involving a Palermo resident or defendant, 1790–1819, LC-CCP, LCC.

[a] The status of another 43 heads of household could not be documented from either land deeds or a Court of Common Pleas suit.

[b] The status of another 174 heads of household could not be documented from either land deeds or a Court of Common Pleas suit.

[c] The status of another 114 heads of household could not be documented from either land deeds or a Court of Common Pleas suit.

Incidents of Extralegal Violence
Associated with the Land Controversies

Each entry lists: Date. Town or settlement / current town name [if different] (backcountry or frontcountry), county [in 1820]. Details. Source.

Note: because documentation for incidents before 1790 and after 1819 is so sparse, they have not been included in the calculations of the distribution of extralegal violence that appear in the text.

1761(?). Pownalborough North Parish / Alna (frontcountry), Lincoln County. At night a band of Indian-garbed settlers harass Dr. Silvester Gardiner, the principal Kennebeck Proprietor, by howling outside his lodging; frightened, the doctor takes precipitous flight out the back door and out of the valley. [Gershom Flagg], *A Strange Account of the Rising and Breaking of a Great Bubble* (Boston, 1767), 11.

June 25, 1761. Newcastle (frontcountry), Lincoln County. At night about forty men armed with stones, clubs, axes, and firebrands beset the log house of Joseph Hutchens, a supporter of the Kennebeck Proprietors' title; the crowd drives out Hutchens's tenant, destroys the house, his fences, and his supply of lumber. Hutchens to the Kennebeck Proprietors, November 2, 1768, KPP, box 2, MeHS.

December 6, 1768. Woolwich (frontcountry), Lincoln County. About thirty men "disguised in an Indian dress" beset and destroy a log house occupied by tenants holding under the Clarke and Lake proprietors. *Boston Evening Post*, December 26, 1768.

June 1785. Lisbon (backcountry), Lincoln County. Settlers' threats deter Amos Davis's attempted survey for the Pejepscot Proprietors. Davis to Josiah Little, June 22, 1785, PPP, box 17, EI.

1786. Islesborough (frontcountry), Hancock County. A crowd drives away Isaac Winslow, Jr., and Samuel Winslow, two visiting Waldo heirs. Henry Knox to Mrs. Horwood, January 13, 1789, HKP, LII, 9, MHS.

June 1788. Washington Plantation / Mount Vernon (backcountry), Kennebec County. Armed settlers drive out Mr. Sawyer, a surveyor for the Kennebeck Proprietors. Obediah Williams to James Bowdoin, June 9, 1788, KPP, box 3, MeHS.

January 1789. Waldoborough (frontcountry), Lincoln County. A crowd led by John Fitzgerald drives from town George Ulmer, a leading man who supports Henry Knox's claim. Isaac Winslow, Jr., to Henry Knox, January 25, 1789, HKP, XXIII, 84, MHS.

1790. Twenty-Five-Mile Pond settlement / Unity (backcountry), Kennebec County. Settlers armed with muskets interrupt Thomas Stone, a surveyor for the Kennebeck Proprietors, and break his compass. Stone to the Kennebeck Proprietors, April 2, 1806, KPP, box 6, MeHS.

August 1792. Mount Vernon (backcountry), Kennebec County. Settlers destroy the marks made by surveyors for the Kennebeck Proprietors. John Gilman to the Kennebeck Proprietors, August 1792, KPP, box 4, MeHS.

October 1792. Bristol (frontcountry), Lincoln County. Settlers armed with muskets interrupt Elijah Crocker, a surveyor for an Indian deed proprietor. Elijah Crocker deposition, October 24, 1792, provided by Wayne Reilly of Bangor.

January 1793. Danville / Auburn (backcountry), Cumberland County. David Hildreth assaults John Merrill, a neighbor who supports the Pejepscot Proprietors' claim, and steals his logging tools. John Merrill deposition, January 31, 1801, PPP, box 12, EI.

April 28, 1793. Ducktrap Plantation / Lincolnville (frontcountry), Hancock County. Samuel Ely leads a crowd that destroys the milldam belonging to George and Philip Ulmer, leading men who support General Henry Knox's land claim. Ulmer v. Ely, April 1796, HC-CCP Record Book, II, case 197, MeSA.

September 19, 1793. Castine (frontcountry), Hancock County. Armed with a club, Samuel Ely assaults Job Pendleton, a General Knox supporter. Commonwealth v. Ely, box 77, HC-CGSP, MeSA.

January 1, 1794. Islesborough (frontcountry), Hancock County. A crowd armed with clubs and loyal to Samuel Ely assaults Prince Holbrook, a General Knox supporter. Commonwealth v. Williams, 1794, box 77, HC-CGSP, MeSA.

October 1795. Balltown / Jefferson (backcountry), Lincoln County. Settlers armed with muskets interrupt Ephraim Ballard's attempt to survey the Plymouth Patent's southeast corner for the Kennebeck Proprietors. Ballard to the Kennebeck Proprietors, January 1, 1796, KPP, box 4, MeHS.

October 1795. Balltown / Jefferson (backcountry), Lincoln County. Armed settlers interrupt Ephraim Ballard's renewed attempt to survey the Plymouth Patent's southeastern corner. Ballard to the Kennebeck Proprietors, January 1, 1796, KPP, box 4, MeHS.

November 12, 1795. Balltown / Jefferson (backcountry), Lincoln County. A dozen armed and blacked settlers surprise Ephraim Ballard's camp and destroy his survey plans and compass. Ballard deposition, November 20, 1795, Related Papers, January 29, 1799, Resolve, MA.

November 14, 1795. Balltown / Jefferson (backcountry), Lincoln County. Armed settlers obstruct and chase away Benjamin Poor, a surveyor suspected of working for the Kennebeck Proprietors. Poor deposition, November 25, 1795, Related Papers, January 29, 1799, Resolve, MA.

November 1795. Balltown / Jefferson (backcountry), Lincoln County. Armed settlers obstruct Benjamin Poor's renewed attempt to run survey lines. Poor deposition, November 25, 1795, Related Papers, January 29, 1799, Resolve, MA.

November 1795. Balltown / Jefferson (backcountry), Lincoln County. Armed settlers obstruct Benjamin Poor's third attempt to run survey lines. Poor deposition, November 25, 1795, Related Papers, January 29, 1799, Resolve, MA.

November 15, 1795. Balltown / Jefferson (backcountry), Lincoln County. At night, set fires destroy two barns belonging to Jonathan Jones, a supporter of the Kennebeck Proprietors. Jones deposition, February 1796, Related Papers, January 29, 1799, Resolve, MA.

December 23, 1795. Clinton (backcountry), Kennebec County. Settlers destroy survey marks made on behalf of the Kennebeck Proprietors' claim. Gershom Flagg to Joseph North, December 27, 1795, KPP, box 4, MeHS.

December 23, 1795. Clinton (backcountry), Kennebec County. Settlers nocturnally steal a horse belonging to a chainman in a survey party working for the Kennebeck Proprietors. Gershom Flagg to Joseph North, December 27, 1795, KPP, box 4, MeHS.

January 30, 1796. Minot (backcountry), Cumberland County. Settlers harass and plunder loggers working for the Pejepscot Proprietors. Michael Little deposition, December 31, 1796, PPP, box 10, EI.

February 6, 1796. Minot (backcountry), Cumberland County. Settlers set a nocturnal fire that destroys the hay and damages the oxen hovel belonging to loggers working for the Pejepscot Proprietors. Michael Little deposition, December 31, 1796, PPP, box 10, EI.

February 1796. Castine (frontcountry), Hancock County. At night a set fire damages a sawmill belonging to Leonard and Philip Jarvis, proprietors. Isaac Parker to Henry Knox, March 1, 1796, HKP, XXXVIII, 149, MHS.

July 1796. Pittston (frontcountry), Kennebec County. Settlers assault a deputy sheriff bearing writs for the Kennebeck Proprietors. Commonwealth v. Smith, 1797, LC-SJC, box 402, LCC.

July 8, 1796. New Milford / Alna (frontcountry), Lincoln County. Settlers led by Isaac Prince mob John Trueman, an agent for the Draper heirs, and destroy his papers. John Trueman to Governor Adams, October 3, 1796, CF, box 10, MA.

July 14, 1796. Ducktrap / Lincolnville (frontcountry), Hancock County. At night settlers cast loose a boom, setting adrift and scattering spars belonging to George Ulmer, Philip Ulmer, and Henry Knox. George Ulmer to Knox, July 15, 1796, HKP, XXXIX, 112, MA.

September 11, 1796. Ducktrap / Lincolnville (frontcountry), Hancock County. At night settlers cast loose a boom, setting adrift and scattering spars belonging to George Ulmer, Philip Ulmer, and Henry Knox. Knox to George Ulmer, September 14, 1796, HKP, XXXIX, 144, MA.

March 1797. New Milford / Alna (frontcountry), Lincoln County. A crowd of armed settlers extorts provisions from Thomas Fairservice, a proprietary supporter in their community. Fairservice deposition, March 30, 1797, CF, box 11, MA.

March 29, 1797. Wiscasset (frontcountry), Lincoln County. At night a crowd in excess of two hundred settlers from New Milford and Balltown marches into Wiscasset, surrounds the jail, and liberates prisoners suspected of mobbing John Trueman in July 1796. Fannie S. Chase, *Wiscasset in Pownalborough* (Wiscasset, 1941), 130.

May 5, 1797. Wiscasset (frontcountry), Lincoln County. At night settlers from New Milford steal and hold for ransom a horse belonging to Manassah Smith, the lawyer for the Draper heirs. Smith to John Trueman, May 6, 1797, CF, box 11, MA.

May 1797. New Milford / Alna (frontcountry), Lincoln County. At night six to eight men break windows in the house belonging to Stuart Hunt, a leading man who supported the Draper heirs' claim. Manassah Smith to John Trueman, May 6, 1797, CF, box 11, MA.

May 8, 1797. New Milford / Alna (frontcountry), Lincoln County. At night settlers break two windows in the house belonging to Stuart Hunt, a leading man who supported the Draper heirs' claim. Thomas Hunt to Stuart Hunt, May 9, 1797, CF, box 11, MA.

June 1797. Augusta (frontcountry), Kennebec County. Two hillcountry settlers visit Augusta to hurl rocks through the windows of the house belonging to Dr. Daniel Cony, an agent for the Kennebeck Proprietors. Commonwealth v. Fish and Webber, 1798, LC-SJC, box 402, LCC.

November 18, 1797. Pittston (frontcountry), Kennebec County. Settlers from Balltown harass the house of Ebenezer Pratt, a proprietary supporter. Pratt v. Moody, KC-SJC, June 1801, Record Book, I, 102, MeSA.

March 1799. Lewiston (backcountry), Lincoln County. At night seven to eight armed men fire shots outside the house of Amos Davis, a supporter of the Pejepscot Proprietors. Davis deposition, January 29, 1801, PPP, box 12, EI.

September 25, 1799. Danville / Auburn (backcountry), Cumberland County. At night settlers fire shots outside the house of Peter Merrill, a supporter of the Pejepscot Proprietors. Martha Merrill deposition, January 31, 1801, PPP, box 12, EI.

October 1799. Danville / Auburn (backcountry), Cumberland County. A crowd breaks into Peter Merrill's barn to seize and destroy a chaise belonging to Josiah Little, a Pejepscot Proprietor. Martha Merrill deposition, January 31, 1801, PPP, box 12, EI.

May 5, 1800. Greene (backcountry), Kennebec County. More than a dozen men disguised as Indians and armed with muskets obstruct Lothrop Lewis's survey for the Pejepscot Proprietors and erase his memorandum book. Lewis to Josiah Little, May 14, 1800, PPP, box 4, EI.

June 7, 1800. Davistown / Montville (backcountry), Lincoln County. Armed settlers seize, threaten, and release George Ulmer, an agent for Henry Knox. Commonwealth v. Smith, June 1801, HC-SJC, box 167, MeSA.

July 1800. Danville / Auburn (backcountry), Cumberland County. Peter Merrill, a supporter of the Pejepscot Proprietors, is assaulted by settlers led by David Hildreth. Merrill deposition, January 31, 1801, PPP, box 12, EI.

July 1, 1800. Danville / Auburn (backcountry), Cumberland County. At night armed men fire shots outside the house belonging to Peter Merrill, a supporter of the Pejepscot Proprietors. Martha Merrill deposition, January 31, 1801, PPP, box 12, EI.

July 7, 1800. Alna (frontcountry), Lincoln County. Deputy Sheriff Pitt Dillingham is obstructed by armed settlers while serving proprietary writs. Commonwealth v. Davis, 1800, LC-SJC, box 403, LCC.

July 13, 1800. Lewiston (backcountry), Lincoln County. At night settlers plunder the tools from a sawmill leased by Josiah Little of the Pejepscot Proprietors to Stephen Chase, a proprietary supporter. Chase deposition, July 13, 1800, PPP, box 12, EI.

July 14, 1800. Lewiston (backcountry), Lincoln County. At night a shot is fired into the wood house belonging to Amos Davis, a surveyor for the Pejepscot Proprietors. Davis deposition, January 19, 1801, PPP, box 12, EI.

July 14, 1800. Lewiston (backcountry), Lincoln County. At night a shot is fired through the window of a house belonging to Stephen Chase, a supporter of the Pejepscot Proprietors. Chase deposition, January 27, 1801, PPP, box 12, EI.

July 18, 1800. Lincoln Plantation / Thorndike (backcountry), Hancock County. Indian-disguised men fire upon surveyors led by Robert Houston and working for Henry Knox; three men are wounded. Houston deposition, August 14, 1800, Related Papers, November 15, 1800, Resolve, MA.

July 23, 1800. Lewiston (backcountry), Lincoln County. Two shots are fired at night through two windows of the house belonging to Stephen Chase, a supporter of the Pejepscot Proprietors. Chase deposition, January 27, 1801, PPP, box 12, EI.

August 7, 1800. Lewiston (backcountry), Lincoln County. At night a crowd surrounds and fires shots into a house belonging to Robert Anderson, a supporter of the Pejepscot Proprietors. Anderson deposition, January 26, 1801, PPP, box 12, EI.

August 1800. Fairfax / Albion (backcountry), Kennebec County. Armed settlers chase away Nathan Winslow, a surveyor for the Kennebeck Proprietors. *Castine Journal*, September 19, 1800.

August 14, 1800. Lewiston (backcountry), Lincoln County. At night a dozen armed settlers discharge their muskets around the house of Robert Anderson, a supporter of the Pejepscot Proprietors. Jacob Anderson deposition, January 26, 1801, PPP, box 12, EI.

August 14, 1800. Lewiston (backcountry), Lincoln County. At night about twenty armed men discharge muskets outside the house of Stephen Chase, a supporter of the Pejepscot Proprietors. Chase deposition, January 27, 1801, PPP, box 12, EI.

September 16, 1800. Litchfield (backcountry), Lincoln County. Armed men fire shots to frighten away surveyors led by John Torsey and working for a Kennebeck Proprietor. Commonwealth v. Neal, September 1800, KC-SJC, box 72, MeSA.

September 21, 1800. Monmouth (backcountry), Kennebec County. Settlers rescue a comrade arrested on suspicion of firing on John Torsey's survey for a Kennebeck Proprietor. Commonwealth v. Lambert, June 1801, KC-SJC, box 72, MeSA.

September 22, 1800. Lewiston (backcountry), Lincoln County. A crowd of more than twenty disguised and armed men hurl stones and fire shots into the house of Ezra Purrinton, where Josiah Little, the principal Pejepscot Proprietor, is lodging; Little receives slight wounds. Purrinton deposition, January 27, 1801, PPP, box 12, EI.

October 1800. Balltown / Jefferson (backcountry), Lincoln County. John Bumford steals two head of livestock and kills two more, all belonging to a John Parker, a supporter of the Kennebeck Proprietors' claim. Parker v. Bumford, May 1802, LC-SJC, box 413, LCC.

October 1800. Lisbon (backcountry), Lincoln County. Armed settlers obstruct surveyors working for a Kennebeck Proprietor. Charles Vaughan to James Bowdoin, October 16, 1800, KPP, box 4, MeHS.

October 1, 1800. Lewiston (backcountry), Lincoln County. At night a crowd of armed and disguised men fires shots around the house of Ezra Purrinton, a supporter of the Pejepscot Proprietors' claim. Joseph Field deposition, January 29, 1801, PPP, box 12, EI.

October 8, 1800. Lewiston (backcountry), Lincoln County. Several men throw down a fence and gate belonging to Ezra Purrinton, a supporter of the Pejepscot Proprietors' claim. Purrinton deposition, January 27, 1801, PPP, box 12, EI.

October 13, 1800. Lewiston (backcountry), Lincoln County. At night men harass Ezra Purrinton, a supporter of the Pejepscot Proprietors' claim, by throwing down a fence, hurling stones at his house, and making "a Headious Noise." Purrinton deposition, January 27, 1801, PPP, box 12, EI.

November 1, 1800. Lewiston (backcountry), Lincoln County. At night men hurl noise and stones at the house belonging to Ezra Purrinton, a supporter of the Pejepscot Proprietors' claim. Mary Purrinton deposition, January 29, 1801, PPP, box 12, EI.

November 4, 1800. Lewiston (backcountry), Lincoln County. At night a "grate Number of Stons" hurled at the house belonging to Ezra Purrinton, a supporter of the Pejepscot Proprietors' claim. Mary Purrinton deposition, January 29, 1801, PPP, box 12, EI.

November 4, 1800. Lewiston (backcountry), Lincoln County. At night men tear down a fence and hurl stones at a house, both belonging to William Carvill, a supporter of the Pejepscot Proprietors' claim. Carvill deposition, January 27, 1801, PPP, box 12, EI.

November 26, 1800. Lewiston (backcountry), Lincoln County. At night a group of armed settlers hurls stones at the house belonging to Ezra Purrinton, a supporter of the Pejepscot Proprietors' claim. William Carvill deposition, January 27, 1801, PPP, box 12, EI.

December 1800. Little Gore / Auburn (backcountry), Cumberland County. At night several persons fire shots around the house of Peter Merrill, a supporter of the Pejepscot Proprietors' claim. Merrill deposition, January 31, 1801, PPP, box 12, EI.

June 1, 1801. Balltown / Jefferson (backcountry), Lincoln County. John Bumford lets loose cattle to damage crops belonging to John Parker, a supporter of the Kennebeck Proprietors' claim. Parker v. Bumford, May 1802, LC-SJC, box 413, LCC.

June 19, 1801. Lincoln Plantation / Thorndike (backcountry), Hancock County. Armed and Indian-disguised settlers fire on surveyors led by Robert Houston and working for Henry Knox; one man is wounded. Houston to Knox, June 26, 1801, HKP, XLIV, 13, MHS.

June 23, 1801. Twenty-Five-Mile Pond settlement / Unity (backcountry), Kennebec County. Settlers kill a horse belonging to John H. Boody, a neighbor who had assisted Henry Knox's surveys. Boody v. Parkhurst, May 1802, HC-CCP Record Book, IV, case 64, MeSA.

June 26, 1801. Northport (frontcountry), Hancock County. Armed and Indian-disguised settlers from the hillcountry seize a blacksmith to obtain information about comrades arrested and held in adjoining Belfast. Robert Houston to Knox, June 26, 1801, HKP, XLIV, 13, MHS.

July 4, 1801. Davistown / Montville (backcountry), Lincoln County. Several hundred armed men muster and prepare to march on Castine to liberate comrades arrested for firing upon Henry Knox's surveyors. John Scobey deposition, July 9, 1801, HKP, XLIV, 3, MHS.

September 3, 1801. Twenty-Five-Mile Pond settlement / Unity (backcountry), Kennebec County. At night a set fire destroys the barn of Benjamin Bartlett, who had assisted Henry Knox's surveys. George Ulmer to Knox, September 5, 1801, HKP, XLIV, 71, MHS.

September 3, 1801. Lincoln Plantation / Thorndike (backcountry), Hancock County. At night a set fire destroys the barn of Joseph Jones, who had assisted Henry Knox's surveys. George Ulmer to Knox, September 5, 1801, HKP, XLIV, 71, MHS.

September 10, 1801. Jackson (backcountry), Hancock County. Armed settlers burn a stack of hay belonging to the Cates family, who had assisted Henry Knox's surveys. John Cates *et al.* deposition, October 31, 1801, HKP, XLIV, 117, MHS.

September 10, 1801. Jackson (backcountry), Hancock County. Armed settlers systematically destroy the boundary and line markers left by surveyors for Henry Knox. John Gleason to Knox, September 24, 1801, HKP, XLIV, 89, MHS.

November 28, 1801. Balltown / Jefferson (backcountry), Lincoln County. John Bumford sets a fire that destroys the barn, crops, and livestock belonging to John Parker, a supporter of the Kennebeck Proprietors' claim. Parker v. Bumford, May 1802, LC-CCP, box 413, LCC.

August 1802. Balltown / Jefferson (backcountry), Lincoln County. Armed settlers obstruct the attempt by Ephraim Ballard to survey the southeast corner of the Plymouth Patent. January 1803 entry, KPP, Record Book, IV, 13, MeHS.

August 1802. Fairfax / Albion (backcountry), Kennebec County. Armed and Indian-disguised settlers obstruct attempt by Charles Vaughan to run survey lines for the Kennebeck Proprietors. Vaughan to Thomas L. Winthrop, August 29, 1802, KPP, box 5, MeHS.

September 13, 1802. Waldoborough (frontcountry), Lincoln County. Armed settlers disrupt attempt by John Malcom to run lines for Henry Knox. Commonwealth v. Schwartz, June 1803, LC-SJC, Record Book, II, 78, LCC.

October 21, 1802. Sheepscot Great Pond Plantation / Palermo (backcountry), Lincoln County. At night a set fire consumes the barn, stored crops, and livestock belonging to Robert Foye, a supporter of the Kennebeck Proprietors' claim. Daniel Davis to the General Court, n.d., Related Papers, February 10, 1804, Resolve, MA.

October 21, 1802. Wiscasset (frontcountry), Lincoln County. Armed settlers from the hillcountry break open the county jail and set John Bumford free. Daniel Davis to the General Court, n.d., Related Papers, February 10, 1804, Resolve, MA.

April 26, 1803. Balltown / Jefferson (backcountry), Lincoln County. At night, set fires destroy two sawmills belonging to Jeremiah Pearson, a supporter of the Kennebeck Proprietors' claim. Commonwealth v. Preble, LC-SJC, Record Book, II, 215, LCC.

September 1803. Balltown / Jefferson (backcountry), Lincoln County. Armed settlers obstruct attempt by Lothrop Lewis to survey the southeast corner of the Plymouth Patent. Charles Vaughan to Thomas L. Winthrop, September 19, 1803, KPP, box 5, MeHS.

September 1803. Fairfax / Albion (backcountry), Kennebec County. Armed settlers obstruct a Kennebeck Proprietors' survey. Charles Vaughan to Thomas L. Winthrop, September 19, 1803, KPP, box 5, MeHS.

August 18, 1804. Bowdoin (backcountry), Lincoln County. At night a set fire consumes the dwelling house of Francis Nicholas, a supporter of the Kennebeck Proprietors' claim. Commonwealth v. Temple, June 1805, LC-SJC, Record Book, II, 174, LCC.

September 25, 1804. Bowdoin (backcountry), Lincoln County. Settlers steal and mutilate a horse belonging to John Merrill, a surveyor working for Bowdoin College. Silas Lee to Bowdoin College, November 7, 1804, Related Papers, March 1, 1805, Resolve, MA.

September 26, 1804. Bowdoin (backcountry), Lincoln County. Armed settlers fire shots and issue threats to frighten surveyors working for Bowdoin College. Silas Lee to Bowdoin College, November 7, 1804, Related Papers, March 1, 1805, Resolve, MA.

September 27, 1804. Bowdoin (backcountry), Lincoln County. Armed settlers obstruct surveyors working for Bowdoin College; they give up the attempt. Silas Lee to Bowdoin College, November 7, 1804, Related Papers, March 1, 1805, Resolve, MA.

May 1805. Balltown / Jefferson (backcountry), Lincoln County. Armed settlers obstruct Lothrop Lewis's renewed attempt to survey the Plymouth Patent's southeast corner. Charles Vaughan to the Kennebeck Proprietors, May 26, 1805, KPP, box 5, MeHS.

August 10, 1805. Patricktown / Somerville (backcountry), Lincoln County. Rufus Plummer leads an armed settler party that obstructs Deputy Sheriff Josiah Norris and robs him of his writs on behalf of the Kennebeck Proprietors. State of Maine v. Plummer, May 1822, LC-SJC, Record Book, V, 284, LCC.

1806. New Waterford / Windsor (backcountry), Lincoln County. Settlers destroy house belonging to Richard Meagher, a leading man who supports the Kennebeck Proprietors' claim. Meagher to the General Court, February 6, 1809, Unpassed House File 6385, MA.

1806. Monroe (backcountry), Hancock County. Armed settlers obstruct a proprietary survey. *Republican Journal* (Belfast), February 16, 1882.

March 1806. Balltown / Jefferson (backcountry), Lincoln County. Armed settlers obstruct Charles Turner's effort to survey the Plymouth Patent's southeastern corner. Charles Vaughan to the Kennebeck Proprietors, March 21, 1806, KPP, box 6, MeHS.

June 1, 1806. Fairfax / Albion (backcountry), Kennebec County. Nathan Barlow leads a settler party that publicly humiliates John Harvey, a proprietary supporter, by riding him through the settlement on a rail. Harvey v. Fowler, December 1807, KC-CCP, box 9, MeSA.

June 24, 1806. New Waterford / Windsor (backcountry), Lincoln County. Thomas LeBallister leads settlers, who destroy a pile of clapboards belonging to Richard Meagher, a leading man who supports the Kennebeck Proprietors' claim. Commonwealth v. LeBallister, September 1807, LC-SJC, Record Book, III, 134, LCC.

July 15, 1806. Fairfax / Albion (backcountry), Kennebec County. Nathan Barlow leads a settler party that besets the house of John Harvey, a proprietary supporter. Harvey v. Fowler, December 1807, KC-CCP, box 9, MeSA.

September 11, 1806. Lisbon (backcountry), Lincoln County. About sixty armed settlers fire shots to scare away William F. Gilmore, a surveyor for the Kennebeck Proprietors. Commonwealth v. Jones, June 1807, LC-SJC, Record Book, III, 42, LCC.

April 14, 1807. Unity (backcountry), Kennebec County. Armed settlers pull down a log cabin belonging to William Banton, a suspected proprietary sympathizer. Banton v. Brown, August 1807, KC-CCP, Record Book, VII, 213, MeSA.

May 7, 1807. Belgrade (backcountry), Kennebec County. Settlers led by John Locke destroy a mill dam belonging to John Jones, a Kennebeck Proprietor. Commonwealth v. Locke, September 1807, KC-SJC, box 72, MeSA.

June 1807. Litchfield (backcountry), Lincoln County. A party of armed settlers fires shots to frighten away surveyors for the Kennebeck Proprietors. Charles Vaughan to Gov. James Sullivan, June 13, 1807, KPP, box 6, MeHS.

October 1807. Greene Plantation / Belmont (backcountry), Hancock County. Settlers burn an effigy of Brentnall Witherell, a blacksmith who supported the proprietor Benjamin Joy. John Wilson to Joy, November 2, 1807, WKP, box 7, MeHS.

October 1807. Greene Plantation / Belmont (backcountry), Hancock County. Armed and Indian-disguised settlers obstruct Deputy Sheriff Francis Anderson bearing ejectment writs for Benjamin Joy. John Wilson to Joy, November 2, 1807, WKP, box 7, MeHS.

October 1807. Greene Plantation / Belmont (backcountry), Hancock County. A crowd harasses the house where Deputy Sheriff Thomas Cunningham has lodged for the night. John Wilson to Benjamin Joy, November 2, 1807, WKP, box 7, MeHS.

October 1807. Greene Plantation / Belmont (backcountry), Hancock County. Indian-disguised settlers ambush Deputy Sheriff Thomas Cunningham, killing his horse and stealing his ejectment writs. John Wilson to Benjamin Joy, November 2, 1807, WKP, box 7, MeHS.

November 1807. Litchfield (backcountry), Lincoln County. Armed settlers fire shots to frighten the surveyors led by Deacon John Neal for the Kennebeck Proprietors. Neal to the General Court, n.d., Related Papers, March 3, 1810, Resolve, MA.

November 1807. Litchfield (backcountry), Lincoln County. A second day of gunshots induces Deacon John Neal to suspend his survey for the Kennebeck Proprietors. Neal to the General Court, n.d., Related Papers, March 3, 1810, Resolve, MA.

November 1807. Fairfax / Albion (backcountry), Kennebec County. Armed and Indian-disguised settlers stop Deputy Sheriff Jason D. Cony and destroy all his writs of ejectment for the Kennebeck Proprietors. Arthur Lithgow to Gov. James Sullivan, January 7, 1808, CF, box 16, MA.

November 24, 1807. Fairfax / Albion (backcountry), Kennebec County. Armed and Indian-disguised settlers ambush Deputy Sheriff Henry Johnson, wounding him and killing his horse. Johnson deposition, December 14, 1807, CF, box 16, MA.

November 25, 1807. Fairfax / Albion (backcountry), Kennebec County. A party of armed and Indian-disguised settlers temporarily detains Deputy Sheriff Henry Johnson and destroys his saddle, saddlebags, and pistols. Johnson deposition, December 14, 1807, CF, box 16, MA.

December 1807. Greene Plantation / Belmont (backcountry), Hancock County. Settlers shoot at the cattle in a barn belonging to Brentnall Witherell, a blacksmith loyal to the proprietor Benjamin Joy. John Wilson to Joy, January 7, 1807, WKP, box 7, MeHS.

December 28, 1807. Litchfield (backcountry), Lincoln County. A dozen armed and Indian-disguised men visit Deputy Sheriff Hugh Mulloy's farm; they threaten him, fire a shot into his house, and kill his horse. Mulloy petition to the General Court, n.d., Related Papers, March 3, 1810, Resolve, MA.

December 31, 1807. Fairfax / Albion (backcountry), Kennebec County. Armed and Indian-disguised men obstruct Deputy Sheriff John O. Webster, who is bearing writs for the Kennebeck Proprietors. Webster deposition, February 12, 1808, CF, box 16, MA.

July 1808. Gardiner (frontcountry), Kennebec County. A squatter family violently resists ejectment by a posse working for Robert Hallowell Gardiner, a Kennebeck Proprietor. Gardiner v. Dunlap, October 1808, KC-SJC, box 73, MeSA.

February 9, 1808. Fairfax / Albion (backcountry), Kennebec County. Armed and Indian-disguised men obstruct Deputy Sheriff John O. Webster, shoot and eat his horse, and burn his sleigh. Webster deposition, February 12, 1808, CF, box 16, MA.

February 12, 1808. Sidney (frontcountry), Kennebec County. A crowd of armed and Indian-disguised men from the hillcountry call on a Mr. Foster to demand money. Samuel Titcomb to Gov. James Sullivan, February 14, 1808, CF, box 16, MA.

March 15, 1808. Jackson (backcountry), Hancock County. Armed and Indian-disguised men intercept Deputy Sheriff Andrew Grant and destroy his writs. Grant deposition, May 18, 1808, James Sullivan Papers, MHS.

March 16, 1808. Augusta (frontcountry), Kennebec County. Someone sets fire to the Kennebec County courthouse. Joseph North to Gov. James Sullivan, March 19, 1808, Unpassed House File 6382, MA.

March 16, 1808. Bridgestown / Troy (backcountry), Kennebec County. Armed and Indian-disguised men assault Deputy Sheriff John Rodgers. Rodgers's complaint, January 5, 1809, KC-SJC, box 73, MeSA.

March 18, 1808. Lee Plantation / Swanville (backcountry), Hancock County. Armed and Indian-disguised settlers intercept and turn back Deputy Sheriff Andrew Grant. Grant deposition, May 18, 1808, James Sullivan Papers, MHS.

April 1808. Jackson (backcountry), Hancock County. Armed and Indian-disguised men stop Daniel Clary, a man posing as a deputy sheriff to serve his own writs. George Ulmer to Gov. James Sullivan, May 20, 1808, CF, box 17, MA.

April 18, 1808. Fairfax / Albion (backcountry), Kennebec County. Armed and Indian-disguised men led by Nathan Barlow rescue Daniel Brackett from the constable Moses Robinson, whom they strip naked and beat with sticks. John Chandler to Gov. James Sullivan, April 25, 1808, Unpassed House File 6381, MA.

May 1808. Beaver Hill / Freedom (backcountry), Kennebec County. Nathan Barlow leads a party of White Indians to drive out Moses Nelson, a new settler who refused to join the resistance. James W. North, *The History of Augusta . . .* (Augusta, 1870), 357.

May 1, 1808. Belgrade (backcountry), Kennebec County. Armed settlers assault Deputy Sheriff Edward Fuller. Commonwealth v. Sanderson, October 1808, KC-SJC, box 74, MeSA.

June 1808. Belgrade (backcountry), Kennebec County. White Indians ambush Deputy Sheriff Pitt Dillingham, killing his horse. North, *Augusta*, 354.

June 1808. Industry (backcountry), Kennebec County. Armed and

Indian-disguised settlers obstruct Lemuel Perham's attempt to survey for the Kennebeck Proprietors. Perham to Bridge and Williams, August 18, 1808, KPP, box 7, MeHS.

July 1808. Palermo (backcountry), Lincoln County. Armed White Indians obstruct Bradstreet Wiggins's attempt to survey northern Palermo for the Kennebeck Proprietors. Arodi Thayer to Bridge and Williams, August 1, 1808, KPP, Record Book, I, 250, MeHS.

August 1808. Belgrade (backcountry), Kennebec County. Armed White Indians rescue their oxen and assault constable Simon Lord. Lord petition to the General Court, n.d., Related Papers, February 8, 1810, Resolve, MA.

August 29, 1808. Rome (backcountry), Kennebec County. Armed White Indians shoot a horse out from under Deputy Sheriff Jesse Robinson. Robinson petition, n.d., Related Papers, June 14, 1809, Resolve, MA.

November 7, 1808. Litchfield (backcountry), Lincoln County. A set fire destroys the barn of Deacon John Neal, a leading man who had endorsed the Kennebeck Proprietors' survey efforts. Neal to the General Court, n.d., Related Papers, March 3, 1810, Resolve, MA.

December 2, 1808. Palermo (backcountry), Lincoln County. Armed men in Indian disguise search the house of Jonathan Greeley, a leading man who supported the Kennebeck Proprietors' claim, for papers and for a proprietary surveyor; finding nothing, they depart. *Portland Gazette*, December 19, 1808.

December 16, 1808. Northport (frontcountry), Hancock County. At night a set fire destroys the barn of Paul H. Stevens, a deputy sheriff. Commonwealth v. Jackson, JC-SJC, box 167, MeSA.

January 1809. Jackson (backcountry), Hancock County. Armed settlers beat Deputy Sheriff Captain Leavitt and destroy his writs. Philo H. Washburn to George Ulmer, February 27, 1809, CF, box 17, MA.

January 11, 1809. Fairfield (backcountry), Kennebec County. Two men in Indian disguise shoot the horse of Joseph Spaulding, a deputy sheriff. Spaulding deposition, January 18, 1809, Related Papers, March 3, 1809, Resolve, MA.

February 1809. Knox (backcountry), Hancock County. Armed and Indian-garbed settlers obstruct Deputy Sheriff Paul H. Stevens. George Ulmer to Gov. James Sullivan, March 4, 1809, CF, box 17, MA.

June 18, 1809. Carritunk (backcountry), Kennebec County. Armed White Indians harass Charles Pierce, a blacksmith. Commonwealth v. Green, June 1809, KC-SJC, box 74, MeSA.

June 1809. Malta (backcountry), Lincoln County. Armed White Indians break up Isaac Davis's attempt to survey for the Kennebeck Proprietors. Arodi Thayer to Bridge and Williams, July 6, 1809, KPP, Letterbook, I, 303, MeHS.

September 8, 1809. Malta (backcountry), Lincoln County. Armed and Indian-disguised settlers led by Elijah Barton ambush Isaac Davis's renewed attempt to survey for the Kennebeck Proprietors; chainman Paul Chadwick is assassinated. John Merrick, ed., *Trial of David Lynn . . . for the Murder of Paul Chadwick at Malta . . .* (Hallowell, 1809).

October 3, 1809. Augusta (frontcountry), Kennebec County. About two hundred White Indians march to Augusta but are deterred by the militia from entering the town and liberating the prisoners suspected of shooting Chadwick. John Chandler to William King, October 18, 1809, WKP, box 9, MeHS.

November 1809. Monmouth (backcountry), Kennebec County. A set fire destroys the barn and grain belonging to Daniel Cunningham, who had assisted in a survey of Litchfield for the Kennebeck Proprietors. Cunningham petition, May 17, 1810, Unpassed House File 6719, MA.

January 5, 1810. Whitefield (backcountry), Lincoln County. About thirty armed men assault James Marr, a surveyor for the Kennebeck Proprietors. Commonwealth v. Philbrook, September 1810, LC-SJC, Record Book, III, 459, LCC.

August 1810. Jefferson (backcountry), Lincoln County. Armed settlers ambush David Murphy, a deputy sheriff who had served writs for the Kennebeck Proprietors and assisted their surveys; because of a shower that wets the White Indians' gunpowder, their guns fail to discharge. Murphy to the Kennebeck Proprietors, June 7, 1811, KPP, box 7, MeHS.

August 19, 1810. Jefferson (backcountry), Lincoln County. A set fire destroys the barn of David Murphy, a deputy sheriff who had served writs for the Kennebeck Proprietors and assisted their surveys. Murphy to the Kennebeck Proprietors, August 23, 1810, KPP, box 7, MeHS.

August 19, 1810. Jefferson (backcountry), Lincoln County. A set fire destroys the barn of Isaac Davis, a surveyor for the Kennebeck Proprietors. Davis petition, December 12, 1810, Related Papers, February 16, 1811, Resolve, MA.

August 27, 1810. Bristol (frontcountry), Lincoln County. A crowd obstructs James Malcom's attempt to survey for the Brown heirs. John Johnston, *A History of the Towns of Bristol and Bremen . . .* (Albany, N.Y., 1873), 463.

August 27, 1810. Greene Plantation / Belmont (backcountry), Hancock County. White Indians abduct and brutally beat David Sewall, the land agent for the proprietor Benjamin Joy. *American Advocate* (Hallowell), September 13, 1810.

August 29, 1810. Bristol (frontcountry), Lincoln County. A threatening, ridiculing crowd escorts Elliot G. Vaughan, an agent for the Brown heirs, out of town and then besets his lodging by "stoning the house and making almost every noise that can be conceived of." Vaughan to Thomas Cutts, October 30, 1810, Lincoln County Lands miscellaneous box 24, MA.

September 1810. Patricktown / Somerville (backcountry), Lincoln County. Armed settlers obstruct James Marr's attempt to survey for the Kennebeck Proprietors. Arodi Thayer to Bridge and Williams, September 12, 1810, KPP, Letterbook, II, 21, MeHS.

December 1811. Montville (backcountry), Lincoln County. White Indians try to obstruct a legal attachment on some land. Joseph Pierce, Jr., to Joseph Pierce, Sr., December 18, 1811, HAPP, box 3, NEHGSL.

May 4, 1813. Minot (backcountry), Cumberland County. Settlers armed with clubs resist a deputy sheriff's attempt to evict them on behalf of the Pejepscot Proprietors. Josiah Little memorandum, May 4, 1813, PPP, box 5, EI.

July 13, 1814. Belmont (backcountry), Hancock County. At night Indian-disguised settlers break into the house of Ebenezer Newell, beat him, and destroy his furniture. Commonwealth v. Drew, June 1815, HC-SJC, box 167, MeSA.

September 5, 1815. Montville (backcountry), Lincoln County. Armed White Indians from adjoining Montville Plantation break into Marshall Spring's hotel to abduct and threaten Joseph Pierce, Jr., the land agent for the Twenty Associates. Allen Goodwin, "A Mob in Montville," *Republican Journal* (Belfast), February 6, 1908.

September 8, 1815. Montville Plantation / Liberty (backcountry), Lincoln County. A suspect in the Pierce mobbing violently resists arrest. Commonwealth v. Edwards, September 1815, LC-SJC, Record Book, IV, 457, LCC.

October 9, 1815. Montville (backcountry), Lincoln County. A dozen White Indians attempt, in vain, to obstruct James Malcom's survey for the Twenty Associates. Malcom Field Book, October 9, 1815, entry, HAPP, box 2, NEHGSL.

October 19, 1818. Carmel (backcountry), Hancock County. Richard Garlin mutilates the oxen belonging to Paul Ruggles, a neighbor who had informed the proprietors about Garlin's timber piracy. Commonwealth v. Garlin, HC-SJC, box 167, MeSA.

June 16–17, 1820. Freedom (backcountry), Kennebec County. At night a crowd "firing guns and making frightful noises" harasses the lodging of Deputy Sheriff Artemas Kimball, who was in town to impound livestock on behalf of the proprietor, Reuel Williams; during the night the settlers rescue their livestock. Kimball deposition, June 19, 1820, CF, box 1, MeSA.

June 22, 1820. Freedom (backcountry), Kennebec County. Armed and Indian-disguised settlers intervene to rescue livestock impounded by Deputy Sheriff Artemas Kimball for the proprietor, Reuel Williams. Kimball deposition, June 23, 1820, CF, box 1, MeSA.

May 23, 1825. Albion (backcountry), Kennebec County. A set fire consumes the barn on a farm recently recovered in an ejectment by the proprietor, Reuel Williams. Ralph Baker to Williams, May 25, 1825, RWP, box 10, MeHS.

May 24, 1825. Albion (backcountry), Kennebec County. A set fire consumes the barn belonging to a supporter of Reuel Williams's claim and containing a chaise that belongs to his land agent. Ralph Baker to Williams, May 25, 1825, RWP, box 10, MeHS.

The following is a selected bibliography of sources that have figured most prominently in this study. For excellent bibliographies on the early history of Maine, see Charles E. Clark, *Maine during the Colonial Period: A Bibliographical Guide* (Portland, 1974); Edwin A. Churchill, *Maine Communities and the War for Independence* (Augusta, 1976); Ronald F. Banks, comp., *Maine during the Federal and Jeffersonian Period: A Bibliographical Guide* (Portland, 1974); John Eldridge Frost, "Maine Genealogy: Some Distinctive Aspects," *New England Historical and Genealogical Register*, CXXXI (1977), 243–266; Elizabeth Ring, *A Reference List of Manuscripts Relating to the History of Maine*, 3 vols. (Orono, 1938–1941); and Joseph Williamson, *A Bibliography of the State of Maine from the Earliest Period to 1891*, 2 vols. (Portland, 1896).

PRIMARY SOURCES

Manuscript Collections

Unfortunately, almost none of the private correspondence of settler families survives in any archive. Fortunately, the Great Proprietors took great pains to collect and save information—especially depositions—about their opponents, for use in lobbying the authorities or in litigation against the settlers. The Great Proprietors' papers also document their own policies, transactions, and correspondence. The Henry Knox Papers (most in MHS, an important minority at MeHS) are especially voluminous and illuminating because the general saved almost everything that came to hand, including revealing reports from his hillcountry informants and intercepted documents produced by the Liberty Men. The Kennebeck Proprietors' Papers (MeHS) are nearly as valuable, especially for the years 1798–1806, when Charles Vaughan served as their land agent and filed regular, detailed, and perceptive reports. I supplemented this collection with the papers of three individual Kennebeck Proprietors: the Reuel Williams Papers (MeHS), the Vaughan Family Papers (now in the possession of George and Martha Vaughan of Boothbay, but destined for the Bowdoin College Library), and the Robert Hallowell Gardiner Papers (now in the possession of Phyllis Gardiner, Oaklands Farm, Gardiner). The Pejepscot Proprietors' Papers (most in EI, some at MeHS) and Little Family Papers (EI) are especially useful for the confrontations in Lewiston and Greene, 1795–1805. The Henry A. Pierce Papers (NEHGSL) document the activities of Joseph Pierce and the Twenty Associates. The Sheepscot Manuscripts (MeSL) include some of the records and correspondence of the Draper Heirs, whose Indian deed claim to the lower Sheepscot Valley caused the Kennebeck Proprietors grave legal problems. Two rich collections of proprietary papers have been published by two especially thorough and thoughtful editors: Frederick S. Allis, Jr., ed., *William Bingham's Maine Lands, 1790–1820*, 2 vols. (Colonial Society of Massachusetts, *Publications*, XXXVI–XXXVII [Boston, 1954]); and Robert E. Moody, ed., *The*

Saltonstall Papers, 1607–1815, 2 vols. (MHS, *Collections*, LXXX–LXXXI [Boston, 1972, 1974]). The William King Papers (MeHS) contain the correspondence of a man who was a small-scale land speculator as well as the dominant Jeffersonian politician in the District of Maine. The George Thatcher Papers (BPL, MeHs, and EI) document the activities of a leading Federalist. Finally, the Papers of the Society for Propagating the Gospel among the Indians and Others in North America (EI) offer detailed reports by Congregational missionaries.

The Records of the State Government

I also relied heavily upon documents produced or collected by the political institutions of the Commonwealth of Massachusetts. The Eastern Lands Committee Papers (MA) concern the legislative committee charged with surveying and selling the commonwealth's public lands. The Council Files (MA) include the record books of actions taken by the council and the voluminous correspondence received by the councillors, documents that are especially rich for those occasions when Maine magistrates sought permission to mobilize the militia against the Liberty Men. The Papers of the General Court (MA) include abundant petitions and correspondence associated with particular acts and resolves or consigned to the legislative graveyard. Many documents submitted to the General Court during the 1780s and 1790s have been published in *Documentary History of the State of Maine*, 24 vols., Collections of the Maine Historical Society, 2d Ser. (Portland, 1869–1916), esp. XXI, XXII. For legislation, see the annual editions of the *Acts and Laws of the Commonwealth of Massachusetts* (Boston, 1780–1819) and the *Resolves of the General Court of the Commonwealth of Massachusetts* (Boston, 1780–1819). The annual editions of *Fleet's Pocket Almanack and Massachusetts Register* (Boston, 1788–1800) and *The Massachusetts Register and United States Calendar* (Boston, 1801–1821) provide invaluable lists of local lawyers, representatives, justices, sheriffs, militia officers, and churches. (The titles above vary, of course, over the years.) They should be supplemented with *The Civil Officer; or, The Whole Duty of Sheriffs, Coroners, Constables, and Collectors of Taxes* (Boston, 1814).

The papers of the four commissions appointed by the General Court to set compromise land prices in contested areas—the Waldo Patent Commission of 1797 (MA), the Plymouth Patent Commission of 1802–1803 (MA), the Pejepscot Patent Commission of 1804 (MA), and the Lincoln County Commission of 1811–1813 (MA)—include record volumes enumerating settlers and the assessments they were supposed to pay to their proprietors. The last commission also left a book of testimony and three boxes of miscellaneous papers (nos. 23–25) that include revealing correspondence and a lot-by-lot history of land transactions in the town of Jefferson. Some of the testimony was published in *Order of Both Branches of the Legislature of Massachusetts to Appoint Commissioners to Investigate the Causes of the Difficulties in the County of Lincoln; and the Report of the Commissioners Thereon, with the Documents in Support Thereof* (Boston, 1811).

Local Records

For proprietary litigation against settlers and for the commonwealth's prosecution of rioters and arsonists, I turned to the dockets, record books, and files of the commonwealth's three courts. Known as the Supreme Court of Judicature before the Revolution and as the Supreme Judicial Court thereafter, the high court rode an annual or twice-annual circuit through the commonwealth's counties. For trials in mid-Maine counties through 1797, the records are at the Massachusetts Archives in Boston; for litigation after 1797, the court's records may be found either at the Lincoln County Courthouse (for Lincoln County trials) in Wiscasset or at the Maine State Archives in Augusta (for Hancock and Kennebec County trials). Also useful are the papers of the two inferior courts: each county's Court of General Sessions of the Peace and Court of Common Pleas (LCC for Lincoln County, MeSA for Hancock and Kennebec counties).

To study persistence, family size, and sex and age ratios, I relied on U.S., Bureau of the Census, *Heads of Families at the First Census of the United States Taken in the Year 1790: Maine* (Washington, D.C., 1908) and the microfilmed Federal Census Returns for 1800, 1810, and 1820. A portion of the 1800 census has been published in Walter Goodwin Davis, "Part of Hancock County, Maine, in 1800," *New England Historical and Genealogical Register*, CV (1951), 204–213, 276–291.

To study the structure and trends in the distribution of property, I relied on tax lists, especially the commonwealth's tax valuation returns (MSL) that survive for several Maine towns. Taken about every ten years, the returns document taxpayers' improved and unimproved acreage, crops raised, and the number of their mature livestock. I made the greatest use of the returns for Balltown from 1791, 1792, 1801, and 1811 (when Balltown had split into the two towns of Jefferson and Whitefield); for Northport from 1801 and 1811; for Lincolnville in 1811; and for Palermo in 1811. The aggregate valuations for every town in the commonwealth were published in the three editions of the *Report of the Committee of Valuation* (Boston, 1793, 1802, 1811). The 1798 Federal Direct Tax returns (NEHGSL) also survive for a few mid-Maine towns and document the value of taxpayers' buildings and lands; I drew most heavily on the returns for Ducktrap and Northport. An 1815 Federal Direct Tax Roll (MeHS) of taxpayers and the aggregate values of their assessed real estate survives for Hancock County, but apparently for no other Maine county.

Because so few hillcountry families relied on the probate court to enumerate and distribute decedents' property, mid-Maine's probate records cannot systematically be analyzed. William Davis Patterson, ed., *Probate Records of Lincoln County, Maine, 1760–1800* (Portland, 1895), provides a compilation of wills, but not inventories, for one mid-Maine county. Land transactions recorded at each county's registry of deeds (LCC, HCC, KCC) are fuller and more helpful for understanding how the settlers handled property. I made the most systematic use of the transactions involving land in Sheepscot Great Pond settlement (Palermo), recorded in Lincoln County, 1790–1819. For patterns of litigation between creditors and debtors, I turned to the record books of the Courts of Common Pleas for each county (LCC, HCC, KCC). I attempted a systematic analysis of all cases in the three counties involving a Palermo resident, 1790–1819. For the votes from mid-Maine towns, I relied on the Abstract of Votes for Governor and Lieutenant Governor, 1785–1819 (MA).

Contemporary Pamphlets

Unlike other early American agrarians, the Liberty Men were almost all literate and had ready access to printing presses. Consequently, their principal ideologues wrote and published several pamphlets that offer unusual insight into the agrarian persuasion in the early Republic: *An Address to the Inhabitants of Maine, Shewing a Safe and Easy Method of Extracting Good from Evil* (Augusta, 1805); [James Davis and Samuel Ely], *The Appeal of the Two Counties of Lincoln and Hancock, from the Forlorn Hope, or, Mount of Distress; to the General Court, or, to All the World* (Portsmouth, N.H., 1796); Samuel Ely, *The Deformity of a Hideous Monster, Discovered in the Province of Maine, by a Man in the Woods, Looking after Liberty* (Boston, 1797); Samuel Ely, *The Unmasked Nabob of Hancock County; or, The Scales Dropt from the Eyes of the People* (Portsmouth, N.H., 1796); *The Petition and Memorial of the Towns of Bristol, Nobleborough, New-Castle, Edgcomb, and Boothbay, in the County of Lincoln* . . . (Boston, 1811); [James Shurtleff], *A Concise Review of the Spirit Which Seemed to Govern in the Time of the American War, Compared with the Spirit Which Now Prevails* . . . (Augusta, 1798); and [Shurtleff], *The Substance of a Late Remarkable Dream* . . . (Hallowell, 1800). Also valuable is the testimony in John Merrick, ed., *Trial of David Lynn . . . for the Murder of Paul Chadwick at Malta* . . . (Augusta, 1809); and the critique of the agrarian persuasion in [John Merrick], *Remarks on Some of the Circumstances and Arguments Produced by the Murder of Mr. Paul Chadwick, at Malta* . . . [Augusta, 1809].

For the religious thoughts of leading agrarians, see Nathan Barlow, *A Vision Seen by Nathan Barlow of Freetown* . . . (Boston, 1802); Samuel Ely, *Two Sermons Preached at Somers, March 18, 1770* . . . (Hartford, Conn., 1771); William Jones, *The Inconsistency and Deception of the Methodist Ministers* . . . (Bristol, ca. 1808; copy at MeHS); William Jones, *A True Account of All the Presbyterian and Congregational Ministers* . . . (Bristol, 1808; only known copy at the British Library); William Scales, *The Confusion of Babel Discovered* . . . (n.p., 1780); William Scales, *Priestcraft Exposed from Its Foundation* . . . (Danvers, Mass., 1781); and Scales, *The Quintessence of Universal History* . . . ([Boston], 1806). See also the contrasting ideas of Thurston Whiting, a Congregationalist and proprietary agent, expressed in *A Discourse Delivered in the Meeting House in Pownalborough, March 1, 1798* (Wiscasset, 1798); and *An Oration Delivered at the Baptist Meeting House in Thomaston, July 4th 1798* . . . (Hallowell, 1798). For the growth and concerns of the Calvinist Baptists, mid-Maine's predominant denomination, see the annual *Minutes of the Bowdoinham Association* (Boston, Portland, Augusta, 1790–1819); and the annual *Minutes of the Lincoln Association* (Wiscasset, Buckstown, Portland, Castine, Hallowell, 1805–1819) (both titles vary over the years). For the travails of the competing Congregational missionaries, see *An Account of the Massachusetts Society for Promoting Christian Knowledge* (Cambridge, Andover, Mass., 1806, 1815).

Geographical Accounts

Several perceptive travelers—drawn to Maine by their curiosity about the sociology of frontier settlement—published revealing descriptions. The very best are Luigi Castiglioni, *Viaggio: Travels in the United States of North America, 1785–87*, trans. and ed. Antonio Pace (Syracuse, N.Y., 1983); Timothy Dwight, *Travels in New England and New York*, ed. Barbara Miller Solomon, 4 vols. (Cambridge, Mass., 1969; orig. publ. New Haven, Conn., 1821), II, 107–166; Edward Augustus Kendall, *Travels through the Northern Parts of the United States in the Years 1807 and 1808* (New York, 1809), III, 40–170; François Alexandre Frédéric, duc de La Rochefoucault Liancourt, *Travels through the United States of North America . . .* (London, 1799); John Southack, *The Life of John Southack: Written by Himself . . .* (Boston, 1809); and Charles Maurice de Talleyrand-Périgord, "Letter on the Eastern Part of America" (Boston, Sept. 24, 1794), in Hans Huth and Wilma J. Pugh, eds., *Talleyrand in America as a Financial Promoter, 1794–96 (Annual Report of the American Historical Association, 1941,* II [Washington, D.C., 1942]), 69–86.

During the early Republic a new concern for geographical analysis produced several valuable topographical descriptions of Maine locales. The best are Alden Bradford, "A Description of Wiscasset, and of the River Sheepscot," MHS, *Collections*, 1st Ser., VII (Boston, 1801), 163–171; Samuel Deane, *The New England Farmer . . .* (Worcester, Mass., 1790); Moses Greenleaf, *A Statistical View of the District of Maine . . .* (Boston, 1816); Greenleaf, *A Survey of the State of Maine . . .* (Portland, 1829); [Benjamin] Lincoln, "Observations on the Climate, Soil, and Value of the Eastern Counties in the District of Maine," MHS, *Collections*, 1st Ser., IV (Boston, 1795), 142–153; [James Sullivan], "A Topographical Description of Thomaston, in the County of Lincoln, and District of Maine, 1794," MHS, *Collections*, 1st Ser., IV (Boston, 1795), 20–25; Joseph Whipple, *A Geographical View of the District of Maine, with Particular Reference to Its Internal Resources . . .* (Bangor, 1816). There are also valuable accounts of Maine localities in the annual *Papers on Agriculture, Consisting of Communications Made to the Massachusetts Agricultural Society* (Boston, 1799–1811) (title varies over the years). Also useful is the geographical and social analysis of an adjacent and similar region in the third volume of Jeremy Belknap, *The History of New-Hampshire*, 3 vols. (Boston, 1791–1792).

Memoirs

A few of the proprietors, settlers, and missionaries left useful reminiscences of their roles in the settlement of mid-Maine. The proprietor Robert Hallowell Gardiner left two valuable accounts: *Early Recollections of Robert Hallowell Gardiner, 1782–1864* (Hallowell, 1936); and "History of the Kennebec Purchase . . . ," MeHS, *Collections*, 1st Ser., II (Portland, 1847), 269–294. The best recollections by settlers are William Allen, "The Journal of William Allen, Esq.," in William Collins Hatch, *A History of the Town of Industry . . .* (Farmington, 1893); William Allen, "Now and Then," MeHS, *Collections*, 1st Ser., VII (Bath, 1876), 269–287; John Davidson, *Reminiscences of John Davidson, a Maine Pioneer* (Boston, 1916); Levi Leighton, *Autobiography of Levi Leighton . . .* (Portland, 1890); Joseph Plumb Martin, *"Private Yankee Doodle": Being a Narrative of Some of the Adventures, Dangers, and Sufferings of a Revolutionary Soldier*, ed. George F. Scheer (Boston, 1962; orig. publ. Hallowell, 1832); Hezekiah Prince, *Remarks of My Life, 1786–1792* (Rockland, 1979); and Josiah Thompson, comp., *Autobiography of Deacon John Thompson of Mercer, Maine . . .* (Farmington, 1920).

Revealing accounts by or about religious missionaries include William S. Bartlett, *The Frontier Missionary: A Memoir of the Life of the Rev. Jacob Bailey . . .* (Boston, 1853); Paul Coffin, "Memoir and Journals of the Rev. Paul Coffin, D.D.," MeHS, *Collections*, 1st Ser., IV (Portland, 1859), 239–405; John Colby, *Life, Experience, and Travels of John Colby . . .* (Portland, 1815); James Potter, *Narration of the Experience, Travels, and Labours of Elder James Potter . . .* (Boston, 1813); Jotham Sewall,

A Memoir of Rev. Jotham Sewall of Chesterville, Maine (Boston, 1853); Elias Smith, *The Life, Conversion, Preaching, Travels, and Sufferings of Elias Smith* (Portsmouth, N.H., 1816); and Ephraim Stinchfield, *Some Memoirs of the Life, Experience, and Travels of Elder Ephraim Stinchfield* (Portland, 1819).

Newspapers and Magazines

Because newspapers were preoccupied with commercial and international news, they provide very little on local developments. I gleaned some information from *American Advocate* (Hallowell), 1810–1814; *Cumberland Gazette* (Portland), 1786–1791; *Eastern Argus* (Portland), 1803–1820; *Gazette of Maine* (Buckstown), 1805–1812; *Kennebec Gazette* (Augusta), 1800–1810; and *Portland Gazette*, 1798–1819. I made greater use of religious magazines, chiefly *A Religious Magazine . . .* (Portland), 1811–1812; *Christian's Magazine, Reviewer, and Religious Intelligencer* (Portsmouth, N.H.), 1805–1808; *Herald of Gospel Liberty* (Portsmouth, N.H.), 1808–1809; *Massachusetts Baptist Missionary Magazine* (Boston), 1803–1816; and *Massachusetts Missionary Magazine* (Salem, Mass., Boston, 1803–1808). (Some of the titles above vary over the years.)

SECONDARY SOURCES

No satisfactory general history of Maine has been written to supersede the still useful James Sullivan, *The History of the District of Maine* (Augusta, 1970; orig. publ. Boston, 1795); and William D. Williamson, *The History of the State of Maine . . .*, 2 vols. (Augusta, 1966; orig. publ. Hallowell, 1832). As lawyers and Jeffersonian politicians, Sullivan and Williamson brought their inside knowledge of the land controversies into their histories. The best work on Maine before the Revolution can be found in Charles E. Clark, *The Eastern Frontier: The Settlement of Northern New England, 1610–1763* (New York, 1970); Gordon E. Kershaw, *The Kennebeck Proprietors, 1749–1775* (Portland, 1975); and Robert Earle Moody, "The Maine Frontier, 1607 to 1763" (Ph.D. diss., Yale University, 1933). For the political history of Maine in the wake of the Revolution, see Ronald F. Banks, *Maine Becomes a State: The Movement to Separate Maine from Massachusetts, 1785–1820* (Middletown, Conn., 1970); and John O. Noble, Jr., "Messengers from the Wilderness: Maine's Representatives to the Massachusetts General Court, 1760–1819" (Ph.D. diss., University of Maine at Orono, 1975).

William Willis, *A History of the Law, the Courts, and the Lawyers of Maine . . .* (Portland, 1863), is an essential source for understanding the judicial system and the men who staffed it. Two lawyers for the Kennebeck Proprietors wrote legal compilations that are useful to understanding the land laws: Nathan Dane, *A General Abridgement and Digest of American Law . . .*, 9 vols. (Boston, 1823–1829), IV; and James Sullivan, *The History of Land Titles in Massachusetts* (Boston, 1801). Also of interest is Thomas C. Amory, *Life of James Sullivan . . .*, 2 vols. (Boston, 1859); and Asahel Stearns, *A Summary of the Law and Practice of Real Actions . . .*, 2d ed. (Hallowell, 1831).

For religious life on the northeastern frontier, see the fine work by Nathan O. Hatch, "The Christian Movement and the Demand for a Theology of the People," *Journal of American History*, LXVII (1980–1981), 545–567; and Stephen A. Marini, *Radical Sects of Revolutionary New England* (Cambridge, Mass., 1982). There are also some useful materials in Norman Allen Baxter, *History of the Freewill Baptists: A Study in New England Separatism* (Rochester, N.Y., 1957); David Benedict, *A General History of the Baptist Denomination America . . .*, 2 vols. (Boston, 1813); Henry S. Burrage, *History of the Baptists in Maine* (Portland, 1904); Calvin Montague Clark, *History of the Congregational Churches in Maine* (Portland, 1926); Jonathan Greenleaf, *Sketches of the Ecclesiastical History of the State of Maine . . .* (Portsmouth, N.H., 1821); William G. McLoughlin, *New England Dissent, 1630–1833: The Baptists and the Separation of Church and State*, 2 vols. (Cambridge, Mass., 1971); Joshua Millet, *A History of the Baptists in Maine* (Portland, 1845); Stephen Allen and W. H. Pilsbury, *History of Methodism in Maine, 1793–1886* (Augusta, 1887); and Isaac Dalton Stewart, *The History of the Freewill Baptists for Half a Century . . .* (Dover, N.H., 1862).

Few social historians have worked on mid-Maine prior to statehood. There is some useful material in Edward Charles Cass, "A Town Comes of Age: Pownalborough, Maine, 1720–1785" (Ph.D. diss., University of Maine at Orono, 1979); Clarence Albert Day, *A History of Maine Agriculture, 1604–1860* (Orono, 1954); and Adele Edna Plachta, "The Privileged and the Poor: A History of the District of Maine, 1771–1793" (Ph.D. diss., University of Maine at Orono, 1975).

Some town histories provide rich materials for the social historian. Before decaying in the twentieth century, the town history was a noble and useful genre written by local gentlemen determined to preserve the previous generation's oral traditions and documents. The best nineteenth-century works on mid-Maine towns are William Allen, *History of Industry, Maine . . .*, 2d ed. (Skowhegan, 1869); William Allen, *The History of Norridgewock . . .* (Norridgewock, 1849); Harry H. Cochrane, *History of Monmouth and Wales*, 2 vols. (East Winthrop, 1894); David Quimby Cushman, *The History of Ancient Sheepscot and Newcastle . . .* (Bath, 1882); Cyrus Eaton, *Annals of the Town of Warren* (Hallowell, 1877); Cyrus Eaton, *History of Thomaston, Rockland, and South Thomaston*, 2 vols. (Hallowell, 1865); Allen Goodwin, *A History of the Early Settlement of Palermo, Me.* (Belfast, 1896); J. W. Hanson, *History of Gardiner, Pittston, and West Gardiner* (Gardiner, 1852); J. W. Hanson, *History of the Old Towns, Norridgewock and Canaan . . .* (Boston, 1849); William Collins Hatch, *A History of the Town of Industry . . .* (Farmington, 1893); John Johnston, *A History of the Towns of Bristol and Bremen . . .* (Albany, N.Y., 1873); John L. Locke, *Sketches of the History of the Town of Camden, Maine . . .* (Hallowell, 1859); James W. North, *The History of Augusta . . .* (Augusta, 1870); John Langdon Sibley, *A History of the Town of Union . . .* (Boston, 1851); David Thurston, *A Brief History of Winthrop . . .* (Portland, 1855); George Augustus Wheeler and Henry Warren Wheeler, *History of Brunswick, Topsham, and Harpswell, Maine* (Boston, 1878); William White, *A History of Belfast* (Belfast, 1827); and Joseph Williamson, *History of the City of Belfast . . .*, I (Portland, 1877). There is proof that it is still possible to write a valuable town history in the following twentieth-century works on mid-Maine communities: Charles E. Allen, *History of Dresden, Maine . . .* (Augusta, 1931); Millard A. Howard, *An Introduction to the Early History of Palermo, Maine* (Augusta, 1976); Jasper Jacob Stahl, *History of Old Broad Bay and Waldoboro*, 2 vols. (Portland, 1956); and James Berry Vickery, *A History of the Town of Unity, Maine* (Manchester, 1954).

Because the settlers were so successful in avoiding a dramatic confrontation, their resistance has attracted little attention from historians. The best exception is Robert E. Moody, "Samuel Ely: Forerunner of Shays," *New England Quarterly*,

V (1932), 105–134. Also of interest are Lawrence Donald Bridgham, "Maine Public Lands, 1781–1795: Claims, Trespassers, and Sales" (Ph.D. diss., Boston University, 1959); and Thomas A. Jeffrey, "The Malta War" (master's thesis, University of Maine at Orono, 1976).

Historians have been more active in assessing the more conspicuous episodes of agrarian resistance elsewhere in eighteenth- and early nineteenth-century America. The best of the recent work can be found in Richard Maxwell Brown, *The South Carolina Regulators* (Cambridge, Mass., 1963); Brown, "Back Country Rebellions and the Homestead Ethic," in Brown and Don E. Fehrenbacher, eds., *Tradition, Conflict, and Modernization: Perspectives on the American Revolution* (New York, 1977), 73–98; Edward Countryman, "Out of the Bounds of the Law: Northern Land Rioters in the Eighteenth Century," in Alfred F. Young, ed., *The American Revolution: Explorations in the History of American Radicalism* (DeKalb, Ill., 1976), 39–61; A. Roger Ekirch, *"Poor Carolina": Politics and Society in Colonial North Carolina, 1729–1776* (Chapel Hill, N.C., 1981); Theodore Marriner Hammett, "The Revolutionary Ideology in Its Social Context: Berkshire County, Massachusetts, 1725–1785" (Ph.D. diss., Brandeis University, 1976); Gary S. Horowitz, "New Jersey Land Riots, 1745–1755" (Ph.D. diss., Ohio State University, 1966); Barbara Karsky, "Agrarian Radicalism in the Late Revolutionary Period," in Erich Angermann *et al.*, eds., *New Wine in Old Skins: A Comparative View of Socio-Political Structures and Values Affecting the American Revolution* (Stuttgart, 1976), 87–114; Sung Bok Kim, "Impact of Class Relations and Warfare in the American Revolution: The New York Experience," *Journal of American History,* LXIX (1982–1983), 326–346; Kim, *Landlord and Tenant in Colonial New York: Manorial Society, 1664–1775* (Chapel Hill, N.C., 1978); Rachel N. Klein, "Ordering the Backcountry: The South Carolina Regulation," *WMQ,* 3d Ser., XXXVIII (1981), 661–680; Staughton Lynd, *Anti-Federalism in Dutchess County, New York: A Study of Democracy and Class Conflict in the Revolutionary Era* (Chicago, 1962); Eldridge Honaker Pendleton, "The New York Anti-Rent Controversy, 1830–1860" (Ph.D. diss., University of Virginia, 1974); Thomas L. Purvis, "Origins and Patterns of Agrarian Unrest in New Jersey, 1735 to 1754," *WMQ,* 3d Ser., XXXIX (1982), 600–627; David P. Szatmary, *Shays' Rebellion: The Making of an Agrarian Insurrection* (Amherst, Mass., 1980); and James P. Whittenburg, "Planters, Merchants, and Lawyers: Social Change and the Origins of the North Carolina Regulation," *WMQ,* 3d Ser., XXXIV (1977), 215–238. Ekirch, Kim, and Purvis stress the "conservatism" of early American agrarians, in contrast to Countryman, Karsky, Lynd, and Szatmary, who detect much behavior and thought that can be called "radical."

In addition to the work on rural resistance, I have drawn on the proliferating studies by social historians of rural life in early New England. For my purposes, the most interesting and useful are Richard L. Bushman, "Family Security in the Transition from Farm to City, 1750–1850," *Working Papers from the Regional Economic History Research Center,* IV, no. 3 (1981), 27–43; Bushman, *From Puritan to Yankee: Character and the Social Order in Connecticut, 1690–1765* (New York, 1970); Christopher Clark, "The Household Economy, Market Exchange, and the Rise of Capitalism in the Connecticut Valley, 1800–1860," *Journal of Social History,* XIII (1979–1980), 169–189; Edward M. Cook, Jr., *The Fathers of the Towns: Leadership and Community Structure in Eighteenth-Century New England* (Baltimore, 1976); William Cronon, *Changes in the Land: Indians, Colonists, and the Ecology of New England* (New York, 1983); Charles S. Grant, *Democracy in the Connecticut Frontier Town of Kent* (New York, 1961); James A. Henretta, "Families and Farms: Mentalité in Pre-Industrial America," *WMQ,* 3d Ser., XXXV (1978), 3–32;

Christine Leigh Heyrman, *Commerce and Culture: The Maritime Communities of Colonial Massachusetts, 1690–1750* (New York, 1984); Stephen Innes, *Labor in a New Land: Economy and Society in Seventeenth-Century Springfield* (Princeton, N.J., 1983); Christopher M. Jedrey, *The World of John Cleaveland: Family and Community in Eighteenth-Century New England* (New York, 1979); Kenneth Lockridge, "Land, Population, and the Evolution of New England Society, 1630–1790," *Past and Present*, no. 39 (Apr. 1968), 62–80; Robert Mutch, "Yeoman and Merchant in Pre-Industrial America: Eighteenth-Century Massachusetts as a Case Study," *Societas*, VII (1977), 279–302; Gregory H. Nobles, *Divisions throughout the Whole: Politics and Society in Hampshire County, Massachusetts, 1740–1775* (New York, 1983); Bettye Hobbs Pruitt, "Self-Sufficiency and the Agricultural Economy of Eighteenth-Century Massachusetts," *WMQ*, 3d Ser., XLI (1984), 333–364; Randolph A. Roth, *The Democratic Dilemma: Religion, Reform, and the Social Order in the Connecticut River Valley of Vermont, 1791–1850* (New York, 1987); Laurel Thatcher Ulrich, *Good Wives: Image and Reality in the Lives of Women in Northern New England, 1650–1750* (New York, 1982); and John J. Waters, "Family, Inheritance, and Migration in Colonial New England: The Evidence from Guilford, Connecticut," *WMQ*, 3d Ser., XXXIX (1982), 64–86. I am especially impressed with the strategies for combining detailed research on social structures with a lively narrative style advanced by Robert A. Gross, *The Minutemen and Their World* (New York, 1976); and Paul E. Johnson, "The Modernization of Mayo Greenleaf Patch: Land, Family, and Marginality in New England, 1766–1818," *New England Quarterly*, LV (1982), 488–516.

I have also learned much from recent studies of the early Republic's frontier. The best are Richard R. Beeman, *The Evolution of the Southern Backcountry: A Case Study of Lunenburg County, Virginia, 1746–1832* (Philadelphia, 1984); Don Harrison Doyle, *The Social Order of a Frontier Community: Jacksonville, Illinois, 1825–70* (Urbana, Ill., 1983); John Mack Faragher, *Sugar Creek: Life on the Illinois Prairie* (New Haven, Conn., 1986); and Steven Hahn, *The Roots of Southern Populism: Yeoman Farmers and the Transformation of the Georgia Upcountry, 1850–1890* (New York, 1983). Especially pertinent to my study are two books written by historians concerned with the frontier legacy of the American Revolution: Andrew R. L. Cayton, *The Frontier Republic: Ideology and Politics in the Ohio Country, 1780–1825* (Kent, Ohio, 1986); and Thomas P. Slaughter, *The Whiskey Rebellion: Frontier Epilogue to the American Revolution* (New York, 1986). See also John L. Brooke, "Society, Revolution, and the Symbolic Uses of the Dead: An Historical Ethnography of the Massachusetts Near Frontier, 1730–1820" (Ph.D. diss., University of Pennsylvania, 1982); Dorothy Elaine Fennell, "From Rebelliousness to Insurrection: A Social History of the Whiskey Rebellion, 1765–1802" (Ph.D. diss., University of Pittsburgh, 1981); and Mark Haddon Jones, "Herman Husband: Millenarian, Carolina Regulator, and Whiskey Rebel" (Ph.D. diss., Northern Illinois University, 1983).

In addition to the work by social historians on rural resistance, rural New England, and the early American frontier, I have drawn on the ideas of several political and political-intellectual historians. For politics in the commonwealth during the early Republic, see Paul Goodman, *The Democratic Republicans of Massachusetts: Politics in a Young Republic* (Cambridge, Mass., 1964); and James M. Banner, Jr., *To the Hartford Convention: The Federalists and the Origins of Party Politics in Massachusetts, 1789–1815* (New York, 1969). Also important are the wider-ranging works of Richard E. Ellis, *The Jeffersonian Crisis: Courts and Politics in the Young Republic* (New York, 1971); David Hackett Fischer, *The Revolution of American Conservatism: The Federalist Party in the Era of Jeffersonian Democracy* (New

York, 1965); Jackson Turner Main, *The Antifederalists: Critics of the Constitution, 1781–1788* (Chapel Hill, N.C., 1961); and Alfred F. Young, *The Democratic Republicans of New York: The Origins, 1763–1797* (Chapel Hill, N.C., 1967). On the ideological legacy of the Revolution, the best work is Joyce Appleby, *Capitalism and a New Social Order: The Republican Vision of the 1790s* (New York, 1984); Eric Foner, *Tom Paine and Revolutionary America* (New York, 1976); Drew R. McCoy, *The Elusive Republic: Political Economy in Jeffersonian America* (Chapel Hill, N.C., 1980); Samuel Eliot Morison, ed., "William Manning's *The Key of Libberty*," *WMQ*, 3d Ser., XIII (1956), 202–254; Gordon S. Wood, *The Creation of the American Republic, 1776–1787* (New York, 1969); and, especially, Richard L. Bushman, *King and People in Provincial Massachusetts* (Chapel Hill, N.C., 1985); and Marvin Meyers, *The Jacksonian Persuasion: Politics and Belief* (Stanford, Calif., 1960).

ABBREVIATIONS

APS	American Periodical Series, microfilm
BHM	*Bangor Historical Magazine*, 7 vols. (1885–1892)
BPL	Boston Public Library (Boston)
CCP	Court of Common Pleas
CF	Council Files
CGSP	Court of General Sessions of the Peace
E	Evans microfilm no. (Charles Evans, comp., *American Bibliography* . . . , 12 vols. [reprint, New York, 1941–1942])
EI	Essex Institute (Salem, Mass.)
ELC	Eastern Lands Committee Papers
GTP	George Thatcher Papers
HAPP	Henry A. Pierce Papers
HC-CCP	Hancock County Court of Common Pleas
HC-CGSP	Hancock County Court of General Sessions of the Peace
HC-SJC	Hancock County Supreme Judicial Court
HKP	Henry Knox Papers
KCC	Kennebec County Courthouse (Augusta)
KC-CCP	Kennebec County Court of Common Pleas
KC-CGSP	Kennebec County Court of General Sessions of the Peace
KCD	Kennebec County Deeds
KCRD	Kennebec County Registry of Deeds
KC-SJC	Kennebec County Supreme Judicial Court
KPP	Kennebeck Proprietors' Papers
LCC	Lincoln County Courthouse (Wiscasset)
LC-CCP	Lincoln County Court of Common Pleas
LC-CGSP	Lincoln County Court of General Sessions of the Peace
LCD	Lincoln County Deeds
LC-SJC	Lincoln County Supreme Judicial Court
LFP	Little Family Papers
MDH	*Documentary History of the State of Maine*, 24 vols., Collections of the Maine Historical Society, 2d Ser. (Portland, 1869–1916)
MeHS	Maine Historical Society (Portland)
MeSA	Maine State Archives (Augusta)
MeSL	Maine State Library (Augusta)
MHS	Massachusetts Historical Society (Boston)
MA	Massachusetts State Archives (Boston)
MSL	Massachusetts State Library (Boston)
NA	National Archives (Washington, D.C.)
NEHGSL	New England Historic Genealogical Society Library (Boston)
PPP	Pejepscot Proprietors' Papers
RWP	Reuel Williams Papers
SCJ	Superior Court of Judicature
SJC	Supreme Judicial Court
SM	Sheepscot Manuscripts
SPG	Society for Propagating the Gospel
S-S	Shaw-Shoemaker microfilm no. (Ralph R. Shaw and Rich-

	ard H. Shoemaker, comps., *American Bibliography* . . . , 22 vols. [New York, 1958–1966])
UMO	University of Maine, Orono
WCD	Waldo County Deeds
WCRD	Waldo County Registry of Deeds (Belfast)
WDWTP	William D. Williamson Town Papers
WKP	William King Papers
WMQ	*William and Mary Quarterly*

NOTES

INTRODUCTION

1. "A Waldo County Centenarian," *Republican Journal* (Belfast), Nov. 26, 1885; *The Town of Liberty: Its History and Geography* (Thorndike, 1927), 40. By "mid-Maine" I refer to the three 1827 counties of Lincoln (formed in 1760), Kennebec (organized in 1799), and Waldo (set off from western Hancock County in 1827). In 1760 mid-Maine consisted of the western half of massive Lincoln County (the half west of the Penobscot River). In 1789 the Massachusetts General Court subdivided Lincoln County in three by setting off Washington County in easternmost Maine and Hancock County on both banks of the Penobscot. So, in 1790 mid-Maine consisted of Lincoln and the western half of Hancock County (that half west of the Penobscot River). In 1799 the General Court again divided Lincoln County by setting off its northern half as Kennebec County. Thus, in 1800 mid-Maine consisted of Lincoln County, Kennebec County (excluding the northernmost towns subsequently set aside for Somerset County in 1811), and the western half of Hancock County. At the first federal census in 1790 mid-Maine's then 60 constituent communities possessed a population of 30,406. By 1820 the settlement of 24 more communities and a 257% population growth increased the region's inhabitants to 108,532 dwelling in 84 communities. In the process mid-Maine's proportion of Maine's population rose from 23% in 1790 to 36% in 1820. In 1790 Maine's population was 96,540; in 1820 it was 298,335. See U.S., Bureau of the Census, *Historical Statistics of the United States: Colonial Times to 1957* (Washington, D.C., 1960), 13.

2. "A Waldo County Centenarian," *Republican Journal*, Nov. 26, 1885. On Liberty's harsh conditions, see James Malcolm *et al.* to the Maine state legislature, ca. Jan. 1824, envelope 17, box 28, Legislative Graveyard, MeSA; they insisted that Liberty had "a large proportion of waste land in it and is thinly inhabitted by people who appear to be very poor." Tibbetts's memory must have erred regarding the hilling of 3,200 hills of corn in one day: an impossible feat.

3. Allen Goodwin, "A Mob in Montville," *Republican Journal*, Feb. 6, 1908; a more fanciful version based on oral tradition appears in *The Town of Liberty*, 31–32.

4. Goodwin, "A Mob in Montville," *Republican Journal*, Feb. 6, 1908.

5. *Ibid.*; Commonwealth v. Joel Clark *et al.*, Sept. 1815, Lincoln County SJC Record Books, IV, 458, V, 4, LCC; Council Records, Feb. 14, 1816, XXXVIII (1814–1816), 298–299, MA (quote).

6. Gary S. Horowitz, "New Jersey Land Riots, 1745–1755" (Ph.D. diss., Ohio State University, 1966); Thomas L. Purvis, "Origins and Patterns of Agrarian Unrest in New Jersey, 1735–1754," *WMQ*, 3d Ser., XXXIX (1982), 600–627; Robert L. Meriwether, *The Expansion of South Carolina, 1729–1765* (Kingsport, Tenn., 1940), 95–96, 107; Irving Mark, *Agrarian Conflicts in Colonial New York, 1711–1775* (New York, 1940); Staughton Lynd, *Anti-Federalism in Dutchess County, New York: A Study of Democracy and Class Conflict in the Revolutionary Era* (Chicago, 1962); Edward Countryman, *A People in Revolution: The American Revolution and Political Society in New York, 1760–1790* (Baltimore, 1981), 46–54; Sung Bok Kim,

Landlord and Tenant in Colonial New York: Manorial Society, 1664–1775 (Chapel Hill, N.C., 1978), 281–415; Eldridge Honaker Pendleton, "The New York Anti-Rent Controversy, 1830–1860" (Ph.D. diss., University of Virginia, 1974); A. Roger Ekirch, *"Poor Carolina": Politics and Society in Colonial North Carolina, 1729–1776* (Chapel Hill, N.C., 1981), 132–147; William S. Powell *et al.*, eds., *The Regulators in North Carolina: A Documentary History, 1759–1776* (Raleigh, N.C., 1971), 4–12; Peter S. Onuf, *The Origins of the Federal Republic: Jurisdictional Controversies in the United States, 1775–1787* (Philadelphia, 1983), 49–73; Edward Countryman, "Out of the Bounds of the Law: Northern Land Rioters in the Eighteenth Century," in Alfred F. Young, ed., *The American Revolution: Explorations in the History of American Radicalism* (DeKalb, Ill., 1976), 39–61; Dorothy Elaine Fennell, "From Rebelliousness to Insurrection: A Social History of the Whiskey Rebellion, 1765–1802" (Ph.D. diss., University of Pittsburgh, 1981), 25–37; Robert L. Brunhouse, *The Counter-Revolution in Pennsylvania, 1776–1790* (Harrisburg, Pa., 1942), 127–128; Randolph C. Downes, "Ohio's Squatter Governor: William Hogland of Hoglandstown," *Ohio Archaeological and Historical Quarterly*, XLIII (1934), 273–282; Elizabeth K. Henderson, "The Northwestern Lands of Pennsylvania, 1790–1812," *Pennsylvania Magazine of History and Biography*, LX (1936), 131–160; Paul Demund Evans, *The Holland Land Company* (Buffalo Historical Society, *Publications*, XXVIII [Buffalo, N.Y., 1924]), 397–427.

7. George William Franz, "Paxton: A Study of Community Structure and Mobility in the Colonial Pennsylvania Backcountry" (Ph.D. diss., Rutgers University, 1974); Marvin L. Michael Kay, "The North Carolina Regulation, 1766–1776: A Class Conflict," in Young, ed., *American Revolution*, 73–106; James P. Whittenburg, "Planters, Merchants, and Lawyers: Social Change and the Origins of the North Carolina Regulation," *WMQ*, 3d Ser., XXXIV (1977), 215–238; Ekirch, *"Poor Carolina,"* 161–210; Rachel N. Klein, "Ordering the Backcountry: The South Carolina Regulation," *WMQ*, 3d Ser., XXXVIII (1981), 661–680; Richard Maxwell Brown, *The South Carolina Regulators* (Cambridge, Mass., 1963); Larry R. Gerlach, *Prologue to Independence: New Jersey in the Coming of the American Revolution* (New Brunswick, N.J., 1976), 185–192; Matt B. Jones, *Vermont in the Making, 1750–1777* (Cambridge, Mass., 1939), 255–275; Robert J. Taylor, *Western Massachusetts in the Revolution* (Providence, R.I., 1954), 75–101; Robert E. Moody, "Samuel Ely: Forerunner of Shays," *New England Quarterly*, V (1932), 105–134; David P. Szatmary, *Shays' Rebellion: The Making of an Agrarian Insurrection* (Amherst, Mass., 1980); Thomas P. Slaughter, *The Whiskey Rebellion: Frontier Epilogue to the American Revolution* (New York, 1986); Barbara Karsky, "Agrarian Radicalism in the Late Revolutionary Period, 1780–1795," in Erich Angermann *et al.*, *New Wine in Old Skins: A Comparative View of Socio-Political Structures and Values Affecting the American Revolution* (Stuttgart, 1976), 87–114.

8. On the post-1760 surge into the backcountry, see Bernard Bailyn, *Voyagers to the West: A Passage in the Peopling of America on the Eve of the Revolution* (New York, 1986), chap. 1; William Wyckoff, *The Developer's Frontier: The Making of the Western New York Landscape* (New Haven, Conn., 1988), 103. On property as culturally variable, see William Cronon, *Changes in the Land: Indians, Colonists, and the Ecology of New England* (New York, 1983), 58, 69. Surely, Frederick Jackson Turner was correct in identifying the frontier as the locus of, in Richard Hofstadter's words, "certain repetitive sociological and economic processes that have refashioned man and institutions in the American environment." See Richard Hofstadter, "Introduction," in Hofstadter and Seymour Martin Lipset, eds., *Turner and the Sociology of the Frontier* (New York, 1968), 4–7 (quote, 5). I would

identify the creation and distribution of property as two of those fundamental processes. As a result of extensive migration to the frontier, most of the population increase in the United States during that generation occurred in new counties virtually unpopulated by whites in 1760. In 1790 those counties claimed one-third of the nation's population; 10 years later that share exceeded two-fifths. During the 1790s the post-1760 frontier region's population grew five times faster than the longer-settled seaboard's. On America's non-Indian population in 1760, see J. Potter, "The Growth of Population in America, 1700–1860," in D. V. Glass and D. E. C. Eversley, eds., *Population in History: Essays in Historical Demography* (Chicago, 1965), 638. I derived my figures for 1790 and again in 1800 by selecting those counties that lay beyond the frontier line for 1760 delineated in Lester J. Cappon *et al.*, eds., *Atlas of Early American History: The Revolutionary Era, 1760–1790* (Princeton, N.J., 1976), 22. For county-by-county population totals in 1790, see Evarts B. Greene and Virginia D. Harrington, *American Population before the Federal Census of 1790* (Gloucester, Mass., 1966; orig. publ. New York, 1937). For county-by-county population totals in 1800, see *Return of the Whole Number of Persons within the Several Districts of the United States . . .* (Washington, D.C., 1802; S-S 3442). My rough calculations conclude that in 1800 the pre-1760 settled area had a population of 3,045,784 (57% of the nation's total, a 15% growth over that area's 1790 population) and the post-1760 settled areas had a population of 2,262,999 (43% of the nation's total, a 78% growth over its 1790 population). In 1760 the colonies' non-Indian population equaled 1,610,000, indicating that by 1800 the pre-1760 settled areas increased by 1,435,484, or fewer than the 2,262,999 resident in post-1760 settled areas.

9. Frederick J. Turner, "Contributions of the West to American Democracy," *Atlantic Monthly*, XCI (Jan.–June 1903), 91; Richard Maxwell Brown, "Back Country Rebellions and the Homestead Ethic in America, 1740–1799," in Brown and Don E. Fehrenbacher, eds., *Tradition, Conflict, and Modernization: Perspectives on the American Revolution* (New York, 1977), 79–82; Edmund S. Morgan, "Conflict and Consensus in the American Revolution," in Stephen G. Kurtz and James H. Hutson, *Essays on the American Revolution* (Chapel Hill, N.C., 1973), 298–301.

10. Thomas Fitzsimons in the "Debate on the Supplement to the Confirming Act," Nov. 16, 1787, in Julian P. Boyd *et al.*, eds., *The Susquehannah Company Papers*, 10 vols. (Ithaca, N.Y., 1930–1971), IX, 278; Jeremy Belknap, *The History of New-Hampshire*, 3 vols. (Boston, 1791–1792), II, 459–460; Timothy Dwight, *Travels in New England and New York*, ed. Barbara Miller Solomon, 4 vols. (Cambridge, Mass., 1969; orig. publ. New Haven, Conn., 1821), II, 323. For the fundamental distinction between gentlemen and other Americans, see Jackson Turner Main, *The Antifederalists: Critics of the Constitution, 1781–1788* (Chapel Hill, N.C., 1961), 3; Gordon S. Wood, "Interests and Disinterestedness in the Making of the Constitution," in Richard Beeman *et al.*, eds., *Beyond Confederation: Origins of the Constitution and American National Identity* (Chapel Hill, N.C., 1987), 85. For the Federalist attempt to tame the Revolution and cultivate hierarchy, see Slaughter, *The Whiskey Rebellion*, 134; and Peter S. Onuf, "Liberty, Development, and Union: Visions of the West in the 1780s," *WMQ*, 3d Ser., XLIII (1986), 179–192.

11. John McFarland to James Duane, Dec. 21, 1771, quoted in Patricia U. Bonomi, *A Factious People: Politics and Society in Colonial New York* (New York, 1971), 203 n; Jack P. Greene, "Independence, Improvement, and Authority:

Toward a Framework for Understanding the Histor*ies* of the Southern Back-country during the Era of the American Revolution," in Ronald Hoffman *et al.*, eds., *An Uncivil War: The Southern Backcountry during the American Revolution* (Charlottesville, Va., 1985), 11–12; Bailyn, *Voyagers to the West*, 637; Countryman, *A People in Revolution*, 48–49; Richard L. Bushman, "Massachusetts Farmers and the Revolution," in Jack P. Greene *et al.*, *Society, Freedom, and Conscience: The American Revolution in Virginia, Massachusetts, and New York*, ed. Richard M. Jellison (New York, 1976), 77–124.

12. I owe much to the discussion in Eric Foner, *Tom Paine and Revolutionary America* (New York, 1976), xviii–xix; and in Michael Merrill and Sean Wilentz, "Class and Democracy in Revolutionary America: The Life and Writings of William Manning, 1747–1814," in Alfred F. Young, ed., *Beyond the American Revolution: Further Explorations in the History of American Radicalism* (DeKalb, Ill., forthcoming).

13. For the whigs, see Bernard Bailyn, *The Ideological Origins of the American Revolution* (Cambridge, Mass., 1967). For dismissals of agrarian rhetoric, see Richard Hofstadter, *The Age of Reform: From Bryan to F.D.R.* (New York, 1955), chap. 1; Charles S. Grant, *Democracy in the Connecticut Frontier Town of Kent* (New York, 1961), 12–23; Bernard Bailyn, *The Peopling of British North America: An Introduction* (New York, 1986), 65. On Ethan Allen, see Brown, "Back Country Rebellions," in Brown and Fehrenbacher, eds., *Tradition, Conflict, and Modernization*, 87. See also Boyd *et al.*, eds., *Susquehannah Company Papers*, XI, xxxiv–xxxvi. On the links between social circumstance and heated rhetoric, see Gordon S. Wood, "Rhetoric and Reality in the American Revolution," *WMQ*, 3d Ser., XXIII (1966), 3–32. On the social trends, see Kenneth A. Lockridge, "Social Change and the Meaning of the American Revolution," *Journal of Social History*, VI (1972–1973), 403–439.

14. Alan Taylor, "The Early Republic's Supernatural Economy: Treasure Seeking in the American Northeast, 1780–1830," *American Quarterly*, XXXVIII (1986), 6–34. On the attempt to perpetuate a democratic capitalism of small producers, see Drew R. McCoy, *The Elusive Republic: Political Economy in Jeffersonian America* (Chapel Hill, N.C., 1980). For the small producers' ideology elsewhere in rural America, see Gregory H. Nobles, *Divisions throughout the Whole: Politics and Society in Hampshire County, Massachusetts, 1740–1775* (New York, 1983); Ruth Bogin, "New Jersey's True Policy: The Radical Republican Vision of Abraham Clark," *WMQ*, 3d Ser., XXV (1978), 104–106; and James P. Walsh, "'Mechanics and Citizens': The Connecticut Artisan Protest of 1792," *WMQ*, 3d Ser., XLII (1985), 66–89.

15. David Cobb to Charles W. Hare, Nov. 10, 1810, in Frederick S. Allis, Jr., ed., *William Bingham's Maine Lands, 1790–1820*, 2 vols. (Colonial Society of Massachusetts, *Publications*, XXXVI–XXXVII [Boston, 1954]), II, 1235–1236. See Chapter 2 for further details.

16. Frederick Jackson Turner, "The Significance of the Frontier in American History," in Turner, *The Frontier in American History* (New York, 1920), 1, 38; Richard Hofstadter, *The American Political Tradition and the Men Who Made It*, 2d ed. (New York, 1973), 38–39. The ideas in this paragraph owe much to a letter from Marta Wagner. On the role of land scarcity (relative to population) in the transition to a capitalist labor market, see Christopher Clark, "The Household Economy, Market Exchange, and the Rise of Capitalism in the Connecticut Valley, 1800–1860," *Jour. Soc. Hist.*, XIII (1979–1980), 176–180.

17. Richard L. Bushman, "Family Security in the Transition from Farm to

City, 1750–1850," *Working Papers from the Regional Economic History Research Center*, IV, no. 3 (1981), 27–43; John J. Waters, "Family, Inheritance, and Migration in Colonial New England: The Evidence from Guilford, Connecticut," *WMQ*, 3d Ser., XXXIX (1982), 64–86; Christopher M. Jedrey, *The World of John Cleaveland: Family and Community in Eighteenth-Century New England* (New York, 1979), 58–94.

18. For the transformation of the early Republic, see Joyce Appleby, *Capitalism and a New Social Order: The Republican Vision of the 1790s* (New York, 1984); Steven Watts, *The Republic Reborn: War and the Making of Liberal America, 1790–1820* (Baltimore, 1987).

CHAPTER ONE

1. William Jones's testimony, May 2, 1811, Lincoln County Commissioners' Records, 5–7, MA. The epigraphs are from Elisha Sylvester to the Pejepscot Proprietors, Jan. 19, 1801, PPP, box 12, folder 1800–1801, EI; and Henry Knox to William Bingham, Nov. 11, 1795, in Frederick S. Allis, Jr., ed., *William Bingham's Maine Lands, 1790–1820*, 2 vols. (Colonial Society of Massachusetts, *Publications*, XXXVI, XXXVII [Boston, 1954]), I, 589 (hereafter cited as Allis, ed., *Bingham's Maine Lands*).

2. John Johnston, *A History of the Towns of Bristol and Bremen . . .* (Albany, N.Y., 1873), 264–280, 380; William Willis, "Scotch-Irish Immigrations to Maine, and a Summary History of Presbyterianism," MeHS, *Collections*, 1st Ser., VI (Portland, 1859), 18; Robert Earle Moody, "The Maine Frontier, 1607 to 1763" (Ph.D. diss., Yale University, 1933), 324–342, 387, 396–405; David Quimby Cushman, *The History of Ancient Sheepscot and Newcastle . . .* (Bath, 1882), 49–54, 65–70, 90–93, 105–106; Robert E. Moody, "The Proposed Colony of Georgia in New England, 1713–1733," Col. Soc. Mass., *Pubs.*, XXXIV, *Transactions, 1937–1942* (Boston, 1943), 265–267; David Dunbar to Secretary Popple, Sept. 15, 1730, *MDH*, XI, 47–52; James Sullivan, *The History of the District of Maine* (Boston, 1795; reprint ed., Augusta, 1970), 149.

3. Gordon E. Kershaw, *The Kennebeck Proprietors, 1749–1775* (Portland, 1975), 7–12; Sullivan, *History of Maine*, 150; Jasper Jacob Stahl, *History of Old Broad Bay and Waldoboro* (Portland, 1956), I, 41; Moody, "Maine Frontier," 368–369; Georgia Drew Merrill, ed., *History of Androscoggin County, Maine* (Boston, 1891), 56–60.

4. The nine claims based on 17th-century Indian deeds were: the Draper, Phillips-Toppan, Ludgate, Vaughan, Noble, Wiscasset, Brown, Hathorne, and Clark and Lake claims. See Cushman, *Ancient Sheepscot*, 1–13, 43–48, 95–99, 108–109, 114–115; Francis B. Greene, *History of Boothbay, Southport, and Boothbay Harbor, Maine* (Portland, 1906), 164–167; Sullivan, *History of Maine*, 140–142, 148; Roy Hidemichi Akagi, *The Town Proprietors of the New England Colonies: A Study of Their Development, Organization, Activities, and Controversies, 1620–1770* (Gloucester, Mass., 1963; reprint of Philadelphia, 1924), 5–9, 27; Charles Thornton Libby, ed., *Province and Court Records of Maine* (Portland, 1931), II, xxiv; Stahl, *Old Broad Bay*, I, 38. For the Indians' property notions, see William Cronon, *Changes in the Land: Indians, Colonists, and the Ecology of New England* (New York, 1983), 62–69. For survey chicanery, see *Report of the Committee for the*

Sale of Eastern Lands . . . (Boston, 1795; E 29044), 2; William Ladd, "Annals of Bakerstown, Poland, and Minot," MeHS, *Colls.*, 1st Ser., II (Portland, 1847), 111.

5. James Sullivan, *The History of Land Titles in Massachusetts* (Boston, 1801; S-S 1375), 91–92, 331–332; Isaac Collier *et al.*, petition to the General Court (quote), ca. Nov. 1800, Related Papers, Resolve CXLIII (Mar. 5, 1801), MA. In 1811 a General Court investigative committee attributed the settlers' legal woes to the lack of any "mode under the existing laws, to compel the proprietors to settle between themselves, as it respects their several titles"; see *Order of Both Branches of the Legislature of Massachusetts to Investigate the Causes of the Difficulties in the County of Lincoln* . . . (Boston, 1811; S-S 23314), 27.

6. Robert Hallowell Gardiner, *Early Recollections of Robert Hallowell Gardiner, 1782–1864* (Hallowell, 1936), 62; Cushman, *Ancient Sheepscot*, 114, 162–163; John Noble, "Land Controversies in Maine, 1769–1772," Col. Soc. Mass., *Pubs.*, VI (Boston, 1900), 24; Job Averell to Samuel Whittemore, Sept. 18, 1760, SM, MeSL; Boothbay's petition to King George III, June 1772, *MDH*, XIV, 168. For the earliest violence, see Alan Taylor, "'A Kind of Warr': The Contest for Land on the Northeastern Frontier, 1750–1820," *WMQ*, 3d Ser., XLVI (1989), 3–26.

7. Richard L. Bushman, "Massachusetts Farmers and the Revolution," in Jack P. Greene *et al.*, *Society, Freedom, and Conscience: The American Revolution in Virginia, Massachusetts, and New York*, ed. Richard M. Jellison (New York, 1976), 77–124; Richard L. Bushman, *King and People in Provincial Massachusetts* (Chapel Hill, N.C., 1985), 198–205; Richard M. Brown, "Back Country Rebellions and the Homestead Ethic," in Brown and Don E. Fehrenbacher, eds., *Tradition, Conflict, and Modernization: Perspectives on the American Revolution* (New York, 1977), 73–98; Harry J. Carman, ed., *American Husbandry* (New York, 1939), 52–53. On most Scotch-Irish emigrants as tenants fleeing food shortages and rack-renting, see R. J. Dickson, *Ulster Emigration to Colonial America, 1718–1775* (London, 1966), 10–15, 29–30. On the persistent class struggle between tenants and landlords in England over rents, labor boons, fines, and use rights, see C. E. Searle, "Custom, Class Conflict, and Agrarian Capitalism: The Cumbrian Customary Economy in the Eighteenth Century," *Past and Present*, no. 110 (Feb. 1986), 106–133.

8. Bushman, *King and People*, 176–210; Robert A. Gross, *The Minutemen and Their World* (New York, 1976), 74–88, 105–107; Christopher M. Jedrey, *The World of John Cleaveland: Family and Community in Eighteenth-Century New England* (New York, 1979), 73, 95, 131–132; Gregory H. Nobles, *Divisions throughout the Whole: Politics and Society in Hampshire County, Massachusetts, 1740–1775* (New York, 1983), 155–186; Kenneth Lockridge, "Land, Population, and the Evolution of New England Society, 1630–1790," *Past and Present*, no. 39 (Apr. 1968), 62–80.

9. Adele Edna Plachta, "The Privileged and the Poor: A History of the District of Maine, 1771–1793" (Ph.D. diss., University of Maine at Orono, 1975), 28; Greene, *Boothbay*, 227; John L. Locke, *Sketches of the History of the Town of Camden, Maine* . . . (Hallowell, 1859), 30; Jonathan Greenleaf, *Sketches of the Ecclesiastical History of the State of Maine* . . . (Portsmouth, N.H., 1821), 135–136; William Allen, *The History of Norridgewock* . . . (Norridgewock, 1849), 91; Robert H. Gardiner, "History of the Kennebec Purchase . . . ," MeHS, *Colls.*, 1st Ser., II (Portland, 1847), 287; Oscar Handlin and Mary Flug Handlin, *Commonwealth: A Study in the Role of Government in the American Economy: Massachusetts, 1774–1861* (Cambridge, Mass., 1969), 9–12. In Sept. 1783, Thomaston's selectmen reported that their town was "mainly settled by those who were put to straights by the late

public calamity by reason of other callings failing." See Thomaston's selectmen to the General Court, Sept. 13, 1783, *MDH*, XX, 260. Balltown's settlers described themselves as poor men who returned "from a dissolved army to our naked wives and children and the young men to their parents and relatives in the same condition." See Balltown Plantation's petition to the General Court, ca. Jan. 1808, Related Papers, Act LXXIV (Mar. 2, 1808), MA. An examination of Balltown's 152 heads of household in 1790 reveals 69 veterans (45.4%) and 83 nonveterans. Because the sources for war service are incomplete, these figures probably underestimate the number of veterans. I compiled the Balltown figures from [Jefferson Historical Society], *Jefferson, Touchstone of Democracy* ([Lewiston], 1976), 89–97. On town incorporations and population in 1790, see John O. Noble, Jr., "Messengers from the Wilderness: Maine Representatives to the Massachusetts General Court, 1760–1819" (Ph.D. diss., University of Maine at Orono, 1976), 288–292. The annual tax lists for Hallowell-Augusta show that the tempo of influx to that Kennebec Valley community increased during the 1780s; during the five years 1775–1779, about 10 new families joined the tax rolls every year. During the next decade, 1780–1789, that rate more than doubled to an average of 21 new taxpayers per year; see James W. North, *The History of Augusta . . .* (Augusta, 1870), 109–220. In 1800, 43,236 of 52,826 (81.8%) mid-Maine residents dwelled in post-1770 incorporated communities.

10. William Rogers testimony, May 3, 1811, Lincoln County Commissioners Records, 25, MA; Jonathan Bagley to Moses Little, Mar. 8, 1780, LFP, box 1, folder 2, EI; William Gardiner to Silvester Gardiner, Nov. 16, ca. 1783, Gardiner Family Papers, Oaklands, Gardiner; Gardiner, "Kennebec Purchase," MeHS, *Colls.*, 1st Ser., II (1847), 287–288; William Allen, *History of Industry, Maine . . .*, 2d ed. (Skowhegan, 1869), 5. For proprietary and court paralysis, see Stahl, *Old Broad Bay*, I, 529–533; Kershaw, *Kennebeck Proprietors*, 275–285; North, *Augusta*, 279–280; Lincolnshire Company Records, 143–144 (Sept. 7, 1774–Mar. 23, 1785), MHS. During the prewar decade, 1765–1774, proprietors conducted at least 40 trespass and ejectment suits against settlers in Lincoln County before the Supreme Judicial Court. During the subsequent wartime decade, 1775–1784, that court did not hear a single proprietary case. See the Record Books of the Supreme Judicial Court for Lincoln County, 1765–1784, MA.

An 1812 investigation into the history of eastern Balltown's 251 farms revealed the Revolution's importance in disrupting the courts and proprietary supervision, throwing open the backcountry to possession claimants. More than half of the farms dated their original possession to the four years 1774–1777, when the closed courts, absent proprietors, and rumors the state would confiscate the patents signaled a land rush by downriver inhabitants. By war's end in 1783, only a few scattered pockets remained unclaimed. Possession claims averaged only 6 per year during the 13 years prior to 1774 but surged to 14 per year during the 11-year interregnum in proprietary supervision, 1774–1784. See James Sinclair and Joseph Weeks, "Statement of Jefferson Inhabitants' Titles for Submission to the Lincoln County Commissioners," 1812, miscellaneous box 25 ("Settlers' Evidences"), MA. The eastern half of Balltown was incorporated as the town of Jefferson in 1807.

11. John H. Cary, "'The Juditious are Intirely Neglected': The Fate of a Tory," *New England Historical and Genealogical Register*, CXXXIV (1980), 113–114; William Frost to George Thatcher, Feb. 7, 1788, GTP, BPL. These descriptions of an intellectual ferment that combined religious and political persuasion and that occurred among the poorer folk parallel in a very striking manner what Christo-

pher Hill found for the English Revolution of the mid-17th century, in *The World Turned Upside Down: Radical Ideas during the English Revolution* (New York, 1972).

12. "A Member of the Watchful Clubb," *Boston Gazette, and the Country Journal,* Nov. 29, 1779; Item 12 of the draft constitution printed in the *Boston Gazette,* July 19, 1779; *Boston Gazette,* June 19, 1780 (quote); Handlin and Handlin, *Commonwealth,* 81; John Murray, *Jerubbaal; or, Tyranny's Grove Destroyed, and the Altar of Liberty Finished* (Newburyport, Mass., 1784; E 18618), 56–57; "Scribble-Scrabble," *Cumberland Gazette* (Falmouth [now Portland]), June 8, 1786. See also Nathaniel Niles, *Two Discourses on Liberty; Delivered . . . June 5, 1774 . . .* (Newburyport, Mass., 1774; E 13502), 10–11; Van Beck Hall, *Politics without Parties: Massachusetts, 1780–1791* (Pittsburgh, Pa., 1972), 126; Bushman, *King and People,* 237–239; Bushman, "Massachusetts Farmers and the Revolution," in Greene *et al., Society, Freedom, and Conscience,* ed. Jellison, 111–113.

13. Thurston Whiting and Benjamin Brackett to Henry Knox, Sept. 7, 1801, HKP, LII, 87, MHS; Elisha Sylvester to the Pejepscot Proprietors, Jan. 19, 1801, folder 1800–1801, PPP, box 12, EI.

14. On the discredited notions, see Henry Knox to George Washington, Oct. 23, 1786, in Francis S. Drake, *Life and Correspondence of Henry Knox, Major-General in the American Revolutionary Army* (Boston, 1873), 91; Samuel Savage to George Thatcher, Mar. 7, 1788, GTP, BPL; William Plumer, "Letters of William Plumer, 1786–1787," Col. Soc. Mass., *Pubs.,* XI, *Transactions, 1906–1907* (Boston, 1910), 392. On "Libertymount" (Davistown), see the intentions of marriage of Nathaniel Hause and Hannah Davis, Feb. 4, 1787, *BHM,* VII, 21. Fairfax's petition (Peter Chalmers *et al.*) to the General Court, ca. Jan. 1808, Related Papers, Act LXXIV (Mar. 2, 1808), MA.

15. Elliot G. Vaughan to Colonel Thomas Cutts, Oct. 30, 1810, in miscellaneous box 24 ("Papers Relating to Lands in Lincoln County"), MA; part of the document appears in Johnston, *History of Bristol and Bremen,* 485.

16. North Callahan, *Henry Knox: General Washington's General* (New York, 1958), 338–364; Marvin S. Sadik, *Colonial and Federal Portraits at Bowdoin College* (Brunswick, 1966), 40–46; George Thomas Little, *The Descendants of George Little, Who Came to Newbury, Massachusetts, in 1640* (Auburn, 1882), 40–42, 109–110. For the incomplete confiscations, see Thomas Rice (Lincoln County's registrar of deeds) to Nathan Dane, Apr. 27, 1793, Nathan Dane Papers, box 6, folder Apr.–May 1793, MHS: "Libels were filed against many Estates in this County for the purpose of confiscation but the Peace intervening put an End to the business so that no Judgment of confiscation was entered against any Lands in this county." For the Waldo Patent, see Henry Knox to Mrs. Horwood, Jan. 13, 1789 (quotes), and Knox memo, Oct. 31, 1789, HKP, LII, 9, 26, MHS; Henry Knox to the General Court, ca. 1785, HKP, LI, 84, MHS; Eastern Lands Committee Report, July 7, 1784, *MDH,* XX, 354–356; William Wetmore to Samuel Phillips, Oct. 21, 1784, ELC, box 53, MA; July 4, 1785, Resolve, in *Resolves of the General Court of the Commonwealth of Massachusetts . . . 1785* (Boston, 1785; E 19090), 61; Resolve VIII (Nov. 1, 1788), in *Resolves of the General Court of the Commonwealth of Massachusetts . . . [Oct.–Nov. 1788]* (Boston, 1788; E 21248), 41; William Wetmore to Henry Knox, Aug. 19, 1785, HKP, LI, 86, MHS, explains the haste. For the Kennebeck Proprietors' confirmation, see Kershaw, *Kennebeck Proprietors,* 290–302; North, *Augusta,* 146, 287; Gardiner, "Kennebec Purchase," MeHS, *Colls.,* 1st Ser., II (1847), 286–287. For the Pejepscot Patent, see Little, *The Descendants of George Little,* 40–41, 109–110; James Sullivan to William King, Feb. 17, 1806, WKP, box 5, MeHS; Elisha Sylvester *et al.* to the Eastern

Lands Committee, June 9, 1789, ELC, box 10, MA; quote from John Daggett *et al.* to the General Court, Dec. 29, 1791, Related Papers, Resolve CXXXIV (Mar. 6, 1792), MA; Commonwealth v. Pejepscot Proprietors (May 1813), Cumberland County Supreme Judicial Court Records, III, 552.

17. Waterman Thomas's Feb. 1795 petition to the General Court is reprinted in Stahl, *Old Broad Bay*, I, 541. On political apathy and powerlessness in frontier Maine, see Plachta, "The Privileged and the Poor"; Hall, *Politics without Parties*, 13, 67, 69; and Ronald F. Banks, *Maine Becomes a State: The Movement to Separate Maine from Massachusetts, 1785–1820* (Middletown, Conn., 1970), 24–25. For the representatives, see *Fleets' Pocket Almanack . . . 1788* (Boston, 1788; E 20361), 52.

18. East of Union River petition, Aug. 17, 1786, *MDH*, XXI, 325; John Allan to Governor Hancock, July 1, 1782, *MDH*, XX, 54; Daniel Cony to George Thatcher, Mar. 15, 1788, GTP, BPL; Alexander Baring to Hope and Company, Dec. 3, 1796, in Allis, ed., *Bingham's Maine Lands*, II, 765; "Ancient Land Grants East of Penobscot River," *BHM*, I, 31; Allis, ed., *Bingham's Maine Lands*, I, 31, 50; *Report of the Committee for the Sale of Eastern Lands*, 2.

19. Resolve CLXIX, Mar. 22, 1784, *Resolves of the General Court of the Commonwealth of Massachusetts . . . [Jan.–Mar. 1784]* (Boston, 1784; E 18601), 139–140; Allis, ed., *Bingham's Maine Lands*, I, 24–27, 36–37; Resolve CIII (July 9, 1784), in *Resolves of the General Court of the Commonwealth of Massachusetts . . . [May–July 1784]* (Boston, 1784; E 18602), 49; [Benjamin] Lincoln, "Observations on the Climate, Soil, and Value of the Eastern Counties in the District of Maine . . . ," MHS, *Collections*, 1st Ser., IV (Boston, 1795), 152.

20. Allen, *Norridgewock*, 51–52, 60; North, *Augusta*, 84; Locke, *Camden*, 53; Gardiner, "Kennebec Purchase," MeHS, *Colls.*, 1st Ser., II (1847), 284–287. The few backcountry towns included in the liberal policies—Chesterville, Winthrop, Readfield, Harlem (China), Union, and Hope—held back from their neighbors' resistance (see Map 5). Only along the Lincoln County coast around Pemaquid—where proprietary claims were most overlapping and proprietary generosity was least evident—did frontcountry towns participate in the resistance. The 1800 federal census recorded populations for 36 communities located along navigable waters and 39 in the backcountry. In 1802 the General Court's valuation committee assessed taxes on all 36 frontcountry communities but exempted 11 of the 39 backcountry settlements. According to the committee, the average frontcountry taxpayer was worth $24.20, compared to $18.88 for his counterpart in those backcountry towns prosperous enough to pay any taxes. William Allen, Jr., of Industry explained that the backcountry drew its inhabitants from "persons who had no property" who gambled "that they might gain a title by possession"; see Allen, *Industry*, 5, 9, 42–43. In 1800, three-fourths of mid-Maine's backcountry settlements (30 of 39) participated in the resistance; those 30 represented more than three-quarters (30 of 38) of the militant communities. Conversely, three-fourths of mid-Maine's towns that held back from the resistance lay along navigable rivers or the coast (28 of 37). Almost all (130 of 148) of the documented confrontations of the resistance during the years 1790–1819 occurred in the backcountry. At least 9 of the 18 incidents in the frontcountry involved backcountry settlers temporarily venturing out to harass a land agent or break open a jail. I define an incident as any illegal act committed against proprietors, their agents, or their supporters. I sought incidents that could be linked to the land unrest in the Waldo, Plymouth, and Pejepscot patents and in the Indian deed claims along the Lincoln County coast: Lincoln, Kennebec, and western Hancock (now Waldo) counties, and the Cumberland County towns in

the Androscoggin Valley. The calculations are confined to those incidents occurring 1790–1819, when documentation is most complete. See Maps 3–4, Figure 1, and Appendix 3.

21. Gardiner, "Kennebec Purchase," MeHS, *Colls.*, 1st Ser., II (1847), 284–294.

22. James Bowdoin to Daniel Cony, Feb. 20, 1799, James Bowdoin Papers, Bowdoin College; John Chandler to Gov. James Sullivan, Apr. 18, 1808, House File (unpassed) 6385, MA; Lothrop Lewis to Josiah Little, May 14, 1800 (Pejepscot Patent settlers quoted), PPP, box 4, Letters to Josiah Little folder, EI. For the proprietors' control over judicial patronage in the Eastern Country, see also Samuel Merrill to Josiah Little, Oct. 30, 1793, LFP, box 3, folder 8, EI; Solomon Lombard to John Pitts, Oct. 24, 1777, KPP, box 3, MeHS; Silvester Gardiner to Jacob Bailey, Oct. 30, 1760, Jacob Bailey Papers, Library of Congress; Benjamin Vaughan to Charles Vaughan, Jan. 17, 1798, Charles Vaughan Papers, box B, folder 2, Bowdoin College; Mason Wheaton to Knox, Mar. 1, 1798, and Knox to the governor, June 22, 1798, HKP, XXLI, 76, 132, MHS. On the settlers' legal disadvantage, see Libby, ed., *Province and Court Records of Maine*, II, xxiii–xxxi; Ducktrap residents to Henry Knox, Oct. 18, 1788, HKP, XXII, 164, MHS; and Joseph H. Pierce, Jr., to Joseph Sprague, Aug. 3, 1821, HAPP, box 3, NEHGSL.

23. Isaac Parker's charge to the jury, in John Merrick, ed., *Trial of David Lynn . . . for the Murder of Paul Chadwick at Malta . . .* (Augusta, 1809; S-S 18778), 42. For the Kennebeck Proprietors' suits, see the Supreme Judicial Court Record Books for Kennebec and Lincoln counties, MeSA. The proprietors prevailed in 39 of the 42 suits decided by juries, in the 12 cases where the defendant failed to appear in court, and in all 9 cases submitted to court-appointed referees.

24. John Page to the Kennebeck Proprietors, May 1805, KPP, box 5, MeHS ("grand axis"); David Cobb to William Bingham, Sept. 7, 1797, in Allis, ed., *Bingham's Maine Lands*, II, 859; Isaac Parker to Henry Knox, Feb. 21, 1804, HKP, XLV, 140, MHS.

25. The quotes are in David Sewall's deposition, Apr. 27, 1797, Bakerstown volume, PPP, EI. See also James Sullivan to William King, Feb. 17, 1806, WKP, box 5, MeHS; and the July 15, 1797, entry in Josiah Little's memo book, PPP, "1782–1829 Books" box, EI.

26. Josiah Little memo, July 16, 1799, Bakerstown volume, PPP, EI; James Sullivan to William King, Feb. 17, 1806, WKP, box 5, MeHS; Resolve, LXIV (June 29, 1798), in *Acts and Laws of the Commonwealth of Massachusetts, 1798–1799* (Boston, 1897), 208–209; the commission's awards are in "Settlers on Pejepscot Lands," July 12, 1804, MA; the 405 settlers included 77 from Leeds, 109 from Greene, 78 from Lewiston, 22 from Little River (Lisbon), 46 from Durham, 58 from Pejepscot (Auburn), and 15 from a gore of land. For example, in the town of Leeds the commissioners awarded quieting terms to 77 settlers, but the Pejepscot Proprietors issued deeds to only 24. The Leeds deeds from Josiah Little are dated Dec. 14–18, 1805, and located in KCD, XII, 567–587, XXXI, 110. For the Supreme Judicial Court ruling, see Josiah Little to Daniel Humphries, Jan. 11, 1808, PPP, box 4, EI. See also Nathaniel Dummer to William King, Feb. 18, 1806, WKP, box 5, MeHS; *Eastern Argus* (Portland), Mar. 28, 1806; and chapter CXLIII (Mar. 5, 1801), in *Acts and Laws of the Commonwealth of Massachusetts, 1801* (Boston, 1897), 223–226.

27. Abraham Welch to George Ulmer, July 11, 1801, HKP, XLIV, 24, MHS; Hugh Mulloy's petition to the General Court, ca. Jan. 1810, Related Papers, Resolve CXLIV (Mar. 3, 1810), MA.

28. Sally Falk Moore, *Law as Process: An Anthropological Approach* (London, 1978), 26, 51, 64, 78.

29. Asahel Stearns, *A Summary of the Law and Practice of Real Actions . . .* , 2d ed. (Hallowell, 1831), 49–55; Sullivan, *History of Maine*, 140–142.

30. Job Averell to Samuel Whittemore, Sept. 29, 1743, SM, MeSL; Wilson quoted in James McFarland deposition, Sept. 17, 1768, SCF 139339, DCCCLXXXVIII, MA; Thomas Fayerweather to ———, Mar. 3, 1795, Lincolnshire Company Papers, in William H. Prescott Collection, MHS; Robert Greenhalgh Albion, *Forests and Sea Power: The Timber Problem of the Royal Navy, 1652–1862* (Hamden, Conn., 1965; orig. publ. Boston, 1926), 242, 259; Charles E. Clark, *The Eastern Frontier: The Settlement of Northern New England, 1610–1763* (New York, 1970), 129; Charles F. Carroll, *The Timber Economy of Puritan New England* (Providence, R.I., 1973), 104–114.

31. Sheepscot settlers quoted in Nehemiah Turner's deposition, June 1767, and Samuel Goodwin's deposition, May 12, 1768, SCF 139350, DCCCLXXXIX, MA.

32. In 1791 among Balltown's taxpayers, the top fifth held almost half the assessed property, and the bottom fifth had only 2%. Similarly, in 1798 the top fifth among Ducktrap-Northport's taxpayers owned half the assessed wealth in contrast to the 5% held by the poorest fifth. The degree of inequality matched that of New England's older rural communities, but the absolute amount of property was much less; so a top-quintile taxpayer in a Maine settlement would have been a relatively humble man in a Massachusetts town. See the 1791 Balltown tax valuation, MSL; and the 1798 Direct Tax returns for Ducktrap and Northport, NEHGSL. See Tables 1 and 3.

33. Jonathan Jones's deposition, June 8, 1797, ELC, box 53, MA; Samuel E. Dutton's minutes, Sept. 1803, HKP, XLV, 115, MHS; Benjamin Trask's deposition, Aug. 24, 1804, Benjamin Kinney's deposition, May 11, 1805, in Colburn v. Parsons, LC-SJC Files, box 420 (1805), LCC; Ladd, "Annals of Bakerstown," MeHS, *Colls.*, 1st Ser., II (1847), 130; William Morris to Theophile Cazenove, Dec. 9, 1792, in Allis, ed., *Bingham's Maine Lands*, I, 201; François Alexandre Frédéric, duc de La Rochefoucault Liancourt, *Travels through the United States of North America . . .* (London, 1799), I, 429–430; Nathaniel C. Allen's deposition, May 19, 1806, Related Papers, Resolve LX (Feb. 24, 1807), MA.

34. Samuel Ely, *The Deformity of a Hideous Monster, Discovered in the Province of Maine, by a Man in the Woods, Looking after Liberty* (Boston, 1797; E 32081), 26. On Williams, see the depositions by Noah Dodge (quote), and Samuel Pendleton, July 1, 1794, SCF 141008, CMXXI, MA; and *BHM*, I, 168, IV, 114–115.

35. Samuel E. Dutton's minutes, Sept. 1803, HKP, XLV, 115, MHS. In 1812, selectmen investigated the history of Jefferson's 251 farms and listed the owner, the original settler, the year of first possession, and the intermediate owners, if any. Most of the town's homesteads were 35–40 years old. Only about a fifth (57 of 251) belonged to the original possessor or someone with the same surname. Eighty different individuals staked the original claims to Jefferson's 251 farms. Most (48 of 80) were small operators who claimed only 1 or 2; only one-fifth (16 of 80) staked more than 4 claims. But there were two important exceptions; Jonathan Jones and John Weeks claimed 29 lots as partners, and 9 more individually. Jones and Weeks persisted in the settlement, selling off most of their claims and developing substantial farms of their own, but most of the small claimers quickly sold out and moved on. Only 38 of the 80 appeared on the first federal census in 1790 for Balltown (as Jefferson was known before incorpora-

tion). See James Sinclair and Joseph Weeks, "Statement of Jefferson Inhabitants' Titles for Submission to the Lincoln County Commissioners," 1812, miscellaneous box 25, MA.

36. In 1797 the Waldo Patent Land Commission found that original settlers (or their heirs) possessed 35 of the 44 lots settled during the 1790s, but only 32 of the 72 settled during the 1780s and only 9 of the 33 settled in the 1770s. In 1792 Ebenezer Farwell discovered that original settlers or their heirs held only 8 of Jones Plantation's 23 lots settled before 1780. See the Waldo Patent Commission Settler Submissions, I, II, MA; Ebenezer Farwell to the Kennebeck Proprietors, May 8, 1792, KPP, box 3, MeHS. See also Park Holland's 1802 Bangor settler list, HKP, XLV, 74, MHS. For insistence on having already paid for their possessions, see the Ducktrap residents' petition to Henry Knox, Oct. 18, 1788, XXII, 164, HKP, MHS; and the Waldoborough Gore petition to the General Court, Nov. 1803, ELC, box 53, MA. For the decadal persistence rates, see Table 2.

37. Thomas L. Purvis, "Origins and Patterns of Agrarian Unrest in New Jersey, 1735 to 1754," *WMQ*, 3d Ser., XXXIX (1982), 600–627; Oscar Handlin, "The Eastern Frontier of New York," *New York History*, XVIII (1937), 50–75; Matt B. Jones, *Vermont in the Making, 1750–1777* (Cambridge, Mass., 1939); Julian P. Boyd *et al.*, eds., *The Susquehannah Company Papers*, 10 vols. (Ithaca, N.Y., 1930–1971), V, xxi–lii; Elizabeth K. Henderson, "The Northwestern Lands of Pennsylvania, 1790–1812," *Pennsylvania Magazine of History and Biography*, LX (1936), 131–160. For the possession speculator elsewhere on the American frontier, see Paul W. Gates, "The Role of the Land Speculator in Western Development," in Gates, *Landlords and Tenants on the Prairie Frontier: Studies in American Land Policy* (Ithaca, N.Y., 1973), 50.

CHAPTER TWO

1. The epigraphs are from Alden Bradford, *A Sermon Delivered before the Congregational Society at Thomaston, (Maine) November 2, 1806* . . . [Wiscasset, 1806], 14; Samuel Thatcher's eulogy, Oct. 28, 1806, *BHM*, V, 133; [James Davis and Samuel Ely], *The Appeal of the Two Counties of Lincoln and Hancock, from the Forlorn Hope, or, Mount of Distress; To the General Court, or, to All the World* (Portsmouth, N.H., 1796; E 31477), 19. Thomas Barnard, *A Sermon Preached in Boston, New-England, before the Society for Encouraging Industry, and Employing the Poor, September 20, 1758* (Boston, 1758; E 8078), 17; Gary B. Nash, *Urban Crucible: Social Change, Political Consciousness, and the Origins of the American Revolution* (Cambridge, Mass., 1979), 189–193.

2. The Gentlemen Subscribers included Charles Apthorp, Charles Ward Apthorp, James Bowdoin, William Brattle, Dr. Silvester Gardiner, John Hancock, Thomas Hancock, Benjamin Hallowell, Briggs Hallowell, James Pitts, Henry Vassall, and Jacob Wendell of the Kennebeck Proprietors; Thomas Brindley, Middlecott Cooke, William Molineux, and Richard Saltonstall of the Twenty Associates; Thomas Flucker, Isaac Winslow, and Francis Waldo of the Waldo Heirs; and Thomas Hutchinson and Isaac Royall of the Pejepscot Proprietors. The subscribers are listed in Society for Encouraging Industry and Employing the Poor, *Rules of Incorporation* . . . (Boston, 1754; E 7155), 7–12. For the Great Proprietors, see Robert Earle Moody, "The Maine Frontier, 1607 to 1763"

(Ph.D. diss., Yale University, 1933), 357; Roy Hidemichi Akagi, *The Town Proprietors of the New England Colonies: A Study of Their Development, Organization, Activities, and Controversies, 1620–1770* (Gloucester, Mass., 1963; reprint of Philadelphia, 1924), 245–246; James Sullivan, *The History of the District of Maine* (Augusta, 1970; reprint of Boston, 1795), 163–165; Gordon E. Kershaw, *The Kennebeck Proprietors, 1749–1775* (Portland, 1975), 43–61, 79–98, 329–332; Marvin S. Sadik, *Colonial and Federal Portraits at Bowdoin College* (Brunswick, 1966), 57, 79; Joseph Williamson, *History of the City of Belfast . . .* , I (Portland, 1877), 80 n.

3. Clifford K. Shipton, *Biographical Sketches of Those Who Attended Harvard College . . . [Sibley's Harvard Graduates]*, 14 vols. (Cambridge, Mass., Boston, 1933–1975), IX, 120–127.

4. Barnard, *A Sermon Preached in Boston*, 10, 13, 19, 20. In 1748 William Douglass, another Boston gentleman, wrote of northern New England, "Idleness and intemperance, the bane of all our plantations, especially considering the nature of the first settlers of this place, are more dangerous than any parcels of despicable straggling Indians." See William Douglass, *A Summary, Historical and Political, of the First Planting, Progressive Improvements, and Present State of the British Settlements in North-America*, II (Boston, 1751; E 6663), 7 n.

5. Drew R. McCoy, *The Elusive Republic: Political Economy in Jeffersonian America* (Chapel Hill, N.C., 1980), 115, 122; J. E. Crowley, *This Sheba, Self: The Conceptualization of Economic Life in Eighteenth-Century America* (Baltimore, 1974), 83.

6. Barnard, *A Sermon Preached in Boston*, 13. McCoy, *The Elusive Republic*, 105–119, discusses the increased use of this rhetoric during the economic hard times of the 1780s.

7. Nathaniel Appleton to David Fales, May 5, 1769, and Appleton to William Minot, June 18, 1770, Lincolnshire Company Record Book, 116, MHS; Henry Alline, Jr., to Briggs Hallowell, May 4, 1768 ("sobriety"), Alline to Peter Haywood and Oliver Wright, Sept. 6, 1769, KPP, Letterbook I, 15, 24, MeHS.

8. Nathaniel Fales to Henry Knox, Jan. 14, 1785, HKP, XVII, 161, MHS. See also Peter S. Onuf, "Liberty, Development, and Union: Visions of the West in the 1780s," *WMQ*, 3d Ser., XLIII (1986), 193–203; McCoy, *The Elusive Republic*, 122; Thomas P. Slaughter, *The Whiskey Rebellion: Frontier Epilogue to the American Revolution* (New York, 1986), 134–135; and Andrew R. L. Cayton, *The Frontier Republic: Ideology and Politics in the Ohio Country, 1780–1825* (Kent, Ohio, 1986), 16–19.

9. Shipton, *Sibley's Harvard Graduates*, XVII, 280.

10. *Ibid.*; James W. North, *The History of Augusta . . .* (Augusta, 1870), 389–390. For the frontier reform impulse among enlightened 18th-century gentlemen, see Lester H. Cohen, "Eden's Constitution: The Paradisiacal Dream and Enlightenment Values in Late Eighteenth-Century Literature of the American Frontier," *Prospects: An Annual of American Cultural Studies*, III (1977), 86–88; Cayton, *The Frontier Republic*, 13.

11. Samuel Vaughan to Charles Vaughan, Apr. 20, 1789, Samuel Vaughan to Frances Western Apthorp, Charles Vaughan Papers, box A, George and Martha Vaughan Papers destined for Special Collections, Bowdoin College.

12. Samuel Vaughan to Charles Vaughan, Feb. 13, 1793; C. Vaughan to S. Vaughan, Mar. 19, 1793, quoted in S. Vaughan to C. Vaughan, June 30, 1793; S. Vaughan to C. Vaughan, June 30, 1793; S. Vaughan to C. Vaughan, Feb. 3, 1794; C. Vaughan's incautious quote repeated in Benjamin Vaughan to C. Vaughan, Dec. 15, 1797, Charles Vaughan Papers, box A, Bowdoin College. See also North, *Augusta*, 389–390.

13. William Allen, "Now and Then," MeHS, *Collections*, 1st Ser., VII (Bath,

1876), 279–280; North, *Augusta*, 390; David Cony to David Cobb, Mar. 14, 1801, quoted in David Cobb to William Bingham, Apr. 7, 1801, in Frederick Allis, Jr., ed., *William Bingham's Maine Lands, 1790–1820*, 2 vols. (Colonial Society of Massachusetts, *Publications*, XXXVI–XXXVII [Boston, 1954]), II, 1114 (hereafter cited as Allis, ed., *Bingham's Maine Lands*); and Charles Vaughan to the Kennebeck Proprietors, Feb. 13, 1805, KPP, box 5, MeHS (academies quote); Charles Maurice de Talleyrand-Périgord, "Letter on the Eastern Part of America" (Boston, Sept. 24, 1794), in Hans Huth and Wilma J. Pugh, eds., *Talleyrand in America as a Financial Promoter, 1794–96* (*Annual Report of the American Historical Association, 1941*, II [Washington, D.C., 1942]), 74 (hereafter cited as Talleyrand, "Letter"); Charles Vaughan to James Bowdoin, Jan. 15, 1801, KPP, box 4, MeHS (quotes on agriculture); on the Kennebeck Proprietors' "interest" in the Kennebeck Agricultural Society, see Benjamin Vaughan to David Cobb, Apr. 30, 1800, in Allis, ed., *Bingham's Maine Lands*, II, 1043.

14. Quote from Robert Hallowell Gardiner, *Early Recollections of Robert Hallowell Gardiner, 1782–1864* (Hallowell, 1936), 63; Robert Hallowell Gardiner, "Jones Eddy," MeHS, *Colls.*, 1st Ser., IV (Portland, 1859), 46; Allen, "Now and Then," MeHS, *Colls.*, 1st Ser., VII (1876), 279–281; Charles Vaughan to the Kennebeck Proprietors, Sept. 1, 1807, KPP, box 6, MeHS.

15. "The Will of General Henry Knox, of Thomaston," *BHM*, V, 140.

16. Charles Royster, *A Revolutionary People at War: The Continental Army and American Character, 1775–1783* (Chapel Hill, N.C., 1979), 79–95, 353–357; Cayton, *The Frontier Republic*, 18.

17. On the values of the Federalist gentry, see John Brooke, "Society, Revolution, and the Symbolic Uses of the Dead: An Historical Ethnography of the Massachusetts Near Frontier, 1730–1820" (Ph.D. diss., University of Pennsylvania, 1982), 435–436; Cayton, *The Frontier Republic*, 43.

18. Joseph W. Porter, "Memoir of General Henry Knox," *BHM*, V, 121–124; North Callahan, *Henry Knox: General Washington's General* (New York, 1958); Allis, ed., *Bingham's Maine Lands*, I, 37–38.

19. Jasper Jacob Stahl, *History of Old Broad Bay and Waldoboro*, 2 vols. (Portland, 1956), I, 379, 530–531; Joseph Williamson, *History of the City of Belfast . . .*, I, (Portland, 1877), 45 n; Hannah Flucker to Henry Knox, July 23, 1784, HKP, LI, 62, MHS; Resolve XLVIII (June 28, 1784), in *Resolves of the General Court of the Commonwealth of Massachusetts . . . [May–July 1784]* (Boston, 1784; E 18602), 27.

20. Henry Knox to Mrs. Horwood, Jan. 13, 1789 (quote), and Knox memo, Oct. 31, 1789, HKP, LII, 9, 26, MHS; Henry Knox to the General Court, ca. 1785, HKP, LI, 84, MHS; Eastern Lands Committee Report, July 7, 1784, *MDH*, XX, 354–356; William Wetmore to Samuel Phillips, Oct. 21, 1784, ELC, box 53, MA; July 4, 1785, Resolve, in *Resolves of the General Court of the Commonwealth of Massachusetts . . . [May–July 1785]* (Boston, 1785; E 19090), 61; Resolve VIII (Nov. 1, 1788), in *Resolves of the General Court of the Commonwealth of Massachusetts . . . [Oct.–Nov. 1788]* (Boston, 1788; E 21248), 41; William Wetmore to Henry Knox, Aug. 19, 1785, HKP, LI, 86, MHS. For the legislative intrigue, see Henry Jackson to Henry Knox, Feb. 13, 1791, XXVII, 140; Jackson to Knox, Feb. 20, 1791, XXVII, 148; Jackson to Knox, Mar. 6, 1791, XXVII, 156; Joseph Pierce to Knox, Feb. 15, 1791, XXVII, 142; Pierce to Knox, June 22, 1794, XXXV, 139; Pierce to Knox, June 29, 1794, XXXV, 145; Pierce to Knox, Feb. 15, 1795, XXXVII, 33; Pierce to Knox, Feb. 23, 1795, XXXVII, 38; Pierce to Knox, Mar. 19, 1795, XXXVII, 51; and Samuel Breck to Knox, Feb. 15, 1791, XXVII, 149, all HKP, MHS.

21. Henry Knox's deed to Oliver Smith, July 2, 1791, HCD, I, 346, HCC; Oliver Smith's deed to Henry Jackson, Dec. 1, 1791, HCD, II, 142, HCC; Henry Knox to Mrs. S. L. Flucker, May 15, 1788, Knox to Mrs. Horwood, Jan. 13, 1789, HKP, XXII, 41, LII, 9, MHS; Joseph Pierce to Henry Knox, June 14, 1791, HKP, XXIX, 106, MHS; Stahl, *Old Broad Bay*, I, 535–536. On Dr. Oliver Smith as an "old friend" of Knox's brother William, see William Knox to Henry Knox, Aug. 4, 1790, HKP, XXVI, 116, MHS. For one of the misleading advertisements, see Mar. 21, 1791, LII, 344, HKP, MHS. For the scheme, see Joseph Pierce to Henry Knox, June 23, July 3, 1791, HKP, XXVIII, 131, 164, MHS; Knox to Dr. Oliver Smith, June 26, 1791, HKP, XXVIII, 145, MHS. On buying out the other heirs, see Henry Knox to Samuel Winslow, Isaac Winslow, Jr., Samuel Waldo, and George Erving, Feb. 20, 1793, Knox to John Steele Tyler and Ebenezer Vesey, Oct. 20, 1793, HKP, XXXIII, 147, XXXIV, 126, MHS; John Steele Tyler to Henry Jackson, Oct. 31, 1793, HKP, XXXI, 129, MHS; Stahl, *Old Broad Bay*, I, 536.

22. Allis, ed., *Bingham's Maine Lands*, I, 36–37; Henry Knox and William Duer to Henry Jackson and Royal Flint, June 2, 1791, in Allis, ed., *Bingham's Maine Lands*, I, 45.

23. *Ibid.*, I, 39–66, 78, 90, 98, 102, II, 911–912; Henry Jackson to Henry Knox, Feb. 15, Dec. 2, 1792, HKP, XXX, 101, XXXIII, 36, MHS.

24. Cyrus Eaton, *History of Thomaston, Rockland, and South Thomaston* . . . (Hallowell, 1865), I, 212–213, 224; Cyrus Eaton, *Annals of the Town of Warren* (Hallowell, 1877), 265–267; Henry Knox to William Bingham, Nov. 11, 1795, Alexander Baring to Hope and Company, Dec. 3, 1796, in Allis, ed., *Bingham's Maine Lands*, I, 588, II, 770, 791 (quote); Henry Jackson to Henry Knox, Mar. 27, 1794, HKP, XXXV, 74, MHS; in Henry Knox to Benjamin Lincoln and Henry Jackson, July 3, 1804, HKP, XLV, 163, MHS, Knox denied their charges that he demanded too high a price from his settlers. For patron-client roles in frontier development, see Stephen Innes, *Labor in a New Land: Economy and Society in Seventeenth-Century Springfield* (Princeton, N.J., 1983), 17–42.

25. Gardiner, *Early Recollections*, 107. On Montpelier, see Joseph Pierce to Henry Knox, Dec. 28, 1794, XXXVI, 134, HKP, MHS; Henry Jackson to Knox, May 8, 1794, XXXV, 99, HKP, MHS; Eaton, *Thomaston*, I, 209–210; Leverett Saltonstall's travel journal, Aug. 26, 1806, entry, in Robert E. Moody, ed., *The Saltonstall Papers, 1607–1815*, 2 vols. (MHS, *Collections*, LXXX–LXXXI [Boston, 1972, 1974]), II, 333 (hereafter cited as Moody, ed., *Saltonstall Papers*); Alexander Baring to Hope and Company, Dec. 3, 1796, in Allis, ed., *Bingham's Maine Lands*, II, 770; Lucy Flucker Knox quoted in Thomas Morgan Griffiths, *Maine Sources in "The House of Seven Gables"* (Waterville, 1945), 8–9.

26. Eaton, *Thomaston*, I, 209; Callahan, *Henry Knox*, 345–348.

27. Callahan, *Henry Knox*, 210–219, 238–239, 281; Thomas B. Wait to George Thatcher, Feb. 7, 1790, Henry Sewall to Thatcher, Mar. 20, 1790, both in GTP, BPL; Royster, *A Revolutionary People at War*, 353–358.

28. Gardiner, *Early Recollections*, 107; Francis S. Drake, *Life and Correspondence of Henry Knox, Major-General in the American Revolutionary Army* (Boston, 1873), 115; Knox to David Cobb, Apr. 24, 1800, in Allis, ed., *Bingham's Maine Lands*, II, 1041.

29. Henry Knox to Stephen Higginson, Jan. 28, 1790, Knox to Rufus King, Mar. 28, 1785, both quoted in Callahan, *Henry Knox*, 235, 246; Knox ("the evils") quoted in Cayton, *The Frontier Republic*, 23.

30. Knox, Samuel Winslow, and Isaac Winslow, Jr., to Thomaston's Land Com-

mittee, Aug. 26, 1786, Related Papers, Mar. 9, 1797, Resolve, MA; Henry Knox to Governor Caleb Strong, Aug. 1, 1800, Knox to Robert Houston, Dec. 10, 1801, HKP, XLIII, 75, XLIV, 156, MHS.

31. Eaton, *Thomaston*, I, 181, 240–241; Henry Knox and Ezekiel G. Dodge, "Memorandum of Agreement," Oct. 31, 1795, HKP, box 3, MeHS; "Persons in Thomaston who are usurpers," Aug. 6, 1801, under letter "T" in Land Record Book, HKP, MeHS.

32. Henry Knox to William Molineux, Aug. 27, 1797, HKP, box 4, MeHS; Frederick Reed to Henry Knox, May 3, 1799, HKP, XLII, 80, MHS; Reed to Knox, May 27, 1800, HKP, box 6, MeHS; Dodge v. Reed, Oct. 1802, LC-SJC Record Book, II, 38, LCC; Ezekiel G. Dodge's petition for partition, Sept. 1797, LC-CCP Record Book, X, 38, LCC; Eaton, *Thomaston*, I, 256. For the similar arrangement by the Twenty Associates (Lincolnshire Company) with William Molineux of Camden, see Lincolnshire Company Records, 186 (Nov. 28, 1787), 198 (Jan. 31, 1789), MHS. Knox could also be blind to how devious he was in dealing with fellow gentlemen. After borrowing a confidential report from the Philadelphia land speculator Theophile Cazenove, Henry Knox wrote to his partner William Bingham, "I have taken a copy without requesting leave, therefore I request you sacredly to keep it to yourself." See Knox to Bingham, Jan. 8, 1793, in Allis, ed., *Bingham's Maine Lands*, I, 99.

33. Callahan, *Henry Knox*, 285; Henry Knox to Thomas Jefferson, Mar. 19, 1801, quoted in Thomas Morgan Griffiths, *Major General Henry Knox and the Last Heirs to Montpelier*, ed. Arthur Morgan Griffiths (Monmouth, 1965), 39; William Bingham to David Cobb, May 1, 1800, in Allis, ed., *Bingham's Maine Lands*, II, 1046. In his will, Knox drastically reduced his son's inheritance, explaining, "My son, Henry Jackson Knox, has involved me in the payment of large sums of money by his thoughtless extravagance"; see "The Will of General Henry Knox of Thomaston," *BHM*, V, 140.

34. Griffiths, *Major General Henry Knox*, ed. Griffiths; see also Nathaniel Hawthorne, *The American Notebooks*, ed. Randall Stewart (New Haven, Conn., 1932), Aug. 12, 1837, entry, 23. For the Lucy Knox anecdote, see Eaton, *Thomaston*, I, 221–222.

35. George Thomas Little, *The Descendants of George Little, Who Came to Newbury, Massachusetts, in 1640* (Auburn, 1882), 40–42, 109–110; Cotton quoted in an undated anonymous informant's memo in the box entitled "From Little Family Papers," PPP, EI.

36. Sept. 23, 1800, entry, Josiah Little memo books, PPP, box 5 ("1782–1829 Books"), EI.

37. Josiah Little to Moses Little, Feb. 28, 1778, box 1, folder 4, LFP, EI; Josiah Little to Mr. Stearns, Mar. 31, 1807, folder 9, box 3, LFP, EI. See also Shipton, *Sibley's Harvard Graduates*, XVII, 492, 499, on the generous charity of James Bowdoin III on behalf of Boston's dependent poor, especially in founding Massachusetts General Hospital.

38. William Minot to Leverett Saltonstall, Aug. 10, 1802, in Moody, ed., *Saltonstall Papers*, II, 87; James Bowdoin to Thomas Reed, Feb. 1793, James Bowdoin's Letterbook I, Bowdoin College; James Bowdoin quoted in Shipton, *Sibley's Harvard Graduates*, XVII, 491 (his second quote); Leverett Saltonstall's travel journal, Sept. 4, 1806, entry, in Moody, ed., *Saltonstall Papers*, II, 335–337.

39. Talleyrand, "Letter," 81–83; William Morris to Theophile Cazenove, Dec. 9, 1792, in Allis, ed., *Bingham's Maine Lands*, I, 194; Edward Augustus Kendall, *Travels through the Northern Parts of the United States in the Years 1807 and 1808*

(New York, 1809), III, 74–75; Alexander Baring to Hope and Company, Dec. 3, 1796, in Allis, ed., *Bingham's Maine Lands*, II, 786; L. H. Cohen, "Eden's Constitution," *Prospects*, III (1977), 83. I have drawn on the unusually detailed travelers' accounts of conditions in the Eastern Country during the 1790s and early 19th century to supplement proprietary opinions. As enlightened gentlemen, the travelers held opinions that mirrored those of the proprietors who wrote their letters of introduction and hosted their visits. One of the travelers, Alexander Baring, became a proprietor of Maine lands, and three others—Talleyrand, La Rochefoucault Liancourt, and William Morris—came to investigate Maine lands for European land speculators. Naturally, their reports addressed proprietary concerns. Although neither proprietors nor land scouts, Timothy Dwight and Edward Augustus Kendall were staunch Federalists who explicitly sympathized with the Great Proprietors and denounced the resistance. See Talleyrand, "Letter," 69; Allis, ed., *Bingham's Maine Lands*, I, 188. For Talleyrand's letter of introduction from the Kennebeck Proprietor Dr. Benjamin Vaughan to his brother Charles Vaughan, see B. Vaughan to C. Vaughan, Feb. 20, 1794, Charles Vaughan Papers, box A, in the possession of George and Martha Vaughan of Boothbay (destined for Bowdoin College's Special Collections); Timothy Dwight, *Travels in New England and New York*, ed. Barbara Miller Solomon, 4 vols. (Cambridge, Mass., 1969; orig. publ. New Haven, Conn., 1821), II, 150–151; and Kendall, *Travels*, II, 160.

40. Talleyrand, "Letter," 73, 75, 80, 82; François Alexandre Frédéric, duc de La Rochefoucault Liancourt, *Travels through the United States of North America . . .* (London, 1799), I, 427, 436–439; Alexander Baring to Hope and Company, Dec. 3, 1796, in Allis, ed., *Bingham's Maine Lands*, II, 786–788; Gardiner, *Early Recollections*, 204; Dwight, *Travels*, ed. Solomon, II, 327. For the similar views by agricultural reformers and genteel travelers of Illinois settlers in the 1820s, see John Mack Faragher, *Sugar Creek: Life on the Illinois River* (New Haven, Conn., 1986), 97–98.

41. David Cobb to William Bingham, Oct. 5, 1795 ("If a people"), Cobb to Henry Knox, Oct. 10, 1795 ("Every inhabitant"), Alexander Baring's "Instructions," Feb. 1798, William Bingham to Cobb, June 26, 1800, in Allis, ed., *Bingham's Maine Lands*, I, 541–542, 545, II, 925, 1056.

42. For complaints of settler cunning, see Kendall, *Travels*, III, 87; Talleyrand, "Letter," 83; William Morris to Theophile Cazenove, Dec. 9, 1792, in Allis, ed., *Bingham's Maine Lands*, I, 200; and "Everyone to His Trade," *Castine Journal*, Nov. 15, 1799.

43. Alexander Baring's "Instructions," Feb. 1798, in Allis, ed., *Bingham's Maine Lands*, II, 924–925; Arodi Thayer to Charles Vaughan, Sept. 1, 1802, KPP, Letterbook I, 153, MeHS. Henry Knox's correspondence and Land Record Book reveal a similar preoccupation with assessing newcomers' appearance to calibrate what they would be permitted to buy; see Henry Jackson to Henry Knox, Sept. 7, 1790, HKP, XXVII, 2, MHS; Land Record Book, entries for June 21, 1800 ("Mr. Lee"), May 4, 1802 ("Mr. Epes"), and May 7, 1802 (another "Mr. Lee").

44. Thomas Vose to Henry Knox, Dec. 14, 1789, HKP, LII, 28, MHS; George Ulmer to Henry Knox, Nov. 30, 1799, HKP, box 5, MeHS; Ulmer to Knox, May 8, 1790, HKP, XXVI, 45, MeHS; La Rochefoucault Liancourt, *Travels*, I, 429–430, 444; George Ulmer's report, ca. 1797, but filed under "1795" in HKP, box 3, MeHS; for an example of a permit, see George Ulmer to Jacob Ames, July 8, 1795, HKP, XXXVII, 136, MeHS.

45. Land Record Book, Nov. 8, 1799 (memo regarding Samuel Patterson), Nov. 25, 1799 (John Heel), Dec. 5, 1799 (Jonathan Clark), Jan. 3, 1801 (Edward Carter), Oct. 17, 1801 (Rena Knight), Nov. 6, 1801 (Gideon Haskel), n.d. (under letter "P," for James Perkins, Jr., includes quote), HKP, MeHS; George Ulmer to Henry Knox, Oct. 23, 1795, HKP, box 4, MeHS; Thomas Knowlton to Knox, Mar. 22, 1798, HKP, box 5, MeHS; Ulmer to Knox, Nov. 19, 1801, HKP, box 6, MeHS; for another proprietor's problems with settlers' speculating in his permits, see Alexander Shepard, Jr., to Col. Merrill, Feb. 25, 1779, folder 1770–1779, PPP, box 10, EI.

46. The Knox quotes regarding Lothrop are from Land Record Book, Dec. 25, 1800 (under letter "S," for Col. Benjamin Shute), HKP, MeHS; John Rynier to Henry Knox, Dec. 31, 1797, HKP, box 4, MeHS ("found him"); Rynier to Knox, Mar. 17, 1798, HKP, XLI, 87, MHS ("saying"); and Rynier's draft agreement with Zenas Lothrop, n.d., HKP, XLI, 94, MHS; see also Rynier to Knox, Sept. 26, 1797, HKP, box 4, MeHS.

47. Talleyrand, "Letter," 84–86. Henry Knox was particularly fond of Adam Smith, owning two copies of *The Wealth of Nations* (see the catalog to his library at the Boston Athenaeum) and citing Smith in "For Sale Lots or Tracts of Land," May 1, 1801, MeHS.

48. La Rochefoucault Liancourt, *Travels*, I, 426, 433–434; Henry Knox to William Bingham, Nov. 11, 1795, in Allis, ed., *Bingham's Maine Lands*, II, 588. One of central New York's great proprietors, Judge William Cooper of Cooperstown, published a guide to successful land management that stressed the importance of inculcating the division of labor among settlers; see [William] Cooper, *A Guide in the Wilderness; or, The History of the First Settlement in the Western Counties of New York, with Useful Instructions to Future Settlers* (Rochester, N.Y., 1897; reprint of Dublin, Ireland, 1810), 14–16.

49. John Conner's deposition, Nov. 22, 1810, miscellaneous box 24 ("Papers Relating to Lands in Lincoln County . . ."), MA.

50. David Cobb to Henry Knox, Aug. 30, 1795 ("poor ignorants"), William Bingham to Cobb, Nov. 7, 1795 ("respectable"), Cobb to Bingham, Dec. 8, 1796 ("explaining" and "in a short time"), Cobb to Knox, Aug. 15, 1797 ("preaching"), Cobb to Charles W. Hare, Oct. 29, 1809 ("Yahoos") in Allis, ed., *Bingham's Maine Lands*, I, 534, 552, II, 821, 858, 1231.

51. David Cobb to Henry Knox, Dec. 13, 1796 ("boors"), Cobb to William Bingham, Oct. 28, 1797 ("vilest insults"), Cobb to Bingham, Jan. 31, 1799, Cobb to Isaac Parker, Apr. 12, 1799 ("sword"), in Allis, ed., *Bingham's Maine Lands*, II, 824, 878, 951, 958.

52. Alexander Baring to Hope and Company, May 26, 1796, David Cobb to William Bingham, Jan. 30, 1797, Cobb to Bingham, Apr. 9, 1797 ("setts down" and "a curse"), Bingham to Cobb, June 26, 1800 ("removed"), in Allis, ed., *Bingham's Maine Lands*, I, 654, II, 832–833, 845, 1057; on the reluctance of the "better class" of settlers to confront the wilderness, see Moses Greenleaf, *A Statistical View of the District of Maine . . .* (Boston, 1816, S-S 37745), 150. On the failure of their plans, see William Bingham to David Cobb, May 1, 1800, Alexander Baring to Hope and Company, July 9, 1812, in Allis, ed., *Bingham's Maine Lands*, II, 1046, 1240.

53. Knox quoted in Anthony F. C. Wallace, *The Death and Rebirth of the Seneca* (New York, 1970), 218; Henry Knox to Thomas Vose, Jan. 10, 1789, XXIII, 70, HKP, MHS. In Oct. 1788 Knox persuaded about half the Waldo Patent's settlers to pay him 4s. ($.67) an acre for their homesteads; he then promptly raised his

price for future sales to between 6s. and 10s. ($1.00–$1.67) and promised another price increase in the near future. Similarly, in retailing his Waldo Patent backlands in 1800–1801, the general shrewdly promised that the first 20 settlers per township who submitted could buy 200 acres apiece at $2–$3 per acre, while subsequent purchasers would have to pay $5–$6 per acre. Knox advised the first submittees to ally with him to capitalize on rising land values; by subsequently selling half of their 200-acre "double lots" at enhanced prices, they could pay for the other half, retained as a homestead. See Henry Knox to Mrs. Horwood, Jan. 13, 1789, HKP, LII, 9, MHS; Waldo heirs to Capt. George Ulmer, Sept. 29, 1788, HKP, LII, 162, MHS; Waldo heirs' "Notification," Oct. 1, 1788, ELC, box 53, MA; Knox to Isaac Winslow, Jr., June 28, 1789, HKP, XXIV, 68, MHS; indenture of Henry Knox with George Ulmer and Benjamin Smith, May 22, 1800, and Smith and Ulmer to Knox, May 25, 1800, both in Land Record Book, HKP, MeHS.

54. Knox to James Treadway, Nov. 7, 1799 ("certificates"), under letter "T" in Land Record Book, HKP, MeHS; on Knox's attention to rumors, see the Oct. 7, 1801 ("pest"), and July 18, 1804, entries in Henry Knox's Land Record Book, MeHS. A grand jury indicted John Drew for participating in a July 13, 1814, assault on a house belonging to a proprietary sympathizer; June 1815 indictment of John Drew, HC-SJC Files, box 167, MeSA.

55. Henry Knox to George Ulmer, Sept. 13, 1794, XXXVI, 52, HKP, MHS; Knox, Samuel Winslow, and Isaac Winslow, Jr., to Thomaston's land committee, Aug. 26, 1786, Related Papers, Resolve, Mar. 9, 1797, MA; and Knox to Northport's selectmen, Apr. 2, 1796, XXXIX, 15, HKP, MHS.

56. Henry Knox to Joseph Pierce, July 5, 1794, XXXV, 151, HKP, MHS ("respectable Emigrants"); Henry Knox, *Advertisement: For the Benefit of Those, Whom It May Concern* (Wiscasset, 1801; S-S 772) ("on principles"); Henry Knox's notice, May 26, 1800, HKP, LII, 79, MHS ("every regular"); [John Merrick], *Remarks on Some of the Circumstances and Arguments Produced by the Murder of Mr. Paul Chadwick, at Malta . . .* ([Augusta, 1809]; S-S 18491), 13. See also Leverett Saltonstall's travel journal, Aug.–Sept. 1806, in Moody, ed., *Saltonstall Papers*, II, 342. On Merrick, see North, *Augusta*, 391–392; and Rev. D. R. Goodwin, "Notice of John Merrick," MeHS, *Colls.*, 1st Ser., VII (1876), 379–402. For the similar views expressed by the Friends of Government in 1786, see David P. Szatmary, *Shays' Rebellion: The Making of an Agrarian Insurrection* (Amherst, Mass., 1980), 73.

57. Pitt Dillingham to Arthur Lithgow, Jan. 30, 1808, Related Papers, Resolve LV (June 19, 1809), MA.

CHAPTER THREE

1. The epigraph is from [Gershom Flagg], *A Strange Account of the Rising and Breaking of a Great Bubble* (Boston, 1767; E 10778), 21–22. Nathaniel Ames quoted in Gregory H. Nobles, *Divisions throughout the Whole: Politics and Society in Hampshire County, Massachusetts, 1740–1775* (New York, 1983), 110; B[enjamin] Lincoln, "Copy of a Letter from the Hon. General Lincoln, on the Religious State of the Eastern Counties in the District of Maine," MHS, *Collections*, 1st Ser., IV (Boston, 1795), 155; earl of Sterling's advertisement quoted in William Otis Sawtelle, "Sir Francis Bernard and His Grant of Mount Desert," Colonial Society

of Massachusetts, *Publications, Transactions*, XXIV (Boston, 1923), 238; Henry Knox's broadside of May 1, 1801, MeHS. See also Moses Greenleaf, *A Statistical View of the District of Maine* . . . (Boston, 1816; S-S 37745), 72.

2. William Allen, *History of Industry, Maine* . . . , 2d ed. (Skowhegan, 1869), 40; Charles F. Allen, "William Allen," MeHS, *Collections*, 2d Ser., II (Portland, 1891), 377–379: "Notes on Compton, Township in Newport County, State of Rhode-Island, September, 1803," MHS, *Colls.*, 1st Ser., IX (Boston, 1804), 203; Alexander Baring to Hope and Company, Dec. 3, 1796, in Frederick S. Allis, Jr., ed., *William Bingham's Maine Lands, 1790–1820*, 2 vols. (Col. Soc. Mass., *Pubs.*, XXXVI–XXXVII [Boston, 1954]), II, 788 (hereafter cited as Allis, ed., *Bingham's Maine Lands*); Peres Fobes, "A Topographical Description of the Town of Raynham, in the County of Bristol, Feb. 6, 1793," MHS, *Colls.*, 1st Ser., III (Boston, 1794), 167. See also William Douglass, *A Summary, Historical and Political, of the First Planting, Progressive Improvement, and Present State of the British Settlements in North-America* (Boston, 1750–1751; E 6307, 6663), I, 537–540, II, 50; Samuel Tenney, "A Topographical Description of Exeter in New Hampshire," MHS, *Colls.*, 1st Ser., IV (Boston, 1795), 90–95; and Robert A. Gross, *The Minutemen and Their World* (New York, 1976), 68–108.

3. For the Hancock County census data, see the Second Census of the United States, 1800, Microfilm Series M32, reel 7; a partial published transcription of the census return appears in Walter Goodwin Davis, "Part of Hancock County, Maine, in 1800," *New England Historical and Genealogical Register*, CV (1951), 204–213, 276–291. For 89 of the householders I could identify their fathers' birthplaces and their location in 1790 (or their prior place of death). Most fathers (those of 61 householders) began life in southern New England, and only 5 householders were the sons of men born in mid-Maine or the Maritimes. But most fathers moved northeastward into Maine or New Hampshire by death or 1790 ($N = 71$). On links between poverty and out-migration in New England's 18th-century towns, see Douglas Lamar Jones, "Poverty and Vagabondage: The Process of Survival in Eighteenth-Century Massachusetts," *NEHGR*, CXXXIII (1979), 243–254; and Greenleaf, *A Statistical View of the District of Maine*, 150. For the 1771 tax valuation, see Bettye Hobbs Pruitt, "Self-Sufficiency and the Agricultural Economy of Eighteenth-Century Massachusetts," *WMQ*, 3d Ser., XLI (1984), 338–341. On 20 improved acres (or more) as the threshold of comfort, see Percy Wells Bidwell and John I. Falconer, *History of Agriculture in the Northern United States, 1620–1860* (Washington, D.C., 1925), 120 (20–26 acres); Gross, *Minutemen*, 213–214 (25 acres); and Christopher M. Jedrey, *The World of John Cleaveland: Family and Community in Eighteenth-Century New England* (New York, 1979), 63 (40 acres).

Seeking most of the settlers on hometown valuations would be either fruitless or misleading. Because most of the settlers were young men just starting out in life, few would be found on the valuations before their migration. Those who could be found would often give a misleadingly poor impression of their prospects. Young men in 18th-century rural New England ordinarily began their adult lives with very little property but gradually acquired some through hard work and inheritance. As a result, picking newly independent young men off the tax rolls would generally underestimate the prosperity that might have been theirs as children and that would probably accrue to them within a decade. Their fathers' assessed property affords a much more comprehensive and accurate assessment of the settlers' backgrounds and prospects. Therefore, with the exception of settlers who were over 45 in 1800, I sought out their fathers on any surviving valuation taken between 1771 and 1801, giving preference, whenever possible, to the 1784 or 1792 valuations as offering a property assessment closest in time to the point when the settlers migrated. Linkage with surviving tax valuations identifies the economic backgrounds for 89 of the roughly 150 settlers whose fathers dwelled within the commonwealth during the period 1771–1801. Either the failure of genealogical identification or the lack of a surviving valuation list for a given town accounts for those who cannot be found (see Tables 1–4). The 1771 valuation list for Massachusetts and Maine towns has been edited, indexed, and published by Bettye Hobbs Pruitt: *The Massachusetts Tax Valuation List of 1771* (Boston, 1978). The other valuations are available on microfilm at MSL.

Employing a different methodology, John W. Adams and Alice Bee Kasakoff reached a different conclusion—that "a stratum of comparatively poor people had crystallized in Massachusetts and Maine who were restricted in their opportunities to move the long distances to reach the cheaper land on the frontier." Studying the male patrilineal descendants of nine New England families whose ancestors immigrated to Massachusetts before 1650, Adams and Kasakoff found 104 on the Massachusetts tax valuation lists for 1771. On the basis of assessed real property, they divided the group into quartiles and found that members of the top and bottom quartiles did not move as far during their lives as did the men in the middle. My findings differ because (a) as they note, their method equating all long moves with movement to the frontier discounts those poorer folk already dwelling close to the frontier (for example, those dwelling in southwestern Maine in 1771, as were many of my group), and (b), as a group, their 104 were relatively poor (an average 971d. annual real estate value versus an average of 1,229.9d. for the entire valuation), so their "middling" taxpayers were poorer than the mean for the commonwealth as a whole. In terms of the 1771 tax valuation (rather than just in terms of their study group), their frontier migrants were relatively poor. Although I think that the 18th-century Maine frontier did provide a haven for marginal men, I suspect that they are quite right that more distant (and more promising) frontier districts (that is, those other than Maine) were beyond the range of eastern Massachusetts' poorest families. See John W. Adams and Alice Bee Kasakoff, "Wealth and Migration in Massachusetts and Maine, 1771–1798," *Journal of Economic History*, XLV (1985), 363–368.

4. Timothy Dwight, *Travels in New England and New York*, ed. Barbara Miller Solomon, 4 vols. (Cambridge, Mass., 1969; orig. publ. New Haven, Conn., 1821), I, 151; François Alexandre Frédéric, duc de La Rochefoucault Liancourt, *Travels through the United States of North America* ... (London, 1799), I, 416; Joseph Whipple, *A Geographical View of the District of Maine, with Particular Reference to Its Internal Resources* ... (Bangor, 1816; S-S 39802), 38; Robert Earle Moody, "The Maine Frontier, 1607 to 1763" (Ph.D. diss., Yale University, 1933), 261–264; [Benjamin] Lincoln, "Observations on the Climate, Soil, and Value of the Eastern Counties in the District of Maine," MHS, *Colls.*, 1st Ser., IV (Boston, 1795), 143–149; [James Sullivan], "A Topographical Description of Thomaston, in the County of Lincoln, and District of Maine, 1794," MHS, *Colls.*, 1st Ser., IV (Boston, 1795), 20–25.

5. Nathaniel Dudley to Charles Vaughan, Mar. 7, 1792 (Mount Vernon settler), KPP, box 3, MeHS; John Southack, *The Life of John Southack: Written by Himself* ... (Boston, 1809; S-S 18663), 16; Condeskeag Plantation (Penobscot Valley) petition to the General Court, Dec. 31, 1789, *BHM*, VI, 171; Nor-

ridgewock petition to the General Court, Aug. 20, 1788, in William Allen, *The History of Norridgewock* . . . (Norridgewock, 1849), 95–96.

6. On family considerations in migration, see Levi Leighton, *Autobiography of Levi Leighton* . . . (Portland, 1890), 15; Gross, *Minutemen*, 82; and Richard Easterlin, "Population Change and Farm Settlement in the Northern United States," *Jour. Econ. Hist.*, XXXVI (1976), 45–75.

7. W. Allen, *Industry*, 40; Charles F. Allen, "William Allen," MeHS, *Colls.*, 2d Ser., II (1891), 377–379; William Allen, "The Journal of William Allen, Esq.," in William Collins Hatch, *A History of the Town of Industry* . . . (Farmington, 1893), 72–74; Thomas M. Prentiss, *The Maine Spelling Book* . . . *to Which Is Annexed a Concise Geographical Description of Maine* . . . (Leominster, Mass., 1799; E 36156), 115–116; Timothy W. Robinson, *History of the Town of Morrill in the County of Waldo and State of Maine*, ed. Theoda Mears Morse (Belfast, 1944), 5, 106; Samuel Deane, *The New-England Farmer* . . . (Worcester, Mass., 1790; E 22450), 272; John Langdon Sibley, *A History of the Town of Union* . . . (Boston, 1851), 97–98; William Morris to Theophile Cazenove, Dec. 9, 1792, in Allis, ed., *Bingham's Maine Lands*, I, 201; Whipple, *A Geographical View*, 13.

8. W. Allen, *Industry*, 40; W. Allen, "Journal," in Hatch, *Industry*, 72–74. On the driver-tree technique, see Sibley, *Union*, 98–99, 105–106.

9. W. Allen, *Industry*, 40; W. Allen, "Journal," in Hatch, *Industry*, 72–74. For the good burn method, see Isaac Parsons, "An Account of New Gloucester," MeHS, *Colls.*, 1st Ser., II (Portland, 1847), 151; W. Allen, *Norridgewock*, 71, 74; David Thurston, *A Brief History of Winthrop* . . . (Portland, 1855), 15; Moses Greenleaf, *A Survey of the State of Maine* . . . (Portland, 1829), 87; Cyrus Eaton, *History of Thomaston, Rockland, and South Thomaston* . . . (Hallowell, 1865), I, 89; Deane, *New-England Farmer*, 57 (quote), 141. On the higher yields of newly burned lands, see Whipple, *A Geographical View*, 15; and Charles Maurice de Talleyrand-Périgord, "Letter on the Eastern Part of America" (Boston, Sept. 24, 1794), in Hans Huth and Wilma J. Pugh, eds., *Talleyrand in America as a Financial Promoter, 1794–96* (*Annual Report of the American Historical Association, 1941*, II [Washington, D.C., 1942]), 73 (hereafter cited as Talleyrand, "Letter"). On the dark day, see Alden Bradford, *History of Massachusetts* . . . (Boston, 1835), 192; and Jeremy Belknap, *The History of New-Hampshire*, 3 vols. (Boston, 1791–1792), III, 27.

10. W. Allen, *Industry*, 40; C. F. Allen, "William Allen," MeHS, *Colls.*, 2d Ser., II (1891), 377–379; W. Allen, "Journal," in Hatch, *Industry*, 72–74; William Allen, "Now and Then," MeHS, *Colls.*, 1st Ser., VII (Bath, 1876), 275.

11. W. Allen, "Journal," in Hatch, *Industry*, 76–77; this cabin was unusually large: see Luigi Castiglioni, *Luigi Castiglioni's Viaggio: Travels in the United States of North America, 1785–87*, trans. and ed. Antonio Pace (Syracuse, N.Y., 1983), 30. Apparently, the Allens' cabin proved unmanageable for the Allen family because, when they built a new cabin in 1797, it was smaller.

12. W. Allen, "Journal," in Hatch, ed., *Industry*, 77–78.

13. *Ibid.*, 78, 79–80 (second quote); W. Allen, "Sandy River Settlements," MeHS, *Colls.*, 1st Ser., IV (Portland, 1856), 39; W. Allen, "Now and Then," MeHS, *Colls.*, 1st Ser., VII (1876), 272 (first quote); Sibley, *Union*, 55 n; W. Allen, *Industry*, 22–23; Greenleaf, *A Survey of the State of Maine*, 216; Norridgewock to the General Court, Aug. 20, 1788, in W. Allen, *Norridgewock*, 93; Alexander Baring to Hope and Company, Dec. 3, 1796, in Allis, ed., *Bingham's Maine Lands*, II, 787–788; Talleyrand, "Letter," 82; James Bridge and Reuel Williams to Henry Jackson, Apr. 8, 1803, RWP, box 1, MeHS.

14. David Cobb to C. W. Hare, Nov. 10, 1810, in Allis, ed., *Bingham's Maine Lands*, II, 1235–1236; Belknap, *New-Hampshire*, III, 90, 147, 150; Sibley, *Union*, 395–402; Cyrus Eaton, *Annals of the Town of Warren* (Hallowell, 1877), 223–224, 258; Hatch, *Industry*, 263.

15. David Cobb to William Bingham, July 1, 1795, in Allis, ed., *Bingham's Maine Lands*, I, 525–528; Allen, "Journal," in Hatch, *Industry*, 78; Belknap, *New-Hampshire*, III, 259; Sibley, *Union*, 56; Leighton, *Autobiography*, 32; Thomas Vose to Henry Knox, May 30, 1796, HKP, box 4, MeHS.

16. Charles E. Allen, *History of Dresden, Maine* . . . (Augusta, 1931), 18; Eaton, *Warren*, 147–148; Eaton, *Thomaston*, I, 99; William Ladd, "Annals of Bakerstown, Poland, and Minot," MeHS, *Colls.*, 1st Ser., II (Portland, 1847), 114; Isaac Parsons' return, in *Papers; Consisting of Communications Made to the Massachusetts Society for Promoting Agriculture . . . [1807]* (Boston, 1807; S-S 13037), 32–33; Deane, *New-England Farmer*, 152; Lincoln County petition to the General Court, Nov. 19, 1779, *Maine Historical and Genealogical Recorder*, III, 173–176.

17. David C. Smith *et al.*, "Climatic Stress and Maine Agriculture, 1785–1885," in T.M.L. Wigley *et al.*, eds., *Climate and History: Studies in Past Climates and Their Impact on Man* (Cambridge, 1981), 450–464; "To Farmers," *Kennebeck Intelligencer* (Hallowell), June 16, 1797; *Portland Gazette*, June 30, 1806; James W. North, *The History of Augusta* . . . (Augusta, 1870), 343; Deane, *New-England Farmer*, 75–76; Sibley, *Union*, 55; Paul Coffin, "Memoir and Journals of Rev. Paul Coffin, D.D.," MeHS, *Colls.*, 1st Ser., IV (Portland, 1859), 341; Surry assessors to the General Court, Nov. 1, 1811, Surry valuation return, 1811, microfilm box 400, MSL.

18. Gouldsborough assessors to the valuation committee, n.d., Gouldsborough valuation return, 1801, and Cornville assessors to the valuation committee, Sept. 25, 1801, microfilm box 397, MSL; Raymondtown petition to the General Court, Feb. 26, 1788, *MDH*, XXI, 440–441; John Rynier to Henry Knox, Mar. 17, 1798, HKP, XLI, 87, MHS; "Substitute for Hay," *Wiscasset Eastern Repository*, Mar. 27, 1804; Thomas Vose to Henry Jackson, May 14, 1794, HKP, XXXV, 106, MHS.

19. Belknap, *New-Hampshire*, III, 19; Deane, *New-England Farmer*, 180; Reuel Williams to Thomas L. Winthrop, Mar. 21, 1805, RWP, box 2, MeHS.

20. William Crosby, "Annals of Belfast," 20–21, MS, MeHS; La Rochefoucault Liancourt, *Travels*, I, 436; Edward Augustus Kendall, *Travels through the Northern Parts of the United States in the Years 1807 and 1808* (New York, 1809), III, 72; Leighton, *Autobiography*, 16, 22; William Frost to George Thacher, Apr. 30, 1787, Samuel Nasson to Thatcher, June 3, 1789, Nathaniel Wells to Thatcher, Apr. 24, 1789, all in GTP, BPL.
In their petitions to the General Court, the settlers usually described themselves as principally younger married couples with large families of young children. Travelers saw many young children in and around the settlers' cabins (see Talleyrand, "Letter," 79). Census figures bear them out. In 1800 only 10% of mid-Maine's population was 45 years of age or older, in contrast to 16% for Massachusetts. There was little difference between the two areas in the percentage of people in their prime, those aged 16–44 (Massachusetts, 39%; mid-Maine, 38%). But children under 16 composed 53% of mid-Maine's population versus only 45% in Massachusetts. The gap was greatest among the youngest children, those under the age of 10; they composed 38% of mid-Maine's population, compared to 30% of Massachusetts'. Data for mid-Maine communities (towns in Lincoln, Kennebec, and western Hancock counties) compiled from

Return of the Whole Number of Persons within the Several Districts of the United States (Washington, D.C., 1802; S-S 3442). See Table 10.

21. W. Allen, "Sandy River," MeHS, *Colls.*, 1st Ser., IV (1856), 39; W. Allen, "Now and Then," MeHS, *Colls.*, 1st Ser., IV (1856), 271; Blue Hill assessors to the valuation committee, June 25, 1792, Blue Hill valuation return, 1792, microfilm box 395, MSL; Sibley, *Union*, 67; North, *Augusta*, 189; Thurston, *Winthrop*, 62–63. On work and diet, see David C. Smith, "Maine's Changing Landscape to 1820," in Charles E. Clark *et al.*, eds., *Maine in the Early Republic: From Revolution to Statehood* (Hanover, N.H., 1988), 23.

22. Thomas Vose to Henry Knox, Sept. 9, 1789, HKP, box 1, MeHS; Nathaniel Barrell to George Thatcher, Mar. 11, 1790, Henry Sewall to Thatcher, Mar. 20, 1790, GTP, BPL; Samuel Nasson to Thatcher, Mar. 12, 1790, GTP, box 2, MeHS; Thomas Vose to Henry Knox, Mar. 30, 1790, HKP, XXVI, 12, MHS; Samuel Goodwin to George Thatcher, Apr. 16, 1790, Daniel Cony to Thatcher, Apr. 24, 1790, Nathaniel Wells to Thatcher, June 4, 1790, John Hobby to Thatcher, July 31, 1790, GTP, BPL; Richard F. Cutts petition to the General Court, June 1790, *MDH*, XXII, 366; York County petition to the General Court, June 1790, *MDH*, XXII, 367.

23. Ezekiel Knowlton to Mary Knowlton, Apr. 14, 1795, in *The Town of Liberty: Its History and Geography* (Thorndike, 1927), 112. See also William Allen, "Somerset County," MS, MeHS; Dwight, *Travels*, ed. Solomon, II, 322. On the importance of female networks in 18th-century New England, see Laurel Thatcher Ulrich, "'A Friendly Neighbor': Social Dimensions of Daily Work in Northern Colonial New England," *Feminist Studies*, VI (1980), 392–405; Ulrich, "Housewife and Gadder: Themes of Self-sufficiency and Community in Eighteenth-Century New England," in Carol Groneman and Mary Beth Norton, eds., "*To Toil the Livelong Day*": *America's Women at Work, 1780–1980* (Ithaca, N.Y., 1987), 21–34; and Sibley, *Union*, 38.

24. William Scales to the General Court, Feb. 14, 1790, *MDH*, XXII, 325, 329; Bristol selectmen to the valuation committee, Sept. 22, 1791, Bristol valuation return, microfilm box 395, MSL; Canaan Plantation to the General Court, Dec. 16, 1786, *MDH*, XXI, 318; Gray petition to the General Court, Oct. 15, 1788, *MDH*, XXII, 61–62; Condeskeag petition to the General Court, Dec. 31, 1789, *BHM*, VI, 171.

25. List of taxes abated by the General Court, Oct. 8, 1782–Jan. 16, 1790, *MDH*, XXII, 310. See also the list of unpaid 1786 taxes as of July 3, 1787, *MDH*, XXI, 229–230.

26. Van Beck Hall, "Appendices to *Politics without Parties: Massachusetts, 1780–1791*," MS, 2–17 (filed at Hillman Library, University of Pittsburgh); *Report of the Committee of Valuation* (Boston, 1802; S-S 2625), 6–14. In 1801 mid-Maine had 11,474 polls and $257,417.87 in aggregate wealth. Massachusetts had 93,415 polls and $4,330,753.40 in aggregate wealth. See Table 8.

27. For denials of white poverty, see Harry J. Carman, ed., *American Husbandry* (New York, 1939), 52–53; Dwight, *Travels*, IV, 238; G. B. Warden, "Inequality and Instability in Eighteenth-Century Boston: A Reappraisal," *Journal of Interdisciplinary History*, VI (1975–1976), 585–620; and Robert E. Brown, *Middle-Class Democracy and the Revolution in Massachusetts, 1691–1780* (Ithaca, N.Y., 1955). For the flaws in the travelers' perception, see Percy Wells Bidwell, *Rural Economy in New England at the Beginning of the Nineteenth Century* (Connecticut Academy of the Arts and Sciences, *Transactions*, XX [New Haven, Conn., 1916]), 368–370. Jacob Bailey quoted in William S. Bartlett, *The Frontier Missionary: A Memoir of the*

Life of the Rev. Jacob Bailey . . . (Boston, 1853), 88. A 1766 tax list for Bailey's parish confirms that most of the dwellings were one-room log cabins without cellars, chimneys, or windowglass (see the valuation list in C. Allen, *Dresden*, 268–271). William Bentley, *The Diary of William Bentley, D.D., Pastor of the East Church, Salem, Massachusetts*, 4 vols. (Gloucester, Mass., 1962; reprint of Salem, Mass., 1905–1914), I, 64; La Rochefoucault Liancourt, *Travels*, I, 443; Southack, *Life of Southack*, 16; Kendall, *Travels*, III, 83. La Rochefoucault Liancourt's words must have been painful for Henry Knox to read, for the duc had been his guest and had left the obliging impression that he was "highly impressed in favor of [Maine], and wishes to establish himself here" (see Henry Knox to David Cobb, Oct. 28, 1795, in Allis, ed., *Bingham's Maine Lands*, I, 550–551).

28. W. Allen, *Norridgewock*, 71. The 1791 and 1801 Balltown valuation returns are available on microfilm at the MSL. Of the 128 persisting taxpayers, 86 increased their improved acreage, 16 decreased or stayed the same, and the returns of 26 are illegible; 80 increased their mature livestock, 33 decreased or stayed the same, 15 returns are illegible; and 74 increased their grain production, 43 decreased or stayed the same, 11 returns are illegible. On average the 128 holdovers added 8.8 improved acres at the expense of 10.8 woodland acres. On average the holdovers increased their mature livestock by 2.7 head. Most of the increase was in oxen (1.0 head) and mature cattle (1.0 head). The increases in mature horses (.3 head) and pigs (.5 head) were slight. See also Tables 3–7. For early Americans' fundamental drive to secure economic independence, see Stephen Innes, *Labor in a New Land: Economy and Society in Seventeenth-Century Springfield* (Princeton, N.J., 1983), 77; and Jack P. Greene, "Independence, Improvement, and Authority: Toward a Framework for Understanding the Histories of the Southern Backcountry during the Era of the American Revolution," in Ronald Hoffman *et al.*, eds., *An Uncivil War: The Southern Backcountry during the American Revolution* (Charlottesville, Va., 1985), 12.

29. W. Allen, *Industry*, 40; W. Allen, "Journal," in Hatch, *Industry*, 79–80.

30. W. Allen, "Journal," in Hatch, *Industry*, 80–83; William Allen, "How I Began Farming," *Maine Farmer* (Winthrop), Sept. 10, 1870; Leighton, *Autobiography*, 29–37.

31. For proprietary support of agricultural improvement (especially the cultivation of winter wheat) to increase land values, see Charles Vaughan to James Bowdoin, Jan. 15, 1801, KPP, box 4, MeHS; Robert Hallowell Gardiner to William D. Williamson, Nov. 13, 1820, under "Gardiner," WDWTP, MeHS; Talleyrand, "Letter," 74; William Morris to Theophile Cazenove, Dec. 9, 1792, Benjamin Vaughan to David Cobb, Apr. 30, 1800, and David Cobb to C. W. Hare, Oct. 29, 1809, in Allis, ed., *Bingham's Maine Lands*, I, 195, II, 1043, 1231.

32. Balltown's 1791 valuation return (and 1792 aggregate), MSL. See Tables 3–5, 7. *Papers to the Massachusetts Society for Promoting Agriculture [1807]*, 11–13, provides returns from various parts of the commonwealth setting the proportion of tilled land at generally from 1/8th to 1/12th of a farmer's land. For the 30-bushel standard for family subsistence, see Pruitt, "Self-Sufficiency," *WMQ*, 3d Ser., XLI (1984), 332–364; and Douglas Lamar Jones, *Village and Seaport: Migration and Society in Eighteenth-Century Massachusetts* (Hanover, N.H., 1981), 8. Families that raised potatoes could subsist on less grain, but, unfortunately, the valuations do not measure that crop. It seems likely, however, that almost all of the taxpayers raised potatoes, because every description of agriculture in the Eastern Country stresses their importance.

33. Nehemiah Smith to the U.S. Commissioner of Patents, Dec. 28, 1851, in

Millard A. Howard, *An Introduction to the Early History of Palermo, Maine* (Augusta, 1976), 62; Deane, *New-England Farmer*, 139–141, 238; Sibley, *Union*, 99, 105–106; Thurston, *Winthrop*, 15; Greenleaf, *A Survey of the State of Maine*, 87; Eaton, *Thomaston*, I, 89; Jasper Jacob Stahl, *History of Old Broad Bay and Waldoboro* (Portland, 1956), I, 306; Smith, "Climatic Stress," in Wigley *et al.*, eds., *Climate and History*, 451.

34. Deane, *New-England Farmer*, 85; Tenney, "Exeter," MHS, *Colls.*, 1st Ser., IV (1795), 92; and Belknap, *New-Hampshire*, III, 137–138. See also William Tudor, *Letters on the Eastern States . . .* (Boston, 1821), 249–251; Susan Geib, "'Changing Works': Agriculture and Society in Brookfield, Massachusetts, 1785–1820" (Ph.D. diss., Boston University, 1981), 40–64; Robert A. Gross, "Culture and Cultivation: Agriculture and Society in Thoreau's Concord," *Journal of American History*, LXIX (1982–1983), 42–61; Rodolphus Dickinson, *A Geographical and Statistical View of Massachusetts Proper* (Greenfield, Mass., 1813; S-S 28328), 8.

35. W. Allen, "Journal," in Hatch, *Industry*, 81; W. Allen, "How I Began," *Maine Farmer*, Sept. 10, 1870; W. Allen, *Industry*, 24; Belknap, *New-Hampshire*, III, 124; Deane, *New-England Farmer*, 203; La Rochefoucault Liancourt, *Travels*, I, 424. Historians who emphasize the entrepreneurial dimension in rural America include Charles S. Grant, *Democracy in the Connecticut Frontier Town of Kent* (New York, 1961), 29–31; Winifred B. Rothenberg, "The Market and Massachusetts Farmers, 1750–1855," *Jour. Econ. Hist.*, XLI (1981), 283–284; Robert D. Mitchell, *Commercialism and Frontier: Perspectives on the Early Shenandoah Valley* (Charlottesville, Va., 1977); and James T. Lemon, *The Best Poor Man's Country: A Geographical Study of Early Southeastern Pennsylvania* (Baltimore, 1972). Historians who stress the limits of commercialization in rural America include James A. Henretta, "Families and Farms: *Mentalité* in Pre-Industrial America," *WMQ*, 3d Ser., XXXV (1978), 3–32; and Robert Mutch, "Yeoman and Merchant in Pre-Industrial America: Eighteenth Century Massachusetts as a Case Study," *Societas*, VII (1977), 281–282.

36. On the seasonal cycle, see Sibley, *Union*, 100–102, 261, 387–393, 413–419; Greenleaf, *A Survey of the State of Maine*, 104, 253–254; Charles Vaughan to the Kennebeck Proprietors, Nov. 24, 1803, May 26, 1805, KPP, box 5, MeHS; John Linn to Thomas L. Winthrop, Mar. 1807, KPP, box 6, MeHS. On preindustrial work rhythms, see E. P. Thompson, "Time, Work-Discipline, and Industrial Capitalism," *Past and Present*, no. 38 (Dec. 1967), 56–97; and Eric Foner, *Tom Paine and Revolutionary America* (New York, 1976), 36–39.

37. Robert Huston *et al.* to the General Court, Dec. 22, 1807, unpassed legislation, House File 5996, MA (regarding William How); William Allen, "Sandy River," MeHS, *Colls.*, 1st Ser., IV (1856), 38. On the interplay of self-sufficiency and the market, see Pruitt, "Self-Sufficiency," *WMQ*, 3d Ser., XLI (1984), 354–355; and Richard L. Bushman, "Family Security in the Transition from Farm to City, 1750–1850," *Working Papers from the Regional Economic History Research Center*, IV, no. 3 (1981), 30–34.

38. Elwell v. Callahan, box 404 (1799), Lincoln County SJC Files, LCC.

39. Leighton, *Autobiography*, 11, 30; "To the Neighbor," *Castine Journal*, Nov. 15, 1799; John Low to William D. Williamson, Dec. 18, 1819 (filed under Parsonsfield), A. H. Giddings to Williamson, Nov. 6, 1826 (Danville), and Dr. Porter quoted in Amos Cook to Williamson, Apr. 7, 1821 (Fryeburg), WDWTP, MeHS.

40. Kendall, *Travels*, III, 86. For a fuller description and analysis of treasure-seeking, see Alan Taylor, "The Early Republic's Supernatural Economy: Trea-

sure-Seeking in the American Northeast, 1780–1830," *American Quarterly*, XXXVIII (1986), 6–34.

41. Taylor, "The Early Republic's Supernatural Economy," *Am. Qtly.*, XXXVIII (1986), 13–14.

42. William Scales to Henry Knox, July 29, 1805, XLVI, 67, HKP, MHS; Coffin, "Journals," MeHS, *Colls.*, 1st Ser., IV (1859), 392. See also Eaton, *Warren*, 155–156; George Augustus Wheeler and Henry Warren Wheeler, *History of Brunswick, Topsham, and Harpswell, Maine* (Boston, 1878), 220; Sibley, *Union*, 228–229; Stover v. Estes, July 1789, SJC Record Book, May–Nov. 1789, 228, MA; Harry H. Cochrane, *History of Monmouth and Wales* (East Winthrop, 1894), I, 214–218; Amos Davis to Josiah Little, Mar. 20, 1784, folder 1782–1799, PPP, box 17, EI.

43. Kendall, *Travels*, III, 96. See also Gordon S. Wood, "Evangelical America and Early Mormonism," *New York History*, LXI (1980), 363–370.

44. Kendall, *Travels*, III, 87; William Scales to the General Court, Nov. 14, 1796, Senate Unpassed File 2134/1, MA.

45. John W. Hanson, *History of the Old Towns of Norridgewock and Canaan* (Boston, 1849), 150–151; Samuel Weston *et al.* to the General Court's valuation committee, Oct. 20, 1801, Canaan valuation, 1801 Maine valuations (reel 397), MSL.

46. Kendall, *Travels*, III, 96. See also Richard L. Bushman, *Joseph Smith and the Beginnings of Mormonism* (Urbana, Ill., 1984), 71–72.

47. John Marden's reminiscences, June 7, 1855, in Allen Goodwin, *A History of the Early Settlement of Palermo, Me.* (Belfast, 1896), 9; Sibley, *Union*, 71; Dwight, *Travels*, ed. Solomon, II, 328. For the culture of mutuality elsewhere in rural America, see Steven Hahn, *The Roots of Southern Populism: Yeoman Farmers and the Transformation of the Georgia Upcountry, 1850–1890* (New York, 1983), 52; and John Mack Faragher, *Sugar Creek: Life on the Illinois Prairie* (New Haven, Conn., 1986), 132.

48. W. Allen, "Sandy River," MeHS, *Colls.*, 1st Ser., IV (1856), 40; Eaton, *Warren*, 181, 294, 302; Hatch, *Industry*, 53; Stahl, *Old Broad Bay*, I, 312, 485; Sibley, *Union*, 56, 407; *Kennebeck Intelligencer*, June 14, 1799; Thurston, *Winthrop*, 63–64. On "changing works," see Ephraim Sheldon deposition, Jan. 6, 1796, Barrett v. Cary and Smith, LC-CCP Files, box 343 (1796), LCC; Gross, "Culture and Cultivation," *JAH*, LXIX (1982–1983), 51–52; and Geib, " 'Changing Works.' "

49. Hezekiah Prince's "Travel Journal," Nov. 9, 1793, entry, in Prince, *Remarks of My Life, 1786–1792* (Rockland, 1979), 24; John Pendleton Farrow, *History of Islesborough* (Bangor, 1893), 73; Thurston, *Winthrop*, 67; Ulrich, "Housewife and Gadder," in Groneman and Norton, eds., *"To Toil the Livelong Day,"* 25.

50. Eaton, *Warren*, 264; Eaton, *Thomaston*, I, 117; Sibley, *Union*, 48 n; Cochrane, *Monmouth*, I, 186; Robinson, *Morrill*, 107–108; Leighton, *Autobiography*, 22; Coffin, "Journals," MeHS, *Colls.*, 1st Ser., IV (1859), 394, 403.

51. Eaton, *Warren*, 353; W. Allen, *Norridgewock*, 110; Belknap, *New-Hampshire*, III, 263; Kendall, *Travels*, III, 81; Wheeler and Wheeler, *Brunswick*, 221; Sibley, *Union*, 230–231 n; "On the Use of Rum," *Falmouth Gazette* (Portland), Feb. 19, 1785; Joseph Tucker to George Thatcher, Feb. 10, 1791, GTP, BPL; *Independent Chronicle* (Boston), Feb. 9, 1786. See also W. J. Rorabaugh, *The Alcoholic Republic: An American Tradition* (New York, 1979).

52. Eaton, *Warren*, 270, 353–354; W. Allen, *Norridgewock*, 110; Leighton, *Autobiography*, 22; Sibley, *Union*, 230–231 n, 356; Robinson, *Morrill*, 88–90, quote 88; William Jones, *A True Account of All the Presbyterian and Congregational Minis-*

ters . . . (Bristol, 1808), 56. On belittling humor, see Cochrane, *Monmouth*, 189–193; Eaton, *Thomaston*, I, 254.

53. Benjamin Lincoln, "Observations on the Eastern Country," KPP, box 3, MeHS; [David Cobb] to William D. Williamson, ca. 1820, filed under "Gouldsborough" in WDWTP, MeHS (the handwriting, style, and sentiments are unmistakably those of Cobb, who then resided in Gouldsborough); Kendall, *Travels*, III, 81; Alden Bradford, "A Description of Wiscasset, and of the River Sheepscot," MHS, *Colls.*, 1st Ser., VII (Boston, 1801), 170; Jonathan Ellis, "A Topographical Description of Topsham . . . ," MHS, *Colls.*, 1st Ser., III (Boston, 1794), 144; "Philo Patria," *Cumberland Gazette* (Portland), Oct. 2, 1788.

54. For the backcountry dread of wooden shoes and uncombed hair, see A. Roger Ekirch, *"Poor Carolina": Politics and Society in Colonial North Carolina, 1729–1776* (Chapel Hill, N.C., 1981), 190; David P. Szatmary, *Shays' Rebellion: The Making of an Agrarian Insurrection* (Amherst, Mass., 1980), 5–6; Robert Maxwell Brown, "Back Country Rebellions and the Homestead Ethic in America, 1740–1799," in Brown and Don E. Fehrenbacher, eds., *Tradition, Conflict, and Modernization: Perspectives on the American Revolution* (New York, 1977), 78–79; and Thomas P. Slaughter, *The Whiskey Rebellion: Frontier Epilogue to the American Revolution* (New York, 1986), 63–74.

55. Ducktrap residents to Henry Knox, Oct. 18, 1788, HKP, XXII, 164, MHS; Waterman Thomas *et al.* to the General Court, Jan. 2, 1789, HKP, LII, 7, MHS. See also the Waldo Patent petition to the General Court, Oct. 8, 1793, HKP, LII, 50, MHS; written by Samuel Ely, the document insists that two-thirds of the settlers were "so poor in purse and property that 'tis beyond their present ability and to human probability will remain so during their lives, to purchase or pay for their premises."

56. On the New Milford "frolic," see Asa Andrews's deposition, winter 1797, in Council Files, box 12 (Mar. 1799–Oct. 1801), MA; Stephen Chase to Josiah Little, Dec. 22, 1800, PPP, box 4, "Letters to Josiah Little" folder, EI; Liberty Man quoted in Thurston Whiting and Benjamin Brackett to Henry Knox, Aug. 26, 1801, HKP, XLIV, 54, MHS. The 1765 rioters against Scarborough merchant Richard King also referred to their riot as a "frolic"; see Silas Burbank deposition, June 28, 1773, in L. Kinvin Wroth and Hiller B. Zobel, eds., *Legal Papers of John Adams* (Cambridge, Mass., 1965), I, 122.

CHAPTER FOUR

1. The epigraph is from Samuel Ely, *The Deformity of a Hideous Monster, Discovered in the Province of Maine, by a Man in the Woods, Looking after Liberty* (Boston, 1797; E 32081), 14. Henry Knox's notice, May 26, 1800, HKP, LII, 79, MHS; Robert Houston's deposition, Aug. 14, 1800, Bradstreet Wiggins's deposition, Aug. 15, 1800, and George Ulmer to Henry Knox, July 23, 1800, Related Papers, Resolve of Nov. 15, 1800, MA; George Ulmer *et al.* deposition, Oct. 31, 1801, HKP, box 6, MeHS; Thurston Whiting and Benjamin Brackett to Henry Knox, Sept. 7, 1801, HKP, LII, 87, MHS; Robert Houston and George Ulmer to Gov. Caleb Strong, Aug. 12, 1800, Related Papers, Resolve of Nov. 15, 1800, MA; Henry Knox to George Ulmer, July 11, 1801, HKP, XLIV, 25, MHS.

2. Thurston Whiting and Benjamin Brackett to Henry Knox, Aug. 28, 1801,

Sept. 7, 1801, HKP, XLIV, 66, LII, 87, MHS; Whiting and Brackett, "Journal," Aug. 28, 1801, entry, HKP, XLIV, 54, MHS; Isaac Parker to Henry Knox, Mar. 1, 1796, HKP, XXXVIII, 149, MHS.

3. LC-CGSP Record Book II, 143, Sept. 8, 1795, LCC; the settler (John Marden) quoted in Allen Goodwin, *A History of the Early Settlement of Palermo, Me.* (Belfast, 1896), 9; Paul Coffin, "Memoir and Journals of Rev. Paul Coffin, D.D.," MeHS, *Collections*, 1st Ser., IV (Portland, 1859), 322–323; William Crosby quoted in Joseph Williamson, *History of the City of Belfast . . .* , I (Portland, 1877), 200. See also Coffin, "Memoir and Journals," 318 (Aug. 2, 1796), 323 (Aug. 8, 1796); John Hills to Henry Knox, Aug. 15, 1793, HKP, XXXIV, 69, MHS; John Langdon Sibley, *A History of the Town of Union . . .* (Boston, 1851), 273; William Allen, *The History of Norridgewock . . .* (Norridgewock, 1849), 132; Cyrus Eaton, *Annals of the Town of Warren* (Hallowell, 1877), 254–255, 263; and Moses Greenleaf, *A Survey of the State of Maine . . .* (Portland, 1829), 105.

4. Thomas Vose to Henry Knox, Apr. 27, 1796, HKP, XXXIX, 49, MHS; Reuel Williams to Thomas L. Winthrop, Nov. 14, 1803, RWP, box 1, MeHS; Reuel Williams to the Kennebeck Proprietors, Mar. 20, 1806, RWP, box 2, MeHS; Charles Vaughan to James Bowdoin, Jan. 19, 1801, KPP, box 4, MeHS.

5. A. H. Giddings to William D. Williamson, Nov. 6, 1826, WDWTP (filed under "Danville"), MeHS; Alfred Johnson to Jedediah Morse, Oct. 27, 1806, SPG, box 3, folder 1, EI. I compiled the number of Congregational churches in 1800 and their location from Jonathan Greenleaf, *Sketches of the Ecclesiastical History of the State of Maine . . .* (Portsmouth, N.H., 1821). I compiled the justices of the peace from *Fleets' Register, and Pocket Almanack for the Year of Our Lord 1800* (Boston, [1799]; E 35487), 138–142.

6. Timothy Dwight, *Travels in New England and New York*, ed. Barbara Miller Solomon, 4 vols. (Cambridge, Mass., 1969; orig. publ. New Haven, Conn., 1821), II, 162, 322–323. For a frustrated radical shoemaker (Walter Brewster) fleeing Connecticut for the Ohio frontier, see James P. Walsh, " 'Mechanics and Citizens': The Connecticut Artisan Protest of 1792," *WMQ*, 3d Ser., XLII (1985), 66–89.

7. Amos Barrett and James Malcom to Knox, Sept. 8, 1794, Noah Miller to Knox, Sept. 8, 1794, HKP, XXXVI, 41, 42, MHS; Charles Vaughan to James Bowdoin, Jan. 4, 1802, KPP, box 4, MeHS; "Communication," *Edes' Kennebec Gazette* (Augusta), Oct. 1, 1802; David Cobb to C. W. Hare, Aug. 22, 1810, in Frederick F. Allis, Jr., ed., *William Bingham's Maine Lands, 1790–1820*, 2 vols. (Colonial Society of Massachusetts, *Publications*, XXXVI–XXXVII [Boston, 1954]), II, 1232–1233 (hereafter cited as Allis, ed., *Bingham's Maine Lands*). For emissaries, see Thurston Whiting and Benjamin Brackett to Henry Knox, Sept. 7, 1801, HKP, LII, 87, MHS; and Knox to Charles Vaughan, July 5, 1801, HKP, XLIV, 17, MHS.

8. Thurston Whiting and Benjamin Brackett to Henry Knox, Sept. 7, 1801, HKP, LII, 87, MHS; Whiting and Brackett, "Journal," Aug. 28, 1801, entry, HKP, XLIV, 54, MHS.

9. Thurston Whiting and Benjamin Brackett to Henry Knox, Sept. 7, 1801, HKP, LII, 87, MHS. For similar ideas elsewhere in rural America, see Gregory H. Nobles, *Divisions throughout the Whole: Politics and Society in Hampshire County, Massachusetts, 1740–1775* (New York, 1983), 124; Ruth Bogin, "New Jersey's True Policy: The Radical Republican Vision of Abraham Clark," *WMQ*, 3d Ser., XXXV (1978), 104–106; and Walsh, " 'Mechanics and Citizens,' " *WMQ*, 3d Ser., XLII (1985), 75, 84.

10. In interpreting agrarian resistance, we should avoid two common misconceptions: that settlers were a proletariat and that there can be no class conflict without a proletariat. For the argument that there could not have been class conflict in rural America for lack of a proletariat, see Edmund S. Morgan, "The American Revolution: Who Were 'The People'?" *New York Review of Books*, Aug. 5, 1976, 31. For class conflict without a rural proletariat, see Jackson Turner Main, *The Antifederalists: Critics of the Constitution, 1781–1788* (Chapel Hill, N.C., 1961), esp. 10–11, 15–106, 129–130; and Main, *Political Parties before the Constitution* (Chapel Hill, N.C., 1973), 261–262. For the argument that hardship does not automatically produce resistance (in the absence of legitimating ideas), see E. J. Hobsbawm and George Rudé, *Captain Swing* (London, 1969), 56; and E. P. Thompson, "The Moral Economy of the English Crowd in the Eighteenth Century," *Past and Present*, no. 50 (Feb. 1971), 76–79.

11. At Knox's instigation, 45 armed volunteers marched under Captain Thomas Knowlton into the backcountry to arrest suspected Liberty Men on the night of June 25, 1801. Most of the volunteers were Belfast newcomers who arrived after the 1800 federal census. Of the 30 who appeared on Belfast's 1801 tax valuation, 21 possessed no improved land; 16 owned no land at all. Indeed, 12 possessed no ratable property of any sort, paying tax only on their poll. Half (15 of 30) were not present in 1800, almost half (13 of 30) were gone by 1810. See George Ulmer to Henry Knox, June 26, 1801, HKP, box 6, MeHS; Captain Thomas Knowlton and Lieutenant Jonathan Wilson to Gov. Caleb Strong, Jan. 25, 1802, Related Papers, Resolve of Mar. 4, 1802, MA; Robert Houston to Knox, June 26, 1801, HKP, XLIV, 13, MHS; Belfast Valuation, 1801, box 397, MSL; Belfast Federal Census Returns, Second Census of the United States, 1800, microfilm series M32, reel 7, NA; Resolve CXI (Mar. 4, 1802), in *Resolves, etc. of the General Court of Massachusetts . . . [Jan.–Mar. 1802]* (Boston, [1802]; S-S 2626), 58 (list of Knowlton's men). Poor transients also predominated among the 51 chainmen and guards employed by Knox to survey his backcountry claim in 1800–1801. Only 4 appeared on the 1800 federal census returns for Hancock County. The largest contingent came from Belfast, where 19 appeared on the 1801 tax list; 15 of the 19 were landless. See the surveying account, Sept. 26, 1801, and "List of Persons Employed in Surveying Business in July 1800 and May and June 1801," HKP, box 6, MeHS. The calculations exclude the 6 leaders: John Gleason, Robert Houston, Philip Ulmer, George Ulmer, Bradstreet Wiggins, and Jonathan Wilson. In 1801, 57 of 174 (33%) Belfast taxpayers were landless, 17 of Northport's 108 (16%), and 40 of Balltown's 279 (14%). The 1801 valuation lists for Balltown, Belfast, and Northport are on microfilm, boxes 397–398, MSL. For the refusal of most Lincolnville-Northport inhabitants to assist the posses or surveyors, see George Ulmer to Henry Knox, June 28, 1801, HKP, XLIV, 14, MHS.

12. The 1800 federal census for Northport and Ducktrap–New Canaan identifies the place of origin for 84 men who signed Samuel Ely's petitions against Henry Knox, and for 20 proprietary allies (Ducktrap and Northport returns, Second Census of the United States, 1800, microfilm series M32, reel 7, NA). Two-thirds (55 of 84) of the resisting settlers came either from elsewhere in mid-Maine, principally the Lincoln County coast, or from Nova Scotia, compared to but half (10 of 20) of those who stood by Knox. Prior frontier experience apparently taught men to distrust proprietors and encouraged settlers to trust in their ability successfully to resist proprietary power. On the recruits' southwestern Maine origins, see Sept. 8, 1801, list, HKP, Land Records Book, MeHS (Lim-

ington, Standish, Gorham, and North Yarmouth supplied the greatest numbers) and the Nov. 1, 1799, and Oct. 1800 entries, HKP, Land Records Book, MeHS. For Knox's wage rate, see the surveying account dated Sept. 26, 1801, HKP, box 6, MeHS.

13. John Hunter to Henry Knox, Oct. 7, 1801, HKP, XLIV, 101, MHS, recorded the conversation. The blacksmith shop may have belonged to George Carr, who lived in Belfast and had participated in Knox's surveys. Hunter, who shared Stewart's sentiments, had been one of Knox's survey assistants. See also David P. Szatmary, *Shays' Rebellion: The Making of an Agrarian Insurrection* (Amherst, Mass., 1980), 86–89; and Thomas P. Slaughter, *The Whiskey Rebellion: Frontier Epilogue to the American Revolution* (New York, 1986), 214–217. The most expensive of Knox's backcountry surveys, the final, triumphant survey in Sept. 1801, cost the general $142.53—less than the subsequent receipts for a single 100-acre lot, and the surveys sliced the Waldo Patent backlands into more than 800 lots. See the surveying account, Sept. 26, 1801, HKP, box 6, MeHS.

14. Elisha Sylvester to the Pejepscot Proprietors, Jan. 19, 1801, PPP, box 12, folder 1800–1802, EI.

15. *History of Litchfield and an Account of Its Centennial Celebration, 1895* (Augusta, 1897), 305; Benjamin Shurtleff, comp., *Descendants of William Shurtleff of Plymouth and Marshfield, Massachusetts*, 2 vols. (Revere, Mass., 1912), I, 70–71; Bettye Hobbs Pruitt, *The Massachusetts Tax Valuation List of 1771* (Boston, 1978), 656; Ebenezer Macomber's deposition, Feb. 25, 1799, in Blanchard v. Beal, LC-SJC files, box 406 (1800), LCC ("poor"); Litchfield valuation return for 1810, Maine tax valuations for 1810, box 399, MSL.

16. [James Shurtleff], *A Concise Review of the Spirit Which Seemed to Govern in the Time of the Late American War, Compared with the Spirit Which Now Prevails . . .* (Augusta, 1798; E 34548), 29.

17. *Ibid.*, 18–24, 26; Plymouth Gore petition (William Cunningham *et al.*) to the Eastern Lands Committee, ELC, box 18, MA. For confirmation of the proprietors' post-Revolutionary reluctance to assist settlement financially, see Moses Greenleaf, *A Statistical View of the District of Maine . . .* (Boston, 1816; S-S 37745), 107–114. William Bingham's investments to promote his lands were exceptional; ironically, his lands were so poorly situated that the improvements attracted few migrants and he lost money; see Bingham to David Cobb, Mar. 25, 1795, in Allis, ed., *Bingham's Maine Lands*, I, 503–508.

18. [J. Shurtleff], *Concise Review*, 19; John Locke, *Two Treatises of Government* (1698), ed. Peter Laslett (Cambridge, 1960), 303–320; C. B. MacPherson, *The Political Theory of Possessive Individualism: Hobbes to Locke* (Oxford, 1962), 199–201; "To James Shurtleff," *Kennebeck Intelligencer*, Jan. 30, 1798, faults Shurtleff's reading of Locke. Shurtleff had not read Locke, but relied on the discussion in James Sullivan, *The History of the District of Maine* (Augusta, 1970; orig. publ. Boston, 1795), 110, 131–139. During the Revolutionary era, Philadelphia's artisans and merchants also differed in their interpretation of Locke's theory of property, with artisans stressing the origins of value in labor while merchants dwelled on the inviolability of property; see Eric Foner, *Tom Paine and Revolutionary America* (New York, 1976), 40.

19. Bowdoin's petition to the General Court, Jan. 21, 1789, *MDH*, XXII, 142; Prospect Land Committee to the Waldo Patent Commissioners, Feb. 16, 1798, ELC, box 53, MA; Isaac Collier *et al.* to the General Court, ca. Nov. 1800, Related Papers, Resolve CXLIII (Mar. 5, 1801), MA; [William Scales], "Kind Sir," folder 1782–1799, PPP, box 17, EI (the handwriting and sentiments match

the separate cover letter, William Scales to Col. Josiah Little, Apr. 23, n.y., LFP, box 3, folder 8, EI).

20. Pejepscot Patent petition to the General Court, n.d., WKP, box 10, MeHS; [J. Shurtleff], *Concise Review*, 46.

21. [J. Shurtleff], *Concise Review*, 11, 21–22, 30; Sullivan, *History of Maine*, 62, 127, 134–135.

22. [J. Shurtleff], *Concise Review*, 5, 20–23. For Americans' dread of "slavery," see Gordon S. Wood, "Rhetoric and Reality in the American Revolution," *WMQ*, 3d Ser., XXIII (1966), 3–32; Christopher M. Jedrey, *The World of John Cleaveland: Family and Community in Eighteenth-Century New England* (New York, 1979), 134; and, especially, Richard L. Bushman, "Massachusetts Farmers and the Revolution," in Jack P. Greene *et al.*, *Society, Freedom, and Conscience: The American Revolution in Virginia, Massachusetts, and New York*, ed. Richard M. Jellison (New York, 1976), 77–124.

23. Ely, *Deformity*, 24; Robert E. Moody, "Samuel Ely: Forerunner of Shays," *New England Quarterly*, V (1932), 105–134; "Samuel Ely," in Franklin Bowditch Dexter, *Biographical Sketches of the Graduates of Yale College . . .* , III (New York, 1903), 67–69 (Dexter pronounced Ely the most "infamous" of all Yale graduates, no small accomplishment); Dwight, *Travels*, ed. Solomon, II, 189.

24. Samuel Ely to the General Court, Jan. 2, 1797, HKP, XL, 42, MHS; Henry Knox to George Ulmer, Mar. 12, 1797, HKP, XL, 80, MHS. The survival of Ely's last petition in Henry Knox's papers, rather than in the files of the House where legally it belonged, is interesting. Knox avidly collected all the documents he could find relating to Ely.

25. Dexter, *Graduates of Yale*, III, 67; Moody, "Samuel Ely," *NEQ*, V (1932), 105–106; Dwight, *Travels*, ed. Solomon, II, 188–189.

26. Moody, "Samuel Ely," *NEQ*, V (1932), 106; Dexter, *Graduates of Yale*, III, 67; Samuel Ely, *Two Sermons Preached at Somers, March 18, 1770 . . .* (Hartford, Conn., 1771; E 12036), 3–58.

27. Moody, "Samuel Ely," *NEQ*, V (1932), 107. The International Genealogical Index at the NEHGSL lists no Massachusetts births for Samuel Ely offspring but three daughters born in Somers, Connecticut, to him and Beulah Billings Ely: Dina, Beulah, and Clarissa in 1772, 1774, and 1777; apparently Ely remarried, for his wife in Maine during the 1790s was named "Temperance." Dexter, *Graduates of Yale*, III, 67, says that Ely also had a son.

28. Oscar Handlin and Mary Flug Handlin, *Commonwealth: A Study of the Role of Government in the American Economy: Massachusetts, 1774–1861* (Cambridge, Mass., 1969), 33; Joseph Hawley to Caleb Strong, June 22, 1782, reprinted in Moody, "Samuel Ely," *NEQ*, V (1932), 107–113.

29. Moody, "Samuel Ely," *NEQ*, V (1932), 108–116; Resolve CLVIII (Mar. 17, 1783), in *Resolves of the General Court of the Commonwealth of Massachusetts . . . [May 1782–Mar. 1783]* ([Boston, 1783]; E 18026), 198; John L. Brooke, "Society, Revolution, and the Symbolic Uses of the Dead: An Historical Ethnography of the Massachusetts Near Frontier, 1730–1820" (Ph.D. diss., University of Pennsylvania, 1982), 556–561.

30. U.S., Bureau of the Census, *Heads of Families at the First Census of the United States Taken in the Year 1790: Maine* (Washington, D.C., 1908), 43; J. Williamson, *Belfast*, I, 229; John L. Locke, "Sketches of the Early History of Belfast," *Republican Journal* (Belfast), May 29, 1856; Commonwealth v. Ely, July 1794, in 1794 SJC Record Book, MA. For Ely's influence, see James Nesmith to Isaac Parker, Mar. 7. 1796. HKP, XXXVIII, 160, MHS.

31. Ely, *The Deformity*, 5, 9–13.

32. *Ibid.*, 23; [J. Shurtleff], *Concise Review*, 38; [James Davis and Samuel Ely], *The Appeal of the Two Counties of Lincoln and Hancock, from the Forlorn Hope, or, Mount of Distress; to the General Court, or, to All the World* (Portsmouth, N.H., 1796; E 31477), 22. For Abraham Clark's similar views, see Bogin, "New Jersey's True Policy," *WMQ*, 3d Ser., XXXV (1978), 106. The North Carolina Regulator Herman Husband similarly argued that laws were invalid when they were "against God's Law or principalls of Nature"; see Mark Haddon Jones, "Herman Husband: Millenarian, Carolina Regulator, and Whiskey Rebel" (Ph.D. diss., Northern Illinois University, 1983), 166.

33. Jasper Jacob Stahl, *History of Old Broad Bay and Waldoboro* (Portland, 1956), I, 488, 501; "Civis," *Wiscasset Telegraph*, Oct. 23, 1798; Allen, *Norridgewock*, 106. For the protection covenant, see Richard L. Bushman, *King and People in Provincial Massachusetts* (Chapel Hill, N.C., 1985), 37–46; T. H. Breen, *The Character of the Good Ruler: A Study of Puritan Political Ideas in New England, 1630–1730* (New Haven, Conn., 1970).

34. Wadsworth quoted in James S. Leamon, "The Search for Security: Maine after Penobscot," *Maine Historical Society Quarterly*, XXI (1982), 123; Samuel Nasson to George Thatcher, Mar. 12, 1790, GTP, MeHS; Ephraim Rollins to William D. Williamson, May 12, 1821, filed under "Nobleborough," in WDWTP, MeHS.

35. The Blue Hill settler is quoted in Leamon, "The Search for Security," *Maine Hist. Soc. Qtly.*, XXI (1982), 140; *Falmouth Gazette* (Portland), Jan. 15, 1785; Thomas B. Wait to George Thatcher, Jan. 8, 1788, Silas Lee to Thatcher, May 9, 1788, GTP, BPL; Benjamin Lincoln to James Bowdoin, Sept. 19, 1786, *MDH*, XXI, 245.

36. Charles Maurice de Talleyrand-Périgord, "Letter on the Eastern Part of America" (Boston, Sept. 24, 1794), in Hans Huth and Wilma J. Pugh, eds., *Talleyrand in America as a Financial Promoter, 1794–96* (*Annual Report of the American Historical Association, 1941*, II [Washington, D.C., 1942], 84; Benjamin Lincoln to James Bowdoin, Sept. 19, 1786, *MDH*, XXI, 245; Massachusetts Votes for Governor and Lieutenant Governor, MA; on low Massachusetts voter turnout, see Van Beck Hall, *Politics without Parties: Massachusetts, 1780–1791* (Pittsburgh, Pa., 1972), 92; on political apathy and powerlessness in frontier Maine, see Adele Edna Plachta, "The Privileged and the Poor: A History of the District of Maine, 1771–1793" (Ph.D. diss., University of Maine at Orono, 1975); Ronald F. Banks, *Maine Becomes a State: The Movement to Separate Maine from Massachusetts, 1785–1820* (Middletown, Conn., 1970), 24–25. I calculated the turnout by dividing the votes by the 5,071 adult polls in Lincoln County towns in 1784, which undoubtedly overestimates the turnout, since Maine was growing rapidly during the 1780s and by 1787 the number of adult polls was undoubtedly greater. On Massachusetts' turnout in the same election, see J. R. Pole, *Political Representation in England and the Origins of the American Republic* (Berkeley, Calif., 1971), 240.

37. On extreme local autonomy, see Main, *Political Parties*, 395, 403; Slaughter, *The Whiskey Rebellion*, 72; Richard E. Ellis, *Jeffersonian Crisis: Courts and Politics in the Young Republic* (New York, 1971), 250–265. For fear of "great men," see Nobles, *Divisions throughout the Whole*, 185–186; Bogin, "New Jersey's True Policy," *WMQ*, 3d Ser., XXXV (1978), 105–106; Edward Countryman, "Out of the Bounds of the Law: Northern Land Rioters in the Eighteenth Century," in Alfred F. Young, ed., *The American Revolution: Explorations in the History of American Radicalism* (DeKalb, Ill., 1976), 49; Bushman, *King and People*, 235–237.

38. On the defensive nature of early modern protest in Europe and America, see E. P. Thompson, "Eighteenth-Century English Society: Class Struggle with-

out Class?" *Social History*, III (1978), 154–155; Foner, *Tom Paine*, 53–54; Charles Tilly, "Collective Violence in European Perspective," in Hugh Davis Graham and Ted Robert Gurr, eds., *Violence in America: Historical and Comparative Perspectives* (Beverly Hills, Calif., 1979), 83–97; E. J. Hobsbawm, *Primitive Rebels: Studies in Archaic Forms of Social Movement in the Nineteenth and Twentieth Centuries* (Manchester, Eng., 1959), 81–92; and Christine Leigh Heyrman, *Commerce and Culture: The Maritime Communities of Colonial Massachusetts, 1690–1750* (New York, 1984), 87–94.

39. [J. Shurtleff], *Concise Review*, 8, 22; Ely, *Deformity*, 15; for the Davistowners' words (probably drafted by James Davis of Davistown with Samuel Ely's assistance, and endorsed by a settlement meeting), see [Davis and Ely], *The Appeal*, 17, 22.

40. Ely, *Deformity*, 5; R. J. Dickson, *Ulster Emigration to Colonial America, 1718–1775* (London, 1966), on Nova Scotia Gov. Charles Lawrence's offering free land to Scotch-Irish and Yankee settlers before the Revolution. Some Ducktrap-Northport settlers were Revolutionary war refugees from Nova Scotia, men who had received free grants there and expected the same reward from the commonwealth for their patriotism; see Robert Charles Anderson, "David Gay (1739–ca. 1815) of Onslow, Nova Scotia and Lincolnville, Maine," *National Genealogical Society Quarterly*, LXVII (1979), 85–97.

41. Thomas Vose to Henry Knox, Mar. 6, 1796, HKP, XXXVIII, 158, MHS.

42. [J. Shurtleff], *Concise Review*, 11–12, 15; Ely, *Deformity*, 5.

43. William Scales to Josiah Little, Apr. 23, n.y., LFP, box 3, folder 8, EI; [J. Shurtleff], *Concise Review*, 10.

44. Ely, *Deformity*, 16; Brown quoted in Gershom Flagg to Joseph North, Dec. 27, 1795, Related Papers, Resolve of Feb. 27, 1796, MA; Benjamin Poor's deposition, Nov. 25, 1795, Related Papers, Jan. 29, 1799, Resolve, MA. In Sept. 1788 John Fitzgerald, an Irish-born Revolutionary war veteran and settler leader in Waldoborough, told the Waldo heirs "that he had fought for the land and that he should think it a great hardship if he should be compelled to pay for it." Fitzgerald quoted in the first of Henry Knox's "Three Books on the Waldo Patent," Sept. 18, 1788, entry, MHS.

45. David Quimby Cushman, *The History of Ancient Sheepscot and Newcastle . . .* (Bath, 1882), 233–234, misdates this incident to 1800; Lovett Vining's deposition, Apr. 3, 1797, Asa Andrews's deposition, winter 1797, CF, boxes 11 (1797–1799), 12 (1799–1801), MA; John Trueman to the Governor and Council, Oct. 3, 1796, CF, box 10 (1795–1797), MA.

46. John Trueman to the Governor and Council, Oct. 3, 1796, CF, box 10 (1795–1797), MA; Lovett Vining's deposition, Apr. 3, 1797, Thomas Fairservice to Stuart Hunt, Mar. 30, 1797, Daniel Silvester's warrant for the arrest of the rioters, Mar. 10, 1797, CF, box 11 (1797–1799), MA; Asa Andrews's deposition, winter 1797, CF, box 12 (1799–1801), MA.

47. Thomas Fairservice to Stuart Hunt, Mar. 30, 1797, Daniel Silvester's Mar. 10, 1797, warrant for the arrest of the rioters, CF, box 11 (1797–1799), MA; "Rights of Man Exercised at Wiscasset," from *Porcupine's Gazette*, reprinted in Fannie S. Chase, *Wiscasset in Pownalborough* (Wiscasset, 1941), 130; *Wiscasset Telegraph*, Apr. 1, 1797; John Gleason to Henry Knox, Apr. 2, 1797, HKP, XL, 90, MHS; Cushman, *Ancient Sheepscot*, 233; Asa Andrews to Gov. Caleb Strong, July 12, 1800, CF, box 12 (1799–1801), MA.

48. Asa Andrews to Gov. Caleb Strong, July 12, 1800, CF, box 12 (1799–1801), MA; Thomas Hunt to Stuart Hunt, May 9, 1797, Manassah Smith to John

Trueman, May 6, 1797, John Trueman to the Governor and Council, June 14, 1797, CF, box 11 (1797–1799), MA.

49. John Trueman to the Governor and Council, June 14, 1797, CF, box 11 (1797–1799), MA.

50. Winslow Ames quoted in Stephen Chase's deposition, Jan. 27, 1801, PPP, box 12, folder 1800–1802, EI.

51. Samuel Crocker's deposition, Dec. 31, 1796, Joseph Eveleth's deposition, Jan. 2, 1797, PPP, box 10, 1796–1799 folder, EI; Peter Merrill's deposition, Jan. 31, 1801, Martha Merrill's deposition, Jan. 31, 1801, Stephen Chase's deposition, Jan. 27, 1801, Jacob Anderson's deposition, Jan. 26, 1801, Robert Anderson's deposition, Jan. 26, 1801, Amos Davis's deposition, Jan. 29, 1801, all PPP, box 12, folder 1800–1802, EI. For the Green Mountain Boys, see John Munro's deposition, May 30, 1771, Philip Nichols's deposition, Apr. 28, 1773, Jeremiah Gardner's deposition, Aug. 3, 1774, E. B. O'Callaghan, *The Documentary History of the State of New-York*, IV (Albany, N.Y., 1851), 710–712, 830, 879–880.

52. Lothrop Lewis to Josiah Little, May 14, 1800, PPP, box 4, "Letters to Josiah Little" folder, EI; Apr. 21–May 9, 1800, entries of Josiah Little's memo book, PPP, box 5 ("1782–1829 Books"), EI.

53. Ezra Purinton's deposition, Jan. 27, 1801, Mary Purinton's deposition, Jan. 29, 1801, William Carvill's deposition, Jan. 27, 1801, John Field's deposition, Jan. 31, 1801, Joseph Field's deposition, Jan. 29, 1801, PPP, box 12, 1800–1802 folder, EI.

54. I define "incident" as any illegal act committed against proprietors, their agents, their supporters, or authorities enforcing the land laws. I confined my search for incidents to the three mid-Maine counties—Hancock, Lincoln, and Kennebec—and to the years 1790–1820, when documentation is most complete. See Appendix 2. For similar activities elsewhere in rural America, see Jonathan Wheat's deposition, May 29, 1771, David Wooster's deposition, Feb. 20, 1773, O'Callaghan, *The Documentary History of the State of New-York*, IV, 780–781, 824–827 (on Vermont); Slaughter, *The Whiskey Rebellion*, 115–189; Eldridge Honaker Pendleton, "The New York Anti-Rent Controversy, 1830–1860" (Ph.D. diss., University of Virginia, 1974), 80–81; Nathaniel Allen to Col. Jenkins, June 25, 1804, in Louise Welles Murray, *A History of Old Tioga Point and Early Athens, Pennsylvania* (Athens, Pa., 1908), 419–420; Timothy Beach to Robert H. Rose, Aug. 1, 1803, in Julian P. Boyd et al., eds., *The Susquehannah Company Papers* (Ithaca, N.Y., 1930–1971), XI, 401–402.

55. [Davis and Ely], *The Appeal*, 13–21; Robert H. Gardiner, "History of the Kennebec Purchase . . . ," MeHS, *Colls.*, 1st Ser., II (Portland, 1847), 288; Martha Merrill's deposition, Jan. 31, 1801, Peter Merrill's deposition, Jan. 31, 1801, PPP, box 12, folder 1800–1802, EI. Islesborough's "people's committee" is well documented in the depositions by Anthony Coombs, Fields Coombs, Hosea Coombs, John Gilkey, Ellison Lassell, and Noah Miller, Apr. 19, 1794, SCF 141008, CMXXI, MA. On written bonds, see Abraham Welch to George Ulmer, July 11, 1801, HKP, XLIV, 24, MHS; Silas Lee to Bowdoin College's trustees, Nov. 7, 1804, Related Papers, Resolve CIX (Mar. 1, 1805), MA; George Ulmer to Henry Knox, Mar. 3, 1797, HKP, XL, 72, MHS; Thomas Vose to Henry Knox, Feb. 10, 1796, CF, box 10 (Mar. 1795–Feb. 1797), MA; Michael Little to Josiah Little, May 26, 1800, PPP, box 4, "Letters to Josiah Little" folder, EI; [John Merrick], *Remarks on Some of the Circumstances and Arguments Produced by the Murder of Mr. Paul Chadwick, at Malta . . .* ([Augusta, 1809]; S-S 18491), 6.

56. Richard Meagher to Deacon Samuel Goodwin, Dec. 29, 1808 (quote), and

Meagher to the General Court, House File 6385 (unpassed), MA. There was some continuity between the war's loyalists and the resistance's "Tories." Henry Knox's Davistown spy, Dr. Abner Meiggs, and Plymouth Company surveyors, Ephraim Ballard and John Jones, were harassed during the war for loyalism and during the resistance for supporting the proprietors. Perhaps their bad wartime experiences with crowd discipline contributed to their subsequent distrust of the enforced solidarity of the resistance. On Meiggs, see Henry B. Meigs, *Record of the Descendants of Vincent Meigs* (Baltimore, 1901), 43; and Otis F. R. Waite, *History of the Town of Claremont, New Hampshire* . . . (Manchester, N.H., 1895), 22. For Jones and Ballard, see James W. North, *The History of Augusta* . . . (Augusta, 1870), 110, 295; Robert Hallowell Gardiner, "Jones Eddy," MeHS, *Colls.*, 1st Ser., IV (Portland, 1859), 45. For the cornhusking incident, see D. R. Goodwin, "Notice of John Merrick," MeHS, *Colls.*, 1st Ser., VII (Bath, 1879), 389; Harvey v. Fowler, writ, Mar. 27, 1807, KC-CCP, box 9, MeSA; the surveyor's quote comes from Benjamin Poor's deposition, Nov. 25, 1795, Related Papers, Resolve for Jan. 29, 1799, MA. On barn burnings, see Joseph Jones's petition to the General Court, ca. Jan. 1802, Related Papers, Mar. 1, 1802, Resolve, MA; David Murphy to the Kennebeck Proprietors, Aug. 23, 1810, June 7, 1811, Isaac Davis to the Kennebeck Proprietors, June 8, 1811, KPP, box 7, MeHS; Isaac Davis to the General Court, Dec. 12, 1810, David Murphy to the General Court, Jan. 10, 1811, Related Papers, Feb. 16, 1811, Resolve, MA.

57. A. Mann to Gov. James Sullivan, Feb. 15, 1808, Lemuel Paine to Sullivan, Feb. 15, 1808, Henry Johnson's deposition, Feb. 15, 1808, Pitt Dillingham's deposition, Feb. 15, 1808 (quote), CF, box 16, MA. For the similar use of tin horns among New York's Anti-Renters, see Pendleton, "The New York Anti-Rent Controversy," 107–108. For similar forms of agrarian resistance in the Georgia hills, see William F. Holmes, "Moonshining and Collective Violence: Georgia, 1889–1895," *Journal of American History*, LXVII (1980–1981), 589–611.

58. Henry Johnson's deposition, Feb. 15, 1808, Pitt Dillingham's deposition, Feb. 15, 1808, CF, box 16, MA; Abraham Welch to George Ulmer, July 11, 1801, Thurston Whiting and Benjamin Brackett to Henry Knox, Aug. 28, 1808, HKP, XLIV, 24, 61, MHS; John Johnston, *A History of the Towns of Bristol and Bremen* . . . (Albany, N.Y., 1873), 368; Charles Vaughan to the Kennebec Proprietors, May 29, 1801 ("fire"), Vaughan to James Bowdoin, Sept. 26, 1801, KPP, box 5, MeHS; Vaughan to the Kennebeck Proprietors, Apr. 10, 1808, KPP, box 6, MeHS ("as a gift"); Benjamin Hallowell to Thomas L. Winthrop, Aug. 29, 1802, KPP, box 5, MeHS; John Chandler to Gov. James Sullivan, Apr. 18, 1808, House File 6385 (unpassed), MA.

59. Ely, *Deformity*, 25; Charles Vaughan to Henry Knox, Apr. 8, 1806, KPP, box 6, MeHS; Thurston Whiting and Benjamin Brackett, "Journal," Aug. 26, 1801, entry, HKP, XLIV, 54, MHS; Charles Thornton Libby, ed., *Province and Court Records of Maine* (Portland, 1931), xxiii–xxxi; Kennebeck Proprietors to the General Court, Jan. 1803, KPP, Record Book IV, 132, MeHS. On destroyed survey marks, see John Gilman to the Kennebeck Proprietors, ca. 1792, KPP, box 4, MeHS; Nathan Dane to Thomas L. Winthrop, Feb. 6, 1808, KPP, box 6, MeHS; James Malcom's field notes, Sept. 29, 1803, and Joseph H. Pierce to Timothy Copp, Aug. 26, 1811, HAPP, NEHGSL. Illinois squatters also destroyed surveyors' marks; see John Mack Faragher, *Sugar Creek: Life on the Illinois Prairie* (New Haven, Conn., 1986), 43.

CHAPTER FIVE

1. The epigraphs are from Timothy Dwight, *Travels in New England and New York*, ed. Barbara Miller Solomon, 4 vols. (Cambridge, Mass., 1969; orig. publ. New Haven, Conn., 1821), II, 162–163; John Buzzell, ed., *Religious Magazine . . .* (APS 2, reel 202), I (1811–1812), 31. For the vision, see Nathan Barlow, *A Vision Seen by Nathan Barlow, of Freetown . . .* (Boston, 1802; S-S 1838), 3–4. For Barlow's White Indian activities, see Moses Robinson's petition to the General Court, Feb. 14, 1809, Related Papers, Resolve XCIII (Feb. 25, 1809), MA; James W. North, *The History of Augusta . . .* (Augusta, 1870), 357.

2. Laura Campbell Hawkins and Emma Campbell Devries, "Barlow and Allied Families," 57–60, typescript, NEHGSL; Sandwich Tax Valuations, 1784 (microfilm box 382), 1791 (box 384), 1792 (box 387), Massachusetts Town Tax Valuations, MSL; "Submissions of Settlers, Kennebeck Purchase," I, 27, MA; Philbrook v. Barlow, June 1799, LC-CCP, Record Books, XI, 44, LCC; Whitwell v. Barlow, Aug. 1803, KC-CCP, Record Books, III, 172, MeSA; Breed v. Barlow, Dec. 1803, KC-CCP, Record Books, III, 245, MeSA; Barlow to Breed, Jan. 11, 1804, KCD, VI, 90, KCRD; Commonwealth v. Barlow, Sept. 1803, KC-SJC, Record Books, II, case 91, and KC-SJC files, box 70, MeSA.

3. Harlem, Lincoln County return, Massachusetts-Maine returns, Federal Direct Tax, 1798, NEHGSL; *Castine Journal*, Mar. 27, 1801; Barlow to Breed, Bragg, and Colbey, KCD, VI, 162, 336, IX, 142, KCRD; inventory of Nathan Barlow's estate, Apr. 9, 1817, Kennebec County Registry of Probate, Augusta.

4. For peasant rebels, see E. J. Hobsbawm, *Primitive Rebels: Studies in Archaic Forms of Social Movement in the Nineteenth and Twentieth Centuries* (Manchester, Eng., 1959), 108–124; and George Rudé, *Paris and London in the Eighteenth Century: Studies in Popular Protest* (New York, 1970), 17–34. For New Jersey land rioters' notion of the king as their protector, see Thomas L. Purvis, "Disaffection along the Millstone: The Petition of Dollens Hegeman and Anti-Proprietary Sentiment in Eighteenth-Century New Jersey," *New Jersey History*, CI, nos. 3–4 (Fall / Winter 1983), 61–82. For the rumors in Maine, see Charles Vaughan to Thomas L. Winthrop, Oct. 10, 1803, KPP, box 5, MeHS (chief justice); James Nesmith to Isaac Parker, Mar. 7, 1796, HKP, XXXVIII, 160, MHS (Waldo Patent); Thurston Whiting and Benjamin Brackett, "Journal," Aug. 26, 1801, entry, HKP, XLIV, 54, MHS (Gilpatrick quoted); Thomas Fillebrown to the Governor's Council, Aug. 18, 1820, Secretary of State's Correspondence, box 1, folder 4, MeSA (Freedom).

5. William Willis, *A History of the Law, the Courts, and the Lawyers of Maine . . .* (Portland, 1863), 107–108; Jackson Turner Main, *The Antifederalists: Critics of the Constitution, 1781–1788* (Chapel Hill, N.C., 1961), 65; "Scribble-Scrabble" [George Thatcher], *Cumberland Gazette* (Portland), June 8, 1786; George Thatcher to Sarah Thatcher, Apr. 26, 1789, GTP, MHS (quote).

6. Robert E. Moody, "George Thacher" [a variant spelling], *Dictionary of American Biography*; Joseph Gales, Sr., comp., *The Debates and Proceedings in the Congress of the United States . . . [Annals of Congress]*, *Fifth Congress* (Washington, D.C., 1851), First Session, 426 ("Foreigners"); Second Session, 1032–1033 (Quaker petitions), 1081 (stamp tax), 1114 ("democratic mobs"); Third Session, 2450, 2454 ("moral information"), 2462 ('spectacles'), 2899, 2902 (Alien and Sedition Acts). For settler antipathy to Thatcher, see Moses Dennett to William King, Nov. 30, 1811, WKP, box 7, MeHS; Pejepscot settlers' petition, Jan. 1812, WKP,

box 11, MeHS; Aaron Blaney, Jr., to Aaron Blaney, Sr., Nov. 1810, in Miscellaneous Lincoln County Papers and Deeds, MeHS; and John Johnston, *A History of the Towns of Bristol and Bremen* . . . (Albany, N.Y., 1873), 482–484.

7. George Thatcher to Nathaniel Cross, May 10, 1817, GTP, Letterbook, 2, EI (first two quotes); Thatcher to Cross, Aug. 4, 1817, GTP, Letterbook, 3, EI (last quote).

8. George Thatcher to Nathaniel Cross, Aug. 4, 1817, GTP, Letterbook, 3, EI.

9. On the Standing Order, see William G. McLoughlin, *New England Dissent, 1630–1833: The Baptists and the Separation of Church and State* (Cambridge, Mass., 1971), I, 124–127; Robert A. Gross, *The Minutemen and Their World* (New York, 1976), 18–29; Richard D. Brown, "Spreading the Word: Rural Clergymen and the Communication Network of Eighteenth-Century New England," in Élise Marienstras and Barbara Karsky, eds., *Autre temps, autre espace / An Other Time, an Other Space* (Nancy, 1986), 53–65. For the destitute parishes, see Stephen A. Marini, *Radical Sects of Revolutionary New England* (Cambridge, Mass., 1982), 36; B[enjamin] Lincoln, "Copy of a Letter from the Hon. General Lincoln, on the Religious State of the Eastern Counties in the District of Maine," MHS, *Collections*, 1st Ser., IV (Boston, 1795), 154–155. For New England's spiritually restless heading to the frontier, see Whitney R. Cross, *The Burned-Over District: The Social and Intellectual History of Enthusiastic Religion in Western New York, 1800–1850* (Ithaca, N.Y., 1950), 6. For the absence of orthodox preaching and Bibles in the Eastern Country, see Daniel Little to Peter Thacher, Feb. 17, 1792, SPG Papers, EI, box 3, folder 5; Dwight, *Travels*, ed. Solomon, II, 162; François Alexandre Frédéric, duc de La Rochefoucault Liancourt, *Travels through the United States of North America* . . . (London, 1799), I, 447; and Van Beck Hall, *Politics without Parties: Massachusetts, 1780–1791* (Pittsburgh, Pa., 1972), 174. I compiled the number of churches by denomination and their date of origin from *Minutes of the Annual Conference of the Methodist Episcopal Church*, I, *For the Years 1773–1828* (New York, 1840); Stephen Allen and W. H. Pilsbury, *History of Methodism in Maine, 1793–1886* (Augusta, 1887); Jonathan Greenleaf, *Sketches of the Ecclesiastical History of the State of Maine* . . . (Portsmouth, N.H., 1821); Isaac Dalton Stewart, *The History of the Freewill Baptists for Half a Century* . . . (Dover, N.H., 1862); and *Minutes of the Bowdoinham Association, Held at Harpswell, September 29th and 30th, 1790* (Boston, 1790; E 22372). "Mid-Maine" refers to those towns within the 1827 boundaries of Kennebec, Lincoln, and Waldo counties. See Map 1.

10. Stephen Chapin, *The Immoral Tendency of Error in Sentiment* . . . (Amherst, N.H., 1809), 26; David Thurston, *A Sermon Delivered in Saco, June 26, 1816, before the Maine Missionary Society, at the Ninth Annual Meeting* (Hallowell, 1816; S-S 389087), 8–9.

11. Daniel Little to Peter Thacher, Feb. 17, 1792, SPG Papers, box 3, folder 5, EI; "Statement of William Hasey of Bangor," *BHM*, VII, 148 (quotes regarding Noble); "Early Settlement of Bangor," *BHM*, IV, 194; William D. Williamson, "Annals of the City of Bangor, Maine," *BHM*, IX, 8–13; "Rev. John Urquhart of Union River," *BHM*, IV, 77; Hezekiah Prince to William D. Williamson, ca. 1820, filed under "Thomaston," WDWTP, MeHS; Commonwealth v. Nathaniel Whitaker, July 6, 1790, LC-SJC Record Book for 1790, 151, LCC. James McLachlan, *Princetonians, 1748–1768: A Biographical Dictionary* (Princeton, N.J., 1976), 62–63; J. Greenleaf, *Sketches of the Ecclesiastical History*, 84 (the Bath impostor); Timothy W. Robinson, *History of the Town of Morrill in the County of Waldo and State of Maine*, ed. Theoda Mears Morse (Belfast, 1944), 88 (Johnson).

12. Paul Coffin, "Memoir and Journals of Rev. Paul Coffin, D.D.," MeHS,

Collections, 1st Ser., IV (Portland, 1859), 307 (July 8, 1796); the Reverend Daniel Little, "1787 Journal," 108, Kennebunk Unitarian Church; Alexander MacLean to Jedediah Morse, Oct. 31, 1805, SPG Papers, box 3, folder 7, EI.

13. William Jones, *A True Account of All the Presbyterian and Congregational Ministers . . .* (Bristol, ca. 1808), 44, 73, 87; William Jones, *The Inconsistency and Deception of the Methodist Ministers . . .* (Bristol, ca. 1810; copy at MeHS), 15–16 (block quote); James Potter, *Narration of the Experience, Travels, and Labours of Elder James Potter . . .* (Boston, 1813), 27–28; Ephraim Stinchfield, *Some Memoirs of the Life, Experience, and Travels of Elder Ephraim Stinchfield* (Portland, 1819; S-S 49511), 5–24; David Stewart, "Memoir of Jonathan Stewart, 1769–1848," MS, Robinson Room, Colby College Library, Waterville.

14. Marini, *Radical Sects*, 36, 53–56; Cyrus Eaton, *History of Thomaston, Rockland, and South Thomaston . . .* (Hallowell, 1865), I, 169; Isaac Backus, *A Church History of New-England*, II, *Extending from 1690 to 1784* (Providence, R.I., 1784), 483–484; Potter, *Narration of the Experience*, 8–13; J. Greenleaf, *Sketches of the Ecclesiastical History*, 153. For a similar interpretation of the role of marginality and mutuality, see Rhys Isaac, *The Transformation of Virginia, 1740–1790* (Chapel Hill, N.C., 1982), 24, 164–165.

15. For the evangelical perspective, see Marini, *Radical Sects*, 136–143; Norman Allen Baxter, *History of the Freewill Baptists: A Study in New England Separatism* (Rochester, N.Y., 1957), 57; Allen and Pilsbury, *History of Methodism in Maine*, 7–11; Nathan O. Hatch, "The Christian Movement and the Demand for a Theology of the People," *Journal of American History*, LXVII (1980–1981), 545–567; and Potter, *Narration of the Experience*, 8–13. For the orthodox perspective, see Alexander MacLean's Journal, entries for Feb. 16, 1802, July 4, 1805, SPG Papers, box 3, folder 7, EI; *Massachusetts Missionary Magazine* (Salem, Mass.; APS 2, reel 25), [II] (May 1804), 24–25; *Massachusetts Missionary Magazine*, I (1803–1804), [260]; and *Connecticut Evangelical Magazine* (APS 2, reel 14), I (1800–1801), 394–395, II (1801–1802), 97, 421–422.

16. Jones, *True Account*, 35, 44, 57; Buzzell, *Religious Magazine*, I (1811–1812), 31; Alfred Johnson to Jedediah Morse, Oct. 27, 1806, SPG Papers, box 3, folder 1, EI.

17. Marini, *Radical Sects*, 117–119; Stewart, *The History of the Freewill Baptists*, 99, 129, 132, 190–192; Jones, *True Account*, 57.

18. Elias Smith, ed., *Herald of Gospel Liberty* (APS 2, reel 19), I (1808–1809), 87, 104; Hatch, "The Christian Movement," *JAH*, LXVII (1980–1981), 551; Daniel Oliver to Jedediah Morse, Aug. 10, 1805, SPG Papers, box 3, folder 14, EI.

19. Alexander MacLean to Jedediah Morse, June 5, 1805, SPG Papers, box 3, folder 7, EI; Daniel Little, "Missionary Journal for 1774," 123, Kennebunk Unitarian Church; Turner quoted in [Massachusetts Society for Promoting Christian Knowledge], *An Account of the Massachusetts Society for Promoting Christian Knowledge* (Andover, Mass., 1815; S-S 35224), 70; Coffin, "Journals," MeHS, *Colls.*, 1st Ser., IV (1859), 316, 348, 391; Asa Rand, *Two Sermons on Christian Fellowship, Preached at Gorham, October 20, 1816* (Portland, 1817; S-S 41926), 22, 33.

20. Stephen Chapin's Report, Dec. 12, 1808, SPG Papers, box 1, folder 18, EI; Paul Coffin to Peter Thacher, Nov. 8, 1797, Oct. 20, 1800, SPG Papers, box 1, folder 22, EI.

21. Coffin, "Journals," MeHS, *Colls.*, 1st Ser., IV (1859), 301, 306–308, 310, 356 (quote); Richard Hazeltine to Jedediah Morse, May 25, 1812, Morse Papers, New-York Historical Society (my thanks to Richard "Pete" Moss of Colby College for providing this citation); Daniel Little to Samuel Phillips, Feb. 18, 1788, box 9,

Benjamin Lincoln Papers, MHS; Rand, *Two Sermons*, 25–30; Calvin Montague Clark, *History of the Congregational Churches in Maine* (Portland, 1926), I, 2–22.

22. Daniel Little to Peter Thacher, Feb. 17, 1792, SPG Papers, box 3, folder 5, EI; Alexander MacLean to Jedediah Morse, May 10, 1803, Mar. 15, 1804 (quote), June 26, 1804, SPG Papers, box 3, folder 7, EI; Alfred Johnson to Morse, Oct. 27, 1806, SPG Papers, box 3, folder 1, EI. Most of the settlements that MacLean identified as in the greatest need of subsidized schoolteaching were centers of the resistance. At least two of those communities (Smithtown and New Waterford) refused to accept Congregational subsidies. See MacLean to Morse, Sept. 4, 1804, SPG Papers, box 3, folder 7, EI.

23. Cyrus Eaton, *Annals of the Town of Warren* ((Hallowell, 1877), 289; Rand, *Two Sermons*, 16–23; Marini, *Radical Sects*, 105; Elias Smith, ed., *Christian's Magazine, Reviewer, and Religious Intelligencer* (APS 2, reel 11), I (1807), 254–255; Coffin, "Journals," MeHS, *Colls.*, 1st Ser., IV (1859), 345.

24. The Reverend Seth Payson to the Society, Jan. 15, 1803, SPG Papers, box 4, folder 1, EI. In 1810, 22 of the 36 frontcountry towns had an orthodox church, versus only 6 of the 47 backcountry settlements. In 1790, 21 of mid-Maine's then 60 communities had at least 1 organized church; 10 years later, 51 of 75 did; in 1810, 66 of 73 did. I determined the distribution of churches from *Minutes of the Annual Conference of the Methodist Episcopal Church*, I; Allen and Pilsbury, *History of Methodism in Maine*; J. Greenleaf, *Sketches of the Ecclesiastical History*; Stewart, *The History of the Freewill Baptists*; *Minutes of the Bowdoinham Association, Held at the Baptist Meeting-House in Green, August 27 and 28, 1800* (Portland, 1800; E 37027); *Minutes of the Bowdoinham Association, Held at the Baptist Meeting-House, in Livermore, September 26th, and 27th, 1810* (Portland, 1810; S-S 19430); *Minutes of the Lincoln Association, Held at the Baptist Meeting-house in Vassalborough, September, 19th and 20th, 1810* (Buckstown, 1810; S-S 19432). See Map 10. For a similar pattern of Congregationalism in a valley's prosperous towns, surrounded by newer evangelical churches in the hills' many small, penurious towns, see Randolph A. Roth, *The Democratic Dilemma: Religion, Reform, and the Social Order in the Connecticut River Valley of Vermont, 1791–1850* (New York, 1987).

25. Jotham Sewall's reports in *Massachusetts Missionary Magazine*, I (1803–1804), 477–478, III (1805–1806), 6–7, IV (1806–1807), 74–75, V (1807–1808), 36; Stinchfield, *Memoirs*, 79, 81–82.

26. Alexander MacLean to Jedediah Morse, June 5, 1805, SPG Papers, box 3, folder 7, EI; Jonathan Huse to Morse, Aug. 1806, SPG Papers, box 2, folder 22, EI.

27. Potter, *Narration of the Experience*, 8–13; William D. Williamson, "Condition of the Religious Denominations of Maine at the Close of the Revolution," MeHS, *Colls.*, 1st Ser., VII (Bath, 1876), 226; Baxter, *History of the Freewill Baptists*, 38–39; Allen and Pilsbury, *History of Methodism in Maine*, 31, 82; Marini, *Radical Sects*, 85; Joshua Millett, *A History of the Baptists in Maine* (Portland, 1845), 104; Alexander MacLean to Jedediah Morse, Sept. 4, 1804, SPG Papers, box 3, folder 7, EI.

28. J. Greenleaf, *Sketches of the Ecclesiastical History*, 288; Stewart, *The History of the Freewill Baptists*, 61, 180; Marini, *Radical Sects*, 88.

29. John Colby, *Life, Experience, and Travels of John Colby . . .* (Portland, 1815; S-S 34388), 15–17, 23; Stewart, *The History of the Freewill Baptists*, 79 (circular letter quoted); Potter, *Narration of the Experience*; Isaac, *The Transformation*, 168; Robert Foster, ed., *Christian Herald* (APS 2, reel 79), I (1818–1819), 188–189; Hatch, "The Christian Movement," *JAH*, LXVII (1980–1981), 553–554.

30. Stewart, *The History of the Freewill Baptists*, 48–49, 119, 205–206, 211; Coffin, "Journals," MeHS, *Colls.*, 1st Ser., IV (1859), 382–383; William Allen, "The Journal of William Allen, Esq.," in William Collins Hatch, *A History of the Town of Industry* . . . (Farmington, 1893), 85.

31. Stephen Chapin's Report, Dec. 12, 1808, SPG Papers, box 1, folder 18, EI; Edmund Eastman to Jedediah Morse, Oct. 18, 1808, SPG Papers, box 2, folder 3, EI. I am grateful to Stephen A. Marini for his generosity in directing me to Chapin's report.

32. My perspective owes much to Christopher Hill, *The Religion of Gerrard Winstanley* (*Past and Present*, supp. no. 5 [London, 1978]), 21–23.

33. [James Shurtleff], *The Substance of a Late Remarkable Dream* . . . (Hallowell, 1800; E 38584), 8, 14; Joel Thompson quoted in Stephen Chase to Josiah Little, Dec. 22, 1800, Letters to Josiah Little folder, PPP, box 4, EI; Bristol settler quoted in Elliot G. Vaughan to Thomas Cutts, Oct. 30, 1810, miscellaneous box 24 ("Papers Relating to Lands in Lincoln County . . ."), MA.

34. The agrarian resistance produced five protest pamphlets. All used a religious language of persuasion. The five pamphlets are Samuel Ely, *The Deformity of a Hideous Monster, Discovered in the Province of Maine, by a Man in the Woods, Looking after Liberty* (Boston, 1797; E 32081); [Samuel Ely], *The Unmasked Nabob of Hancock County; or, The Scales Dropt from the Eyes of the People* (Portsmouth, N.H., 1796; E 31477); [James Davis and Samuel Ely], *The Appeal of the Two Counties of Lincoln and Hancock from the Forlorn Hope, or, Mount of Distress; to the General Court, or, to All the World* (Portsmouth, N.H., 1796; E 31477, paired with *Unmasked Nabob*); [James Shurtleff], *A Concise Review of the Spirit Which Seemed to Govern in the Time of the Late American War, Compared with the Spirit Which Now Prevails* . . . (Augusta, 1798; E 34548); and [J. Shurtleff], *The Substance*. For the role of religious thinkers in other agrarian resistances, see David Joseph Goodall, "New Light on the Border: New England Squatter Settlements in New York during the American Revolution" (Ph.D. diss., State University of New York at Albany, 1984); and Mark Haddon Jones, "Herman Husband: Millenarian, Carolina Regulator, and Whiskey Rebel" (Ph.D. diss., Northern Illinois University, 1983).

35. Johnston, *History of Bristol and Bremen*, 380–381, 394; Jones, *Inconsistency*, 1–5, 21, 43; *Debates, Resolutions, and Other Proceedings of the Convention of the Commonwealth of Massachusetts, Convened at Boston, on the 9th of January, 1788* . . . (Boston, 1808; S-S 15516), 157 (Jan. 30, 1788); *Order of Both Branches of the Legislature of Massachusetts to Appoint Commissioners to Investigate the Causes of the Difficulties in the County of Lincoln* . . . (Boston, 1811; S-S 23314), 146.

36. Jones, *True Account*, 56, 73–74, 80.

37. George Ulmer to Henry Knox, July 11, 1801, HKP, XLIV, 27, MHS; Coffin, "Journals," MeHS, *Colls.*, 1st Ser., IV (1859), 318–319; Jotham Sewall, "Diary," Oct. 20, 1801, entry, MeHS; Jotham Sewall quoted in James Berry Vickery, *A History of the Town of Unity, Maine* (Manchester, 1954), 58. For the similar thoughts of religious radicals in 17th-century England and New England, see Christopher Hill, *The World Turned Upside Down: Radical Ideas during the English Revolution* (New York, 1972); and Philip F. Gura, *A Glimpse of Sion's Glory: Puritan Radicalism in New England, 1620–1660* (Middletown, Conn., 1984), 49–92.

38. Coffin, "Journals," MeHS, *Colls.*, 1st Ser., IV (1859), 318–320 (Aug. 2–3, 1796); Jotham Sewall's diary, entries for Oct. 21–22, 1801, Oct. 12, 1802, MeHS; Vickery, *Unity*, 58–61; Jotham Sewall to the editors, Aug. 16, 1805, *Massachusetts*

Missionary Magazine, III (1805–1806), 180; Alexander MacLean's Journal, July 17, 1805, entry, SPG Papers, box 3, folder 7, EI.

39. Alexander MacLean to Jedediah Morse, Apr. 5, 1806, SPG Papers, box 3, folder 7 (first quote), EI; Alexander MacLean's Journal, Feb. 6, 1802, entry, SPG Papers, box 3, folder 7 (second quote), EI; Alexander MacLean's Schedule, Feb. 27, 1805, SPG Papers, box 3, folder 7, EI. See also Seth Payson to Jedediah Morse, Jan. 15, 1803, SPG Papers, box 4, folder 1, EI; Alfred Johnson to Abiel Holmes, May 17, 1805, SPG Papers, box 3, folder 1, EI; Coffin, "Journals," MeHS, *Colls.*, 1st Ser., IV (1859), 351. For Captain John Harvell, a recent arrival from Amherst, New Hampshire, see Daniel F. Secomb, *History of the Town of Amherst, Hillsborough County, New Hampshire* (Concord, N.H., 1883), 268, 430, 619–620; Carleton E. Fisher and Sue G. Fisher, comps., *Soldiers, Sailors, and Patriots of the Revolutionary War: Maine* (Louisville, Ky., 1982), 346. For the Christian Connection, see N. O. Hatch, "The Christian Movement," *JAH*, LXVII (1980–1981), 545–567.

40. Chapin quoted and analyzed in Stephen A. Marini, "The Standing Order and the Northern Frontier: The Missionary Report of Stephen Chapin from the District of Maine, December 12, 1808," Dec. 15, 1969, MS, 7, 45.

41. Eliphalet Gillet, *A Discourse Delivered on the Annual Fast in Massachusetts, April 7, 1808* (Augusta, 1808), 20; Edward Payson, *A Discourse, Delivered at Portland, May 5, 1814; Before the Bible Society of Maine, at Their Annual Meeting* (Portland, 1814; S-S 32446), 21.

42. Lincoln, "Copy of a Letter," MHS, *Colls.*, 1st Ser., IV (1795), 155; Daniel Little to Henry Knox, June 8, 1789, HKP, LII, 17, MHS; Eaton, *Thomaston*, I, 223; Knox to Samuel Lane, Apr. 16, 1797, in "Oeconomics and Improvements" book, HKP, box 12, MeHS; Alfred Johnson to Peter Thacher, Mar. 23, 1796, SPG Papers, box 3, folder 1, EI; Alfred Johnson to Jedediah Morse, Oct. 27, 1806, SPG Papers, box 3, folder 1, EI; Silas Warren to Jedediah Morse, Oct. 10, 1809, May 28, 1812, SPG Papers, box 5, folder 6, EI.

43. John Scales, ed., "Some Descendants of William Scales of Rowley, Massachusetts, 1640," *New England Historical and Genealogical Register*, LXVI (1912), 43–46; Clifford K. Shipton, *Biographical Sketches of Those Who Attended Harvard College . . . [Sibley's Harvard Graduates]*, 14 vols. (Cambridge, Mass., Boston, 1933–1975), XVII, 626–627; William Scales to the General Court, Nov. 14, 1796, Senate Unpassed 2134/1, MA ("dead languages"); William Scales, *Priestcraft Exposed from Its Foundation . . .* (Danvers, Mass., 1781; E 44057), ii, 14–16 (remaining quotes). Scales's classmates included two sons of Kennebeck Proprietors—James Bowdoin, Jr. (ranked second in a class of 56), and William Vassal (sixth)—as well as Samuel Phillips, Jr. (fifteenth), the future chair of the General Court's Eastern Lands Committee. The class ahead of Scales included a Waldo heir named William Wetmore and Thurston Whiting, who would become a minor land speculator and one of Henry Knox's agents. Scales's roommate could hardly have been more incompatible; appointed Harvard's Hollis Professor of Religion in 1792, David Tappan became a staunch defender of Calvinist orthodoxy and the Congregational establishment as well as a firm Federalist who denounced the French Revolution and pronounced the funeral sermon of Samuel Phillips, Jr. See Shipton, *Sibley's Harvard Graduates*, XVII, 447–451, 452, 466–467, 487–500, 593–604, 653–654; *Massachusetts Missionary Magazine*, V (1807–1808), 41.

44. Shipton, *Sibley's Harvard Graduates*, XVII, 627–628; James Bowdoin *et al.* memorial to the General Court, ca. Oct. 1782, Ebenezer Temple *et al.* to the

General Court, Jan. 21, 1789, Jesse Davis *et al.* to the General Court, Feb. 14, 1790, *MDH*, XX, 121, XXII, 142, 324–326; William Scales to the General Court, Nov. 4, 1796, Senate Unpassed 2134/1, MA.

45. William Scales, *The Confusion of Babel Discovered* . . . (n.p., 1780; E 16989), iii, 46–47, 63, v, in sequence of quotation. For Congregational antipathy to these notions, see Rand, *Two Sermons*, 20–21. For the similar views of Samuel Gorton, a 17th-century Rhode Island religious radical, see Gura, *A Glimpse of Sion's Glory*, 59–61, 291–301; David S. Lovejoy, *Religious Enthusiasm in the New World: Heresy to Revolution* (Cambridge, Mass., 1985), 95. For the similar views of Gerrard Winstanley, see Hill, *The World*, 112–119.

46. William Scales to Josiah Little, Apr. 23, n.y., LFP, box 3, EI, is the cover letter for the unsigned essay that begins "Kind Sir" and is located in PPP, box 17, folder 1782–1799, EI. The two documents are written in the same hand, and the first refers to a separate document. The quote is from "Kind Sir." Because of the document's laudatory reference to the French Revolution, it probably dates to the early 1790s.

47. William Scales to the General Court, June 21, 1790, *MDH*, XXII, 392; William Scales to Josiah Little, Apr. 23, n.y., LFP, box 3, folder 8, EI. On madness as social protest, see Hill, *The World*, 223–229.

48. Scales, *The Confusion of Babel*, vii; William Bentley, *The Diary of William Bentley, D.D., Pastor of the East Church, Salem, Massachusetts*, 4 vols. (Gloucester, Mass., 1962; reprint of Salem, Mass., 1905–1914), I, 146 (Feb. 16, 1790).

49. Robert A. Gross, "Lonesome in Eden: Dickinson, Thoreau, and the Problem of Community in Nineteenth-Century New England," *Canadian Review of American Studies*, XIV (1983), 1–17; Henry David Thoreau, *Walden and Civil Disobedience*, ed. Michael Meyer (New York, 1983), 372–373.

50. Shipton, *Sibley's Harvard Graduates*, XVII, 452–454; Eaton, *Warren*, 187–188; Eaton, *Thomaston*, I, 234–235; Sheldon S. Cohen, "The Turkish Tyranny," *New England Quarterly*, XLVII (1974), 568–574. For Cushing and Bowman, see Shipton, *Sibley's Harvard Graduates*, XIII, 546–549, 564, XVII, 454–455.

51. Shipton, *Sibley's Harvard Graduates*, XVII, 455–456; J. Greenleaf, *Sketches of the Ecclesiastical History*, 106, 152, 173; Jones, *True Account*, 35, 43–44; Alexander Bird to Thurston Whiting and Moses Copeland, Jan. 1786, LCD, XIX, 2, LCC; William Scales to the General Court, Nov. 14, 1796, Senate Unpassed 2134/1, MA. For Whiting's electioneering, see Jeremiah Hill to George Thatcher, Feb. 12, 1791, GTP, BPL. During the years 1775–1799, in five purchases with stipulated bounds, Whiting obtained 553.5 acres for $2,498.50, or $4.51 per acre. During the same period his 11 sales involved 421 acres (and a half interest in his Warren gristmill) for $3,379.23, or $8.03 per acre. At the end of the period he stood $880.73 and 132.5 acres ahead of where he started. The remaining seven deeds consisted of two mortgages given by Whiting (worth $2,500), two received ($2,100), two token releases for mortgagers, and one proprietary investment ($832.50) in a tract with unknown boundaries. Whiting's purchases and sales are recorded in LCD, LCC. By contrast, Scales recorded no deeds in either Kennebec or Lincoln county.

52. Thurston Whiting, *A Discourse Delivered in the Meeting House in Pownalborough, March 1, 1798* (Wiscasset, 1798; E 35021), 8 ("something charming"); Thurston Whiting, *An Oration Delivered at the Baptist Meeting House in Thomaston, July 4th 1798* . . . (Hallowell, 1798; E 35022), 18 ("state of savage").

53. Thurston Whiting and Benjamin Brackett to Henry Knox, Sept. 7, 1801, HKP, LII, 87, MHS.

54. Thurston Whiting and Benjamin Brackett, "Journal," Aug. 27, 1801, entry, HKP, XLIV, 54, MHS. Whiting and Brackett said the pamphlet was by "Old Davis of Davistown," which means it must have been [Davis and Ely], *The Appeal.*

CHAPTER SIX

1. The epigraphs are from Timothy Dwight, *Travels in New England and New York*, ed. Barbara Miller Solomon, 4 vols. (Cambridge, Mass., 1969; orig. publ. New Haven, Conn., 1821), II, 163; and Samuel Ely, *The Deformity of a Hideous Monster, Discovered in the Province of Maine, by a Man in the Woods, Looking after Liberty* (Boston, 1797; E 32081), 20. For Ulmer's visit, see Isaac Winslow, Jr. (quoting William Molineux), to Henry Knox, Jan. 25, 1789, HKP, XXIII, 84, MHS; Knox to Winslow, Mar. 1, 1789, HKP, XXIII, 115, MHS.

2. Dwight, *Travels*, ed. Solomon, II, 321; Moses Greenleaf, *A Statistical View of the District of Maine* . . . (Boston, 1816; S-S 37745), 86; Charles Maurice de Talleyrand-Périgord, "Letter on the Eastern Part of America" (Boston, Sept. 24, 1794), in Hans Huth and Wilma J. Pugh, eds., *Talleyrand in America as a Financial Promoter, 1794–96 (Annual Report of the American Historical Association, 1941*, II [Washington, D.C., 1942]), 81.

3. "General George Ulmer," *Hancock Gazette* (Castine), Jan. 11, 1826; Jasper Jacob Stahl, *History of Old Broad Bay and Waldoboro* (Portland, 1956), I, 297, 394–396, 510–511; François Alexandre Frédéric, duc de La Rochefoucault Liancourt, *Travels through the United States of North America* . . . (London, 1799), I, 431; anonymous to Henry Knox, Dec. 1, 1785, HKP, box 2, MeHS; James Getchal to Philip Ulmer, Sept. 23, 1784, LCD, XVII, 126, LCC; Getchal to George Ulmer, Sept. 23, 1784, LCD, XVII, 126, LCC. See also Alan Taylor, "The Rise and Fall of George Ulmer: Political Entrepreneurship in the Age of Jefferson and Jackson," *Colby Library Quarterly*, XXI (1985), 51–66.

4. William Lithgow to the Kennebeck Proprietors, Oct. 29, 1765, KPP, box 2, MeHS; Robert Earle Moody, "The Maine Frontier, 1607 to 1763" (Ph.D. diss., Yale University, 1933), 264; Stahl, *Old Broad Bay*, I, 64, 100; Gordon E. Kershaw, *The Kennebeck Proprietors, 1749–1775* (Portland, 1975), 30, 52, 152–154; Robert H. Gardiner, "History of the Kennebec Purchase . . . ," MeHS, *Collections*, 1st Ser., II (Portland, 1847), 280.

5. Henry Knox to Mrs. S. L. Flucker, May 15, 1788, HKP, XXII, 41, MHS; La Rochefoucault Liancourt, *Travels*, I, 422; Henry Knox, Samuel Winslow, and Isaac Winslow, Jr., to Thomaston's land committee, Aug. 26, 1786, Related Papers, Mar. 9, 1797, Resolve, MA.

6. Henry Knox to Mrs. Horwood, Jan. 13, 1789, HKP, LII, 9, MHS; Lower Neck agreement, Sept. 10, 1788, HKP, LI, 144, MHS; Thomaston agreement, Sept. 12, 1788, HKP, LI, 148–149, MHS; Ducktrap and New Canaan agreement, Sept. 23, 1788, HKP, LI, 154, MHS; Frankfort agreement, Sept. 27, 1788, HKP, LI, 161, MHS; Owl's Head agreement, Oct. 2, 1788, HKP, LI, 164, MHS; the second of Henry Knox's "Three Books on the Waldo Patent," Oct. 4, 1788, entry, MHS (quote). In all, 289 families embraced the heirs' offer, signing for 32,784 acres, which at four shillings per acre promised the heirs a return of $21,856.

7. Anonymous to Henry Knox, Dec. 1, 1785, HKP, box 2, MeHS; "Agreement

at Ducktrap, 1788," HKP, LII, 5, MHS; Jacqueline June Watts, ed., *Lincolnville Early Days* (Camden, 1976), I, 19–23 (for the toll bridge); Ducktrap return, Massachusetts and Maine 1798 Federal Direct Tax valuations, I, NEHGSL; Paul Coffin, "Memoir and Journals of Rev. Paul Coffin, D.D.," MeHS, *Colls.*, 1st Ser., IV (Portland, 1859), 325. In Ducktrap-Northport, Philip and George Ulmer bought 3,668 acres from Knox for $5,230: 18% of the land sold in those two communities, for only 14% of the moneys Knox received. Despite the superior value of their lands, the brothers paid just $1.42 per acre, compared to the $1.85 per acre paid by all others. The 137 deeds issued by Knox to Northport and Lincolnville lands, 1795–1804, sold a total of 20,475 acres for $36,335 (from Hancock and Lincoln County Registries of Deeds). For Knox's patronage (especially justices' commissions), see La Rochefoucault Liancourt, *Travels*, I, 430, 434, 443; William Wetmore to Knox, Aug. 19, 1785, HKP, LI, 86, MHS; Knox to Jonathan Wilson, Sept. 12, 1801, HKP, Deeds Folder, box 2, MeHS; Wilson to Knox, Dec. 7, 1801, June 5, 1805, HKP, boxes 6, 8, MeHS; Knox to Wilson, Jan. 8, 1806, HKP, box 10, MeHS; Mason Wheaton to Knox, Mar. 1, 1798, HKP, XLI, 76, MHS; James Malcom to Knox, Apr. 17, 1805, Jonathan Wilson to Knox, June 15, 1805, Robert Houston to Knox, Sept. 23, 1805, HKP, box 9, MeHS; J. Jackson to Knox, Apr. 17, 1802, HKP, XLV, 16, MHS. For George Ulmer's pension, see Related Papers, Resolve CXIV (Mar. 15, 1786), MA; and the Sept. 27, 29, 1788, entries in the second of Henry Knox's "Three Books on the Waldo Patent," MHS.

8. Sept. 23, 24, 29, and 30, 1788, entries in second of Henry Knox's "Three Books on the Waldo Patent," MHS; "Agreement at Ducktrap, 1788," HKP, LII, 5, MHS; "Lists of Names who have signed General Knox's Proposals Since he left Ducktrap," HKP, box 11, MeHS; "Subscribers in New Canaan, Northport and Ducktrap," in Henry Knox's Land Records Book, MeHS.

9. Oliver Parker's justice's court, Apr. 13, 1793, HC-CGSP Files, box 77, MeSA (for Ulmer striking Ely); Philip and George Ulmer v. Samuel Ely, Apr. 1796, in HC-CCP Record Book, II, case 197, McSA (on the dam); Robert E. Moody, "Samuel Ely: Forerunner of Shays," *New England Quarterly*, V (1932), 123; Ebenezer Jennison's survey journal, July 2, 1793, entry, HKP, LII, 53, MHS. For the events of Mar. 1796, see George Ulmer to Henry Knox, Mar. 18, Apr. 7, 1796, HKP, XXXVIII, 171, XXXIX, 23, MHS; Ulmer to Thomas Vose, Mar. 18, 19, 1796, HKP, XXXVIII, 172–173, MHS; Knox to Ulmer, July 6, 1796, HKP, box 4, MeHS; Isaac Parker to Henry Knox, Mar. 1, 1796, HKP, XXXVIII, 149, MHS; Jan. 26, Feb. 23, 1796, entries, Council Records, XXXII (1793–1797), 330, 345–347, MA; Resolve CIV (Feb. 27, 1796), in *Resolves of the General Court of the Commonwealth of Massachusetts . . . [Jan.–Feb. 1796]* (Boston, 1796; E 30764), 43–44; Henry Knox to Thomas Vose, Feb. 28, 1796, HKP, XXXVIII, 147, MHS.

10. George Ulmer to Henry Knox, Mar. 3, 1797, HKP, XL, 72, MHS; George Ulmer's court, Mar. 1, 1797, HC-CGSP files, box 77, MeSA. Apparently Ransom was eventually released without trial, and by the 1800 census he removed to Waldoborough, a community where opposition to Knox remained ascendant. Ransom and his wife Hannah drifted southwest to Portland, Maine's principal seaport, where he earned his living as a day laborer. In Mar. 1802, Ransom convinced several inhabitants of nearby Freeport that he could extract (nonexistent) silver ore from the vicinity but needed cash in advance to produce the necessary "dreggs." He collected $3,000 but, before he could abscond, was arrested, tried, convicted, and sentenced to an hour in Portland's public pillory

and six months in the county jail. Commonwealth v. Ransom, and Commonwealth v. Graves, both May 1803, Cumberland County SJC, I, 432, 456, MeSA. For Ely's disappearance, see Alan Taylor, "The Disciples of Samuel Ely: Settler Resistance against Henry Knox on the Waldo Patent, 1785–1801," *Maine Historical Society Quarterly*, XXVI (1986–1987), 88.

11. John Harkness to the Waldo Patent Commission, Jan. 1, 1798, ELC, box 53, MA; George Ulmer to Henry Knox, Feb. 4, 1798, HKP, box 5, MeHS; Henry Knox to George Ulmer, Mar. 12, 1797, HKP, XL, 80, MHS; Knox to Major Robert Treat, Sept. 23, 1801, HKP, box 6, MeHS; Knox to Charles Vaughan, Sept. 3, 1802, HKP, XLV, 44, MHS; Resolve LX (Mar. 9, 1797), in *Resolves of the General Court of the Commonwealth of Massachusetts . . . [Jan.–Mar. 1797]* ([Boston, 1797]; E 32449), 72; Waldo Patent Commission Submissions (1797), 2 vols., MA; Henry Knox to Lucy Knox, Dec. 13, 1801, HKP, XLIV, 169, MHS. Writing from Ducktrap on July 9, 1801, Ulmer told Knox, "The people this way favour the insurgents very much and but few will take an active part against them." See Ulmer to Knox, July 9, 1801, HKP, XLIV, 22, MHS.

12. John Lillie to Henry Knox, May 21, 1797, HKP, XL, 125, MHS; Ulmer to Knox, June 20, 1801, HKP, LXIV, 8, MHS; Knox to Joseph Pierce, July 28, 1801, HKP, box 6, MeHS; Henry Knox to Joseph Pierce, Nov. 9, 1801, HKP, XLIV, 124, MHS; Charles Vaughan to Thomas L. Winthrop, Aug. 24, 1802, KPP, box 5, MeHS. See also Colonel William Jones's testimony, May 2, 1811, Lincoln County Commissioners' Records, 8, MA; Charles Vaughan to James Bowdoin, June 17, 1801, KPP, box 5, MeHS; and Henry Knox to John Rynier, Aug. 30, 1799, HKP, XLII, 121, MHS.

13. Reuel Williams to Thomas L. Winthrop, Mar. 21, 1806, RWP, box 2, MeHS; Henry Jackson to Henry Knox, Oct. 26, 1803, HKP, XXXIV, 128, MHS; Joseph Pierce to Silas Lee, Dec. 15, 1806, HAPP, Deed Book A, 132, NEHGSL; Joseph H. Pierce, Jr., to Joseph H. Pierce, Sr., Dec. 10, 1811, HAPP, box 3, NEHGSL.

14. For the nature of political leadership in 18th-century New England towns, see Robert Zemsky, *Merchants, Farmers, and River Gods: An Essay on Eighteenth-Century American Politics* (Boston, 1971), 28–38; Edward M. Cook, Jr., *The Fathers of the Towns: Leadership and Community Structure in Eighteenth-Century New England* (Baltimore, 1976), 23–118; Robert A. Gross, *The Minutemen and Their World* (New York, 1976), 10–15; Charles S. Grant, *Democracy in the Connecticut Frontier Town of Kent* (New York, 1961), 143–167; and Christopher M. Jedrey, *The World of John Cleaveland: Family and Community in Eighteenth-Century New England* (New York, 1979), 121–123. For the yeomanry's fears, see *Debates and Proceedings in the Convention of the Commonwealth of Massachusetts Held in the Year 1788, and Which Finally Ratified the Constitution of the United States* (Boston, 1856), 60, 67, 70, 137, 157, 175; Samuel Eliot Morison, ed., "William Manning's *The Key of Libberty*," *WMQ*, 3d Ser., XIII (1956), 202–254; "Yankee," *Kennebeck Intelligencer* (Augusta), Feb. 9, 1799 (quote).

15. On crowds and the protection covenant, see Richard L. Bushman, *King and People in Provincial Massachusetts* (Chapel Hill, N.C., 1985), 37–46; John Howe, "Attitudes toward Violence in the Pre-War Period," in John Parker and Carol Urness, eds., *The American Revolution: A Heritage of Change* (Minneapolis, Minn., 1975), 84–95; Christine Leigh Heyrman, *Commerce and Culture: The Maritime Communities of Colonial Massachusetts, 1690–1750* (New York, 1984), 304–329. For the King incident, see Silas Burbank's deposition, June 28, 1773, and Jonathan Wingate's deposition, June 16, 1773, in L. Kinvin Wroth and Hiller B. Zobel, eds., *Legal Papers of John Adams* (Cambridge, Mass., 1965), I, 121, 125;

James S. Leamon, "The Stamp Act Crisis in Maine: The Case of Scarborough," MeHS, *Newsletter*, XI (1971–1972), 74–93. For the luckless deputy, see Artemas Kimball's deposition, June 23, 1820, Maine Executive Council Files, box 1, folder 10, MeSA.

16. Henry Knox's notice, May 26, 1800, HKP, LII, 79, MHS.

17. Henry Knox memo, ca. 1801, HKP, LII, 81, MHS. I derived the list of gentlemen by examining all the court cases and recorded deeds for the two communities for the period 1790–1810, LCD, LCC. It is noteworthy that, unlike most of his neighbors, who were Calvinist Baptists (including insurgent brother Jacob), Jonathan Greeley was a Congregationalist. See Jonathan Cogswell, *A Sermon Delivered in Augusta, June 23, 1819, before the Maine Missionary Society at Their Twelfth Anniversary* (Hallowell, 1819; S-S 47656), 38; *Minutes of the Lincoln Association, Held at the Baptist Meeting-House, in Thomaston, September 20th, and 21st, 1809* (Portland, 1809; S-S 16917) (Jacob Greeley appears as one of the Palermo Second Baptist Church's emissaries).

18. The six Palermo leaders were Jacob Greeley, Captain Daniel Clay, Jonathan Bartlett, Benjamin Turner, David Turner, and Stephen Marden. For the identifications, see Thurston Whiting and Benjamin Brackett, "Journal," Aug. 25–27, 1801, entries, HKP, XLIV, 54, MHS; and Henry Knox memo, ca. 1801, HKP, XLII, 81, MHS. For the 1806 tax list, see Millard Howard, *An Introduction to the Early History of Palermo, Maine* (n.p., 1976), 28–31; Palermo valuation list, 1811, box 400 (microfilm), MSL. In Aug. 1801 Abraham Welch, a spy for Henry Knox, reported that Twenty-Five-Mile Pond settlement's two preeminent men, Deacon Stephen Chase and Squire Ezekiel Pattee, led the White Indians there. Captain John Hills, one of Knox's surveyors, reported that Chase possessed "as good a farm as any in the State of Massachusetts"; its 400 acres yielded 60 tons of English hay annually and supported 40 cattle and 30 sheep. See Abraham Welch to George Ulmer, July 11, 1801, HKP, XLIV, 24, MHS; John Hills to Henry Knox, Aug. 15, 1793, HKP, XXXIV, 69, MHS; George Ulmer to Henry Knox, Dec. 15, 1800, HKP, XLIII, 131, MHS; James Berry Vickery, *A History of the Town of Unity, Maine* (Manchester, 1954), 58.

19. George Ulmer to Henry Knox, Dec. 29, 1800, under letter "D" in Land Records Book, HKP, MeHS; Ulmer to Knox, Nov. 15, 1801, Knox to Ulmer, Nov. 16, 1801, HKP, XLIV, 133, 134, MHS.

20. See Table 11. On the similar sociology of resistance among western Pennsylvania's Whiskey Rebels, see Thomas P. Slaughter, *The Whiskey Rebellion: Frontier Epilogue to the American Revolution* (New York, 1986), 168, 175–189; and among northwest Georgia's "white-cappers," see William F. Holmes, "Moonshining and Collective Violence: Georgia 1889–1895," *Journal of American History*, LXVII (1980–1981), 599. The larger unimproved landholdings (but fewer livestock) of "Tories" suggest that they tended to be petty local speculators willing to cut a deal with the proprietors as the best means to preserve their claims, which exceeded the community norm, from squatter intrusion. This was the case with Jonathan Jones, the principal proprietary ally in Balltown, the insurgent headquarters. See Thurston Whiting and Benjamin Brackett, "Journal," Aug. 25, 1801, entry, HKP, XLIV, 54, MHS; Ephraim Ballard to the Kennebeck Proprietors, Jan. 1, 1796, KPP, box 4, MeHS.

21. The 1800 federal census divides adult male heads of household into three broad age groups: 16–25, 26–44, and 45 and older. Table 12 displays the younger distribution of "Indians" in contrast to "Chiefs" and "Tories." Younger men with newly established households had fewer children than older men with longer-established households. In 1800, Indians ($N = 127$) averaged 4.4 chil-

dren, compared to the Chiefs' 5.4 ($N = 32$) and the Tories' 5.8 ($N = 41$). In further testimony to the Indians' greater youth, they added children during the decade, whereas the families of Chiefs and Tories tended to shrink. The 113 Indians who can be found in both the 1800 and the 1810 federal census returns dramatically increased their children (from 4.4 to 5.9), whereas the families of Chiefs (from 5.3 to 4.9) and Tories (from 5.7 to 5.3) dwindled. Because federal census returns survive for all mid-Maine towns but tax valuations for only a minority, the census statistics involve more cases than the tax data. Second and Third Census of the United States, returns for Lincoln, Hancock, and Kennebec counties in the District of Maine, 1800 (microfilm series M32, reels 6, 7), and 1810 (M252, reels 11, 12), NA. On the correlation of property accumulation with age in 18th-century New England, see Jedrey, *The World of John Cleaveland*, 58–94; John J. Waters, "Patrimony, Succession, and Social Stability: Guilford, Connecticut in the Eighteenth Century," *Perspectives in American History*, X (1976), 131–160; Waters, "Family, Inheritance, and Migration in Colonial New England: The Evidence from Guilford, Connecticut," *WMQ*, 3d Ser., XXXIX (1982), 64–86. For the New England Regulators, see Gregory H. Nobles, "Shays's Neighbors: The Context and Consequences of Rebellion in Pelham, Massachusetts, 1780–1815" (paper presented at American Historical Association annual meeting, Dec. 29, 1984), 20–21.

22. Thurston Whiting and Benjamin Brackett to Henry Knox, Sept. 7, 1801, HKP, LII, 87, MHS; Pitt Dillingham to Arthur Lithgow, Jan. 25, 1808, A. Mann (the Winslow resident) to Gov. James Sullivan, Feb. 15, 1808, CF, box 16 (Aug. 1807–May 1808), MA; Charles Vaughan to James Bowdoin, Oct. 16, 1800, July 9, 1801, KPP, box 4, MeHS; Vickery, *Unity*, 39; Charles Turner, Jr., survey notes, Mar.–Apr. 1806, Plymouth Company Line, Area 21, Range 20, Land Office Records, box 2, folder 27, MeSA (I am grateful to Lawrence M. Sturtevant of Belgrade for alerting me to this document).

23. Pitt Dillingham to Arthur Lithgow, Jan. 30, 1808, Related Papers, Resolve LV (June 19, 1809), MA; George Bender, Jr., deposition, Feb. 13, 1808, CF, box 16 (Aug. 1807–May 1808), MA.

24. Thurston Whiting and Benjamin Brackett, "Journal," Aug. 31, 1801, entry, HKP, XLIV, 54, MHS; Robert Hallowell Gardiner, *Early Recollections of Robert Hallowell Gardiner, 1782–1864* (Hallowell, 1936), 62–71; [Samuel Ely], *The Unmasked Nabob of Hancock County; or, The Scales Dropt from the Eyes of the People* (Portsmouth, N.H., 1796; E 31477), 3–8; Charles Vaughan to Robert Hallowell, Aug. 6, 1802, KPP, box 5, MeHS; Benjamin Whitwell, *Certain Statements First Published in the Kennebec Gazette . . .* (Augusta, 1810; S-S 22051), 7.

25. Charles Vaughan to the Kennebeck Proprietors, Nov. 24, 1803, KPP, box 5, MeHS; Thurston Whiting and Benjamin Brackett, "Journal," Aug. 27, 1801, HKP, XLIV, 54, MHS.

26. Elisha Sylvester to Josiah Little, Oct. 20, 1792, folder 1782–1799, PPP, box 17, EI; Sylvester to Little, July 10, 1806, folder PPP, box 17, 1806–1810, EI.

27. Thurston Whiting and Benjamin Brackett to Henry Knox, Sept. 7, 1801, HKP, LII, 87, MHS.

28. *History of Bedford, New Hampshire, from 1737 . . .* (Concord, N.H., 1903), 294–298; Edward L. Parker, *The History of Londonderry, Comprising the Towns of Derry and Londonderry, N.H.* (Boston, 1851), 193.

29. David Quimby Cushman, *The History of Ancient Sheepscot and Newcastle . . .* (Bath, 1882), 279–280; Rufus K. Sewall, "An Account of the History of the Edgecomb Congregational Church," Rufus K. Sewall Papers, MeHS. Pickles is

first mentioned as living in Davistown in a Nov. 16, 1799, deed, which described his status as "Master of Arts"; see Pickles to Avery, Nov. 16, 1799, LCD, XLVII, 53, LCC.

30. Abraham Welch to George Ulmer, July 11, 1801, HKP, XLIV, 24, MHS; Simon Towle to Captain Hunter, Sept. 16, 1801, HKP, XLIV, 82, MHS; John Scobey to George Ulmer, July 9, 1801 [misdated June 9, 1801], HKP, XLIV, 3, MHS; George Ulmer to Henry Knox, July 11, 1801, and Knox to Ulmer, July 22, 1801, HKP, XLIV, 27, 34, MHS; Ulmer *et al.* deposition, Oct. 31, 1801, HKP, box 6, MeHS; recognizances of Joshua Smith, James Smith, and Jonathan Spaulding, July 3, 1801, HC-SJC Files, box 167, MeSA; *Castine Journal*, July 10, 1801.

31. George Ulmer to Henry Knox, June 20, July 11, Nov. 6, 1801, HKP, XLIV, 8, 27, 121, MHS; John Scobey to George Ulmer, July 9, 1801 [misdated June 9, 1801], HKP, XLIV, 3, MHS; Thurston Whiting and Benjamin Brackett, "Journal," Aug. 27, 1801, entry, HKP, XLIV, 54, MHS.

32. Daniel Davis to Henry Knox, Oct. 1, 1801, HKP, XLIV, 98, MHS; Twenty Associates v. Ezekiel Knowlton, Twenty Associates v. William Clark, Oct. 1802, LC-SJC Record Book, II, 42, LCC; Arodi Thayer to Charles Vaughan, Sept. 16, 1802, KPP, Letterbook, I, 156, MeHS; Vaughan to Henry Knox, Aug. 25, 1802, HKP, XLV, 40, MHS; Ephraim Ballard and Phillip Bullen, "Field Notes," Oct. 20, 1803, "Minutes of the Settlers' Lots," Feb. 14, 1804, HAPP, box 1, NEHGSL (for the survey).

33. Pickles left Davistown sometime before Aug. 1808, when a court case referred to him as "late of Montville." See HC-CCP Record Book, X, 169, HCC. He died in Corinth, Vermont, ca. 1812. His widow Margaret returned to Montville, where she was recorded on the 1813 tax list (Allen Goodwin Papers, UMO) and on the 1820 federal census. See also Silas McKeen to Margaret Pickles, July 13, 1813, in possession of Grace Hatch of Bangor, who graciously sent me a copy. For Copp's marriage, see Montville's Vital Records, 29, MeSA.

34. Daniel Davis to the General Court Committee on Robert Foye's petition, ca. Jan. 1804, Related Papers, Resolve LXXXV (Feb. 10, 1804), MA; Howard, *Palermo*, 11; Allen Goodwin notes on Robert Foye, Allen Goodwin Papers, UMO; Palermo Valuation List, 1811, box 400 (microfilm), MSL; Thurston Whiting and Benjamin Brackett, "Journal," Aug. 27, 1801, entry, HKP, XLIV, 54, MHS; Samuel Mooers and Humphrey Hook's appraisal, ca. Jan. 1804, Related Papers, Resolve LXXXV (Feb. 10, 1804), MA.

35. Daniel Davis to the General Court Committee on Robert Foye's petition, ca. Jan. 1804, Samuel Mooers and Humphrey Hook's appraisal, ca. Jan. 1804, Robert Foye to the General Court, ca. Jan. 1804, Related Papers, Resolve LXXXV (Feb. 10, 1804), MA; Kennebeck Proprietors to the General Court, Jan. 1803, KPP, Record Book, IV, 131, MeHS; Allen Goodwin's notes on Robert Foye, Allen Goodwin Papers, UMO; John Parker's complaint, Jan. 1802, LC-CGSP files, box 5 (1802), LCC; Commonwealth v. Bumford, June 1802, LC-SJC Record Book, II, 32, LCC; Lincoln County Gaol Book, June 16, 1802, entry, LCC; the General Court compensated Foye $800 of his estimated $900 loss; see Resolve LXXXV (Feb. 10, 1804), in *Resolves, etc. of the General Court of Massachusetts . . . [Jan.–Mar. 1804]* (Boston, 1804; S-S 6741), 51.

36. Howard, *Palermo*, 9; Allen Goodwin, "The Bartlett Family of Montville," Allen Goodwin Papers, UMO; Charles Vaughan to the Kennebeck Proprietors, July 9, 1806, KPP, box 6, MeHS. I culled the deeds and court cases for Bartlett and Foye during the period 1790–1820 from LCD, and LC-CCP, LCC.

37. Charles Vaughan to the Kennebeck Proprietors, Mar. 21, 1806, KPP, box 6, MeHS; Thurston Whiting and Benjamin Brackett, "Journal," Aug. 26, 27, 1801, entries, HKP, XLIV, 54, MHS. When Captain Willing Blake and Rufus Gilmore visited Sheepscot Great Pond in mid-Sept. as emissaries and spies for Henry Knox, they found that Bartlett had become much more taciturn: "He did not seem willing to talk much. They seemed to dislike communicating before strangers." See Blake and Gilmore to Knox, ca. Sept. 1801, HKP, XLVII, 32, MHS.

38. Charles Vaughan to James Bowdoin, Sept. 26, 1801, Jan. 4, 1802, KPP, box 5, MeHS; Arodi Thayer to the General Court, Jan. 21, 1802, Record Book, KPP, IV, 33, MeHS.

39. Gardiner, "Kennebec Purchase," MeHS, *Colls.*, 1st Ser., II (1847), 288–290; Charles Vaughan to James Bowdoin, Jan. 4, 1802, Vaughan to Robert Hallowell, Aug. 6, 1802, Vaughan to Thomas L. Winthrop, Aug. 22, 24, 29, Sept. 22, 1802, Benjamin Hallowell to Winthrop, Aug. 29, 1802, KPP, box 5, MeHS; Arodi Thayer to the General Court, Jan. 21, 1802, KPP, Record Book, IV, 33, MeHS; Resolve LXXXIV (Feb. 19, 1802), in *Resolves, etc. of the General Court of Massachusetts . . . [June–Mar. 1802]* (Boston, 1802; S-S 2626), 47–49; Elijah Brigham *et al.* to Gov. Caleb Strong, Feb. 24, 1804, CF, box 14 (1803–1805), MA (quote). William Allen, Jr., of Industry, considered the commissioners "a very unfortunate committee for the poor settlers" because they were "high-toned Federalists" of "the patrician grade." They held "high aristocratic notions" and "inflexible opinions as to the rights of freeholders; with no sympathy for trespassers or squatters as the settlers were called." See William Allen, "The Journal of William Allen, Esq.," in William Collins Hatch, *A History of the Town of Industry . . .* (Farmington, 1893), 84; and William Allen, *History of Industry, Maine . . .* (Skowhegan, 1869), 7.

40. Charles Vaughan to Judge Foster and Kilbourne Whitman, ca. Feb. 1803 [misfiled under 1790], KPP, box 3, MeHS; Allen, "Journal," in Hatch, *Industry*, 84–85; Allen, *Industry*, 8–9. I calculated the per-acre figure for Industry submissions by aggregating the 78 submissions from that town recorded in the volumes of Plymouth Patent Commission Settler Submissions (1802–1803), I–III, MA (for Allen's Oct. 19, 1802, submission, see III, 770); those 78 settlers submitted for 7,425 acres and were assessed $8,763.75 in payments.

41. Allen, "Journal," in Hatch, *Industry*, 84–85; William Allen, "Mercer, Somerset County, Maine," MS, William Allen Papers, MeHS, maintains that things were equally bad in that town for the submitting settlers. The difference between the $190 of Allen's award and the $207 he paid represents fees, interest, and the cost of forwarding the money to Boston. Allen's resentment is particularly striking because he expressed it later in life, after he had received substantial patronage from Charles Vaughan to survey his proprietary lands. William Allen, Jr., had better reason to forget his disappointment than almost any other settler, but he did not.

42. Seventy-nine Sheepscot Great Pond settlers submitted, of a probable population of 92 households in 1802. The numbers are derived from Plymouth Patent Commission Settler Submissions (1802–1803), I–III, MA; see also Howard, *Palermo*, 13–16. I calculated the 13 holdouts by noting those on the 1800 federal census return for Sheepscot Great Pond who did not submit for their lands but reappeared on the 1806 Palermo highway tax (reprinted in Howard, *Palermo*, 28–31). The 13 holdouts were Christopher Erskine, Jeremiah Bran, James Brown, Joseph Hutchens, John James, Jonathan Bartlett, Benjamin

Turner, David Turner, Stephen Bowler, Nathaniel Bradstreet, Leonard Anderson, Rufus Plummer, and David Hutchens. The last nine appear on Knox's lists of White Indians; for their concentration in Sheepscot Great Pond's southwestern corner around Jonathan Bartlett, see Millard Howard's "Partial Key to Bradstreet Wiggins's Survey of Palermo," MS, and Howard's copy of Wiggins's 1808 survey map. Mr. Howard generously shared these with me. On Joseph Hutchens's predicament, see Charles Vaughan to the Kennebeck Proprietors, June 13, 1806, KPP, box 6, MeHS.

43. Charles Vaughan to the Kennebeck Proprietors, Mar. 1804, and Vaughan to Thomas L. Winthrop, Aug. 11, 1803, KPP, box 5, MeHS; Charles Vaughan's Feb. 19, 1803, report to the Kennebeck Proprietors, quoted in Charles Thornton Libby, ed., *Province and Court Records of Maine*, II (Portland, 1931), xxx; Charles Vaughan to Thomas L. Winthrop, Mar. 26, 1804, Vaughan to the Kennebeck Proprietors, Mar. 1804, May 26, 1805, KPP, box 5, MeHS; Arodi Thayer to Charles Vaughan, Apr. 16, Sept. 27, 1804, KPP, Letterbook, I, 179, 184, MeHS; Plymouth Company vote, Aug. 5, 1805, KPP, Record Book, IV, 198, MeHS; State of Maine v. Rufus Plummer, May 1822, LC-SJC Record Book, 284, LCC; Arodi Thayer to Charles Vaughan, Jan. 27, Mar. 7, 1806, Vaughan to the Kennebeck Proprietors, Mar. 21, 1806, KPP, box 6, MeHS.

44. Charles Vaughan to the Kennebeck Proprietors, June 13, 1806, Mar. 31, 1807, KPP, box 6, MeHS.

45. *Ibid.*; Kennebeck Proprietors v. Jonathan Bartlett *et al.*, LC-CCP, Aug. 1807, Record Book, XIX, 173, LCC; Jonathan Bartlett's agreement with Charles Vaughan, June 10, 1806, KPP, box 6, MeHS; Mar. 6, 1807, vote, KPP, Record Book, IV, 240, MeHS.

46. Survey notes of Charles Turner, Jr., Mar.–Apr. 1806, Plymouth Company Line, Area 21, Range 20, Land Office Records, box 2, folder 27, MeSA; Charles Vaughan to the Kennebeck Proprietors, June 13, Oct. 10, 1806, Mar. 31, 1807, KPP, box 6, MeHS; Arodi Thayer to Charles Vaughan, Aug. 21, 1806, Feb. 5, 1807, KPP, Letterbook, I, 215, MeHS. For Bartlett's belated grant, see Grant Books, VI, 124 (Feb. 3, 1818), KPP, MeHS.

47. On Bartlett's control, see Charles Vaughan to the Kennebeck Proprietors, June 13, 1806, KPP, box 6, MeHS. Plummer does not appear as a household head in the 1800 Federal Census Return for Sheepscot Great Pond, apparently because he and his wife lived in his father's household. Rufus Plummer to Reuel Williams, Jan. 26, 1808, RWP, box 3, MeHS; Commonwealth v. Rufus Plummer, June 1809, LC-SJC Record Book, III, 251–252, LCC; John Dole's Justice of the Peace docket, Jan. 14, 1809, entries 8–9, LCC; Lincoln County Gaol Calendar, Jan. 14, 1809, entry, LCC. Thereafter Plummer was an unwanted man in the area. When he returned in 1822, he was quickly arrested and sentenced to another year in jail for his resistance 17 years earlier to Norris's service of the Kennebeck Proprietors' writ. This was an unprecedented revival of a long-dormant charge that he could have been tried for in 1809 when first apprehended, a charge that many others could also have been prosecuted for. That and the unusually heavy sentence attest that this prosecution was highly selective and intended to remove Plummer from the area. Learning his lesson, Plummer lived out the rest of his life alone on Isle au Haut in Penobscot Bay. See State of Maine v. Rufus Plummer, May 1822, LC-SJC Record Book, V, 284, LCC; for Plummer's release in Sept. 1823, see LC-SJC Record Book, VI, 83, LCC. For genealogical information on Rufus Plummer, I am indebted to Carolyn Ballantine of Palermo.

48. Palermo Valuation List, 1811, box 400 (microfilm), MSL; Palermo, Maine, return, Fourth Census of the United States, 1820, microfilm series M33, reel 36.

49. Jonathan Bartlett to Washington Plummer, Aug. 4, 1829, WCD, VI, 237, WCRD; Bartlett to Peasley Plummer, Aug. 4, 1829, WCD, IV, 337, WCRD; Peasley Plummer to Bartlett, Aug. 4, 1829, WCD, V, 59, WCRD; Probate Records, I, 512, 565, 643, II, 89, Waldo County Registry of Probate, Belfast; on Tidd, see Allen Goodwin, "The Bartlett Family," Allen Goodwin Papers, Special Collections, UMO; and Richard J. Hinton, *John Brown and His Men* (New York, 1968; reprint of New York, 1894), 559–567.

50. Charles Vaughan to the Kennebeck Proprietors, Apr. 8, Oct. 10, 1806, KPP, box 6, MeHS; Plymouth Company votes, Aug. 17, Nov. 5, 1807, KPP, Record Books, IV, 267, 282, MeHS.

51. Edward Augustus Kendall, *Travels through the Northern Parts of the United States in the Years 1807 and 1808* (New York, 1809), III, 85–86; J. W. Hanson, *History of the Old Towns, Norridgewock and Canaan . . .* (Boston, 1849), 148–150. Kendall, who visited Canaan and Norridgewock in 1807, dates the episode to 1804. At a much later date an eyewitness to the affair, William Allen, Jr., of Industry, penned his reminiscences and dated the episode to 1801. Kendall must be correct, because court records indicate Lambert's presence in Canaan until 1804. See William Allen, Jr., "Pittsfield, Maine," in William Allen, Jr., Papers, MeHS; and Hodge v. Lambert and Kincaid, June 1802, LC-SJC, II, 18, LCC. In 1798 Daniel Lambert owned 100 acres of barely developed land, dwelled in a log cabin judged worthless by the direct tax assessors, and ranked 60th among Canaan's 106 taxpayers. Three years later a state valuation return found that Lambert still lived in a log cabin, possessed no barn, and owned 100 acres, only 2 of which were improved and 49 of which (half the homestead) were judged "unimprovable." He owned no horse, no oxen, but a single cow, and a lone pig. See Canaan's returns in the Massachusetts-Maine 1798 Direct Tax Returns, NEHGSL; and in the Massachusetts-Maine 1801 Tax Valuation Returns, MSL.

52. Submissions to the Plymouth Patent Commission, V, MA; Balltown 1791 tax list, MSL.

53. Kendall, *Travels*, III, 87–89; J. W. Hanson, *History of Gardiner, Pittston, and West Gardiner* (Gardiner, 1852), 168; Hanson, *Norridgewock*, 148–150. The fact that the English-born Kendall left the beaten path to travel to Canaan, Maine, suggests that he was related to Abiatha Kendall, an English-born settler, who was probably his chief informant. For the Kendall family in Canaan, see Clarence I. Chato, "History of Canaan," MeSL.

54. Kendall, *Travels*, III, 87–91; W. Allen, "Pittsfield, Maine," 17, sets the date of repayment as June 20. Hanson insists it was Sept. 1. Kendall sets it as "in September."

55. Kendall, *Travels*, III, 92–93; and W. Allen, "Pittsfield, Maine," 17. Daniel Lambert escaped three suits recently decided against him. See Jewett v. Lambert ($36.07), Currier v. Lambert *et al.* ($58.55), Fowler v. Lambert ($152.27), all Aug. 1804, KC-CCP, IV, 6, 36, 177, MeSA. Of the 60 area settlers who submitted, 16 defaulted. This compares to only 4 of 79 submittees who defaulted in Sheepscot Great Pond settlement. See James Bridge and Reuel Williams's 1808 account of settlers who failed to pay their awards, KPP, MS 00-43, MeHS.

56. Kendall, *Travels*, III, 93–95. There seems to have been an association between militant agrarianism and treasure-seeking. See Steven C. Bullock, "Joshua Belding's Visions: Family, Economy, and Culture in Post-Revolutionary

Rural New England," 7, MS; Clark Jillson, *Green Leaves from Whitingham, Vermont* . . . (Worcester, Mass., 1894), 119–121. Also note Harris Ransom's treasure scheme; see Commonwealth v. Ransom, Commonwealth v. Graves, both May 1803, Cumberland County SJC, I, 432, 456, MeSA.

CHAPTER SEVEN

1. Lemuel Paine to Gov. James Sullivan, Feb. 13, 1808, CF, box 16 (Aug. 1807–May 1808), MA (the epigraph); James W. North, *The History of Augusta* . . . (Augusta, 1870), 847.

2. Thomas A. Jeffrey, "The Malta War" (master's thesis, University of Maine, Orono, 1976); Arthur Lithgow's memorial to the Governor and Council, Feb. 1808, CF, box 16 (Aug. 1807–May 1808), MA; North, *Augusta*, 357; Arthur Lithgow's Account of 1807–1808 expenses, Related Papers, Resolve LV (June 19, 1809), MA; Bridge and Williams's Account, Nov. 8, 1810, KPP, box 7, MeHS. For the Embargo's impact, see Cyrus Eaton, *Annals of the Town of Warren* (Hallowell, 1877), 306; *Portland Gazette*, Nov. 2, 1807, Jan. 25, 1808; Japhet C. Washburn to Thomas L. Winthrop, Dec. 7, 1810, KPP, box 7, MeHS.

3. In 1806–1807 the Calvinist Baptists' net gain in mid-Maine was 62; before 1807–1808 the greatest net gain ($N = 328$) came in 1798–1799. See the annual *Minutes of the Bowdoinham Association* . . . (title varies), 1790, 1792–1810 (E 22372, 24140, 25221, 26693, 28328, 30113, 31858, 33442, 35224, 37027, S-S 114, 1818, 3731, 5779, 7924, 9893, 12048, 14423, 16916, 19430), and the *Minutes of the Lincoln Association*, 1805–1806, 1808–1810 (S-S 7925, 9894, 14424, 16917, 19432); John Buzzell, ed., *Religious Magazine* . . . (1811–1812; APS 2, reel 202), I (Oct. 1812), 270, 274; Ephraim Stinchfield, *Some Memoirs of the Life, Experience, and Travels of Elder Ephraim Stinchfield* (Portland, 1819; S-S 49511), 79–82, 99–100; the Reverend Daniel Merrill to Boston's Baptist ministers, May 13, 1808, reprinted in *Massachusetts Baptist Missionary Magazine*, II (1808–1810), 68–70. The Stinchfield quote is from his letter of June 20, 1808, in Elias Smith, ed., *Herald of Gospel Liberty* (APS 2, reel 19), I (1808–1809), 3; the letter is anonymous, but the information matches Stinchfield's *Memoirs*.

4. Lemuel Paine to Gov. James Sullivan, Feb. 13, 1808, CF, box 16 (Aug. 1807–May 1808), MA; Arthur Lithgow to the Governor and Council, Feb. 1808, Related Papers, Resolve LV (June 19, 1809), MA; Lithgow to Gov. James Sullivan, Jan. 23, 25, 1808, CF, box 16 (Aug. 1807–May 1808), MA; "Sheriff's Proposals," ca. Jan. 1808, CF, box 16 (Aug. 1807–May 1808), MA; and Pitt Dillingham to Arthur Lithgow, Jan. 30, 1808, Related Papers, Resolve LV (June 19, 1809), MA.

5. Pitt Dillingham to Arthur Lithgow, Jan. 30, 1808, Related Papers, Resolve LV (June 19, 1809), MA; Pitt Dillingham's deposition, Feb. 15, 1808, Dillingham to Nathan Weston, Feb. 4, 1808, CF, box 16 (Aug. 1807–May 1808), MA.

6. The original document signed "Teckarb Leinad" and inscribed "Indian Advertisement" on its reverse side can be found in the cluster of papers relating to Arthur Lithgow, CF, box 16 (Aug. 1807–May 1808), MA. It is reprinted in Alan Taylor, "'Stopping the Progres of Rogues and Deceivers': A White Indian Recruiting Notice of 1808," *WMQ*, 3d Ser., XLII (1985), 102–103. See also Arthur Lithgow's account of expenses, n.d., Related Papers, Resolve LV (June 19, 1809), MA.

7. Herbert I. Brackett, *Brackett Genealogy: Descendants of Anthony Brackett of Portsmouth and Captain Richard Brackett of Braintree* . . . (Washington, D.C., 1907), 214–219; Joseph Jones, list of "Indians" seen at Sandy Stream, Sept. 10, 1801, HKP, XLIV, 75, MHS; Daniel Brackett, Jr., indictment, May 1808, KC-SJC Files, MeSA; on Whitney, see Isaac Dalton Stewart, *The History of the Freewill Baptists for Half a Century* . . . (Dover, N.H., 1862), 206; Paul Coffin, "Memoir and Journals of Rev. Paul Coffin, D.D.," MeHS, *Collections*, 1st Ser., IV (Portland, 1859), 318–319. In Oct. 1802 Daniel Brackett submitted to the Plymouth Patent Commission, which ruled that he should pay the Kennebeck Proprietors $160 for his lot. But he was apparently unable to procure the cash, for in 1808 the Kennebeck Proprietors' lawyers listed Daniel Brackett as a defaulter. See Plymouth Patent Commission Submissions, I, 74 (Oct. 19, 1802), MA; "Abstract of the Names etc. of Settlers who Submitted to the Awards of Commissioners, but have not Purchased their Deeds," 1808, KPP, MS 00-43, MeHS.

8. Taylor, "'Stopping the Progres,'" *WMQ*, 3d Ser., XLII (1985), 102.

9. *Ibid.*, 103; E. J. Hobsbawm and George Rudé, *Captain Swing* (London, 1969); Thomas P. Slaughter, *The Whiskey Rebellion: Frontier Epilogue to the American Revolution* (New York, 1986), 184.

10. Taylor, "'Stopping the Progres,'" *WMQ*, 3d Ser., XLII (1985), 99, 102–103. Christopher M. Jedrey, *The World of John Cleaveland: Family and Community in Eighteenth-Century New England* (New York, 1979), xiii, points out the persistence of a militant Protestant worldview in rural New England into the late 18th century. The similarity of this rhetoric to that treated by Christopher Hill, in *The World Turned Upside Down: Radical Ideas during the English Revolution* (New York, 1972), is very striking. For the imagery of "kings" in an 18th-century English forest insurgency, see E. P. Thompson, *Whigs and Hunters: The Origin of the Black Act* (London, 1975), 81, 142–146; see also George Rudé, *The Crowd in History: A Study of Popular Disturbances in France and England, 1730–1848* (New York, 1964), 227–228; and E. J. Hobsbawm, *Primitive Rebels: Studies in Archaic Forms of Social Movement in the Nineteenth and Twentieth Centuries* (Manchester, Eng., 1959), 108–124. For other White Indians referring to settlers as "Englishmen," see Jonathan Vining's testimony in John Merrick, ed., *Trial of David Lynn . . . for the Murder of Paul Chadwick at Malta* . . . (Augusta, 1809; S-S 18778), 8, 11.

11. Pilsbury's circular letter appears in *Minutes of the Lincoln Association, Held at the Meeting-House, in Ballstown, September 21st and 22d, 1808* (Buckstown, 1808; S-S 14424).

12. Taylor, "'Stopping the Progres,'" *WMQ*, 3d Ser., XLII (1985), 102–103. For similar agrarian notions of class struggle in the 1790s and 1880s, see Samuel Eliot Morison, ed., "William Manning's *The Key of Libberty*," *WMQ*, 3d Ser., XIII (1956), 202–254; and Lawrence Goodwyn, *The Populist Moment: A Short History of the Agrarian Revolt in America* (New York, 1978), esp. 20–54.

13. On the myth, see Samuel Ely, *The Deformity of a Hideous Monster, Discovered in the Province of Maine, by a Man in the Woods, Looking after Liberty* (Boston, 1797; E 32081), 17. On the costumes, see *Boston Evening Post*, Dec. 26, 1768; Pitt Dillingham to Arthur Lithgow, Jan. 30, 1808, Related Papers, Resolve LV (June 19, 1809), MA. On mock Indian dialect, see *Portland Gazette*, Dec. 19, 1808; and Hugh Mulloy's petition to the General Court, n.d., Related Papers, Mar. 3, 1810, Resolve, MA; Allen Goodwin, "A Mob in Montville," *Republican Journal* (Belfast), Feb. 6, 1908. On Whiskey Rebels, see Slaughter, *The Whiskey Rebellion*, 113, 115, 188, 208–211; on Vermont, see Samuel Gardenier's deposition, Sept. 21, 1771, in E. B. O'Callaghan, *The Documentary History of the State of New-York* (Albany,

N.Y., 1851), IV, 724–729; on the Wild Yankees, see David Craft, *History of Bradford County, Pennsylvania* (Philadelphia, 1878), 49.

14. Taylor, "'Stopping the Progres,'" *WMQ*, 3d Ser., XLII (1985), 94–108; Eldridge Honaker Pendleton, "The New York Anti-Rent Controversy, 1830–1860" (Ph.D. diss., University of Virginia, 1974), 38–40.

15. On the brutality of whites and Indians toward one another on the northeastern frontier during the mid-18th century, see B. J. Whiting, "Incident at Quantabacook, March, 1764," *New England Quarterly*, XX (1947), 169–196; David Quimby Cushman, *The History of Ancient Sheepscot and Newcastle . . .* (Bath, 1882), 134; and Jeremy Belknap, *The History of New-Hampshire* (Boston, 1791–1792; E 23166, 24087, 24088), II, 47, 82, 280, III, 369; Belknap notes the rescue riots to liberate whites accused of killing Indians. On Samuel Ball, see Thomas Hutchinson, *The History of the Colony and Province of Massachusetts-Bay* (Cambridge, Mass., 1936), III, 3. For the near-extinction of Maine's Indians, see James Sullivan, *The History of the District of Maine* (Boston, 1795; reprint ed., Augusta, 1970), 96; Sullivan estimated that there were only about 300 Indians left in mid-Maine by 1795. For the mobbing of an Indian guide, see James Irish to the Massachusetts land agent, Apr. 8, 1825, ELC, box 22, item 14, MA.

16. For elite outsiders' dismissing settlers as near-savages, see H.A.S. Dearborn, "The Life of Major General Henry Dearborn," MS, 30–34, MeHS; Charles Maurice de Talleyrand-Périgord, "Letter on the Eastern Part of America" (Boston, Sept. 24, 1794), in Hans Huth and Wilma J. Pugh, eds., *Talleyrand in America as a Financial Promoter, 1794–96* (*Annual Report of the American Historical Association, 1941*, II [Washington, D.C., 1942]), 83; *Edes' Kennebec Gazette* (Augusta), Sept. 24, 1802.

17. George Ulmer to Henry Knox, Mar. 18, 1796, HKP, XXXVIII, 171, MHS; Stephen Chase to Josiah Little, Feb. 2, 1801, PPP, box 4, Letters to Josiah Little folder, EI; Thurston Whiting and Benjamin Brackett to Henry Knox, Aug. 28, Sept. 7, 1801, HKP, XLIV, 60, LII, 87, MHS; Whiting and Brackett, "Journal," Aug. 27–28 entries, HKP, XLIV, 54, MHS.

18. John Rynier to Henry Knox, Dec. 31, 1797, HKP, box 4, MeHS; Robert Hallowell Gardiner, *Early Recollections of Robert Hallowell Gardiner, 1782–1864* (Hallowell, 1936), 71. On female networks, see Laurel Thatcher Ulrich, "'A Friendly Neighbor': Social Dimensions of Daily Work in Northern Colonial New England," *Feminist Studies*, VI (1980), 392–405. For women's prominence in European food riots, see George Rudé, *Paris and London in the Eighteenth Century: Studies in Popular Protest* (New York, 1970), 17–34; Charles Tilly, "Collective Violence in European Perspective," in Hugh Graham and Ted R. Gurr, eds., *Violence in America: Historical and Comparative Perspectives* (Beverly Hills, Calif., 1979), 83–93; E. P. Thompson, "The Moral Economy of the English Crowd in the Eighteenth Century," *Past and Present*, no. 50 (Feb. 1971), 116; John Walter, "Grain Riots and Popular Attitudes to the Law: Maldon and the Crisis of 1629," in John Brewer and John Styles, eds., *An Ungovernable People: The English and Their Law in the Seventeenth and Eighteenth Centuries* (New Brunswick, N.J., 1980), 47–83.

19. Thurston Whiting and Benjamin Brackett, "Journal," Aug. 26–27, 30–31 entries, HKP, XLIV, 54, MHS.

20. North, *Augusta*, 358, 373; John Neal to the General Court, ca. Jan. 1809, Related Papers, Mar. 3, 1810, Resolve, MA; Charles Vaughan to Thomas L. Winthrop, Aug. 22, 1802 ("literal warfare"), KPP, box 5, MeHS; Vaughan to the Kennebeck Proprietors, Feb. 12, 1806, Mar. 9, 1806, KPP, box 6, MeHS. On

similar anonymous threatening letters associated with agrarian unrest and food riots in England, see E. P. Thompson, "The Crime of Anonymity," in Douglas Hay *et al.*, *Albion's Fatal Tree: Crime and Society in Eighteenth-Century England* (New York, 1975), 255–307.

21. Ephraim Ballard to the Kennebeck Proprietors, Jan. 1, 1796, KPP, box 4, MeHS; Elliot G. Vaughan to Col. Thomas Cutts, Oct. 30, 1810, miscellaneous box 24 ("Papers Relating to Lands in Lincoln County . . ."), MA; on the English crowd's blasphemous style, see E. P. Thompson, "The Crime of Anonymity," in Hay *et al.*, *Albion's Fatal Tree*, 306; and Hobsbawm and Rudé, *Captain Swing*, 211–212; on Vermont's Green Mountain Boys, see Samuel Gardenier's deposition, Sept. 21, 1771, and Charles Hutchesson's deposition, Nov. 12, 1771, in O'Callaghan, *The Documentary History of the State of New-York*, IV, 724–729, 745–796.

22. Thurston Whiting and Benjamin Brackett, "Journal," Aug. 26, 27, 31, 1801, entries, HKP, XLIV, 54, MHS; Whiting and Brackett to Henry Knox, Sept. 7, 1801, HKP, LII, 87, MHS; George Ulmer to Henry Knox, June 28, 1801, HKP, XLIV, 14, MHS; Slaughter, *The Whiskey Rebellion*, 185–187; James E. Crowley, "The Paxton Disturbance and Ideas of Order in Pennsylvania Politics," *Pennsylvania History*, XXXVII (1970), 317–339; Oscar Handlin, "The Eastern Frontier of New York," *New York History*, XVIII (1937), 69; suits involving a Belfast resident culled from the HC-CCP and LC-CCP Record Books for 1796–1805, MeSA, LCC. Of the 134 Belfast debt cases, in 119 the Belfast resident was the plaintiff, and in 78 of the 119 was of high status.

23. On the Augusta courthouse fire, see Joseph North *et al.* to Gov. James Sullivan, Mar. 19, 1808, House File 6382, MA; North, *Augusta*, 354–357. For barn burning, see Joseph Jones's petition to the General Court, ca. Jan. 1802, Related Papers, Mar. 1, 1802, Resolve, MA; David Murphy to the Kennebeck Proprietors, Aug. 23, 1810, June 7, 1811, Isaac Davis to the Kennebeck Proprietors, June 8, 1811, KPP, box 7, MeHS; Isaac Davis to the General Court, Dec. 12, 1810, David Murphy to the General Court, Jan. 10, 1811, Related Papers, Feb. 16, 1811, Resolve, MA. For the New York Anti-Renters' restraint, see Pendleton, "The New York Anti-Rent Controversy," 75, 78, 81, and on their barn burning, see 110–111. On the restraint of English crowds, see Hobsbawm and Rudé, *Captain Swing*, 212; Thompson, "The Moral Economy of the English Crowd," *Past and Present*, no. 50 (Feb. 1971), 76–136.

24. [John Merrick], *Remarks on Some of the Circumstances and Arguments Produced by the Murder of Mr. Paul Chadwick, at Malta . . .* ([Augusta, 1809]; S-S 18491), 20; see also Manassah Smith to John Trueman, May 6, 1797, CF, box 11 (1797–1799), MA. For the New England Regulators, see David P. Szatmary, *Shays' Rebellion: The Making of an Agrarian Insurrection* (Amherst, Mass., 1980).

25. On the insurrection act, see Gov. James Sullivan to John Chandler, Apr. 2, 1808, House File (unpassed) 6311, MA; and Sullivan to Chandler, Apr. 29, 1808, House File (unpassed) 6380, MA. For examples of the settlers' tactics, see Silas Lee to the trustees of Bowdoin College, Nov. 7, 1804, Related Papers, Act CIX (Mar. 1, 1805), MA; Charles Vaughan to James Sullivan, June 13, 1807, KPP, box 6, MeHS; John Johnston, *A History of the Towns of Bristol and Bremen . . .* (Albany, N.Y., 1873), 486; "The Early History of Monroe," *Republican Journal*, Feb. 16, 1882.

26. Charles Hayden to Gov. Sullivan, Feb. 13, 1808, George Bender's deposition, Feb. 13, 1808, CF, box 16 (Aug. 1807–May 1808), MA. For Lithgow's removal, see Thomas C. Amory, *Life of James Sullivan . . .* (Boston, 1859), II, 273–275.

27. John Chandler to Gov. James Sullivan, Apr. 25, 1808, House File (un-passed) 6381, MA.

28. Pitt Dillingham to Nathan Weston, Feb. 4, 1808, CF, box 16 (Aug. 1807–May 1808), MA; Philip Bullen to Charles Vaughan, Nov. 20, 1809, KPP, box 7, MeHS.

29. Benjamin Whitwell to Theophilus Parsons, Aug. 13, 1804, quoted in Richard E. Ellis, *Jeffersonian Crisis: Courts and Politics in the Young Republic* (New York, 1971), 225–226. For Whitwell, see William Willis, *A History of the Law, the Courts, and the Lawyers of Maine . . .* (Portland, 1863), 243. For the "Greene Indian War," see Timothy W. Robinson, *History of the Town of Morrill in the County of Waldo and State of Maine*, ed. Theoda Mears Morse (Belfast, 1944), 51; William Crosby, "Annals of the Town of Belfast," MS, 13, MeHS.

30. Writ, in Commonwealth v. James Smith, June 1801, box 167, HC-CCP files, MeSA; George Ulmer to Henry Knox, June 20, 1801, HKP, XLIV, 8, MHS; Robert Houston to Henry Knox, June 26, 1801, HKP, XLIV, 13, MHS.

31. Gov. James Sullivan to Edmund Bridge, June 24, 1808, ELC, box 45, MA; see also Samuel Titcomb to Sullivan, Feb. 14, 1808, CF, box 16 (Aug. 1807–May 1808), MA.

32. Henry Knox to George Ulmer, July 11, 1801, HKP, XLIV, 25, MHS; Knox to Ulmer and Robert Houston, Aug. 23, 1801, HKP, LII, 86, MHS; Knox to Ulmer, Sept. 22, 1801, HKP, XLIV, 86, MHS; [Merrick], *Remarks on Some of the Circumstances*, 19; North, *Augusta*, 354.

33. John Conner's deposition, Nov. 22, 1810, miscellaneous box 24 ("Papers Relating to Lands in Lincoln County . . ."), MA; Artemas Kimball's deposition, June 23, 1820, Executive Council Files, box 1, folder 10, MeSA.

34. Henry Johnson's deposition, Dec. 14, 1807, CF, box 16 (Aug. 1807–May 1808), MA.

35. Moses Robinson's petition to the General Court, Feb. 14, 1809, Related Papers, Resolve CCXCIII (Feb. 25, 1809), MA.

36. John Chandler to Gov. James Sullivan, Apr. 25, 1808, House File (un-passed) 6381, MA; E. W. Ripley to Arodi Thayer, May 9, 1808, KPP, box 6, MeHS; witness list in Commonwealth v. Barlow, KC-SJC Files, box 73, MeSA; Robert H. Gardiner, "History of the Kennebec Purchase . . . ," MeHS, *Colls.*, 1st Ser., II (Portland, 1847), 290–294; *Portland Gazette*, June 6, 1808; on the Fairfax survey, see Reuel Williams's account with the Kennebeck Proprietors, Mar. 1, 1811, KPP, box 7, MeHS.

37. Job Chadwick to the Kennebeck Proprietors, Mar. 7, 1807, KPP, box 6, MeHS; "Chadwicks in America," 13, 17, 24, typescript, MeSL. For the offer, see Thayer to Bridge and Williams, Apr. 27, 1809, KPP, Letterbook, I, 297, MeHS; for the "turbulent township," see Thayer to Bridge and Williams, Oct. 24, 1808, KPP, Letterbook, I, 263, MeHS. Alexander MacLean to Jedediah Morse, July 18, 1804, SPG Papers, box 3, folder 7, EI (first two quotes); Job Chadwick's missionary report for 1804, SPG Papers, box 1, folder 17, EI.

38. Arodi Thayer to James Bridge and Reuel Williams, Mar. 15, 1808, KPP, Letterbook, I, 235, MeHS; Thayer to Bridge and Williams, July 6, 1809, KPP, Letterbook, I, 303, MeHS; Thayer to Bridge and Williams, Aug. 17, 1809, KPP, Letterbook, II, 5, MeHS; North, *Augusta*, 373–374; Merrick, ed., *Trial of David Lynn*, 1–11, including the witnesses' quotes, 8 (Jonathan Vining and George Mason).

39. "Chadwicks in America," MS, 13, MeSL; North, *Augusta*, 374–376. The quotes are from Owen Clark's petition to the General Court, Jan. 26, 1810,

Related Papers, Resolve XCIII (Feb. 5, 1810), MA; and Reuben Fairfield's testimony in Merrick, ed., *Trial of David Lynn*, 12.

40. [Merrick], *Remarks on Some of the Circumstances*, 12. See "The Early History of Monroe," *Republican Journal*, Feb. 16, 1882, for an example of a leading man's bringing his neighbors to accept proprietary terms.

41. [Merrick], *Remarks on Some of the Circumstances*, 9, 13–14, 16, 20. For Massachusetts authorities' similar legal strategy toward the New England Regulators, see Gregory H. Nobles, "Shays's Neighbors: The Context and Consequences of Rebellion in Pelham, Massachusetts, 1780–1815" (paper presented at American Historical Association meeting, Dec. 29, 1984); for New York authorities' similar legal strategy toward the Anti-Renters, see Pendleton, "The New York Anti-Rent Controversy," 153.

42. North, *Augusta*, 375–376; Gardiner, "Kennebec Purchase," MeHS, *Colls.*, 1st Ser., II (1847), 290; Rev. D. R. Goodwin, "Notice of John Merrick," MeHS, *Colls.*, 1st Ser., VII (Bath, 1876), 387–388. In midtrial one of the defendants, Jonas Proctor, suddenly agreed to testify for the prosecution, only to insist in his testimony that he knew nothing about the murder and saw no one commit it. See Merrick, ed., *Trial of David Lynn*, 13.

43. Gardiner, "Kennebec Purchase," MeHS, *Colls.*, 1st Ser., II (1847), 290; Kennebeck Proprietors' grant to Lois Chadwick, Feb. 14, 1811, KPP, Grant Book, IV, 488–489, MeHS; Job Chadwick's mortgage to Robert Hallowell Gardiner, May 22, 1810, KCD, XVII, 425, KCRD; Chadwick to Gardiner, Dec. 27, 1814, KCD, XXIII, 527, KCRD.

44. Pendleton, "The New York Anti-Rent Controversy," 38, 56–58; Robert Hallowell Gardiner to William Tudor, Mar. 23, 1808, Oct. 21, 1809, folder 1, box 2, Gardiner Family Papers, Oaklands, Gardiner. The assault on David Sewall offers an example of the unusual violence that sometimes attended the resistance's decay. In Aug. 1810 the White Indians of Greene Plantation felt deeply frustrated at their inability to intimidate David Sewall, Benjamin Joy's land agent, with their menaces. Unwilling to concede, they felt driven to act. At night about 50 disguised men seized Sewall at Manassah Sleeper's tavern and dragged him outside. After one man knocked Sewall to the ground with the butt end of a musket, the party stripped the agent to the waist and carried him off to a secluded spot, where they beat him badly with their fists. When they returned him to the tavern, he was unconscious and covered with bruises and clotted blood. See John Conner's deposition, Nov. 22, 1810, David Sewall to Gov. Elbridge Gerry, Nov. 15, 1810, both in miscellaneous box 24 ("Papers Relating to Lands in Lincoln County . . ."), MA.

45. Pitt Dillingham to Arthur Lithgow, Jan. 30, 1808, Related Papers, Resolve LV (June 19, 1809), MA; Pitt Dillingham's deposition, Feb. 15, 1808, George Bender, Jr.'s, deposition, Feb. 13, 1808, CF, box 16 (Aug. 1807–May 1808), MA. For the two faces of the 18th-century English crowd, see Thompson, "The Crime of Anonymity," in Hay *et al.*, *Albion's Fatal Tree*, 307.

46. Ronald F. Banks, *Maine Becomes a State: The Movement to Separate Maine from Massachusetts, 1785–1820* (Middletown, Conn., 1970), 133; John Davis *et al.* petition to the General Court, ca. Jan. 1808, Related Papers, Act of Mar. 2, 1808, MA.

47. See Table 6 on the settlers' increasing investment in permanent structures on their property.

48. Over the two-decade period, settlers' ownership of oxen (1.4 per taxpayer in 1791, 1.4 in 1811) and cattle (2.5 in 1791, 2.3 in 1811) stagnated, possession

of pigs increased modestly (.9 in 1791, 1.3 in 1811), but horse ownership more than doubled (.3 in 1791, .7 in 1811). In 1791, 63 of 190 taxpayers owned horses, 101 of 213 in 1801, 234 of 376 in 1811. Jefferson and Whitefield valuation lists, 1811, box 400 (microfilm), MSL.

Palermo settlers' court cases provide other measures of the backcountry's increasing integration into the wider economy. The number of cases involving residents leapt from a mere 34 in the 1790s to 244 during the next decade. This was not simply a consequence of local population growth, for the 618% increase far outstripped the town's 80% growth in households, from 71 in 1800 to 128 in 1810. No longer did Palermo's settlers live virtually beyond the county courts. As in the previous decade, residents rarely sued outsiders and almost never one another. Informality, good neighborhood, and a community consensus against internal suits continued to prevail in Palermo, but external transactions involved unprecedented numbers in litigation with outsiders. In the 1790s about one-sixth of the community's residents appeared in court as defendants; in the 1800s that doubled to more than a third. Palermo residents were defendants in 190 of 244 (77.9%) of the cases and in 172 of those 190 cases confronted an outside plaintiff. Residents sued outsiders in 47 of 244 (19.3%) of the cases and one another in 18 of 244 (7.4%) of the cases. In the 1790s, 10 of 91 (11.0%) decadal residents (all those known to have resided in Palermo at some point during the decade) brought suits, and 4 of 18 (22.2%) who resided in the community throughout the decade (those present in 1790 and in 1800, a subset of the decadal residents). In the 1800s, 35 of 230 (15.2%) decadal residents and 13 of 40 (32.5%) full-timers brought suits. In the 1790s, 16 of 91 (17.6%) decadal residents and 4 of 18 (22.2%) full-timers appeared as defendants. In the 1800s, 80 of 230 (34.8%) decadal residents and 17 of 40 full-timers (42.5%) appeared as defendants. All of these suits were for unpaid debts.

Two-thirds of the outsiders who sued Palermo residents hailed from front-country towns. Almost all Palermo defendants were men of modest status—yeomen, artisans, or laborers—rather than high-status traders, doctors, gentlemen, merchants, and esquires. But Palermo defendants usually confronted high-status plaintiffs. Palermo plaintiffs sued other backcountry residents in 29 of 54 cases (the remaining 25 were against frontcountry residents). Frontcountry residents were the plaintiffs against Palermo defendants in 114 of 190 (60.0%) of the cases. Low-status men were Palermo's defendants in 168 of 190 (88.4%) cases (high-status plaintiffs accounted for the balance, 22 of 190, 11.6%). Palermo defendants confronted high-status plaintiffs in 112 of 190 (58.9%) of the cases.

Most cases indicate where the defendant had signed the note that he had failed to pay. The percentage and the absolute number of documented notes signed by Palermo defendants in frontcountry towns increased steadily during the period 1790–1810. During the 1790s Palermo defendants signed almost three-fifths (7 of 12, 58.3%) of their documented notes in frontcountry towns. During the next five years, 1800–1804, Palermo residents signed a little more than three-fifths (23 of 37, 62.2%) of their documented notes in frontcountry towns. That rose to more than two-thirds (85 of 124, 68.5%) in the succeeding five years, 1805–1809. In sum, over time, Palermo residents tended to appear more frequently in the courts as defendants sued by high-status outsiders for debts that had been contracted in frontcountry towns; this trend attests to the backcountry settlers' increased involvement in external transactions. Palermo residents participated in 93 cases during the first half of the decade 1800–1809 and in 151 cases in the second half. Palermo residents were defendants in 71% (66 of 93) of the early-decade cases and in 82% (124 of 151) of the late-decade cases. As defendants, Palermo residents confronted frontcountry residents in half (33 of 66, 50%) of the early cases and in almost two-thirds (81 of 124, 65%) of the late-decade cases. During the early years of the decade Palermo defendants confronted elite plaintiffs only half the time (33 of 66, 50%); this proportion rose to almost two-thirds of the cases in the later years of the decade (79 of 124, 63%).

Finally, the court cases usually indicated when the plaintiff was not the original creditor, but someone who had purchased the debtor's note from that original creditor or an intermediate party. The degree to which Palermo residents' notes ended up in third-party hands provides another measure of their growing involvement in the wider economy. Third parties figured in none of the 11 cases with this documentation from the 1790s. Instead, in every case the Palermo defendant confronted his original creditor. But, because an increasing number of notes given by Palermo residents entered wider circulation, during the following decade third-party plaintiffs appeared in one-fifth (31 of 141) of the appropriately documented cases involving Palermo defendants. Documentation of note exchange is lacking for 23 of the 34 cases from the 1790s and for 49 of the 190 cases from the 1800s where Palermo residents were defendants. The cases were collected from the LC-CCP Record Books, LCC.

49. John Wilson to Benjamin Joy, Jan. 7, 1808, WKP, box 7, MeHS.

CHAPTER EIGHT

1. The epigraphs are from Samuel Ely, *The Deformity of a Hideous Monster, Discovered in the Province of Maine, by a Man in the Woods, Looking after Liberty* (Boston, 1797; E 32081), 16; and William Allen, Jr., "Bingham Lands," MeHS, *Collections*, 1st Ser., VII (Bath, 1876), 358. For a similar interpretation of Vermont's Jeffersonians, see Randolph A. Roth, *The Democratic Dilemma: Religion, Reform, and the Social Order in the Connecticut River Valley of Vermont, 1791–1850* (New York, 1987), 68–70.

2. H.A.S. Dearborn, "The Life of Major General Henry Dearborn," MS, 19–23, MeHS; Harry H. Cochrane, *History of Monmouth and Wales* (East Winthrop, 1894), I, 63–76; Robert Hallowell Gardiner, *Early Recollections of Robert Hallowell Gardiner, 1782–1864* (Hallowell, 1936), 79–80; Paul Goodman, *The Democratic-Republicans of Massachusetts: Politics in a Young Republic* (Cambridge, Mass., 1964), 122–123; Ronald F. Banks, *Maine Becomes a State: The Movement to Separate Maine from Massachusetts, 1785–1820* (Middletown, Conn., 1970), 48–49; George Augustus Wheeler and Henry Warren Wheeler, *History of Brunswick, Topsham, and Harpswell, Maine . . .* (Boston, 1878), 758. Banks and the Wheelers take at face value King's subsequent (and politically useful) assertion that he was a self-made man who arrived barefoot in Topsham to commence his fortune. On King's wealthy father, see James S. Leamon, "The Stamp Act Crisis in Maine: The Case of Scarborough," MeHS, *Newsletter*, XI (1971–1972), 72–93.

3. My interpretation of the Jeffersonians relies on Joyce Appleby, *Capitalism and a New Social Order: The Republican Vision of the 1790s* (New York, 1984); Appleby, "Commercial Farming and the 'Agrarian Myth' in the Early Republic,"

Journal of American History, LXVIII (1981–1982), 833–849; Appleby, "What Is Still American in the Political Philosophy of Thomas Jefferson?" *WMQ*, 3d Ser., XXXIX (1982), 287–309. Appleby dissents from those historians who portray the Jeffersonians as nostalgic agrarians and civic humanists fearful of commercial development. For the latter perspective, see Lance Banning, *The Jeffersonian Persuasion: Evolution of a Party Ideology* (Ithaca, N.Y., 1978); Banning, "Jeffersonian Ideology Revisited: Liberal and Classical Ideas in the New American Republic," *WMQ*, 3d Ser., XLIII (1986), 3–19. On the commonwealth's Jeffersonians, see Goodman, *The Democratic-Republicans*, 97–127; James M. Banner, Jr., *To the Hartford Convention: The Federalists and the Origins of Party Politics in Massachusetts, 1789–1815* (New York, 1969), 168–215. Cyrus Eaton, *History of Thomaston, Rockland, and South Thomaston* . . . (Hallowell, 1865), I, 260.

4. Joyce Appleby, "What Is Still American?" *WMQ*, 3d Ser., XXXIX (1982), 307–308; Gordon S. Wood, "Interests and Disinterestedness in the Making of the Constitution," in Richard Beeman *et al.*, eds., *Beyond Confederation: Origins of the Constitution and American National Identity* (Chapel Hill, N.C., 1987), 69–112. By "Federalists" I refer to the "Old Federalists" of David Hackett Fischer, *The Revolution of American Conservatism: The Federalist Party in the Era of Jeffersonian Democracy* (New York, 1965).

5. Eaton, *Thomaston*, I, 260; Joseph W. Porter, "Memoir of General Henry Knox," *BHM*, V, 129.

6. Of the 75 mid-Maine communities detected by the 1800 federal census, 55 voted in 1803, and 20 did not; 29 of 55 towns cast 90% of their ballots for one candidate, 26 of those 29 for the Federalist Caleb Strong. The Federalists won majorities in 44 of 55 towns and 2,861 of the 4,005 votes. In the 17 towns *with* a Congregational church, the Federalists polled 1,284 votes (78.3%) versus 344 (21.0%) for the Jeffersonian Republicans, with 12 votes scattered. This compares to the 38 towns *without* a Congregational church, where the Federalists won 1,577 votes (66.7%) to the Republicans' 783 (33.1%), with 5 votes scattered. In the 37 towns *with* a squire in 1800, the Federalists captured 2,288 votes (74.3%) versus 777 (25.3%) for the Republicans, with 13 votes scattered. In the 18 towns *without* a justice, the Federalists polled 575 votes (61.1%) to the Republicans' 350 (37.7%), with 4 votes scattered. In the 24 voting towns involved in the resistance in 1800, the Federalists reaped 1,073 votes (67.1%) to 524 (32.8%) for the Republicans, with 1 scattered vote. This compares to the 31 nonresisting towns, which cast 1,788 (74.3%) Federalist votes to 603 (25.1%) for the Republicans, with 16 scattered votes. The 1803 votes from mid-Maine towns are recorded in "Abstract of Votes for Governor and Lieutenant Governor, 1785–1819," MA; James Shurtleff, *The Substance of a Late Remarkable Dream* . . . (Hallowell, 1800; E 38584), 15, 19.

7. Henry Knox's draft of the committee report, ca. 1803, HKP, XLV, 135, MHS.

8. *Eastern Argus* (Portland), Mar. 15, 1805 ("Turn Out!"), July 5, 1805 ("supercilious"); William G. McLoughlin, *New England Dissent, 1630–1833: Baptists and the Separation of Church and State* (Cambridge, Mass., 1971), II, 1065–1083, 1122–1126. On p. 1078, McLoughlin speaks of James Sullivan's "studied ambiguity on the question of religious taxes"; the same could be said of the Jeffersonians' positions, in general, and on the land issue, in particular. James Sullivan, *The History of the District of Maine* (Augusta, 1970; reprint of Boston, 1795), 62, 110, 139, seems to attack proprietary patents; but on p. 127 Sullivan argues that proprietary grants were essential to control frontier society. David Crowell

354 Notes to pp. 212–214

to William D. Williamson, May 5, 1821, filed under "Whitefield," WDWTP,
MeHS; James Robinson, Jr., to Williamson, ca. 1820, filed under "Jefferson,"
WDWTP, MeHS.

9. *Gazette of Maine* (Buckstown), Apr. 10, 1806; Banks, *Maine Becomes a State,*
41–47; George Ulmer to William King, Mar. 17, 1807, WKP, box 6, MeHS;
William Allen, *History of Industry, Maine* . . . (Skowhegan, 1869), 20; vote totals
for Maine's counties calculated from the "Abstract of Votes for Governor and
Lieutenant Governor, 1785–1819," MA.

10. Eaton, *Thomaston,* I, 260; Henry Jackson Knox to Henry Knox, Mar. 28,
1805, HKP, XLVI, 38, MHS; Henry Knox to John Gleason, Apr. 24, 1806, HKP,
XLVI, 132, MHS. Eaton mistakenly identifies Bernard as the winner in 1804;
for Adams as, in fact, the winner, see *The Massachusetts Register and United States
Calendar: For the Year of Our Lord 1805* . . . (Boston, 1804; S-S 6750), 35.

11. Henry Knox to Israel Thorndike, Aug. 14, 1805, HKP, XLVI, 74, MHS;
"Statement of Purchases of Land from Henry Knox, Esq. to Israel Thorndike,
David Sears, and William Prescott," July 25, 1806, HKP, XLIX, 151, MHS; J. D.
Forbes, *Israel Thorndike: Federalist Financier* (New York, 1953), 94–95; Joseph
Williamson, *History of the City of Belfast* . . . , I (Portland, 1877), 48; Cyrus Eaton,
Annals of the Town of Warren (Hallowell, 1877), 300; Charles Willing Hare to the
Trustees of the Bingham Estate, Feb. 11, 1807, in Frederick S. Allis, Jr., ed.,
William Bingham's Maine Lands, 1790–1820, 2 vols. (Colonial Society of Massa-
chusetts, *Publications,* XXXVI–XXXVII [Boston, 1954]), II, 1215 (hereafter
cited as Allis, ed., *Bingham's Maine Lands*); on Knox's death, see Henry Jackson
Knox to Henry Jackson, Oct. 28, 1806, HKP, XLVI, 155, MHS; on Knox's insol-
vency, see Lucy Knox's petition to the Supreme Judicial Court, Sept. 1809, LC-
SJC Record Book, III, 329, LCC; and "Inventory of Henry Knox's Estate," June
17, 1807, HKP, XLIX, 164, MHS.

12. In 1814 Henry Knox's widow, Lucy, sued Dodge in a vain attempt to
recover payment for some of the general's land that the doctor had acquired.
See Knox v. Dodge, Aug. 1814, LC-CCP, XXVIII, 81, LCC; on the passage of
the "old Federalists," see Fischer, *The Revolution of American Conservatism,* 1–17,
250–251.

13. The proportion of Federalist votes in a town's total in 1807 correlates
strongly and positively with its total valuation in 1802 (r^2 = .27) and with possession of a Congregational church, as a dichotomous variable (r^2 = .28). Naturally, the proportion of Republican votes in a town's total correlates strongly but
negatively with those same variables (r^2 = .28, r^2 = .28). The Federalist proportion correlates strongly but negatively with a town's year of incorporation (r^2 =
.23) and the Republican proportion strongly but positively (r^2 = .23), indicating
that the Federalists did better in the older towns, Republicans better in the
newer ones. In the 16 towns with a Congregational church by 1810 and no
Calvinist Baptist church by 1810, the Federalists prevailed; 1,333 (52.0%) Federalist to 1,221 (47.6%) Republican (10 scattered votes). In the 12 towns with both
Congregational and Calvinist Baptist churches, the Federalists lost: 838 (44.4%)
Federalist to 1,038 (55.0%) Republican (10 scattered votes). In the 30 towns
with a Calvinist Baptist church but no Congregational church, the Republicans
crushed the Federalists: 864 (27.0%) Federalist to 2,326 (72.6%) Republican (12
scattered votes). Finally, in the 7 towns with neither a Calvinist Baptist church
nor a Congregational church, the Republicans did still better: 108 (17.3%) Federalist to 626 (82.1%) Republican. In towns that had a justice of the peace in
1800, the Federalists were more competitive—2,487 (43.2%) Federalist to 3,245
(56.3%) Republican (27 scattered votes)—than in the towns without a justice of

the peace in 1800: 656 (26.0%) Federalist to 1,854 (73.6%) Republican (9 scattered votes). "Abstract of Votes for Governor and Lieutenant Governor, 1785–1819," MA; *Report of the Committee of Valuation* (Boston, 1802; S-S 2625). For the presence of a denomination's church in a given town, see the sources listed in Chapter 5, n. 24, above. For the justices in 1800, see *Fleets' Register, and Pocket Almanack for the Year of Our Lord 1800* (Boston, [1799]; E 35487).

14. I estimated the adult male electorate in Hancock, Kennebec, and Lincoln counties in 1800 from the federal census returns as 14,267 by adding half of the males in the age 16–25 category to the totals in the 26–44 and 45-plus categories. The 4,202 votes cast in 1800 represented 30% of that estimated electorate. In 1810 the same method yielded a potential electorate of 23,380. The 12,241 votes cast in 1810 represented 52% of that estimated electorate. By contrast, the same method applied to Massachusetts counties in 1800 indicates that 31,001 of 90,942 voted, for a 34% turnout. In 1810, 56,518 of 94,408 voted, for a 64% turnout. In 1800, 154 of Massachusetts' 276 (56%) towns sent at least one representative to the General Court. In 1810, 255 of Massachusetts' 285 (90%) towns sent at least one representative to the General Court. (For mid-Maine the figures are, for 1800, 20 of 75, and, for 1810, 48 of 83.) This demonstrates that, although mid-Maine's political participation increased dramatically, it still lagged behind that of more populous and more prosperous Massachusetts. For the votes from mid-Maine towns, see the 1800 and 1810 returns in the "Abstract of Votes for Governor and Lieutenant Governor, 1785–1819," MA; for town representation see, *Fleets' Register, 1800*; *The Massachusetts Register and United States Calendar; for the Year of Our Lord, 1810 . . .* (Boston, [1809]; S-S 18057). In 1800 mid-Maine had a population of 52,826 and sent 20 representatives; in 1810 it had a population of 84,976 and sent 58 representatives.

15. For the justices, see *Fleets' Register, 1800*; *The Massachusetts Register, 1810.* The quote is from the Kennebec County petition of John Davis *et al.*, ca. Jan. 1808, Related Papers, Betterment Act of Mar. 2, 1808, MA; Davis was the petition's author, clerk of the Kennebec Court of Common Pleas, and a local Jeffersonian leader; unlike petitions by settlers, this is written in a fine script and is replete with florid phrases. In 1800, 9 of 39 backcountry communities had a squire; in 1810, 30 of 47.

16. For a Federalist's criticism of Dearborn's popular style, see "A Soldier," *Kennebeck Intelligencer* (Hallowell), Oct. 29, 1796; Samuel S. Wilde to David Cobb, Jan. 2, 1802, in Allis, ed., *Bingham's Maine Lands*, II, 1141–1142.

17. James Sullivan, *The Path to Riches . . .* (Boston, 1792; E 24829). On the Jeffersonians' internal split between commercial and agrarian wings, see Richard E. Ellis, *The Jeffersonian Crisis: Courts and Politics in the Young Republic* (New York, 1971), 207–217. In 1807, 30 of the resisting communities (as of 1800) voted 2,318 (67.9%) Republican, versus 1,080 (31.7%) Federalist (14 votes scattered). This contrasted with 35 nonresisting communities (as of 1800) that voted 2,781 (57.2%) Republican, versus 2,063 (42.4%) Federalist (with 22 scattered votes). The votes were collected from "Abstract of Votes for Governor and Lieutenant Governor, 1785–1819," MA. On the Republicans' failure to alter the commonwealth's land policies when in power, 1807–1809, see "A Friend to the Interests of Maine," *Bangor Weekly Register*, Apr. 6, 1816; and Moses Greenleaf, *A Statistical Survey of the District of Maine . . .* (Boston, 1816; S-S 37745), 93–99.

18. Goodman, *The Democratic Republicans*, 161–162; Ellis, *Jeffersonian Crisis*, 224–229; Joseph Foxcroft to William King, Dec. 5, 1807, Abijah Richardson to King, Jan. 17, 1808, WKP, box 7, MeHS.

19. On Sullivan, see Joseph Pierce to Henry Knox, June 5, 1791, HKP, XXIX,

86, MHS; "Memoir of Governor James Sullivan," *BHM*, VII, 36–39; Thomas C. Amory, *Life of James Sullivan* . . . , 2 vols. (Boston, 1859). For Dearborn, see H.A.S. Dearborn, "Major General Henry Dearborn," 19–23; Cochrane, *Monmouth*, I, 70; Gardiner, *Early Recollections*, 79, 190; Marvin S. Sadik, *Colonial and Federal Portraits at Bowdoin College* (Brunswick, 1966), 151; J. W. Hanson, *History of Gardiner, Pittston, and West Gardiner* (Gardiner, 1852), 144–145. For Morton, see Clifford K. Shipton, *Biographical Sketches of Those Who Attended Harvard College* . . . [*Sibley's Harvard Graduates*], 14 vols. (Cambridge, Mass., Boston, 1933–1975), XVII, 555–561; for Morton's land agency, see the advertisement in *Independent Chronicle* (Boston), May 19, 1791. For Eustis, see Henry Jackson to Knox, Jan. 17, 1790, Mar. 7, 1790, HKP, XXV, 100, 162, MHS; Ellis, *Jeffersonian Crisis*, 208.

20. Henry Knox to George Ulmer, Oct. 28, 1801, HKP, box 2 (Deeds), MeHS; Ulmer to Knox, Oct. 30, Nov. 13, 1801, HKP, box 6, MeHS; Knox to Ulmer, Nov. 16, 1801, HKP, XLIV, 134, MHS; and (for the quote) Ulmer to Knox, Nov. 15, 1801, HKP, XLIV, 133, MHS. Ulmer's final account as Knox's land agent is Dec. 4, 1801, HKP, XLIV, 153, MHS.

21. "General George Ulmer," *BHM*, II, 118; Amory, *Life of James Sullivan*, II, 275; *Eastern Argus*, Apr. 6, 1808; Alan Taylor, "The Rise and Fall of George Ulmer: Political Entrepreneurship in the Age of Jefferson and Jackson," *Colby Library Quarterly*, XXI (1985), 58–59.

22. The voting figures are derived from "Votes for Senators, 1805," Council Records, MA.

23. George Ulmer to Henry Knox, Apr. 12, 1806, HKP, XLVI, 129, MHS; Knox to Ulmer, May 11, 1806, HKP, XLVI, 135, MHS.

24. Allis, ed., *Bingham's Maine Lands*, II, 1173–1177; Harrison Gray Otis to Charles Willing Hare, June 22, 1805, David Cobb to Charles Willing Hare, Mar. 2, 1806, Alexander Baring to Hope and Company, July 9, 1812, *ibid.*, II, 1189–1190, 1193–1194, 1240.

25. David Cobb to Charles Willing Hare, Mar. 2, 1806, Hare to Harrison Gray Otis, Jan. 7, 1807, General Court Resolve of Jan. 17, 1807, Hare (quote) to the Trustees of the Bingham Estate, Feb. 11, 1807, in Allis, ed., *Bingham's Maine Lands*, II, 1194, 1212–1217.

26. William King to Nathaniel Dudley, Jan. 21, 1815, Mar. 18, 1816, *Maine Historical and Genealogical Recorder*, I (1884), 100–101; Allen, "Bingham Lands," MeHS, *Colls.*, 1st Ser., VII (1876), 358.

27. Banks, *Maine Becomes a State*, 55; George Ulmer to William King, Mar. 17, Sept. 11, 1807, WKP, box 6, MeHS; "Abstract of Votes for Governor and Lieutenant Governor, 1785–1819," MA; Waterman Thomas to William King, June 2, 1807, WKP, box 7, MeHS.

28. James Berry Vickery, *A History of the Town of Unity, Maine* (Manchester, 1954), 42; "To the Settlers on the Plymouth Patent," *Portland Gazette*, Feb. 22, 1808; Benjamin Whitwell, *Certain Statements First Published in the Kennebec Gazette* . . . (Augusta, 1810; S-S 22051), 3; Kennebeck Proprietors, *A Few Facts, Stated by the Proprietors of Land in the County of Kennebeck, Tending to Show the Injustice of the Present Trespassers on Said Land* (Boston, 1808; copy in KPP, box 7, MeHS).

29. Banks, *Maine Becomes a State*, 55–56; Amory, *Life of James Sullivan*, II, 277; Betterment Act, Chapter LXXIV (Mar. 2, 1808), in *Laws of the Commonwealth of Massachusetts* . . . [*1806–1809*] (Boston, 1808; S-S 15525), 290–292. Kentucky's 1797 "occupying claimants law" may have been a model for King's bill; see Paul W. Gates, "Tenants of the Log Cabin," in Gates, *Landlords and Tenants on the Prairie Frontier: Studies in American Land Policy* (Ithaca, N.Y., 1973), 13–47.

30. Robert Gould Shaw to James Bridge and Reuel Williams, Feb. 20, 1808 (includes Otis quote), RWP, box 3, MeHS; "The Proprietors," *Boston Gazette*, Jan. 28, 1808; "Standing Laws," *Boston Gazette*, Feb. 1, 1808; the Kennebeck Proprietors' Memorial to the General Court, Feb. 8, 1808, in the Related Papers, Act LXXIV (Mar. 2, 1808), MA; Betterment Act, Chapter LXXIV (Mar. 2, 1808), in *Laws of the Commonwealth of Massachusetts, [1806–1809]*, 290–292. On the defeat of the agrarian legal program and its consequences for the resistance, see Ellis, *Jeffersonian Crisis*, 221–223, 229. For favorable proprietary impressions of the Betterment Act, see Arodi Thayer to Charles Hayden, Mar. 7, 1808, Thayer to James Bridge and Reuel Williams, July 7, 1808, KPP, Letterbook, I, 228, 245, MeHS; Samuel Spear to James Bridge and Reuel Williams, Nov. 1, 1808, RWP, box 3, MeHS; Joseph H. Pierce, Jr., to Major Eusebius Fales, July 8, 1825, HAPP, box 1, folder 3, NEHGSL.

31. By 1810 most settlers who had been on the land for a decade or more had accumulated enough invested labor in their lands to achieve their coveted competency. Those settlers resident in Balltown (Jefferson and Whitefield) in 1800 who persisted to their towns' 1811 tax lists (158 of 289) owned an average of 119 acres of land—including 15 improved acres—raised 31 bushels of grain and 8 head of mature livestock. Three-quarters of these settlers lived in frame houses (119 of 158) rather than log cabins, and another three-quarters (118 of 158) housed their grateful livestock in barns. Most had attained the 30-bushel annual grain production necessary for family subsistence. The more labor they put into their homesteads and the higher the resistance's stakes mounted, the more anxious they became over their lack of secure title. Younger men needed time to replicate the longer residents' success. On the 1811 tax lists for Jefferson and Whitefield, new taxpayers (post-1800) owned two-thirds as much land (79 acres), possessed about half the improved acreage (8), annually raised less than half as much grain (13 bushels), and sustained half as many mature livestock (4) as taxpayers resident since 1800. Where three-quarters of the persisters had frame houses and barns, fewer than half the new taxpayers did (100 of 219). Possessing fewer resources to pay the proprietors and having less at risk should the resistance fall short, these settlers were less tempted to reach an accommodation. For the Jefferson-Whitefield holdovers from 1800: acres of improved land (2,267 sum, 156 observations, 10.9 standard deviation), homestead size (18,606 sum, 156 observations, 89.3 standard deviation), head of mature livestock (1,201 sum, 156 observations, 4.5 standard deviation), and bushels of grain (4,831 sum, 156 observations, 20.1 standard deviation). For the newcomers: acres of improved land (1,762 sum, 220 observations [1 missing observation], 11.3 standard deviation), homestead size (17,316 acres sum, 220 observations [1 missing observation], 80.6 standard deviation), head of mature livestock (949 sum, 220 observations [1 missing observation], 4.0 standard deviation), and bushels of grain (2,777 sum, 221 observations, 18.2 standard deviation). Jefferson and Whitefield valuation lists, 1811, box 400 (microfilm), MSL. Elisha Sylvester to Josiah Little, July 10, 1806, PPP, box 17, folder 1806–1810, EI. The deeds from Little to Greene settlers during the period Dec. 1805–May 1808 are KCD, IX, 118, 478, 512, X, 56, 59, 160, XI, 42 (x 3), 143, XIII, 293, XV, 607, XVII, 166, 190, 438, 494, XXI, 86, XXIII, 33, 228 (x 2), XXIV, 342, KCRD; they total 1,271.5 acres for $5,331.01.

32. James Shurtleff to William King, Jan. 11, 1808, Litchfield, Bowdoin, and Wales petition to the General Court, May 1, 1808, John Neal to King, Mar. 21, 1808, WKP, box 7, MeHS; the Sept. 27, 1800, writ for the arrest of Calvin Hall, Lemuel Neal, and others, KC-SJC files, box 72, MeSA; Cochrane, *Monmouth*, II,

524, presents a misdated and erroneous account of the Lemuel Neal incident; Walter Goodwin Davis, *The Ancestry of Joseph Neal, 1769–1835, of Litchfield* (Portland, 1945), 5, 9–10, 13; *History of Litchfield and an Account of Its Centennial Celebration, 1895* (Augusta, 1897), 234–235.

33. Amory, *Life of James Sullivan,* II, 278; Charles Vaughan to the Kennebeck Proprietors, Mar. 19, 1808, KPP, box 6, MeHS; John Chandler to Gov. James Sullivan, Mar. 18, 1808, Apr. 18, 1808, in House Files (unpassed) 6384, 6385, MA; *Portland Gazette,* June 6, 1808; James Shurtleff to William King, Jan. 11, 1808, WKP, box 7, MeHS; John Neal to William King, Mar. 21, 1808, WKP, box 7, MeHS; John Neal to the General Court, ca. Jan. 1810, Related Papers, Resolve CXLVII (Mar. 3, 1810), MA ("rowaring"). On the costs of Betterment Act suits, see the Kennebeck Proprietors to the General Court, Feb. 24, 1810, KPP, Record Book, IV, 414, MeHS. Defendants who invoked the Betterment Act obtained only limited protection. In Oct. 1810 the Supreme Judicial Court ruled on the most important ejectment cases brought by the Kennebeck Proprietors in their struggle to regain legal control over the Sheepscot backcountry. The seven defendants dwelled in Beaver Hill (Freedom), long the most isolated and most militant settlement in the Plymouth Patent. Four of the defendants were their settlement's original settlers, leading Liberty Men, and brothers: James, John, Joshua, and Stephen Smith. When the four Smiths and another defendant invoked the Betterment Act, the jury assessed the land at $2.00–$2.50 per acre and valued their improvements at $300 (Joshua Smith), $300 (John Smith), $325 (James Smith), $600 (Benjamin Cummings), and $650 (Stephen Smith). Instead of buying the improvements, the Kennebeck Proprietors chose payments from the five for the land value and for court costs that averaged $99 per defendant. On average, this raised the five settlers' price to secure their homesteads to $3.26 per acre. If the settlers' own legal fees matched the proprietors', their total price rose to $4.00 per acre, no bargain where unoccupied land usually sold for about $3.00 per acre. The four Smiths apparently could not afford to pay within the three-year period, for in Feb. 1816 the Kennebeck Proprietors sold their unpaid-for homesteads to Robert Hallowell Gardiner. Because they had not been on the land for the requisite six years, the two younger defendants—James Smith, Jr., and John Rider—could not even enjoy the Betterment Act's limited protection; they defaulted, losing their homesteads as well as their costs of court. The Kennebeck Proprietors repossessed the land but probably did not attempt to collect the legal costs from young Smith and Rider. See James Bridge and Reuel Williams, memorandum on the Kennebeck Proprietors' legal cases, Oct. 1810, KPP, box 7, MeHS; Reuel Williams *et al.* to the Kennebeck Proprietors, ca. 1811, KPP, Record Book, V, 12–13, MeHS; on the Smiths' failure to pay, see KPP, Grant Books, VI, 11 (Feb. 22, 1811), MeHS.

34. Act LXXXIII (Mar. 2, 1810), Act CXXII (Mar. 6, 1810), in *Laws of the Commonwealth of Massachusetts . . . [1809–1811]* (Boston, 1811); S-S 23309), 121–122, 218–221; Aaron Blaney, Jr., to Aaron Blaney, Sr., Nov. 1810, in Lincoln County Miscellaneous Papers and Deeds, MeHS.

35. Vickery, *Unity,* 43; Charles Vaughan *et al.* to the Kennebeck Proprietors, Oct. 13, 1809, Oct. 23, 1810, Reuel Williams's Account, Mar. 1, 1811, KPP, box 7, MeHS; Aug. 28, 1810, entry, KPP, Grant Books, IV, 363, MeHS; Isaac Davis's Account, Jan. 23, 1811, KPP, box 8, MeHS; Commonwealth v. John Philbrook *et al.,* Sept. 1810, LC-SJC Record Book, III, 459, LCC. On Palermo, see *Portland Gazette,* Dec. 19, 1808; Arodi Thayer to James Bridge and Reuel Williams, Aug. 1, 1808, Oct. 24, 1808, Feb. 2, 1809 (quotation), KPP, Letterbook, I, 250, 263, 284, MeHS. Marsh's testimony appears in John Merrick, ed., *Trial of David Lynn*

... *for the Murder of Paul Chadwick at Malta* ... (Augusta, 1809; S-S 18778), 14; Parker's charge to the jury appears on p. 42.

36. N. E. Wells, "The Early Settlers of Montville," *Republican Journal* (Belfast), Feb. 5, 1885; Matthew Randall to William D. Williamson, ca. 1820, filed under "Freedom," WDWTP, MeHS; Report on Land Divisions, Nov. 17, 1810, KPP, Record Book, IV, 459–460, MeHS; on the number of incidents, see Figure 1. For animal mutilations, see the papers relating to Commonwealth v. Richard Garlin, box 167, HC-SJC files, MeSA; Commonwealth v. Richard Garlin, June 1818, HC-SJC Records, IV, 4, MeSA; Kennebeck Proprietors v. John Clark, Oct. 1821, LC-SJC Records, V, 264, LCC. It is revealing that the General Court's strict Mar. 1805 "Incendiary Act" targeted against the resistance contained no penalties against maiming livestock. But in Feb. 1821, after the organized resistance had faded, the new Maine State Legislature passed an incendiary law that essentially copied its 1805 predecessor. The sole addition stipulated a fine of $500 or up to six months solitary confinement, followed by three more years imprisonment at hard labor for anyone who "wilfully and maliciously, passionately, cruelly, or barbarously [did] kill, wound, maim, or disfigure any one or more of the horses, sheep, or cattle of another." This suggests that livestock maiming became far more common between 1805 and 1821, a period associated with the resistance's decline. See The Massachusetts Incendiary Act, Chapter LXXXV (Mar. 16, 1805), in *Acts and Laws Passed by the General Court of Massachusetts [Jan.–Mar. 1805]* ([Boston, 1805]; S-S 8856), 661–662; the Maine Incendiary Act, Chapter 4 (Feb. 24, 1821), in *Laws of the State of Maine, from the Separation to 1833 Inclusive* ..., 2d ed. (Hallowell, 1834), I, 58.

37. Jonathan Mower, Jr., *et al.*, petition to the General Court, ca. Dec. 1806, Related Papers, Resolve LX (Feb. 24, 1807), MA; "Truth," *Eastern Argus*, Mar. 26, 1807; Resolve LX (Feb. 24, 1807), in *Resolves of the General Court of the Commonwealth of Massachusetts ... [Jan.–Feb. 1807]* (Boston, 1807; S-S 13029), 41–42; Luther Robbins to William King, Nov. 30, 1810, "Pejepscot Petition," ca. Jan. 1812, WKP, box 10, MeHS; Commonwealth v. Pejepscot Proprietors, Cumberland County SJC Record Book, III, 552, MeSA.

38. Memorandum of Joseph H. Pierce, Jr., ca. 1810, Winthrop Family Letters, II, 96, BPL ("to remove"); Joseph H. Pierce, Jr., to Joseph H. Pierce, Sr., Dec. 18, 1811, HAPP, box 3, NEHGSL ("wretchedness").

39. Aug. 28, 1810, grants to Malta settlers, KPP, Grant Books, IV, 383–415, MeHS. These totaled $8,997.13 for 3,510.5 acres, all within the survey completed Apr. 14, 1810, by Isaac Davis and James Marr. The deeds from Little to Greene residents, Aug. 1813–Jan. 1818 are KCD, XXI, 572, XXIII, 20, 33, 64, 132, 159, 160, 334, 382, 383, 403, 413, 492, 493, 500, 546, 547, XXIV, 15, 37, 71, 136, 160, 168, 170, 307, XXV, 319, 352, 353, 380, 402, 421, XXVIII, 58, 238, 239, 274, 322, 324, 325, 329, 344, 362, XXIX, 140, 164, 165, 166, 210, 211, 228, 283, 294, 394, 412, 420, 421, XXX, 27, 42, 46, 173, 205, 220, 221, 478, 480, XXXI, 106, 131, XXXIII, 254, 327, XXXIV, 75, 202, 271, KCRD. Of the deeds, 7 give no acreage, so the calculations are based on the 62 that do. Because of the War of 1812 and the cold year of 1816, land may have been less valuable in 1813–1818 than in 1805–1808, although Col. Little did not see it that way. Josiah Little's memo book, Sept. 3, 1814, entry, PPP, box 5 ("1782–1829 Books"), EI.

40. "A Friend to Justice," *Independent Chronicle*, Dec. 13, 1810; John Johnston, *A History of the Towns of Bristol and Bremen* ... (Albany, N.Y., 1873), 482–484; Aaron Blaney, Jr., to Aaron Blaney, Sr., Nov. 1810, in Lincoln County Miscellaneous Papers and Deeds, MeHS; Elliot G. Vaughan's statement to the Lincoln

County Grand Jury, ca. Oct. 1810, in miscellaneous box 23 ("Papers Relating to the Tappan and Drowne Claims . . ."), MA; Report of the Committee considering Judge Thatcher's Letter to Gov. Elbridge Gerry, Oct. 26, 1810, Council Records, XXXVI (1810–1811), MA; Johnston, *History of Bristol and Bremen*, 487–489; Elliot G. Vaughan to Col. Thomas Cutts, Oct. 30, 1810, James Malcom to George Thatcher, Oct. 23, 1810, Silas Lee to Gov. Elbridge Gerry, Nov. 15, 1810, Alden Bradford to George Thatcher, Oct. 17, 1810, all in miscellaneous box 24 ("Papers Relating to Lands in Lincoln County . . ."), MA.

41. Johnston, *History of Bristol and Bremen*, 482, 489–496; John Hannibal Sheppard, *The Life of Samuel Tucker . . .* (Boston, 1868), 212–213; George Thatcher to Elbridge Gerry, Oct. 30, 1810, in miscellaneous box 24 ("Papers Relating to Lands in Lincoln County . . ."), MA; Committee Report on Judge Thatcher's letter to Gov. Elbridge Gerry, Oct. 26, 1810, Council Records, XXXVI (1810–1811), MA; Samuel Reed to William King, Jan. 11, 1811, WKP, box 10, MeHS; *Order of Both Branches of the Legislature of Massachusetts to Appoint Commissioners to Investigate the Causes of the Difficulties in the County of Lincoln . . .* (Boston, 1811; S-S 23314); Robert H. Gardiner, "History of the Kennebec Purchase . . . ," MeHS, *Colls.*, 1st Ser., II (1847), 292; Act CXXI (Feb. 28, 1811), in *Laws of the Commonwealth of Massachusetts, [1809–1811]*, 371.

42. "Lincoln County Settlers," 1813, MA; Resolve of Feb. 25, 1813, in *Resolves of the Commonwealth of Massachusetts . . . [1812–1815]* (Boston, 1812–1815; S-S 26023), 203–205; Ephraim Rollins to William D. Williamson, May 1821, filed under "Nobleborough," WDWTP, MeHS; Sheppard, *Samuel Tucker*, 215.

43. For Federalist land speculation, see Malcolm J. Rohrbough, *The Land Office Business: The Settlement and Administration of American Public Lands, 1789–1837* (New York, 1968), 19–21; Andrew R. L. Cayton, *The Frontier Republic: Ideology and Politics in the Ohio Country, 1780–1825* (Kent, Ohio, 1986), 33–50. On the differing Federalist and Republican styles in dealing with popular protest, see Thomas P. Slaughter, *The Whiskey Rebellion: Frontier Epilogue to the American Revolution* (New York, 1986), 105, 225–227.

44. Ellis, *Jeffersonian Crisis*, 262–265; Richard Buel, Jr., *Securing the Revolution: Ideology in American Politics, 1789–1815* (Ithaca, N.Y., 1972), 137–240; John R. Howe, Jr., "Republican Thought and the Political Violence of the 1790s," *American Quarterly*, XIX (1967), 147–165; Banning, "Jeffersonian Ideology Revisited," *WMQ*, 3d Ser., XLIII (1986), 11–13; Joyce Appleby, "Republicanism in Old and New Contexts," *WMQ*, 3d Ser., XLIII (1986), 20–34.

45. Richard Hofstadter, *The American Political Tradition and the Men Who Made It*, 2d ed. (New York, 1973), 45–49; Richard L. Bushman, *King and People in Provincial Massachusetts* (Chapel Hill, N.C., 1985), 235–251. It is revealing that mid-Maine's resistance persisted longest in Freedom, where the inhabitants clung to the archaic language of the protection covenant into the 1820s. In an Aug. 1820 letter to the governor's council on behalf of his neighbors in Freedom, Thomas Sinclair deferentially addressed the councillors as "wise men who are able to correct our mistaks, before whom we lay our selves open to Conviction and reproof, from whom we hope to recive instruction." The settlers sought "friendly admonition from those who have the rule over us." Thomas Sinclair to Col. Thomas Fillebrown, Aug. 16, 1820, Secretary of State's Correspondence, box 1, folder 4, MeSA.

46. Gates, "Tenants of the Log Cabin," in Gates, *Landlords and Tenants*, 24, 43; Slaughter, *The Whiskey Rebellion*, 226; Rohrbough, *The Land Office Business*, 23–31; Paul Demund Evans, *The Holland Land Company* (Buffalo Historical Society, *Publications*, XXVIII [Buffalo, N.Y., 1924]), 122–169; Elizabeth K. Henderson,

"The Northwestern Lands of Pennsylvania, 1790–1812," *Pennsylvania Magazine of History and Biography*, LX (1936), 131–160; Julian P. Boyd *et al.*, eds., *The Susquehannah Company Papers* (Ithaca, N.Y., 1930–1971), XI, xv–xxviii; Louise Welles Murray, *A History of Old Tioga Point and Early Athens, Pennsylvania* (Athens, Pa., 1908), 449–450; Alfred F. Young, *The Democratic Republicans of New York: The Origins, 1763–1797* (Chapel Hill, N.C., 1967), 205–206, 533–535; David Maldwyn Ellis, *Landlords and Farmers in the Hudson-Mohawk Region, 1790–1850* (Ithaca, N.Y., 1946), 35–36, 151–154.

47. Richard E. Ellis, "The Persistence of Antifederalism after 1789," in Beeman *et al.*, eds., *Beyond Confederation*, 295–315; Banning, *The Jeffersonian Persuasion*, 273–302.

CHAPTER NINE

1. The epigraphs are from James Robinson, Jr., to William D. Williamson, ca. 1820, WDWTP, filed under "Jefferson," MeHS; and Walter Lindley Mower, *Sesquicentennial History of the Town of Greene, Androscoggin County, Maine . . .* ([Auburn], 1938), 4. Palermo selectmen's petition to the General Court, Jan. 20, 1812, WKP, "Miscellaneous Political Papers" box, MeHS. The 1811 tax list for Palermo reveals that various Kennebeck Proprietors still held 9,958 acres, about two-fifths of the town's total area (25,866 acres). Palermo's 1811 Valuation Return, box 400 (microfilm), MSL. The Kennebeck Proprietors' records indicate that the company or individual members held 13,247 acres there in Nov. 1810. See the KPP, Record Book, V, 16, MeHS; KPP, Grant Book, IV, 291–306, 348, 363–375, 380–381, V, 26–27, 32, 45, 54, 73, 82, 87, 93, 99, 106, 111, 114, 120, 125, 126, 133, 152, 161, 169, 183, 187, 196, 212, 223, 233, 238, 246, 362, VI, 9, 10, 17, 22, 26, 29, 42, MeHS. According to the Plymouth Company's records, during the period July 1, 1809–Dec. 31, 1811, the 36 sales to Palermo settlers averaged $3.24 per acre. Where all but 4 of the 79 submittees of 1802–1803 had fulfilled their payments, 11 of the 36 purchasers fell short and had their grants canceled; the canceled grants accounted for 36% of the acres and 38% of the moneys covered by the 1809–1811 sales. The 36 sales amounted to an aggregate 3,686.5 acres for $11,948.46. For submittees who did not pay, see Arodi Thayer to James Bridge and Reuel Williams, July 13, 1809, KPP, Letterbook, II, 1, MeHS. After 1811 the Kennebeck Proprietors sold their land off very slowly; in 1834 more than half (5,090 acres) of their 1811 acreage remained in the hands of nonresident proprietors, meaning that land sales averaged only 212 acres per year during the 23-year interim. The 1834 Palermo tax list is in the possession of Millard Howard of Palermo, who generously allowed me to copy it.

Palermo's out-migration had increased dramatically, particularly among the young men. Ready access to wild land encouraged almost two-thirds of the 1800 heads of household (45 of 72) and about half of their sons (30 of 59) who came of age during the 1800s to persist to 1810. But only half the 1810 heads of household (66 of 129) and but two-fifths of their sons (43 of 108) who came of age during the 1810s remained in 1820. See the 1800 return for Sheepscot Great Pond, Lincoln County, Second Census of the United States, 1800, M32, reel 6; the 1810 return for Palermo, Lincoln County, Third Census of the United States, 1810, M252, reel 12; the 1820 return for Palermo, Lincoln County, Fourth Census of the United States, 1820, M33, reel 36, NA.

Tax lists confirm that poorer, younger men tended to flee Palermo, leaving their more prosperous parents behind. Of the 1806 taxpayers, 78 persisted to 1811, and 32 departed. On average, those 1806 taxpayers who remained in 1811 paid almost twice as high a tax ($3.33) as those who departed by 1811 ($1.76). Similarly, the 1811 taxpayers who persisted to 1820 possessed an average of 100 acres (10 of them improved), 7 head of mature livestock, and 15 bushels of grain. In contrast, those who left town by 1820 possessed only 55 acres (4 of them improved), 4 head of mature livestock, and a meager 4 bushels of grain. Of the 1811 taxpayers, 81 persisted from 1811 to 1820, and 66 departed. Two-thirds of the 1811–1820 persisters owned frame houses (53 of 81) and barns (54 of 81), compared to only one-third of those who departed (25 of 66, 22 of 66). Because the poorer, younger sort who had supported the resistance tended to depart, only 11 of the town's 27 identifiable Liberty Men remained in 1820. See the Palermo 1806 Highway Tax list, reprinted in Millard A. Howard, *An Introduction to the Early History of Palermo, Maine* (Augusta, 1976), 28–31; the 1811 Palermo Valuation Return, box 400 (microfilm), MSL.

It is revealing that nearby Jefferson—the lone backcountry community to escape proprietary land payments—was better able to retain its inhabitants. Two-thirds of Jefferson's 1810 heads of households persisted to 1820, compared to only half of Palermo's. And where Palermo's out-migrants were starkly poorer than that town's persisters, only slight property distinctions differentiated those who left Jefferson from those who stayed. In contrast to Palermo, Jefferson's poor young men did not feel pushed to leave, probably because nonresident proprietors did not hold two-fifths of the township's land, as was the case in Palermo. The 1820 Federal Census Return for Jefferson; the 1811 Valuation Returns for Jefferson, microfilm box 400 (1811 Valuation Returns from Maine Towns), MSL; Table 1.

2. Boardman Johnson to William D. Williamson, Dec. 13, 1819, filed under "Jackson," A. H. Giddings to William D. Williamson, Nov. 6, 1826, filed under "Pejepscot," WDWTP, MeHS. Congregational missionaries, who ordinarily sympathized with the Great Proprietors, agreed that they demanded unrealistic prices that undercut local development. See Alfred Johnson to Abiel Holmes, Oct. 31, 1814, Nov. 22, 1814, SPG Papers, box 3, folder 1, EI; Silas Warren to the Society, June 15, 1821, SPG Papers, box 5, folder 6, EI. Moses Greenleaf of Williamsburg, a resident proprietor and land agent, calculated that the region lost at least $458,000 annually in payments to nonresident proprietors. See Moses Greenleaf, *A Statistical View of the District of Maine . . .* (Boston, 1816; S-S 37745), 93–99, quote on 97. Fifteen signed copies of the May 1820 petition (a total of 862 signatures) survive in 1820 Public Law Documents, box 2, envelope 24, MeSA; 21 signed copies of the Jan. 1821 petition (a total of 869 signatures) survive in 1821 Public Law Documents, box 13, envelope 29, MeSA. The petitions protested how some particularly clever proprietary lawyers manipulated the Betterment Act. The Supreme Judicial Court allowed a proprietor to bring two separate suits against the same settler: one for the small improved portion of his homestead and the other for the woodland. By this stratagem the proprietor could, in one suit, completely recover the unimproved woodland without paying the settler anything, while, in the other, oblige the settler to pay the wild land value to secure the handful of improved acres. This deprived the defendant of most of his acreage, leaving him with only the small, unviable plot immediately around his cabin. He had to meet his proprietor's terms to repossess the surrounding woodlot. See also Abram Choate *et al.*, petition to the

General Court, ca. 1811, House File (unpassed) 6908, MA; for a proprietor's admission of the practice, see John Johnson, Jr., to Thomas Johnson, Jan. 6, 1809, Lincoln County Courthouse Collection, box I-18, folder 4, Lincoln County Cultural and Historical Society, Wiscasset.

3. Reuel Williams to Gov. William King, June 26, 1820, Artemas Kimball's deposition, June 19, 1820, Artemas Kimball's deposition, June 23, 1820, Executive Council Files, box 1, MeSA; Thomas Sinclair to Thomas Fillebrown, Secretary of State's Correspondence, box 1, MeSA; Ralph Baker to Reuel Williams, May 25, 1825, Joel Wellington to Williams, May 26, 1825, RWP, box 10, MeHS. For the Freedom settlers' deeds, see KCD, XXXVII, 198, 200, XL, 35, XLIII, 66, 188, 231, 235, XLIV, 111, 112, XLV, 50, 340, XLVI, 76, XLVIII, 405, LVII, 266, LX, 407, KCRD.

4. Michael Smith's deposition, June 9, 1787, PPP, box 20, "Bakerstown, 1780–1794" folder, EI. For proprietors' problems with timber trespasses and town tax assessments, see William Allen, "Ripley and Cambridge," MS, MeHS; Arodi Thayer to James Bridge and Reuel Williams, Apr. 24, 1809, KPP, Letterbook, I, 296, MeHS; James Temple Bowdoin's petition, Dec. 1812, KC-CCP Records, XV, 295, MeSA; Robert E. Moody, ed., *The Saltonstall Papers, 1607–1815*, 2 vols. (MHS, *Collections*, LXXX–LXXXI [Boston, 1972, 1974]), II, 309, 342; Charles Vaughan to Reuel Williams, Jan. 3, 1824, RWP, box 10, MeHS; Joseph H. Pierce, Jr., to William Parkman, Mar. 15, 1816, Pierce to Timothy Copp, July 13, 1821, Pierce to David Fales, Aug. 15, 1821, Pierce to Montville's Assessors, Aug. 22, 1821, HAPP, box 3, NEHGSL.

5. For the boundary resolutions, see Arodi Thayer to Samuel S. Wilde, July 14, 1808, KPP, Letterbook, I, 248, MeHS; Thomas Francis to William D. Williamson, Jan. 12, 1820, filed under "Leeds," WDWTP, MeHS. The distribution of wealth in mid-Maine's backcountry in the 1810s was about the same as it had been in the 1790s. In rural towns six of seven men owned land, and most farms were modest—50–100 acres. Status was similarly stable in the backcountry. In Palermo during the 1810s, about nine tenths of the men considered their status modest—either yeoman or artisan—with fewer than a tenth claiming higher status as gentleman, trader, doctor, or esquire; these proportions matched those of the two preceding decades. Because local resources were limited and out-migration to the frontier drew off the young without property, inequality did not worsen over time in the rural town. Men either inherited landed independence or moved on; those who stayed could expect stability but no riches. See Tables 1, 2, 6; Mighill Parker to Williamson, Mar. 8, 1821, WDWTP, filed under "Islesborough," MeHS; Hal S. Barron, "Staying down on the Farm: Social Processes of Settled Rural Life in the Nineteenth-Century North," in Steven Hahn and Jonathan Prude, eds., *The Countryside in the Age of Capitalist Transformation: Essays in the Social History of Rural America* (Chapel Hill, N.C., 1985), 327–343.

6. William G. McLoughlin, *New England Dissent, 1630–1833: The Baptists and the Separation of Church and State* (Cambridge, Mass., 1971), II, 1107–1113; David Benedict, *A General History of the Baptist Denomination in America* . . . (Boston, 1813; S-S 27873), II, 457, 463–464, 468, 471–472; Joshua Millett, *A History of the Baptists in Maine* (Portland, 1845), 193–194, 246–247; Stephen A. Marini, *Radical Sects of Revolutionary New England* (Cambridge, Mass., 1982), 121–122; Minton Thrift, ed., *Memoir of the Rev. Jesse Lee, with Extracts from His Journals* (New York, 1823; reprint ed., New York, 1969), 204 (Nov. 17, 1794, entry).

7. Millett, *History of the Baptists in Maine*, 120, 459; Sylvanus Boardman's circular letter, in *Minutes of the Bowdoinham Association, Held at the Baptist Meeting-House*

in Readfield, September 26th and 27th, 1804 (Portland, 1804; S-S 5779), 7; Benedict, *General History of the Baptist Denomination*, II, 471; *Minutes of the Lincoln Association, Held at the Baptist Meeting-house, in Vassalborough, September 19th and 20th, 1810* (Buckstown, 1810; S-S 19432), 12; John Neal to the General Court, ca. Jan. 1810, Related Papers, Resolve CXLVII (Mar. 3, 1810), MA; Henry Kendall to the editor, May 23, 1810, in *Massachusetts Baptist Missionary Magazine*, II (1808–1810), 345–346. See the similar findings in Eldridge Honaker Pendleton, "The New York Anti-Rent Controversy, 1830–1860" (Ph.D. diss., University of Virginia, 1974), 294–295.

8. John Baker's circular letter in *Minutes of the Lincoln Association, 1810*, 9–15; Isaac Case to the editor, Dec. 25, 1811, in *Massachusetts Baptist Missionary Magazine*, III (1811–1813), 201–202. For Job Chadwick's conservative notions, see his circular letter, in *Minutes of the Bowdoinham Association Held at the Baptist Meeting House in Vassalborough, September 28th and 29th, 1803* (Portland, 1803; S-S 3731).

9. Frederick J. Turner, "Contributions of the West to American Democracy," *Atlantic Monthly*, XCI (Jan.–June 1903), 91. See Table 7. Brothers William and Joshua Davis, their brothers-in-law Samuel Henry and Samuel Morgaridge, and their cousin Levi Davis had all served in Davistown's Liberty Men and all emigrated to become the first settlers of Windsor Township, Morgan County (now in Noble County), and the founders of its Baptist church. At the same time, Hollis Hutchens and his four White Indian sons, Hollis, Jr., David, John, and Daniel, settled nearby Olive Township (Morgan County). See Charles Robertson, *History of Morgan County, Ohio* (Chicago, 1886), 392, 398, 401–402, 412–414; *History of Noble County, Ohio, with Portraits and Biographical Sketches of Some of Its Pioneers and Prominent Men* (Chicago, 1887), 118, 314. On the role of out-migration in stifling the New York antirent resistance and the Pennsylvania Whiskey Rebellion, see Pendleton, "The New York Anti-Rent Controversy," 244, 282; Thomas P. Slaughter, *The Whiskey Rebellion: Frontier Epilogue to the American Revolution* (New York, 1986), 224.

10. David C. Smith *et al.*, "Climatic Stress and Maine Agriculture, 1785–1885," in T.M.L. Wigley *et al.*, eds., *Climate and History: Studies in Past Climates and Their Impact on Man* (Cambridge, 1981), 459; Cyrus Eaton, *History of Thomaston, Rockland, and South Thomaston . . .* (Hallowell, 1865), I, 270; Clarence Albert Day, *A History of Maine Agriculture, 1604–1860* (Orono, 1954), 110; James W. North, *The History of Augusta . . .* (Augusta, 1870), 409, 427–429; Moses Greenleaf, *A Survey of the State of Maine . . .* (Portland, 1829), 137–138; Alibeus Partridge to anonymous sons, Apr. 26, 1813, Camden Historical Society; William Parkman, Jr., to William Parkman, Sr., Sept. 1814, Concord Public Library, Concord, Mass.; William D. Williamson, *The History of the State of Maine . . .* (Augusta, 1966; orig. publ. Hallowell, 1832), II, 671.

11. Howard Alexander Carter, *History of Isaac P. Carter Family and Their Descendants* (Washington, Iowa, 1905), 4; Cyrus Eaton, *Annals of the Town of Warren* (Hallowell, 1877), 322; Joseph Whipple, *A Geographical View of the District of Maine, with Particular Reference to Its Internal Resources . . .* (Bangor, 1816), 22, 41, 43; Day, *A History of Maine Agriculture*, 111; Greenleaf, *A Survey of the State of Maine*, 137–139; Williamson, *The History of the State of Maine*, II, 665. The General Court also blamed high land prices in Maine for the out-migration. To retain settlers in Maine, the legislators adopted a new public land policy that favored direct sales in modest parcels to actual settlers; in eight selected townships the first 50 settlers could obtain 100 acres for a mere five dollars by erecting a house and barn within one year and clearing 10 acres within five years. But by 1816 this was too little, too late, for the remaining public lands lay

far in the interior, remote from market, and the new policy did nothing for mid-Maine's settlers who dwelled within proprietary claims. See Williamson, *The History of the State of Maine*, II, 662; Day, *A History of Maine Agriculture*, 112–113; "A Friend to the Real Interests of Maine," *Bangor Weekly Register*, Apr. 6, 1816; and Greenleaf, *A Statistical View of the District of Maine*, 54–55, 107–114.

12. Robert Hallowell Gardiner to Dr. Petty, June 10, 1815, in Gardiner Family Papers, box 2, folder 7, Oaklands, Gardiner. In two communities (selected because they had been important resistance centers), between a fourth and a third of the settlers defaulted on their contracts with Gardiner: 8 of 29 in Malta (27.6%) and 14 of 49 in Freedom (28.6%). The statistics apply only to original sales, that is, not to subsequent resales of repossessed lots in the two communities, both of which came to terms after 1809. See Gardiner's Land Record Book, 235–238, 247–251, Oaklands, Gardiner. Gardiner subsequently reported, "The fulling mill, oakum mill, furnace, forge, nail factory, spike factory, and other smaller concerns all proved failures, and the losses on several of them were heavy." See Robert Hallowell Gardiner, *Early Recollections of Robert Hallowell Gardiner, 1782–1864* (Hallowell, 1936), 217.

13. The deeds: Daniel Brackett to Daniel Brackett, Jr., June 4, 1807, Daniel Brackett, Jr., to John Bradstreet, June 7, 1808, KCD, XIII, 39, 248, KCRD; May 1808 arrest warrant for Daniel Brackett, Jr., endorsed by Deputy Sheriff James Norris as unsatisfied, May 30, 1809, KC-SJC files, box 74, MeSA; writ for the arrest of Thomas Brackett, May 1808, KC-SJC files, box 73, MeSA; Herbert I. Brackett, *Brackett Genealogy: Descendants of Anthony Brackett of Portsmouth and Captain Richard Brackett of Braintree . . .* (Washington, D.C., 1907), 220–221; Libbeus Collemore v. Daniel Brackett, Aug. 1813, KC-CCP, XV, 561, MeSA, indicates that the latter then dwelled in Waterford in Oxford County and had left unpaid an Aug. 1811 court judgment for $26.42 in damages and $12.48 in costs from when he had lived in Lincoln Plantation (Thorndike). For Bradstreet's involvement in the resistance, see the writ for his arrest, in Harvey v. Barlow, Dec. 1807, KC-CCP files, box 9, MeSA. David Sturges Copeland, *History of Clarendon [N.Y.] from 1810 to 1888* (Buffalo, N.Y., 1889), 1, 14–16; William F. Peck, "An Historical Sketch of Monroe County and the City of Rochester," in *Landmarks of Monroe County, New York . . .* (Boston, 1895), 407.

14. Daniel Brackett's application for a pension, Nov. 8, 1820, M804, roll 313, NA; Isaac S. Signor, ed., *Landmarks of Orleans County, New York . . .* (Syracuse, N.Y., 1894), 573, 579.

15. Arad Thomas, *Pioneer History of Orleans County, New York . . .* (Albion, N.Y., 1871), 199; Signor, ed., *Landmarks*, 562, 573, 579, 586–587.

16. Ronald F. Banks, *Maine Becomes a State: The Movement to Separate Maine from Massachusetts, 1785–1820* (Middletown, Conn., 1970), 67–149; Frederick S. Allis, Jr., ed., *William Bingham's Maine Lands, 1790–1820*, 2 vols. (Colonial Society of Massachusetts, *Publications*, XXXVI–XXXVII [Boston, 1954]), II, 1222 n. For earlier agrarian separationists (especially Brigadier General Samuel Thompson of Brunswick), see Henry Knox to Rufus King, June 13, 1785, Isaac Winslow to Knox, Sept. 13, 1785, HKP, LI, 82, 87, MHS.

17. David C. Smith, "Maine and Its Public Domain: Land Disposal on the Northeastern Frontier," in David M. Ellis, ed., *The Frontier in American Development: Essays in Honor of Paul Wallace Gates* (Ithaca, N.Y., 1969), 114–125; "An Act for the Limitations of Actions Real and Personal" (Mar. 19, 1821), "An Act for the Settlement of Certain Equitable Claims Arising in Real Estate" (June 27, 1821), in *Laws of the State of Maine, from the Separation to 1833 Inclusive . . .* (Hallowell, 1834), I, 240–241, II, 150–153; Asahel Stearns, *A Summary of the Law*

and Practice of Real Actions . . . , 2d ed. (Hallowell, 1831), 201–203. The revised betterment law allowed the defendant to request that the jury determine the full extent of his possession and oblige the plaintiff to include it within his suit. To discourage expensively prolonged litigation meant to intimidate settlers, the new law allowed the defendant, at the start of a suit, to propose in open court the prices he would either pay for the land value or sell his improvements for; if the plaintiff ignored the offer, proceeded with his suit, and the jury decided on a higher improvement value and a lower wild land value, then he had to bear the full cost of the suit (paying the defendant's legal fees as well as his own). For the new trespass act, see "An Act Directing the Proceedings against Forcible Entry and Detainer" (Feb. 5, 1821), in *Laws of the State of Maine, from the Separation to 1833*, I, 293.

18. Malta, Kennebec County, Maine, Third Census of the United States, 1810, M252, reel 11, Fourth Census of the United States, 1820, M33, reel 35, NA; Malta selectmen's petition to the Maine State Legislature, Jan. 1821, Public Special Legislation, box 9, envelope 140, MeSA. Today few in mid-Maine know anything about the resistance, and most of the region's towns bear names that honor the Great Proprietors (Bowdoin, Bowdoinham, Pittston, Gardiner, Vassalboro, Waldoboro, Lincolnville, Appleton, Searsmont, Waldo, Swanville, Knox, Jackson, Thorndike, Dixmont, and Nobleboro) or that express the search for distinction; only three towns, all located deep in what was once the militant backcountry, preserve names originally chosen to express their settlers' commitment to the resistance: Liberty, Freedom, and Unity.

19. Nathaniel Hawthorne, *The American Notebooks*, ed. Randall Stewart (New Haven, Conn., 1932), 23; Alexis de Tocqueville, *Democracy in America*, ed. Phillips Bradley (New York, 1945), I, 48–56.

20. Thomas Morgan Griffiths, *Major General Henry Knox and the Last Heirs to Montpelier*, ed. Arthur Morgan Griffiths (Monmouth, 1965); Thomas Morgan Griffiths, *Maine Sources in "The House of the Seven Gables"* (Waterville, 1945); Nathaniel Hawthorne, *The House of the Seven Gables* (New York, 1961; orig. publ. Boston, 1851), 12–25; Robert Clark, *History and Myth in American Fiction, 1823–1852* (New York, 1984), 54–55.

21. On *The House of the Seven Gables* as reflecting Hawthorne's rebellion against his family heritage, see Frederick C. Crews,"A Psychoanalytical Interpretation," in Roger Asselineau, ed., *The Merrill Studies in "The House of the Seven Gables"* (Columbus, Ohio, 1970), 33–49; on the novel as rebellion against "a rising commercialism," see Henry Nash Smith, *"The House of the Seven Gables* as Social History," in Asselineau, ed., *The Merrill Studies*, 50–55. Julian Hawthorne, *Nathaniel Hawthorne and His Wife: A Biography* (Boston, 1885), 25–26, notes the connection between the Hathorne claim and the fictional Pyncheon claim but confuses the Hathorne claim to Edgecomb and Boothbay with the Manning family's interest in Raymond. On Colonel John Hathorne, see Sidney Perley, *The History of Salem, Massachusetts* (Salem, Mass., 1924), I, 284 n. 1, II, 238, III, 257–290, 336–337. For the Hathorne claim, see Francis B. Greene, *History of Boothbay, Southport, and Boothbay Harbor, Maine* (Portland, 1906), 167. For Hawthorne's youth, see Robert Cantwell, *Nathaniel Hawthorne: The American Years* (New York, 1971), 3, 13, 18, 29, 35–46, 59.

22. Hawthorne, *American Notebooks*, ed. Stewart, 7–11, both quotes 11; Cantwell, *Nathaniel Hawthorne*, 216–217.

23. North, *Augusta*, 178–179, 507, 571–577, 814; William Willis, *A History of the Law, the Courts, and the Lawyers of Maine* . . . (Portland, 1863), 154–157 (quote

157), 694; Paul Coffin, "Memoir and Journals of Rev. Paul Coffin, D.D.," MeHS, *Colls.*, 1st Ser., IV (Portland, 1859), 377.

24. Richard L. Bushman, *King and People in Provincial Massachusetts* (Chapel Hill, N.C., 1985), 235–251 (quote 240); Allen, *Norridgewock*, 107. For producers' movements and ideology in 19th-century America, see Sean Wilentz, *Chants Democratic: New York City and the Rise of the American Working Class, 1788–1850* (New York, 1984), 172–216, 326–359; Allan Dawley and Paul Faler, "Working-Class Culture and Politics in the Industrial Revolution: Sources of Loyalism and Rebellion," *Journal of Social History*, IX (1975–1976), 466–480; Steven Hahn, *The Roots of Southern Populism: Yeoman Farmers and the Transformation of the Georgia Upcountry, 1850–1890* (New York, 1983), 269–289; John Mack Faragher, *Sugar Creek: Life on the Illinois Prairie* (New Haven, Conn., 1986), 132, 181; Lawrence Goodwyn, *The Populist Moment: A Short History of the Agrarian Revolt in America* (New York, 1978). On the yeoman myth, see Richard Hofstadter, *The Age of Reform: From Bryan to F.D.R.* (New York, 1955), 23–59.

25. Joseph Plumb Martin, *"Private Yankee Doodle": Being a Narrative of Some of the Adventures, Dangers, and Sufferings of a Revolutionary Soldier*, ed. George F. Scheer (Boston, 1962; orig. publ. Hallowell, 1832), xii–xiv, 281–283; Manoah Ellis *et al.* to the General Court, May 26, 1790, *BHM*, III, 44; Submissions to the Waldo Patent Commission, II, 65, MA.

26. Joseph Plumb Martin to Henry Knox, Dec. 22, 1801, Knox to Martin, Dec. 29, 1801, HKP, XLIV, 165, XLIII, 172, MHS. Martin's Sept. letter does not survive in Knox's papers at either MHS or MeHS. Prospect Tax Valuation for 1811, microfilm box 400, MSL; Martin's deposition quoted by George F. Scheer in his introduction to Martin, *"Private Yankee Doodle,"* xiv–xv.

27. Martin, *"Private Yankee Doodle,"* ed. Scheer, 95, 147–148, 150–152, 182–184, 186, 190–191 (first three quotes), 193 (last quote), 279–280. For confirmation of Martin's observations about the officers, see Charles Royster, *A Revolutionary People at War: The Continental Army and American Character, 1775–1783* (Chapel Hill, N.C., 1979), esp. 79–96.

28. Martin, *"Private Yankee Doodle,"* ed. Scheer, 283–284, 287–288.

INDEX

Adams, John, 211
Adams, Joshua, 213
African-Americans, 48–49, 53
Agrarianism, 6–8, 14, 16–18, 28, 94–96, 100–114, 150, 186–189, 216, 222, 229–230
Agrarian laws, 16
Agriculture, 1, 64–65, 70, 74–77, 256–259; reform of, 36–37, 55–56, 75–77; livestock in, 37, 65, 66, 68–69, 74, 206–207, 257; and crop parasites, 67–68, 70
Albion, 235, 279. See also Fairfax; Freetown
Alcohol, 36, 37, 84–85
Allen, Abel, 117
Allen, Ethan, 7, 193
Allen, Nathaniel C., 28
Allen, William, 62–66, 74, 173
Allen, William, Jr., 65–66, 69–70, 74, 77, 78, 142, 173–174, 179, 209, 247
Alna, 108, 171, 251, 268. See also New Milford
American Revolution, 14–18; legacy of, 5–6, 9, 38, 84, 93–94, 95–96, 104–105, 111, 112–114, 116, 119, 131–132, 139, 143, 144, 147, 156–157, 185, 187, 229, 235, 246–249
Ames, Nathaniel, 61
Ames, Winslow, 117
Anderson, Francis, 273
Anderson, Robert, 117, 269
Andrews, Asa, 108, 115–116
Androscoggin River valley, 103
Antifederalists, 129, 144, 190, 216, 232
Antinomianism, 137, 145–147, 149, 237–238
Anti-Renters (New York), 4, 229, 231
Appleton, 161, 226, 251
Apthorp, John, 35
Aristocracy, fear of, 13–14, 177–178, 187, 211–212, 236

Auburn. See Danville
Augusta, 90, 147–148, 173, 181–182, 193, 195, 204, 235, 245–246, 252, 267, 275, 277
Averell, Job, 13, 25

Backcountry resistance: in Maine, 2–3, 114–121, 164–166, 264–279; in New Jersey, 4, 5; in South Carolina, 4, 5; in North Carolina, 4; in New York, 4; in Pennsylvania, 4, 5; in Vermont, 4, 5, 107; in Ohio, 4, 45; in Massachusetts, 5, 107
Bagley, Jonathan (of Davistown), 163
Bagley, Jonathan (Pejepscot Proprietor), 15
Bailey, Jacob, 73
Baker, John, 238
Bakerstown, 236. See also Minot
Ball, Samuel, 190
Ballard, Ephraim, 193, 265–266, 271
Ballstown. See Balltown
Balltown, 17, 29, 74, 75, 90, 100, 114, 119, 171, 174, 176, 178, 187, 190, 193, 206–207, 212, 254, 255, 256, 257, 258–259, 265, 266, 267, 269, 270, 272, 273. See also Jefferson (Maine); Whitefield
Bangor, 133. See also Condeskeag
Banton, William, 273
Baptists: Calvinist, 101, 135, 137, 182, 183, 187, 212, 214, 223, 237–238; Freewill, 135, 136, 140, 141, 142, 146, 183, 238. See also Evangelicals
Baring, Alexander, 50, 52, 56, 62, 66
Barlow, Anson, 235
Barlow, James, 235
Barlow, Nathan, 119, 123, 128–129, 144, 201–202, 225–226, 235, 238, 240, 273, 275
Barlow, Obed, 128
Barnard, Thomas, 31–33, 246
Bartlett, Benjamin, 271